ARISTOTLE TRANSFORMED

'Aristotle and Alexander of Aphrodisias', bronze plaquette by Ulocrino (see Donald R. Morrison's note on pp. 481-4). Reproduced by courtesy of the Victoria and Albert Museum, London.

Aristotle Transformed

THE ANCIENT COMMENTATORS
AND THEIR INFLUENCE

EDITED BY

Richard Sorabji

Cornell University Press

ITHACA, NEW YORK

First published 1990 Cornell University Press

Library of Congress Cataloging-in-Publication Data

Aristotle transformed : the ancient commentators and their influence /
    edited by Richard Sorabji.
        p.   cm.
    Includes bibliographical references.
    ISBN 0-8014-2432-1
    1. Aristotle—Criticism and interpretation—History.   I. Sorabji,
Richard.
B485.A655   1990
185—dc20   89-37190

Printed in Great Britain

Contents

Preface

The story of the ancient commentators on Aristotle has not previously been told at book length. Here it is assembled for the first time by drawing both on some of the classic articles translated into English or revised and on the very latest research. Some of the chapters will be making revisionary suggestions unfamiliar even to specialists in the field. The philosophical interest of the commentators has been illustrated elsewhere.[1] The aim here is not so much to do this again as to set out the background of the commentary tradition against which further philosophical discussion and discussions of other kinds can take place.

The importance of the commentators lies partly in their representing the thought and classroom teaching of the Aristotelian and Neoplatonist schools, partly in the panorama they provide of the 1100 years of Ancient Greek philosophy, preserving as they do many original quotations from lost philosophical works. Still more significant is their profound influence, uncovered in some of the chapters below, on subsequent philosophy, Islamic and European. This was due partly to their preserving anti-Aristotelian material which helped to inspire medieval and Renaissance science, but still more to their presenting an Aristotle transformed in ways which happened to make him acceptable to the Christian Church. It is not just Aristotle, but this Aristotle transformed and embedded in the philosophy of the commentators, that lies behind the views of later thinkers.

Many of the commentaries are being translated in the series 'The Ancient Commentators on Aristotle', published by Duckworth and Cornell University Press from 1987 onwards (general editor: Richard Sorabji). The present book will also serve as an introduction to them.

Chapters 1, 4, 10, 11, 19 and 20 are new; 2, 6, 8 and 12 are translated; 5, 9, 14, 15 and 18 are substantially revised. Others are revised in more minor ways; Greek and Latin passages are translated throughout. The original articles appeared as follows:

Chapter 2: Karl Praechter, 'Die griechischen Aristoteleskommentare', *Byzantinische Zeitschrift* 18, 1909, 516-38.
Chapter 3: Hans B. Gottschalk, pp. 1089-112 and 1150-1 of

---

[1] For example, *Time, Creation and the Continuum* and *Matter, Space and Motion*, and in a related volume *Philoponus and the Rejection of Aristotelian Science*, London and Ithaca N.Y. 1983, 1988, 1987.

'Aristotelian philosophy in the Roman world from the time of Cicero to the end of the second century AD', in W. Haase (ed.), *Aufstieg und Niedergang der römischen Welt* II, 36.2, Berlin 1987.

Chapter 5: H.J. Blumenthal, 'Themistius, the last Peripatetic commentator on Aristotle?', in *Arktouros, Hellenic Studies presented to Bernard M.W. Knox on the occasion of his 65th birthday*, Berlin 1979.

Chapter 6: Pierre Hadot, 'L'harmonie des philosophies de Plotin et d'Aristote selon Porphyre dans le commentaire de Dexippe sur les *Catégories*', in *Plotino e il Neoplatonismo in Oriente e in Occidente*, Problemi attuali di scienza e di cultura 198, Accademia Nazionale dei Lincei, Rome 1974, 31-47.

Chapter 7: Sten Ebbesen, *Commentators and Commentaries on Aristotle's Sophistici Elenchi*, 3 vols, vol. 1 = *Corpus Latinum Commentariorum in Aristotelem Graecorum (CLCAG)*, vol. 7, part 1, Brill, Leiden 1981, 133-70.

Chapter 8: H.D. Saffrey, 'Comment Syrianus, le maître de l'école néoplatonicienne d'Athènes, considerait-il Aristote?', in Jürgen Wiesner (ed.), *Aristoteles: Werk und Wirkung*, vol. 2, Berlin 1987.

Chapter 9: Richard Sorabji, 'Infinite power impressed: the transformation of Aristotle's physics and theology', in Sarah Hutton and John Henry (eds), *New Perspectives in Renaissance Thought: Essays in the History of Science, Education and Philosophy in memory of Charles B. Schmitt*, London 1989.

Chapter 12: Ilsetraut Hadot, 'La vie et l'oeuvre de Simplicius d'après des sources grecques et arabes', in *Simplicius – sa vie, son oeuvre, sa survie*, Peripatoi 15, Berlin 1987, 3-39.

Chapter 13: H.J. Blumenthal, 'Neoplatonic elements in the *de Anima* commentaries', *Phronesis* 21, 1976, 64-87.

Chapter 14: L.G. Westerink, *Anonymous prolegomena to Platonic Philosophy*, Amsterdam 1962, Introduction, xxxii.

Chapter 15: James Shiel, 'Boethius' commentaries on Aristotle', in R. Hunt, R. Klibansky, L. Labowsky (eds), *Medieval and Renaissance Studies* 4, 1958, 217-44.

Chapter 16: Sten Ebbesen, 'Boethius as an Aristotelian scholar', in Jürgen Wiesner (ed.), *Aristoteles: Werk und Wirkung*, vol. 2, Berlin 1987.

Chapter 17: Robert Browning, 'An unpublished funeral oration on Anna Comnena', *Proceedings of the Cambridge Philological Society* n.s. 8, 1962, 1-12.

Chapter 18: H.P.F. Mercken, *The Greek Commentaries on the Nicomachean Ethics of Aristotle in the Latin Translation of Robert Grosseteste*, vol. 1 = *Corpus Latinum Commentariorum in Aristotelem Graecorum(CLCAG)*, vol. 6, part 1, Brill, Leiden 1973, Introduction, *3-*29.

Acknowledgments

I wish to thank the following for their generous permission to print, and in some cases to translate, earlier work:

Chapter 2: BSB B.G. Teubner Verlagsgesellschaft, Leipzig.
Chapter 3: the editors of *Aufstieg und Niedergang der römischen Welt*.
Chapters 4, 8, 12, 16: Walter de Gruyter and Co., Berlin.
Chapter 6: Accademia Nazionale dei Lincei, Rome.
Chapters 7 and 18: Professor G. Verbeke, director of the *Corpus Latinum Commentariorum in Aristotelem Graecorum*.
Chapter 9: the organisers of the Charles B. Schmitt Memorial Symposium held at the Warburg Institute on 20-1 February 1987.
Chapter 13: van Gorcum, Assen – The Netherlands.
Chapter 14: North Holland Publishing Co., Amsterdam.
Chapter 15: the editors of *Medieval and Renaissance Studies*.
Chapter 17: the Cambridge Philological Society.

The work on this book, like that on the translations in the series 'The Ancient Commentators on Aristotle', has been generously funded by the following sources: the National Endowment for the Humanities, an independent federal agency of the USA, the Leverhulme Trust, the British Academy, the Jowett Copyright Trustees, the Royal Society (UK), Centro Internazionale A. Beltrame di Storia dello Spazio e del Tempo (Padua), Mario Mignucci (Padua) and Liverpool University.

For an enormous investment of work on the typescripts, including electronic wizardry, I am indebted to John Ellis, Duran Dodson and Eric Lewis, and for the indexing to John Ellis, Duran Dodson, Lars Mortensen and Jean-Pierre Schneider. For his role in the preparation of the King's College bibliography on the commentators, I am grateful to Titos Christodoulou. The three translations from French and one from German were all executed by Victor Caston. The typing kindly undertaken by Gertrud Watson and D. Woods was exceptionally difficult because of the extensive revision of some chapters. Thanks are due to them and not least to Deborah Blake at Duckworth, whose patience and editorial skill has brought this book and the related volumes of translation to light.

Contributors

Dr Henry J. Blumenthal   Department of Greek, Liverpool University

Professor Robert Browning   Dumbarton Oaks, Washington D.C.

Professor Sten Ebbesen   Institut for Middelalderfilologi, University of Copenhagen

Dr Hans B. Gottschalk   School of Classics, Leeds University

Dr Ilsetraut Hadot   Directeur de Recherches, C.N.R.S., Paris

Professor Pierre Hadot   Collège de France (emeritus)

Dr H. Paul F. Mercken   Filosofisch Instituut, Rijksuniversiteit, Utrecht

Professor Donald R. Morrison   Department of Philosophy, Rice University

Professor Ian Mueller   Department of Philosophy, University of Chicago

Professor Karl Praechter   1858-1933

le Père H.D. Saffrey   Couvent St Jacques, Paris

Dr Robert W. Sharples   Department of Greek, University College, London

Dr James Shiel   Sussex University (emeritus)

Professor Richard Sorabji   Department of Philosophy, King's College, London

Dr Koenraad Verrycken   University of Antwerp

Professor L.G. Westerink   State University of New York at Buffalo

CHAPTER ONE

The ancient commentators on Aristotle

Richard Sorabji

Two impulses: Andronicus and Porphyry

Cicero reports in the *Topics* (ch. 3), written in 44 BC, that Aristotle is
ignored by all but a few philosophers, and indeed his own knowledge of
Aristotle does not extend far beyond the early dialogue works. Yet even
before the time he was writing, as Gottschalk argues in Chapter 3 below,
a new explosion of interest in Aristotle was under way, which was to
occupy the rest of the century. Whether in Rome or more probably in
Athens, Andronicus of Rhodes had begun his work on the great edition of
Aristotle which forms the basis of today's editions, and he had
accompanied some of the treatises with commentaries. Altogether five
different commentaries were produced on Aristotle's *Categories* by the
end of the century, along with a Doric version of the *Categories*
purporting to be the work of the old Pythagorean Archytas, and two
compendia of the Philosophy of Aristotle. The commentaries are lost,
except for fragments, notably those preserved in Simplicius' commentary
on the *Categories*, and the next comparable boost to Aristotelian studies
would not come until Porphyry in the third century AD. But the tradition
of commentary on Aristotle had begun.

The earliest surviving commentaries come from Aristotelians of the
second century AD, culminating at the end of that century and the
beginning of the next in the commentaries of the greatest expositor and
elaborator of Aristotle's thought within the Aristotelian tradition,
Alexander of Aphrodisias (appointed to his Aristotelian Chair between
198 and 209).

Outside the Aristotelian schools, the chief interest in the first two
centuries AD still focused on Aristotle's *Categories*. The work seems to
have acted as a catalyst, attracting commentaries from three schools, the
Stoic, Platonist and Aristotelian. Gottschalk suggests below that it was
the Aristotelians who first described the Stoic scheme as one of
'categories', but that the comparison forced them in return to establish a
correct order for their own scheme of categories, since order was

important to the Stoic scheme in a way that Aristotle never took it to be important.

Arguments raged for and against the viability of Aristotle's categorial scheme, and the arguments against might well have won. For in Rome Plotinus (c. 205-260), whom we tend to regard, following a modern classification, as the founder of Neoplatonism, sided with the arguments against in *Enneads* 6.1-3. But on this issue, Porphyry (232-309), his disciple, biographer and editor, resisted him (P. Hadot, Chapter 6 below).[1] Platonists should not complain with Plotinus that Aristotle's categories fail to take account of the Platonic Ideas, for the *Categories* is not about things, but only about words insofar as they signify things,[2] and words get applied primarily to things in the sensible world, not to the Ideas in the intelligible realm.[3] Porphyry's pupil Iamblichus (c. 240-c. 325) went further with his 'intellective theory' (*noera theôria*). He tried to show how the categories, properly understood, apply first and foremost to the intelligible realm. The category of place, for example, understood as a boundary which embraces and holds something together, applies most fully there.[4] Iamblichus' pupil Dexippus (c. 330), perhaps drawing on Porphyry, adds that the reason why the *Categories* is not directly about things is that it is designed for beginners.[5] And he shows how Aristotle's account of substances may still apply in an analogous way to intelligible as well as to sensible substances.[6]

Porphyry's intervention was decisive. He is credited with a work in seven books entitled *On the School of Plato and Aristotle Being One* and (if it is distinct) one *On the Difference between Plato and Aristotle*. Some of the contents are preserved in an Arabic treatise by al-'Almirî.[7] From there on, the study of Aristotle was assured. For the unity of Platonism and Aristotelianism meant that Aristotle's logic and a wide selection of his other texts became a standard prerequisite for Platonic studies in the Neoplatonist schools, and Neoplatonism was now the dominant philosophy. Porphyry himself wrote an introduction to the *Categories* called the *Isagoge* (Introduction) or *Quinque Voces* (Five Terms), two *Categories* commentaries, of which one is extant, one fragmentary, and half a dozen or

---

[1] See also A.C. Lloyd, 'Neoplatonic logic and Aristotelian logic', *Phronesis* 1, 1955-6, 58-79 and 146-60.

[2] Porphyry *in Cat.* 57,7-8; 58,5-7; 91,19; ap. Simplicium *in Cat.* 10,22-3.

[3] Porphyry *in Cat.* 91,19-27.

[4] Iamblichus ap. Simplicium *in Cat.* 363,29-364,6; general programme at 2,13.

[5] Dexippus *in Cat.* 40,19-25.

[6] Dexippus *in Cat.* 41,18-42,3, discussed by P. Hadot in Chapter 6. However, if Dexippus (*in Cat.* 44) rejects the view of Iamblichus (ap. Simplicium *in Cat.* 116,25) that intelligible substances also satisfy the criterion of admitting opposites, this may lend support to Sten Ebbesen's suggestion in ch. 20 that we can see (at 17,1) some impatience directed against Iamblichus by Dexippus.

[7] *As-Saâdah Wa'l-Isâd (On Seeking and Causing Happiness)*, M. Mînuvî (ed.), Wiesbaden 1957.

more other commentaries on Aristotle, for some of which fragments survive.[8]

The harmony of Plato, Aristotle and other Greek philosophers

The harmony of Plato and Aristotle was accepted to a larger or smaller extent by all commentators in the Neoplatonist tradition, and the great bulk of the ancient commentators, Christians included, are in that tradition. Among the major commentators after Porphyry, there are only two exceptions. Themistius, so Blumenthal argues in Chapter 5, remained more Aristotelian than Platonist.[9] And in the twelfth-century revival of commentary writing in the circle of Anna Comnena, while Eustratius observes the traditional 'harmony',[10] Michael of Ephesus reverts to the Aristotelian tradition represented by Alexander of Aphrodisias.

On the harmony of Plato and Aristotle, Iamblichus of the Syrian school (c. 240-c. 325) was accused of going too far and denying that Aristotle contradicted Plato's theory of Ideas.[11] In fifth-century Alexandria, Hierocles also espoused a thorough-going version of harmony and made Plato and Aristotle agree on the subject of Creation.[12] He credited the general thesis of harmony to his teacher Plutarch of Athens (died 432) and to his Alexandrian forebear Ammonius Saccas, who taught Plotinus in the third century. A more nuanced view was taken in Athens by Plutarch's other pupil, Syrianus (died c. 437), and their common pupil Proclus (c. 411-485). They accepted harmony in many areas,[13] but could see that there was disagreement on the theory of Ideas (H.D. Saffrey, Chapter 8) and also on the issue of whether God was causally responsible for the existence of the physical world, which Aristotle denied. But back in Alexandria, Proclus' pupil Ammonius (434/45-517/26) was to claim harmony even on these issues, and, though the debate was not

---

[8] See Francesco Romano, *Porfirio e la fisica aristotelica*, Catania 1985, for a collection of the *Physics* fragments in Italian translation. The named fragments of the lost *Categories* commentary are being assembled and edited by Andrew Smith. The tentative list of ten commentaries and related works in Romano, p. 33, is augmented by Ebbesen's suggestion of an *in SE*, in Chapter 7 below.

[9] The chapter incorporates a response to the opposing view of E.P. Mahoṇ̇v. 'Themistius and the agent intellect in James of Viterbo and other thirteenth-century philosophers (Saint Thomas Aquinas, Siger of Brabant and Henry Bate)', *Augustiniana* 23, 1973, 422-67, at 428-31; id., 'Neoplatonism, the Greek commentators and Renaissance Aristotelianism', in D.J. O'Meara (ed.), *Neoplatonism and Christian Thought*, Albany 1982, 169-77 and 264-82, esp. n. 1, 264-6. Some Platonist influence is cited too in Robert Todd, introduction to translation of Themistius *in DA* 3, 4-8, in Frederick Schroeder and Robert Todd, *Two Greek Aristotelian Commentators on the Active Intellect*, Toronto, forthcoming.

[10] A.C. Lloyd, 'The Aristotelianism of Eustratios of Nicaea', in Jürgen Wiesner (ed.), *Aristoteles Werk und Wirkung*, Berlin 1987, 341-51.

[11] Elias *in Cat.* 123, 1-3.

[12] Photius *Bibliotheca* (Bekker) 171b33ff.

[13] Syrianus *in Metaph.* 80,4-7; Proclus *in Tim.* 1. 6,21-7,16.

clear-cut,[14] his claim was to prevail. Aristotle, he maintained, accepted Plato's Ideas,[15] at least in the form of principles (*logoi*) in the divine Intellect, and these principles were in turn causally responsible for the beginningless existence of the physical world. Ammonius wrote a whole book to show that Aristotle's God was thus an efficient cause of the world's existence. The book is lost, but some of its principal arguments are preserved by Simplicius.[16] Ammonius' interpretation of Aristotle's God as Sustainer of the world was passed on through Farabi's *Harmony of Plato and Aristotle*, and eventually influenced the Christian writers of the thirteenth century, including Thomas Aquinas. It was the Aristotle of the Alexandrian commentators (and of certain spurious works) that they inherited. Hence, by an irony, what started in Ammonius as a desire to harmonise Aristotle with Plato finished in the thirteenth century by helping to make Aristotle safe for Christianity (Richard Sorabji, Chapter 9). In Simplicius (writing after 532), who goes furthest of all, it is a formally stated duty of the commentator to display the harmony of Plato and Aristotle 'in most things'.[17] Philoponus (c. 490-570) who with his independent mind had thought better of his earlier belief in harmony, is castigated by Simplicius for neglecting this duty (Koenraad Verrycken, Chapter 11).[18]

The idea of harmony was also extended beyond Plato and Aristotle to embrace the Presocratics. Plato's pupils Speusippus and Xenocrates saw Plato as being in the Pythagorean tradition.[19] And this view gained support from pseudo-Pythagorean forgeries of the third to first centuries BC, which drew on the ideas of Plato and Aristotle, but embedded them in works purporting to come from an earlier period and to be written by Pythagoras and his pupils.[20] These works, though not deceiving everyone,[21] were taken by the Neoplatonists as genuine. Plotinus saw the

[14] Asclepius sometimes accepts Syrianus' interpretation (*in Metaph.* 433,9-436,6), which is, however, qualified, since Syrianus thinks Aristotle is really committed willy-nilly to much of Plato's view (*in Metaph.* 117,25-118,11; ap. Asclepium *in Metaph.* 433,16; 450,22). Philoponus repents of his early claim that Plato is not the target of Aristotle's attack, and accepts that Plato is rightly attacked for treating Ideas as independent entities outside the divine Intellect (*in DA* 37,18-31; *in Phys.* 225,4-226,11; *contra Procl.* 26,24-32,13; *in An. Post.* 242,14-243,25). Elias also thinks (*in Cat.* 123,1-3) there is some disharmony on the theory of ideas.

[15] Asclepius *in Metaph.* from the voice of (i.e., from the lectures of) Ammonius 69,17-21; 71,28; cf. Zacharias *Ammonius PG* vol. 85, col.952 (Colonna).

[16] Simplicius *in Phys.* 1361,11-1363,12, translated in Richard Sorabji, *Matter, Space and Motion*, London and Ithaca NY 1988, ch. 15.

[17] Simplicius *in Cat.* 7,23-32.

[18] Simplicius *in Cael.* 84,11-14; 159,2-9.

[19] See e.g. Walter Burkert, *Weisheit und Wissenschaft*, Nürnberg 1962, translated as *Lore and Science in Ancient Pythagoreanism*, Cambridge Mass. 1972, 83-96.

[20] See Holger Thesleff, *An Introduction to the Pythagorean Writings of the Hellenistic Period*, Åbo 1961; Thomas Alexander Szlezàk, *Pseudo-Archytas über die Kategorien*, Peripatoi vol. 4, Berlin and New York 1972.

[21] Themistius recognised the spuriousness of pseudo-Archytas' version of the *Categories* (Boethius *in Cat.*, PL 64, 162A).

Presocratics as precursors of his own views,[22] but Iamblichus went far beyond him by writing ten volumes on Pythagorean philosophy and making maximum use of the pseudo-Pythagorean writings.[23] Thereafter Proclus sought to unify the whole of Greek philosophy by presenting it as a continuous clarification of divine revelation,[24] and Simplicius argued for the same general unity in order to rebut Christian charges of contradictions in pagan philosophy,[25] charges which had been provoked *inter alia* by Porphyry's earlier complaints of conflicts in Christianity.[26] Not for the only time in the history of philosophy (the condemnation of 219 propositions in 1277 provides another example), a perfectly crazy position (harmony) proved philosophically fruitful. To establish the harmony of Plato and Aristotle, philosophers had to think up new ideas, and the result was an amalgam different from either of the two original philosophies.

Neoplatonist school practices

The Neoplatonist commentaries increasingly come to reflect a teaching curriculum. Under Iamblichus, twelve dialogues of Plato were selected for study in a set order, culminating in the two 'theological' dialogues, the *Timaeus* and the *Parmenides*.[27] Syrianus had Proclus study Aristotle as the 'Lesser Mysteries' serving to introduce the 'Greater Mysteries' of Plato. As a very quick student, he took two years over Aristotle.[28] Proclus' pupil Ammonius and subsequent commentators make it explicit in their introductions to the *Categories* commentaries that the eventual purpose of embarking on a study of Aristotle is to be carried up to the supreme Neoplatonist God, the One.[29] This ascent to God would presumably be achieved only when the Greater Mysteries of Plato's *Timaeus* and *Parmenides* were revealed.

Much of the relevant information is found in the ten-point introductions to Aristotle's philosophy which are prefixed to *Categories* commentaries from Ammonius onwards, and which are described by Praechter in Chapter 2 and Westerink in Chapter 14 below. The ten points were already laid down, we are told, by Proclus in his *Sunanagnôsis* (reading of a text with a master).[30] One of the standard ten

[22] Plotinus e.g., 4.8.1; 5.1.8 (10-27); 5.1.9.
[23] See Dominic O'Meara, *Pythagoras Revived: mathematics and philosophy in late antiquity*, forthcoming.
[24] See Christian Guérard, 'Parménide d'Elée selon les Néoplatoniciens', forthcoming.
[25] Simplicius *in Phys*, 28,32-29,5; 640,12-18. Such thinkers as Epicurus and the Sceptics, however, were not subject to harmonisation.
[26] Probably in his lost treatise *Against the Christians*.
[27] *Anonymous Prolegomena to Platonic Philosophy*, L.G. Westerink (ed. & tr.), Amsterdam 1962, ch. 26 (new, revised edition, translated into French, Collection Budé, forthcoming).
[28] Marinus, *Life of Proclus*, ch. 13.
[29] Ammonius *in Cat*. 6,9-16.
[30] Elias *in Cat*. 107,24-6.

points is the aim of studying Aristotle, ascent to God, an idea still found in Eustratius' twelfth-century commentary on the *Nicomachean Ethics* (Mercken, Chapter 18), and two others are the means to that end, which determines the canon to be studied, and what part of that canon is to be taken first. The student is to start with the logical works of Aristotle, and then move on through ethics, physics, mathematics and theology. Logic is important as the starting point, but no longer has the monopoly it enjoyed at the time of the very earliest commentaries.

One of the ten points is devoted to the qualities demanded of a commentator. It is here that a complete knowledge of Aristotle is demanded, and that Simplicius requires the commentator to track down the harmony of Plato and Aristotle in most things, while Elias complains that Iamblichus took the harmonisation too far. On the other hand, when Alexander denies that for Aristotle man's rational soul is immortal, Elias does not view that as a legitimate assertion of disharmony between Plato and Aristotle, but as opposition to his own school.[31]

Another introductory heading concerns the reason for Aristotle's obscurity of style, which Ammonius explains as designed so that 'good people may for that reason stretch their minds even more, whereas empty minds that are lost through carelessness will be chased away by the obscurity when they encounter sentences like these'.

The tenth introductory heading breaks up into six or more points about the particular treatise to follow, the *Categories*. Ammonius says that each and every treatise of Aristotle should be introduced by such a set of six points,[32] but Philoponus holds that the points should be made only where called for.[33] One of the six points concerns the authenticity of the ensuing treatise, a question which Andronicus had had to address, when he constructed the first edition of Aristotle's works.[34]

Even before the ten points on Aristotle's philosophy, Ammonius and his successors provide a commentary on Porphyry's *Isagoge* (Introduction to the *Categories*), and preface it in turn with an account of philosophy in general. The definition of philosophy as contemplation of death provides the occasion for a disquisition on suicide. Peter Brown has observed in conversation that the Greeks would have been very shocked by the Latin-speaking circle of Ambrose and Augustine, which seized on Greek philosophical texts as they became available in Latin, and read them in any order. This is the antithesis of Proclus' 'reading of a text with a master'. However, the formal scheme of the six-point introduction (along with some material from the ten points and a definition of philosophy)

---

[31] Elias *in Cat.* 123,1-7. Alexander is also accused of introducing his own doctrines into his commentaries on Aristotle by Plutarch of Athens, ap. Philoponum *in DA* 21,20-3. Another aspect of the discussion of the qualities of commentator and audience in Elias and Olympiodorus concerns the adage that Socrates or Plato are dear, but the truth is dearer. For this see L. Tarán, 'Amicus Plato, sed magis amica veritas', *Antike und Abendland* 30, 1984, 93-124.

[32] Ammonius *in Cat.* 7,7-14.   [33] Philoponus *in Cat.* 8,7-8.

[34] For a history of the study of authenticity in connexion with Aristotle's works, see Jill Kraye, *Pseudo-Aristotelian Studies*, London, forthcoming.

was eventually passed on to the Latin world in the sixth century by
Boethius in his commentaries on Aristotle's logical works (Shiel, Chapter
15). And the influence of Boethius' introduction on twelfth-century Latin
texts has been detected in fields as far apart as Rhetoric, Grammar,
Literature, Medicine, Law and Theology.[35] It is an irony that the
Neoplatonists lavished so much attention on the written text, when Plato
preferred the spoken word on the mistaken ground that you cannot ask a
text questions.

I. Hadot has argued, contrary to the suspicions voiced by Praechter,
that a formalised set of six points can be traced back as far as the
Christian theologian Origen in the third century AD in his Commentary
on the *Song of Songs*.[36] The points correspond to various items in the
ten-point and six-point scheme of Alexandrian Neoplatonism. In fact, a
number of the points are discussed in the earliest *Categories*
commentaries, as also are the question of the order of the categories, and
whether they apply to the intelligible world of Ideas (Gottschalk,
Chapter 3). Earlier than that again, we find the tendency to harmonise
the various schools in the work of the Platonist Antiochus (died c. 67 BC).
But, as Saffrey points out in Chapter 8, harmony was easier to maintain
before Andronicus' edition, when Aristotle was known chiefly by his early
dialogue works, written while he was still a member of Plato's Academy. ·

School practices are revealed not only in the introductions to
commentaries, but also in the use of the expression 'from the voice of'.
Nearly all of Ammonius' commentaries are described in the manuscripts
as being 'from the voice of' or 'from the seminars of' Ammonius. In other
words, they are Ammonius' lectures written up as commentaries by his
students.[37] Sometimes the name of the student, Ascelpius or Philoponus,
is supplied, and in three of the four cases where Philoponus is mentioned,
we are warned that he has added 'some reflections of his own',[38] so that it
becomes much harder to decide what belongs to Ammonius. The tradition
of encouraging students to write up one's lectures and comments is found
as early as Plutarch of Athens and Syrianus. Plutarch read the *Phaedo*
with Proclus, encouraging him to take notes, so that there might
eventually be a commentary by Proclus on the *Phaedo*, while Proclus'
Timaeus commentary represents his record of Syrianus' teaching, along
with his own critical remarks.[39]

[35] A.J. Minnis, *Medieval Theories of Authorship*, London 1984, citing R.W. Hunt,
'Introductions to the *Artes* in the twelfth century', *Studia Mediaevalia*, Festschrift for R.J.
Martin, Bruges 1948, 85-112; E.A. Quain, 'The medieval accessus ad auctores', *Traditio* 3,
1945, 243-56. Praechter (Chapter 2) finds Boethius' influence as late as the sixteenth century.

[36] I. Hadot, 'Les introductions aux commentaires exégétiques chez les auteurs
néoplatoniciens et les auteurs chrétiens', in M. Tardieu (ed.), *Les régles de l'interpretation*,
Paris 1987.

[37] The classic article on this is M. Richard, '*Apo phônês*', *Byzantion* 20, 1950, 191-222
(unpublished English translation by Victor Caston), although the explanation is already
given by Praechter in Chapter 2.

[38] The four commentaries are *in An. Pr., in An. Post., in DA, in GC*. The last three warn of
Philoponus' additions.

[39] Marinus, *Life of Proclus*, chs 12 and 13.

Relations between teacher and pupil were close in other ways. The philosophical chairs in Athens and Alexandria were latterly passed from teacher to pupil. Plutarch of Athens taught Syrianus (his successor) and Proclus. Syrianus taught his own successor Proclus and Hermeias who took the chair at Alexandria. Proclus taught Hermeias' successor, Ammonius, while Ammonius taught Damascius, who held the chair at Athens, and Olympiodorus, an indirect successor of his own, as well as the two non-chair-holders, Philoponus and Simplicius. These ties were in some cases cemented by family connexions. Hermeias married a relative of Syrianus, originally intended for Proclus, while Ammonius was Hermeias' son.

The *Physics* commentary of Philoponus is not described as being 'from the seminars of Ammonius', but, according to Verrycken in Chapter 11, it incorporates an early redaction heavily influenced by Ammonius. É. Évrard has shown that it already exemplifies the custom of double discussion later systematised in Olympiodorus, Elias, David and Stephanus, and the same can be said of Philoponus' *de Anima* commentary, which is described as being from the seminars of Ammonius with the addition of personal reflections by Philoponus.[40] Here, indeed, we even have a technical name for the first of the two discussions: *protheôria* – a preliminary general discussion of doctrine (424, 4 and 13). The institution of a general discussion gives the inventive Philoponus a grand opportunity to introduce his own ideas. The general discussion is followed by a textual discussion (called by later commentators *exêgêsis tês lexeôs*) of the same portion of Aristotle. Unlike the medieval Latin question commentaries and literal commentaries,[41] the two discussions in the Greek tradition are intended for the same audience. Of the two discussions the general one is preceded by a single lemma or quotation from Aristotle, while the textual discussion may have several lemmata, which are sometimes wrongly printed in the *CAG* edition, as if they were part of the discussion. Readers of these commentaries should be alerted to look up both discussions, in order to discover Philoponus' full view, as well as consulting such major digressions as the corollaries on place and vacuum, which interrupt the *Physics* commentary.

Évrard finds that the commentary is divided into portions which would take about an hour each to deliver, regardless of whether that splits up or bundles together the topics which Aristotle is discussing. These hour-long portions must correspond to a single lecture or lesson (later called a *praxis*). If Praechter (in Chapter 2) finds less evidence of hour-long portions in commentaries by some later authors, it may be that they have

[40] Philoponus' general discussion of touch, for example, runs from *in DA* 407,18 to 422,10 (although the editor, Hayduck, does not put a proper break here), the exegesis of text from 422,11 to 436,33. For the *Physics* commentary, see E. Evrard, *L'école d'Olympiodore et la composition du 'commentaire à la physique' de Jean Philopon*, Diss., Liège 1957.

[41] On these see Anthony Kenny and Jan Pinborg, 'Medieval philosophical literature', in Norman Kretzmann, Anthony Kenny, Jan Pinborg (eds), *The Cambridge History of Later Medieval Philosophy*, Cambridge 1982, 11-42.

been written up in a way that disguises the lecture presentation more fully. As Praechter noted elsewhere,[42] the commentaries of Simplicius do not exhibit the lecturing structure, and this, along with his references to readers, rather than to an audience, has suggested that he was writing outside of a classroom context.

An idea of the *topography* of a school may be gained from the excavation by Jean and Janine Balty at Apamea, which literary evidence favours as the city where Iamblichus taught,[43] with Dexippus among his pupils. The Baltys have suggested that the beautiful mosaic of Socrates marked the site of the school and was installed by the Emperor Julian, thirty-five years after Iamblichus' death and after the dispersal of his best associates.[44] If this is right, I would suggest that the mosaic found next to it[45] represents rhetoric, rather than philosophy, classes (see illustration). It shows Persuasion (*Peithô*) and Judgment (*Krisis*) awarding a beauty contest to Cassiopeia, who is disrobing to display a comely body that does not immediately suggest the spiritual philosophy of Iamblichus. In the conventional story, Cassiopeia was disqualified, and it was a standard part of a rhetorical student's training to be given a theme from mythology and told to argue that the verdict should have gone the other way. The total area of mosaic seems too vast for the needs of a philosophy school alone, and rhetoric classes might well go on side by side with philosophy classes. Charlotte Roueché has drawn my attention to a later analogue in fifth-century Alexandria. There we learn that, although lecturers often taught in their homes on Fridays, a philosophy class could be going on in the central school within earshot of a philology

[42] Karl Praechter, 'Simplikios', *RE* 3A, 1 (2nd series) 1927, cols 204-13.

[43] See, for example, John Dillon, 'Iamblichus of Chalcis (c. 240 – 325 A.D.)', in Wolfgang Haase (ed.) *Aufstieg und Niedergang der römanischen Welt*, II 36.2, Berlin 1987, 862-909, at 869-70.

[44] Jean-Charles Balty, 'Julian et Apameé, aspects de la restauration de l'Hellénisme et de la politique antichrétienne de l'empéreur', *Dialogues d'histoire ancienne*, 1974, 267-304; Janine et Jean-Charles Balty, 'Un programme philosophique sous la cathédral d'Apameé; l'ensemble néoplatonicien de l'empéreur Julien', in *Texte et Image, Actes du colloque international de Chantilly (13-15 Octobre 1982)*, Paris 167-76. I am deeply indebted to the Baltys for their hospitality at the site.

[45] The mosaics are also displayed consecutively in the museum at Apamea.

class.[46] At Alexandria, someone like Philoponus would be likely to teach both philosophy and philology, though holding a chair only in the latter. Similarly at Apamea, Iamblichus and his associates might well have helped in the rhetoric teaching. Iamblichus himself wrote a rhetorical work, as did two of his associates. For the general student, rhetoric would have been the more vocational and popular course, but it was also considered a necessary complement to philosophical studies, since even in those days the philosopher's powers of expression left room for improvement.[47]

If the connexion with rhetoric is made out, this will bear on the survival of the school at Apamea. A larger institution involving rhetoric as well as philosophy would have been better able to survive the persecution of pagan philosophers under the Christian Emperor Constantine. Those teachers who stayed, even the rhetoricians, could, some of them, have been used to teaching philosophy. Hence at the time of Julian's munificence, philosophy classes would either have been continuing, or at least revivable. And Julian will have had more incentive to install the mosaics, if he was not merely in the position of honouring the memory of his favourite philosopher, the pagan Iamblichus, but attempting to restore to an ongoing school its former prestige in philosophy, as part of his short-lived drive to restore paganism.

I do not think we have to suppose that philosophy teaching at Apamea was even interrupted, although the standard view is that Aedesius moved Iamblichus' school to Pergamum at a time of repression under the Christian Emperor Constantine and his successors.[48] In fact, Eunapius says less than this. He mentions the well-known suppression of pagan temples and disapproval of the philosopers' rites,[49] and he says that Iamblichus' former pupils were dispersed all over the Empire.[50] But he does not say that the dispersal was due to repression, and he may intend it rather as a sign of the school's influence. As for Aedesius, he says that he inherited Iamblichus' school, that out of conviction he turned to the holier life of a goatherd or cowherd, apparently in Cappadocia, and that he was persuaded to return to philosophy, after which he set up a chair in Pergamum.[51] This is not to say that he moved Iamblichus' school there. He may have left it functioning when he took up the life of a herdsman.

The commentators and Christianity

The story of Iamblichus' school is, however, interesting as a phase in the long history of interaction between the Neoplatonist commentators and

[46] Zacharias, *Life of Severus*, p. 23.

[47] See I. Hadot in Chapter 12, 300-1, and further references there. Iamblichus' rhetorical work is recorded in Syrianus, *in Hermogenem*, I, 9, 10ff.

[48] e.g. John Dillon, op. cit., 871.

[49] Eunapius, *Lives of the Sophists*, 461; 471; 472 (Wrights' Loeb translation is bound with Polystratus).

[50] Eunapius 461; 462.

[51] Eunapius 461; 464-5; 469.

Christianity. To see the sun rise behind the colonnades at Apamea is to be reminded of Iamblichus' insistence on performing the traditional animal sacrifices. Eunapius portrayed him sacrificing at dawn in one of his suburban villas, accompanied by his associates who had urged him to admit them to his private rites.[52] In sacrificing animals, he was going not only against the Christian Church, which reaffirmed its opposition to animal sacrifice at the Council of Nicaea in 325 AD, the probable year of his death, but also against his own pagan teacher Porphyry. For Porphyry had written a whole book against the sacrifice and eating of animals.[53] On the other hand Porphyry's attack on animal sacrifice, congenial as it would have been to Augustine,[54] does not show him to be a friend of the Christians. On the contrary, his onslaught on them in *Against the Christians*, and still more in *Philosophy from Oracles*, was considered the most formidable assault from the side of pagan Greek thought in the whole of antiquity. His books were burnt both by Constantine and, a hundred years later, by Theodosius, and he was answered by many of the main Christian theologians, including Augustine. Augustine's own conversion to Christianity was as much a conversion to Neoplatonism. He describes in *Confessions* VII 9 the revelation provided by some 'books of the Platonists' which he obtained in Latin translation, and for a long time he saw no obvious difference between Neoplatonism and Christianity. But in the *City of God*, which began to appear in 413, he is aware that there is much in Porphyry with which he must disagree, even if he concurs with Porphyry on other points, including, apparently, the right attitude to sacrifice.

Later in the century, the Neoplatonist commentator Proclus had to leave Athens for a year, to avoid persecution at the hands of Christians for impiety.[55] He followed Iamblichus[56] in seeing theurgic practice as the route to mystical union with the gods. He could not foresee that within 25 years of his death pseudo-Dionysius would appropriate his ideas for

---

[52] Eunapius 458-9.

[53] Porphyry, *On Abstinence from Animal Food* (English translation by Thomas Taylor). Iamblichus on the other side claims Pythagoras' support for the view that human souls do not transmigrate into the bodies of sacrificial animals, so that these can be killed and eaten (Iamblichus, *Life of Pythagoras*, ch. 18, 85). Indeed, he denies that human souls transmigrate into any animals at all (Aeneas of Gaza, *Theophrastus*, PG 85, 893A-B; Nemesius *Nat. Hom.* 51, p. 117 Matthaei). But whether this too contradicts Porphyry depends on one's interpretation of Porphyry (see W. Deuse, *Untersuchungen zur mittelplatonischen und neoplatonischen Seelenlehre*, Mainz, Wiesbaden 1983, 129-167, and the briefer overview in Andrew Smith, 'Porphyrian Studies since 1913', in *Aufstieg und Niedergang*, as above, II, 36.2, 717-73, at 725-7, with further literature cited there).

[54] Porphyry's preference for a spiritual sacrifice (*Abst.* 2.61) fits perfectly with Augustine's quotation from Psalms 51,18 (*City* 10,4-6). On vegetarianism, however (*City* 1,20), Augustine seems to reflect the arguments which Porphyry ascribes to his opponents (*Abst.* 1.6; 1.18), despite doubts that have been expressed about his knowledge of this particular treatise of Porphyry (see P. Courcelle, *Late Latin Writers and their Greek Sources*, Cambridge Mass. 1969, p. 188, n.177, translated from *Les lettres grecques en Occident*, Paris 1948).

[55] Marinus, *Life of Proclus*, 15.

[56] e.g. Iamblichus *de Mysteriis* 2.11.

Christianity and even apply his word 'theurgy' to the Christian sacraments.[57] Proclus' writings do not appear to contain many remarks on the Christians, but Alan Cameron has drawn attention to the use among later Neoplatonists of coded references to Christian domination,[58] and, exploiting these, Saffrey has enlarged the count of barbed references to the Christians in Proclus.[59] One style of reference, 'the prevailing circumstances', will be encountered below.

Coded references are subsequently used by Damascius, the last head of the Neoplatonist school in Athens. He recounts with pride the story of Proclus' contemporary Hierocles of Alexandria, who ran up against 'those in power' in Constantinople, spattered with his own blood the (Christian) magistrate who had him beaten, and called him a Cyclops.[60] Damascius further complains bitterly that the Neoplatonist professor in Alexandria, Ammonius, had come to some discreditable agreement with the bishop in charge of 'the prevailing opinion' in the 490s for financial reasons.[61] It has proved difficult to discover what the concession was. Westerink (in Chapter 14) rejects the suggestion that Ammonius agreed to stop teaching Plato, while his own suggestion that Ammonius agreed to be silent on the pagan belief in the eternity and divinity of the world is discarded by Verrycken (in Chapter 10). But I think there is no need to assume that the concession bore on Ammonius' teaching. It might have involved an agreement not to parade worship of the pagan gods, and theurgic belief and practice, in the way that Ammonius' teacher Proclus had done in Athens and Iamblichus in Syria, or more simply not to make trouble with Christians, if he wanted funding.

In a seminal article, Karl Praechter argued that the Alexandrian school made concessions to Christian monotheism, abandoning the Neoplatonist distinction between a supreme God, the One, and a second God, the Intellect.[62] He further argued that this concession was already made by the earlier Alexandrian, Hierocles, in the first half of the fifth century, and that it was continued by Simplicius, whose commentary on Epictetus he took to be written in Alexandria under the supervision of Ammonius. The thesis about Simplicius and Hierocles has already been overturned by I. Hadot,[63] but its application to Ammonius is now challenged (in

---

[57] pseudo-Dionysius, *Letter* 9.1, *PG* 3, 1108A. This and many other references to Christian theurgy are cited by H.D. Saffrey, 'New objective links between the pseudo-Dionysius and Proclus', in D.J. O'Meara (ed.) *Neoplatonism and Christian Thought*, Albany NY 1982, 64-74 and 246-8, at 71-2.

[58] Alan Cameron, 'The last days of the Academy at Athens', *Proceedings of the Cambridge Philological Society* n.s. 15, 1969, 7-29. Verrycken, however, points out in Chapter 11 that the same phrases were sometimes used by Christians.

[59] H.D. Saffrey, 'Allusions antichrétiennes chez Proclus le diadoque Platonicien', *Revue des sciences philosophiques et théologiques* 59, 1975, 553-63.

[60] Damascius *Life of Isidore* 83, 5-11 (Zintzen).

[61] Damascius *Life of Isidore* 250,2; 251, 12-14.

[62] Karl Praechter, 'Richtungen und Schulen im Neuplatonismus', *Genethliakon für Carl Robert*, Berlin 1910.

[63] I. Hadot, *Le problème du néoplatonisme Alexandrin: Hiéroclès et Simplicius*, Paris 1978.

Chapter 10) by Verrycken. Ammonius openly recognises the pagan distinction between the One and the Intellect. He even ascribes such a distinction to Aristotle, although both divinities, so Verrycken suggests, may be contained within Aristotle's idea of the unmoved mover.

Ammonius' pupil Philoponus was a Christian, and his view that the physical world, including prime matter itself, had a beginning was a distinctively Christian one. Residing in Alexandria, he eventually worked out a comprehensive alternative to Aristotelian physics, a scientific world view tailored to cohere with his Christian beliefs.[64] What Verrycken argues in Chapter 11, however, is that these ideas involve a complete volte-face on Philoponus' part. Though a Christian from the start, he was content at first to reproduce in his commentaries the ideas of Ammonius. We can see him changing his mind on the eternity of the world, on Aristotle's arguments about the need for an infinite force, on the definition of place, on the impossibility of a vacuum, on the necessity for a fifth element to constitute the rotating heavens and on the harmony of Plato and Aristotle. Verrycken further conjectures that these changes came fairly late in Philoponus' career, starting with the treatise *Against Proclus on the Eternity of the World* in 529. Thereafter the commentaries on the *Posterior Analytics*, the *Physics* and probably the *Meteorology* were revised. At any rate, they all contain expressions of the later view, but, in the first two cases at least, these are found alongside unrevised expressions of the earlier view.

Verrycken's case for a volte-face and for a revision of at least two commentaries is impressively documented. I believe the *de Anima* commentary may also prove to contain a later stratum, if there is a reference to the Christian Creator at 330,24, to earlier lectures on the *Meteorology* at 339,35 and to the *Categories* commentary at 391,32.[65] Whether or not the change began in 529, that year was certainly a significant one. Not only did Philoponus publish his onslaught on Proclus, the greatest of the Athenian Neoplatonists, in defence of the Christian view, attacked by Proclus, that the physical universe had a beginning, but 529 was the year in which the Christian Emperor Justinian finally closed the pagan Neoplatonist school in Athens. Damascius, the head, along with Simplicius, Priscian and four others, left shortly afterwards for the court of Khosroes in Ctesiphon, in present-day Iraq, and archaeological evidence, admittedly conjectural, has been offered to suggest that they did not return. At any rate, if the house excavated in Athens is really the one handed down by Plutarch of Athens to his Neoplatonist successors, the

[64] Richard Sorabji, 'John Philoponus', in id. (ed.), *Philoponus and the Rejection of Aristotelian Science*, London and Ithaca NY 1987.

[65] Henry J. Blumenthal, however, following Koenraad Verrycken, takes it to be wholly early in 'Simplicius and others on Aristotle's discussions of reason', in *Gonimos, Neoplatonic Studies Presented to Lendeert G. Westerink at 75, Arethusa*, Buffalo NY 1988, 103-19.

statues carefully placed down a well were never recovered by them.[66]

No wonder Simplicius, who was one of the seven philosophers, employs such bitter invective in his attacks on Philoponus.[67] He sees Christianity and Philoponus its representative as thoroughly irreverent. They deny the divinity of the heavens, and glorify the things of the body above the things of the mind by the revolting habit of preserving the relics of martyrs. His own commentaries, in contrast to the sober and argumentative tone of the Christian Philoponus, culminate in devout prayers.

In Alexandria, unlike Athens, Neoplatonist teaching continued with little disturbance for the rest of the sixth century. Westerink describes in Chapter 14 the open way in which the pagan professor Olympiodorus addresses the Christian pupils in his class. When he speaks of guardian spirits or demons, they are to think of angels, or of conscience. This he describes, using a code word, as an interpretation adapted to 'the prevailing circumstances'. Olympiodorus was the last of the pagan commentators in Alexandria. The next commentators, Elias, David, pseudo-Elias and Stephanus were all Christians. But, as Westerink shows, though using the traditional format and formulae, they did not address themselves in Olympiodorus' explicit way to the relation between pagan and Christian belief.[68]

The most important remaining example of interaction with Christianity concerns the Christian Boethius, who wrote in Latin at the beginning of the sixth century, and passed the commentary tradition on to the Latin-speaking world. Like the early Augustine, he writes as if there were no difference between Christianity and Neoplatonism. Some of his treatises are works of Christian theology, while his commentaries on Aristotle's logic are works of Neoplatonism. In his *Consolation of Philosophy*, paganism and Christianity are combined. The *Consolation* has indeed been viewed as a pagan work, on the grounds that it makes the world eternal. But quite apart from the fact that some Christians accepted this view, I think that Boethius merely described the eternity of the world as a hypothesis of Plato and Aristotle.[69]

In this survey of the relations between the Neoplatonist commentators and Christianity, we have found a wide spectrum and even a progression of attitudes. There is Porphyry's offensive against Christianity, the commitment of Iamblichus in Syria and Proclus in Athens to pagan ritual

---

[66] Alison Frantz, 'Pagan philosophers in Christian Athens', *Proceedings of the American Philosophical Society* 119, 1975, 29-38. The identification is, however, conjectural, and it had been doubted that the scratch marks defacing the floor represent crosses superimposed by Christian occupiers.

[67] Philippe Hoffmann, 'Simplicius' polemics', in Richard Sorabji (ed.), *Philoponus and the Rejection of Aristotelian Science*, London and Ithaca NY 1987, 57-83.

[68] I am not persuaded by the examples of 'Christianising' in David offered by Haig Khatchadourian and A.K. Sanjian, which pertain to ethics and at *Prolegomena* 115,12-13 (cf. 129,8-10) to the Creation of man. See the interesting discussion in A.K. Sanjian (ed.), *David Anhaght', the 'Invincible' Philosopher*, Atlanta 1986, 55 and 109.

[69] Richard Sorabji, *Time, Creation and the Continuum*, London and Ithaca NY 1983, 196.

under increasing pressure, the vehemence of Damascius and the bitterness of Simplicius when the Athenian school was closed. We have seen the Christian counter-attack by Philoponus in Alexandria and the pacific agreement to differ of the Alexandrians Ammonius and Olympiodorus. Finally there was the undramatic absorption of the Alexandrian chair by Christian professors. The Latin-speaking Christian Boethius stands aside from this progression, since he was one of those who saw Neoplationism as one with Christianity and helped it to penetrate deep into Christian sensibility.

Dangers in reading the commentators

Evidently, the theological motive of the Neoplatonist curriculum and the pressure to harmonise Plato with Aristotle creates dangers, if the commentaries are read as straightforward guides to Aristotle, without due allowance being made. Nor is it safe to extract from them the fragments of the Presocratics, or of other authors, without taking account of the Neoplatonist background against which the fragments were originally selected for discussion. For different reasons, analogous caveats apply to fragments preserved by the pre-Neoplatonist commentator Alexander.[70] Henry Blumenthal warns in Chapter 14 of the amount of Neoplatonist doctrine to be found in the *de Anima* commentaries, and shows that Anglo-Saxon scholars have often been unaware of the Neoplatonist bias. The opposite danger, exemplified by Cousin and Ravaisson, is accepting the harmony of Plato and Aristotle as literal truth.

The distorting Neoplatonist context, however, does not prevent the commentaries from being incomparable guides to Aristotle. The commentators' introductions to Aristotle's philosophy insist that the commentator must have minutely detailed knowledge of the entire Aristotelian corpus, and this they certainly have. Moreover, commentators are enjoined neither to accept nor to reject what Aristotle says too readily, but to consider it in depth and without partiality. The commentaries draw one's attention to hundreds of phrases, sentences and ideas in Aristotle, which one could easily have passed over, however often one read him. The scholar who makes the right allowance for the distorting context will learn far more about Aristotle than he would on his own.

The *de Anima* commentaries, which Blumenthal studies, are likely to involve more distortion than logical commentaries, or than the non-theological parts of *Physics* commentaries, just because Plato had less to say on logic and physics. In fact, the Neoplatonist distortion is so much greater in the *de Anima* commentary ascribed to Simplicius than in his other commentaries that this has been given as one of several reasons

---

[70] For Alexander's treatment of the Stoics, see Robert B. Todd, *Alexander of Aphrodisias on Stoic Physics*, Leiden 1976, 24-9.

for suspecting that it may be by another author (Priscian). But this hypothesis is contested by I. Hadot in Chapter 12 below.[71]

The individual commentators

Having described some of the overall trends, I turn now to the individual commentators. Those whose commentaries we possess fall into three main groups. First there are the second- and early third-century Aristotelians, Aspasius, someone using Adrastus, Alexander of Aphrodisias, and, writing in the same tradition but at a later date, Themistius. Then there is the largest group, the commentators writing in the Neoplatonist manner, some of the later ones Christians, between 250 and about 610, when Stephanus was called from Alexandria to Constantinople. Finally, there was a revival of commentary-writing in eleventh-century Byzantium, which reached its peak in the commentaries of Eustratius and Michael of Ephesus in the twelfth century.

Some of the earliest commentary we have is on Aristotle's *Nicomachean Ethics*. Earliest of all is that of Aspasius of Athens from the first half of the second century AD, covering Books 1-4, 7 and 8. Then there is the commentary on *EN* 2-5, printed in *CAG* 20, which may derive from Adrastus of Aphrodisias.[72] Although Gottschalk[73] and in (Chapter 18) Mercken reject the hypothesis that it is actually by Adrastus, Mercken believes that it too may be as early as the second century AD. Both commentaries are described by Mercken below.

Alexander of Aphrodisias, taught among others by Aspasius' pupil Herminus, was appointed to a chair of Aristotelian philosophy some time between 198 and 209. This may have been a chair in Athens, one of the four founded for the four main philosophical schools by Marcus Aurelius (Emperor 161-180). The satirist Lucian in *The Eunuch* represents these

---

[71] The hypothesis is that of F. Bossier and C. Steel, in 'Priscianus Lydus in de "In de anima" van Pseudo(?)-Simplicius', *Tijdschrift voor Philosophie* 34, 1972, 761-822, repeated in C. Steel, *The Changing Self*, Brussels 1978. The point about the special character of *de Anima* commentaries is made by I. Hadot in the appendix to her *Le problème du néoplatonisme Alexandrin: Hiéroclès et Simplicius*, Paris 1978, where she resists all but one of the arguments of Bossier and Steel. In Chapter 12 below, she resists the remaining argument, and the conclusion as well. But one issue, not previously mentioned, on which the *de Anima* commentary may differ at least from the *Physics* commentary is whether it is qualities (*in Phys.* 623,11-18) or matter (*in DA* 134,6) by which bodies are prevented from occupying the same place. It may also be wondered how the doubt that light is a body (*in DA* 134,13-20) is to be squared with the endorsement of Plato's definition of light as a kind of fire (*in Cael.* 12,28; 16,20-1; 130,31-131,1; but cf. *in DA* 133,32; 134,6). See Richard Sorabji, *Matter, Space and Motion*, London and Ithaca NY 1988, 106-7; 108. It may also be wondered why the *de Anima* commentary at 141,15-38, does not, like Priscian *Metaphrasis* 14,10-12, credit the wave theory of sound to Theophrastus.

[72] Paul Moraux, *D'Aristote à Bessarion*, Laval Quebec 1970, 24f; *Der Aristotelismus bei den Griechen*, vol. 2, Berlin 1984, 323-30.

[73] Hans Gottschalk, in another part of the work from which Chapter 3 is a revised extract: 'Aristotelian philosophy in the Roman world from the time of Cicero to the end of the second century AD', in W. Haase (ed.), *Aufstieg und Niedergang der römischen Welt* II 36,2, 1155, n. 363, commenting on Kenny, *The Aristotelian Ethics*, Oxford 1978, 37 n. 3.

chairs as open to competition among any exponents of the relevant schools who submitted themselves to examination by a committee of first citizens.[74] In Lucian's version, a eunuch is a leading competitor. Alexander's brilliance at filling out Aristotle's ideas to obtain a coherent Aristotelian position can be illustrated from many examples. One (not from a commentary) which I have given elsewhere is his defence of Aristotle's claim that space is finite against the objection that an edge of space is conceptually problematic.[75] The need for an edge in a finite universe was not finally circumvented until the invention of Riemannian geometry in the nineteenth century.

In fourth-century Constantinople, Themistius (fl. late 340s to 384 or 385) saw himself as the inventor of paraphrase, wrongly thinking that the job of full-scale commentary was completed.[76] His paraphrases, however, contained a substantial amount of interpretation, including a whole excursus on the active intellect, and they were widely used in later times. It has been estimated that Philoponus' *Physics* commentary draws silently on Themistius 600 times,[77] and he had a great influence on Renaissance Platonism.[78]

In connexion with the Neoplatonist commentaries, we have already seen how Porphyry (232-309) put the study of Aristotle on a sure footing within Neoplatonism, insisting on the compatibility with Plato of Aristotle's categorial scheme, while his pupil Iamblichus (c. 240-c. 325) confirmed this harmonisation with his 'intellective theory' of the categories. Iamblichus' commentaries on Aristotle are lost, but a collection of surviving fragments has been made by Larsen.[79] The only pupil of Iamblichus from whom a commentary on Aristotle survives is Dexippus (c. 330: see Chapter 6).[80] His *Categories* commentary shares with Porphyry's surviving one the special characteristic of being in dialogue form.

The house used by the late Athenian Neoplatonists, claimed by Alison Frantz to be identical with the one excavated by her, was bequeathed to the school by Plutarch of Athens (died 432). No commentary of Plutarch's on Aristotle survives, but the evidence for a *de Anima* commentary is discussed by Blumenthal in Chapter 13 below. In fact, most of the

[74] Lucian's evidence is used by John P. Lynch, *Aristotle's School*, Berkeley, Los Angeles 1972, 169-73.

[75] Richard Sorabji, *Matter, Space and Motion*, London and Ithaca NY 1988, ch. 8.

[76] Themistius *in An. Post.* 1,2-12. See H.J. Blumenthal, 'Photius on Themistius (Cod. 74): did Themistius write commentaries on Aristotle?', *Hermes* 107, 1979, 168-82.

[77] H. Vitelli *CAG* 17, p. 992, s.v. Themistius.

[78] This is brought out in the articles by E.P. Mahoney, which Blumenthal discusses in Chapter 5.

[79] Bent Dalsgaard-Larsen, *Jamblique de Chalcis*, Aarhus 1972, gives fragments of the commentaries on the *Categories* and *Prior Analytics*, along with others of uncertain origin. There was also a commentary on the *de Interpretatione*, perhaps on the *de Caelo*, but probably not on the *de Anima*; see John Dillon, 'Iamblichus of Chalcis (c. 240-325 AD)', in W. Haase (ed.), *Aufstieg und Niedergang der römischen Welt* II 36.2, Berlin 1987, 862-909, at 872 and 877.

[80] The commentary is translated by John Dillon, London and Ithaca NY 1989.

Aristotle commentaries of the Athenian school are lost. This applies to the commentaries of Syrianus (died c. 437), apart from that on *Metaphysics* 3, 4, 13, 14, and to those of Proclus (c. 411-485) and of Damascius, who was head at the time of closure in 529.[81]

The Alexandrian commentators Ammonius (435/45-517/26) and Philoponus (c. 490 to 570s) have already been described. Philoponus' most scintillating arguments turn the tables on the 800-year-old Aristotelian tradition by arguing that on the Creation of the world Christianity must be right. If the physical universe had no beginning, it would already have passed through a more than finite number of years, and Aristotle declared that passing through an infinity was impossible. Moreover, the number of years traversed by next year would be greater than infinity. It would be another eight hundred years before medieval philosophy had even assembled the materials to cope with the latter point.[82]

I think that Justinian's closure of the school in Athens was effective.[83] But it has remained a mystery where Simplicius went to write his commentaries. They seem to have been composed after the brief stay of the seven Athenian philosophers at Ctesiphon came to an end, as it did by 532. In Chapter 12, I. Hadot backs the thesis which has been argued by Michel Tardieu in a series of three writings, that Simplicius went to Ḥarrân (Carrhae), in present-day Turkey near the Iraq border.[84] Some of Tardieu's best evidence is the occurrence of place-names from the region of Ḥarrân in Simplicius' commentaries, and some part of his further evidence is recorded by I. Hadot below. There is testimony preserved in Syriac of a Neoplatonist school flourishing in Ḥarrân as late as 943, and more than seventy years before that, it was from Ḥarrân that Ṭâbit b. Qurra went to found the Platonising school in Baghdad, which became the driving force behind the diffusion of Greek Philosophy in the Arabic world. If Tardieu is right, the Athenian Neoplatonist school did not after all disappear from the map of history. It survived in Ḥarrân through Simplicius, accompanied, so Tardieu has suggested orally, by Damascius and Priscian. And it was this school's teaching which Ṭâbit b. Qurra transported to Baghdad. At the same time, if all this is correct, it may still be wondered if Simplicius' role in the school will have been that of a

---

[81] For the other Aristotle commentaries of Syrianus, as known from fragments, see Loredana Cardullo, 'Syrianus' lost commentaries on Aristotle', *Bulletin of the Institute of Classical Studies* 33, 1986, 112-24. For the evidence on Proclus' Aristotle commentaries, see L.G. Westerink in Chapter 13, n. 18, for that on Damascius', L.G. Westerink, *The Greek Commentaries on Plato's Phaedo.* vol. 2, Damascius, Amsterdam 1977, 11-12.

[82] Richard Sorabji, 'Infinity and the Creation', inaugural lecture 1982, repr. in id. (ed.), *Philoponus and the Rejection of Aristotelian Science*, London and Ithaca NY 1987, 164-78.

[83] The best case against was made by Alan Cameron, 'The last days of the Academy at Athens', on which I have commented in *Time, Creation and the Continuum*, 199-200.

[84] M. Tardieu, 'Ṣâbiens coraniques et "Ṣâbiens" de Ḥarrân', *Journal Asiatique* 274, 1986; id., 'Les Calendriers en usage à Ḥarrân d'après les sources arabes et le commentaire de Simplicius à la *Physique* d'Aristote', in I. Hadot (ed.), *Simplicius – sa vie, son oeuvre, sa survie*, Berlin 1987; id. *Coutumes nautiques mésopotamiennes chez Simplicius* in preparation.

teacher, given the absence of signs of a teaching context in his commentaries.

The continuation of the commentary tradition in Alexandria by Olympiodorus (495/505-after 565), Elias, David, pseudo-Elias and Stephanus is described by Westerink in Chapter 14. To the commentaries which he surveys, L. Tarán has added an edition of an anonymous commentary from this period on the *de Interpretatione*.[85] Stephanus was called to a chair in Constantinople in 610 or soon after, and this is usually considered as marking the end of the Alexandrian school. In a forthcoming article, however,[86] Mossman Roueché argues that pseudo-Elias and David may have followed Olympiodorus rather than preceding him. Although pseudo-Elias was at one time writing outside Alexandria, probably in Constantinople,[87] he could subsequently have moved to Alexandria, and the Alexandrian school could have continued into the period of the Arab capture of the city in 640. Such a time scale would be facilitated by Westerink's new refusal below to date Elias' activity as early as 541.

Much more important than the work of the last Alexandrians was the slightly earlier activity of Boethius in Rome, who sought to make Aristotle accessible to the Latin-speaking world. He announced a plan in his second commentary on the *de Interpretatione* for translating all the Aristotle he could lay hands on and Plato into Latin, with commentary.[88] He got as far as translating all or nearly all of Aristotle's logical works, equipping some logical works and the *Physics* with selective scholia or full commentaries and writing monographs on the syllogism covering the *de Interpretatione* and *Prior Analytics*. But then he was executed, on a charge which he denied, at about the age of 44 or 45 in 525 or 526. His *Consolation of Philosophy* is a reflection written in prison, while awaiting execution, on whether life is governed by fate, chance, or providence. Its poignancy was to inspire English translations or paraphrases by King Alfred, Chaucer and Queen Elizabeth I.

As Ebbesen explains in Chapter 16, some commentary had been available in Latin before Boethius. There had in the fourth century AD been an earlier Latin adaptation of the *Isagoge* and commentary on the *Categories* by Marius Victorinus, a paraphrase of the *Categories* (*Decem Categoriae*) and Latin translations by Praetextatus of Themistius' paraphrases of the *Prior* and *Posterior Analytics*.[89] Still earlier, in the second century, Apuleius wrote a Latin exposition of the *de Interpretatione*.[90] But it was predominantly Boethius who handed on the commentary tradition

---

[85] L. Tarán (ed.), *Anonymous Commentary on Aristotle's De Interpretatione (Codex Parisinus Graecus 2064)*, Meisenheim am Glan, 1978.

[86] Mossman Roueché, 'The definitions of Philosophy and a new fragment of Stephanus of Alexandria'.

[87] L.G. Westerink, *Pseudo-Elias (Pseudo-David), Lectures on Porphyry's Isagoge*, Amsterdam 1967.

[88] Boethius *in Int.*[2] (Meiser), 79,9-80,1.

[89] See P. Hadot, *Marius Victorinus*, Paris 1971.

[90] See J. Isaac, *Le Peri Hermeneias en occident de Boèce à saint Thomas*, Paris 1953; M.W. Sullivan, *Apuleian Logic*, Amsterdam 1967.

to the Latin world from the sixth to the twelfth century. Not only does he preserve six standard points in his introduction to the first commentary on the *Isagoge* and to the *Categories* commentary,[91] he also gives in his *Isagoge* commentaries a definition and division of philosophy,[92] and describes the eventual goal of philosophical study as contemplation of God,[93] while in his second commentary on the *de Interpretatione*, he expresses the intention of demonstrating the harmony of Plato and Aristotle.[94] He views Aristotle's *Categories* as only an introduction for beginners, the heights of philosophy being reserved by Aristotle for his *Metaphysics*.[95] Although only one *Categories* commentary exists, Boethius planned a second one, to show the higher meaning of the *Categories*. It was to draw on Pythagorean science, he says, and so presumably would have followed the model of Iamblichus' 'intellective theory'.[96] A reconstruction of the projected commentary is offered by Ebbesen in Chapter 16. Boethius' other extant Aristotelian commentaries do in fact come in pairs. There are two on Porphyry's *Isagoge* and two on Aristotle's *de Interpretatione*. In each case, the first commentary is the more elementary. These commentaries between them cover the syllabus which in the Latin West came to be called the Logica Vetus, or Old Logic.

The late Alexandrian commentaries and prolegomena of Elias, David and Stephanus were read in the Byzantine world for some centuries after c.610, when Stephanus left Alexandria for Constantinople, and the results are evident in various compendia.[97] But the tradition of Greek commentary writing was revived in that world only in the eleventh century. Of more than a dozen late Byzantine commentators described in Hunger's *Byzantinisches Handbuch*, the *CAG* has edited only three.[98] Of these by far the most important are Eustratius (1050/1060-c. 1120) and Michael of Ephesus. Robert Browning has transformed understanding (Chapter 17) by redating Michael and showing that both commentators

---

[91] Boethius *in Isag.*[1] I. 1, 4,17-5,10 (Schepss-Brandt); *in Cat. PL* 64, 161A-162A; most of the points are also found in *in Int.*[2] (Meiser), 1-13.

[92] Definition, Boethius *in Isag.*[1] I. 3, 7,11-16; division, *in Isag.* [1] I. 3, 7, 11-12, 9; *in Isag.*[2] I. 1-3, 135,5-143,7.

[93] *in Isag.*[1] I. 3, 8,6-19.

[94] Boethius *in Int.*[2] (Meiser), 80,1-6.

[95] Boethius *in Cat. PL* 64, 252 B-C.

[96] Boethius *in Cat. PL* 64, 160A-B.

[97] See Mossman Roueché, 'Byzantine philosophical texts of the seventh century', *Jahrbuch der Österreichischen Byzantinistik* 23, 1974, 61-76; 'A middle Byzantine handbook of logical terminology', ibid. 29, 1980, 71-98.

[98] Besides Eustratius and Michael, Sophonias is included from the thirteenth century. H. Hunger's survey is in *Die hochsprachliche profane Literatur der Byzantiner*, vol. 1 (=*Byzantinisches Handbuch*, part 5, vol.1), Munich 1978, 25-41. He does not include the paraphrase commentary unreliably attributed to the otherwise unknown Heliodorus of Prusa (*CAG* 19.2) of which all we can say is that it must antedate 1366 (see R.A. Gauthier in R.A. Gauthier and J.Y. Jolif, *Aristote, L'ethique à Nicomaque* 2, Paris 1970, introduction 106-7).

belonged to a circle organised by the Princess Anna Comnena in twelfth-century Byzantium. Accordingly the completion of Michael's commentaries should be put at 1138 or later instead of 1040. Sten Ebbesen's study of Michael's commentary on the *Sophistici Elenchi* shows him 'vacuuming' earlier scholia, amending them and stitching them skilfully together, to make one recension after another, the earliest being perhaps for a class attended by Anna herself. At the end of the process Ebbesen finds no personal slant imposed by Michael himself.[99] On the other hand, in his commentaries on the animal works and on the *Politics*, one would conjecture that he had fewer scholia to rely on.[100] In every case, his concern (Mercken, Chapter 18) is simply to expound Aristotle. Eustratius, by contrast, is distinctive for his defence of Christianity and of Platonism along with his penchant for syllogisms, all described by Mercken.

Michael's commentaries seem designed partly to cover areas where gaps had been left, and this may have been at Anna's direction. Not all of the gap-fillers are extant, but we have commentaries on the great corpus of biological works (*Parts of Animals, Motion of Animals, Progression of Animals, Generation of Animals, Parva Naturalia*)[101] and a small fragment of one on the *Politics*. The lost *Rhetoric* commentary had a few antecedents, but the *Rhetoric* too had been comparatively neglected.[102] It was probably in this circle that a composite commentary was constructed on the *Nichomachean Ethics* (*CAG* 19.1, pp. 158-86; *CAG* 20; *CAG* 22.3), using Eustratius for Book 1, the second-century derivative of Adrastus for Books 2 to 5, Eustratius for 6, Aspasius for 8, Michael for 9, 10 and a further commentary on 5, and a makeshift for the remaining Book 7 (Mercken, Chapter 18, Ebbesen, Chapter 19).[103] There is controversy over Praechter's view that Michael also supplied the pseudo-Alexandrian commentary on *Metaphysics* 6-14, which completes Alexander's own

---

[99] Sten Ebbesen, *Commentators and Commentaries on Aristotle's Sophistici Elenchi, Corpus Latinum Commentariorum in Aristotelem Graecorum* 7.1 (*CLCAG*), 268-85.

[100] For the biological commentaries in general, see the introduction to A. Preus, *Aristotle and Michael of Ephesus on the Movement and Progression of Animals*, Hildesheim 1981.

[101] For the *Parva Naturalia*, there is a commentary on its first treatise, the *de Sensu*, extant by Alexander. The paraphrase in Arabic of Aristotle's *History, Generation* and *Parts of Animals*, which A. Badawi has translated into French and identified as a translation of Themistius, may, according to others, be merely an Arabic summary of the Arabic translation of those three works of Aristotle. See A. Badawi, *Commentaires sur Aristote perdus en grec et autres epîtres*, Beirut 1971, and the review of it by F.W. Zimmermann and H.V.B. Brown, 'Neue arabischen Übersetzungen aus dem Bereich der spätantiken griechischen Philosophie', *Der Islam* 50, 1973, 313-24, at 323-4.

[102] See C.A. Brandis, 'Über Aristoteles' Rhetorik und die griechischen Ausleger derselben', *Philologus*, 1849, 34ff., and other references given by Gottschalk in Chapter 3, n.67.

[103] Ebbesen sees Michael as a likely compiler, Mercken thinks this quite possible.

commentary on 1-5, although Ebbesen tells me that he still[104] agrees with Praechter, as does Mercken in Chapter 18.

About this same time (1130), James of Venice went to Byzantium, perhaps visiting Michael, as Browning suggests and Ebbesen agrees (Chapters 17 and 19), and thereafter translated into Latin a commentary derived from Philoponus on the *Posterior Analytics*, and scholia on the *Topics* and *Sophistici Elenchi*, as well as writing his own commentaries on the *Sophistici Elenchi* and *Posterior Analytics*. In the same century, Gerard of Cremona (died 1187) translated Greek commentaries from the Arabic versions: Themistius on the *Posterior Analytics*, Alexander on the *de Sensu*, as well as Alexander's treatises *On the Intellect* (= *Mantissa* 106-113) and *On Time*. In the next century, the thirteenth, translations from both Greek and Arabic became a flood, and the Latin world was no longer confined to Boethius' repertoire. Grosseteste and William of Moerbeke both translated from the Greek, while from the Arabic side, translations were made not only of Greek commentaries but also of works influenced by the Greek commentaries, including commentaries on Aristotle by Averroes in the thirteenth century, and non-commentary works by Avicenna and Ghazali in the twelfth.[105]

This volume

Six of the chapters in this volume are new (1, 4, 10, 11, 19 and 20). Four are translated for the first time from French or German (2, 6, 8; 12). Six are substantially revised (3, 5, 9, 14, 15, 18). Others are revised in more minor ways, except that in all Greek and Latin quotations have been translated, and where these quotations formed a substantial part of the original (15, 17), the change is significant. After my introductory Chapter 1, I have included a translation of Praechter's monumental review of *CAG* (Chapter 2), which anticipated in outline much of the scholarly research

---

[104] The similarities to Syrianus (died c. 437) have suggested to some that it predates Syrianus (most recently Leonardo Tarán, review of Paul Moraux, *Der Aristotelismus*, vol. 1, in *Gnomon* 46, 1981, 721-50 at 750), to others that it draws on him (most recently P. Thillet, in the Budé edition of Alexander *de Fato*, p. lvii). Praechter ascribed it to Michael of Ephesus in his review of *CAG* 22.2 in *Göttingische Gelehrte Anzeigen* 168, 1906, 861-907. For Ebbesen, see *Commentators and Commentaries on Aristotle's Sophistici Elenchi* (= *CLCAG*, vol. 7), part 3, p. 87.

[105] For Grosseteste, see Mercken, Chapter 18. For Moerbeke, see P. Thillet, *Alexandre d'Aphrodise de Fato ad Imperatores, version de Guillaume de Moerbeke*, Paris 1963, with bibliography. For James of Venice, see Ebbesen, Chapter 19, and L. Minio-Paluello, 'Jacobus Veneticus Grecus', *Traditio* 8, 1952, 265-304; id., 'Giacomo Veneto e l'Aristotelismo Latino', in Pertusi (ed.), *Venezia e l'Oriente fra tardo Medioevo e Rinascimento*, Florence 1966, 53-74, both reprinted in his *Opuscula*, 1972. For Gerard of Cremona, see M. Steinschneider, *Die europäischen Übersetzungen aus dem arabischen bis Mitte des 17 Jahrhunderts* (repr. Graz 1956); E. Gilson, *History of Christian Philosophy in the Middle Ages*, London 1955, 235-6 and more generally 181-246. For the translators in general, see Bernard G. Dod, 'Aristoteles Latinus', in N. Kretzmann, A. Kenny, J. Pinborg (eds), *The Cambridge History of Later Medieval Philosophy*, Cambridge 1982. Note that in translating Islamic dates based on Hegira, it is necessary to take account of the Muslim year being shorter by 10 or 11 days.

that has been conducted since. In Chapter 3, Gottschalk has added some new reflections on Stoic categories to his work on the beginning of of the commentary tradition. Sharples in Chapter 4 explores the little-known persona of Alexander, and considers to what extent his commentaries and *Quaestiones* may reflect his teaching practices. Blumenthal has revised his presentation of Themistius as the last of the Aristotelians, to take account of Mahoney's evidence of a rival Neoplatonist influence on him. P. Hadot's Chapter 6 on Porphyry and Dexippus represents one of the most important treatments of the harmony of Plato and Aristotle. In Chapter 7, Ebbesen attempts a reconstruction of Porphyry's semantics and his theory of concept formation. In Chapters 8 and 9, Saffrey and Sorabji take the question of the harmony of Plato and Aristotle from Syrianus and Proclus, who were still partly sceptical, on to Ammonius who extended harmonisation to Aristotle's theology, and handed down the idea of Aristotle's God as a Platonic Creator through the Arabs to the thirteenth-century West. Verrycken presents an entirely new view of Ammonius and Philoponus in Alexandria (Chapters 10 and 11), conceding to Praechter only that Ammonius simplified Neoplatonist theology, by cutting out the henads and triads of his teacher Proclus. I. Hadot provides a comprehensive account of Simplicius in Chapter 12, and establishes his Aristotle commentaries as being *in Cael., in Phys., in Cat.,* in that order, with a lost *in Metaph.* and, after the *Physics* and *Metaphysics* commentaries, *in DA*. Westerink's masterly survey of the Alexandrians and their introductions is brought up to date in Chapter 14, and Blumenthal's warning of Neoplatonist influence in the *de Anima* commentaries is updated by his note in Chapter 13 on the authenticity of Simplicius *in DA*.

All discussion of Boethius' commentaries is indebted to Shiel's exhaustive comparison of the relevant texts, which are here presented by him for the first time in translation. There has been less accord over the startling conclusion he drew from that comparison, that Boethius was quite lacking in originality. According to Shiel, Boethius simply borrowed his comments from Greek annotations in the margin of his copy of Aristotle, translating into Latin as he went, and in Chapter 15 Shiel explains why he is unmoved by subsequent objections to his interpretation. In Chapter 16, I have included a presentation by Ebbesen of the opposing case for Boethius' originality.

Browning's work on the circle of Anna Comnena altered the picture of the late Byzantine commentators, and in Chapter 17 he has translated the funeral oration from which he drew his evidence. In Chapter 18, Mercken gives an account of the main *Ethics* commentaries, a corpus which, on his dating, includes the earliest extant commentaries, written by Aristotelians of the second century AD, and then leaps to some of the latest Greek commentaries from the hands of Eustratius and Michael in the twelfth century.[106] Mercken further brings out the influence these commentaries

---

[106] The *Ethics* commentary assigned to Heliodorus of Prusa is probably later. It belongs to any time up to the fourteenth century.

exerted on Albert the Great and Bonaventure, once they had been translated into Latin by Grosseteste.

Ebbesen takes a dim view of the logic in the Neoplatonist commentaries, but none the less stresses its influence (Chapter 19). As in Averroes' Arabic commentaries (Sorabji, Chapter 9), so here, the work of Philoponus got misascribed to Alexander. Philoponus' comments on the *Posterior Analytics*, thus disguised, were picked up by James of Venice, perhaps from the library of Michael of Ephesus, and so promoted thirteenth-century realism about the objects of scientific knowledge. By contrast the nominalism characteristic of the eleventh to twelfth centuries was partly encouraged by the tradition of Porphyry and Boethius, that Aristotle's *Categories* is about *words*, insofar as they signify things. This is in spite of the fact that Porphyry and Boethius themselves are better described as conceptualists[107] than as nominalists.

This completes the study of the individual commentators. Chapter 20 represents a harvest of another kind. Study of the commentators makes it possible to trace for the first time the development of concepts and theories very different from Aristotle's, and in Chapter 20, Mueller is able to chart the evolution of the view that mathematical objects have their being in the mind.

The importance of the commentaries

The 15,000 pages of the *CAG* are the longest corpus of Ancient Greek philosophy that has not previously been translated into English or other modern European languages. But a programme is now under way which aims to translate a substantial proportion, including all the most important Greek commentaries, with fragments preserved in Arabic and other languages, and with related texts.[108]

I have already explained the value of the works as commentaries, but it will now be clear that they are much more than commentaries. Commentary writing was one of the ways of doing philosophy, and the works therefore represent the thought of the Neoplatonist and Aristotelian schools, as well as expounding Aristotle. Furthermore, they embed fragments from all periods of Ancient Greek philosophical thought. That is how many of the Presocratic fragments were assembled, for example, and the interest of these is widely known. But the other fragments that remain provide a panorama of every period of Ancient Greek philosophy.

The commentaries represent a missing link in the history of philosophy. The Latin-speaking Middle Ages obtained their knowledge of Aristotle at least partly through the medium of the commentaries. We have already seen how that medium could pass on a transformed

[107] For conceptualism in other senses, see Mueller in Chapter 20 and Mercken in Chapter 18, reporting A.C. Lloyd on Eustratius' conceptualism.

[108] This is the series 'The Ancient Commentators on Aristotle', edited by Richard Sorabji, published by Duckworth and Cornell University Press, from 1987 onwards.

Aristotle, one whose God has become a Creator of the world, and whose active intellect, it may be added, provides the hope of immortality for the human soul. Without knowledge of the commentaries, we cannot understand the Aristotle of the later Middle Ages. Again, the ancient commentaries are the unsuspected source of ideas which have been thought, wrongly, to originate in the later medieval period. It has been supposed, for example, that Bonaventure in the thirteenth century invented the ingenious arguments based on the concept of infinity which attempt to prove the Christian view that the universe had a beginning. In fact, Bonaventure is merely repeating arguments devised by the commentator Philoponus 700 years earlier and preserved in the meantime by the Arabs.[109] Bonaventure even used Philoponus' original examples. Again, the introduction of impetus theory into dynamics, which has been called a scientific revolution, has been held to be an independent invention of the Latin West, even if it was earlier discovered by the Arabs or their predecessors. But recent work has traced a plausible route by which it could have passed from Philoponus, via the Arabs, to the West.[110]

The new availability of the commentaries in the sixteenth century, thanks to printing and to fresh Latin translations, helped to fuel the Renaissance break from Aristotelian science. For the commentators record not only Aristotle's theories, but also rival ones, while Philoponus as a Christian devises rival theories of his own and accordingly is mentioned in Galileo's early works more frequently than Plato.[111]

The commentaries are also a source, we have seen, for the history of school practices in the Neoplatonist period. Much of their significance was already foreseen in Karl Praechter's seminal review of *CAG*, here translated from the German of 1909 as Chapter 2. He adds their utility as evidence for changes in grammar and vocabulary. As regards the latter, the indices of the current translation series are designed to help keep track of changes in word-meaning.

Readers will find in Simplicius' commentaries not only a record of earlier Greek thought, but also, in the case of the *Categories* commentary, an admirable gymnastic for students. For the *Categories* is a central, and apparently simple, metaphysical text of Aristotle's, but the commentary tradition represented by Simplicius takes it apart with a thoroughness unmatched in modern discussions, and forces the reader to think through the very basis of the metaphysics. It is of immediate philosophical interest and requires no background knowledge, to join in the ancient

[109] Richard Sorabji, *Time, Creation and the Continuum*, London and Ithaca NY 1983, ch. 14.

[110] Fritz Zimmermann, 'Philoponus' impetus theory in the Arabic tradition', in Richard Sorabji (ed.), *Philoponus and the Rejection of Aristotelian Science*, London and Ithaca NY 1987, 121-9.

[111] William A. Wallace, Prelude to Galileo, *Essays on Medieval and Sixteenth-Century Sources of Galileo's Thought*, Dordrecht 1981, 136 (contrast 196-7); Charles Schmitt, 'Philoponus' commentary on Aristotle's *Physics* in the sixteenth century', in Richard Sorabji (ed.), *Philoponus and the Rejection of Aristotelian Science*, 1987.

discussion of whether Aristotle's other categories can all be reduced to relatives, or whether the definition of relatives can itself be made water-tight. Philosophical work on these ancient debates is just beginning to come out in quantity, and it is the mirror image of modern work on whether relational properties can be eliminated as merely supervenient, or whether quantum physics proves the contrary.[112]

As the commentators become more accessible, I expect more information to come to light on the history of concepts and theories. In forthcoming work, John Ellis tells the story of a perceived clash between Aristotle's *Categories* and his *de Anima*.[113] Individual qualities cannot exist separately from what they are in, according to the *Categories*. But cannot an apple's individual fragrance float off into the surrounding air? Only if accompanied by some of the apple's substance, Ammonius suggests. But this conflicts, as Philoponus comes to see, with the *de Anima*'s insistence that our sense of smell does not operate by direct contact with the apple's substance.

This provides only one instance of a wholesale re-evaluation of Aristotle's treatment of the five senses, in which I see two major tendencies.[114] First, the commentators dematerialised Aristotle's account of the sensory processes: the eye jelly does not become coloured; sound involves only a wave, not a moving block of air. Secondly, they came to notice that the sensory processes are much more diverse (witness smell) than Aristotle had allowed in their degree of materiality. To the move towards dematerialisation the Arabic writers, Avicenna in particular, contributed the idea of an intention, understood by him, and still by Thomas Aquinas, as some kind of meaning or message. But by the time of Brentano in the nineteenth century, the idea of *awareness* of that message had become prominent. Thus it was only through a series of distortions by the commentators that Brentano was able to read into Aristotle's treatment of sense perception his own seminal idea of an intentional object. He thought of an intentional object, like a hoped-for fortune, as an object which does not have to exist in reality in order to serve as the object of which our mind is aware. By reading this influential idea into Aristotle, he lent authority to it, and to his proposal that the mental could be distinguished from the physical by the fact of its being directed to intentional objects of this kind. This little story illustrates that the role of the best commentators is to reinterpret rather than to reflect Aristotle, and that, as in the case of Brentano, reinterpretation can prove more fruitful than fidelity.

Philosophical commentary is important also in the Islamic and Indian

---

[112] Paul Teller, 'Relational holism and quantum mechanics', *British Journal for the Philosophy of Science* 38, 1987, 71-81, and for work on the ancient debates see the number of publications since 1985 in the bibliography under Logic – *Categories* and *Isagoge*.

[113] John Ellis, 'Can an apple's fragrance be separated from it?', in preparation.

[114] Richard Sorabji, 'Aristotle's theory of sense perception', in M. Nussbaum and A. Rorty (eds), *Aristotle's de Anima*, forthcoming Oxford 1990; 'From Aristotle to Brentano: the development of the concept of intentionality', in H.J. Blumenthal and H.M. Robinson (eds), volume on Aristotle and the Aristotelian traditions, forthcoming 1991.

traditions; indeed the whole of traditional Indian philosophy takes the form of commentary. A recent conference assessed whether commentary was compatible with originality and found that in all three traditions it was.[115] There is originality not only of interpretation, but also of ideas. From the Greek commentaries we may recall Philoponus' introduction into dynamics of impetus theory, which has been called a scientific revolution, his defence, endorsed by Galileo, of motion in a vacuum as not implying infinite speed, and his stunning objections to an infinite past. We may recall Simplicius' treatment of prime matter as an extension which, when endowed with properties, constitutes body, and Alexander's explanation of the edge of space. There is the discussion in Syrianus and Proclus of whether bodies can coincide in exactly the same place and the debate in many commentators on the reduction of other properties to relatives.[116]

The *CAG* texts

I shall conclude with a list of the commentaries on Aristotle in the *CAG* edition and a list of the principal commentators with dates.

I   Alexander *in Metaphysica* (*in Metaph.*) 1-5 and ps.-Alexander *in Metaph.* 6-14, M. Hayduck, 1891.

II   1   Alexander *in Analytica Priora* (*in An. Pr.*), M. Wallies, 1883.

       2   Alexander *in Topica* (*in Top.*), M. Wallies, 1891.

       3   ps.-Alexander (Michael of Ephesus) *in Sophisticos Elenchos* (*in SE*), M. Wallies, 1898. (But see S. Ebbesen's edition in *Corpus Latinum Commentariorum in Aristotelem Graecorum* 7.2, 153-99, of an earlier version also by Michael.)

III   1   Alexander *in de Sensu* (*in Sens.*), P. Wendland, 1901.

       Alexander *in Meteorologica* (*in Meteor.*), M. Hayduck, 1899.

       Fragments of Alexander's commentaries have now been collected as follows:

       2   Alexander on the intellect from *in de Anima* (*in DA*), in Paul Moraux, *Alexandre d'Aphrodise, Exégète de la Noétique d'Aristote*, Liège and Paris 1942, 203-21.

       Alexander *in Analytica Posteriora* (*in An. Post.*), in Paul Moraux, *Le Commentaire d'Alexandre d'Aphrodise aux Secondes Analytiques*, Peripatoi 13, Berlin 1979.

IV   1   Porphyry *Isagoge* (*Isag.*) and *in Categorias* (*in Cat.*), A. Busse, 1887.

       2   Dexippus *in Cat.*, A. Busse, 1888.

       3   Ammonius *in Porphyrii Isagogen* (*in Isag.*), A. Busse, 1895.

---

[115] Conference held by Professor Daya Krishna in Jaipur, India, 10-14 March 1989, under the auspices of the Indian Council of Philosophical Research.

[116] I have written about all except the last in the following places: *Time, Creation and the Continuum*, ch. 14; *Philoponus and the Rejection of Aristotelian Science*, chs 1 and 9; *Matter, Space and Motion*, chs 1, 7, 8, 9 and 14.

4 Ammonius *in Cat.*, A. Busse, 1895.
5 Ammonius *in de Interpretatione* (*in Int.*), A. Busse, 1897.
6 Ammonius *in An. Pr.*, M. Wallies, 1899.

V   1 Themistius *in An. Post.*, M. Wallies, 1900.
     2 Themistius *in Physica* (*in Phys.*), H. Schenkl, 1900.
     3 Themistius *in DA*, R. Heinze, 1899.
     4 Themistius *in de Caelo* (*in Cael.*), Latin and Hebrew, S. Landauer, 1902.
     5 Themistius *in Metaph. 12*, Latin and Hebrew, S. Landauer, 1903.
     6 ps.-Themistius (Sophonias) *in Parva Naturalia* (*in PN*), P. Wendland, 1903.

VI   1 Syrianus *in Metaph. 3, 4, 13, 14*, W. Kroll, 1902.
     2 Asclepius *in Metaph. 1-7*, M. Hayduck, 1888.

VII 1 Simplicius *in Cael.*, J.L. Heiberg, 1894. (New edition in preparation, P. Hoffmann).

VIII Simplicius *in Cat.*, C. Kalbfleisch, 1907.

IX   Simplicius *in Phys. 1-4*, H. Diels, 1882. (New edition in preparation, L. Tarán).

X   Simplicius *in Phys. 5-8*, H. Diels, 1895. (New edition in preparation, L. Tarán).

XI   Simplicius (?) *in DA*, M. Hayduck, 1882.

XII   1 Olympiodorus *Prolegomena* (*Proleg.*) and *in Cat.*, A. Busse, 1902.
     2 Olympiodorus *in Meteor.*, W. Stuve, 1900.

XIII 1 Philoponus *in Cat.*, A. Busse, 1898.
     2 Philoponus *in An. Pr. 1*, Philoponus (?) *in An. Pr. 2*, M. Wallies, 1905.
     3 Philoponus *in An. Post. 1*, Philoponus (?) *in An. Post. 2*, Anon. *in An. Post. 2*, M. Wallies, 1909.

XIV 1 Philoponus *in Meteor.*, M. Hayduck, 1901.
     2 Philoponus *in de Generatione et Corruptione* (*in GC*), H. Vitelli, 1897.
     3 ps.-Philoponus (Michael of Ephesus) *in de Generatione Animalium* (*in GA*), M. Hayduck, 1903.

XV   Philoponus *in DA 1-2*, Philoponus (?) *in DA 3*, M. Hayduck, 1897.

XVI   Philoponus *in Phys. 1-3*, H. Vitelli, 1887.

XVII Philoponus *in Phys. 4* and fragments, H. Vitelli, 1888.

XVIII 1 Elias *in Isag.* and *in Cat.*, A. Busse, 1900.
     2 David *Proleg.* and *in Isag.*, A. Busse, 1904.
     3 Stephanus *in Int.*, M. Hayduck, 1885.

XIX 1 Aspasius *in Ethica Nicomachea* (*in EN*), G. Heylbut, 1889.
     2 Heliodorus (?) *in EN*, G. Heylbut, 1889.

XX   Composite commentary on *EN*, G. Heylbut, 1892:
     Eustratius *in EN 1, 6*.
     Derivative of Adrastus *in EN 2-5*.
     Anon. *in EN 7*.

Aspasius *in EN 8* is printed in XIX, 1.
Michael of Ephesus *in EN 9-10*.

XXI   1 Eustratius *in An. Post. 2*, M. Hayduck, 1907.
      2 Anonymous Neobarii and Stephanus *in Rhetorica (in Rhet.)*, H. Rabe, 1896.
XXII 1 Michael of Ephesus *in PN*, P. Wendland, 1903.
      2 Michael of Ephesus *in de Partibus Animalium (in PA), in de Motu Animalium (in MA), in de Incessu Animalium (in IA)*, M. Hayduck, 1904.
      3 Michael of Ephesus, *in EN 5*, M. Hayduck, 1901.
XXIII 1 Sophonias paraphrase *in DA*, M. Hayduck, 1883.
      2 Anon. paraphrase *in Cat.*, M. Hayduck, 1883.
      3 Incert. paraphrase *in An. Pr.*, M. Wallies, 1884.
      4 Anon. paraphrase *in SE*, M. Hayduck, 1884.

Supplement

I   2 Priscian of Lydia *Metaphrasis in Theophrastum (in Theophr.)* and *Solutiones ad Chosroem (Chosr.)*, I. Bywater, 1886.
II   1 Alexander *de Anima (DA)* and *Mantissa (Mant.)*, I. Bruns, 1887.
     2 Alexander *Quaestiones (Quaest.), de Fato (Fat.)*, and *de Mixtione (Mixt.)*, I. Bruns, 1892.

Principal Greek commentators

Andronicus of Rhodes	edition perhaps 60 BC
Boethus	Andronicus' pupil, first century BC
Lucius and Nicostratos	Platonist critics, early second century AD
Adrastus	first half of second century AD
Aspasius	first half of second century AD
Alexander of Aphrodisias	appointed to chair between 198 and 209 AD
Porphyry	232-309 AD
Iamblichus	c. 240-c.325 AD
Dexippus	fl. c. 330 AD
Themistius	fl. late 340s to 384 or 385 AD
Plutarch of Athens	died 432 AD
Syrianus	died c. 437 AD
Proclus	c. 411-485 AD
Ammonius	435/45-517/26 AD
Damascius	head of Athenian school at time of closure, 529 AD
Philoponus	c. 490-570s AD
Simplicius	wrote after 529 AD
Olympiodorus	495/505 – after 565 AD
Elias	probably a pupil of Olympiodorus
Stephanus	called to Constantinople in, or soon after, 610 AD
pseudo-Elias	either before or after Stephanus

David	akin to pseudo-Elias, and close in date, but not his source
Eustratius	1050/1060 – c. 1120 AD
Michael of Ephesus	commentaries completed 1138 AD or later

CHAPTER TWO

Review of the *Commentaria in Aristotelem Graeca**

Karl Praechter

The Berlin Academy is about to finish a tremendous undertaking which developed organically from their edition of Aristotle, itself appearing between 1831 and 1870 and now the basis of all Aristotelian studies. Even in organising that earlier edition, the significance of the commentators for the *recensio* as well as for the interpretation of the Aristotelian texts could not remain unnoticed. Hence extracts from some of the commentary literature were compiled under Brandis' supervision in a fourth volume. In the framework of the Aristotle edition, they occur only as a side concern. The commentators – they could not have been otherwise in this context – appear only as a tool for research on the Philosopher, without regard to their own value for the most diverse areas of study. Yet the preface to the fifth volume already betrays a change in attitude towards the commentary literature. We learn there that the remaining excerpts Brandis collected did not go to press because a sampling of individual chapters simply could not be a replacement for the commentaries in full, and a critical edition of the latter was still, as before, lacking. Thus, instead of continuing these extracts, Syrianus' commentary on the *Metaphysics* appeared complete – as much as is extant, at any rate – in the fifth volume, edited by Usener. It was with this in mind that the Academy decided in 1874 to produce a new and independent edition of the Greek commentators on Aristotle. A committee consisting of Bonitz, Zeller (who put forward the proposal), and Vahlen was entrusted with management of the enterprise and Adolf Torstrik with the redaction (after Torstrik's death in 1877, Hermann Diels took his place). For the preparation, selection, and survey of the extant tradition, and the collation of manuscripts, as well as for editing the individual parts of the corpus, a circle of colleagues who had been schooled proficiently in philology was assembled immediately and extended over the years. The execution of the plan went forward at a swift and sure pace. In 1882, the first volume, comprising xxxiii plus 800 pages, had already resulted from their edition of Simplicius on the *Physics*. By 1892, H. Usener was able to review eighteen prepared and edited parts of

* Translated by Victor Caston.

the collection,[1] and today the last part is in press.

The scholarly work whose precipitate is contained in this considerable series of volumes represents an imposing amount of self-discipline. For all the works which are included here, everything had to be built from the ground up. The examination of the tradition's often truly entangled relationships, which in many cases posed very difficult riddles concerning the question of authorship, had to be handled everywhere *ex integro*. Even where an *editio princeps* did not have to be prepared, earlier editions offered only minimal help, as they rested on unsatisfactory foundations. Usener's own very meritorious edition did not remove the need for a new foundation, as the collation of relevant manuscripts at his disposal had been inaccurate. Considering how great the danger is of endlessly postponing the conclusion with work as vast as that which had to be conducted here, by a series of men and with the complicated organisation of such an undertaking, one must express the highest admiration for Diels. His talent for organisation above all takes the credit for this great project not only being finished, but even having reached its conclusion within a very short allotment of time (relatively speaking); and yet he found both the energy and the time to supervise the entire undertaking step by step, indicating the way, checking and advising at every point, with the most faithful care. The pleasant uniformity of the entire corpus is a closely related benefit of this working procedure. In spite of the considerable number of co-workers and the freedom which obviously had to be granted to those involved to fulfil their tasks in detail, the collection has the appearance of the work of a single hand; this not only affords aesthetic pleasure, but also uncommonly facilitates the use of the commentaries. On a single point only it would have been preferable, and also possible, to have kept the army of compilers within certain bounds through more definite marching orders: I have in mind the arrangement of the indices verborum. For external reasons, it was of course unavoidable that these indices should be limited to a selection of what is lexically and grammatically important.[2] Viewpoints, however, often differ on the ranking of importance, in accordance with the subjective perception of the editor. To exclude this subjective element completely and to regulate uniformly the production of these indices in detail, for authors of very different periods and diverse idiosyncracies, would be inconceivable. Nevertheless, it is an avoidable inconvenience when the indices to the different works of a single author (as, for example, with Michael of Ephesus) or different books of a single work (as, for example, with Michael's commentary on the *Ethics*) exhibit considerable variations between editors and lack the idiosyncratic expressions[3] and philosophical terms (such as *dikaiosunê* in the *Ethics*) recorded there.

---

[1] *Gött. gel. Anz.*, 1892, 1000f.

[2] Grammatical matters are in general taken up only where they can be assigned to a particular Greek entry (where *an* is missing with the optative, *ean* with the indicative, and so on).

[3] See *Gött. gel. Anz.*, 1906, 879, n. 1.

This is a point, however, of minor significance. Whoever utilises these indices for grammatical and terminological studies and for questions of literary criticism should simply keep this state of affairs in mind, so as not to be led to false conclusions *ex silentio*.

As for the rest, these editions deserve the highest praise in every respect for their external arrangement as much as for their internal realisation. The extremely practical organisation of reports on the manuscript tradition and other aids which come into consideration for the *recensio* is especially to be commended. This has been a persistently weak point in our editing methods. Many otherwise excellent editions suffer from an aggravating clumsiness in the organisation of the *praefatio*, with the result that the user who has been led only occasionally in the course of his work to the writer in question and who wants to form his own judgment on the authentic text of some passage or other must unfortunately work through an introduction of fifty or more closely printed pages, just to obtain a glimpse of the elementary facts of the tradition and to be able to make use of the apparatus for a questionable passage. This precipice has been circumvented with great skill in the commentary collection. The *praefatio* of each part reports in the most concise manner, essentially indicating only the results of the investigation, the worth and interrelationship of the textual sources employed for the constitution of the text and represented in the apparatus by its sigla. A *supplementum praefationis* adds a description of the collected manuscripts that were not considered or mentioned in the *praefatio* and were not used for the *recensio* (which are characterised, so far as is possible, by lists of variations for particular sections), and gives more detailed reports on translations and editions. This method, which is adhered to throughout the entire corpus (with trivial discrepancies in the distribution of material between the *praefatio* and *supplementum*), unites splendidly the possibility of a quick and convenient overview with a thorough introduction to the tradition, and should be considered an exemplar for editions of ancient authors.[4]

These prefaces deserve as much recognition for their content as for their form. Concerning the appraisal of some of the tradition's sources, of course, one may differ. There is evidence everywhere, however, of the industrious and conscientious investigation and survey of the material, and of sensible judgment. The same holds true for the editing of the author's text which follows the *praefatio* and *supplementum*. What deserves special notice above all is the distancing from wilful conjecture, a superiority all the more worthy of recognition, since these texts – which as regards grammar are based in essence on the ancient tradition, yet in detail make the numerous concessions of its late period – are often a truly great temptation for critical emendation among philologists used to working on [earlier] antiquity. In this regard, these editions ought to

[4] Gratifyingly, Ernst Diehl has followed a similiar procedure in his edition of Proclus' commentary on Plato's *Timaeus*, which was suggested by Diels and supported by the Berlin Academy.

provide a methodological precedent, and editors of Byzantine texts especially should be directed to the cautious and circumspect procedure followed here.

Separate indices of words, names, and passages cited from Plato and Aristotle conclude the volumes (or their sections), all of which we can be very thankful for, as they provide access for the first time to much which the text offers that is valuable regarding language and content.

The final verdict to be pronounced on the whole Greek commentator corpus must be that a model edition has been produced, which should be greeted most enthusiastically and gratefully as such and for the influence which it is bound to exercise on the art of editing and on philological methods.[5]

Yet we must welcome it not only for this reason. This collection is also of the greatest importance because of the authors represented here. It is not yet the moment to measure the profit which various fields of study will derive from it, since its exploitation has hardly begun and a long time will pass before it reaches a final conclusion. There is, however, much of a general nature that can be recognised even now. From the ore of precious Presocratic fragments, which is currently minted in Diels' edition of the Presocratics, one can foresee what the history of Ancient Greek philosophy has yet to gain from fragments of Theophrastus, Eudemus, Epicurus, the Stoics, etc. The abundant advantages which Aristotelian textual criticism also gains from the commentators does not concern us here. For this and several other points, Usener's thorough review (mentioned above) should be consulted.[6] It is our concern here only to emphasise what the new corpus offers to Byzantine studies, which carry off the lion's share, so to speak. If one places the beginning of the Byzantine period of Greek literature in the time of Constantine I (as has been argued convincingly by K. Krumbacher),[7] all of the authors included here – excluding Aspasius, Alexander of Aphrodisias and Porphyry – belong to the Byzantine period, and, of the three just named, Porphyry influenced the Byzantine school for centuries with his introductory logical work, thus forging, through his being frequently commented upon and excerpted, the first link in a long chain of Byzantine publications. Our corpus also immediately confirms Krumbacher's division of epochs rather than the one previously customary, which recognises the year 529 as the border between antiquity and the Byzantine Middle Ages. Porphyry does not in fact belong to the Constantinian period, but his life extends quite close to it, and with him a new direction begins. A deep chasm separates him from Alexander of Aphrodisias, something without analogy in the sixth century. Alexander's interest still lies in puzzles, and, although he wishes only to be an interpreter of Aristotle, he not infrequently arrives at perceptions of his own which deviate from

---

[5] [New editions are, however, being prepared of Simplicius *in Phys.* by L. Tarán, and of Simplicius *in Cael.* by P. Hoffmann. – Ed.]

[6] See n. 1.

[7] *Gesch. d. byz. Litt.*[2], 2.

Aristotle. For Porphyry, in contrast,[8] it is merely a matter of making accessible to the understanding of a wider circle what was recognised as logic *par excellence*, that is, Aristotelian logic, and above all else of making it useful for school – hence his short, introductory handbook on the Five Terms (*pente phônai*); hence the new pedagogical experiment of his *Categories* commentary in the form of a catechetical dialogue. This pedagogical interest in the development of new methods for making Aristotle accessible persisted. Dexippus uses a different form of dialogue-exegesis, while Themistius in his [use of] paraphrase brings an old form of explanation to a new level of respectability.[9] Something of the spirit of Scholasticism already breathes in these works: Aristotelianism has grown stiff, but new life stirs in the manner in which it is handed on. The combination of Aristotelian logic with the Neoplatonic system, however, is entirely scholastic, and though first championed by Porphyry, it endures from then on, finding its perpetuation in the linkage of Aristotelianism with Christian dogma. Of course, this combination was not suddenly engendered by Porphyry without preparation from those who came before. Middle Platonism of the second century AD, as Albinus demonstrates, had already incorporated Aristotelian logic into its system, but in such a way that it was attributed to Plato. From the fact that Plato on occasion made use of this or that form of argument, it was taken as proof that he had also established this form theoretically; and in this manner they succeeded, beginning with these few points, in claiming essentially all of Aristotelian logic as Plato's. It is with this that Porphyry broke. Now Aristotelian logic as such, and not covered in Platonic colours, formed the basis for the study of philosophy in the schools of the Neoplatonists as well, and thus the exegesis of Aristotle also came to hold an extremely important place in the Platonic school, which it never lost.

Thus we find traces in our commentaries of an important change that was complete by the third century AD and causes us to mark a break in the development of commentary activity before Porphyry. In contrast, the closing of the Athenian school in the sixth century left no trace at all in the commentaries. On the contrary, the works of this century are inseparably connected to one another, and nowhere does there split even the most insignificant seam which could be used for the division of two epochs. In particular, the opposition between pagan and Christian is not at all prominent and forms no boundary. Within the school of Ammonius Hermeiou, Ammonius, Asclepius and Simplicius are pagan; no definite conclusion can be reached concerning Olympiodorus; and Philoponus is a

---

[8] [For warnings about Porphyry's supposed neutrality in the logical commentaries, see now P. Hadot in Chapter 6. *De Anima* commentaries are, of course, less neutral still, see Henry J. Blumenthal, Chapter 13 and I. Hadot, *Le problème du néoplatonisme Alexandrin: Hiéroclès et Simplicius*, Paris 1978, appendix 193-202. – Ed.]

[9] This methodological effort issues in a late second blossoming in Sophonias. Cf. the beginning of his paraphrase of the *de Anima*.

Christian. Yet their commentaries give no indication of it.[10] If the *Categories* commentaries of Simplicius, Olympiodorus and Philoponus are compared with each other, the stamp of the same school is recognisable even down to details. The same holds true for the next generation of Olympiodorus' students, Elias and David. Their names suggest a Christian confession of faith. Their work remains wholly within the tradition of Ammonius' school.

On yet another point, the commentator corpus reflects a fundamental characteristic of Byzantine literature. If we disregard those pieces which cannot be attributed to a specific author or precisely dated, the entire collection falls chronologically into two groups which are very unequal in extent. The first group consists of the following: from the Peripatos, Aspasius (in the second quarter of the second century AD;[11] XIX 1 of the commentary collection), Alexander of Aphrodisias (who was Professor of Peripatetic Philosophy in Athens between 198 and 211; I, II, III), and Themistius (from the second decade until the end of the fourth century AD; V); from the Neoplatonic school, Porphyry (232 or 233 until 301; IV 1), Dexippus (about the middle of the fourth century; IV 2), Syrianus (who became the Diadochus of the Platonic school in 431/2; VI 1), Ammonius (a student of Proclus, who died in 485; IV 3-6) and his school: Asclepius (VI 2), Simplicius (VII-XI), Olympiodorus (XII), John Philoponus (XIII-XVII), and Elias and David (XVIII). Somewhat later still than David is Stephanus, whom the Emperor Heraclius called to Constantinople soon after 610.[12] We thus have an uninterrupted sequence of literary publications from the second century until into the seventh, and between the lifetimes of the men named above there is hardly the space of a generation which, here or there, is not covered. Yet with Stephanus the thread breaks off suddenly, to be spun again only centuries later. The great hole, which gapes throughout Byzantine intellectual life from the middle of the seventh century onwards, also makes itself noticeable in the commentary literature. Only here it extends even further than it does in other areas. In the ninth century, when new life stirred elsewhere, here there reigned a perfect silence – and for long afterwards. It revives only in Psellos' period. The date of Michael of Ephesus (II 3, XIV 3, XX, XXII; he is also the pseudo-Alexander of *in Metaph.* I; cf. *Gött. gel. Anz.* 1906, pp. 882ff) cannot be determined with certainty, to be sure, but in all probability he belongs to

[10] [For Olympiodorus' paganism, see now L.G. Westerink, pp. 331ff, and for pagan and Christian controversy in the commentaries of Simplicius and Philoponus see K. Verrycken, Chapter 10 and P. Hoffmann, 'Simplicius' polemics', in Richard Sorabji (ed.), *Philoponus and the Rejection of Aristotelian Science*, London and Ithaca NY 1987. For David's Christianising tendency, see Haig Khatchadourian, 'Universals in David, Boethius and al-Farabi's summary of Porphry's *Isagoge*', in Avedis K. Sanjian (ed.), *David Anhaght̕, the 'Invincible Philosopher'*, Atlanta, Georgia 1986. It is not clear whose pupil David was. – Ed.]

[11] The dating is taken from Zeller here and in what follows.

[12] cf. H. Usener, *de Stephano Alexandrino*, Bonner Lektionskatal. Summer 1879, 5. [Whether Stephanus is later than David is questioned by Mossman Roueché: see Chapter 1 – Ed.]

the eleventh century,[13] and only with difficulty to an earlier period. He is also probably the contemporary of Eustratius (XX, XXI 1).[14] Aside from these two men, the Byzantine renaissance is also represented in our corpus by Sophonias (at the turn of the thirteenth and fourteenth centuries;[15] V 6, XXIII 1).[16]

How will Byzantine studies profit from the collection of the commentators on Aristotle?

First of all, material will become available which is invaluable for the history of the Greek language, for the lexicon as well as for grammar. Without exception, every author included in the collection has in general become accessible to linguistic research for the first time in these editions, which have been neatly and conscientiously prepared on the basis of a careful survey of the tradition. An abundance of grammatically significant writings can now be traced through the centuries in almost uninterrupted continuity. Peculiarities of the later language have long been known from more or less secure examples, but no judgment was possible concerning their currency and significance, as, for example, with the absence of *an* with the optative and in the apodosis of counterfactual hypothetical sentences, *hotan* and *ean* with the indicative and the optative, *hote, hênika, heôs, hou, prin* with the subjunctive, the confusion in the use of negatives (*oute* for *oude*, etc.), and peculiar uses and placements of *de*. All of these can now be observed within a larger context. It is clear that textual criticism of Byzantine writers must cull diverse advantages from the insights to be gained here. Literary criticism does not leave empty-handed either, as is demonstrated by the question concerning the pseudo-Alexander of the *in Metaph.* and his relation to Syrianus; with the help of the linguistic indices, it allows of a definite solution. It can only be hoped that these commentaries will soon be exploited for their grammatical significance in earnest. Obviously, it is not merely a matter of establishing the specific deviations from classical grammar; it should also be considered how individual authors place the forms accepted by classical grammar next to one another and opposite the changes. Another interesting problem would be the relationship between contemporary writers in other areas and these men, who, on the one hand, are led by their subject and tradition to a linguistic conservatism, and yet, on the other hand, are led to a certain vital sense of the language through the oral lecture style.

The commentator corpus will greatly advance work on the philosophical lexicon. Diels' work on *elementum* and *stoikheion* ('element'), the paradigm of a history of philosophical terms, still stands entirely alone. Further investigations are without question needed for

[13] cf. *Gött. gel. Anz.*, 1906, 902ff; Arist., *Pol.*, O. Immisch (ed.), Leipzig 1909, xviif. [But see now Robert Browning, p. 399, for the twelfth-century date – Ed.]

[14] cf. K. Krumbacher, *Gesch. d. byz. Litt.*[2], 430.

[15] ibid.

[16] The name Heliodorus, which appears as the author of a commentary on the *Ethics* (XIX 2), rests on a falsification. Cf. L. Cohn, *Berl. philol. Woch.*, 1889, col. 1419.

the preparation of the Greek Thesaurus. For a delimited, yet still quite broad area, the Aristotle commentaries provide abundant material. A lexicon of philosophical terms built on this foundation could form the basis for further investigations into the philosophical terminology of late antiquity and the Middle Ages, and would prove especially useful for theology.

If we proceed from language to literary form, then the Berlin Academy's undertaking valuably enriches our knowledge here as well. The Aristotle commentaries are in large part transcripts from oral lectures and thus were not originally conceived as written works, but became such only subsequently. Owing to their origin, such works exhibit certain peculiarities that have occupied philology repeatedly in recent years,[17] since the interest shown in Cynic-Stoic diatribe necessarily leads to it. In particular, H. von Arnim's thorough investigation of the works of Dio Chrysostom was of as great consequence to his diatribes as to his sophistic speeches.[18] New light was shed especially on the duplicates in Dio's work, which von Arnim attributed to the repetition of the same lecture, thus connecting them with the peculiar origin of this literature. In the same way, the peculiarities of the composition, language and style of the oral lectures which became written works through transcription have also begun to be traced in the area of Christian sermon literature.[19] The Academy's commentary collection draws our attention to a new species of this genre, namely, the lecture transcribed from the lectern.[20] Generally, in a version of these notes produced with the aim of publication, the tangible traces of the oral lecture have been effaced, such as any reference to the audience as companions (*hetairoi*) or the use of address in the second person plural, while changes which indicate written composition, such as 'we write (*graphomen*)' and the like, are introduced. Nevertheless, the original state of affairs is frequently betrayed in the occasional overlooked passage:[21] numerous items in the collection already confirm in their titles that the *viva vox* of a lecturer is recorded here with the phrase 'from the mouth of so-and-so (*apo phônês tou deinos*)'.[22] Next to the name of the professor, the name of the audience member himself may appear in the heading as well, as in the transcription which Asclepius made from Ammonius' series of lectures on the *Metaphysics*. Indeed, it could also happen that the student disseminated his transcription solely in his own name, without thereby committing a transgression in the eyes of his teacher. When the not yet twenty-year-old Proclus read Plato's *Phaedo* with the elderly Plutarch (of Athens), he was encouraged by Plutarch to write down the exegesis, and

[17] References to the literature can be found in P. Wendland, *Gött. gel. Anz.*, 1901, 780, n. 1.
[18] *Leben und Werke des Dio von Prusa*, Berlin 1898, 171ff, 282ff.
[19] P. Wendland, *Gött. gel. Anz.*, 1901, 780ff.
[20] cf. also Freudenthal, *Hellenistische Studien* III, 303 on lecture notes in antiquity.
[21] cf. *Gött. gel. Anz.*, 1905, 518f; ibid. 1906, 903.
[22] [See M. Richard, '*Apo phônês*', *Byzantion* 20, 1950, 191-222. – Ed.]

egged on by the remark that then there would be a *Phaedo* commentary in circulation under Proclus' name too.[23] By this indifference to intellectual property, we can explain a discrepancy between David's and Elias' introductions to philosophy. In response to Callimachus' epigram (Wilamowitz) 23, David (XVIII 2, p. 31,34) cites two verses under Olympiodorus' name ('to which the philosopher Olympiodorus said [*pros touto de eipen Olumpiodôros ho philosophos]*'), which in Elias (XVIII 1, p. 14,8) are ascribed to the speaker himself ('I would say to him the contrary, in the following words [*egô de ta'nantia ekeinôi phêmi epê houtôs]*'). Although according to the title[24] the commentary appeared as his own, Elias has made a literal transcription here and adopted the 'I (*egô)*' of his teacher, while David has substituted 'Olympiodorus the philosopher'. It is clear that in this branch of transcribed literature, namely, in the exegetical lectures of the philosophical schools, duplicates must have appeared very frequently. Few professors caused as much confusion as the Alexandrian Hierocles, whose lecture series on the *Gorgias* was transcribed twice by Theosebios, with the result that when the versions were compared with each other, it was felt that, apart from the fundamentally Platonic character of the exegesis, nothing was the same.[25] In any event, what usually occurred was that the same notes formed the basis for the lecture's repetition, at which point changes of detail could be transcribed into the text or on inserted leaves, or even given merely oral expression. At this point, one can imagine that a series of lectures might be transcribed not only from different repetitions, but also copied down on each occasion by several listeners, of whom one may have perhaps followed the lecture word for word, while others

[23] Marinus, *Vita Procli* sec. 12. The inclusion of both names in the title, as in Asclepius' case, is of course not entirely impossible here either. According to Porphyry's *Vita Plotini* sec. 3 (at the end), Amelius dedicated his transcript of Plotinus' lectures to Ustillianus Hesychius, thus laying claim to it as his own literary property. Whether Plotinus was mentioned as the originator, we do not know. In the *Phaedrus* commentary that is extant under the name of Hermeias (ed. P. Couvreur, Paris 1901), the discussion is interrupted at 92,6 by the report of an objection raised by 'our companion Proclus (*ho hetairos Proklos)*'. Then it is recounted what 'the philosopher (*ho philosophos)*' responded to this objection. This 'philosopher' can only be Syrianus, with whom Proclus and Hermeias studied together. The entire section interrupted by the objection belongs to Syrianus, and since this does not in any way stand out from the rest of the commentary, it is likely the whole commentary belongs to Syrianus as well. Objections and refutations are brought forward in identical circumstances, 154,21ff, 28ff.

[24] On the title, cf. A. Busse, praef., vff. If the form of the title accepted by Busse on p. vii ('Introduction, by the grace of God, to Porphyry's *Isagoge* from the mouth of the philosopher Helios (*Prolegomena sun theôi tês Porphuriou eisagôgês apo phônês Heliou philosophou)*') were correct, then it would indeed be possible to suppose an analogous title (with 'from the mouth of (*apo phônês)*') for the preceding 'Introduction to Philosophy (*Prolegomena tês philosophias)*'. Then one would have to assume that Elias read his literal transcription from Olympiodorus to the listeners of his own lecture series, which is very unlikely. The 'from the mouth of (*apo phônês)*' of the Laurentianus MS could easily have arisen, however, from the effect of the preceding 'from the mouth of David (*apo phônês Dabid)*'. The tradition that Busse rests his text on does not recognise it.

[25] Phot. *Bibl.* 338b35ff. B.

paraphrased it in different ways, combining their transcriptions later before publication. One can also further imagine that the teacher's expanded and revised notes may have been at the disposal of some of the students, and finally that the activity of the listener himself also made itself noticeable in additions, elaborations, transpositions, and the like. In this way, much of what strikes the reader of the commentaries can be explained: contradictions (apart from those which have their origin in the impulsiveness of an oral lecture, or, as with Proclus' commentary on Plato's *Timaeus*, in the stirring, colourful manner of the commentator[26]); appending the same discussion in one transcript to one point, and in another transcript to another point of the presentation;[27] the greater completeness of the commentary of a later generation in contrast with that of an earlier one;[28] and above all the duplicates, which abound in many of these Aristotle commentaries. It goes without saying that athetising in order to eliminate such unevenness is completely inadmissable in these circumstances. Our task rather can only be to establish all the publications for each work in detail, to examine their special peculiarities case by case, and to trace the ramifications of this for each commentary, for each commentary series (such as the succession of *Categories* commentaries in Ammonius' school), and ultimately for the entire literary genre (which raises questions of language and the form of presentation). If Olympiodorus can, after discussing the views of the Peripatetics and Stoics on the place of logic in Plato's philosophy, say 'In my eyes you are both right' (*Proleg.* 17,20),[29] then here the freedom and informality of oral speech are clearly revealed. Likewise, Michael of Ephesus in *Nic. Eth.* X, p. 598,19ff.[30]

The close relation between the commentaries and the oral lecture brings us to another point: the commentator corpus furthers our

[26] cf. *Gött. gel. Anz.*, 1905, 533. As regards contradictions, see also 1908, 234.
[27] cf. ibid. 1908, 228f.
[28] cf. ibid. 1904, 377ff.
[29] 'The arguments of the Peripatetics and the Stoics have this character, while the divine Plato thinks it (sc. logic) a part and a tool (sc. of philosophy), from which [it follows that] there is no need of preparation, *"for as far as I am concerned,"* he says, *"you both win"*. For you both get a rich supply of proofs, just because etc. (*Hoi men oun tôn Peripatêtikôn kai tôn Stôkôn logoi touton ekhousi ton tropon. Ho de theios Platôn kai meros autên* (sc. *tên logikên*) *oietai einai kai organon* (sc. *tês philosophias*), *hothen ou deitai kataskeuês· amphoteroi gar, phêsin, emoi nikate· dia touto gar epikheirêmata euporeite hekateroi, dioti k.t.l.*)'.
[30] Here the audacity is admittedly diminished by an addition, which I have italicised: 'He (sc. Aristotle) says, *once the omissions and that which must be supplied from elsewhere are brought together*, that in accordance with the assumptions of the Epicurean and later Stoic philosophers concerning happiness, one can attribute a share of happiness even to the non-rational animals, while according to myself and Plato and others who along with us would place happiness in the intellective life, it is impossible for the non-rational animals to be happy in that way, etc. (*legei de* (sc. *ho Aristotelês*) *hôs sullexamenous ta paraleleimmena kai hôn prosüpakouein exôthen khrê, hoti kata men tas tôn allôn philosophôn Epikoureiôn te kai tôn husteron Stoikôn peri eudaimonias hupolêpseis dunatai tis eudaimonian metadidonai kai tois alogois zôiois kat' eme de kai Platôna kai tous allous hosoi tên eudaimonian en noerai zôêi histômen, adunaton kata tautên eudaimonein ta aloga tôn k.t.l.*)'.

knowledge of *philosophical, and especially exegetical, teaching.* However pressing its need, a history of philosophical instruction still eludes us. Such a history alone could teach us to understand how ancient philosophy was able to fulfil the vast cultural mission which befell it in antiquity as sovereign in the realm of *Weltanschauung,* and in the Middle Ages as the 'handmaiden of theology'. Ivo Bruns' monograph on the activity of Epictetus' school[31] demonstrates how a great deal of valuable material still lies fallow even with much-read authors. As philosophical instruction after the second century AD was essentially exegetical, the commentaries immediately come to the centre of our attention. To elucidate their method, and thus the teaching method of the philosophical schools, is a pressing task. Of course, if its method is to be properly understood, the philosophical commentary should not be isolated from the context of commentary literature as a whole. Nevertheless, the investigation might well begin with the philosophical commentary, since massive amounts lie before us, thus offering a firm foundation for research. At the forefront stands the Aristotle commentary. For study began with Aristotle, with the aim of progressing towards Plato.[32] Among Aristotle's works, the logical ones were put first, and among these again, the *Categories.*[33] Still before these, Porphyry's *Isagoge* served as the classic preparation for the *Categories.* Its exegesis initiated the course.[34]

---

[31] *de Schola Epicteti,* Kiel 1897.

[32] Marinus, *Vita Procli* sec. 3: 'at least, in less than two full years, Syrianus read through all of Aristotle's philosophy together with Proclus ... and having been sufficiently led through these as through a kind of preliminary initiation and lesser mysteries, he began to lead him into the initiation of Plato *(en etesi goun oute duo holois pasas autôi* (sc. *tôi Proklôi) tas Aristotelous sunanegnô* (sc. *ho Surianos) pragmateias ... akhthenta de dia toutôn hikanôs hôsper dia tinôn proteleiôn kai mikrôn mustêriôn eis tên Platônos êge mustagôgian)'.* Cf. also the sequence in sec. 12: 'So, he read Aristotle's *de Anima* and Plato's *Phaedo* with Plutarch *(anaginôskei oun para toutôi* (sc. *tôi Ploutarkhôi) Aristotelous men ta peri psukhês, Platônos de ton Phaidôna)'.* Elias, *in Cat.* 123,9: 'It is necessary for him (sc. the interpreter of Aristotle) to know everything of Plato's so that he may demonstrate Plato's self-consistency, making Aristotle's philosophy an introduction to Plato's *(dei auton* (sc. *ton Aristotelous exêgêtên) panta eidenai ta Platônos hina sumphônon heautôi ton Platôna apodeixêi ta Aristotelous tôn Platônos eisagôgên poioumenos)'.* For the later period, cf. perhaps the Byzantine school dialogue, *Byz. Zeitschr.* II, 1893, 99, l. 79; Theodor. Prodr. Speech on Isaac Komn., *Byz. Zeitschr.* XVI, 1907, 115, ll. 118, 123 (previously, 'the divine Plato *(Platôn ho theios)'* represented the highest level of philosophy). Treatise on the philosopher Joseph, *Byz. Zeitschr.* VIII, 1899, 11, ll. 15, 19.

[33] Ammonius, *in Cat.* 6,2ff; Simplicius, *in Cat.* 6,2f; Philoponus, *in Cat.* 5,15ff; Olympiodorus, *in Cat.* 8,29ff; Elias, *in Cat.* 117,17ff (in the last three, there are also several views which deviate somewhat from those of the former).

[34] Porphyry himself designated his *Isagoge* [Introduction] as a prerequisite for the study of the *Categories (Isag.* 1,3). Its position at the beginning of the entire course of study is clear in Ammonius' explication of *The Five Terms (pente phônai,* as Porphyry's *Isagoge* was called) 1,2 (cf. also 13,10 introductory lectures *[eisagôgikais akoais]);* 22,23: 'This is first in order, for if it leads into Aristotle's *Categories,* which is about the simple terms *(phônai)* which themselves are the beginning of logic, it is clear that this is first in order in logic *(prôton de esti têi taxei· ei gar eis tas Aristotelous Katêgorias eisagêi, hai peri tôn haplôn eisi phônôn, hautai de tês logikês eisin arkhai, dêlon hoti prôton esti têi taxei tês logikês)'.* Here too the ancient tradition was preserved in the Middle Ages: Nicephorus Blemmydes'

42 *Karl Praechter*

From here it was thus a short step to preface this series of lectures with a general introduction, containing discussions on the concept and division of philosophy and similar questions, as was done by Ammonius (IV 3), Elias (XVIII 1) and David (XVIII 2). It is surely no accident that, among the extant commentaries, only those to Porphyry's *Isagoge* provide such general prolegomena, while those on Aristotle and Plato contain introductions specifically relating only to Aristotle and Plato and their works. Ammonius provides the simplest of these general introductions. It has become so elaborate in Elias and David, his pupils at one remove, that it has developed into a special segment of the lecture series with its own title, though its affiliation to the exegesis of Porphyry is assured by references. The complete course of lectures might, in keeping with modern custom, perhaps be entitled *Explanation of Porphyry's Isagoge with an Introduction to Philosophy*. This general introduction is matched by a special introduction to the study of Aristotle at the opening of the *Categories* lecture series,[35] which is divided into two parts:[36] the first concerns the philosophy and writings of Aristotle in general, the second the *Categories* in particular. The first comprises ten points, which are enumerated by Ammonius, Simplicius, Olympiodorus, Philoponus and Elias, in varying sequence and somewhat different formulations. The differences need not be mentioned here; it is sufficient to elaborate the points according to Simplicius (VIII 3,20ff; the sequence in Ammonius is palpably false): (1) 'In how many and what sorts of ways did the philosophical schools get their names? (*kata posous kai poious tropous tas onomasias eskhon hai kata philosophian haireseis*)'; (2) 'What is the division of the Aristotelian treatises (so that it becomes clear where in the

Autobiography (Heis.) 2,28: 'completely educated as regards terms (*phônai*), categories (*katêgoriai*), and on interpretation (*hermêneia*)'. Cf. further *Byz. Zeitschr.* II, 1893, 98, l.16

[35] cf. the beginning of Philoponus' commentary to the *Categories*: 'Just as when we began the *Isagoge* [only Porphyry's *Isagoge* could be meant; the plural occurs also at 12,19], we spoke of what pertains to all philosophy, and then marked off the object of the book then before us, so too as we now begin before the first (*prôtou*) Aristotelian treatise, let us speak of what pertains to all Aristotelian philosophy, and then we will define the object of the present book, the *Categories* (*Kathaper arkhomenoi tôn Eisagôgôn elegomen ta pros pasan philosophian sunteinonta, epeita aphorizometha ton skopon tou prokeimenou bibliou, houtô kai nun arkhomenoi pro tou* (*prôtou?*) *Aristotelikou sungrammatos eipômen ta pros pasan philosophian sunteinonta tên Aristotelikên philosophian, eith' houtôs ton skopon tou prokeimenou tôn Katêgoriôn bibliou diorisômetha)*'.

[36] Olympiodorus has three parts at 1,7 and accordingly in the exposition as well (3ff): Aristotelian philosophy, logic, categories. The second section contains the discussion of the question whether logic is a part (*meros*) or a tool (*organon*) of philosophy. That this is a subsequent elaboration of the original bi-partite schema becomes quite apparent from the fact that section III immediately picks up where section I leaves off. The tenth and last point in section I raises the question (1,23 = 12,18): 'How many and what sorts of things must be said about each treatise beforehand? (*posa kai tina dei hekastou sungrammatos prolegesthai)*'. The usual points are under discussion: theme (*skopos*), utility (*khrêsimon*), order (*taxis*), title (the reason for the title) (*epigraphê* (*hê tês epigraphês aitia*)), author (whether the book is authentic) (*sungrapheus* (*ei gnêsion to biblion*)), structure (the division into chapters) (*diaskeuê* (*hê eis ta kephalaia diairesis*)). Section III begins with the application of these points to the *Categories*, and section II intrusively intervenes. In Simplicius (8,9ff; 9,4ff), the original sequence is clearly recognisable.

sequence we should place the present book)? (*tis hê diairesis tôn Aristotelikôn sungrammatôn (hina kai to prokeimenon hopou khôrou taxômen genêtai dêlon))*'; (3) 'Where should one begin Aristotle's treatises? (*pothen arkteon tôn Aristotelous sungrammatôn*)'; (4) 'What is the end of Aristotle's philosophy? (*ti to telos estin tês Aristotelous philosophias*)'; (5) 'What leads us to this end? (*tina ta agonta hêmas pros to telos*)'; (6) 'What is the style of the Aristotelian treatises? (*ti to eidos tôn Aristotelikôn sungrammatôn*)'; (7) 'Why did the Philosopher choose unclear diction? (*dia ti tên asapheian epetêdeusen ho philosophos*)'; (8) 'What sort of interpreter is required for such arguments? (*poion dei ton exêgêtên einai tôn toioutôn logôn*)'; (9) 'What sort of audience should be admitted? (*poion dei ton akroatên paralambanesthai*)'; (10) 'How many chapters should one expect for each Aristotelian treatise, of what sort, and on what ground? (*posa dei prolambanein hekastês Aristotelikês pragmateias kephalaia kai poia kai dia poian aitian*)'.[37] In this list, two things ought to surprise us. First, why should there be a chapter here on the names of the philosophical schools, which contrasts so oddly with all the other sections? Naturally, it chiefly concerns only the name (of Aristotle's school) 'Peripatetic'. Its explanation has given rise to the entire chapter, which, incidentally, is very old, judging from its content.[38] While this state of affairs has become obscured in Ammonius (1,4.13ff) and Olympiodorus (1,16; 3,8ff), it is quite evident in Simplicius (3,19) and Elias (107,8). Philoponus (1,7) also emphasises the Aristotelian point of departure, although admittedly in a very clumsy manner.[39] Elias even considers it necessary to justify the extension of the inquiry to the names of all schools.[40] In any event, the first point can be formulated on Elias' model: 'Why is Aristotle's philosophy named thus, viz. "Peripatetic"? (*dia ti houtôs ônomasthê he Aristotelous philosophia, Peripatetikê*)'. With that, however, the matter is not yet closed. Whoever reads through the list of ten problems will ask himself, 'Why, alongside questions which concern Aristotle and Aristotelian studies in general, does there arise this detail

---

[37] According to Elias [*in Cat.* 107,24-6 – Ed.], this schema dates back to Proclus. Some traces can be found in Proclus' commentary on the *Timaeus*: I 348,15ff: 'secondly, he differentiated the arguments, thirdly he prepares the listener in such a way that the subsequent arguments will be accepted (*deuteron ton tropon aphôrisato tôn logôn, triton parakeuazei ton akroatên, hopôs prosêkei tous mellontas hupodekhesthai logous*)'; 355,3f: 'and such is the form of the arguments and such is the listener (*kai hopoion tôn logôn eidos kai hopoios ho akroatês*)'.

[38] cf. Diels *Dox. Gr.*, 246.

[39] 'Firstly, in how many ways the philosophical schools are named, so that we will know to which school the Philosopher belonged (*Prôton kata posous tropous onomazontai hai tôn philosophôn haireseis, hina gnômen ek poias haireseôs ên ho philosophos*)'.

[40] 'And the first of these ten is, why is Aristotle's philosophy named thus, viz. "Peripatetic". But since this is particular and unphilosophical (for the philosopher is fond of the universal), the general features must be looked into as for what and how many reasons the philosophical schools are named (*Kai prôton esti tôn deka, dia ti houtôs ônomasthê hê Aristotelous philosophia, Peripatêtikê. all' epeidê touto merikon kai aphilosophon (philokatholou gar ho philosophos), ta katholou zêteisthô dia tinas kai posas aitias ônomasthêsan hai kata philosophian haireseis*)'.

of language, which contrasts so strikingly with the remaining nine points?' There must be a hundred more such questions of detail, all with the same right to be considered. Why were not all of them handled or none at all? I mention the entire question only because it is an example of how our commentaries further scholarly research that has been concerned with other problems in recent years, and in turn how new light is thrown on our commentaries by such publications. The discovery of Didymus' commentary on Demosthenes' speeches[41] has provided an opportunity for discussions that frequently touch on general questions concerning the method of ancient commentaries. In this connection, Fr. Leo[42] emphasises that the actual commentary (*hupomnêma*) was intended to be read together with the text of the author, that it is only a portion of the book, of the commented edition. Here lies the solution, I believe, to the puzzle mentioned above. What holds true for the written commentary (*hupomnêma*) also holds true for the transcribed oral commentary. It presupposes that there is in the lecturer's hands a text of the writer to be explicated, which, as a part of the school library, is also available to the audience. The exegesis refers to this text step by step. Obviously, the text also traditionally contains the author's biography and a list of his writings as an introduction. Here, the lecturer only needs to add what seems appropriate to him. The section on the names of the Peripatetics and of other philosophical schools is probably such an addition, in fact, to a biographical introduction. Perhaps the origin of the name 'Peripatetic' was not mentioned at all in the introduction, or perhaps it was mentioned in isolation but the speaker thought it appropriate to set it in the context of the names of the schools and so to add this customary chapter here.

In the same way, the second shock the ten membered schema delivers is also softened. The second point concerns the question of how to divide Aristotle's writings. Nowhere is there offered what one would immediately expect, namely, a list of these writings. The individual works, as a rule preceded by 'as (*hôs*)' or 'such as are (*hoia estin*)', rather appear only as examples for the rubrics of the division (*diairesis*), in which the individual commentators vary in comprehensiveness when citing them. Surely the school library's text of Aristotle contained a list of writings, but one without an easily recognisable or memorable principle of organisation (just like the lists which have come down to us from Diogenes Laertius, the Anonymous Menagii and Ptolemy), and the division (*diairesis*) given by the commentators was intended to bring organisation and perspicuity to the collection.[43] The first and second

---

[41] *Berliner Klassikertexte, herausg. v. d. Generalverwaltung der Kgl. Museen zu Berlin,* Heft I, Berlin 1904.

[42] *Nachrichten von der Kgl. Gesellsch. d. Wiss. z. Gött.,* philol.-hist. Klasse 1904, 258.

[43] Fr. Littig, *Andronikos von Rhodes,* II Teil, Erlangen 1894 (Progr.), 16ff, traces this division back to Andronicus, but his demonstration of this does not seem successful to me. I would not, of course, offer as a successful counterargument that the Aristotelian treatise *de Interpretatione,* which was rejected by Andronicus (see the entry in Littig III 1895, 28ff), is

points are thus only supplements to the Aristotle edition. To combine these two points (especially the first) with the remaining ones, which are of a completely different nature, into a unbroken unity through a consecutive numbering was surely foolish. What can be offered in its defence, however, is the attempt, on the one hand, not to complicate the arrangement of the introduction further by distinguishing between matters supplementary to the edition and questions for independent discussion; and, on the other hand, to establish by the introduction of the same continuous numbering an easily surveyable correspondence between the overview of the problem and its detailed treatment (e.g. in Ammonius 1,4ff; 1,13ff; 3,21ff; 5,31ff; Olympiodorus 1,15; 3,8ff; 8,29ff; etc.).

The schema which provides the basis for the special introduction to the *Categories* which follows the general introduction to Aristotle also occurs in the introduction to other works and obviously at some point in time possessed a general validity.[44] It comprises the following points: the aim of the writing in question (*ton skopon*),[45] its authenticity (*to gnêsion*), its order in the list of readings (*tên taxin tês anagnôseôs*), the reason for its title (*tên aitian tês epigraphês*), its division into chapters (*tên eis kephalaia diairesin*), and the question as to which part of philosophy (or

---

considered here as genuine, since this work was taken from the list of writings in use and could have been inserted into Andronicus' division. On the Arabic sources in which the same principle of division is carried out, see Fr. Littig, *Andronikos von Rhodos*, I Teil, Munich 1890 (Progr.), 20ff. On this question, cf. also A. Baumstark, *Aristoteles bei den Syrern vom V.-VIII. Jahr.*, I, Leipzig 1900, 70ff.

[44] cf. Ammonius, *in Porph. Isag.* 21,6ff: 'We should also mention the things which the philosophers call prolegomena or technical preliminaries in every book (*dei de hêmas eipein kai ta pros tôn philosophôn houtô prosagoreuomena prolegomena êtoi protekhnologoumena epi pantos bibliou*)'. These prolegomena can be cited with great frequency in the commentary literature after Ammonius. Outside the *CAG*, for example, Olympiodorus, *in Gorg.* (Jahn) 108ff, *in Alcib.* (Creuzer) 3ff (3 aim (*skopos*), 9 utility (*khrêsimon*), 10 order (*taxis*), 11 division into chapters or parts (*eis ta kephalaia êtoi merê diaireseôs*)) can be cited. These points also extended to Latin commentary literature, as, for example, in Boethius, *in Isag.* (Brandt) 14,17. Thomas Aquinas can also be cited as an example from a later period, cf. *in Aristot. de Anima* 2a: 'One renders one's hearers well disposed by showing the *usefulness* of the knowledge, by first stating the *order* and *division* of the treatise (*benevolum ... reddit ostendendo utilitatem scientiae, docilem praemittendo ordinem et distinctionem tractatus*)'. Further: *In Boethii Severini de philosophiae consolatione opus Iohannis Murmellii Ruraemundensis praelibatio* (1514, printed in the Boethius edition, Basel 1570), 898: 'There are some things to be studied first with which the minds of students are fittingly prepared for what is to be treated; and these are Boethius' life, *the title of the work, the quality of the style* [by which surely the manner of instruction (*tropos tês didaskalias*) is meant], *the intention of the writer, the number of books, what the purpose of the work is, and to what part of philosophy it is to be assigned (... quaedam praelibanda sunt quibus studiosorum animi ad ea quae tractanda sunt non incongrue praeparentur. sunt autem haec: Boethii vita, titulus operis, styli qualitas, scribentis intentio, numerus librorum, quae sit operis utilitas et ad quam id philosophiae partem referatur*)'.

[45] [*Skopos*, literally 'aim', and accordingly Praechter translates it *Zweck*. But in fact it is used, like *prothesis*, for the theme, and this would have been a more helpful rendering. As noted above, the introductions do ask about the aim or end of Aristotle's philosophy, but the word there used is *telos*. – Ed.]

of the particular field of study in question) the writing concerned belongs (*hupo poion meros anagetai to paron sungramma*). Occasionally, the method of instruction (*ho tropos tês didaskalias*) occurs as a further subject of discussion. The order and formulation of this chapter vary;[46] the complete list, even apart from the the method of instruction (*tropos tês didaskalias*), is not always considered, and at times it is explicitly stated that one of the points can be left aside in consideration of special circumstances, while at other times this restriction intervenes silently.

The material which the Aristotle commentaries provide offers an opportunity for the investigation of this schema's history, something which is highly desirable. Fr. Littig traces its first instantiation to the new founder of Aristotelian studies in the first century BC, Andronicus of Rhodes.[47] What militates against this, however – at least, if my observations are correct – is the fact that then the schema would have disappeared from the literature for centuries, only to surface again in Ammonius' time.[48] Of course, it must be admitted that some of the points unified in the schema are mentioned several times after Andronicus. The question concerning the aim of the writings is very widespread. Andronicus spoke of the purpose (*prothesis*) of the *Categories*, according to *Schol. in Aristot.* (Brandis) 81a27; cf. also Alexander, *in An. Pr.* 8,2ff, 9,5. The aim (*skopos*) of Platonic dialogues plays a major role in Iamblichus' exegesis,[49] and his successors, such as Proclus (and later Olympiodorus) emphasised this point heavily. Alexander also mentions the reason for the title (*aitia tês epigraphês*), *in An. Pr.* 42,23 (cf. also *in de Sens.* 2,1: 'Even the title of the book reveals the purpose of the treatise itself (*dêloi de kai hê epigraphê tou bibliou tên prothesin tês kat' auto pragmateias*)'). Alexander puts purpose (*prothesis*) and utility (*khrêsimon*) together, at *in Top.* 1,3 (here the use (*khrêsimon*) was given by Aristotle himself); cf. also 26,24; 125,4-8. The sequence in which the Platonic writings should be read is an old problem (Albinus, *Isag.* 4; Diogenes Laertius 2,62; and so on). Calcidius combines the writer's purpose (*scriptoris propositum*) and the order (*ordinatio*) (*in Tim.* 4; the division into chapters is meant in the last expression, cf. ch. 7), while Dexippus combines aim (*skopos*) and title (*epigraphê*) (*in Cat.* 5,26-30); both of these men belong to the fourth century. Hierocles combines aim (*skopos*), order (*taxis*) and name (*epônumia*), *in Carm. Aur.*

---

[46] The compilation given in the text above is that of Ammonius, *in Porph. Isag.* 21,8ff. The manner of teaching (*tropos tês didaskalias*) (the phrase is from Plato, *Cratylus* 435E) is in Ammonius, *in Porph. Isag.* 23,18; 26,5; *in Cat.* 66,6 (cf. 80,15); Philoponus, *in Cat.* 102,16; Elias, *in Porph. Isag.* 35,7; 40,8; *in Cat.* 129,1; David, *in Porph. Isag.* 80,14; 93,25; 95,10 (cf. also p. x, 2 lines from the bottom, in the preface to David's commentary on the *Categories*); Anon., *in de Interp.*, schol. in Aristot. (Brandis), 93a11; Proclus, *in Resp.* II. 8,8f; Anon., *Proleg. Phil. Platon.* (Herm) 27. 220,27f.

[47] *Andronikos von Rhodos* II. 19f.

[48] [But see now Hans B. Gottschalk, in Chapter 3, and I. Hadot, 'Les introductions aux commentaires exégétiques chez les auteurs néoplatoniciens et les auteurs chrétiens', in Michel Tardieu (ed.), *Les règles de l'interprétation*, Paris 1978. – Ed.]

[49] cf. *Gött. gel. Anz.*, 1905, 526f.

(Mullach) 417a.[50] I have not, however, encountered the set schema mentioned above anywhere before Ammonius.[51] If further investigations do confirm it to be of later origin, this schema will be useful for literary criticism.

The inauthentic Hippolytus fragment 7 from the introduction to the Psalms is ascribed to Origen in the Syrian Ambros., while the other three Greek MSS used by H. Achelis provide no name. It begins: 'And this is the aim and *utility* of the book; but the *reason for its title* is this. (*Kai houtos men tês bibliou ho skopos kai to khrêsimon. hê de aitia tês epigraphês hautê)*'. If fr. 9 – which according to Barber. III 59 likewise belongs to Origen and is again left anonymous by the three Greek MSS – is of the same origin, then the order (*taxis*) may be added to the three points (140,17 Ach; what precedes is a discussion of the number of the Psalms, which could correspond to the division into chapters (*eis kephalaia diairesis*), but the technical expression is not used). The combination of the three points (still more, if four) arouses the most lively suspicion against its being attributed to Origen, since the prolegomena schematism is unlikely, even thus abridged, for the beginning of the third century. A Latin commentary by Oribasius on the Hippocratic Aphorisms[52] would also be revealed as a forgery because the preface immediately mentions the aim[53] of the writing ('... to this he has directed his study (*...eo studium suum dirigit)'*, p. 6), then its utility ('it is useful (*utilem vero)'*, p. 7), and its authenticity (p. 7), after which the rest of the usual questions follow: 'to what part of the medical art is this book to be assigned? (*in quam partem artis medicae liber hic redigatur)'* (p. 8); 'if you ask in what order the rest is to be read (*caeterum si quo ordine legendus sit quaeras)'* (p. 9); 'then if one asks of the method of instruction (*ho tropos tês didaskalias) (modus doctrinae si quaeritur)'* (p. 9); 'But in how many parts is the present book divided? What is its title (*aitia tês epigraphês*)? (*at in quot partes praesens liber dividitur? quid est aphorismus?)'*.

If we proceed from the introduction to the actual commentary, we find – in Olympiodorus, Elias and David, in the third book of Philoponus' commentary on the *de Anima*[53a] and in Stephanus – an organisation of

---

[50] 'And this is the *object* of the epic verses and the *order*: to present the philosophical character to the listeners before the other lessons [i.e. the order (*taxis*) of the poems is that they should be read before any other reading, and their aim is to represent the philosophical character (*kharaktêr philosophos*) to the listeners]; they are called "golden" because of their being, as far as epic poems go, the best and divine (*Kai houtos men ho skopos tôn epôn, kai hê taxis, kharaktêra philosophon pro tôn allôn anagnôsmatôn ektheinai tois akroatais khrusa de tên epônumian eskhe dia to hôs en epesin arista einai kai theia)'*.

[51] In whose time it appears to have been rather generally widespread already; see nn. [37 and] 44.

[52] *Oribasii medici clarissimi commentaria in Aphorismos Hippocratis hactenus non visa, Ioannis Guinterij Andernaci doctoris medici industria velut e profundissimis tenebris eruta et nunc primum in medicinae studiosorum utilitatem aedita*. Basileae. Ex officine And. Cratandri. 1535 I must thank my friend in Bern, S. Singer, for verifying the title of the Berner Stadtbibliothek's text (no. 133).

[53] [See n. 45 above. – Ed.]

[53a] [Now commonly, but not with certainty, ascribed to Stephanus. – Ed.]

the content which is instructive with respect to commentary methods and teaching. A lesson (*praxis*)[54] is divided, insofar as the material allows, into two parts, a general discussion (*theôria*) and an explanation of the text (*lexis*), of which the first provides an exegesis of a portion of text as regards its main content and its larger context, while the second provides a detailed exegesis focusing on individual sentences and words.[55] With the paucity of immediate testimonies concerning the external conditions of teaching, the question arises as to whether knowledge can perhaps be gained from the written transcripts of the lessons (*praxeis*) as to the extent and duration of the lecture. Was it fixed to a determinate period, corresponding to our class hour, or in delimiting it was it primarily finishing the subject matter that was decisive? (Although even in this case the duration of time could not go completely unnoticed, since a seminar (*sunousia*) could not possibly last an entire day or longer). The significant difference in the size of individual lessons (*praxeis*) within one and the same commentary seems to suggest the latter alternative.[56] Yet the transcript's asymmetries could be in play here too. It is, for example, quite natural that there is less to be taken down in a class hour in which a small number of facts are proved in detail through examples, than in a lecture which is saturated from start to finish with important and well integrated material. We must therefore look for more reliable criteria. As such, the following considerations come to mind. (1) The treatment of a lemma in a general discussion (*theôria*) and an exegesis of text always ends together with the full lesson (*praxis*), not even occasionally in the middle of one so as to make the general discussion (*theôria*) of a new portion of text begin in the middle of the lesson (*praxis*) in question. The latter might be thought to be the case if the lecturer had to fill out a determinate period of time with his lecture. Judging from the overall character of these lectures, it is difficult to believe that an agreement between the lecture's constraints on content and time was worked out through previous experiment or calculation. (2) There are also never two groups comprising general discussion (*theôria*) and *lexis* interpretation

---

[54] *Prattein* as a scholastic term means 'to treat exegetically': *Proleg. Plat. Phil.* (Herm.) 26, 219,29f: 'Of these [certain Platonic dialogues], it is worthwhile to inquire about the order because everybody expects these to be treated exegetically also. First then one should explain the *Alcibiades* (*toutôn de axion esti tên taxin zêtêsai, dioti kai toutous êxiôsan pantes prattesthai. prôton toinun dei ton Alkibiadên prattein)'*. 220,13f: 'But since some think it worthwhile to give an exegesis of the *Laws* and the *Republic*... (*epeidê de kai tous Nomous kai tas Politeias prattein axiousi tines)'*. When used absolutely, it means 'to perform an exegesis'. *Praxis* as 'exegesis' is broader in meaning than the individual exegetical lecture or its lecture plan; cf. Marinus, *Vita Procli* 22: 'For with measureless love of toil, he used to give five exegeses, and sometimes even more, in the same day, usually writing about 700 lines (*philoponiai gar ametrôi khêsamenos exêgeito tês autês hêmeras pentê, hote de kai pleious praxeis kai egraphe stikhous ta polla amphi tous heptakosious)'*.

[55] For further details, cf. *Gött. gel. Anz.*, 1904, 382ff; 1905, 532f; 1906, 898f; 1908, 222ff.

[56] [É. Évrard contrasts Philoponus' *Physics* commentary, in which lessons last about an hour, regardless of the divisions of the subject: *L'école d'Olympiodore et la composition du 'commentaire à la Physique' de Jean Philopon*, Diss. Liège 1957. This commentary provides an earlier use of the format than those listed by Praechter above. – Ed.]

joined together in a single lesson (*praxis*), as would be expected occasionally if the lesson (*praxis*) had to fill a certain amount of time. (3) The close of a lesson (*praxis*) is announced by a reference to the subject matter. Thus Stephanus, *in Int.* 34,1ff: 'But this suffices for the present general discussion. We will learn how he does this [the solution of a puzzle by Aristotle], with the grace of God, in another general discussion. *With the text clear and all that is in it well discussed here, we shall bring the present lesson to a close (all' arkei tauta tēi parousēi theōriāi. pōs gar touto poiei en heterai theōriāi sun theōi mathēsometha. saphous de tēs lexeōs ousēs kai pantōn tōn en autēi kalōs theōrēthentōn en toutois tēnde tēn parousan praxin katapausōmen)*'. If all these facts militate against an analogy to our class hour, then, on the other hand, natural limitations on a lecture suggest certain temporal boundaries arising from the circumstances themselves, in that very extensive general discussions (*theōriai*) can be divided into several lessons (*praxeis*) and after a long general discussion (*theōria*) the interpretation of the text (*lexis*) assigned to the following lesson (*praxis*).[57]

These are only a few of the numerous questions concerning commentary method and the organisation of teaching whose investigation the new commentators' texts will encourage. Of others, I will mention only the coexistence of dialogue-[58] and lecture-commentaries, which are likewise a reflection of two forms of teaching, having their parallel in the seminars and lectures of university instruction. The dialogue-commentary of the sort found in Porphyry's *in Cat.* is at once related to the catechising also represented in other areas of ancient and Byzantine literature[59] and to the oral examination.[60] The different types of commentaries (as regards content and form) should be recalled as they are mentioned in the *loci classici*, Simplicius, *in Cat.* 1,8ff and Sophonias, *in DA* 1,4ff. Among them, the paraphrase, as uniquely depicted by Sophonias (1,11ff), is a remarkable example, even in this purely technical literature, of the Greeks' surviving feeling for style, which objects to the disunity and disharmony of the commentary's usual form, owing to the alternation from the author's words in the lemma to the commentator's subsequent explanation, and to his tearing the writer's text to pieces.[61]

If we turn to the commentaries' significance for our understanding of

---

[57] Supporting evidence can be found in *Gött. gel. Anz.*, 1908, 222-4.

[58] Porphyry's and Dexippus' commentaries on the *Categories*, and Boethius' first commentary on Porphyry's *Isagoge*.

[59] cf. e.g. Cicero, *de Partitione Oratoria*; Philo, *Quaestiones in Genesim* and *in Exodum*; C. Chirius Fortunatianus, *Ars Rhetorica*; Bakcheius, *Eisagōgē technēs mousikēs*; Manuel Moschopulos, *erōtēmata grammatika* and *peri skhedōn*.

[60] *Byz. Zeitschr.* II, 1893, 97ff.

[61] Sophonias, *in de An.* 1,11ff: 'But pretending to be Aristotle himself and using his own voice as a mask *in order that the whole may be seen as one and not cut apart*, they [namely, the paraphrasts] have left his own text aside, neither dividing it nor unifying it in their treatises (*auton gar hupoduntes Aristotelēn kai tōi tēs autaggelias proskhrēsamenon prosōpeiōi, hōs eusunopton kai to pan hen eiē kai mē diakoptoito, tēn men lexin parēkan autēn, oute diēirēmenēn outh' hēnōmenēn tois hupomnēmasi suntaxamenoi)*'.

philosophy in late antiquity and the Byzantine period, then it is to be highly valued here as well. The development of philosophical ideas in this period was realised essentially in the form of exegesis. This is a sufficient reason for writers of the history of philosophy to regard it primarily from this point of view, and to direct their attention to the different methods and changing principles of exegesis and the correspondingly varying conception the authors have of Plato and Aristotle. Proclus' commentary on Plato's *Timaeus*, for example, contains an abundance of material for the history of exegesis that is still little used; the Aristotle commentaries are likewise very fertile. When this task is approached one day in earnest, there will develop a sharper eye for fine distinctions, and the individual features of commentators who for us still disappear in the great mass will become recognisable, affording a glance into the development of the exegesis of Aristotle, and thereby into the development of philosophical views as well. Elsewhere,[62] I have attempted to show that we obtain a new image of Iamblichus as soon as we investigate his principles of exegesis, a depiction which helps us to understand the powerful inspiration with which this man inflamed his students. With respect to exegesis, Syrianus, Ammonius, Asclepius and Simplicius are also fascinating.[63] Above all, however, the impressive corpus of Aristotle commentators will teach us to depart from the one-sidedness which is still predominant in the writing of the history of Greek philosophy, and which has completely assimilated the philosophical development from the third century AD onwards to the on-going formation of the Neoplatonic system.[64] Even E. Zeller has been influenced by this tendency. For example, he discusses Themistius under the Neoplatonists, even though admittedly none of Neoplatonism's distinguishing characteristics are evident in him.[65] It is simply that under the prevailing paradigm no other lodging is to be found. This is the punishment for having held the significance of exegesis in too little esteem. For the philosophers of this time, it is not at all a matter of system building, of the quest for truth on the path of independent speculation. Plato and Aristotle are to be explained – the truth lies resolved in their works. Thus, the emphasis of Aristotle exegesis lay in itself, even where influenced by Neoplatonic views. Yet frequently this influence also retreats entirely, especially in the area of logic, which is neutral by its own nature. This non-partisan commentary activity, which is independent of the religio-philosophical tendencies of Neoplatonism, is of immense importance to the greater historical context. It paves the way for ancient philosophical instruction in the Christian world. With exegesis conducted in this way, there was little or nothing to prune away for it to be acceptable to the adherents of the new religion too. With all the

[62] *Gött. gel. Anz.*, 1905, 525ff.

[63] ibid. 1903, 526.

[64] On this matter, Paul Tannery has made some excellent remarks in his essay, 'Sur la période finale de la philosophie grecque', *Revue philosophique* XLII, 1896, 266ff.

[65] [But cf. Henry J. Blumenthal in Chapter 13. – Ed.]

fanatical hatred with which the adherents of the old and new religions battled, here was a field on which they could in fact meet in peace. Thus, the philosophical schools were able to become Christian. How peaceful the completion of this transition may have been is demonstrated by the relation of Philoponus, David and Elias to Ammonius, Simplicius and Olympiodorus.[66] Ammonius' course on the *Categories* could be read before Christians as much as Elias' course before pagans. In this way the Aristotle commentaries lead us unnoticeably to Christian scholasticism. Boethius, the founder of Aristotelian studies in the Christian West, belongs by nature to our commentators series, though his language separates him.[67] The continuing effect of the Greek commentators on Byzantine intellectual life – which must have been mediated by teaching during centuries of literary unproductivity as well – can now be traced with the help of these new complete texts. Interest in Aristotle led to the creation of new commentaries during the Byzantine renaissance, from which the Academy edition has brought to life a truly respectable interpreter of Aristotle in Michael of Ephesus.[68] The multifaceted character of his Aristotelian studies is noteworthy. Only now can that be judged. The new edition offers for the first time a more reliable foundation for the several commentaries which do not appear in the tradition as his work (or not incontestably) and could only be attributed to him on the basis of research into their language and content. Michael commented on the most varied writings in the Aristotelian corpus, as few before him had done. From the Organon, he worked on the *Prior* and *Posterior Analytics*, the *Topics*, the treatise *de Interpretatione* (cf. *CAG* IV 5, p. xlv), and the *Sophistici Elenchi* (contained in *CAG* II 3); from the *Metaphysics*, he commented upon books 7-14 (according to his *in Parva Naturalia*, *CAG* XXII 1, p. 149,15), while books 6-14 are extant under Alexander of Aphrodisias' name in *CAG* I;[69] of the works on natural science, he commented on the *Physics* and the *de Caelo*. He did not halt, as the rest of the Aristotle interpreters did (with few exceptions),[70] before

[66] [But for Simplicius, see P. Hoffmann, n. 10 above and for Philoponus, K. Verrycken, Chapter 11. – Ed.]

[67] The Wiener Akademie has included him in the plan of the *Corpus scriptorum ecclesiasticorum Latinorum*, and in 1883 the edition was commissioned to G. Schepss. Cf. praef., p. v, of the first volume which has appeared in the meantime: *Ancii Manlii Serverini Boethii in Isagogen Porphyrii commenta. Copiis a Georgio Schepss comparatis suisque usus rec. Samuel Brandt*, Vindob. Lips. 1906 (*Corp. script. eccl. Lat.*, vol. 48). This supplements Usener's note, *Gött. gel. Anz.*, 1892, 1008.

[68] For details on Michael and his works, cf. *Gött. gel. Anz.*, 1906, 879ff; O. Immisch (ed.), *Pol.*, xviff.

[69] [The ascription of 6-14 to Michael is still controversial. See e.g. Leonardo Tarán, review of Paul Moraux, *Der Aristotelismus* vol. 1 in *Gnomon*. L.6, 1981, 721-50, at 750; P. Thillet in the Budé edition of Alexander *de Fato*, p. lvii; Sten Ebbesen, *Commentators and Commentaries on Aristotle's Sophistici Elenchi*, Corpus Latinum Commentariorum in Aristotlem Graecorum 7.3, Leiden 1981, 87. – Ed.]

[70] Boethius at least planned a translation and exegesis of all Aristotelian works (according to the second edition of the commentary on the *de Interpretatione* (Meiser) 79,16ff). Georgios Pachymeres treated the works on natural science: *in de Gen. Anim.* and *in*

the anthropological and zoological writings, with their abundance of
details from natural history. It appears that it was a medical and
scientific interest, due to either predisposition or career, which led him to
be active exegetically here as well. His commentary on the *Parva
Naturalia* is extant. According to a list of Aristotle exegetes contained in
a manuscript,[71] he commented on the *Historia Animalium*. While
nothing is otherwise known of these works, we do nevertheless have his
commentaries on the *de Generatione Animalium* (XIV 3), the *de Partibus
Animalium*, the *de Motu Animalium* and the *de Incessu Animalium*. A
further work (proposed by Michael at *in Parv. Nat.* 149,16, but cited as
complete in the manuscript list) dealt with the *de Coloribus*. Michael's *de
Anima* was probably also a commentary. The commentary to books 5, 9
and 10 of the *Nichomachean Ethics* are also extant. Finally, Michael gave
his attention to two works, of which the first has rarely and the second (as
far as we know) has never been commented on in the Greek language: the
Rhetoric and the *Politics*. That Michael was involved with the latter has
only recently been ascertained. O. Immisch, in the appendix to his edition
of Aristotle's *Politics*, published the scholia of *cod. Hamiltonianus*,[72]
whose author refers (ad loc. 1282a3ff) to his exegesis of the treatise *de
Partibus Animalium*. The conclusion which Immisch drew from this (p.
xvi), namely, that we are dealing with Michael of Ephesus here, can be
confirmed. Aside from him, Georgios Pachymeres is the only other
commentator on the *de Partibus Animalium* we know of.[73] The few
indeterminate allusions to contemporary affairs[74] are insufficient to draw
a conclusion, but the language is sufficient. A whole series of Michael's
idiosyncracies recur in this small scholia selection.[75] Immisch (p. xviii)
has already indicated the cultural-historical significance of this
commentary on the *Politics*. Aristotle's *Politics* was made accessible to
the West in the thirteenth century and formed the foundation for the
development of political theory, which was based on Aristotle for
centuries thereafter. The Byzantine renaissance, as regards interest in

de Part. Anim. are known from the library catalogue of *cod. Paris* 2328, according to
Cramers *Anec Paris*. I 393; and Theodorus Metochites did as well, cf. K. Krumbacher, *Gesch.
d. byz. Lit.*[2], 552f.

[71] In *cod. Marc.* 203 (H. Usener, *Rhein Mus.* XX, 1865, 135f) and *cod. Vat.* 241 (M.
Hayduck, *CAG* 18.3, p. v).

[72] *Aristotelis Politica*, post F. Susemihlium recog. Otto Immisch, Lipsiae 1909 (Bibl.
Teubn.), 295ff.

[73] See n. 70 above.

[74] Immisch, xviif.

[75] A comparison of the scholia with the compilations in *Gött. gel. Anz.* 1906, 885ff yields
this result. Substantial agreements of characteristic expressions can be demonstrated. 'The
crows among us (*hoi kath' hêmôn korakes*)' of 303,34 (Immisch) can be compared to 'the
crows among us (*tous kath' hêmas korakes*)' of *in Eth.* 587,20. Immisch has already
emphasised (p. xviii) that corresponding to the exegesis of the *Politics* referred to as being in
the future in the commentary on the *Ethics*, there is an exegesis of the *Ethics* cited in our
scholia. Besides, an agreement in diction demonstrates that it is the extant *Ethics*
commentary which is in question: both *in Eth.* X 578,19 and *in Pol.* (Immisch) 305,21, in
deviating from Aristotle, speak of the happy man who is politically active (*politikos
eudaimôn*).

this treatise, is ahead by about two centuries.[75a]

Michael's on the whole sober and intelligent exegesis may have furthered Aristotelian studies considerably in his time and can also provide essential services to the inexperienced reader of Aristotle today. Above all, he seeks to make Aristotle's concise expression more intelligible through paraphrase and to elucidate the context by demonstrating the connection of thought; he also frequently eases one's concentration through examples. Yet he also has value for the experienced reader owing to his preservation of many sorts of valuable materials, however trivial they were to the author's overall historical-philological interests, and owing to the perspective he permits on the philosophical tendencies of his time. It cannot be doubted that such a literarily productive man, who in addition – unless everything is deceptive – held a teaching position, was linked through numerous connections to his contemporaries and their views. It is a sign of how insufficient our knowledge is of the personalities and intellectual life in the eleventh century that we are virtually unable to discover a single one of these connections, and that for us such a man is an almost completely isolated phenomenon, to whom we cannot form ties anywhere and whose date we can supposedly determine according to only very general indices. The century of Michael Psellos, Eustratius, and Ioannes Italos serves as a point of contact for a more detailed characterisation of the philosophical writer, even when it is a commentator working largely with an inherited legacy. Yet the material lies partly unedited in the dust of libraries, partly in editions which are unusable for scholarly purposes, and the rest offers few returns for the moment in its isolation. Acquisition kindles new desires: now that Michael of Ephesus has been given back to us, the more anxious is our longing for the resuscitation of Psellos and his follower, Ioannes Italos. If those men were joined from the following centuries by Nicephorus Blemmydes, Georgios Pachymeres, Theodorus Metochites, and perhaps Leon Magentinos (who was originally accepted in the plan of the Academy's enterprise, but then struck from it) together with their philosophical work, then our knowledge of the philosophy of the later Byzantine period would be placed on a substantially broader and more secure foundation. If we may be permitted to hope that the Academy and the directors of the commentary venture will also expeditiously join in here – as they have often stimulated and supported the editions of related writers in connection with the corpus of Aristotle commentators – then they can be certain of the renewed thanks of all Byzantine specialists.[76]

As an addendum, a few words may be said here as regards the

[75a] [One century, given Browning's redating of Michael to the twelfth century in Chapter 17. This also affects the next paragraph. – Ed.]

[76] As a demonstration that the editions of philosophical comentaries can be of benefit to the exegesis of even quite distant literature, one may be casually directed to *Byz. Zeitschr*. XIV, 1905, 219, ll. 7ff, 490f (the passage of Elias can be found in the Academy edition, 6,32ff; cf. also 24,21ff). The definition of philosophy mentioned in the first passage is one of the six treated in the *Isagoge* commentaries of Ammonius, Elias and David.

Supplementum Aristotelicum. It is intended to complete the Aristotle edition as well as the commentator edition, and it contains, besides the rediscovered Aristotelian *Ath. Pol.* (III 2), a number of writings which, without being in the form of a commentary, belong to the testimonies of Aristotelian studies in antiquity and the Middle Ages. Both parts of the first volume will interest the Byzantine specialist. The writing published in the first part belongs to the encyclopaedic literature which Constantinus Porphyrogenitus engendered. It is a work of zoological excerpts, whose title reports the content and sources as follows: 'Summary of the investigations of land, air, and sea animals, elaborated for Constantine the Great King and Emperor. Aristophanes' [the Alexandrian Philologist's] abridgement of Aristotle's *On Animals*, arranged by animal and what is said about them by Aelianus, Timothy [the Philologist from Gaza about 500 AD] and others (*Sullogê tês peri zôiôn historias khersaiôn ptênôn te kai thalattiôn Kônstantinôi tôi megalôi basilei kai autokratori philoponêtheisa. Aristophanous tôn Aristotelous peri zôiôn epitomê hupotethentôn hekastôi zôiôi kai tôn Ailianôi kai Timotheôi kai heterois tisi peri autôn eirêmenôn)'*. Among the excerpts, those from Timothy deserve special attention for their stylistic character. On this matter, cf. H. Usener, *Gött. gel. Anz.* 1892, p. 1019, where he confirms the observance of the law of sentence conclusions discovered by W. Meyer. The second part of the volume brings us to the period of the Athenian philosophers' emigration to the court of the Persian king Chosroes, after the closing of the school in Athens. Priscian took part in this exodus, and his *Solutiones* is a work that is directly linked with this outcome, but at the same time also deals with the question of the origin of Neoplatonism and makes use of important material. The writing appears here complete for the first time. Also Priscian's Metaphrasis of Theophrastus' *de Sensu et de Imaginatione*, which is of importance primarily for Theophrastus, yet also for Neoplatonism, will become available for the first time with this edition.

Despite its brevity, this survey of the Academy's commentary enterprise may provide some idea of the riches which are here offered to scholarship, while at the same time suggesting the tasks which it incurs. May their resolution be vigorously engaged on all fronts. For their great gift, the highest gratitude is owed to the Academy and all those who worked with the project, and above all to their most deserving and untiring director.

CHAPTER THREE

The earliest Aristotelian commentators*

Hans B. Gottschalk

I

The tradition of writing commentaries on Aristotle's works began about the middle of the first century BC, in a (successful) attempt to revive the Aristotelian school after a period of eclipse lasting a century and a half. The reasons for this eclipse are obscure and probably complex, but one factor which seemed important at the time was the inaccessibility of Aristotle's most important philosophical writings, the so-called *pragmateiai* or 'school-treatises'. Andronicus of Rhodes set out to remedy this by preparing a new, critical edition of these works; he received some help from Tyrannio of Amisus, a well-known grammarian settled at Rome, who supplied him with copies of Aristotelian manuscripts which had found their way into the library of a certain Apellicon and had been taken from Athens to Rome by Sulla after his sack of Athens in 86 BC, but Andronicus seems to have been fully responsible for the editorial work.[1] However, this edition was only one part of a larger scheme aimed at

---

* This is a reprint, with some additions and revisions, of pp. 1089-112 and 1150-1 of an article entitled 'Aristotelian philosophy in the Roman world from the time of Cicero to the end of the second century AD' in *Aufstieg und Niedergang der römischen Welt (ANRW)* II 36 pt. 2, 1079-174. Some of the additional material was first presented in a paper read at the Institute of Classical Studies, London, in February 1988; I am very grateful to Richard Sorabji for his helpful comments on this. The most important general works dealing with this period are E. Zeller, *Die Philosophie der Griechen* III 1⁴, 1909, 641-53; F. Überweg and K. Praechter, *Grundriss der Geschichte der Philosophie des Altertums*, 11th edition, Berlin 1920, 568ff, 12th edition, Berlin 1926, 556ff (the 11th edition contains very full bibliographies up to the time of the First World War, while that of the 12th is more selective); P. Moraux, *Der Aristotelismus bei den Griechen* I-II, Berlin 1973-84 (where no volume number is given, the references are to vol. I). For logic, see K. Prantl, *Geschichte der Logik im Abendlande* I, Leipzig 1855, 582ff and W. and M. Kneale, *The Development of Logic*, Oxford 1962, 181ff. Further references are given by Moraux *passim* and in my *ANRW* article, 1081ff.

[1] cf. *ANRW* 36.2.1083ff. On Andronicus' edition see F. Littig, *Andronicus von Rhodos* I, Munich 1890, II-III, Erlangen 1894-5; M. Plezia, *De Andronici Rhodii studiis Aristotelicis*, Cracow 1946; P. Moraux, *Les listes anciennes des ouvrages d'Aristote*, Louvain 1951, 283ff, *Aristotelismus* I 58ff; I. Düring, *Aristotle in the Ancient Biographical Tradition*, Göteborg 1957, 472ff (this work, a collection of testimonia with commentary, is henceforth abbreviated *AB*).

making Aristotle's writings available in a form which contemporary philosophers would find suitable to their needs and interests. In one sense it was selective: it included the main philosophical school-treatises of Aristotle[2] and some by Theophrastus, but not, it seems, the purely factual writings and collections of material or the published 'exoteric' works by which he was chiefly known to Cicero and his contemporaries.[3] But it was accompanied by commentaries on some treatises and a catalogue which, in the tradition of Callimachus' *Pinakes*, included not only a detailed enumeration of Aristotle's (and Theophrastus') writings, but a certain amount of biographical and other material helpful for understanding Aristotle and his work. Our most important information about the character of the edition comes from a passage of Porphyry's *Life of Plotinus*:

> Since Plotinus had entrusted to me the task of arranging and emending his books ... I decided first of all not to allow them to remain in a random chronological order as they had been issued; but following the example of Apollodorus of Athens and Andronicus the Peripatetic, of whom the first collected (the works of) the comic writer Epicharmus into ten volumes and the other grouped the writings of Aristotle and Theophrastus into treatises, bringing together those on related subjects, in the same way I grouped the fifty-four books of Plotinus I had into six Enneads.[4]

The result can be seen by comparing the catalogue of Aristotle's writings preserved in some Arabic sources,[5] which is derived from that of Andronicus, with the Hellenistic catalogue preserved by Diogenes

---

[2] Excluding the *de Interpretatione*, which Andronicus thought spurious (Ammon. *in Int.* 5,28ff, cf. Philop. *in DA*. 27,21f) and *Metaph.* 2. On the collection of Aristotle's letters he is said to have made see below, p. 58.

[3] cf. Moraux, *Arist.*, 63.

[4] Porph. *Vit. Plot.* 24 – *AB* T 75g; see also ch. 26 fin, about the summaries he added to his edition. Jacoby has doubted the existence of Andronicus' edition, arguing that Porphyry here refers only to his catalogue (*Comm. on FGH* 244 F 213-18, p. 795), but Porphyry was using Andronicus as a precedent for his own edition of Plotinus. Cf. Moraux, *Arist.*, 59, R. Pfeiffer, *History of Classical Scholarship*, Oxford 1968, I 264. On Porphyry's editorial work see now M.-O. Goulet-Cazé, in id., L. Brisson, D. O'Brien et al. (eds), *Porphyre, La Vie de Plotin*, I, Travaux préliminaires (Histoire des doctrines de l'ant. class. VI), Paris 1982, 280ff, and D. O'Brien, ibid. 350ff; on the character of his life in general, H.J. Blumenthal, 'Marinus' Life of Proclus: neoplatonist biography', *Byzantion* 54, 1984, 471.

[5] This catalogue formed part of a *Life* of Aristotle by a certain Ptolemy-al-Ġarîb (P. the Stranger or the Unknown) which until recently was only known from excerpts in later Arabic compilations (edited by Düring, *AB* 185ff); a complete Arabic version has recently turned up in a manuscript at Constantinople, cf. I. Düring, 'Ptolemy's *Vita Aristotelis* rediscovered', in R.B. Palmer, R. Hamerton-Kelly (eds), *Philomathes: Studies... in Memory of P. Merlan*, The Hague 1971, 264-9, and M. Plezia, 'De Ptolemaeo Pinacographo', *Eos* 63, 1975, 37-42 (Prof. Plezia has kindly informed me that he and Prof. J. Bielawski hope to publish a complete edition in the next three years or so). In the preface to this life, published in translation by Düring loc. cit., the writer refers to the work of Andronicus but states that he did not have it to hand at the time of writing (and presumably had to rely on memory and notes made earlier). The writer of the Greek original was until recently taken to have been a Platonist of the fourth century AD; see Plezia loc cit., A. Dihle, 'Der Platoniker Ptolemaios',

Laertius (5.22ff). Ptolemy-al-Ġarîb includes, as items 29-56, nearly all the school-treatises extant today, with the same titles and, except for the *Poetics* and *Metaphysics*, the same number of books. Diogenes lists many of the same writings, but usually as short works of from one to three books, with different titles from those known to us. For example, instead of our eight-book *Physics*, Diogenes has a three-book *Peri phuseôs* (no. 90), one book entitled *Phusikon* (no. 91) and one *Peri kinêseôs* (no. 115); probably all three were books later incorporated in the *Physics*. Diogenes' *Êthika* in five books (no. 38) may be our *Eudemian Ethics* without the three books in common to it and the *Nicomachean Ethics*;[6] Ptolemy has the *Eudemian Ethics*, under that name, in eight books (no. 36). Our *Rhetoric* in three books is catalogued by Ptolemy (no. 39), but Diogenes has a *Tekhnê rhêtorikê* in two books (no. 78) and the third book separately under the title *Peri lexeôs*, divided into two books (no. 87). A particularly striking case is that of the *Prior Analytics*, which Diogenes describes as having no fewer than nine books; it must have consisted of quite short sections which Andronicus collected into the two long books we still have today.[7] Some at least of Theophrastus' writings were treated in the same way. A subscription at the end of book 7 of the *Historia Plantarum* tells us that Andronicus gave it the place and title it has today, while Hermippus knew it (presumably together with book 6) by the title, *On under-shrubs and grasses*.[8]

This process of consolidation did not originate with Andronicus, but can be traced to the beginning of the Peripatetic school. Andronicus himself, when considering the place of the *Postpraedicamenta* in the *Corpus*, referred to earlier attempts to arrange the logical treatises.[9] In Diogenes' catalogue we find the *Politics* already collected into eight books (no. 74), although there can be no doubt that this work consists of parts written at widely different times, and since the author of the catalogue seems unsure whether to attribute it to Aristotle or Theophrastus, it may have

---

Hermes 85, 1957, 314ff (=id. *Antike und Orient. Gesammelte Aufsätze*, V. Pöschl, H. Petersmann (eds), Heidelberg 1984, 9ff), Moraux, *Arist.*, 60 n. 6. But see now M. Plezia, 'De Ptolemaei Vita Aristotelis', in J. Wiesner (ed.), *Aristoteles: Werk und Wirkung, Paul Moraux gewidmet* I, Berlin 1985, 1-11; here he argues persuasively that the author of the *Vita* was a Peripatetic, not a Platonist, and repeats his earlier proof that he was not the main source of the extant Neoplatonic 'Lives' of Aristotle. The identification with P. Chennos, a grammarian and mythographer active in the second century AD, has now been exploded. Cf. below p. 60 and now D. Gutas, 'The spurious and the authentic in the Arabic Lives of Aristotle', in J. Kraye et al. (eds), *Pseudo-Aristotle in the Middle Ages*, London 1986, 15-36.

[6] This is the traditional view (Moraux, *Listes*, 80f), but recently Kenny (*The Aristotelian Ethics*, Oxford 1978, 39ff) has suggested that it may be Books 1-5 of the extant *EE*, while the titles *Peri philias* (no. 24) and *Peri pathôn orgês* (no. 37) represent our books 7(-8) and 6 respectively. On the *EN*, which is found in neither catalogue, see below, p. 68.

[7] cf. Moraux, *Listes*, 87f, *Arist.*, 60ff, with more examples.

[8] *Peri phruganikôn kai poiôdôn*; the title is taken from the opening words of Book 6. The subscription is found in the oldest MS, U, and two later ones; in the Aldine edition it has been transferred to the beginning of Book 8 (see further Regenbogen, *RE* Suppl. VII, 1940, 1373f, 1451f, with references).

[9] Simpl. *in Cat.* 379,8ff, cf. Moraux, *Arist.*, 99 n. 12.

been Theophrastus who first brought them together. Eudemus seems to have done the same for the *Physics*; in his own *Physics* he treated the same topics as Aristotle in much the same order.[10] No doubt they were following lines laid down by Aristotle himself; the cross-references still found in his works, most if not all of which must go back to him, show that he meant them to be seen as parts of a comprehensive scheme. But for whatever reason, the following generations of Peripatetics did not continue the work, and it was left to Andronicus to complete it.

The justification of what he did was contained in his book about Aristotle's writings. Its exact title is not known, but it was a substantial work in at least five books. Its main feature was a catalogue of Aristotle's works, genuine and spurious, which is said to have enumerated no fewer than a thousand books.[11] This part of the work occupied at least three books; Book 3 is quoted as the source of a discussion of Aristotle's *Physics*[12] and Book 5 seems to have contained the list of 'hypomnematic' writings.[13] The logical works will have been dealt with before the physical, either in Book 2 or the earlier part of Book 3. In addition Andronicus' book contained a transcript of Aristotle's will and is quoted as the source of a pair of letters, almost certainly spurious, said to have passed between Aristotle and Alexander the Great;[14] they could have been part of the collection of 'Letters of Aristotle found by Andronicus' listed as item 96 of Ptolemy's catalogue.[15] The presence of these items suggests that the book may also have included a biography of Aristotle, or at least a summary of the main facts of his life, presumably in Book 1.[16] While there is no direct evidence for this in the form of quotations, the parallels favour the inclusion of some biographical data; even if Porphyry's *Life of Plotinus* is not admitted as evidence, some material of this kind seems to have been included in Callimachus' *Pinakes*,[17] and the Neoplatonic *Lives* of Aristotle contain some very valuable information not

[10] See especially Eudemus fr. 98 and Wehrli's commentary, p. 88f; C. Brandis, 'Über die Schicksale der aristotelischen Bücher', *Rh. Mus.* 1, 1827, 281ff.

[11] Elias *in Cat.* 113,17ff, cf. 107,11ff = *AB* T 75p; also the introduction of the Arabic *Life*, cited above, n. 5. For discussion of the content of Andronicus' book see Littig II 18ff, Plezia, *Andronicus*, 26-35, Moraux, *Arist.*, 63-94.

[12] Simpl. *in Phys.* 923,7ff.

[13] It is referred to under item 97 of Ptolemy's catalogue. 'Hypomnematic' is a portmanteau term used to denote collections of material and other writings which are neither systematic school-treatises nor finished literary works; the extant *Problems* and *Mir. Ausc.* are examples of this class of writing. Its earliest extant occurrence in this sense appears to be in the Neoplatonic *Introductions* to Aristotle's philosophy, but it may be earlier. See further P. Moraux, *Les Listes Anciennes d'Ouvrages d'Aristote*, Louvain 1951, 114ff, 145ff, and Düring *AB* 230, 446ff.

[14] Will: *Vita Aristotelis Marciana* 43 (*AB* p. 105). Letters: see below n. 24 and text.

[15] See Plezia, *Arist. Epist. Fr.* (op. cit. n. 24 below) 18, 84ff. According to the Arabic version of Ptolemy, the collection was in twenty 'parts' or 'sections', and Plezia argues that this means that there were twenty letters, not twenty books of letters.

[16] Littig II 18; Plezia, *Andronikos* 18-26 attempts a detailed reconstruction of this biography. But Düring, *AB* p. 422 has denied that Andronicus wrote a Life of Aristotle in any form.

[17] Call. fr. 429, 438 Pfeiffer; Pfeiffer, *Hist. Cl. Schol.* I 129.

preserved anywhere else, e.g. the chronological discussion taken from Philochorus (*Vit. Marc.* 9, 12). Since it is unlikely that the author of their immediate source studied the Hellenistic historians himself, this must have come from a good intermediate source, and Andronicus is the only respectable source he is known to have used.

But the main emphasis was undoubtedly on Aristotle's writings, their authenticity, internal structure, the connection between them and their place in the Aristotelian corpus. Andronicus' purpose must have been to explain his grouping of shorter treatises in *pragmateiai* and the sequence of *pragmateiai* in his edition, and also the relationship of these works to the literary dialogues and the large mass of hypomnematic writings, collections of material and so on, which were listed in his catalogue but apparently not included in his edition. The details, unfortunately, are obscure. We are told that in his view the study of philosophy should begin with logic,[18] and it is reasonable to infer that the logical works, which he first organised as a corpus, stood at the beginning of his edition and headed the list of *pragmateiai* in his catalogue, as they do in Ptolemy's. Attempts have been made to recover more details from the introductions to some of the extant commentaries on Aristotle, particularly from the classification of Aristotle's writings found at the beginning of certain sixth-century commentaries on the *Categories*. But while the questions raised by these commentators and many of the answers they suggest clearly belong to an older tradition, all we can really say about Andronicus is that he probably discussed some of the same topics; we know hardly anything of his treatment or the internal arrangement of his work.[19] We can still see, however, that he employed the techniques of Hellenistic scholarship. His catalogue included incipits and information about the length, in lines, of the works he listed, and letters and personal writings were listed at the end.[20] No doubt he compared different manuscripts, although positive evidence is rare.[21] But he also used the available indirect evidence, both internal and external. He condemned the *de Interpretatione* as spurious because it contains what appears to be a false reference to the *de Anima*,[22] and in connection

---

[18] Philop. *in Cat.* 5,18ff, Elias *in Cat.* 117,24 = *AB* T 75n, 77a (p. 455).

[19] See further Düring, *AB* 444ff, Moraux, *Listes*, 146ff, id., *Arist.* 58ff, with references.

[20] See item no. 97 in Ptolemy's catalogue (*AB* p. 230).

[21] The most definite evidence would be Dexippus *in Cat.* 21,18ff, on *Cat.* 1a1, but comparison with Simplicius' comments on the same passage (29,29ff) suggests that Dexippus may have been mistaken and it was Porphyry who compared manuscripts at this point; cf. Plezia, *Andronikos*, 7; Moraux, *Arist.*, 102. A variant at *Phys.* 202a14 reported by Simpl. *in Phys.* 440,14 as from Andronicus may have been due to conjecture or carelessness, cf. Moraux, *Arist.*, 113ff. The other passages mentioned by Brandis, *Über die Reihenfolge der Bücher des Aristotelischen Organons und ihre griech. Ausleger, Abh. Akad.*, Berlin 1833, 273 are not concerned with textual criticism.

[22] Ammonius *in Int.* 5,28ff; cf. Anon. in C. Brandis, *Scholia gr. in Aristotelem*, Berlin 1836, 94a21ff; Philop. *in DA.* 27,21ff. The passage in question is *de Int.* 16a8, but as the later commentators point out, Andronicus seems to have misunderstood it. Cf. Moraux, 'La critique d'authenticité chez les commentateurs d'Aristote', *Mélanges Mansel*, Ankara 1974, 274ff; id., *Arist.*, 117ff.

with Books 5 and 6 of the *Physics* he cited Eudemus' *Physics* and
correspondence with Theophrastus as well as the cross-references in
Aristotle's other writings.[23] He also quoted a pair of spurious letters said to
have passed between Aristotle and Alexander the Great, with the
intention, seemingly, of emphasising the importance of the 'esoteric'
writings comprised by his edition in comparison with the well-known
'exoteric' literary works.[24] The emphasis throughout was on higher rather
than lower criticism, and we can see why Tyrannio left the work to him;
only an Aristotelian with a full philosophical training could have completed it successfully.

Andronicus is said to have been the eleventh Peripatetic scholarch. The
authority for this is Ammonius, writing in the fifth century AD, and
unfortunately the same Ammonius also tells us that Boethus, Andronicus'
pupil, was eleventh scholarch.[25] The discrepancy has led Düring to reject
Ammonius' testimony altogether, but it is unreasonable to forego the only
evidence we have about Andronicus' position in life for what may be a mere
slip,[26] and Ammonius' information may have come from a good source: he
used the *Life of Aristotle* and catalogue of his writings compiled by
Ptolemy, who for his part used Andronicus' book.[27] So Andronicus, who
must have said something about the history of the Peripatetic school (if
only to explain why the school-treatises had been allowed to fall into
oblivion), may have mentioned his scholarchate himself. If Ammonius and
Elias are right to this extent, it follows that he did his work in Athens, and
this would explain why he had to rely on Tyrannio for copies of the
Apellicon manuscripts. Düring's assertion that he prepared his edition at
Rome is baseless.[28] A fiction also is the 'Roman edition' of Aristotle so
beloved by compilers of handbooks,[29] unless we want to dignify the bad

---

[23] See Simpl. *in Phys.* 923,7ff; Eudemus fr. 6 and 98 Wehrli; *AB* T 75m; cf. Plezia, *Andronikos*, 33ff; Moraux, *Arist.*, 115f.

[24] Aulus Gellius 20.5 = *AB* T 76f; cf. M. Plezia, *Aristotelis Epistularum fragmenta cum Testamento*, Warsaw 1961, 42f, 127ff.

[25] Ammonius *in Int.* 5,24 '(Andronicus), who was eleventh <head of the School> after Aristotle'; id. *in An. Pr.* 31,11 'But Boethus, the eleventh <head of the School> after Aristotle'. Ammonius' statement about Andronicus is repeated by Elias and others (*AB* T 75p), but their testimony has no independent value; cf. Düring, *AB*, 416ff, 420f. Lynch, 204 claims that the second Ammonius passage is 'an obviously apocryphal and harmonising list of *diadochoi*' and that Ammonius 'went on to list as Boethus' followers such men as the Neo-Platonists Porphyry and Iamblichus'. It is clear that he has misunderstood Ammonius' *ekolouthêsen* and knows no more of his text than the brief extract printed by Düring.

[26] One way of reconciling both statements would be to suppose that Ammonius included Aristotle in his count in the first passage and excluded him in the second; cf. Zeller, III 1, 642 n. 5.

[27] cf. Elias *in Cat.* 107,11ff = *AB* T 75 p. 3; Ptolemy's catalogue item 96-7, etc.

[28] *AB* p. 420 and elsewhere. It was swallowed by J.P. Lynch, *Aristotle's School*, Berkeley 1972, 203ff, whose vaunted critical faculty works in a curiously intermittent fashion.

[29] It was invented by H. Usener, 'Ein altes Lehrgebäude der Philologie', in *Kl. Schriften* II,

commercial copies of Apellicon's manuscripts, about which Strabo tells us, with this title.[30]

However, the very existence of the Peripatos at this time has been called into question in two recent books, in which it is argued that all the philosophical schools, with the possible exception of the Epicurean, ceased to exist after Sulla's siege of Athens in 86 BC caused the destruction of their buildings and the dispersal of their members.[31] Thereafter the schools continued in an ideological sense only, with no permanent institutional centre, and their most important representatives spent their working lives in places other than Athens, especially in Rome and the great cities of Syria and Asia Minor. Lynch has succeeded in demonstrating that we have no positive evidence for the existence of the Peripatos in the imperial age and that the men described as scholarchs in modern accounts of this period have no identifiable claim to the honour.[32] But while it is right to suspend judgement where no evidence exists, there is some evidence for the first century BC: not only the report that Andronicus and Boethus were scholarchs, but also a remark in the *Index Academicorum Herculanensis* that Ariston and Cratippus 'abandoned the Academy and became Peripatetics'.[33] This cannot mean merely that they showed an interest in Peripatetic philosophy or that Ariston made a name as a commentator on Aristotle, for Eudorus the Academic and Athenodorus the Stoic did the same without losing their membership of their respective schools. Moreover, since the school of Antiochus recognised no fundamental distinction between Academic and Peripatetic beliefs, it would have been pointless to describe any of its members as apostates for teaching Peripatetic doctrines. The report only makes sense if there was some organisation recognised by contemporaries as the legitimate successor of Aristotle's school and official representative of his teaching, for Ariston and Cratippus to join. Undoubtedly the school's activity must have been inter-

---

Leipzig and Berlin 1913, 306f (first edition in *Sitzungsber. d. philos.-philolog. und hist. Kl. d. Bayer. Ak. d. Wiss.*, 1892, 582-648); *Kl. Schriften* III 150ff, who claims that the main part of the editorial work was done by Tyrannio, acting as literary adviser to Cicero's publisher friend Atticus, for publication by Atticus. For appropriate comment see A.E. Housman in the introduction to his edition of Lucan, pp. xiii-xviii; also Littig, *Andronikos* II, 8ff.

[30] As is done by Littig, *Andronikos* I, 12f. Cf. Strabo 13.1.54 p. 609 C = *AB* T 66b.

[31] Lynch, *Aristotle's School*, 163ff; J. Glucker, *Antiochus and the Late Academy*, *Hypomnemata* 56, Göttingen 1978, 98ff, 330ff.

[32] See *ANRW* 36.2.1080 n. 5.

[33] *Index Acad. Herc.*, col. 35. 10ff, p. 112 Mekler 'Of whom Ariston and Cratippus left the Academy and became Peripatetics'. Glucker 99ff discusses this passage at length and tries to alter the accepted reading in such a way as to support his contention that Antiochus' 'Academy' was something different from the school founded by Plato. This does not concern us here, but he also says (96, 113) that Dio of Alexandria, who is named a few lines previously (col. 35 line 8) went over to the Peripatos with the other two, and this is clearly wrong.

rupted for a time by the siege of Athens and its aftermath,[34] and Andronicus may not have been able to work in the old buildings near the Lyceum, outside the city-wall. But the life of a learned institution does not depend on buildings or even administrative continuity; what matters is that there should be an identifiable body of men whose members feel that they are the heirs and representatives of an intellectual tradition and that their claim should be admitted by those contemporaries who are sufficiently interested to hold any decided view on the matter.[35]

A more difficult question is the date of Andronicus' edition. Düring puts it between 40 and 20 BC;[36] his chief reason for putting it so late is Cicero's silence, which would indeed be inexplicable if the work was done in Rome during his lifetime. But as we have seen, Andronicus almost certainly worked at Athens, and most of the evidence points to an earlier date. Apellicon's library came to Rome about 84 BC, Tyrannio about 71; Sulla's library seems to have been accessible to Sulla's friends, including Cicero, and Tyrannio was highly regarded in their circle,[37] so the rediscovery of Aristotle's manuscripts can hardly have happened later than 60 BC. Andronicus must have been considerably older than Strabo, who was born about 63 BC. Strabo says that he himself was an associate, possibly a pupil, of Boethus, a pupil of Andronicus,[38] and in his enumeration of eminent Rhodians places his name between those of Stratocles, a pupil of Panaetius, and Leonidas, possibly a pupil of Posidonius;[39] he does not name him among his own contemporaries. All this would tend to make Andronicus roughly contemporaneous with Cicero, and one piece of evidence points to an upsurge of activity in the Peripatetic school about 60 BC. Not long after the death of Antiochus of Ascalon, when his brother Aristus was head of the Academy, two of its members, Ariston of Alexandria and Cratippus of Pergamum, went over to the Peripatos; the exact date is unknown, but Antiochus died in 68 BC and Cratippus was an established Peripatetic teacher when Cicero met him in Ephesus in 51.[40]

---

[34] Perhaps this was what induced Andronicus to devote himself to literary work, much as the forced closure of the Neoplatonic school at Athens some six centuries later induced Simplicius to write his invaluable commentaries.

[35] cf. H. Weissert, 'Über Universitätsjubiläen', *Ruperto-Carola* 64, 1980, 5-8, who points out that many universities which claim a history of several centuries have not in fact been continuously active throughout these periods.

[36] Düring, *AB* p. 421; for earlier proponents of this view see Brink, *RE* Suppl. VII, 1940, 938.

[37] See the passages quoted in *AB* T 74c.

[38] Strabo 16.757 = *AB* T 75b 'In my time, famous philosophers born at Sidon are Boethus, with whom I studied Aristotelian philosophy, and...'. Moraux, *Arist.*, 54 argues that *sumphilosophein* with the dative always means 'to be a pupil of ', but the available evidence is not sufficient to allow a firm conclusion. But since Strabo does not refer to anyone else as his teacher, most scholars have understood him to mean that he was a pupil of Boethus; see Zeller III 1, 646 n. 2; Brink 938.62f; F. Susemihl, *Geschichte der gr. Lit. in der Alexandrinerzeit*, Leipzig 1892, 307 n. 354.

[39] Strabo 14.655; cf. Zeller 590n, 606n.

[40] *Index Acad. Herc.* 35.8ff, p. 110ff Mekler. Most of the other evidence has been collected in Mekler's notes ad loc.

Each later became eminent in his own way, Ariston as one of the first
generation of commentators on Aristotle, Cratippus as a popular teacher
whose pupils included Cicero's son Marcus.[41] They must have had a good
reason for transferring their allegiance, and it is a plausible guess that
what attracted them was the renaissance of Aristotelian studies which
seemed likely to result from Andronicus' researches; such a move would
have been a natural outcome of Antiochus' advocacy of a return to the
'ancient' (we might almost say 'classical') thinkers of the fourth century.
Eudorus and Athenodorus, who must have written their commentaries
on the *Categories* after Andronicus' edition had come out, flourished in
the middle of the first century BC; the latter was an old man when he
returned to his native city not long after the battle of Actium.[42] All this
would indicate that Andronicus began his work in the sixties and
published his edition and catalogue, not necessarily all at once, during
the following decades.[43]

One difficulty remains. It is often said that Cratippus was head of the
Peripatos in the mid-forties, when Cicero's son Marcus was his pupil at
Athens.[44] The evidence is supposed to be a remark of Cicero's, who had a
high regard for Cratippus and wrote of him as 'of all the Peripatetics
whom I have heard, in my judgment easily the foremost'.[45] But if Cicero
meant to convey that he was scholarch, this expression would be
strangely inappropriate, like saying that a man is 'easily Vice-Chancellor
of his university', and all the other evidence is against this supposition.[46]
When Cicero first met him in 51, he resided at Mytilene, and he was still

[41] Cic. *de Off*. 1.1.1, etc; see below.

[42] Strabo 14.674. For the chronology of Ariston and Eudoros see P.M. Fraser, *Ptolemaic Alexandria*, Oxford 1972, I 488ff (text), II 707ff (notes), who points out that both men must have been considerably older than Strabo. Unfortunately he is inclined to accept Düring's late date for Andronicus (n. 97) and this forces him to suggest that Ariston and Eudoros may have written their commentaries on the *Categories before* Andronicus. But this is very unlikely, as we shall see.

[43] This would be confirmed if it were certain that Cic. *Orator* 192 refers to Andronicus' edition of Ar. *Rhet*. 3, 1408b32ff, as Usener claimed (*Kl. Schr*. II, 306); but since he does not give a title, it is not certain that the reference is to this book (cf. Düring, 'Notes on the history of the transmission of Aristotle's writings', *Göteborgs Årsskr*. 56, 1950, 3, 38f), and even if it is, Cicero might have used an earlier version, perhaps even one of the bad commercial copies of which Strabo speaks. The earliest extant writer to quote from a certainly Andronicean text of Aristotle seems to be Dionysius of Halicarnassus, who cites passages from *Rhetoric* 3 as standing *en têi tritêi biblôi tôn rhêtorikôn tekhnôn* (*Comp*. c. 25, cf. *Epist ad Amm*. 1.8). Cf. F.H. Sandbach, 'Plutarch and Aristotle', *Illinois Class. Stud*. 7, 1982, 229. Recently Moraux (*Arist*., 57f) has suggested that Andronicus may have begun even earlier, 'soon after the death of Apellicon and the confiscation of his library'. This is not impossible, although Moraux is inclined to discount Plutarch's story that Andronicus received help from Tyrannio; he could have started his work before learning of the papers in Rome, and then asked Tyrannio for copies.

[44] e.g. Fraser I, 489; cf. Littig, *Andronikos* I, 7ff.

[45] Cic. *Tim*. 1; cf. *Off*. 3.2.5: 'My <friend> Cratippus, the foremost philosopher in living memory'; *Off*. 1.1.2: 'The foremost philosopher of this age'. For Cratippus' career, see A. O'Brien-Moore, 'M. Tullius Cratippus, priest of Rome', *Yale Class. Stud*. 8, 1942, 25-8 and Moraux, *Arist*., 223-56.

[46] For the non-specific use of *princeps* qualified by an adverb cf. *Epist. ad fam*. 13.78.1.

there in 48, when he met Pompey fleeing after his defeat at Pharsalus. By 44 we find him at Athens. Through Cicero's good offices he obtained Roman citizenship, but at the same time Cicero persuaded the Council of the Areopagus to pass a special motion requesting him to remain at Athens. These facts do not suggest that he had an official position there, but that he seriously considered moving on to Rome and was with difficulty persuaded to stay.[47] Even at this time, when Marcus Cicero was under his care, his associates were men he had brought with him from Mytilene; and when Cicero's friend C. Trebonius invited Marcus to accompany him to Asia, he proposed to take Cratippus as well so that Marcus' studies would not be interrupted.[48] These passages are enough to indicate what his position was: he was head of a private school of philosophy existing side by side with the official Peripatos, perhaps with a special following among young Romans finishing their education in Athens.[49] His relations with Andronicus and his followers may have been strained. Unlike his fellow-convert Ariston, he took no part in the work on Aristotle's school-treatises, but seems to have been a Peripatetic of the Hellenistic type, teaching rhetoric as well as the more popular kind of philosophy.[50] On the other hand Andronicus must have thought his own work much more important than retailing moral uplift to the gilded youth of Rome. As for Cicero, his predilection for Cratippus and silence about Andronicus can be explained on both intellectual and personal grounds. In spite of his strictures on the Hellenistic Peripatos, the Hellenistic tradition was the one in which he had been brought up.[51] Philosophy for him was a gentlemanly accomplishment, and he knew Aristotle almost entirely from his elegant dialogues. He would have found the school-treatises barely comprehensible and Andronicus' detailed editorial labours abhorrent. At the same time he was a very grand personage. When he visited Greece he did not expect to call on philosophers – they were expected to wait on him. Cratippus made it his business to wait on eminent visitors from Rome and to tell them what they wanted to hear;[52] Andronicus, it seems, did not.

II

Andronicus performed his task well. He not only established the form and

[47] Lynch, 204ff; Moraux, *Arist.*, 223ff; Glucker, *Antiochus*, 114ff, has a different and to my mind far-fetched explanation of this episode.

[48] Marcus Cicero in *Epist. ad Fam.* 16.21.5; Trebonius, ibid. 12.16.2.

[49] It is tempting to speculate that one motive for his migration to Athens was the hope of becoming scholarch, but that he was defeated. In that case the man who vacated the scholarchate in 47 or 46 must have been Andronicus, and his successor Boethus. But this is very uncertain.

[50] cf. Cicero *Brutus* 250, Moraux, *Arist.*, 227ff. This need not invalidate the suggestion made above, that he and Ariston were attracted to the Peripatos by Andronicus' work on the school-treatises; it may only mean that Cratippus found he had bitten off more than he could chew.

[51] His approval of Cratippus may be evidence that he took his opinion of the Hellenistic Peripatos at second hand, perhaps from Antiochus.

[52] Cic. *Tim.* 1; Plut. *Pomp.* 75.

canon of Aristotle's writings which, with comparatively slight modifications, we still use today, but initiated a way of doing philosophy which was to predominate among Aristotelians to the end of antiquity and to spread to the adherents of other schools. Their work was firmly centred on the Aristotelian writings. Much of it consisted of straight exegesis and even where they disagreed with Aristotle's doctrine or were dealing with different problems from his, they often chose to present their views as an interpretation or development of his ideas. Philosophical debate could take the form of an argument over the authenticity or meaning of a text.[53]

Andronicus presented Aristotle's philosophy as a system like those of the Stoics and Epicureans, which his adherents were expected to understand and propagate, with such additions as might be needed from time to time. It has been suggested that this entailed a distortion of Aristotle's thought.[54] But while it is true that many of Aristotle's books were not originally written for the context in which Andronicus placed them, and Andronicus ignored and probably had no means of knowing the dates at which particular books were composed, a systematic tendency was inherent in Aristotle's philosophy from the start. This is not only shown by the elaborate cross-references and the summaries and synopses by which his writings are articulated, but by his use of a limited number of well-established principles to solve the problems presented by his investigation of different areas of reality. In making these tendencies explicit, Andronicus continued a development begun by Aristotle's earliest pupils, as we have seen, and adopted the only way to make Aristotle's teaching fruitful in the circumstances of his time.

One result was to throw up a new set of problems concerning the interrelation of Aristotle's works. They could take several forms. Real or apparent differences of doctrine or terminology between various parts of the Corpus had to be explained and harmonised; this was done in the commentaries written under Andronicus' influence, especially those of Boethus.[55] But there was also the more general question of the way in which the parts of philosophy were connected and the order in which they should be studied. Such questions had long exercised the Stoics, and their

---

[53] cf. R.B. Todd, *Alexander of Aphrodisias on Stoic Physics*, Philosophia Antiqua 28, Leiden 1976, 2ff, 8ff. The same approach can be found among Platonists; see Dörrie, *Platonica Minora*, 308, H.J. Blumenthal, 'Plotinus in later Neoplatonism', in H.J. Blumenthal and R.A. Markus (eds), *Neoplatonic and Christian Thought (Essays in honour of P.H. Armstrong)*, London 1981, 213f, with references, and D.A. Russell, *Plutarch*, London 1973, 64. It is criticised by Seneca *Epist.* 108.23.

[54] Düring, *AB* p. 422f; id., *Aristoteles*, Heidelberg 1966, 42; id., *RE* Suppl. XI, 1986, 199, 319ff; his insistence that Aristotle was a *'Problemdenker'* seems to be derived from N. Hartmann (whose historical essays have been collected in vol. II of his *Kleinere Schriften*, Berlin 1957), but I am not sure that Düring has understood his meaning fully. Cf. J.L. Ackrill, *Aristotle the Philosopher*, Oxford 1981, 1ff.

[55] There is some evidence that such harmonisation may sometimes have led to textual interpolation: see J. Brunschwig, 'Observations sur les manuscrits parisiens des "Topiques"', in G.E.L. Owen (ed.), *Aristotle on Dialectic*, Oxford 1968, 16ff (on *Top.* 120a6-11).

tripartite division of philosophy into logic (*to logikon*), natural philosophy (*to phusikon*) and ethics (*to êthikon*) was the position from which the Aristotelians began; they could do so the more readily because Aristotle occasionally used the same classification.[56] In general, however, Aristotle approached the problem in a different way. His distinction between theoretical, practical and productive 'sciences' was not a division of philosophy only but of all types of intellectual endeavour.[57] Leaving the last aside, the first two coincide reasonably closely with the Stoics' physical and ethical branches of philosophy; but since Aristotle's subdivision of theoretical science (into First Philosophy, Natural Philosophy and Mathematics) left no obvious place for logic, his followers felt free to place it in a separate class, as the Stoics had done. The omission was explained by saying that logic was not a part of philosophy coordinate with the other two, but a tool used in both theoretical and practical philosophy.[58] There is no direct evidence for attributing this argument to Andronicus, but an indirect link can be established. On the related question of the order in which Aristotle's works should be read, Andronicus held that the logical works should come first, on the ground that neither of the other branches of philosophy could be learned properly without a grasp of the basic rules of argument.[59] This implies that he held, and probably originated, the view of logic as a tool. Boethus may have disagreed; he argued that the study of philosophy should begin with physics because it is closest to everyday experience.[60] When he wrote, it seems, opinion in the school was still fluid, but later Andronicus' view became canonical.

As this example shows, Andronicus' decisions were not always taken as the last word, and several additions were made to the Aristotelian canon by his immediate successors. The last six chapters of the *Categories*, the so-called *Postpraedicamenta*, which Andronicus did not regard as

---

[56] Ar. *Top.* 105b19: 'Propositions and subjects of discussion are divided into three: some are ethical, some concerned with natural philosophy, some logical.' Cf. Alex. Aphr., ad loc., p. 93,20ff. The same division is attributed to Plato by writers from Cicero (*Acad. Post.* 1.5.19) to Aristocles of Messene (fr. 1 Heiland = Euseb. *PE* 11.3.6; cf. F. Trabucco, 'Il problema del "De philosophia" di Aristocle di Messene e la sua dottrina', *Acme* 11, 1958, 136f) and to Xenocrates by Sext. Emp. *Adv. Math.* 7.16 (= fr.1 Heinze = 82 Isnardi Parente).

[57] For Aristotle's classification of the sciences and the problems it raises see H.H. Joachim's commentary on the *EN*, Oxford 1951, 1ff.

[58] Alex. Aphr. *in Top.* 74,26ff; 94,8ff, quoting Arist. 104b2f; Ammon. *in Cat.* 4,28ff; Simpl. *in Cat.* 4,22ff; Olympiod. *in Cat.* 7,24ff, Philop. *in Cat.* 4,23ff; Elias *in Cat.* 115,14ff; Anon. *de Arte Logica* (in the preface of Busse's edition of Olympiod. *in Cat.*) p. xif. All these writers describe logic as an *organon* of philosophy and logical writings as *organika*, but the use of 'Organon' as a collective title for Aristotle's logical works seems to have no ancient authority. The summary of Aristotle's philosophy given by Diogenes Laertius 5.28ff (see *ANRW* II, 35.2. 1129) has a different scheme, based on bi-partition: philosophy is divided into practical and theoretical, practical into ethics and politics, and theoretical into physics and logic; but the writer adds that logic is a tool, not a part of philosophy in its own right. Cf. Moraux, 'L'exposé de la philosophie d'Aristote chez Diogène Laërce V, 28-34', *Rev. Philos. de Louvain* 47, 1949, 7ff.

[59] Philop. *in Cat.* 5,18ff; cf. Elias *in Cat.* 117,22ff.

[60] Philop. *in Cat.* 5,16f; Moraux, *Arist.*, 143ff.

belonging to that treatise, were treated as part of it by most subsequent commentators, including Boethus;[61] the only exception of which we know is the anonymous writer of two pseudo-Archytean tracts which together repeat the content of the extant *Categories*, with minor modifications.[62] The *de Interpretatione*, which Andronicus declared spurious, was accepted as genuine by all who came after him.[63] Nicolaus of Damascus, active in the reign of Augustus, referred to two books which Andronicus apparently did not know, Theophrastus' *Metaphysica* and the short essay which today forms the second book (alpha elatton) of Aristotle's *Metaphysics*, but which must have gained its present place after the formation by Andronicus of the thirteen-book *Metaphysics* listed in Ptolemy's catalogue.[64] It is not known how Nicolaus obtained his extra material. He may have found some manuscripts in the libraries of eastern Mediterranean cities, as Drossaart Lulofs has suggested (p. 28); his diplomatic activity on behalf of Herod the Great involved much travelling and may have presented him with good opportunities. But it is also possible that Andronicus' work was continued by members of his school after his death and Nicolaus simply reflects a later stage in its progress. At the level of textual criticism we hear of Andronicean readings which were not accepted by the majority of later commentators.[65] Nevertheless Andronicus' edition was the foundation of all subsequent work, much as I. Bekker's edition of 1831 has been the basis of the scholarly activity of more recent times. No less important was his example. In the ensuing centuries, philosophical discussions among Aristotelians took place against a background of philological and historical criticism.

Aristotle's writings were not all studied with equal intensity. The

[61] The evidence is indirect. Boethus included these chapters in his commentary on the *Categories* (see Simpl. *in Cat.* 433,28ff, on 15b1), while Andronicus is not quoted on this part of Aristotle's work (Simplicius' reference on p. 385,3f is to his views about the categories 'Action' and 'Passion', cf. ibid. 322,15). Cf. Plezia, *Andronicus*, 42; Moraux, *Arist.*, 99, 163; and id., *Mélanges Mansel* (above, n. 22) 276.

[62] See *ANRW* 36.2.1131ff. The fact that ps-Archytas wrote up both sections of the *Categories* is some evidence (but by no means conclus. 'e) that Andronicus accepted both as genuinely Aristotelian, even if he did not believe that they formed a single work. Cf. Moraux, *Arist.*, 99 against Plezia, *Andron.*, 35; but in *Mél. Mansel*, 272 Moraux still accepts the older view that Andronicus probably regarded the *Postpraedicamenta* as spurious. See also Boethius *in Cat.* 1, Migne *PL* 64,162A.

[63] Ammon. *in Int.* 5,28ff, and the parallels cited by Moraux, *Arist.*, ∴ n. 3; cf. Prantl, *Gesch. d. Logik* I, 547; Zeller II 2, 69 n. 1.

[64] See the subscription to Theophr. *Metaph.* = Nic. Damasc. *T* 7.1 (edited by H.J. Drossaart Lulofs, *Nicolaus Damascenus on the Philosophy of Ar.*, *Philosophia antiqua* 13, Leiden 1969) and for Arist. *Metaph.* 2, Nicolaus *F* 21, with Drossaart Lulofs' comments (p. 30, 137, 139). It is not likely that Andronicus knew bk. 2 as part of his version of the *Metaphysics*, as W.W. Jaeger suggests (*Studien zur Entstehungsgesch. d. Metaphysik d. Aristoteles*, Berlin 1912, 178); even if the later commentators, faced with the *fait accompli* that the books of the *Metaphysics* were labelled A-N, occasionally treated bk. 2 as a mere appendage of bk. 1, there would have been no reason for Andronicus to do so when he originated this arrangement. Cf. Plezia, *Andron.*, 53f. The scholia of MS Par. Gr. 1853 on the opening of *Metaph.* 2 have been discussed by S. Bernardinello, 'Gli scolî alla Metafisica di Aristotele nel F 234r del Parisinus Graecus 1853', *Elenchos* 3, 1982, 39-54.

[65] See above, n. 21 and *ANRW* 36.2. 1112.

biological works were almost entirely neglected; the only writer known to have given them more than a passing mention was Nicolaus of Damascus, who included compendia of the zoological works and the *de Plantis* in his summary of Aristotle's philosophy,[66] and no full commentaries were written on any of them in antiquity. The *Politics* received little attention, perhaps because it was too remote from the political realities of the time. The *Rhetoric* and *Poetics* were ignored by the philosophers; their influence, and that of Theophrastus' rhetorical works, has to be traced in the writings of professional rhetoricians.[67] The *fortuna* of the *Ethics* is curious. Ptolemy's catalogue (nos. 35-6) lists the *Eudemian Ethics* in eight books (i.e. including the three books common to it and the *EN*) and the *Magna Moralia*, but omits the *Nicomachean Ethics*. This may be due to an accident of transmission; Arius Didymus refers to the tenth book of the *EN* and Atticus in the second century AD enumerates all three versions,[68] and from this time the Aristotelian commentators concentrate on the *EN* (to which the common books are now assigned) to the exclusion of the others. But a recent study has shown that until then the *Eudemian Ethics* was quoted more often and seems to have enjoyed higher esteem than the *Nicomachean*.[69]

Besides this the *Organon*, the physical works, including the *de Anima* and at least some of the *Parva Naturalia*, and the *Metaphysics* were

[66] See Drossaart Lulofs, p. 9ff.

[67] cf. C.A. Brandis, Über Ar.'s Rhetorik u. d. gr. Ausleger derselben', *Philologus* 4, 1849, 34ff; F. Solmsen, 'The Aristotelian tradition in ancient rhetoric', *AJP* 62, 1941, 35-50, 169-90 = id., *Kleine Schriften* II, Hildesheim 1968, 178-215; R.B. Todd, *Alex. of Aphr. on Stoic Physics*, Leiden 1976, 12ff. Some of these omissions were not made good until the twelfth century, when Michael of Ephesus wrote commentaries on the *PA, IA, MA, GA, Politics* and *Rhetoric*, as well as parts of the *Organon, Ethics* and *Parva Naturalia*, apparently in a deliberate attempt to fill the gap left by earlier commentators; see his commentary on the *Parva Naturalia* (CAG 22.1) 149. R. Browning, 'An unpublished funeral oration on Anna Comnena', *Proc. Cambr. Philol. Soc.* 188, 1962, 6ff (Chapter 17 below), has shown that this was 'part of a cooperative scholarly undertaking conceived and guided by Anna Comnena'. Cf. A. Preus in the introduction to his translation of Michael's commentary on *MA* and *IA*, Hildesheim 1981, p. 8ff; H. Hunger, *Die hochsprachliche profane Literatur der Byzantiner* I, Munich 1978, 34f.

[68] Arius Did. ap. Stob. 2 p. 52.10 (referring to 1172b9); Atticus fr. 2.9 Edouard des Places (ed.) Paris 1977, cf. Moraux, *Listes*, 307. The paraphrase of the *EN* ascribed to Andronicus belongs to a much later period; see Moraux, *Arist.*, 136ff.

[69] Kenny, *Ar. Ethics*, ch. 1; his conclusions have been qualified in a review by D. Charles, *JHS* 100, 1980, 224f. According to Kenny (29ff) the change was due to Aspasius, who believed that the *EE*, including the common books, was the work of Eudemus, but transferred the common books to the *EN* because they seemed necessary to fill a gap whose existence Aspasius inferred from a cross-reference at *EN* 1155b15 (Kenny gives the reference wrongly as 1135b13-16). But Kenny appears to have misread Aspasius (see *ANRW* 36.2. 1158 and n. 375) and as we have seen, Arius already knew the ten-book form of the *EN*. Kenny's attempt (p. 21f) to discredit this evidence by attributing the introduction of Arius' *Epitome* to Stobaeus himself runs counter to everything we know about Stobaeus' method; cf. C.H. Kahn, 'Arius as a doxographer', in W.W. Fortenbaugh (ed.), *On Stoic and Peripatetic Ethics: the work of Arius Didymus*, New Brunswick 1983 (a collection of papers presented at a symposium in 1981), 4 n. 1. – See also R. Bodeus, 'Contribution à l'histoire des oeuvres morales d'Aristote: les Testimonia', *Rev. Philos. de Louvain* 71, 1973, 451ff.

studied systematically. But above all it was the *Categories* which attracted most attention. Simplicius enumerates five 'early commentators' who wrote about this tract and the problems it raised in the years immediately following its publication by Andronicus; they include Eudorus the Academic and Athenodorus the Stoic as well as the Peripatetics Andronicus, Boethus and Ariston.[70] Not much later an unknown hack compiled a version of the *Categories* in the Dorian dialect which he attributed to Archytas of Tarentum, a Pythagorean active in the early fourth century BC.[71] Subsequently almost every Aristotelian of note wrote a commentary or interpretative essay; some Platonists incorporated Aristotle's doctrine into their philosophy,[72] others, notably Plotinus, attacked it.[73] All these efforts were summed up in the great commentaries of Alexander of Aphrodisias and Porphyry;[74] through the latter this work entered the mainstream of the Neoplatonic tradition and went on to become one of the basic philosophical texts of the Middle Ages.

What is remarkable about this is that Aristotle's earliest followers seem to have attached much less importance to this tract. We are told, on late and somewhat dubious authority, that Theophrastus and Eudemus wrote *Categories* in imitation of their master.[75] But since no quotations have come down to us, it seems that any writings of theirs on this subject were regarded as relatively unimportant, and that they did not develop this aspect of Aristotle's teaching to the same extent as other parts of his logic.[76] There is also the fact that the *Categories* is not mentioned in the original versions of the Hellenistic catalogue of Aristotle's writings, unless it is hidden under the mysterious title *Ta pro tôn topôn á*.[77] It

[70] Simpl. *in Cat.* 159,32; cf. Brandis, *Abh. Akad.*, Berlin 1833, 272ff.

[71] See *ANRW* 36.2.1131ff.

[72] e.g. Albinus (Alcinous) *Didascalicus* 6.10 p. 159 Hermann; Anon. *in Plat. Theaet.* 20,34; 40,10; 68,10ff. Cf. Philo *de Decal.* 30; Dörrie, *Platonica Minora*, 300.

[73] Plot. *Enn.* 6.1-3; cf. Simpl. *in Cat.* 2,3. See H.J. Blumenthal, 'Plotinus in the light of twenty years' scholarship, 1951-1971', *ANRW* II, 36.1.547ff; K. Corrigan and P. O'Cleiright, 'The course of Plotinian scholarship from 1971 to 1986', ib. 579ff and S.K. Strange, 'Plotinus, Porphyry and the Neoplatonic interpretation of the "Categories" ', *ANRW* II 36.2.955ff.

[74] See Simpl. *in Cat.* 1,13ff, who goes on to say something about later commentators down to his own day. The commentary of Porphyry here referred to is the one dedicated to Gedalius, now lost; his surviving commentary is a much shorter work intended for beginners (cf. A. Smith, 'Porphyrian studies since 1913', *ANRW* II 36.2.755 and S.K. Strange, 'Plotinus, Porphyry and the Neoplatonic interpretation of the "Categories" ', ib. 956f).

[75] Philop. *in Cat.* 7,20ff; Olympiod. *in Cat.* 13,24ff; David *in Isag.* 102,4ff = Theophrastus fr. 1-2 Repici, Eudemus fr. 7-8 Wehrli (the second passage cited here has been omitted in both editions). Cf. L. Repici, *La logica di Teofrasto*, Bologna 1977, 179f; M. Frede, 'Titel, Einheit und Echtheit der aristotelischen Kategorienschrift', in P. Moraux and J. Wiesner (eds), *Zweifelhaftes im Corpus Aristotelicum*, *Peripatoi* 14, Berlin 1983, 22ff; H.B. Gottschalk, 'Did Theophrastus write a *Categories*?', *Philologus* 181, 1987, 245-53.

[76] cf. Brandis, 1833, 268ff. I.M. Bochenski, *La logique de Théophraste*, Fribourg 1947, 31f, 37 thinks that Theophrastus did not write a *Categories* and this is an argument against the authenticity of the Aristotelian work. He is probably right on the first point, but the second does not necessarily follow.

[77] Diog. Laert. no. 59 = Hesychius no. 57; cf. Moraux, *Listes*, 58ff, id., *Arist.*, 99ff. Its occurrence among the collections of material near the end of the list is the result of a late interpolation, cf. Moraux, *Listes*, 131, Düring, *AB* p. 69.

would appear to have fallen into even deeper oblivion than most of the other books of the Aristotelian corpus, until Andronicus brought it into prominence by placing at at the head of his edition.

It would be interesting to know why the *Categories* came to exercise so much fascination, but there is no evidence. What we can do is to see what kind of question the early commentators asked and how they set about answering them. Many of their queries concerned points of detail and some were trivial and even perverse, but they also raised the problems which later generations of interpreters regarded as important and anticipated many of the solutions they proposed.[78] Perhaps the most fundamental is the one with which the student is faced at the outset: what is the subject-matter of the *Categories*? Is Aristotle saying something about terms, or the things signified by terms? There are good arguments on both sides: Aristotle's language is ambiguous, and while most of the distinctions he makes are more appropriate to things than verbal expressions, he arrives at his classification by analysing the expressions which can be meaningfully applied to things.[79] A minority of ancient interpreters came down decisively on one side or the other; thus Plotinus insisted that the *Categories* deals with the classification of real things, and his critique was given the title *On the classes of being*.[80] On the other hand the Stoics, Athenodorus and Cornutus seem to have treated the essay as an attempt to analyse language and criticised Aristotle for not including some parts of speech, such as conjunctions, and grammatical distinctions in his discussion.[81] This is in accord with their formalistic view of logic[82] as well as their nominalist interpretation of Plato's Forms,[83] but implies that they regarded Aristotle's system of categories as something very different from their own, which they certainly looked upon as a classification of real things.[84] These are the extreme positions. Most interpreters accepted a compromise which seemed to do justice to all the arguments: the *Categories* is about simple terms considered not as terms (i.e. in a way appropriate to grammatical science) but as signifying things. This solution was given its classical formulation by Porphyry, but was already hit upon by Boethus and accepted by such eminent Peripatetics as Herminus, Alexander of Aigai and Alexander of Aphrodisias.[85]

---

[78] The main source of our knowledge is Simplicius' commentary on the *Categories*, occasionally supplemented by those of Porphyry, Dexippus and Ammonius. On their inter-relationship see Praechter, 'Nikostratos der Platoniker', in H. Dörrie (ed.), *Kleine Schriften*, *Collectanea* 7, Hildesheim and New York 1973, 123-8 (first published in *Hermes* 57, 1922, 481-517).

[79] The controversy is summarised by Simpl. *in Cat.* 9-13.

[80] *Peri tôn genôn tou ontos* = *Enn.* 6.1-3; the title was devised by Porphyry, but is amply justified by the opening words of the treatise. Cf. Simpl. *in Cat.* 2,3, 16,17ff.

[81] Porph. *in Cat.* 59,10ff, 86,20ff; Simpl. 18,26ff.

[82] e.g. Galen *Inst. Log.* 3.5, 4.6.

[83] Zeno fr. 65 (*SVF* 1 p. 19.27); cf. Syrian. *in Metaph.* 105,21ff = *SVF* 2.364.

[84] *SVF* 2.369ff; cf. J.M. Rist, 'Categories and their uses', in A.A. Long (ed.), *Problems in Stoicism*, London 1971, 38ff, who refers to other discussions, and below, p. 78.

[85] Porph. *in Cat.* 58,5ff, 59,5ff; Simpl. *in Cat.* 10,20ff, 11,23ff, 13,13ff, 41,28ff; cf. Moraux, *Arist.*, 148ff. Different aspects of the problem are discussed by K. v. Fritz, 'Der Ursprung der

Connected with this was another controversy, as to how many categories were to be postulated and the order in which they were to be placed.[86] In general, those who favoured a verbalist interpretation tended to regard Aristotle's analysis as incomplete, because it made no provision for grammatical inflections and such words as conjunctions. Besides Athenodorus and Cornutus, this criticism is attributed to the Platonists Lucius and Nicostratus.[87] But although it persisted into the second century, it was already refuted by Boethus, who pointed out that the parts of speech omitted by Aristotle were irrelevant because they only function in sentences and do not signify anything by themselves. Presumably his objections were directed at Athenodorus; we do not know if Cornutus and the rest modified his position in order to meet Boethus' arguments.[88] Others wanted to reduce the number of categories. Thus Andronicus is said to have held that the ten categories could be reduced to two, the self-subsistent and the relative.[89] According to Simplicius, Andronicus was here following the lead of Xenocrates, but whereas his classification is connected with his derivation of existing things from the One and Indefinite Dyad,[90] it is impossible that it should have had the

---

aristotelischen Kategorienlehre', *Arch. Gesch. Philos.* 40, 1931, 449-96 (revised: id., *Schriften zur griechischen Logik*, II: *Logik, Ontologie und Mathematik, Problemata 71*, Stuttgart 1978, 9-52) and A.C. Lloyd, 'Neoplatonic logic and Aristotelian logic', *Phronesis* 1, 1956, 58-79, 146-60. It is instructive to compare the ancient discussions with their counterparts in modern textbooks and commentaries; while opinions differ on many points, the arguments used and the range of possible views have not changed significantly.

[86] Simpl. *in Cat.* 18,22ff, 62,24ff.

[87] Simpl. *in Cat.* 18,28ff, 62,24ff, 64,13ff. For Nicostratus, see K. Praechter, *Kleine Schriften*, Hildesheim 1973, 101ff; Lucius is only known through his association with him. See below, p. 80.

[88] Simpl. *in Cat.* 11,23ff. Moraux, *Arist.*, 150 thinks that Athenodorus wrote after Boethus and Boethus' criticism is directed against an earlier Stoic or even Andronicus. But if Athenodorus is to be identified with the son of Sandon and teacher of Octavian, as is generally believed, he was an old man when he returned to his native Tarsus and entered local politics there shortly after the battle of Actium (Strabo 14.674f); so his philosophical activity must have fallen into the years 60-30 BC and be contemporaneous with that of Boethus. Moraux's reasons for thinking that Andronicus favoured a verbalist interpretation are quite insufficient; see below.

[89] 'For the followers of Xenocrates and Andronicus seem to comprehend everything under the in-itself and the relative, so that according to them such a crowd of categories is excessive', Simpl. *in Cat.* 63,22 = Xenocr. fr. 12 Heinze = 95 Isnardi Parente; cf. Moraux, *Arist.*, 103f. The last clause (*hôste...plêthos*) seems to be Simplicius' own conclusion. J. Dillon, *The Middle Platonists*, London 1977, 133 and H. Dörrie, *Platonica Minora*, Munich 1976, 300 claim that Eudoros took the same view, but the passages they adduce (Simpl. *in Cat.* 174,14ff, Dillon, 256,16ff, Dörrie) do not bear them out, and elsewhere Eudoros writes as if he accepted all ten categories; see below, p. 77f. The same division is used in the anonymous commentary on Plato's *Theaetetus*, col. 20.34 and 40.10; contrast 68.10ff.

[90] In their commentaries Heinze (p. 37ff.) and Isnardi Parente (p. 327ff, 439ff) refer to Hermodorus ap. Simpl. *in Phys.* 248,2ff (= Hermodorus fr. 7 Isn. Parente) and Sext. Emp. *Adv. Math.* 10.263ff. Cf. K. Gaiser, 'Platons Menon und die Akademie', *Arch. Gesch. Philos.* 46, 1964, 243f (reprinted in J. Wippern (ed.), *Das Problem der ungeschriebenen Lehre Platons, Wege der Forschung* 186, Darmstadt 1972, 329-93). The twofold division of *onta* is also found in the *Divisiones Aristoteleae* (Diog. Laert. 3.108f = Cod. Marc. no. 67, p. 39f Mutschmann); here substances are said to differ from relatives inasmusch as the terms

same metaphysical significance for Andronicus. It is not even certain that Andronicus was directly influenced by Xenocrates at this point, for the connection between them may have been made by Simplicius himself or an intermediate source, perhaps Porphyry. In another part of his commentary (p. 342,24), Simplicius admits that Andronicus 'maintained the tenfold number of genera', and he has much to say about his detailed modifications of Aristotle's teaching about particular categories. So it appears that Andronicus did little more than point up the fundamental distinction, clearly drawn by Aristotle himself,[91] between the category of Substance, whose members subsist in their own right, and the remaining categories, which depend on substances for their being, without wishing to obliterate the differences between the latter. Indeed, he seems to have made an attempt to order them according to the degree to which they were essential to substances, and to have placed Relation last because its connection with Substance was loosest.[92] Here his treatment could have been influenced by Stoic notions[93] and seems to imply a 'realist' interpretation of Aristotle's doctrine.

The other fragments of Andronicus' commentary are concerned with details.[94] In his paraphrase he tried to clarify Aristotle's thought by expanding his text where it seemed unduly compressed or by slight changes of wording; occasionally he replaced a loose expression by a more formally correct one.[95] On occasion, however, he can interpret Aristotle

---

denoting the latter, but not the former, 'require some explanation' (*deitai tinos hermêneias*) to make them meaningful, e.g. 'larger' must be larger than something. Tarán, rev. of Moraux, *Arist.*, *Gnomon* 53, 1981, 741 thinks that Andronicus was influenced by the Stoics as well as Xenocrates and offers a different interpretation of his doctrine, but the balance of the evidence does not support his view.

[91] Arist. *Cat.* 2a34, etc., cf. *An. Post.* 83a25ff. The same point is made very clearly by ps-Archytas *Peri tô katholou logô* p. 31,6ff. Thesleff, cf. p. 32,7f. (cf. Simpl. *in Cat.* 76,1ff) and Boethus *de Trin.* ch. 4. Cf. K. v. Fritz, 'Der Ursprung der aristotelischen Kategorienlehre', *Arch. Gesch. Philos.* 40, 1931, 462, 478ff, 487ff; revised: id., *Schriften zur griechischen Logik*, II: *Logik, Ontologie und Mathematik, Problemata* 71, Stuttgart 1978, 20, 35ff, 43ff; H.W.B. Joseph, *An Introduction to Logic*, Oxford 1916 etc., 49ff; W.K.C. Guthrie, *A History of Greek Philosophy* VI, Cambridge 1982, 142; Prantl I 564 claims to find a similar doctrine in Galen *Meth. Med.* 2.7 (X 129 Kuhn), but Galen is not concerned with the doctrine of categories at this point; in the *Institutio Logica* he refers to all ten categories and even claims to have discovered an eleventh; see *ANRW* II 36.2.1170.

[92] Simpl. *in Cat.* 157,18ff; his reasoning is based on Ar. *EN* 1096a21ff, cf. *Metaph.* 1088a23; Joseph 51 n. 1, Moraux, *Arist.*, 107ff. Similar reasoning was used by Eudoros ap. Simpl. 206,10ff and ps-Archytas p. 23,17ff; cf. T.A. Szlezák, 'Ps.-Archytas über die Kategorien', *Peripatoi* 4, Berlin 1972, 110.

[93] cf. Simpl. *in Cat.* 166,8ff = *SVF* 2.403.

[94] Littig's collection (*Andronikos* III, 14ff) is almost complete; additional passages are Simpl. *in Cat.* 154,3ff and 332,14f. For a full discussion see Moraux, *Arist.*, 101ff; cf. Prantl I, 537ff; Plezia, *Andron.*, 6ff, 36ff.

[95] e.g. at 8a31f, where Aristotle defines relatives (*ta pros ti*) as things whose being consists

more freely. Two instances deserve mention here. One concerns the difference between substance and attribute. Aristotle distinguished between the two kinds of predication of which 'Socrates is a man' (or 'animal') and 'Socrates is a philosopher' are instances: the first tells us the species or genus to which Socrates belongs, and the universals, 'man' or 'animal' themselves belong to the category Substance; the second states one of his attributes and belongs to Quality. Aristotle tries to describe the difference by saying that the first kind of universal, the 'second substance', is predicated of (*kata*) the concrete individual while the second inheres in (*en*) the individual.[96] But according to Simplicius, Andronicus claimed that some attributes are predicated of their subject, e.g. 'philosopher' of Socrates.[97] We are not told the reasoning which led Andronicus to adopt this position or the criteria by which he decided which attributes fell into this class,[98] but it is clear that it entailed some blurring of the distinction between 'second substances' and qualities. We shall find a similar tendency in Boethus; it may be the result of Stoic influence.

The second innovation of Andronicus I shall consider here concerns the categories which modern writers generally call Time and Place. Aristotle did not use nouns to designate them, but the adverbs 'When' (*pote*) and 'Where' (*pou*) and treated time and place as kinds of extension belonging to the category Quantity (*Cat.* 5a6ff). Andronicus, however, decided that time and place exist in their own right and 'when' and 'where' are their attributes; he therefore renamed the categories 'Time' (*khronos*) and 'Place' (*topos*) and assigned 'when' and 'where' subordinate places within them.[99] His view is discussed and criticised by Simplicius (pp. 342-64) at

---

in standing in some relation (*pros ti*) to something, Andronicus objected that his definition contains the definiendum and proposed to substitute *pros heteron* for *pros ti*, using the term employed by Aristotle at 6a37 (there is no need to invoke Stoic influence here, with Tarán, 742). He was followed by Boethus and Ariston; Achaicus, a Peripatetic probably of the second century AD, tried to show that the change was unnecessary, but formally Andronicus is right, although the point is trivial. The source for all this is Simpl. *in Cat.* 201,34ff.

[96] cf. G.E.L. Owen, 'Inherence', *Phronesis* 10, 1965, 97ff.

[97] Arist. *Cat.* 1a20ff, cf. 2a18ff; Simpl. 54,8ff; cf. Moraux, *Arist.*, 104f.

[98] Simplicius seems to say that it included all attributes of which we can say that e.g. 'Socrates is x', where 'x' can be construed as a noun in apposition to 'Socrates', but this is clearly too wide, as it would cover relative terms like 'husband of Xanthippe'.

[99] Simpl. *in Cat.* 347,6: 'But Archytas and Andronicus, supposing that time exists independently (i.e. not as an aspect of quantity), placed When in the same category, as existing within the ambit of time. For it is his rule to take as principal the leading first genera in each <kind of> existence, in whose ambit the others exist; since therefore Time precedes When and Place precedes Where in respect of <their> very being, he rightly treats them as genera in a leading sense. So it has been shown above that Aristotle puts When in a different category <from time> because he concentrates on the differences in the meanings <of the terms>, but Archytas placed When in the same category as Time because he paid more attention to the kinship of the things <they signify>.' 357,28: 'Archytas and Andronicus placed When with Time and Where with Place and established the two categories in this way. But Aristotle, for the reasons stated above, made Time and Place

considerable length, but it is not certain how much of his argumentation goes back to Andronicus himself. One point, however, is clearly made by Simplicius: here as elsewhere Andronicus inclined towards a realist interpretation of the categories; he and ps-Archytas differed from Aristotle because they were thinking primarily of the relationships between things falling under the categories, whereas Aristotle concentrated on the meanings of the terms used to denote them.

The most elaborate of the early commentaries was the one written by Boethus of Sidon which, as well as line-by-line exegesis and textual criticism, included in-depth examinations of some of the problems Aristotle raised; Boethus devoted a whole book to the category of Relation, but we are not told whether this was part of his commentary or a separate essay.[100] Apparently his intention was to set the *Categories* in the context of Aristotle's philosophy as a whole and of the Academic-Peripatetic tradition. He quoted extensively from Aristotle's writings and those of other Academics and Peripatetics.[101] Where Aristotle's treatment was or appeared to be incomplete, he tried to fill the gap with material drawn from other parts of the corpus; thus his commentary on the categories Time, Action and Passion, which Aristotle did not discuss in detail, includes a great deal of matter based on the *Physics* and *Metaphysics*.[102] In general his attitude was conservative. He rejected many of Andronicus' innovations and refuted many of the objections which had been brought against Aristotle, especially by Stoic writers.[103] His counter-arguments were not always accepted by Aristotle's opponents, and many of the criticisms he refuted were repeated by later writers, including Plotinus, to be refuted again by others reusing many of Boethus' arguments.[104] We cannot usually tell what modifications, if any, the arguments on both sides underwent in the course of this process, but there can be no doubt that Boethus was largely responsible for the scholasticism which is such a marked feature of subsequent Aristotelian philosophy.

---

belong to Quantity and set up two different categories of When and Where.' 'Archytas' here means ps-Archytas *Peri tô katholou logô* p. 26,10ff Thesleff; cf. Szlezák, ad loc., p. 126f; Littig III, 25ff, Moraux, *Arist.*, 111ff. The same terminology is used by Philo, *Decal.* 30; cf. Eudoros ap. Simpl. *in Cat.* 206,13ff.

[100] Simpl. *in Cat.* 1,17, 163,6. For a full discussion see Moraux, *Arist.*, 147-64; Prantl I, 540ff. Textual variants or conjectures are mentioned by Simpl. 29,29ff, 58,27ff; cf. Moraux, 150, 153. A full edition of Boethus' fragments is a desideratum of scholarship.

[101] Aristotle: ap. Simpl. *in Cat.* 65,21 (*An. Post.*); 50,2ff, 302,15ff (*Phys.*); 78,6, 302,15 (*Metaphysics*); 42,1 (*de Anima*). Plato: 159,14, 163,6. Speusippus: 36,28, 38,19 (cf. L. Tarán, 'Speusippus and Aristotle on homonymy and synonymy', *Hermes* 106, 1978, 75ff). He also used the writings of Theophrastus and Strato. Besides this it is of little significance that he missed some passages in Aristotle which might have been relevant to his argument: see Porphyry ap. Simpl. *in Cat.* 36,27 (cf. Moraux, 151). A misquotation of Plato *Rep.* 438A noted by Simpl. 159,16 may be due to his quoting from memory.

[102] ap. Simpl. *in Cat.* 348,22ff, 433,28ff.

[103] See Simpl. *in Cat.* 167,22, 373,7, and above n. 88.

[104] See, besides the passages quoted in the last note, Simpl. *in Cat.* 25,10ff, 58,15ff, 187,24ff, 302,5ff, 338,21ff, 433,20ff; cf. Moraux, *Arist.*, 147f, 150, 160f, 163f.

Work of this kind does not lend itself to detailed discussion in a survey such as the present one, but two examples may serve to illustrate Boethus' way of thinking. One is his extraordinarily subtle treatment of time and its relationship to both movement and rest. Aristotle's dictum that the contrary of movement as such is rest, but the contrary of any particular movement is movement in the opposite direction, gave rise to a fair amount of controversy, some points of which were taken up later by Plotinus. Boethus tried to explain it by introducing the notion of time as a coordinate of both movement and rest. Time, he argued, being in constant flux, is a concomitant (*sumparêkei*) of both movement and rest; when objects are in movement, they stand in the same relationship to time as to the space they traverse (or, if the movement is one of qualitative change, to the spectrum of qualities within which the change takes place), but when they are at rest, their relationship to time is the contrary of their relationship to space etc., in that the former is still changing while the latter is not. Thus movement and rest can be seen as contrary relationships to time.[105] This implies a certain view of time: not as the 'number' or 'measure' of movement, but as the quantitative or extensional aspect of movement and rest – a view similar to that of Theophrastus' successor Strato or of the Stoics.[106] It follows that time is an objective reality, independent of the existence of a subject to perceive it,[107] and belongs, together with place, in the category Quantity. Boethus agreed with Aristotle, against Andronicus, in making When and, by analogy, Where, into separate categories.[108]

Even more revealing is his discussion of Substance. He began by denying the relevance of a question raised by a previous writer, perhaps

---

[105] Arist. *Cat.* 15b1ff, Simpl. ad loc. p. 432,24ff; Plotinus' view (*Enn.* 6.3.27) is quoted at p. 433,20ff, Boethus at 433,28ff. Cf. Moraux, *Arist.*, 163f.

[106] Strato fr. 76-8 F. Wehrli (*Die Schule d. Aristoteles* V, Basel 1952 etc.), and ap. Simpl. *in Cat.* 346,14 (omitted by Wehrli), 'Strato, saying that time is the quantity of movement, supposed that it is something inseparable from movement'. Stoics: *SVF* 1.93, 2.509-16.

[107] Themistius *in Phys.* 160,26f, 163,6ff = Simpl. *in Phys.* 759,18ff, 766,18ff. Here Boethus contradicted Arist. *Phys.* 223a21ff; later Alexander of Aphrodisias tried to defend Aristotle's position (ap. Simpl. *in Phys.* 759,20ff). Cf. Moraux, *Arist.*, 170f.

[108] Simpl. *in Cat.* 348,2ff. A similar doctrine is found in an essay *Peri tês tou pote katêgorias* preserved in a Florentine manuscript (Laur. 71.32) and printed by Waitz in the introduction of his edition of the Organon, Leipzig 1844, I, 19-23 and by P.M. Huby, 'Boethus of Sidon's Commentary', *CQ* n.s. 31, 1981, 398ff, who claims that it is nothing less than an excerpt from Boethus' commentary on the *Categories*. This is an attractive hypothesis, but there are difficulties. Simplicius *in Cat.* 347,22-36, in a passage apparently borrowed from Iamblichus, defines the category 'When' as the relation between time and the things in time. The same definition is found in the anonymous work (p. 22 init. Waitz), where it is illustrated by means of an example which Simplicius ascribes to Boethus a few lines later (348,2); but since he introduces his quotation with the words 'Boethus also...supposes...', it does not look as if he found the definition and the illustration together in his source. Furthermore the anonymous writer tries to reconcile his theory with the notion that time is the number of movement, but our authorities seem to imply that Boethus refused to do this; see Simpl. *in Cat.* 434,18f (Huby, 407 takes a different view of this passage) and Themistius *in Phys.* 163,6 = Simpl. *in Phys.* 766,18. While the anonymous tract contains much that can be traced back to Boethus, it would not be safe to ascribe anything to him which is not attributed to him by name in an ancient source.

Eudorus,[109] whether the category Substance was meant to embrace intelligible as well as sensible substances, but then went on to raise a problem of his own. In the *Categories* (2a11ff) Aristotle distinguished two kinds of substance, concrete individuals and the species or genera to which they belong; the second kind he refers to here, but nowhere else, as 'second substances' (2a14). In the *Metaphysics* (1028b33ff etc.), however, he says that 'substance' can mean one of three things: matter, form or universal, or the concrete individual composed of both. Boethus asked how these classifications are related and pointed out that the definition of substance given in the *Categories* (2a11), 'That which is neither in something else nor predicated of something else', fits matter and concrete individuals but would exclude the form or universal, because it is predicated of the individual. Therefore, he concludes, forms or 'second substances' do not belong to Substance but to a different category, such as Quality or Quantity.[110] Consistently with this view he held that the unity of individuals is due to their form 'in as much as the form is limited and made numerically one' by being included in matter.[111] In this way Boethus, as Dexippus says, affirmed the priority of the concrete individual over the universal. He could have found support for his opinion in such passages as *Cat.* 3b15 or *Metaph.* 1033b22 and his interpretation points forward to that of Alexander, but one cannot avoid the suspicion that it was influenced by Stoic doctrines.[112] But Boethus took care to base his argument on a painstaking analysis of Aristotle's own words. His intention was not to mediate or compromise, and in other contexts he shows himself a true Aristotelian. For example, he refuted those who wanted to subsume Action and Passion under a single category Movement by pointing out that the distinction is required by Aristotle's doctrine of a first mover who is active but not moved;[113] the view he refuted was taken up again later by Plotinus (*Enn.* 6.1.15), but originated among Stoic opponents of Aristotle.[114] Boethus wanted nothing more

---

[109] Simpl. *in Cat.* 78,4ff, cf. T.A Szlezák, *Pseudo-Archytas über die Kategorien*, Berlin and New York 1972, 105. The problem was taken up again by Nicostratus and Plotinus (*Enn.* 6.1.2, cf. Simpl. *in Cat.* 76,13ff) and is presupposed by ps-Archytas *Peri tô katholou logô* p. 22,31ff Thesleff, cf. Simpl. 76,19ff, 77,8ff.

[110] Simpl. *in Cat.* 78,5ff, Dexippus *in Cat.* 45,27ff; cf. ps-Archytas *Peri tô katholou logô* p. 24,17ff. Th. See further Prantl I, 541ff, Moraux, *Arist.* 155ff, G. Movia, *Anima e Intelletto*, Padua 1968, 194ff. The question whether the specific differentia qualifies the genus or species (ap. Simpl. *in Cat.* 97,28ff), which Prantl connects with this doctrine, belongs to a different discussion.

[111] Simpl. *in Cat.* 104,26f, cf. Dexippus 45,22ff.

[112] *SVF* 2.369ff, cf. Prantl I, 430ff, Zeller III 1,95ff, Rist (above, n. 84), 43ff.

[113] Simpl. *in Cat.* 302,12ff, cf. 306,13ff; cf. Szlezák, *Pseudo-Archytas über die Kat.*, 126; Moraux, *Arist.*, 160. Note the implication: in this case, at least, Boethus applied the doctrine of categories to an intelligible substance.

[114] However Aristotle himself names *Kinêsis* as a category at *Metaph.* 1029b25, and at *EE* 1217b29 has two categories *kinein* and *kineisthai*. Cf. v. Fritz, 'Der Ursprung der aristotelischen Kategorienlehre', *Arch. Gesch. Philos.* 40, 1931, 451, 465, 484 (revised: id., *Schriften zur griechischen Logik*, II: *Logik, Ontologie und Mathematik, Problemata* 71, Stuttgart 1978, 11, 24, 40).

than to be a faithful exponent of Aristotelianism. He tried to keep the discussion within an Aristotelian framework and saw his main task as explaining the real or apparent discrepancies he found in Aristotle's writings. But he could not altogether escape the influences which had established themselves in the centuries after Aristotle's death.

The other 'early commentators' on the *Categories* are less important, at least for their contribution to the knowledge of Aristotle. Only one, Ariston of Alexandria, was a professed Aristotelian. Two of his comments are recorded, both concerned with Relation; one echoes a remark of Andronicus and Boethus,[115] the other raises the question whether 'cosmos' is a relative term and what its correlate might be. It has been variously interpreted and may have been distorted in the course of transmission, but the problem seems to hinge on the ambiguity of the expressions *kosmos* and *to en kosmôi*.[116] Eudorus, his fellow Alexandrian and rival,[117] tried to determine the correct order in which the categories should be placed. Arguing that every substance must have some properties and extension, he placed Quality and Quantity immediately after Substance; after these came Time and Place which, though extrinsic to substances, are necessary for their existence.[118] This is something to which Aristotle seems to have attached little importance; the order in which the categories are enumerated at *Cat.* 1b26f differs from that in which they are discussed in the body of that work, and different arrangements are found in his other writings. It is characteristic both of Eudorus and the intellectual climate in which he worked that he should have devoted so much effort and ingenuity to this task. His decisions may have been influenced by Aristotelian and

---

[115] See above n. 95.

[116] Simpl. *in Cat.* 188,31ff = fr. 2 Mariotti. See Zeller III 1, 649; Prantl I, 546; Moraux, *Arist.*, 183-5; I. Mariotti, *Aristone d'Alessandria*, Bologna 1966, 48-57 tries to explain it by reference to the Stoic distinction between *to holon* and *to pan*, but this is far-fetched. The difficulty arises from the fact that the terms employed by Ariston in this context include three neologisms whose exact meaning is not clear (*kosmôtos, geôtos, aerôtos*), as well as the ambiguous *to en kosmôi*.

[117] According to Strabo 17.790C, both published books about the source of the Nile whose content was so similar that Eudorus accused Ariston of plagiarism. See further Zeller III 1, 633ff; Dillon, *Middle Platonists*, London 1977, 115ff (on the *Categories*, 133ff); H. Dörrie, 'Der Platoniker Eudoros von Alexandreia', *Hermes* 79, 1944, 25-38 = id., *Plat. Min.*, 297-309; Praechter, *Kl. Schr.*, 130f (see n. 78); Fraser, *Ptolem. Alexandria* I,489; II,708f; Moraux, *Arist.* II, 509-27.

[118] Simpl. *in Cat.* 206,10ff; cf. ps-Archytas *Peri tô katholou logô* p. 23,17-24,16 Thesleff, with Szlezák's notes, pp. 108-18; this is the earliest extant attempt to fix the order of the categories and clearly owes much to Eudorus, although their conclusions differ in some respects. W. Theiler, *Unters. zur antiken Lit.*, Berlin 1970, 489f, followed by Szlezák 116, claims that Eudoros also influenced the lists of categories given by Philo Alexandrinus, *de Decalogo* 30 and Boethius *de Trinitate* ch. 4 init, although both, like Arist. 1b26, place Relation fourth, after Substance, Quality and Quantity, Philo puts Time and Place last, and Boethius retains the terms *Ubi* and *Quando* (Where and When). Theiler's assertion that Boethius placed Relation last is wrong; his order is *Substantia, Qualitas, Quantitas, Ad aliquid, Ubi, Quando, Habere, Situm esse, Facere, Pati*, i.e. essentially the same as in Aristotle 1b26.

perhaps even Platonic precedents,[119] or by metaphysical considerations like those used by ps-Archytas for the same purpose,[120] but that the question was raised at all may have been due to the Stoics, in whose system it was more important;[121] indeed Aristotle's seeming neglect of it may have been one of their reasons for interpreting his doctrine as a classification of terms rather than things. – The other comments on the *Categories* ascribed to Eudorus are petty and pedantic to the point of captiousness; most of them are concerned with the sub-divisions of the category Quality, one with a detail in Relation.[122]

The last of the 'old commentators' was a Stoic, Athenodorus, who wrote a book entitled *Against Aristotle's Categories*; he is generally quoted together with Cornutus, another Stoic active in the middle of the first century AD.[123] As we have seen already, they thought that the *Categories* is concerned with language and criticised Aristotle for unduly restricting the scope of his analysis (above, p. 70). Their remaining comments were less far-reaching. Athenodorus held that weight should be regarded as a third subdivision of the category Quantity, together with number and extension; Cornutus disagreed, preferring to place weight, i.e. heaviness and lightness, in the category Quality.[124] Both agreed in denying that objects such as heads or wings could fall into the category Relation, although they gave different reasons for this.[125] Probably it was Athenodorus who suggested substituting a single category Movement for the Aristotelian Action and Passion, the idea refuted by Boethus.[126] Some remarks about Time and Place are attributed to Cornutus alone.[127]

These writers did little for the elucidation of Aristotle, but their attitude raises an interesting problem. The Stoics appear to have been hostile to Aristotle's doctrine from the start and, unlike the Platonists, made no attempt later to incorporate it in their system; apparently their

---

[119] Szlezák, 110 thinks that Eudorus placed Quality next to Substance because he was influenced by the Platonic distinction between *ousia* or *ti estin* and *poion ti* (on which see K. Gaiser, *Arch. Gesch. Philos.*, 243f), but this would at most account for the placing of one category, and the same order is found at *Metaph.* 1017a25.

[120] Szlezák, 116 has some interesting speculations on this point.

[121] Simpl. *in Cat.* 165,32ff = *SVF* 2.403; cf. Rist (above, n. 84) 54f.

[122] See the index to Simpl. *in Cat.*; Prantl I, 539f, Zeller III 1, 633.

[123] See the index to Kalbfleisch's edition of Simpl. *in Cat.* The title of Athenodorus' book *Pros tas Aristotelous katēgorias*, is given by Simpl., 62,25; Cornutus' book was entitled *Pros Athēnodōron kai Aristotelēn* (ibid. 62,28, Porph. *in Cat.* 86,23), but we only hear of one substantial disagreement; Cornutus also criticised Aristotle's *Categories* in a *Tekhnē Rhētorikē*. See further Brandis (1833), 275, Prantl I, 538f; Zeller III 1, 607f; Praechter, *Kl. Schr.*, 128 (see n. 78); for Athenodorus' date see above, n. 88.

[124] For Athenodorus see Simpl. 128,7; he is associated with ps-Archytas (p. 25,1-3 Th.) and Ptolemy the astronomer; cf. Szlezák, 120f, Sambursky, *The Physical World of Late Antiquity*, London 1962, 83. For Cornutus see Simpl. 129,1ff; he is joined with Porphyry. The statement of Brandis and Prantl (539 n. 20) that Cornutus agreed with Athenodorus on this point is based on a wrong reading in the old editions of Simplicius' commentary.

[125] Simpl. *in Cat.* 187,28ff.

[126] See above, p. 76. Since Aristotle himself seems to do this at *Metaph.* 1029b25, this may be evidence that Athenodorus had read the *Metaphysics*.

[127] Simpl. *in Cat.* 351,21ff, 359,1ff, 15ff.

chief concern was to emphasise the differences between Aristotle's teaching and their own. Yet they took an active part in the debate sparked off by Andronicus and seem to have exercised some influence on him and the other early commentators. All this suggests that they were resisting an attempt to find Aristotelian ideas in their teaching. All the ancient authorities who write about a Stoic doctrine of 'Categories' as if it were a mere variant of the Aristotelian one are late commentators on Aristotle,[128] and there is no good evidence that the early Stoics used the term 'category' in anything like its Aristotelian (and modern) sense. Thus it would appear that the 'Stoic doctrine of Categories', about which so much has been written, originated in an attempt by Andronicus, or possibly Eudorus, to read Aristotelian notions into Stoicism.[129] If this is correct, Athenodorus was right to object: the assimilation of the Stoic classification to the Aristotelian Categories has caused nothing but confusion.[130]

The burst of activity following the publication of Andronicus' edition was succeeded by a lull. We know the names of many Peripatetic commentators active in the first century AD, but the paucity of quotations suggests that their work was not highly regarded by later authorities, and we hear of no commentaries on Aristotle by members of other schools. It was not until the middle of the second century AD that there was a revival, associated with the names of Aspasius, Adrastus, Herminus and Sosigenes, the last two being teachers of Alexander of Aphrodisias. The work of Aspasius, Adrastus and Alexander will be discussed elsewhere in this book; it remains for me to mention what little we know of commentators active in this period who did not belong to the Peripatetic school. Only three men have to be considered, all of them Platonists: Atticus, Lucius and Nicostratus. Atticus, who lived under the emperor Marcus Aurelius, is chiefly known for a series of intemperate attacks on Aristotle and all his works preserved by Eusebius,[131] but other sources attribute two remarks to him concerning Aristotle's definitions of homonyms and synonyms at the beginning of the *Categories* which his latest editor, des Places, has taken as evidence that he wrote a commentary on that work.[132] However, no comments on the doctrine of categories itself or any other logical question are attributed to him, and

---

[128] Plotinus, whose critique of the Stoic doctrine (*Enn.* 6.1.25ff) is the most comprehensive account of it extant today, leaves us in no doubt that it differed fundamentally from Aristotle's.

[129] The doctrine of 'Body going through body', on which see Todd (op. cit. in n. 67 above) 73ff, would be an analogous case.

[130] In passing, let me point out one difference which has generally been overlooked. The Stoic terms *hupokeimenon, poion, pôs ekhon* and *pros ti pôs ekhon* are adjectives, while the names of the Aristotelian categories are nouns or adverbs construed as nouns.

[131] Eusebius *PE* 11.1.15.4-9, 12-13. The fragments have been collected (with some omissions) by E. des Places, Paris 1977. See further Dillon, 247-58; Düring *AB* p. 325ff; M. Baltes in *Jahrb. für Antike u. Christentum*, Ergänzungsband 10, Münster 1983, 38-57; C. Moreschini, *ANRW* II 36.1.477-91.

[132] Simpl. *in Cat.* 30,16ff; 32,19ff ~ Porph. *in Cat.* 66,34ff, incompletely reported as fr. 41-2 des Places. Cf. Brandis, *Abh. Akad.*, Berlin 1833, 279.

there is nothing in his longer fragments to suggest that he had studied any Aristotelian treatise at first hand; so des Places' claim must remain very doubtful. The first of these remarks is a footling criticism, but the second raises a question about the relationship of the analogical and metaphorical use of terms which, while only remotely connected with what Aristotle says, is not without interest. The first one is said to be an elaboration of an objection by Nicostratus, who seems to have been about a generation older than Atticus. This philosopher, who is known from a Delphian honorific inscription and from the pages of Aulus Gellius, is said by Simplicius to have been the author of a treatise containing objections to nearly everything said in the *Categories*, written in a 'hostile and impudent' manner; it was based on a similar work by an otherwise unknown Lucius.[133] They are quoted together half a dozen times, Lucius alone three times and Nicostratus alone twelve times; eight of these quotations are in the section dealing with the *Postpraedicamenta*, and it looks as if Lucius may not have included these chapters in his purview. But it is generally assumed that most of the other criticisms of Aristotle's doctrine, which are mentioned and refuted by Simplicius and the other commentators without their authors being named, were taken from Nicostratus, and that his book was nothing less than a collection of all possible objections to Aristotle's teaching on this subject.[134] Nicostratus for his part used older material, including Stoic arguments which he sometimes misunderstood.[135] Like Athenodorus and Cornutus, Lucius and Nicostratus complained that Aristotle's list of Categories omitted some terms which should have been included, and claimed that weight should be counted as a third sub-division, with number and extension, of the category Quantity (this point was also made by ps-Archytas).[136] Like ps-Archytas again Lucius (and probably Nicostratus also) argued that Quality should come before Relation, as it does in Aristotle's list of Categories at 1b26, but not in his detailed treatment in the body of his work (ch. 7-8); here Simplicius admits that they have a case.[137] They also raised a problem which would have appeared fundamental to Platonists,

---

[133] Simpl. *in Cat.* 1,18ff; for other quotations see the index of the Berlin ed. s.v. See further, for Nicostratus, K. Praechter, 'Nikostratos der Platoniker', *Hermes* 57, 1922, 481-517 = id., *Kl. Schr.*, 101-37; K. v. Fritz, 'Nikostratos' no. 26, *RE* XVII 1, 1936, 547-51; Dillon, 233-6. For Lucius, W. Capelle 'Lukios' no. 1, *RE* XIII 2, 1927, 1791-7; Praechter, op. cit., 502 n. 1. Cf. L. Deitz, 'Bibliographie du platonisme impérial antérieur à Plotin: 1926-1986', *ANRW* II 36.1.154.

[134] Many of the arguments attributed to Lucius and/or Nicostratus by Simplicius are quoted anonymously by the other commentators, Porphyry, Dexippus and Ammonius, and are also found in Plotinus (*Enn.* 6.1); see Praechter, 501 (=121ff). Porphyry seems to have made a point of refuting all of them in his lost large commentary on the *Categories*; cf. Simpl. 21,4; 29,29 etc.

[135] See Praechter, 488 (=108ff) on Simpl. *in Cat.* 406,6ff.

[136] Simpl. 62,28ff, 64,13ff, 128,5ff; ps-Archytas p. 25,2, 28,4 Th. For Athenodorus see above, p. 78. Nicostratus, ap. Simpl. 368,12ff criticises Aristotle for not providing a discussion of the category *ekhein* which would include all the uses of that word enumerated in the *Postpraedicamenta* (15b17ff).

[137] Simpl. 156,16ff; cf. ps-Archytas p. 23,21ff Th.; above, p. 77.

whether the Categories are found in the intelligible as well as the sensible world; this was already considered by ps-Archytas and was later taken up by Plotinus, and it is impossible to tell for certain how much Lucius and Nicostratus contributed to the discussion.[138] The other criticisms attributed to either are minor quibbles about Aristotle's use of particular words[139] or other details. In one place Nicostratus pointed out a discrepancy between the accounts of movement given in the *Categories* and the *Physics*, showing that he was acquainted with this work.[140] Nevertheless it seems that his critique was entirely destructive and neither he nor his predecessor made any positive suggestions; the best that can be said for them is that they raised difficulties which it was useful to clear up once and for all. But the trouble they took to refute Aristotle suggests that they must have regarded his teaching as a serious threat to the Platonist position.

[138] Simpl. 73,28ff, 76,14ff; cf. Plot. *Enn.* 6.1.1-2; ps-Archytas p. 22,31ff; 30,19ff Th., with Szlezák, ad loc.; above, p. 76 (with n. 109).
[139] e.g. *poson*, Simpl. 127,30; *diathesis*, 231,20.
[140] Simpl. 428,3ff, comparing *Cat.* 15a13 with *Phys.* 225a25ff.

CHAPTER FOUR

The school of Alexander?*

Robert W. Sharples

I

Alexander of Aphrodisias was appointed by the emperors as a public teacher of Aristotelian philosophy at some time between 198 and 209 AD.[1] As a public teacher it is likely that he had, in some sense, a school.[2] But trying to establish what happened in that school and how it functioned is comparable to the task we would have if we had to establish what went on in a philosophy department in a modern university on the basis of a selection of books by the professor and a confused collection of his papers, the notes from which he lectured and the essays of his students, with no obvious indication of which were which.

We know a considerable amount about the Neoplatonic schools of the fifth and sixth centuries AD and the study of Aristotle's writings in them; we know the place they had in the curriculum, the order in which they were read, and we can compare the ways in which different commentators approached the question of the relation between the works of Aristotle and those of Plato. We can trace relations between teachers and their pupils, and we are sometimes told that a particular text is a pupil's record of his teacher's utterances. The very organisation of the commentaries sometimes reflects and makes clear the requirements of the teaching context, in the division of a commentary into separate lectures and the placing of a general summary of a section of argument before the discussion of particular points. For the medieval period, too, we

---

* Full details of modern works referred to in the notes by author's name (and in some cases date) only are given in the References on p. 111. It will be immediately obvious how much the present discussion owes, particularly where Alexander's use of his predecessors is concerned, to the work of Paul Moraux and in particular to the first two volumes of his study *Der Aristotelismus bei den Griechen* (Moraux 1973 and 1984); extensive use has also been made of the word-searching facilities afforded by the Thesaurus Linguae Graecae CD-ROM disc and the Ibycus Scholarly Computer kindly loaned to the Institute of Classical Studies, London, by Professor David Packard.

[1] cf. Todd 1976, 1 n. 3.

[2] But not the Aristotelian Lyceum, which had probably ceased to exist in 86 BC; cf. Lynch, 192-207. We do not even know whether Alexander taught in Athens, though this seems likely and Todd 1976, 1 n. 2 notes the reference at *in Metaph.* 415,29-31 to Aristotle's statue there.

have copious information on the organisation of teaching and study.[3]

With Alexander matters are very different. We know the names of some of his teachers,[4] and his surviving works give us evidence for his disagreements with them.[5] We also know something of his disagreements with other philosophers of his own generation or the generation before;[6] and we can trace, however controversially, his influence on later thinkers.[7] But we do not know the name of a single one of his immediate pupils,[8] and for all that we can tell the influence of other writers on him might have been largely, and his influence on other writers entirely, through the medium of writing rather than personal encounter. We are after all explicitly told that Alexander's commentaries were among those *read* in Plotinus' school.[9]

It is however in principle unlikely that any thinker in the ancient world would have communicated entirely through the written, rather than the spoken word. And some of the writings attributed to Alexander are most naturally seen in the context of his teaching activities or of debates within his circle.

These writings include commentaries on Aristotelian works, treatises or monographs on particular topics such as those *On the Soul*[10] and *On Fate*, and also numerous short discussions.[11] Three books of these collected discussions are entitled *phusikai skholikai aporiai kai luseis*, 'School-discussion problems and solutions on nature'; a fourth is titled 'Problems on Ethics' but sub-titled, no doubt in imitation of the preceding three books when it was united with them,[12] *skholikai êthikai aporiai kai luseis*,

---

[3] cf. especially the account in A. Kenny and J. Pinborg, 'Medieval philosophical literature', in N. Kretzmann, A. Kenny and J. Pinborg (eds), *The Cambridge History of Later Medieval Philosophy*, Cambridge 1982, 11-42.

[4] Namely Herminus (c. 120-180 or 190 AD, Moraux 1984, 361-3; Alexander ap. Simplicium *in Cael.* 430,32ff) and Sosigenes (similar in date; Alexander *in Meteor.* 143,13); possibly also Aristoteles of Mytilene (died between 165 and 180 AD, Moraux 1984, 400; cf. Galen *Scr. Min.* vol. 2 (Müller) 11,4f; Alexander *Mant.* 110,4; and below n. 42).

[5] cf. below at nn. 20-47.

[6] Below at nn. 58-89.

[7] cf. Sharples 1987, 1220-4, with references there.

[8] H.J. Blumenthal has pointed out that it is wrong to describe Alexander as the last *Peripatetic* – as opposed to Neoplatonist – commentator on Aristotle (Chapter 5 below, and 'Alexander of Aphrodisias in the later Greek commentators on Aristotle's *De anima*', in J. Wiesner (ed.), *Aristoteles Werk und Wirkung, Paul Moraux gewidmet*, vol. 2, Berlin 1987, 90-106, at 100. But Alexander does seem, as far as our information goes, to stand at the end of a distinctively Peripatetic *tradition*. On alleged Peripatetic teachers later than Alexander (Ammonius and Prosenes) cf. Lynch, 213.

[9] Porphyry, *Life of Plotinus*, 14.

[10] To be distinguished from Alexander's commentary, now lost, on Aristotle's *de Anima*.

[11] The lost and surviving works attributed to Alexander are listed, with bibliography, at Sharples 1987, 1182-94. The authorship of many of the short texts is open to debate; in what follows I will on occasion use 'Alexander' for convenience to refer to the authors of these texts without necessarily thereby implying any view on the question of authenticity.

[12] So Bruns 1892, v.

'school-discussion problems and solutions on ethics'.[13] A further collection was transmitted as the second book of Alexander's treatise *On the Soul*, and labelled *mantissa* or 'makeweight' by the Berlin editor Bruns. Other texts essentially similar to those in these collections survive in Arabic though not in Greek; and there is evidence to suggest that there were other collections now lost.[14] The circumstances in which these collections were put together are unclear; it was not always expertly done, and while some of the titles attached to particular pieces seem to preserve valuable additional information, others are inept or unhelpful.[15] Nor is it clear at what date the collections were assembled.[16]

It is not my concern here to give a full enumeration of the works attributed to Alexander or to classify them in detail. That has been done elsewhere both by myself and by others. Rather, I will proceed to a discussion of what the works can tell us about the context in which they arose. It will be helpful to start with consideration of the relation of Alexander's works to those of his predecessors, teachers and contemporaries.

II

Assessment of Alexander's use of earlier Aristotelian commentators is rendered more problematic by the fact that the only earlier commentaries which survive entire are on the *Nicomachean Ethics*.[17] While Alexander was certainly interested in that work, as the collection of *Ethical*

---

[13] I am currently preparing translations of the *Quaestiones, Ethical Problems and Mantissa* for publication in the series of translations of the Greek commentators on Aristotle edited by Professor Sorabji.

[14] 'Scholia logica' are referred to in what may be a gloss at Alexander *in An. Pr.* 250,2; and an 'Explanation and summary of certain passages from (Aristotle's) *de Sensu*', which Moraux suggests may have been a similar collection, is referred to by a scholion on *quaestio* 1.2. Cf. Moraux 1942, 24; Sharples 1987, 1196.

[15] cf. the discussion at Bruns 1892, xi.

[16] Alexander's commentary on the *de Sensu* cites not only the lost *de Anima* commentary (167,21) but also a section of the *Mantissa* (*in Sens.* 31,29, citing *Mantissa* 127-130; cf. P. Wendland, preface to *CAG* 3,1, v; Moraux 1978, 297 n. 71), cf. also below, n. 98.

[17] Namely the commentary on the *Ethics* by Aspasius (*CAG* vol. 19) and the anonymous scholia on books 2-5 published in *CAG* vol. 20, which incorporate material by Adrastus of Aphrodisias; cf. P. Mercken, *The Greek Commentaries on the Nicomachean Ethics of Aristotle*, Leiden 1973 (*Corp. Lat. Comm. in Arist. Graec.* 6.1) 1.14*-22*, and Moraux 1984, 323-30. A. Kenny, *The Aristotelian Ethics*, Oxford 1978, 37 n. 3, suggests that the commentary itself is by Adrastus, but this is difficult to reconcile with the ancient evidence for Adrastus' work; cf. H.B. Gottschalk, 'Aristotelian philosophy in the Roman World' in W. Haase (ed.), *Aufstieg und Niedergang der römischen Welt*, Teil II 'Principat', Bd. 36.2 'Philosophie und Wissenschaften', Berlin 1987, 1079-174, at 1155 and n. 363.

Problems shows,[18] it is not clear whether he wrote a complete commentary on it or not.[19]

Not surprisingly, Alexander refers in several places to his own teachers. According to Philoponus,[20] Alexander in his (lost) monograph *On the disagreement between Aristotle and his followers concerning syllogisms with mixed premisses*[21] referred to Sosigenes' interpretation of Aristotle, *Prior Analytics*, 1.9, 30a15-23. In his commentary on the *Meteorology* Alexander cites Sosigenes on the explanation of the solar and lunar halo, agreeing with Sosigenes in supporting the position of Aristotle and Posidonius against rival theories.[22] Sosigenes' general interest in the theory of vision is reflected in Alexander's works,[23] and Moraux has suggested that Alexander was Themistius' source for Sosigenes' explanation of phosphoresence.[24]

[18] The *Ethical Problems* are admittedly chiefly interested in the solution of difficulties in the application of logical distinctions to ethical subject-matter (for example, the way in which pleasure and pain are opposites; see below at n. 167, and for another example below at nn. 39-41) and in topics (such as responsibility for actions) which Alexander dealt with in independent treatises. On the general character of the *Ethical Problems*, cf. A.J. Madigan, 'Alexander of Aphrodisias: the book of *Ethical Problems*', in W. Haase (ed.), *Aufstieg und Niedergang der römischen Welt*, vol. II.36.2, Berlin 1987.

[19] That he did so is suggested by a reference to '*hupomnêmata* on the *Ethics*' at Alexander *in Top*. 187,9-10; but this is the only evidence. Cf. Sharples 1985, at 113.

[20] Philoponus *in An. Pr*. 126,20-3. Cf. also [Ammonius] *in An. Pr*. 39,24-6; Moraux 1984, 339-44. Below, n. 25.

[21] That is, on syllogisms with mixed modal premisses. Cf. Alexander *in An. Pr*. 125,30ff; Moraux 1984, 393.

[22] Alexander *in Meteor*. 143,13; Moraux 1984, 335. Sosigenes' opinion is cited, it may be noted, *not* from a commentary but from his 'eighth book *On Sight*'.

[23] cf. Alexander *de Anima* 42,4-46,19; *Mantissa* 127,20-150,18; *Quaestiones* 1.2 and 1.13. At *de Anima* 43,16 Alexander refers to 'enquiries about how we see', but the points he there mentions cannot all be related to the *Mantissa* discussion. Cf. Bruns 1887 ad loc.

[24] Themistius *in DA* 61,22ff, from Sosigenes' third book *On Sight*; cf. Philoponus *in DA* 348,10-19. Moraux 1984, 359. – When Simplicius in his *de Caelo* commentary (503,35) cites Alexander and Porphyry as concerned about a passage of Aristotle where Sosigenes preferred to suppose an error by a copyist rather than a confusion by Aristotle himself, it might seem reasonable to suppose that Alexander's (lost) *de Caelo* commentary, which Simplicius cites extensively, discussed Sosigenes' view and was Simplicius' source for it. However, Th.-H. Martin, 'Questions connexes sur deux Sosigène et sur deux péripatéticiens Alexandre', *Annales de la Faculté de lettres de Bordeaux* 1, 1879, 174-87, at 176-7, argues that Simplicius, who cites Sosigenes only on the topic of the heavenly spheres, is drawing directly on a treatise by Sosigenes *On the Counteracting Spheres* (cf. Proclus *Hypotyp*. (Manitius) 4.98, 130,7-23; Moraux 1984, 344-58). It is for the *same* point, it may be noted, that pseudo-Alexander *in Metaph*. cites Sosigenes at *CAG* vol.1 706,13; it could be the genuine commentary by Alexander that was the pseudo-Alexander's source, but it seems equally likely that pseudo-Alexander derived the information from Simplicius. (Cf., on another similar case, P. Merlan, 'Ein Simplikios-Zitat bei ps.-Alexandros und ein Plotinus-Zitat bei Simplikios', *Rh. Mus*. 89, 1935, 154-60; but also, challenging the generally accepted late dating of the section of the *Metaphysics* commentary not by Alexander himself, and its attribution to Michael of Ephesus, L. Tarán at *Gnomon* 53, 1981, 750, reviewing Moraux 1973). Elsewhere the pseudo-Alexander uses Sosigenes' name simply as an example (466,17, 663,2); this may be an attempt to create an impression of authenticity, as with his use of Alexander himself as an example (cf. M. Hayduck, preface to *CAG* vol.1, vi, and the references in his index). – The Sosigenes referred to at Alexander *Mixt*. 3 216,12 is a Stoic,

Alexander argued against his teacher Herminus in the monograph on mixed modal syllogisms and similarly in the commentary on the *Prior Analytics*, without naming him in the latter.[25] In his *de Caelo* commentary, too, Alexander disagreed with Herminus' views on the parts played by the nature of the heavenly body on the one hand, and its soul on the other, in explaining the heavenly motion.[26] Simplicius quotes a passage in which Alexander states that he heard Herminus' explanation of Aristotle's claim that acceleration of the heavens would imply unnatural retardation.[27] Simplicius himself remarks that Alexander was the first to understand Aristotle's argument here correctly,[28] and it seems likely that here too Alexander developed his view in conscious opposition to that of Herminus.

Simplicius refers to Alexander's statement of Herminus' position as 'in accordance with Aspasius', and concludes the citation with 'this is what Herminus said in accordance with Aspasius'.[29] Aspasius was earlier than Herminus;[30] Simplicius' remarks indicate that he took the statement of Herminus' view from Alexander – specifically from the lost *de Caelo* commentary – and that Alexander, in stating his teacher's view, remarked on its similarity to that of Aspasius.[31] Aspasius and Alexander are cited together several times in Simplicius' *Physics* commentary, sometimes as agreeing,[32] sometimes as disagreeing,[33] and once Simplicius tells us that Alexander knew of the reading of the Aristotelian text adopted by Aspasius, but preferred another.[34] It seems likely that

---

not Alexander's teacher; cf. Martin, op. cit., 177-8.

[25] The view reported from Herminus by pseudo-Ammonius *in An. Pr.* 39,31 corresponds to that criticised by Alexander at *in An. Pr.* 125,3-6. (While Alexander does not there name Herminus, he does call his view 'ridiculous', 125,16). Moraux 1984, 391-4 notes the connection between the two passages and suggests that pseudo-Ammonius is using Alexander's monograph, rather than the commentary, as his source. Herminus is also referred to at Alexander *in An. Pr.* 72,27; 89,34; 91,2; *in Top.* 569,3; 574,26.

[26] For Alexander the nature and the soul of the heavens are identical. Cf. Simplicius *in Cael.* 380,5, who notes that Alexander replies to the views of Herminus but not to those of Julianus of Tralles; Merlan, op. cit. in n. 24, and id., 'Plotinus *Enneads* 2.2', *TAPhA* 74, 1943, 179-91; Sharples 1987, 1214 n. 153, and references there.

[27] Aristotle *Cael.* 2.6, 288b22; Simplicius *in Cael.* 430,32ff.

[28] Simplicius *in Cael.* 430,29. At *in Int.* (*ed. sec.*) 272,14ff Boethius reports Alexander as supposing a textual corruption in Aristotle *Int.* 10,19b29-30, but argues (274,12) that Alexander was wrong and that the interpretation of Herminus and Porphyry is to be preferred.

[29] Simplicius *in Cael.* 430,32-431,11; cf. Moraux 1984, 240ff.

[30] Galen, who was born in 129, was taught by one of Aspasius' pupils (Galen *Scripta Minora* (Marquardt) vol. 1 32,5-7). Aspasius' philosophical activity is to be placed in the first half of the second century AD: Moraux 1984, 226.

[31] So Moraux 1984, 361 n. 5. The alternative would be to interpret Simplicius as saying that Alexander cited Herminus' views *according to* Aspasius, that is that Aspasius was his source; but even without the chronological difficulty it would be odd if Alexander had to use Aspasius as a source for the views of his, Alexander's, own teacher.

[32] Simplicius *in Phys.* 547,11; 727,35; 752,15.

[33] Simplicius *in Phys.* 131,15ff (where Alexander argued against Aspasius at length; cf. Moraux 1984, 235-6); 558,34; 728,5.

[34] Simplicius *in Phys.* 422,25.

Simplicius is throughout citing Aspasius' commentary from quotations in Alexander's.[35] Aspasius is cited in Alexander's *Metaphysics* commentary[36] and in that on the *de Sensu*;[37] and it seems that Alexander also cited Aspasius extensively in his *de Interpretatione* commentary.[38]

One of the short texts attributed to Alexander, *Ethical Problem* 11, adopts a similar solution to Aspasius', though without referring to him by name, to the problem that 'involuntary' appears to have two senses while its opposite 'voluntary' has only one.[39] The anonymous commentary on *Nicomachean Ethics* Book 3, which has been linked with Adrastus of Aphrodisias, adopts a different view; unfortunately it is not clear whether Alexander in the *Ethical Problem* is replying to Adrastus, or whether this particular material in the anonymous *Ethics* commentary is later and is drawing in a confused way on the *Ethical Problem*.[40] Similar issues are discussed in two passages of Alexander's *Topics* commentary, again without explicit reference to any of his predecessors.[41]

Alexander's third teacher apart from Sosigenes and Herminus, Aristoteles of Mytilene (if Moraux's view is accepted[42]) is referred to at *Mantissa* 110,4, a section of a text which may or may not be by Alexander himself.[43] It seems likely that both the general account of Aristotle's doctrine of intellect entering human beings 'from outside' (*nous thurathen*) at 110,4-112,5, and the following reply to the objection that intellect cannot be said to 'come from outside' if it is incorporeal and

[35] So Diels in the *index nominum* to *CAG* vols 9-10 s.v. 'Aspasios', citing Simplicius *in Phys.* 131,14; 547,11; 558,34 (the last passage is particularly noteworthy; Simplicius says that he *thinks* that Aspasius' position was as he described it, and immediately goes on to cite Alexander). On the other hand, if all Simplicius' references to Aspasius by name do come from Alexander, we would have to suppose that Alexander cited Aspasius (and other predecessors) by name in his lost *Physics* commentary rather more than is his practice in the extant commentaries; he is much more sparing in his references to predecessors by name there than is Simplicius. (The references to Theophrastus and Eudemus in the *Prior Analytics* commentary, below nn. 48-9, are perhaps a special case). Aspasius is referred to in about 20 separate contexts in Simplicius' *Physics* commentary, but only three times in Alexander's *Metaphysics* commentary, a difference which cannot entirely be explained by difference in length between the two works. (Alexander is regularly mentioned in close proximity to the references to Aspasius in Simplicius' *Physics* commentary; there are exceptions, but failure to mention Alexander cannot prove that he was not the source.)

[36] cf. Aspasius ap. Alexander *in Metaph.* 41,27ff and 379,3ff; in the latter passage Alexander disagrees with Aspasius, though not explicitly. Cf. Moraux 1984, 246-9; also below n. 62.

[37] Alexander, *in Sens.* 10,2 (disagreement); also (without Aspasius being named explicitly) ibid. 82,16-17. Moraux 1984, 244-5.

[38] So Moraux 1984, 231.

[39] Aspasius *in EN* 59,2-11. Sharples 1985, 110.

[40] Anon. *in EN* (*CAG* vol. 20) 141,10-20. Sharples (1985) 111. Cf. also Alexander, *P. Eth.* 27 154,15-155,5 and 155,29-156,9 with Anon. *in EN*, *CAG*, vol. 20, 133,35-134,4 and 134,9-21 respectively.

[41] Alexander *in Top.* 99,2-20; 100,31-101,14; cf. also 181,21-187,9. Sharples 1985, 112.

[42] cf. P. Moraux, 'Aristoteles, Der Lehrer Alexanders von Aphrodisias', *AGPh* 49, 1967, 169-82, and id. 1984, 399-401; *contra*, P. Thillet, *Alexandre d'Aphrodise: Traité du Destin*, Paris, Budé, 1984, xv-xix.

[43] cf. Sharples 1984, 1213-14 and references there.

hence cannot move (112,5-113,12),[44] are to be interpreted as accounts of Aristotle's views; it is the latter section that the author of the *Mantissa* passage proceeds to attack. Both he and Aristoteles of Mytilene accept as given the identification of the 'intellect from outside' of Aristotle's *Generation of Animals* with the active intellect of *de Anima* 3.5.[45] Alexander also cited Aristoteles of Mytilene's views on *de Caelo* 1.4[46] and on *Metaphysics* Book 2, in the latter case referring to Aristoteles' interpretation as 'rather dialectical, though relevant'.[47]

Of earlier Peripatetics, Alexander refers extensively to Theophrastus[48] and Eudemus.[49] He argues against Andronicus for the authenticity of the *de Interpretatione*[50] and also against Sotion[51] and Xenarchus;[52] he used the commentaries of Boethus, apparently,[53] and of his namesake

[44] The objectors are referred to in the third person (*epipherousin*, 112,6), but not further identified; however, see below at n. 68. The attribution of both 110,4-112,5 and 112,5-113,12 to the same author has been disputed; cf. Sharples, op. cit., 1212 and references in nn. 134-6 there.

[45] Sharples 1987, 1212 and references in nn. 137-9 there. I am grateful to Victor Caston for emphasising the importance of this point. At *Quaest.* 2.3 48,18-22 it is taken as established (*ekeito*) that divine providence, acting through the influence of the heavenly bodies on the sublunary, is the cause of some creatures' possessing more soul-faculties than others, and in particular of man's possessing reason. Moraux 1967, at 163-4 n. 2, compares this passage to *Mant.* 113,6-12, and argues from this that *Quaest.* 2.3 is an early work of Alexander's.

[46] Alexander ap. Simplicium *in Cael.* 153,16ff; Moraux 1984, 401-2.

[47] Alexander *in Metaph.* 166-19-167,3, referring to 'our Aristotle' by contrast with the Stagirite; noted by P. Accattino, 'Alessandro di Afrodisia e Aristotele di Mitilene', *Elenchos* 6, 1985, 67-74, at 73-4.

[48] There are about 50 references to Theophrastus by name in the extant works of Alexander, about half of these being in the *Prior Analytics* commentary.

[49] There are 11 references to Eudemus in Alexander's extant works, again mainly from the *Prior Analytics* commentary (7 of the total). Simplicius *in Phys.* 1355,32 cites Alexander as arguing against Eudemus on the location within the heavenly sphere of the prime mover; cf. 1354,9ff. Alexander is also referred to as citing Eudemus by Simplicius *in Phys.* 133,21ff; Simplicius says that he cannot himself find in Eudemus' commentary the reading of Aristotle cited by Alexander (ibid., 133,24-5). Simplicius notes that Alexander seems to be following Eudemus at *in Phys.* 10,13 (cf. 11,16); a reaction by Alexander to Eudemus is noted at 99,29.

[50] Alexander *in An. Pr.* 161,1.

[51] Alexander *in Top.* 434,2, on whether sleep is a privation.

[52] Alexander is cited as replying to Xenarchus by Simplicius, *in Cael.* 21,33ff (cf. 22,18) and 23,22ff; cf. Moraux 1973, 199f. Alexander also referred to Xenarchus in his *de Anima* commentary (Philoponus *in DA* (Verbeke) 15,65-9; Moraux 1973, 207). Moraux 1942, 211 n. (e) compares with this passage *Mant.* 106,20-3; here too Alexander argues against a literal understanding of material intellect as matter, though without here naming Xenarchus. The interpretation of the associates of Xenarchus and Boethus on what is the *prôton oikeion* according to Aristotle are referred to and criticised at *Mantissa* 151,3ff, as are those of Sosicrates and Verginius Rufus; cf. Moraux 1973, 209, and other references at Sharples 1987, 1190.

[53] At *in Phys.*, 211,13ff Simplicius quotes from Alexander, then from Boethus, and then again from Alexander (below n. 117); cf. Moraux 1973, 170 and n. 1, arguing that Alexander is Simplicius' source. Alexander is also cited by Simplicius *in Phys.* 759,20 as replying to Boethus' claim that movement could be numerable even in the absence of soul; the issue is one that is also discussed in the treatise *On Time* by Alexander preserved in Arabic, and comparison with that suggests that Simplicius in his *Physics* commentary may have taken more from Alexander here than he explicitly acknowledges. Cf. R.W. Sharples, 'Alexander of

Alexander of Aegae,[54] and also seems to have reported views of Nicolaus of Damascus.[55] He referred to the eclectic Potamo;[56] and there is evidence that he knew and made use of the pseudo-Aristotelian *de Mundo*.[57]

Alexander's interest in the views of earlier and near-contemporary philosophers was not however confined to Peripatetics. His controversies with Galen[58] and the extent to which he opposed Stoicism, while nevertheless being influenced by the Stoics both in language and in thought,[59] are well known. But his writings show interest in Platonism and Epicureanism too. It is not, indeed, surprising that he should discuss Plato's Theory of Forms in commenting on Aristotle's criticisms of it in the *Metaphysics*; indeed his *Metaphysics* commentary is the major source of evidence for Aristotle's lost *de Ideis*.[60] His arguments against Xenocrates on the question of the priority of genus to species fall into the same general area,[61] as does his preserving the information, from Aspasius, that the first-century AD Platonist Eudorus altered the text of Aristotle.[62]

In *quaestio* 2.13 Alexander argues that the triangles in Plato's *Timaeus* have a material, rather than a formal role.[63] There is no *explicit*

Aphrodisias, *On Time', Phronesis*, 27 1982, 58-81, at 70-1 and nn. 75-7.

[54] At *in Cat.* 10,19-20 Simplicius cites Alexander of Aphrodisias and then says that Alexander of Aegae said the same; at *in Cat.* 13,11-18 he refers to the view of 'the Alexanders' (Moraux 1984, 222f). Cf. also Simplicius *in Cael.* 430,32, stating that Alexander of Aphrodisias cited Alexander of Aegae on Aristotle's argument at *de Caelo* 2.6, 288b22; above, n. 27, and Moraux 1984, 223-5.

[55] At *in Phys.* 23,14-16 Simplicius successively cites interpretations of Xenophanes by Nicolaus and by Alexander before proceeding to argue against them both; Moraux suggests that Alexander in his commentary argued against Nicolaus, and that it was through his commentary that Simplicius knew of Alexander's views. Cf. Moraux 1973, 451-7, and J.B. McDiarmid, 'Theophrastus on the Presocratic causes', *Harvard Studies in Classical Philology* 61, 1953, 85-156, at 115-20.

[56] Alexander ap. Simplicium *in Cael.* 652,9ff.

[57] So Moraux 1967, 160 n. 2, comparing Alexander ap. Simplicium *in Phys.* 310,25-311,37 with [Aristotle] *de Mundo* 398b16ff.

[58] cf. Sharples 1987, 1179 and nn. 18-21, with references there; also now V. Nutton, 'Galen's philosophical testament: "On my own Opinions" ', in J. Wiesner (ed.), *Aristoteles: Werk und Wirkung, Paul Moraux gewidmet*, vol. 2, Berlin 1987, 27-51, at 45-51.

[59] cf. Sharples 1987, 1178 and nn. 11-13, with references there. Simplicius *in Phys.* 671,4 reports Alexander as commenting that an argument under discussion can also be used against the Stoics; cf. also below n. 98.

[60] Alexander *in Metaph.* 79,3-98,24; cf. W. Leszl and D. Harlfinger, *Il 'De Ideis' di Aristotele e la teoria platonica delle idee*, Florence 1975 (Accademia toscana di scienze e lettere La Colombaria, studi, 40).

[61] Below, n. 139.

[62] Alexander *in Metaph.* 58,31-59,8, on *Metaph.* 1.6, 988a10-11. H. Dörrie, 'Der Platoniker Eudoros von Alexandria', *Hermes* 79, 1944, 25-39, at 34f, 38f, and Dillon, 116 and 128 n. 1. It has generally been thought that Eudorus changed the text to support his own version of Platonism, deriving matter from the One; but Moraux argues against this in 'Eine Korrektur des Mittelplatonikers Eudoros zum Text der Metaphysik des Aristoteles', in *Beiträge zur alten Geschichte und deren Nachleben: Festschrift für Franz Altheim*, Berlin 1969, vol. 1, 492-504.

[63] cf. Plato, *Timaeus* 53Cff. Alexander is cited by Simplicius *in Phys.* 26,13, on the reference in Aristotle *Phys.* 1.2., 184b19 to those who postulated three principles, as

reference by name to Plato or his followers, or to the *Timaeus*, in the text of the *quaestio*; the title describes the text as 'against the Platonists who say that it is the shapes and forms of bodies that are composed of the triangles, not the bodies themselves'. The interpretation advanced by the author of the *quaestio*, implying that it is the Receptacle that plays the role of matter in the *Timaeus*, is like that of Aristotle;[64] it would be difficult to interpret the third-person plural references in the text of the *quaestio* (as opposed to the title) as referring *solely* to non-Platonic interpreters of the *Timaeus*, but the discussion may have as much to do with Peripatetic doubts about how to interpret Plato as with Platonist exegesis.

Quaestio 2.21 is concerned, as Merlan showed,[65] to defend an Aristotelian theory of providence against Platonist critics, and notably the middle-Platonist Atticus, who themselves maintain that the sublunary is a primary concern of the divine, and criticise the Peripatetics for denying divine providence or making it entirely accidental; though in attacking the notion that the sublunary is a *primary* concern of the divine Alexander takes the opportunity to attack the Stoics too.[66] At 66,23 there may be an ironic allusion to the Craftsman of Plato's *Timaeus* as lacking concern for the world himself; this is hardly fair, for as fr. 2 Vitelli (discussed below) shows, Alexander was perfectly well aware that the Craftsman of the *Timaeus* delegates much of his concern for the worlds to lesser gods. Atticus may however not have emphasised this point in the way other contemporary Platonists did.[67] Alexander's, or his predecessors', views on intellect also seem to involve a reaction to Atticus;[68] and Alexander, in attacking Plato's view that the universe is perishable in its own nature but preserved by the divine will,[69] was upholding an Aristotelian position which Atticus had attacked.[70] Alexander appeals in support of his own view to the principle

---

identifying Plato's first principles as matter, the efficient cause and the exemplar; Simplicius criticises Alexander for failing to take account of Plato's final cause, and himself in this context downgrades matter to an auxiliary cause (26,5ff).

[64] Aristotle, *Physics* 4.2, 209b11ff; cf. F.M. Cornford, *Plato's Cosmology*, London 1937, 181 and 187.

[65] Merlan 1967, at 90-1. It is true that the issue could arise within a purely Peripatetic context; that the influence of the heavens on the sublunary may be purely accidental is already suggested by Theophrastus, *Metaphysics* 5b19-26.

[66] cf. *Quaest.* 2.21 70,2-6, against those who say that virtue alone is good, with Alexander *Fat.* 199,14ff.

[67] On Atticus' treatment of divine providence cf. Dillon, 252.

[68] So P.L. Donini, *Tre studi sull' Aristotelismo nel II secolo d.C.*, Turin 1974, 49-50, comparing Atticus fr. 7,75 des Places.

[69] Alexander ap. Simplicium *in Cael*. 358,27ff, and Alexander *Quaest*. 1.18; cf. M. Baltes, *Die Weltentstehung des platonischen Timaios nach den antiken Interpreten*, Leiden 1976, 76-81; Sharples 1983, at 99-102 and nn. Cf. also Alexander *in Metaph*. 212,15.

[70] Atticus, fr. 4,8-17 des Places. On the issue cf. R.R.K. Sorabji, *Time, Creation and the Continuum*, London 1983, 304 n. 47 and references there. Alexander agrees with Atticus that Plato in the *Timaeus* held the ordered cosmos to have a real beginning in time, and attacks Taurus on the issue; cf. Alexander ap. Simplicium *in Cael*. 297,9ff and ap. Philoponum *contra Proclum* (Rabe) 213-16 (from Alexander's *de Caelo* commentary, ibid.,

that what is impossible is impossible even for the gods, and cites Plato, *Theaetetus* 176A in support of this. Other Platonic works referred to by Alexander – often, again, in discussions prompted by Aristotle's references to Plato – include the *Sophist, Timaeus, Laws* 10 and the *Second Epistle*.[71]

In fr. 2 Vitelli, a short text preserved as part of a miscellany of extracts from Alexander in a Florentine MS,[72] Alexander replies to a Stoic philosopher who has criticised Aristotle for disagreeing with Plato on the immortality of the soul and divine providence. Exactly the same criticisms had been made by Atticus. Against the Stoic, Alexander argues that Aristotle did at least make the soul incorporeal, like Plato, even if not imperishable, while for the Stoics it is neither,[73] and also that Plato's view of divine providence is more acceptable than Stoic pantheism, because it does not involve the supreme god directly in mundane affairs (a feature of Stoic doctrine that he objects to elsewhere too[74]). In support of the latter point he alludes, without naming the works in question, to *Timaeus* 42E and *Politicus* 272E.

Alexander's Stoic opponent is not named in the text of the fragment itself. There is however a prefatory note in the MS, which begins as follows.

> By the same Alexander, from the argument against Heraclides; a consideration of what was said by Aristotle about the fifth element. In this (Alexander) argues against a certain Stoic philosopher ...

At first sight the natural way to interpret this is that, in the course of an

---

212,14); Baltes op. cit., 71-6, Dillon, 242-4 and 253-4, and K. Praechter, 'Tauros', *RE* 2 Reihe 5.1, 1934, 68.

[71] There are numerous references to Plato in Alexander's *Metaphysics* commentary (cf. Hayduck's index); notable is *in Metaph.* 59,28ff, citing *Timaeus* 28C and the *Second Epistle*, 312E. Plato is also cited by Alexander ap. Simplicium *in Phys.* 355,13 (citing *Laws* 10); 420,13; 420,18; 454,19 (Plato's *On the good*); 700,19; 705,5; 894,12; 1351,27; by Alexander ap. Simplicium *in Cael.* 276,14 (referring to *Timaeus* 31AB, a passage already discussed by Theophrastus, ap. Proclum *in Timaeum* (Diehl) 1.456.16-18); and by Alexander ap. Philoponum *in Phys.* 81,25 (on the *Sophist* as evidence for Parmenides; cf. Alexander ap. Simplicium *in Phys.* 135,16; 136,10).

[72] Noted by G. Vitelli, 'Frammenti di Alessandro di Afrodisia nel cod. Riccard. 63', *Studi Italiani di Filologia Classica* 3, 1895, 379-91, an elaboration of his account in 'Indice de' codici greci Riccardiani, Magliabechiani e Marucelliani', ibid., 2, 1894, at 515. The fragment was then published by Vitelli in 'Due frammenti di Alessandro di Afrodisia', *Festschrift Theodor Gomperz*, Vienna 1902, 90-3. (Citations according to this article.) The miscellany includes another otherwise unknown text on the *sôrites* argument and a number of extracts from Alexander's *de Anima* with one passage each from the *de Mixtione* and the *Quaestiones*. On the value of the MS for the *de Mixtione*, cf. E. Montanari, 'Per un'edizione del *Peri kraseos* di Alessandro di Afrodisia', *Atti e memorie dell' Accademia toscana di scienze e lettere La Colombaria* 36, 1971, 17-58.

[73] '(Plato) also says that the soul is an incorporeal substance and that it is imperishable; and *one* of these points about it is also made by Aristotle' (93,13-15; my emphasis).

[74] Alexander, *de Prov.* 19,3ff; 25,1ff; 31,16; 53,1ff; 63,7ff in H.-J. Ruland, *Die arabischen Fassungen zweier Schriften des Alexander von Aphrodisias*, diss. Saarbrücken 1976; *Quaest.* 2.21 68,9ff; *Mant.* 113,12ff; *Mixt.* 226,24ff. Cf. [Aristotle] *de Mundo* 6, 397b20ff, 398a5ff; Todd 1976, 226-7.

argument against someone named Heraclides[75] on the topic of the fifth heavenly element, Alexander digressed in order to reply to the attacks of an unnamed Stoic. The argument against Heraclides would have to be either an independent treatise of Alexander's of which no other trace has survived, or else an excursus in one of his commentaries – probably that on the *de Caelo*. Such an excursus would have to be on a very considerable scale for there to be room within it for a further digression in reply to the Stoic; and this makes it all the more odd that no trace of it has survived in Simplicius' *de Caelo* commentary, which cites Alexander's extensively.[76] (The fragment amounts to nearly a page of printed Greek text, and appears to refer back at its outset to preceding exposition of the Stoic's arguments).

The alternative is to suppose that the 'Heraclides' in question is in fact the Stoic referred to in the second sentence of the introduction and in the text itself; for a Stoic might naturally attack the Aristotelian theory of the fifth element.[77] This possibility is the more interesting because in the text itself Alexander says that his adversary is 'leader' (*proïstatai*) of the Stoic school (p. 93,3).[78] The term can indeed just mean 'champion', and is so used later in this text (p. 93,6); but it is the same word *proïstamai* that Alexander uses in speaking of his own appointment as a public teacher of Peripatetic philosophy.[79] Conceivably therefore in Heraclides we have the name of a contemporary holder of the corresponding Stoic position.

It may, moreover, be possible to identify the Stoic in question. Aurelius Heraclides Eupyrides is referred to as a Stoic teacher in one, and possibly two, second-century Athenian inscriptions.[80] Lynch dates him to the

---

[75] One might suppose that the reference is to Heraclides of Pontus. However, Heraclides' views on the fifth element are unclear (cf. H.B. Gottschalk, *Heraclides of Pontus*, Oxford 1980, 106-7); and, significantly, he is not cited on this topic in Simplicius' *de Caelo* commentary, which draws extensively on the commentary by Alexander now lost.

[76] It may be instructive to compare the treatment of Alexander's two digressions in commenting on *An. Pr.* 1.15, 34a10-12, at 177,19-182,8 (on Chrysippus' claim against Diodorus Cronus – and Aristotle – that the impossible can follow from the possible) and on 34a12-16, at 183,34-184,18 (on the Philonian and Diodorean definitions of the possible; cf. below, n. 98). The content of the latter digression is very briefly summarised by Philoponus *in An. Pr.* 169,17-23; it does not appear in [Ammonius] or [Themistius]' *Prior Analytics* commentaries, though similar distinctions *are* drawn in Simplicius' commentary on the *Categories* (195,31ff. cf. Sharples 1982, 93-4). The topic of the former digression is at least mentioned in all the later commentaries, albeit much more briefly than in Alexander (cf. [Ammonius] *in An. Pr.* 50,13-21; [Themistius] *in An. Pr.* 26,31-29,28; Philoponus *in An. Pr.* 165,27-167,30).

[77] Atticus too wrote on this; fr. 5 des Places. It is true that even if Heraclides is identified with the Stoic we would still be faced either with an independent treatise of which no other record has survived or with a lengthy excursus in a commentary which has similarly left no other traces; but at least in the later case it would not be a matter of a digression *within* an excursus.

[78] The rhetorical ploy in 'it is surprising that someone who claims to be a philosopher is not ashamed (*sc.* of arguing like this)' is reminiscent of some of Alexander's remarks against those whose views he attacks in the *de Fato*; cf. especially 171,22ff.

[79] *Fat.* 164,14.

[80] *IG* II² 3801, and also perhaps *IG* II² 3989. S. Follet, *Athènes au IIe et au IIIe siècle après J.-C.*, Paris 1976, 88 points out that the apparent peregrine status of the dedicator

reign of Hadrian (117-138),[81] but this may be much too early. The name Aurelius suggests that this Heraclides received Roman citizenship not before the reign of Marcus Aurelius (161-180),[82] and indeed the receipt of the citizenship may have been the occasion of the setting up of one or both of the honorific inscriptions. The dedicator of the first inscription was a certain Symmachus of Phlya who set up the inscription to Heraclides as his teacher and who may have been the father of two youths who were ephebes between 182 and 191.[83] That suggests that Symmachus was born in around 135, and that he may have been a pupil of Heraclides in about 155-160;[84] Heraclides himself might then have been born in about 115. This would make him approximately the same age as Alexander's teachers.[85] If Alexander was born in about 145-50 it does not seem inconceivable that he might have written our text in about 180-185 while Heraclides was still the principal Stoic teacher; its tone is hardly deferential from a young man to one 30 years or more his senior, but it is not clear that Alexander would feel any obligation to be deferential towards a member of a rival school.

Quaestio 1.13 is a criticism of a claim that Epicurus' account of colour is similar to that of the other schools (sects, *haireseis*). The person who had claimed this is named in the text only as 'someone', *tis*, but the title supplied by the editor – who presumably had independent information[86] – identifies him as 'Censorinus the Academic', apparently not the author of *de Die natali*, who lived in the first half of the third century AD, but an otherwise unknown philosopher.[87] Von Arnim suggests that he is to be dated to the second half of the second century, that is to the time of Alexander or the generation before;[88] if 'Academic' (as opposed to

---

Symmachus in *IG* II² 3801 places that inscription before the granting of universal citizenship in 212. I am grateful to Dr A.J.S. Spawforth for drawing my attention to Follet's discussion.

[81] I am grateful to Dr Spawforth for pointing this out.

[82] Lynch, 190. Ueberweg-Praechter, *Grundriss der griechischen Philosophie* (12th ed., 665) dates our Heraclides rather to the *middle* of the second century AD. A *terminus ante quem* may perhaps be given by another Stoic, Julius Zosimianus, whose funerary inscription is preserved in *IG* II² 11551 and whom both Ueberweg-Praechter and Lynch (loc. cit.) agree in putting later than Heraclides; he seems to have died at the end of the second century AD. Two other philosophers named Heraclides can be excluded: Heraclides (40) in *RE* is a Stoic of the second century BC, but Alexander refers to his adversary in the present tense; Heraclides (41) is a Pyrrhonist of the first century BC.

[83] The suggestion is made by the editors of *IG* II² ad loc. (*IG* II² 2111/2). Follet 81 dates the inscription more precisely to 185/6.

[84] It would be natural, as Dr Spawforth points out, to suppose that Symmachus put up the dedication to his teacher when he ceased to be a pupil, or soon after; however, he *might* have done so years after he had ceased to be a pupil, to mark the grant of citizenship or (perhaps more plausibly) Heraclides' becoming *diadokhos*, if he was not already so when he taught Symmachus.

[85] cf. above, n. 4.

[86] See above, n. 15, and Bruns' discussion cited there which draws attention to the present title.

[87] No. 8 in Pauly-Wissowa, *RE* 3.2, 1899, col. 1910.

[88] In *RE* loc. cit. But this is simply conjecture based on the present text.

'Platonist') indicates an adherent of the *sceptical* Academy, as it regularly does by Alexander's time, the lateness of this Censorinus' date is striking.[89]

Alexander's discussions of pleasure, a major concern of the *Ethical Problems*, are concerned with problems raised by Aristotelian doctrine rather than with specifically anti-Epicurean polemic.[90] Alexander does however criticise the Epicurean view that the universe is infinite;[91] in his commentary on the *Physics*, or perhaps in an independent treatise now lost, he argued against the views of an Epicurean Zenobius on the related question whether an infinite body can be in place.[92]

Other writers referred to by Alexander include Aratus, whose views on which heavenly pole is uppermost he criticised;[93] Euclid, whose first theorem is not, he argued, incompatible with the Aristotelian theory of a finite universe;[94] Hipparchus, against whom he defended the Aristotelian account of the acceleration of falling bodies;[95] and Geminus, whose epitome of Posidonius' *Meteorology* he cited to illustrate the difference between physical explanation and astronomical hypothesis.[96]

III

Alexander's commentaries are not formally arranged, as the Alexandrian Neoplatonist ones were to be, on the basis of a general discussion of each section (*theôria*) followed by comments on details of the text (*lexeis*); he proceeds through Aristotle's text paragraph by paragraph and often sentence by sentence.[97] There are indeed occasions when a particular

[89] The last major figures to whom the term 'Academic' seems to be applied are Plutarch and Favorinus; cf. H. Tarrant, *Scepticism or Platonism: the history of the Fourth Academy*, Cambridge 1985, 97 and 129-35, id. at *Class. Quart.* 33, 1983, 182-3, and J. Glucker, *Antiochus and the Late Academy*, Göttingen 1978 (*Hypomnemata* 56), 213-15, 281.

[90] cf. the article by Madigan cited in n. 18 above.

[91] *Quaest.* 3.12. This text upholds the Peripatetic view, that the universe is finite with *nothing* outside it, both against the Epicurean view that the universe is infinite and against the Stoic claim that there is void outside the finite world-system; cf. R.B. Todd, 'Alexander of Aphrodisias and the case for the infinite universe', *Eranos* 82, 1984, 185-93.

[92] Simplicius *in Phys.* 249,37; 489,20ff. Cf. Todd 1976, 17 n. 80. This is Zenobius no. 3 in *RE* vol. 10A col. 12; no date for him is there suggested. Other references to Epicureanism by Alexander are cited by Simplicius *in Phys.* 372,11; 467,1; 679,12; 679,32, and by Philoponus *in GC* 12,6.

[93] Simplicius *in Cael.* 391,12.

[94] Simplicius *in Phys.* 511,30.

[95] Simplicius *in Cael.* 265,29; cf. 266,29. Cf. S. Sambursky, *The Physical World of Late Antiquity*, London 1962, 78.

[96] Simplicius *in Phys.* 291,21. Cf. Gottschalk, above n. 75, 63-9.

[97] On the arrangement of the Alexandrian Neoplatonist commentaries, cf. L.G. Westerink, *The Greek Commentaries on Plato's Phaedo*, Amsterdam 1976, 25, and references in n. 42 there. It is true that Alexander does sometimes follow a general summary by a fuller discussion (cf. e.g. *in Top.* 181,21ff) or by detailed comments on particular words within a section (e.g. *in Metaph.* 289,29,33). But this is not a general principle of organisation as it is in the later commentaries. Nor is there a division into daily lectures; *proteraia* in the context of a citation of Alexander ap. [Philoponum] *in DA* 470,18 is [Philoponus]' term, not Alexander's.

point prompts an extended discussion, in effect a self-contained excursus;[98] and Alexander does sometimes refer to fuller discussion in another treatise.[99]

The later Neoplatonic commentaries have introductions describing Aristotle's works in the context of a formal curriculum;[100] Alexander's commentary on the *Prior Analytics* does begin with a discussion of whether logic is a part of philosophy or a tool (*organon*),[101] and that on the *Meteorologica* discusses the nature of the subject and the place of the treatise within a general classification of Aristotle's physical works.[102] On the other hand the commentary on the *Metaphysics* plunges immediately into a discussion of the opening sentences of the Aristotelian text, with no preliminary consideration of the nature of metaphysics as a subject, the composition of the Aristotelian treatise, or the authenticity of the books of which it is composed – though it is true that these topics are discussed later.[103] Alexander did discuss the classification of Aristotle's writings[104] and the authenticity of the *de Interpretatione*;[105] he was also influential in establishing Andronicus' title for the work which thus became known as the *Categories*, against the rival title *Before the Topics* (*ta pro tôn topôn*) (supported by Adrastus and Herminus).[106] Nevertheless, the general impression is that Alexander's concerns in this area are scholarly rather than a matter of formal pedagogy.

[98] e.g. *in An. Pr.* 177,19-182,8, on Chrysippus' claim that the impossible can follow from the possible; ibid., 183,34-184,18, on Philonian, Diodorean and Aristotelian definitions of possibility. The example in the latter passage of what is possible for Philo although prevented (it is still possible for chaff divided into atoms, or at the bottom of the sea, to burn) seems to conflate two examples which are distinct in *Quaest.* 1.18 31,9ff (chaff divided into atoms cannot burn, and a pebble at the bottom of the sea cannot be seen). It does not however follow that the discussion in the commentary is later than and derives from that in the *quaestio*, for there could be a common source. Cf. Sharples 1983, 99 and n. 5.

[99] Above, nn. 19, 21.

[100] e.g. Simplicius *in Cat.* 3,18. Cf. Westerink, above n. 97, 28.

[101] Alexander *in An. Pr.* 1,1-6,12. Cf. also the discussion of the subject-matter of the *Categories* by Alexander ap. Simplicium *in Cat.* 10,8-20 (above, n. 54); Moraux 1984, 609.

[102] Alexander *in Meteor.* 1,1-4,11.

[103] The relation between books 1, 2 and 3 is discussed at *in Metaph.* 136,13-138,23 and 196,19-26, and this in itself involves some discussion of the subject of the whole treatise (138,6ff); similarly the discussion of 3 as in a sense the start of the enquiry, 1 being prefatory, leads to discussion of subject of the whole (170,5-171,22). It may be noted, though, that the discussion in the commentary on 3 is attached to the opening section of that book as its lemma, while in the commentary on 2 there is a separate opening section. Alexander is aware both of those who rejected 1 because of 3's appearing like an opening book (172,21-2) and, by implication, of those who found the first-person-plural references to Platonism problematic; cf. 196,20, and W. Jaeger, *Aristotle: fundamentals of the history of his development*, tr. R. Robinson, Oxford 1934, 175 and n.2.

[104] Simplicius *in Cat.* 4,13; Moraux 1973, 75. (However, on this cf. L. Tarán's review of Moraux 1973 at *Gnomon* 53, 1981, 739-40, arguing that the material from Alexander here is heavily overlaid by Simplicius' own later concerns and terminology.)

[105] Alexander *in An. Pr.* 160,32 (against Andronicus); cf. Boethius, *in Int.* (*ed. sec.*) 11,13-15. Moraux 1973, 117 and n. 2.

[106] M. Frede, *Essays in Ancient Philosophy*, Minneapolis 1987, 18-20. Cf. Alexander ap. Boethium *in Int.* (*ed. sec.*) 10,14, on whether the *de Interpretatione* is concerned with philosophy or rhetoric.

Alexander frequently gives alternative explanations of the same point without indicating which he prefers; Moraux has given a list of passages in Simplicius which show that this was the case in Alexander's lost *de Caelo* commentary,[107] and there are examples in the surviving commentaries too.[108] This hardly suggests that the commentaries formed part of a programme of teaching, at least not at any introductory level. There are occasional remarks in the commentaries about the process of teaching, but these are prompted by similar remarks in the Aristotelian text itself and do not give any clear indication of Alexander's own view.[109]

Where there is some evidence of school activity in the form of Alexander's writings is in some of the minor works.[110] In addition to (i) 'problems' in the strict sense with their solutions, these include (ii) expositions (*exêgêseis*) of particularly problematic Aristotelian texts, (iii) short expositions of Aristotelian doctrine on a particular topic, and (iv), straightforward and sometimes tedious paraphrases of passages in Aristotle's writings; both (iii) and (iv) alike seem to be described as *epidromai* or 'summaries'. There are also (v) collections, one might almost say batteries, of arguments for a particular Aristotelian position.[111] It seems likely that (iii), (iv) and (v), in particular, reflect teaching activity; it is difficult in some cases to see why else they might have been written. Some of these texts may be Alexander's own expositions of particular topics, while some may be more in the nature of exercises by his students.[112]

There are certainly, as one might expect, connections between the short texts and the commentaries both in general thought and in particular detail. Aristotle's analogy in his *de Anima* of a point uniting two lines, to illustrate the way in which the 'common sense' perceives the objects of different special senses, is picked up by Alexander in his *de Sensu* commentary, and elaborated into the analogy of the centre of a circle uniting the radii in the *Quaestiones* and *de Anima*.[113] *Quaestio* 3.11 may

[107] Moraux 1967, 169 n. 1.

[108] cf. (e.g.) *in An Pr.* 156,11-157,10; 161,3-26 (cf. Sharples 1982 at 97-9); *in Metaph.* 141,21ff; 159,9; 162,6,10; 164,24; 165,4; 165,21; 169,11; 220,24ff; 337,29.

[109] At *in Metaph.* 167,5ff, on 2.3, 994b32, it is observed that people react to lectures in the light of what they already know; and at ibid., 168,7ff, on 995a10, there is a warning against the danger of giving an impression of hair-splitting.

[110] The following summary account (which is not exhaustive) of the various types of texts to be found among the minor works may be supplemented by the discussion at Bruns 1892, v-xiv; Moraux 1942, 19-28; Sharples 1987, 1194-5.

[111] As Bruns 1892, xii-xiii notes, these are characteristic of the *Mantissa* rather than of the *Quaestiones*; they also occur in the *Ethical Problems*. (*Quaestio* 2.28, however, approaches close to the type.)

[112] cf. Bruns 1892, ix. In the ancient world an 'exercise' would almost certainly be a piece for oral delivery before the teacher. It could in principle be written out beforehand or written up afterwards; but some of the passages do not in themselves seem interesting enough to justify records of them being made for general use after the discussion of which they might have formed part. (There may be exceptions to this; cf. below at n. 174.) Alexander might on the other hand have preserved his own teaching materials for future use even when they were somewhat pedestrian.

[113] Aristotle *DA* 3.2, 427a9ff; Alexander *in Sens.* 164,13ff; *Quaest.* 3.9 96,10ff; *de Anima*

be connected with a possible report of Alexander in Ammonius' *de Interpretatione* commentary,[114] and there are links between *quaestio* 3.12 and Simplicius' reports of Alexander's *de Caelo* commentary.[115] The idea of nature as a force from the gods at Alexander, *in Metaph.* 104,8, should be compared with the discussion in *quaestio* 2.3 of what the divine force (*theia dunamis*) is that comes from the heavens to the sublunary.[116] Simplicius in his *Physics* commentary[117] cites Alexander as saying that matter in itself (as opposed to matter as matter for some thing, i.e. an instance of some particular type of thing) is characterised not by the privation (*sterêsis*) of quality, for privation is in itself a quality, but by the negation (*apophasis*) of it; the same argument is advanced at *quaestio* 2.7 53,9-19.[118]

Sometimes the relation between different works is more problematic. *Quaestio* 2.17 argues that even though fire as we experience it, an effervescence (*zesis*) of fire, is hotter than elemental fire, identified as *hupekkauma*, it does not therefore follow that elemental fire is less hot through admixture of the opposite, coldness. Aristotle in the *Meteorologica*[119] regards the effervescence and excess of heat as real fire, by contrast with what occupies the region above air but below the heavens, which 'we

---

63,8ff. In referring to Aristotle's *de Anima* Alexander's *de Sensu* commentary is picking up Aristotle's own cross-reference at *Sens.* 7, 449a9-10; *Quaest.* 3.9 is a commentary on 427a2-14. Cf. P. Henry, 'Une comparaison chez Aristote, Alexandre et Plotin', in *Les Sources de Plotin (Entretiens Hardt* 5), Geneva 1960, 427-49, at 436-8.

[114] R.B. Todd, 'Alexander of Aphrodisias on *de Interpretatione* 16a26-9', *Hermes* 104, 1976, 140-6, relates *Quaest.* 3.11 to Ammonius *in Int.* 39,17-32, arguing that this comes from Alexander, as does explicitly the syllogism at 39,13-17 to which it is a reply.

[115] Simplicius *in Cael.* 284,25-285,5; 285,21-5; 286,25-7, noted by I. Bruns, *Interpretationes Variae*, Kiel 1893, 4 and 10, and R.B. Todd, 'Alexander of Aphrodisias and the case for the infinite universe', *Eranos* 82, 1984, 185-93.

[116] cf. Sharples 1987, 1188; I am grateful to Professor William E. Dooley for drawing my attention to the *in Metaph.* passage. Such a force plays a central part in Alexander's doctrine of providence, and one might be tempted to think that the *quaestio*, discussing exactly what is due to the force, was a development of the commentary, but in fact Moraux has argued that this *quaestio* is early (cf. n. 45).

[117] Simplicius *in Phys.* 211,20ff (above, n. 53).

[118] For other links between the commentaries and the minor works cf. also nn. 41, 53, 69 and 132. A contrast between the privation, which *per se* is not but *per accidens* is, and matter which *per se* is but *per accidens* is not, is drawn in a similar way in commenting on Aristotle *Physics* 1.8 both by Alexander *Quaest.* 1.24 38,16-19 and by Philoponus *in Phys.* 173,21-6; but Philoponus does not cite Alexander here, and it is not clear whether there is any connection with his lost *Physics* commentary or whether the similarity is simply the result of coincidence. Cf. also Simplicius *in Phys.* 240,19. At *in Phys.* 238,8 Simplicius reports Alexander as presenting alternative interpretations of Aristotle's solution to the problem of coming-to-be, depending in one case on a contrast between *per se* and accidental not-being and in the other on one between *per se* and accidental coming-to-be; Simplicius himself argues against the latter. See above, n. 107. *Quaest* 1.8, 1.17 and 1.26 argue that a form, and in particular the soul of a living creature, cannot be in matter or in a body as in a subject (*hupokeimenon*; see below, n. 178). At *de Caelo* 1.9, 278b1-2, however, Aristotle refers to things that have their being (*ousia*) in some underlying matter (*en hupokeimenêi tini hulêi*); Simplicius, *in Cael.* 279,5ff records Alexander's attempts to explain away this phrase.

[119] Aristotle *Meteor.* 1.3, 340b23.

are accustomed to call fire'. Alexander in his commentary on the *Meteorologica* follows this doctrine, but appears to suggest that the *hupekkauma* below the heavens, though not in fact fire, is nevertheless an element (whereas the effervescence of heat, presumably, is not).[120] The *quaestio* too, in denying that the *hupekkauma* contains an admixture of coldness, is safeguarding its elemental status.

Aristotle says, at *de Caelo* 2.7, 289a20, that the heat and light of the heavenly bodies are caused by the effect they have by friction on the underlying *air*; this is odd, because it should be fire that is next below the heavenly sphere. Simplicius reports that Alexander interpreted this 'air' as the *hupekkauma*, though – he adds – Alexander in putting forward this interpretation also observed that Aristotle elsewhere called this *hupekkauma* elemental *fire*.[121] This corresponds with the *quaestio*, but not, it would seem, with Aristotle's *Meteorology* itself or with Alexander's commentary on it. Perhaps, though, Alexander's point is that Aristotle did elsewhere identify what lay directly beneath the heavens as *fire of a sort* rather than air, whether it was fire in the strict sense or not; Alexander himself is consistent in interpreting the *hupekkauma* as an *element* whether fire in the strict sense is to be identified with it or not. Presumably too for Alexander Aristotle is describing the same *substance* as occupying this region in the *Meteorology* and in the *de Caelo*; it is simply Aristotle's terminology that differs.

In *quaestio* 2.23 it is argued that the attraction of the magnet for the iron is to be likened not to the way in which the womb attracts the seed and the veins nourishment, by drawing in intervening air or moisture, or to the way in which the sun *seems* to attract water by turning it to vapour which naturally rises, but rather to the way in which an object of desire attracts a living creature, the magnet possessing some feature which the iron lacks.[122] Simplicius however reports Alexander in his *Physics* commentary[123] as first asserting that the magnet attracts things by an incorporeal force – which Simplicius rejects as contrary to Aristotle's intention of showing that there is nothing intervening between what

---

[120] Alexander *in Meteor.* 14,25ff, also citing Aristotle *GC* 2.3, 330b25. Alexander here refers to the *hupekkauma* as *to pur tôn stoikheiôn kaloumenon*, 'the one of the elements which is called fire' – implying that it is an element, though it is strictly wrong to call it fire.

[121] Simplicius *in Cael.* 439,14. Simplicius' own answer is that the circular movement of the heavens heats the air as well as the *hupekkauma* above it (439,27-32); an explanation might perhaps be sought in the idea that there is an admixture of fire *and* air even in the celestial sphere (cf. *Meteor.* 1.3, 340b8, and Guthrie's note on *Cael.* 2.7; W.K.C. Guthrie, *Aristotle: On the Heavens*, Loeb ed. 1939, 176-9).

[122] The magnet is described as like iron but lacking moisture (74,26-8), so perhaps it is dryness that the iron desires? Oddly, too, the *quaestio* speaks of the living creature attracting the nourishment that it desires, rather than of the nourishment attracting the living creature (74,20-1); but it is clear that the magnet possesses what the iron lacks, rather than vice versa (74,26).

[123] That the citation is from Alexander's *Physics* commentary is not explicitly stated, but is *prima facie* likely and rendered more so by the fact that Alexander's comments are directed towards the elucidation of a phrase in Alexander's text (Simplicius *in Phys.* 1055,15).

moves and what is moved – and then as saying either that there is after all some corporeal effluence or else that, since the explanation of magnetism is unclear, Aristotle may not be referring to magnetism at all but to cases like that of flames which are attracted by the burning wood and so do not rise up to their natural place.[124] (This, rather than the magnet, is in fact the example which Aristotle himself gives).[125]

Some of the short texts *may* indeed be extracts from the commentaries.[126] However, if the editor who supplied the titles for the *Quaestiones* can be believed, *quaestio* 2.22 differed from the account in Alexander's lost commentary on *de Generatione et Corruptione*.[127] *Quaestiones* 3.10 and 3.14, summaries of sections of Aristotle's *Meteorologica*, can be compared with Alexander's extant commentary on that text, which we have.[128] Some of the short texts relate to issues discussed in Alexander's treatises, rather than directly to Aristotelian texts,[129] but this division is not a hard-and-fast one.

The interest and quality of argument of these texts varies considerably. Some of them are so pedestrian and even turgid that it is difficult to believe that they could have been produced for anything other than a pedagogic purpose.[130] Others show considerable philosophical liveliness and acumen. For our present purpose there are two interconnected questions that are of particular interest. One is whether there are

[124] Simplicius *in Phys.* 1055,24-1056,6, on 7.2, 244a14.

[125] Aristotle *Phys.* 7.2, 244a12-13.

[126] cf. Sharples cited in n. 53 above, at 67-8. *Quaestio* 1.1 indeed corresponds to a section of the commentary on the *Metaphysics* attributed to Alexander, but this commentary is not, at least in its present form, by Alexander himself (above, n. 24); either there is a common source – which could be the genuine commentary – or the compiler of the commentary we have has incorporated the passage from the *quaestio*.

[127] On these titles generally cf. n. 15 above, and on the relation between *quaestio* 1.11 and the *de Anima* commentary see below, n. 142.

[128] 3.10 is very summary in form; its two pages correspond to pages 66-89 of the *Meteorologica* commentary, and while it reports the explanations of the saltiness of the sea that appear in the *Meteorology* itself and in the commentary (and in P.Hibeh 16 = Democritus 68A99a Diels-Kranz), it omits the names of the proponents of the various theories as given in the commentary, though not by Aristotle himself. *Quaestio* 3.14 is a summary of Aristotle (?) *Meteorology* 4, finishing at the end of ch. 7; Alexander's commentary itself devotes 34 pages to 4.1-7 and only 16 to the rest of the book. The *quaestio* has a comment at the end saying that some things are missing 'as he wrote before'; this may be a later addition simply referring to the title at the beginning of the *quaestio*, which describes it as 'incomplete'. The *quaestio* and the commentary are sufficiently close for the former to be emended from the latter (cf. *quaestio* 3.14 109,18 with Bruns ad loc.). Cf. V.C. Coutant, *Alexander of Aphrodisias: Commentary on Book IV of Aristotle's Meteorology*, diss. Columbia 1936, 89 n. 33.

[129] *Quaestio* 3.3 is a turgid and repetitive summary of Aristotle *de Anima* 2.5, which it is difficult to believe can have been written by Alexander himself; strangely, it enjoyed great subsequent popularity, versions surviving both in Arabic and (from the Arabic) in Latin.

[130] cf. Sharples 1987, 1181 and n. 32, with references. The form of many of Alexander's writings – commentaries on works by another author, and short discussions of individual problems – is such as to make a piecemeal approach to problems more likely; but there is also the problem that Alexander characteristically puts forward alternative solutions without indicating a preference between them (cf. nn. 107-8).

discrepancies in doctrine so great that it can be shown that the texts cannot all reflect the viewpoint of a single author; the other is whether any of these texts can be shown to reflect a context of live discussion within Alexander's school.

IV

There are certainly discrepancies both within particular texts and between different texts so great that scholars have been reluctant to accept that all of the views put forward are Alexander's own. The problem is partly that of knowing how systematic a thinker Alexander was, but there is the further problem, where more than one text is concerned, that we are generally ill-informed about the relative chronology of the works attributed to him,[131] and that his views may have changed over time.

Quaestio 1.11 is concerned to explain Aristotle's statement in *de Anima* 1.1, 402b7 that 'the universal living creature is either nothing, or posterior'. The text is transmitted in two versions: the second and longer gives two solutions in full, while the shorter version gives the second solution only and refers for the first – as does also the longer text – to the author's commentary on Aristotle's *de Anima*. The first solution (22,23-23,21) turns on the claim that there is no prior genus of things which form an ordered sequence, as do the faculties of the soul which different creatures possess;[132] the second (23,21-24,22 = 21,19-22,20) argues that the universal is posterior to what falls under it in the sense that, if only one instance of a kind exists, the nature of the kind does indeed exist but need not exist *as a universal*, that is in more than one instantiation,[133] while on the other hand the universal will not (for a Peripatetic) exist if there are no instantiations of it at all.

Moraux in 1942 suggested that the first solution was the genuine solution of Alexander, as expressed in his commentary, and that the second solution was an attempt by a pupil to improve on it; though he insisted on the merits of the second solution as an interpretation of

[131] For a summary of what is known cf. Sharples 1987, 1181 and nn. 35-40 with references there.

[132] For this argument cf. also Alexander *de Anima* 16,18-17,8; 40,4-10; *in Metaph*. 152,6ff; 208,31ff. Moraux 1942, 51-2; R.W. Sharples, ' "If what is earlier, then of necessity what is later?": some ancient discussions of Aristotle, *De generatione et corruptione* 2.11', *Bulletin of the Institute of Classical Studies* 26, 1979, 27-44, at 37 and n. 142. But as Moraux 1942, 57-8 points out, Alexander does argue that there can be a hierarchy within a genus, and gives the example of different types of creature, at *in Metaph*. 210,6-8, against Platonists who deny the existence of a generic idea of number.

[133] 23,25-24,1 = 21,23-30. The point is here put in terms of 'animal' – a generic nature – still existing if there were only one *individual* animal, but it would certainly also apply to a *species* with only one individual member, and to a genus with only one species (see below). If there were only one type of animal, but many instances of that type, the nature 'animal' would presumably possess the accidental property of being a universal with several instances, but not that of being a genus common to several species. – With the following discussion cf. Sharples 1987, 1199-202, and references there.

Aristotle's thought concerning universals in general.[134] (This need not, I think, conflict with Tweedale's view that the first solution is more convincing as an interpretation of Aristotle's thoughts in this particular context[135]). The second solution can however be paralleled elsewhere in the writings attributed to Alexander.[136]

There is, moreover, a difficulty within the second solution itself. A.C. Lloyd, while regarding it as a statement of Alexander's general position, rejected the final part (24,16ff Bruns), which in effect asserts that the universal, while posterior to the nature that happens to be universal, is nevertheless prior to each *individual* particular (sc. in the cases where there *is* a plurality of particulars).[137] This seemed to give the universal nature an unacceptable priority over the particular.[138] However, there are other texts attributed to Alexander where similar points are made about both the genus and the species;[139] and there does not seem anything *paradoxical* in saying (i) that the specific nature of man would still exist even if it were only instantiated in one individual and hence was not a universal (and similarly that the generic nature of animal would still exist, though not *as a genus*, even if only one species of animal actually existed), and yet (ii) that the nature of man as a species is prior to individuals like Socrates and Callias with their individual accidents, snub-nosedness and the rest. (ii) *may* in itself be an unacceptable and un-Aristotelian position (though I do not myself believe so), but that is a different point; it does not in itself seem an impossible one for Alexander to have held sincerely as an interpretation of Aristotle, and it seems to agree not only with other texts attributed to Alexander but also with his treatment of providence, where it is the preservation of the *species* that is the primary concern.[140]

Unfortunately, though, there are yet other texts attributed to Alexander which lay emphasis on the creation of universals by the minds

---

[134] Moraux 1942, 50 62.

[135] M.M. Tweedale, 'Alexander of Aphrodisias' views on universals', *Phronesis* 29, 1984, 279-303, at 284.

[136] *Quaest.* 1.3 8,12ff.

[137] The point is actually stated in terms of the relation between genus and species, but seems to apply to that between species (or genus) and individual too; cf. nn. 133 and 139.

[138] A.C. Lloyd, *Form and Universal in Aristotle*, Liverpool 1980, 51.

[139] Alexander *de Providentia* 89,5 Ruland (above n. 74; cf. P. Thillet, 'Un traité inconnu d'Alexandre d'Aphrodise sur la providence en version arabe', in *L'homme et son destin d'après les penseurs du moyen âge: Actes du 1er congrès international de philosophie médiévale*, Louvain 1960, 313-24, at 321); cf. also Alexander's *Refutation of the assertion of Xenocrates that the species is prior to the genus* (S. Pines, 'A new fragment of Xenocrates and its implications', *Transactions of the American Philosophical Society* 51, 1961, no. 2.) Complaints in authors like Simplicius (*in Cat.* 82,22-8; 85,5-9) and Dexippus (*in Cat.* 45,12-31) that Alexander makes universals posterior to particulars do not conflict with this, for they simply reflect the fact that he did not give the universal form the priority that would satisfy a Platonist, that is regarding the universal as existing even if it has no individual instantiations *at all*. Cf. P.L. Donini, *Le scuole, l'anima, l'impero: la filosofia antica da Antioco a Plotino*, Turin 1982, 222.

[140] *Quaest.* 1.3 8,22-4; 1.25 41,8ff; 2.19 63,15ff; *de Providentia* 33,1ff; 59,6ff; 87,5ff. Sharples 1987, 1216 and n. 170.

that distinguish the specific or generic nature from the individual accidents;[141] it seems difficult to reconcile these with the idea of a specific or generic nature that may or may not be instantiated in several individuals or species, but is at any rate in some sense prior to the individual members of a plurality with their accidents. The question really is, whether we can believe that Alexander's own views can have varied so much as to allow both approaches to be his, or whether rival views were being advanced by different members of his school.[142]

Quaestio 2.9 argues that the Aristotelian definition of soul as the entelechy of a body of a certain sort[143] does not involve making the soul relative to something. For, while the soul is 'of' the body, it is already something in itself first (which seems to contradict Alexander's definition of the soul as the product of the mixture of the bodily elements[144]) just as a head is first of all a thing and (only) then the head of something else (which seems to contradict Aristotle's view that a hand, or any other bodily organ, is only a hand equivocally if it is not the hand of a living creature, in other words that the part has its being in the context of the whole[145]). These remarks in themselves are odd enough; when however the *quaestio* goes on to argue that both soul and head indicate a proper nature and substance which *happens* (*sumbebēken*) to belong to something else, it is difficult to believe that this text can be by Alexander expressing his own views.

V

Since we know so little about the way in which the collections of short

[141] Alexander *de Anima* 90,6-7; *Quaest.* 2.28 78,18-20.

[142] The citation of what must surely be Alexander's *de Anima* commentary, now lost, as the author's own (*eirētai moi*, 21,18 = 22,26) suggests one of three things: (a) the whole text with both solutions is by Alexander himself; (b) the part with the first solution was composed by him (but why, if the point was already discussed in the commentary?) and the second solution added later by someone else; (c) the whole text is by a single author who is not Alexander but, in citing the commentary as his own, wishes to pass himself off as so being (so Moraux 1942, 53, 61). A case where multiple authorship, or at least an addition by the original author but at a later date, does seem likely is the last section of *quaestio* 1.4; cf. R.W. Sharples, 'An ancient dialogue on possibility: Alexander of Aphrodisias, *Quaestio* 1.4', *Archiv für Geschichte der Philosophie* 64, 1982, 23-38, at 37-8, but also M. Mignucci, 'Pseudo-Alexandre, critique des stoïciens (*Quaestiones* 1.4)', in *Proceedings of the World Congress on Aristotle, Thessaloniki August 7-14 1978*, Athens 1981, 198-204.

[143] Aristotle *DA* 2.1, 412a27-8.

[144] Alexander *de Anima* 24,21-3.

[145] cf. Aristotle *Meteor.* 4.12, 389b31; 390a12; *DA* 2.1, 412b21; *PA* 1.1, 641a4; *GA* 1.19, 726b24; 2.1, 734b25, 735a8; *Metaph.* 7.10, 1035b24ff.; *Politics* 1.1, 1253a21. It is true that a head is less obviously an organ used for a certain purpose than is a hand. Admittedly, Aristotle does in *Categories* 7 argue that particular heads and hands, as primary substances, are not relative at all (8a20), and that 'head' and 'hand' as universal, secondary substances (which are the concern of our *quaestio*; 54,23) are relative in the sense that what they belong to enters into their definition, but not in the narrower sense that their very being *consists in* being related to something else in a particular way (8a27ff.). This might perhaps be explained by saying that a bodily organ such as a head or a hand is to be defined in terms of its function, rather than (e.g.) of its position in relation to the whole body. But it still hardly provides a parallel to the use of *sumbebēken* in the *quaestio*.

texts attributed to Alexander were assembled,[146] there is the possibility
that a text whose attribution to Alexander himself is questionable on
doctrinal grounds might be the work of a later scholar who never met him
and knew his views only through his written works. A surer sign of the
origin of a text in a school discussion may be given by phrases like 'it was
said', 'the question was asked', 'the difficulty was raised', and past tense
first person plural endings. Such phrases may indeed simply be
cross-references within the commentaries themselves; the first person
plurals may just express an editorial 'we'. And even when there does seem
to be reference to discussion, it may be a discussion carried on in earlier
tradition rather than in Alexander's own school.

At *in An. Pr.* 191,19ff Alexander is discussing the proof by *reductio* at
1.15, 34a34ff. He first observes that certain people said certain things
(*elegeto oun tina hupo tinôn*, 191,24) to the effect that the conclusion of
the *reductio* is false but not impossible, and so does not generate a
contradiction. To this Alexander responds (*legomen*, 192,4) by appealing
to Aristotle's observation at 34b7ff that assertoric premisses need to be
understood without temporal restriction. A further objection ('to this it
was said in turn', *pros touto elegeto palin*, 193,13) turns on the minor
premiss of the *reductio*, arguing that it is wrong to create a contradiction
by supposing that what was only stated as possible does in fact apply; for,
it is claimed, 'can' is only said of what is not *in fact* the case.[147] Alexander
answers this objection (*luoito*, 193,20) with the observation that there is a
difference between (i) supposing, when something is not in fact realised,
that it is realised, and (ii) supposing that something is realised when it is
not, in the sense of supposing the contradiction that it is simultaneously
realised and not.[148] It seems difficult not to take this as the record of an
actual discussion.

At *in An. Pr.* 218,7ff Alexander is discussing the argument at 1.17,
36b26 that two contingent negative premisses in the second figure yield no
conclusion, because with contingent premisses negative and positive are
convertible, and two positive premisses yield no conclusion in the second
figure.[149] Alexander observes that someone might ask (*epizêtesai d'an tis*)
why a similar argument is not applied, with reverse effect, to positive
contingent premisses that *do* apparently yield a conclusion in other moods.
The first reply, introduced by the words 'it was said first of all' (*elegeto
prôton men*, 218,13) is that such conversion is natural only in the case of
premisses that would not yield a conclusion without it (which seems to beg
the question rather). Alexander then continues with the argument (*eti de*,
218,20) that the contingent premiss is in fact positive rather than
negative in character. Again, it seems natural to interpret 'it was said

---

[146] cf. however above, nn. 14-16.
[147] On this cf. Sharples 1982, at 97 and nn. 91-2.
[148] cf. Aristotle, *SE* 4, 166a24; *Cael.* 1.12, 281b8ff.; *Metaph.* 9.4, 1047b13.
[149] So Alexander. Aristotle's own argument is not that (e.g.) Q(aEb) and Q(aAb) convert,
but that Q(aEb) and Q(bEa) do not; cf. 36b35, and Alexander at 220,3ff.

first of all' as a record of an actual discussion. However, the topic of mixed modal syllogisms was one on which Alexander disagreed with two of his teachers, Sosigenes and Herminus;[150] so in both these passages the discussion referred to could be one in which Alexander participated as a pupil, not one in his own school.[151]

At *in Top.* 133,24, on 2.1, 109a27ff, Alexander says that there was an enquiry (*ezêtêthe*) as to how a *problem* could be false. His reply is that what is false is the actual statement that someone supports and the dialectician tries to refute.[152] There is no 'enquiry' into the point in question in Aristotle's own text; and it seems natural to take 'there was an enquiry' as referring to some discussion at which Alexander was present, rather than to the commentary tradition.[153]

Other *quaestiones* beginning with the statement 'there was an enquiry' (*ezêtêthe*)[154] include 1.9, on the question how, if opposites are the things furthest removed from each other in the same *genus*, it is not disease, rather than poor physical condition, that is the opposite to good physical

---

[150] Above, nn. 20, 25.

[151] At *Quaest.* 2.3 48,18-22 (cf. above, n. 45) the statement that the derivation of human reason from divine providence is established is followed by the remark that for this reason 'it was said' (*elegeto*) that man derives from divine providence everything he has through reason. It is not clear whether 'it was said' refers to the context of a particular discussion, of which this *quaestio* is the only part recorded, or to a more general tradition.

[152] Appropriately enough, Alexander's solution to this general problem about problems is itself introduced by a phrase used to introduce solutions to particular problems, 'may it not be the case that' (*mêpot' oun*, 133,26; cf. Alexander *in Top.* 250,26; *Quaest.* 1.26 42,25; 2.3 48,22; 3.2 81,29; *Mant.* 119,31; 177,5). What would be false in this case, according to his solution, would be not the question 'how can a problem be false' but the assertion 'a problem cannot be false'.

[153] A rather similar case occurs in *Quaest.* 3.2. After citing Aristotle, *DA* 2.5, 417b5, this continues, 'Aristotle having said this, there was a general enquiry by the commentary (*exêgêsis*) whether the transition to actuality is a change'. (The enquiry was 'general' (*katholou*) because it related to transitions to actuality in general, and not just to the actualisation of knowledge in the activity of *theôria*.) 'By the commentary', hardly natural in English, could in principle refer to one particular commentary either as the actions of commenting or as the resultant written work, or, perhaps more naturally, to the tradition of commentary on the passage extending over several generations. However, 'by (*hupo*) the commentary' is only an emendation by Bruns; the MSS have '*from* (*apo*) the commentary'. With this reading it seems more natural to interpret the past tense as referring to consultation of a commentary on a particular occasion, which might or might not be in the context of a discussion actually taking place in the school. But the point at issue is precisely the sort on which, in reading Aristotle's *de Anima*, one would go and look up commentaries on *other* Aristotelian works, if one did not indeed already have to hand a commentary on the *de Anima* that itself discussed the issue in general terms; and in this case the singular 'from *the commentary*' seems odd, unless *exêgêsis* were to have the sense of 'the tradition of commentary on all Aristotle's works in general'.

[154] Such references do not indeed always imply discussion. When in *P. Eth.* 25 the author states that 'we enquired into what happiness is' (*ezêtêsamen ti pote estin hê eudaimonia*), the first person plural verb is most naturally taken as including both the writer and his readers – or the speaker and his audience – as students of the *Nicomachean Ethics* in general, even if the text never actually formed part of an ordered sequence of expositions of the *whole* of that work. (I am grateful to Professor Sorabji for a suggestion that prompted this line of thought.) What follows certainly seems more like a teaching summary based on Aristotelian texts than anything that had its origin in a philosophical debate.

condition, since the later is an *intensification* of mere healthiness,[155] and *Ethical Problem* 17, which considers under which type of good pleasure should be classified.[156] In neither of these passages, again, is there any obvious indication that the enquiry referred to is one in earlier written commentaries, rather than in a discussion in the school; equally, there is no indication that the development of the problem or its solution is *itself* the record of an actual discussion, 'there was an enquiry' simply being the starting point from which the statement of the problem and its solution develops.

In *quaestio* 1.16 citation of Aristotle, *Physics* 1.5, 188a26-30, is followed, in the primary MS, V, and in Bruns' edition, by 'He raised the problem of what was meant by this statement' (inferior MSS and the earlier editions have the passive, 'the problem was raised'). It does not seem easy to interpret 'he raised the problem' as a reference to some other part of Aristotle's own discussion in the *Physics*;[157] it could be a reference to a speaker in a discussion or to some earlier commentator, but in either case the lack of any explicit indication as to who is meant is odd.

Elsewhere too there are problematic references to unidentified persons which could reflect a context of discussion in which the identity of the person meant would be clear.[158] *Ethical Problem* 4 begins by stating an argument the conclusion of which is considered paradoxical: 'there is no opposite to what is an instrument, but there is something opposite to

---

[155] The attempt to reconcile a general Aristotelian principle and an awkward example is characteristic of the *Quaestiones*. The question might indeed arise, in discussion of an Aristotelian text such as *Top.* 8.2, 153b17ff; Alexander's commentary on this passage (*in Top.* 507,10ff) does not contain anything relating closely to the point of the *quaestio*, though the extant version of this section of Alexander's *Topics* commentary may be an abridgement.

[156] The conclusion reached is that, just as pleasures are good only if they accompany activities that deserve to be chosen (cf. *P. Eth.* 2 120,11ff; 16 137,2ff; 19 139,23ff; Aristotle *EN* 10.5, 1175a21ff), so the type of good they fall under will be that under which the activity to which they relate also falls. The classification of goods from which the *quaestio* starts is a familiar one in the Peripatetic tradition; cf. Arius Didymus ap. Stobaeum *Ecl.* 2.7.19 (p. 134,20-1 Wachsmuth); [Aristotle] *MM* 1.2, 1183b19; Aspasius *in EN* 32,10; Moraux 1973, 370; R.W. Sharples, 'The Peripatetic classification of goods', in W.W. Fortenbaugh (ed.), *On Stoic and Peripatetic Ethics, the work of Arius Didymus*, New Brunswick 1983 (*Rutgers University Studies in Classical Humanities* 1), 139-59, at 143 and 151. Indeed, the classification occurs in Alexander's *Topics* commentary (Alexander *in Top.* 242,4 = Aristotle fr. 113 Rose), though without any reference to pleasure.

[157] Aristotle does go on (188a30-1) 'it is also necessary to consider by reference to argument how this comes about', that is (W.D. Ross, *Aristotle's Physics*, 488-9) by argument as well as by appeal to authority. But the discussion in the *quaestio* is an attempt to interpret difficulties in Aristotle's position, not a statement of his argument. 'He raised the problem' in 28,8 appears to be picked up by 'someone might raise the problem' in 28,17; and while *autos* in 28,11 refers to Aristotle, it is Aristotle's apparently conflicting statements, that opposites come from one another (*Phys.* 1.5, 188b21-6 being so interpreted at 28,10-16) and that the principles are opposites but cannot come from each other (188a27-8) that have raised a difficulty in the mind of someone else. The difficulty is noted, without reference to Alexander by name or explicit citation of 188b21-6, by Simplicius (*in Phys.* 182,19-21); his solution (182,21-6) is similar to 28,25-29,2 of the *quaestio*. Cf. also Philoponus *in Phys.* 111,19ff.

[158] cf. also *Mant.* 112,6, above n. 44.

wealth, so wealth is not an instrument', and then continues, 'if *he* supposes that generally no instrument has an opposite ...', where 'he' must be the proposer of the objection.[159] However, when in *Ethical Problem* 14 an extended statement of the problem of how there can be an intermediate state between pleasure and distress on Aristotle's account[160] is followed by the bald statement 'yet they think that there is some condition intermediate between pleasure and distress', 'they' is probably a reference to Aristotelians and other right-thinking people in general – Alexander tending to identify Aristotelian doctrine and common sense[161] – for the problem is that of reconciling Aristotelian theory with accepted opinion, rather than an attempt to find a damaging inconsistency in some opponent's particular position.

VI

Quaestio 2.21, already discussed in the context of Alexander's relations with Platonism, is in the form of a narrated dialogue. The opening deserves extended quotation, as the nearest we have to what at any rate purports to be an account of a discussion between Alexander and his associates:

> Recently I was[162] discussing providence with my companions, and I tried to show both that there is some concern and forethought from the divine beings concerning mortal ones, according to Aristotle, and what it is. I was ready to say in what way it comes about, when one of those who were present said that it was worth learning first what response one should give to those who ask whether one should say that the divinities exercise providence over these things here in a primary way according to us too, or only accidentally ...[163]

The narrator responds by challenging the assumption that primary providence and purely accidental 'providence' are the only two possibilities, arguing that there are several ways in which providence or forethought can be neither primary nor accidental, without indicating which of them actually applies to Aristotelian providence as he understands it.[164] The respondent then asks him to give an account of the Aristotelian position and to say which of the solutions suggested does in

---

[159] 122,34. Bruns 1892, xiv used the fact that the objector is simply referred to in passing in this way to argue that this text was an incomplete fragment of some larger whole; but it is not clear that this is a safe inference. He similarly argues that *P. Eth.* 3 is a fragment, because the Stoics are there referred to simply as 'them', but it is not clear how far 'fragment' is a relevant concept in the case of these short texts whose original context is unclear. Certainly *P. Eth.* 3 and 4 are not fragments in the same sense as *Quaest.* 2.21 (below, n. 166) or *Quaest.* 3.14 (above, n. 128).

[160] Alexander cites Aristotle, *EN* 7.12, 1153a14 and 10.4, 1174b14.

[161] cf. R.W. Sharples, *Alexander of Aphrodisias: On Fate*, London 1983, 18.

[162] The Greek has the plural 'we', presumably the editorial 'we'.

[163] *Quaest.* 2.21 65,18-23.

[164] 66,3-70,6.

fact apply (70,6-11).[165] The narrator protests that this goes beyond his original undertaking (70,11-17), but eventually agrees (70,24-71,2); and at this point the text breaks off. In fact, the narrator had intended to give an account of the Aristotelian position even before 'one of those present' intervened; the point of the exchange at 70,6-17 is presumably to emphasise that the solution will be in terms of the ways found in the intervening discussion of escaping this dilemma, and also to emphasise the difference between finding a number of dialectical solutions to an opponent's objections and giving a positive account of one's own position.

The strategy of the dialogue, in so far as it can be discerned in its incomplete state, was similar to that of the treatise *de Providentia* surviving in Arabic, and the *quaestio* may be an unfinished attempt to develop the ideas of the *de Providentia* in a dialogue form.[166] The dialogue is a literary construction rather than the record of an actual discussion. The introductory section may be purely based on literary models – though Alexander shows little interest in Aristotle's exoteric dialogues.

In *Ethical Problem* 7 the initial statement of the problem how some pleasure can be good and other pleasure bad, if all pain is bad, is in the past tense: 'it was necessary either for pleasure too to be a bad thing ... or for all [pleasure] to be a good thing', because of the apparent paradox in some pleasure being opposed to pain as good to bad, other pleasure as one evil to another. The past 'it was necessary' can be read, and is perhaps most naturally read, as a report of a discussion.[167] What is more striking, however, is that the second and longer of the two solutions offered[168] is introduced not by the customary *ê* ('or rather: ...'), but by 'something of the following sort was also said' (*elegeto de ti kai toiouton*). 'Was said' seems to apply not just to the first sentence that follows it (127,20-3), which could hardly stand on its own as a contribution, but to the whole view developed in the following section;[169] and it seems natural to take this as being a discussion at which the author of the *Problem* was present. The suggestion introduced in this way is after all one of the two main

[165] On this cf. R.W. Sharples, 'Alexander of Aphrodisias on divine providence: two problems', *Class. Quart.* 32, 1982, 198-211, at 204-8.

[166] ibid., 199 and nn. 13-14.

[167] Not all past tenses have this significance, of course. At *P. Eth.* 16 137,9 'the opposite of what is bad was either good or bad' is probably best taken, not as a reference to a discussion, still less as a reference back to other texts (5 125,2ff; 7 127,3ff) in a collection which probably did not exist as such at the time of writing, but rather as a statement of generally accepted doctrine. Cf. also perhaps *P. Eth.* 5 124,29.

[168] The first suggested solution (127,8-20) is that not all pain is in fact bad; pain relating to shameful activities is something deserving to be chosen (in the sense, of course, that we should positively want to find such activities painful, not in the sense that we should want both them and the pain that attaches to them). Another suggestion, which occupies the rest of this text, is then made (127,20ff); essentially, it is that, even if all pain is bad, it is opposed to some pleasures as one evil to another, to others as good to bad. This is really just a restatement of what was found difficult at the beginning of the text (127,5-7), but now at 127,20ff an account of how this can be so is provided by the distinction of different types of pleasures.

[169] The next sentence, 127,23-4, begins 'For' (*gar*).

suggested solutions to the problem, and the one stated at greater length; in other words, it is part of the reason for this text existing at all in its present form.

A similar expression occurs in *Mantissa* 169-72. This text, entitled by the editor '[From] the [teachings] of Aristotle concerning what depends on us', is an attempt to resolve the problem of free human agency in an orderly universe, a problem which the *de Fato* itself does not really deal with in a satisfactory way.[170] Its author takes the bold step of linking responsible human choice with the presence of not-being in the sublunary realm, which risks making it an imperfection in the universe as a whole. (It might be argued that it is nevertheless the highest aspect of *sublunary* nature; but our text does not in fact make this point.[171])

The opening words of this discussion are 'concerning what depends on us, an opinion like the following was also stated (*elegeto tis kai toiade doxa*)'. The argument that neither what depends on nature nor what depends on education can depend on us (169,34-170,2) is then linked with the problem with which the subsequent discussion is chiefly concerned, that of the apparent dilemma of determinism or uncaused motion (170,2-3: 'and this would be a still greater difficulty, if it were the case that nothing comes about without a cause'). The text then comments, 'and this, too, seemed so to everyone (*kai auto hapasin edokei*)', before proceeding to its solution. It is not immediately clear whether 'this seemed so to everyone' refers to a specific occasion or to the opinions of philosophers in general, and whether 'this' is the fact that there would be a difficulty, or the view that nothing comes about without a cause.[172] Nor is it clear whether the initial 'an opinion like the following was also stated' applies just to the indications of the problems, or also to the following solution.[173] If the former, the reference could be to a particular discussion – as 'was *also* stated' perhaps suggests – or to a general tradition; the difficulties raised at the start of the passage are after all ones which would occur naturally enough in any discussion of the problem of free will and determinism. If on the other hand 'an opinion like the following was also stated' refers to the solution as well, the question arises whether the author introduces the solution in this way because he himself does not accept it. This has indeed been the most common interpretation, that Alexander himself reports, because of its interest, a view that he does not himself share.[174]

[170] cf. R.W. Sharples, 'Responsibility, chance and not-being (Alexander of Aphrodisias *Mantissa* 169-172)', *Bulletin of the Institute of Classical Studies* 22, 1975, 37-64, at 42.

[171] Sharples, op. cit. 52 and n. 170; cf. id. 'Responsibility and the possibility of more than one course of action: a note on Aristotle *de Caelo* 2.12', *Bulletin of the Institute of Classical Studies* 23, 1976, 69-72.

[172] It is true that most Greek thinkers had held that nothing came about without a cause, except Epicurus; but his atomic swerve is, oddly, nowhere mentioned in the writings attributed to Alexander. Bruns indeed suggests reading *tisin* for *hapasin*; 'and this, too, seemed so to some'.

[173] However, Professor G.E.R. Lloyd suggested to me that it might be more natural to refer to the statement of the problems alone by *elegeto tis toiade aporia*, rather than *doxa*.

[174] So Bruns 1892, xiii; Merlan 1967, 88. Later ancient and medieval practice might

Ethical Problems 8 and 28 present two different solutions to the same problem, that of the relation of virtue to the various virtues. A cross-reference from one *Problem* to the other has apparently been inserted in the text.[175] There is a temptation to see these two texts as, perhaps, papers prepared for the same seminar; but there could on the other hand have been a considerable lapse of time between their writing. Alternative answers to a single problem occur both in the *Problems* attributed to Aristotle[176] and elsewhere in the texts attributed to Alexander.[177]

Another case in which one text seems to be developing a discussion from another has been brought to my attention by John Ellis. *Quaestio* 1.8 begins by stating the argument that a form cannot be in matter, or a soul in a body, as in a subject (*hupokeimenon*); for a subject must be something that exists in actuality in its own right, but matter cannot exist apart from form (17,8-12). This argument is introduced by 'it was said that' (*ên legomenon hoti*. 17,9). The objection is then made that the argument could equally well be applied to accidents of bodies, since a body cannot exist without shape and colour (17,12-17); and the *quaestio* continues with a reply to this objection (17,17ff). The initial argument at 17,8-12 occurs also in the *Mantissa*,[178] but without the particular objection at 17,12-17 being brought against it. It therefore looks very much as if the *quaestio* may be referring back to, and building on, the discussion in the *Mantissa*.

VII

The impression given by the writings attributed to Alexander is one of lively philosophical discussion. The opinions of his predecessors and of his near-contemporaries from other philosophical schools play a part in this; but it is difficult to believe that some at least of the texts here considered

---

suggest that discussions would have been recorded by a pupil rather than by Alexander himself; but that on its own would not explain the contrast between occasional remarks like 'the following opinion was stated' and solutions which on the face of it seem to be put forward, even if tentatively, by the writer *in propria persona*.

[175] *P. Eth.* 8 128,22, bracketed by Bruns as an editorial addition.

[176] cf. e.g. [Aristotle] *Probl.* 10.18 and 10.54, 10.48 and 34.1, 11.20 and 11.47, 38.1 and 38.11.

[177] The subject matter of *P. Eth.* 13, on differentiation among pleasures, is to some extent similar to that of *P. Eth* 2, 17 and 19, but the argument in 13 that we choose between pleasures and activities in themselves, rather than as means to some further end, seems a distinctive contribution.

[178] At *Mantissa* 119,32-120,9; I am grateful to Mr Ellis for drawing to my attention the significance of the absence of the counter-argument found in *quaestio* 1.8. The text at *Mantissa* 120,1 is corrupt and difficult to interpret, but the general sense is clear. Similar arguments occur also at *Quaest.* 1.17 30,3ff and *Quaest.* 1.26 42,14ff; cf., on Aristotle, G.E.M. Anscombe and P.T. Geach, *Three Philosophers: Aristotle, Aquinas, Frege*, Oxford 1961, 10f, and above n. 118. But the mention of the *soul* suggests that the reference in *Quaest.* 1.8 is to the *Mantissa* rather than to *Quaest.* 1.17 (where the soul is only mentioned at the end), and the emphasis of *Quaest.* 1.26 is rather different.

do not reflect the activity of Alexander's own philosophical school. This makes it all the more odd that we know so little about any pupils of Alexander, and that as far as our information goes he seems to mark the end of a distinctive and continuous Peripatetic tradition.

References

This is a list for the reader's convenience of some works referred to repeatedly in the notes to this article; it is *not* intended as a comprehensive bibliography of the subject.

I. Bruns (ed.), *Supplementum Aristotelicum* 2: 2.1, Berlin 1887, 2.2, Berlin 1892.

J.M. Dillon, *The Middle Platonists*, London 1977.

J.P. Lynch, *Aristotle's School*, Berkeley 1976.

P. Merlan, 'Zwei Untersuchungen zu Alexander von Aphrodisias', *Philologus* 113, 1969, 85-91.

P. Moraux, *Alexandre d'Aphrodise: Exégète de la noétique d'Aristote*, Liège and Paris 1942.

P. Moraux, *Der Aristotelismus bei den Griechen von Andronikos bis Alexander von Aphrodisias*: I, Berlin 1973; II, Berlin 1984.

P. Moraux, 'Alexander von Aphrodisias *Quaest.* 2.3', *Hermes* 95, 1967, 159-69.

P. Moraux, 'Le *De anima* dans la tradition grecque', in G.E.R. Lloyd and G.E.L. Owen, (eds), *Aristotle on Mind and the Senses: Proceedings of the Seventh Symposium Aristotelicum*, Cambridge 1978.

R.W. Sharples, 'Alexander of Aphrodisias, Problems about Possibility I-II', *Bulletin of the Institute of Classical Studies* 29, 1982, 91-108; 30, 1983, 99-110.

R.W. Sharples, 'Ambiguity and opposition: Alexander of Aphrodisias, *Ethical Problems* 11', *Bulletin of the Institute of Classical Studies*, 32, 1985, 109-16.

R.W. Sharples, 'Alexander of Aphrodisias: scholasticism and innovation', in W. Haase (ed.), *Aufstieg und Niedergang der römischen Welt* II.36.2, Berlin 1987, 1176-243.

R.B. Todd, *Alexander of Aphrodisias on Stoic Physics*, Leiden 1976.

CHAPTER FIVE

Themistius: the last Peripatetic commentator on Aristotle?[1]

Henry J. Blumenthal

It may be thought old fashioned to begin with dates, but the fact that Themistius' active career ran from the late 340s to 384 or 5, and that his paraphrases of Aristotle were probably compiled during the earlier part of the period 337-357 is not unimportant.[2] By the end of his life Plutarch the son of Nestorius, arguably the man who restored the study of Platonic philosophy at Athens,[3] will already have been teaching there. By the close of the fifth century the study of Aristotle had become inextricably intertwined with the exposition, as it purported to be, of Plato's thought, and the fifth- and sixth-century commentators whose work we now have were Neoplatonists to a man. The last major commentator before Themistius, over a century before him, was Alexander, who may claim to be a genuine Peripatetic without too much fear of contradiction. Notwithstanding recent attempts to establish that Alexander was influenced by Plato or Platonists on certain important issues,[4] the core of his thought, and so his explanation of Aristotle, is overridingly Peripatetic. That is not to say that there are no ideas in Alexander which are the product of meditation on and argument with other traditions, but he clearly stood apart from the Middle Platonist amalgam of his time.

In between came Plotinus, Porphyry and Iamblichus. By the time of Philoponus and Simplicius Neoplatonism had been dominant for some

[1] References to the Aristotelian commentators are to page and line of the Berlin Academy edition: where unspecified they are to commentaries on the *de Anima*.

[2] For these dates cf. O. Seeck, *Die Briefe des Libanius*, Leipzig 1906, 292f and 306; G. Dagron, *L'Empire Romain d'Orient au IVe Siècle et les Traditions Politiques de l'Hellénisme: Le Témoignage de Thémistius*, Travaux et Memoirs du Centre de Recherche d'Hist. et Civ. Byz. 3, Paris 1968, 5 n. 3 and 12; A.H.M. Jones, J.R. Martindale and J. Morris, *Prosopography of the Later Roman Empire* I, Cambridge 1971, 892 and 889.

[3] cf. É. Évrard, 'Le maître de Plutarque d'Athènes et les origines du néoplatonisme athénien', *Antiquité Classique* 29, 1960, 404-6 and my '529 and its sequel: what happened to the Academy?', *Byzantion* 48, 1978, 373-5; for another view see H.-D. Saffrey and L.G. Westerink (eds), *Proclus, Théologie Platonicienne* 1, Paris 1968, xxxv-xlviii.

[4] cf. P. Merlan, *Monopsychism Mysticism Metaconsciousness. Problems of the soul in the Neoaristotelian and Neoplatonic Tradition*, The Hague 1963, ch. 2; P.L. Donini, *Tre Studi sull'Aristotelismo nel II Secolo d.C.*, Turin 1974, *passim*.

250 years, and independent commentary was a thing of the past. Aristotle was by then almost always read as a thinker who was expressing the Platonic truth, sometimes inadequately or obscurely.[5] These later commentators owe a great deal to Porphyry and Iamblichus, as well as to their successors, and were not ashamed to confess their debt. Since Porphyry and Iamblichus were active before Themistius, it would not be surprising if he too were strongly influenced by Platonism, and yet one's first impression on reading his philosophical work is that he was not. Nevertheless the *Orations* make a number of pronouncements which might point in the opposite direction. So occasionally do the paraphrases. The purpose of this chapter is to look at the evidence on a few points that may be taken as a test of philosophical orientation, in the hope of being able to determine which of these contrary impressions is correct.

Three kinds of evidence are available to help us make this decision. First, Themistius' own statements of his philosophical attitudes. Second, and most important, the substance of his interpretations of Aristotle: does he give what we should regard as a straight reading of Aristotle, or does he prefer the kind of explanation that makes Aristotle a Platonist? Theoretically, we should be able to derive further information on this question from Themistius' comments on previous interpretations, but the paraphrase style of commentary does not normally allow him to discuss them, though it is sometimes clear that he is following Alexander.[6] On the other hand we do have some references to Themistius in the later commentators, who will occasionally take issue with him on whether or not a passage should be read Platonically.

The main source for Themistius' own statements of his orientation is not his philosophical *oeuvre*, but rather his *Orations*. Their reader cannot fail to notice the honorific terms in which he repeatedly refers to Plato. He is divine, all-wise, reverend, most magnificent and, most often, marvellous. In addition, Themistius' admiration for Plato seems to have impressed his correspondents. Gregory of Nazianzus speaks of 'your Plato' (*Ep.* 24), and Libanius attributes to Themistius, as a compliment, the possession of both Plato's faculties, noble teaching and eloquence (*Ep.* 793). Further, Themistius clearly approved of the metaphysical foundation which Plato gave to his politics. In *Or.* 34 he comments on how Plato progressed beyond Socrates and his band, who were concerned with virtue, vice and happiness on the human plane, to attach human to divine goodness, and to model the human polity on that of the universe as a whole; with that disregard of progress in Plato's thought characteristic of antiquity, he sees this as the point of the *Gorgias* as well as the *Republic, Phaedrus* and *Laws*. Themistius seems to prefer this grandiose design to Aristotle's more modest treatment of virtue on the human plane alone (447,29ff Dindorf). Yet at other times he will say that Aristotle's view of philosophy and politics is better than that of Plato, who was too naive in

[5] cf. Chapter 13 below.
[6] cf. esp. Themistius' comments on *nous dunamei* and *nous kath' hexin* and Alexander *de Anima* 80.24ff.

saying that the world's wrongs will not end before philosophers become kings or kings philosophers (*Or.* 8 = 128,19ff D).

One point of particular interest that emerges from the *Orations* is the frequency with which Themistius mentions Plato's views on ethics and politics. Themistius' Plato is that of the philosopher-king and the Cave, not that of the Good beyond being, or the perfect being of the *Sophist*. His Platonic texts – they tend to recur – are predominantly those that might be described as in the Socratic rather than the Pythagorean and metaphysical tradition, and this immediately marks his Plato as very different from that of the Neoplatonists. Plotinus, as W. Theiler once pointed out, gives us a *Plato dimidiatus:*[7] the missing half was that concerned with moral virtue in a city (*polis*) and the organisation and structure of that city. Themistius, who was, after all, a politician and man of affairs, was interested in this other half, in Plato the would-be man of action who went three times to the West (cf. e.g. *Or.* 8 = 125,19-32D), thereby showing at least his independence of the Neoplatonic tradition which concentrated on Plato the metaphysician.

Themistius did not abandon his high regard for Plato when he wrote the paraphrases on Aristotle – he is alleged by Photius in a report, which in other respects is not reliable, to have written paraphrases on Plato too.[8] There, for reasons connected with the type of exposition, explicit references are comparatively rare, but when he does appear Plato is treated no less reverently than in the *Orations* (cf. e.g. 107,22). Probably for this reason Themistius has sometimes been described as a Platonist.[9] But when it comes to actual doctrines, and here we pass to our second heading, reverence for Plato is not translated into that superimposition of Platonism on Aristotelian texts which is the hallmark of the Neoplatonists.

At this stage we must identify some criteria by which the commentaries can be used for our present purpose. If we look primarily at the relatively well-documented tradition stemming from Aristotle's *de Anima* – 'stemming from' to include independent treatises like Alexander's *de Anima* as well as commentaries, whether paraphrases or the more conventional kind – we may take the following points, *exempli gratia*, as reliable indicators:

(1) Do soul and body form a single unit, related as form to matter, or is soul separate, and in control of an ontologically inferior subordinate?

(2) Is the soul a continuum, possibly with a division between intellect

---

[7] 'Plotin zwischen Plato und Stoa', in *Les Sources de Plotin*, Entretiens Hardt 5, Vandoeuvres-Geneva, 1960, 67.

[8] cf. pp. 121-2 below and n. 32.

[9] That he defended some Platonic views against Aristotle, or adopted Neoplatonist doctrines, has been claimed on the basis of texts which will not support it, so. S. Landauer, citing *in Metaph.* 9,3-11 (in his index thereto, s.v. Plato), Schmid-Staehlin, *Gesch. Gr. Lit.*[6] II.ii, Munich 1924, 1011 and n. 8, citing *Or.* 32 = 439,4D and 4 (2 is a misprint) = 61, 28, which are not evidence for Neoplatonism. O. Hamelin, *La Théorie de l'Intellect d'après Aristote et ses Commentateurs*, Paris 1953, 38-43, regards Themistius as an 'Alexandrin'

and reason, a matter on which Aristotle himself is notoriously hesitant, or does it divide at one or more points below this level?

(3) A related question: is the soul seen in Aristotle's way as a structure in which the lower components are pre-requisites for the existence of the higher ones, or as a Neoplatonic 'emanation' where the higher level is given and the lower ones derive from it?

(4) Does the human soul relate to higher reality by being a part, or a product, of it? Here, though as we shall see the answer may not be decisive, we may put the question which became so important later, 'is the agent intellect one or many?'

The most difficult problem for exponents of a Platonist reading of Aristotle was to explain his treatment of the relation between body and soul. This was a crucial issue on which the two traditions were clearly opposed. However one might interpret certain passages from the *Eudemus* and *Protrepticus*,[10] the *de Anima* clearly presents us with a soul indissolubly linked to the body by being its form. While the intellect may be an exception, there is no doubt about the unity of the rest. For a Platonist this view was, of course, totally unacceptable.

Most of Aristotle's discussion of the actual operations of soul could be translated fairly easily into Platonist dualism by a realist reading of texts treating the activities of its faculties.[11] But the explicit discussion of the nature and definition of soul, and its connection with the body, could not be dealt with so easily. In fact Platonists seem to have found this sufficiently difficult for some at least to have read Aristotle as if he were talking about a soul and a body that already had soul: the latter would be the form that makes matter into body, upon which the individual soul was superimposed. This is what we find in the Platonist handbook which appears in Plotinus and Porphyry, and which Themistius too may have used.[12] There this view of soul and body appears as an assumption. The later commentators, whose Platonising of Aristotle was more thorough, tried to show that only the soul below the level of the individual soul was united to the body as form to matter, and argued that this manifestation of soul which gives formless matter the status of body could be described as form and actuality.

Thus Simplicius has *phusis* (nature), a standard term for this level, as an informing cause, *eidêtikê aitia*, to which soul is added (4,14ff). When he comes to the discussion of the soul's definition as the first actuality of a *sôma organikon* he uses, or rather abuses, Aristotle's notion of a first and second actuality to distinguish one which merely gives form and so life to

---

manqué, but he insists on seeing Platonism where it does not, or need not exist, so, e.g., the *aüla* of 115,5 are not evidence for Platonic Ideas.

[10] *Eudemus* fr. 8 Ross, *Protrepticus* fr. 10b Ross.

[11] cf. my *Plotinus' Psychology*, The Hague, 1971, 135ff.

[12] cf. Plotinus 4.7,1-8[5], Porphyry ap. Nemesium *de Nat. Hom.* ch. 2, Themistius 24,22ff and 41,11ff, and *Plotinus' Psychology* 11-13 with nn. 10 and 13; H. Doerrie, *Porphyrios' 'Symmikta Zetemata'*, Zetemata 20, Munich 1959, 111ff.

the body and another which uses that body, so informed, as its instrument, Platonically (90,29ff). Thus he constructively misinterprets *sôma organikon* to mean not a body fully equipped with the necessary parts, but a body which is a tool.[13] This is in line with the Neoplatonist concept of the human soul as a series of strata arranged hierarchically. These layers, in defiance of Aristotle's notion of form, were sometimes described as a series of forms, each being form to the one below, which constituted the matter for its superior. Philoponus, though he tried to provide a less un-Aristotelian solution, approached the same problem with similar preconceptions (cf. 198,22ff).[14] For these men the form was not the essence of any given kind of life which subsumed all lower kinds.

In Themistius there is, with one arguable exception, no sign of any such attempt to avoid the clear import of Aristotle's text, and he gives us both the Aristotelian structure of faculties and its arrangement (e.g. 44,21ff). If it is argued that he was constrained by his genre, and unable to depart radically from Aristotle, this argument cannot be used about his treatment of the notorious comparison of the soul with a sailor (413a8f), where Aristotle's meaning is sufficiently unclear to allow even a mere paraphrase scope for a Platonist reading. Aristotle's hesitation here, his suggestion that perhaps the soul was an actuality of the body like a sailor in a ship, could easily be referred to areas of soul other than the intellect to which Aristotle himself seems in the end to have confined it. This was done by Simplicius and Philoponus, and doubtless by other Neoplatonists whose comments we do not have. Simplicius professed to be puzzled by how Aristotle could entertain any doubt about the separability of the soul: for him it was clearly and indisputably separate (96,8ff). Themistius, on the other hand, perplexed though he seems to be, takes Aristotle's remark as a hesitation, and explains its presence as a feature of the early stage in the investigation. If soul were an actuality like a steersman, he says, and it is clear that this applies to *nous*, then it could be an actuality, but separable. So far the whole soul had been characterised in outline, but not accurately. Up to this point, he continues, the discussion is like a sketch until we turn our attention to all the soul's faculties: that is how we would achieve clarity about whether the whole soul, or some part of it, is a separable form (43,25-34).

Since, as we have mentioned, the soul's activities as described by Aristotle could be taken as compatible with a Platonist view of its relation to the body, there is no special occasion for widespread Neoplatonisation in commenting on the rest of Book 2 or 3.1-2. Difficulties will again present themselves over the imagination, a faculty which may not always or necessarily involve the body in its activity. This could lead to problems both about separability, and about whether or not the soul comes apart, as it did for some Neoplatonists, at this level just because the same sort of activity related both to sense-perception, with its clear links with the

[13] For further discussion cf. my 'Some Platonist readings of Aristotle', *PCPhS*, n.s. 27, 1981, 4-6.
[14] cf. 'Body and soul in Philoponus', *The Monist* 69, 1986, 378-9.

corporeal, and reason and intellection, where these links could be held no longer to apply. This, as I have shown elsewhere, is one point where there is a great deal of discussion of Aristotle in non-Aristotelian ways.[15] In particular we find that the later commentators are much concerned to find clear demarcations between upper and lower soul, a preoccupation of which Themistius is innocent, and whose absence caused Stephanus to find fault with his commentary (508,19-25).[16] That, briefly, is the answer to our second question. The third we have answered in passing, and now we must turn to the fourth, the treatment of Aristotle's chapter on the active intellect.

Here Themistius departs from the paraphrase style and launches on an extended discussion (98,12-109,3), aimed primarily at resolving the status of the active intellect. In particular he is concerned with whether or not it should be identified with the ultimate divine being, the *prôtos theos*, or perhaps some other. This aspect of the problem may be understood in the light of Alexander's well-known view that the active intellect, *nous poêtikos*, was in fact the supreme principle itself. Themistius rejects it (102,30ff). His own suggestion that it might be a god (*theos*) other than the first may most readily be seen as an attempt to place it in the hierarchy of unmoved movers deployed in *Metaphysics* 12.8. By contrast there is nothing about whether it is part of a hypostasis, be it Intellect (*Nous*) or Soul, a question which forms the background to the Neoplatonists' discussions.[17] Though they are of course concerned with Themistius' question whether or not each intellect is internal to the individual, the later commentators 'solve' this problem by saying that Aristotle's active intellect must be part of the individual because the subject, *skopos*, of the *de Anima* is the rational soul.[18] They were all nevertheless much interested in its relation either to the simple series of hypostases of the earlier Neoplatonists, or to the complex system of unparticipated and participated souls and intellects of later Neoplatonism, a system which, let us note, was originated, if not fully developed, by Iamblichus,[19] and so should have been known to Themistius. He was certainly aware of some Neoplatonic thought on these matters, for he refers to a question that was of some importance to them, whether or not all souls were one,[20] as one that was discussed by both earlier and more recent thinkers (cf. 104,15f).

Themistius' stress on the unity of the actual and potential intellects at one point in his discussion seems at first not only to be inconsistent with the view that it was a god – an inconsistency he does not really resolve[21] –

[15] 'Neoplatonic interpretations of Aristotle on *Phantasia*', *Rev. of Metaphysics* 21, 1977, 242-57; for Themistius' deviations from Aristotle see now R.B. Todd, 'Themistius and the traditional interpretation of Aristotle's theory of *phantasia*', *Acta Classica* 24, 1981, 49-59.

[16] cf. 'Neoplatonic interpretations' (n. 15 above), 253-4.

[17] For further details cf. Chapter 13 below, pp. 312-13.

[18] cf. Simplicius 240,2ff, [Philop.] 536,2-5, citing Plutarch.

[19] cf. e.g. R.T. Wallis, *Neoplatonism*, London 1972, 100 and 123-34.

[20] cf. esp. Plotinus 4.9.

[21] On this, and some other points arising from Themistius' treatment of 3.5, cf. P. Moraux,

but also to exclude the Platonist patterns. But we must remember that they did discuss whether the active intellect was or was not part of a fully descended intellect, that is one that is part of the individual soul rather than, as Plotinus and some others maintained, a section of the transcendent intellect itself,[22] though it should be noted that the two 'parts' of intellect they discussed were more often seen as intuitive and discursive intellect. So the type of question Themistius is asking does not in itself exclude Platonist influence on his approach. What he says in the course of answering it is, however, so different from the Platonist treatments as to show that he was not thinking in the same conceptual schemes.[23]

It should nevertheless be noted that this view is not universally shared, and before leaving this matter we should look briefly at the evidence that has been adduced in support of the thesis that, at least in this area of his thought, we are in fact dealing with a commentator influenced by Neoplatonism. The main recent proponent of this view has been E.P. Mahoney. In a 1973 article on Themistius in James of Viterbo and other mediaeval philosophers he drew attention to certain features of Themistius' doctrine of the intellect which could be described as Neoplatonic.[24] These are the apparently hierarchical organisation of the soul's faculties in a matter-form relation on the Plotinian model, the ambiguity about the unicity or otherwise of the agent intellect to which we have already referred, and the description of a plurality of intellects as illuminated and illuminating (*ellampomenoi kai ellampontes*). Several further articles on the influence of Greek commentators on Renaissance philosophy take Themistius as holding these Neoplatonic views, which the later writers followed. The position is restated with further arguments, partly in reply to the original version of this paper, in a long note to the published version of Mahoney's contribution to a 1978 conference.[25] This gives an excellent survey of the opinions on both sides

'Le *de Anima* dans la tradition grecque. Quelques aspects de l'interprétation du traité, de Théophraste à Thémistius', in G.E.R. Lloyd and G.E.L. Owen (eds), *Aristotle on Mind and the Senses*, Cambridge 1978, 309-13.

[22] For a doxography cf. [Philop.] 535,2ff.

[23] A further text from outside the *de Anima* which would give ample scope for Neoplatonising distortion is *Metaph*. 12: Themistius in his paraphrase characterises the human mind as weak and inefficient, which would not be acceptable to a commentator who thought each human mind capable of assimilation to the transcendent *nous*, and of thereby attaining its power, *in Metaph*. 32,18ff.

[24] 'Themistius and the agent intellect in James of Viterbo and other thirteenth-century philosophers', *Augustiniana* 23, 1973, 423-67: on Themistius cf. esp. 428-31. Here, and in 'Neoplatonism, the Greek commentators ...' (see n. 25 below) Mahoney indicates that he started from suggestions made by P.O. Kristeller.

[25] 'Neoplatonism, the Greek commentators, and Renaissance Aristotelianism', in D.J. O'Meara (ed.), *Neoplatonism and Christian Thought*, Studies in Neoplatonism: Ancient and Modern 3, Albany NY 1982, 169-77 and 264-82, cf. esp. n. 1 on pp. 264-6. For his subsequent treatments of the use of the Greek commentators in the Renaissance, cf. 'Philosophy and science in Nicoletto Vernia and Agostino Nifo', in A. Poppi (ed.), *Scienza e filosofia all' Università di Padova nel Quattrocento*, Contributi alla storia dell' Università di Padova 15, Trieste 1983, 135-202; 'Marsilio Ficino's influence on Nicoletto Vernia, Agostino Nifo and

of this question and recommends a compromise view that, while Themistius' work contains some Neoplatonic views, he is not a faithful representative of that philosophy.[26]

While Mahoney's comments have caused me to see that in the original version of this article, as opposed to some earlier discussions of these matters,[27] I had underemphasised the extent to which Themistius uses Neoplatonic vocabulary, I would maintain that this is primarily a matter of language, and that even his noetic, the area in question, is still fundamentally free of Platonism – except, of course, in so far as Aristotle himself was not. To take the points at issue in turn:

(1) The most obviously Neoplatonic-looking part of Themistius' discussion is that in which he talks about the successive faculties of soul being related to those below them in each case as form to matter (100,32-5). That is an idea that can, of course, be found in Plotinus.[28] What is less clear is that it is not a possible interpretation of Aristotle himself: one might think of the relation of wood to matter, plank to wood, and ship to plank. At the very least it is a *possible* Peripatetic solution to the problems, highlighted for example by J.L. Ackrill,[29] inherent in Aristotle's concept of the soul as form of what already has form, though it might be argued on the other side that such a solution would give rise to problems analogous to the notorious difficulty about the plurality of unmoved movers in *Metaphysics* 12.

(2) A better candidate for Neoplatonist influence here is the notion that intellect could be both one and many, a view that is, of course, unproblematical for a Neoplatonist, but has caused sufficient offence to some Aristotelian scholars for them to suggest that the text of Themistius is here corrupt.[30] That, as Mahoney rightly says, is not a satisfactory solution. In any case caution is again called for: what we have could be simply an implication of Alexander's view that there is only one active intellect: in so far as that operates in all individuals it must also, at least conceptually, be plural.

(3) When we come to language, Mahoney rightly points to what is apparently the strongest indication of Neoplatonic ways of thinking, namely the reference to illuminated and illuminating intellects. But on

Marcantonio Zimara', in G.C. Garfagnani (ed.), *Marsilio Ficino e il ritorno del Platonismo*, Florence 1986, 509-31: neither, however, contains direct discussion of the text of Themistius.

[26] Following A. Guzzo and V. Mathieu s.v. 'Intelletto' in vol. 3 of the *Enciclopedia Filosofica*[2], Florence 1967, 963 (Mahoney's reference).

[27] cf. the articles cited in nn. 5 and 15 above.

[28] cf. p. 116 above and the selection of references given by Mahoney, 'Neoplatonism, the Greek commentators ...' (n. 25 above), 266.

[29] 'Aristotle's definitions of *psuchê*', *Proc. Aristotelian Soc.* 73, 1972-3, 122-7, repr. in J. Barnes, M. Schofield and R. Sorabji (eds), *Articles on Aristotle 4. Psychology and Aesthetics*, London 1979, 67-70.

[30] So P. Merlan, *Monopsychism* (see n. 4), 50 n. 3, following A. Kurfess, *Zur Geschichte der aristotelischen Lehre vom sog. NOUS POIĒTIKOS und PATHĒTIKOS*, Tübingen 1911 (repr. in A. Kurfess and I. Düring, *Aristotle and His Influence: two studies*, New York 1985), 23.

closer examination this is less clearly Neoplatonic. In the first place Themistius ties it to Aristotle's comparison of intellect with light in *de Anima* 3.5, and uses the characteristics of illumination to explain Aristotle's choice of light rather than Plato's of the sun in the *Republic* (103,34-5). It might be worth adding that, even though 'illumination' (*ellampsis*) is a Neoplatonic rather than an Aristotelian term, the word does occur once in the Aristotelian corpus.[31] In the work *On Plants* pseudo-Aristotle writes that sense-perception causes the illumination of life: *hê gar aisthêsis aitia estin ellampseôs zôês* (815b33). Though there is no evidence, as far as I know, that this work was familiar to the tradition, it is interesting to note that this is just the sort of remark about the relation of one level of soul to the next that one normally expects to find in a Neoplatonist: we cannot, however, be sure that *ellampsis* was in the original text.

A further item of language, which Mahoney might have added, but perhaps did not because it is not necessarily significant, is the use of the common Neoplatonic terms for the operation of discursive reason in its transition from one object to another, namely *metaballô* and *metabainô* (100,7 and 11). They are to be found over and over again in the later commentators' discussions of reasoning, but not in Aristotle's; what they describe, however, is not in any way un-Aristotelian.

All this shows that such Neoplatonic influence as there may have been was marginal in matters of doctrine, and only a little greater in features of language. These conclusions are reinforced by a wider look at Themistius' language. Any reader familiar with Neoplatonist writing must notice the almost complete absence of typically Platonic and Neoplatonic terminology. While one should not expect the fully developed vocabulary of fifth-century Neoplatonism, there is enough in Plotinus, Porphyry and particularly Iamblichus to obtrude itself if it appeared. It could be objected that the paraphrase form did not lend itself to the introduction of un-Aristotelian terms, but while this objection might apply to the passages on *de Anima* 2, it cannot apply to the discussion of 3.5, where Themistius produces ordinary commentary. Given the control afforded by this chapter, where, if anywhere, one would expect Platonism and Platonist language, we may safely say that their absence is neither insignificant nor fortuitous.

Before turning to the later commentators we should notice a problem which their references to Themistius have been taken to present. Some of them do not correspond closely, or at all, with the text of the paraphrases. On the basis of this difficulty, of a report in Photius that there were commentaries as well, and of remarks by Themistius himself in *Or.* 23, it has been argued that he wrote a series of full commentaries, and that the later commentators sometimes refer to these. If this were correct, it

---

[31] In a work whose original was probably by Nicolaus of Damascus: The extant text is a retranslation from Latin, cf. P. Moraux, *Les listes anciennes des ouvrages d'Aristote*, Louvain 1951, 109.

would have important implications, for clearly in such works Themistius would have had more scope for departures from Aristotelianism than within the constraints of paraphrase. I think, however, that we may safely assume that the picture presented by the extant paraphrases is accurate, and that untraceable references call for other explanations.[32]

One further preliminary point: the commentators' procedures can easily give a misleading impression of their attitudes, since they will most often refer to earlier opinions only when they wish to show that these are mistaken, or use them as ammunition in a controversy. Where a matter is uncontroversial, they will often simply give the standard explanation – a procedure, after all, not unlike ours.

The largest number of later named references to Themistius is in Simplicius' commentary on the *Physics*. Apart from Books 7 and 8, this treatise is not as open as some to Neoplatonising.[33] But it is of interest that only one text in Simplicius' commentary shows Themistius clearly opposed to Aristotle. That is on the independent existence of time (765,31ff). Otherwise Themistius is treated in the same way as Alexander, with whom he is recorded as agreeing and disagreeing more or less equally often.[34] Simplicius himself agrees with him more often than not, but since the points at issue are often philological rather than philosophical, and most of the latter are not relevant to differences between Plato and Aristotle, one can find no evidence here for Themistius as a Platonist. In the *de Caelo* commentary, on the other hand, Simplicius says in so many words that Themistius generally follows Aristotle, but occasionally, as on movement up and down, prefers Plato's account (69,9ff). The remaining references there are to scientific matters. In the *de Anima* commentary, whose different style excludes frequent references to others, there is only a single named reference to Themistius, to his view that the objects of taste are only the painful and pleasant, whereas Simplicius thinks taste gives other kinds of information too.[35]

Philoponus' *Physics* commentary, like Simplicius', gives little that is to

[32] A case for commentaries is made by C. Steel, 'Des commentaires d'Aristote par Thémistius', *Rev. philosophique de Louvain* 71, 1973, 669-80; for a critique cf. my 'Photius on Themistius (*Cod.* 74): Did Themistius write commentaries on Aristotle', *Hermes* 107, 1979, 168-82. Professor Steel has since indicated (by letter) that he no longer believes in the existence of separate commentaries.

[33] As Simplicius noted in his own commentary, 1036,14-17, Themistius did not pay much attention to 7.

[34] On Simplicius' use of Alexander see my 'Alexander of Aphrodisias in the later Greek commentaries on Aristotle's De Anima', in J. Wiesner (ed.), *Aristoteles Werk und Wirkung*, vol. 2, Berlin 1987, 90-106.

[35] The authenticity of this commentary is questioned, and its attribution to Priscian suggested, by F. Bossier and C. Steel, 'Priscianus Lydus en de *in de Anima* van Pseudo(?)-Simplicius', *Tijdschrift voor Filosofie* 34, 1972, 761-822; for another view cf. I. Hadot, *Le problème du néoplatonisme Alexandrin. Hiéroclès et Simplicius*, Paris 1978, 193-202 and my 'The psychology of (?) Simplicius' commentary on the De Anima' in H.J. Blumenthal and A.C. Lloyd (eds), *Soul and the Structure of Being in Late Neoplatonism*, Liverpool 1982, 73-5. Professors Bossier and Steel have both since (1985) told me that they are still fully convinced that this commentary is by another hand.

our purposes, and the few references in *in An. Post.* are also primarily technical, showing no symptoms of Platonising. The part of the *de Anima* commentary written by Philoponus himself is again unhelpful. On whether the sense of touch is one or many, Themistius is reported as disagreeing with Aristotle, and Philoponus follows him, but this has nothing to do with Platonism. The same is true of the question whether flesh is an organ or a medium, where Themistius agrees with Aristotle (418,24f) while Philoponus expresses dissatisfaction with the whole discussion (433,15ff).

The third book of the Philoponus commentary, written by Stephanus, gives us more, and, as we have mentioned, indicates that Themistius' interpretation was seen as inadequately Platonic. One report, on his argument for the need for a soul to have all the irrational faculties before it can have reason, has him giving an argument which is not Aristotelian, but the position it maintains is (450,8ff). All this pertains to the discussion of how many senses we have, and Stephanus himself goes on to offer a professedly more Platonic explanation of why we have five (ibid. 27-33). Another citation, difficult to trace, has Themistius talking of imagination as an active power. This does look like Neoplatonising, but the very fact that it does not appear in the paraphrases excites suspicion that either Stephanus, or a source, has introduced the Neoplatonic element himself. It is interesting that he was not content with Themistius' account, in so far as he, like Aristotle, said sensation and imagination happen together, a view not conducive to the hierarchical picture of the soul favoured by the late commentators. Stephanus proceeds to criticise Themistius for a view he did not express, namely that imagination can only operate simultaneously with sense-perception.[36]

One earlier report should be added. Ammonius, the teacher of both Simplicius and Philoponus, tells us how Julian gave a ruling against Themistius in a dispute on whether 2nd and 3rd figure syllogisms are perfect, in favour of Maximus, who had heard Iamblichus, and followed him and Porphyry (*in An. Pr.* 31,15-22). Even if this is not a matter where a Platonic view could have been adopted, the tale is further evidence for Themistius' independence of the Neoplatonists.

Thus both the content of Themistius' works, and such evidence as we have of the commentators' attitudes to him, show that he was predominantly a Peripatetic. In this he stood out against the tendencies of his time. His frequently expressed admiration for Plato does not invalidate this conclusion. Themistius may rightly claim to have been the last major figure in antiquity who was a genuine follower of Aristotle. For him, unlike his contemporaries, Plato does not surpass the master of those who know but he, and Socrates, 'innanzi agli altri più presso gli stanno'.

---

[36] cf. 508,19ff and n. 16 above.

CHAPTER SIX

The harmony of Plotinus and Aristotle according to Porphyry*

Pierre Hadot

The objections which Plotinus raised against Aristotle's theory of categories have played a major role in the history of logic. They required Neoplatonists wishing to save a place in their system for Aristotelian logic truly to exert themselves in the logical and metaphysical interpretation of the *Categories*.

It is well known that the second and third books of Dexippus' commentary on the *Categories* are almost totally devoted to the resolution of Plotinus' objections. The solutions which Dexippus proposes to Plotinus' objections are borrowed, on the one hand, from the great commentary which Porphyry wrote on the *Categories* and addressed to Gedalius (now unfortunately lost), and, on the other hand, from Iamblichus' commentary on the same work of Aristotle. Unfortunately, when quoting from these two sources, Dexippus does not name them. They can occasionally be identified by comparing his text with that of Simplicius, who generally uses the same authors in commenting on the *Categories*, except that he names them (sometimes, at least). Simplicius tells us (*in Cat.* 2,9) that Iamblichus' commentary often followed Porphyry's word for word, but also corrected it, abridged it, and added to it both important theoretical discussions and, notably, a comparison between Aristotle's *Categories* and the treatise *On the Whole* of Archytas (whom Iamblichus considered to be Aristotle's source). This last feature of Iamblichus' commentary permits us in certain cases to trace its influence.

The present essay is confined to several lines of Dexippus (*in Cat.* 40,13-42,3) which relate to a Plotinian aporia that is particularly important, since it concerns the concept of *ousia* (substance).

Here is the text of Plotinus' objection (from his treatise 'On the genera of being'; 6.1.2.4-8) as Dexippus reports it:

> If there are two *ousiai* (one intelligible, the other sensible), how can they be traced to a single genus? For what do these two *ousiai* have in common as

* Translated by Victor Caston.

regards being? And, even if we assume that there is something in common, it will still be necessary to posit something prior and different from the two, which is neither a body, nor an incorporeal (in order to explain their commonality). It follows from this that either the incorporeal is a body or body is an incorporeal. (Dexippus, *in Cat.* 40,14-18)

To be properly understood, Plotinus' aporia must be placed within its original context. The fundamental question Plotinus poses is the following: How can Aristotelian substance claim to be a single genus? On the one hand, Aristotle does not speak of intelligible substance, even though that is what *is* at the highest level (6.1.1.28). On the other hand, even if one wanted to give intelligible and sensible things both the name 'substance', it would not be possible, for intelligible being is essentially different from sensible being. Moreover, even if it were agreed that the intelligible and the sensible were differentiae of a single genus, it would be necessary to posit something prior to the intelligible and the sensible, which was both intelligible and sensible, incorporeal and corporeal. Yet, even if restricted to sensible substance, it is unacceptable that the concept of substance should be truly common to the realities to which one attributes it. If Aristotle can call form and matter, as well as the composite of the two, *'ousia'*, it must be admitted that these realities are not equally substances, but that form is 'more' substance (6.1.2.8-12). The general sense of Plotinus' objection is the following. If one enumerates all *ousiai* – the intelligible *ousia* (which Aristotle does not mention in the *Categories*, yet recognises elsewhere), the *ousia* which is form or which is matter, the *ousia* which is composed of the two (form and matter) – one must admit that the term *'ousia'* is not employed synonymously (in the same sense), but homonymously (in different senses). These different *ousiai* do not, therefore, belong to the same genus.

To this objection, Dexippus' source gives a preliminary response:

> Obviously, it is easy to respond to these objections by saying that the difficulties Plotinus raises are foreign to the intention of the *Categories*. For in the present case, Aristotle proposed to discuss neither the beings nor the genera of first *ousia*; he has beginners in mind, who can only understand the most basic lessons. Thus, as the actual discussion concerns words which can be said of *ousia* (*kat' ousiôn legesthai*), it is unreasonable of Plotinus to introduce a discussion of beings into a discussion which concerns words. (Dexippus, *in Cat.* 40,19-25)

In this text we find Porphyry's customary argument when refuting objections of this kind: Aristotle's *Categories* is addressed to beginners and only treats meaningful words, not beings (cf. Porphyry *in Cat.* 56,31; Simplicius *in Cat.* 10,20). Yet Dexippus' source wishes to go further in refuting Plotinus and grasp the opportunity which this occasion provides to treat the problem of substance in depth. It does not necessarily follow *a priori* that the author Dexippus copied could not be Porphyry merely from the fact that the author he uses wishes to go beyond arguments based on the intention of the *Categories* and to devote an important discussion to substance considered from a metaphysical point of view. Porphyry's greater commentary on the *Categories* contained investigations of this kind (cf., for example, Simplicius *in Cat.* 158,27). In any case, Dexippus' text continues:

> It does not seem right, however, thus to avoid this extension of the argument, an extension which is well adapted to our present inquiry. On the contrary, it seems desirable to start from the same point as the philosophy of Plotinus does and relate the extension of the present arguments to the whole of his doctrine. Plotinus in fact posits *ousia* as a genus unique among intelligible realities because it procures being for incorporeal forms universally and gives being to all the forms which are sensible and blended with matter. If that is so, the principle of *ousia* extends across all things, taking successively the first, second, and third rank insofar as it gives being to one primarily and to others in another manner. This is why, if everything leads to this principle of *ousia* (since everything is suspended from it), Aristotle's description of *ousia* can also provide a glimpse of the first principle of *ousia*, from which the *ousia* has fallen to its lowest degree. (Dexippus, *in Cat.* 40,25-41,3)

Here we have a fascinating text. It attempts to justify Aristotle with the help of the philosophy of Plotinus and to show that, at bottom, Aristotle's logic can find room within the ambit of the Plotinian system.

To begin with, notice the appearance of the phrase the 'philosophy of Plotinus'. In the Neoplatonic period, it is generally the 'philosophy of Plato' or the 'philosophy of Aristotle' which is spoken of – that is, this phrase is only used for the doctrine of the great masters. The formula which Dexippus uses betrays the enthusiasm of a pupil for his teacher, recalling the title of a work by Amelius in which he speaks in praise of Plotinus' doctrine: 'On the proper character of the philosophy of Plotinus' (Porphyry, *Vita Plotini* 20.101). We can assume that the pupil whose text Dexippus has preserved is Porphyry rather than Iamblichus; the latter in fact had a tendency to distance himself from Plotinus.

This assumption appears to be confirmed by an examination of the text of Simplicius' commentary (*in Cat.* 76,25) which corresponds to the discussion of Dexippus under consideration. In this parallel passage, 'the philosophy of Plotinus' disappears, and the philosopher who posits substance as a genus unique among intelligible realities is no longer Plotinus, but Plato. This substitution seems to have been made in fact to eliminate the overly enthusiastic mention of the 'philosophy of Plotinus' and is quite probably the work of Iamblichus. Note in this regard that the substitution of Plato for Plotinus destroys the force of the argument. It was very interesting to say that Plotinus' own philosophy affords a resolution of Plotinus' objection against Aristotle. Yet it is far more banal to remark, as Simplicius does, that Plato considers substance as an intelligible genus. In wishing to replace Plotinus with Plato, Iamblichus has completely distorted the sense of the reasoning.

Two questions may now be posed: (1) Does Dexippus give us an exact summary of Plotinus' doctrine? and (2) How does this evocation of Plotinus' philosophy permit a resolution of Plotinus' aporia?

To answer the first question is already to answer the second in part. In fact, Plotinus himself had proposed a solution to his own anti-Aristotelian objection, and this solution agrees with the résumé of the Plotinian doctrine of substance which Dexippus offers.

In fact, after having refused to accept that *'ousia'* can be attributed synonymously (in the same sense) to all the *ousiai* Aristotle acknowledges, Plotinus makes the following assumption, representing his attempt to preserve the unity of the concept of *ousia*: 'Yet if we collect the intelligible "substance", the matter, the form, and the composite of the two together, is it not necessary to say that this is a single category? It is in this manner that someone would say that the genus of the Heraclides is a single thing; this sort of unity would not be a common predicate attributed to all, but would result from the fact that all take their origin from a single thing. Intelligible *ousia* in this case would be *ousia* in a primary sense, the others in a derivative and lesser sense' (6.1.3.1-5).

According to the hypothesis which Plotinus proposes, the unity of the concept of substance would thus correspond to the type of unity that exists between terms which are neither totally synonymous nor totally homonymous, but whose common name is based on a single principle (*Metaph.* 4.2, 1003a33; 7.4, 1030a35). The single principle would here therefore be intelligible *ousia*, which would be the source of being for the form, the composite, and the matter. Porphyry's *Isagoge* (1,18 Busse) offers, like Plotinus, the example of the Heraclides in order to define genus: 'One calls genus the collection of certain terms which have a determinate relation with respect to some one thing, and each with respect to the others. It is in this sense that one speaks of the genus of the Heraclides in virtue of their relation to a first (or primary) principle, I mean Heracles.' There will, however, be a certain ambiguity here, since both the group of terms connected by this relation and their principle will equally be called 'genus' (*Isag.* 1,23ff). The genus is therefore both the principle which grounds the community of name and the group of terms which have this name in common. From Plotinus' Platonic perspective, intelligible *ousia* – which is the principle of the community of name between the different *ousiai* – is not just any origin or generator whatsoever; it is a principle because it is *ousia* in itself, it grounds being, because it is the idea itself of *ousia*. It is a genus in the Platonic sense, that is, an intelligible reality which exists in and for itself, which is not attributable to subjects lower than it, but grounds the very possibility of predicates being attributed to subjects in the beings which participate in them.

This conception of *ousia* does exist in Plotinus. One encounters a preliminary version of it in the treatise 'On the *ousia* of the soul' (4.2.1.29ff). There Plotinus comments on *Timaeus* 35A: 'From the *ousia* which is indivisible and always identical with itself and the *ousia* which becomes divisible in the body, the Demiurge makes a third kind of *ousia* by blending them'. Plotinus identifies indivisible *ousia* with intelligible reality, which is compared to the undivided and unmoving centre of a circle, from which the rays shoot forth and derive their being (4.1.27). Divisible *ousia* corresponds to material forms; intermediate *ousia* is the *ousia* of the soul. There is a hierarchy of *ousiai*, therefore, which are grounded in an original *ousia* and progressively descend on account of distance and division. Yet it is above all in the two treatises dedicated to the theme 'That what is one and identical can be at the same time in its entirety everywhere' (6.4-5) that Plotinus develops a doctrine of intelligible *ousia* the most clearly. If we remain at the level of logic, Plotinus tells us (probably with Aristotle's *Categories* in mind), the nature of bodies serves as our model and our principles are taken from there, so that if we come hence to divide *ousia*, we no longer believe in its unity. If, on the contrary, we start from principles proper to intelligible *ousia*, we understand that it is an indivisible unity, which is not divided in the subjects that participate in it, but always remains identical with itself, while being present everywhere in its entirety (6.5.2.1-3, 32). In the same way, in the treatise 'On numbers' (6.6.13.27), Plotinus does not hesitate to affirm that the name '*ousia*' applies to sensible things by derivation from intelligible things. If one applies the category *ousia* to sensible things and to intelligible things, it is nevertheless the latter to which the category is attributed in the highest degree. *Ousia* and being are, by themselves, intelligible and not sensible, even if the sensible participates in them. Lastly, the treatise 'On the genera of being' (6.2.7.6) explicitly presents intelligible *ousia* as a genus along with the other Platonic genera – movement, rest, identity and difference – by specifying (6.2.8.25) that what comes after these genera are the particularised genera: determinate *ousia*, determinate movement, etc.

One can therefore find in Plotinus elements of the doctrine of *ousia* which Dexippus (probably following Porphyry) attributes to him. Yet it must be recognised that the formulas Dexippus uses are not at all the same as those in Plotinus. The text of Dexippus systematises the teaching of Plotinus and, in systematising it, causes it to undergo an important transformation. Intelligible *ousia* is there defined as a principle of *ousia*, that is, as a principle of being in the three degrees (*taxis*) of reality: the intelligible, the psychic, and the sensible levels. To each degree there corresponds a type of being (primary being, derivative being) and a type of *ousia*. As regards this participation of the lower degrees in the principle of *ousia*, it can be said that the principle of *ousia* extends through all things, though this only means that everything has its origin and end in it. The hierarchy of the degrees of being and of *ousia* corresponds to a progressive degradation.

This presentation is completely analogous to the systematisation of Plotinian theses in the theorems of Porphyry's *Sententiae*. It might be worthwhile to emphasise the correspondence between Dexippus' text and certain tendencies that come into relief in the Porphyrian systematisation (in the *Sententiae* and in other works, fragments, and testimonia). The idea of a first substance, a principle of the being of things, appears to be attested under Porphyry's name in John Lydus (*de Mens.* 138,18 Wünsch): 'Hestia is the substance-source, the cause of being for all things, situated in the Father.' The principle of the degradation of *ousia*, as it were, recurs very frequently, as for example in *Sententiae* 13: 'everything engendered is worse in its substance than that which engendered it (*pan to gennôn têi ousiâi autou kheiron autou gennâi)*', and recapitulated in *ad Gaurum* 54.11, 42.18 (Kalbfleisch): 'The products issued from the substance of a thing are always lower in rank with respect to power and substance than that which engendered them; they cannot be of the same *ousia* as the first generators'. This degradation of *ousia* in passing from the generator to the engendered corresponds to a progressive materialisation, as expressed in the following text of Porphyry, cited by Proclus, *in Tim.* 1.439.30 (Diehl): 'To the extent that intelligible *ousia* descends towards the world, it leads to a state of divided, dense, and material multiplicity, although above it was unified, indivisible, and single.' In this regard, *Sententiae* 11.3.5 (Mommert) speaks of a diminution (*huphesis*) of power in the progression towards individuality. The degrees of reality are presented as a hierarchy of *ousiai* (*Sententiae* 5, 10, 17, 22) and great importance is given to the manner in which each degree of *ousia* acquires its being (*kektêtai to einai; Sententiae* 4.9, 6.2, 27.4, 40.7 Mommert). This ontology corresponds rather well to the Porphyrian ontology as characterised by W. Theiler in his work *Porphyrios und Augustin* (Halle 1933, 11ff). It can in fact be traced again in Augustine, for example in the following text, which in a way appears to summarise what we have just read: 'For since God is the *highest essence*, that is to say, he is in the highest sense and is therefore unchangeable, he *gave being* to those things which he created from nothing, though not being in the highest sense (such as his own), but *gave more being* to some and to others less, and so *ordered natures by degrees of being* (*Cum enim deus summa essentia sit, hoc est summe sit, et ideo immutabilis sit, rebus quas ex nihilo creavit esse dedit, sed non summe esse, sicut est ipse, at aliis dedit esse amplius, aliis minus, atque ita naturas essentiarum gradibus ordinavit)*' (*de Civ. Dei* XII.2).

The second question we were to answer was: how does this evocation of the Plotinian doctrine of *ousia* permit the resolution of Plotinus' aporia concerning the unity of the concept of *ousia*? As mentioned above, the Plotinian doctrine of *ousia* allows different *ousiai* to be conceived of as deriving from and referring to a single principle. This is precisely what Dexippus' text asserts: 'If everything leads back to this principle of *ousia* because everything is suspended from it, the description of *ousia* (by Aristotle) can also provide a glimpse of the first principle of *ousia*.' The expressions 'leads back' and 'suspended' evoke the relation 'from one and to one' (*aph' henos kai pros hen*): the different levels of *ousiai* come from a single principle and refer to a single principle. This relation is what makes knowledge by analogy possible, and, as we shall see in the continuation of Dexippus' text, this is in fact the type of knowledge envisaged. This principle of analogy permits Aristotle's description of sensible *ousia* to be used to provide a glimpse of the original *ousia*. It is indeed a matter of description and not of definition (cf. Dexippus, *in Cat.* 44,11; for a clear distinction between definition and description, cf. Porphyry, ap. Simplicium *in Cat.* 30,13-15). The description of *ousia* in question is the one which Aristotle gives at *Categories* 2a11: 'Ousia in the most fundamental, first, and principal sense of the term is that which is neither said of a subject nor in a subject.' Dexippus in fact refers to this text several times when speaking of the description of *ousia* (cf. 42,2; 44,15 and 25). The Aristotelian description 'neither said of a subject nor in a subject' therefore gives us a glimpse of intelligible *ousia*. One can assume that, for Porphyry, these negative phrases take on a positive and fuller sense when referring to intelligible *ousia*. 'Not to be in a subject' means 'to be in itself and by itself', as he states in his *Sententiae* 39.35.2 (Mommert): ' "Being always at rest within itself" is predicated of the real being which subsists by itself (*tou de ontôs ontos kai kath' heauto huphestêkotos aülou to einai aei en heautôi hidrumenon*)'. One encounters traces of this transposition again in Simplicius, *in Cat.* 76,3: 'If the *ousia* which subsists by itself (*kath' hautên huphestôsa*) has need of nothing else and if all others have need of it, if this *ousia* communicates being absolutely to all the others, it is fitting that this *ousia* should be more honoured than the others.' With regard to 'not to be said of a subject', in the case of intelligible *ousia* this phrase means that it is absolutely one and identical, since *Categories* 1b6 states that what is numerically one is never said of a subject. Now, according to Plotinus himself, intelligible *ousia* is 'one and the same in number, not partitioned, but whole (*hen kai tauton arithmôi mê memerismenon, alla holon on*)' (6.5.3.19). One can thus say that the individuality and subsistence of sensible *ousia* are, as it were, only a reflection and trace of the indivisibility and the independence of intelligible *ousia*.

Dexippus' commentary then continues by proposing a new objection and a response to that objection (41,4). They are both inseparable from the discussion just considered. The latter, in fact, showed that from the perspective of Plotinus' philosophy the unity of the concept of *ousia* was acceptable. Yet to this solution Dexippus immediately raises the objection that one would expect, namely, that Plotinus' system has different premises from Aristotle's system. It would be necessary to begin with Aristotelian, and not Plotinian, premises in order to examine whether the Aristotelian concept of *ousia* offers a true unity of content:

> Had Aristotle used the same premises as Plotinus, what was just claimed would appear somewhat reasonable. Yet in actual fact it is by taking [reading *prolabôn* with MSS AM] Plotinus' dogmas for granted that you defend Aristotle. (Dexippus, *in Cat.* 41,4-6)

The answer to this objection will consist in showing that, correctly understood, Aristotle's philosophy agrees with Plotinus' philosophy, and that there is in Aristotle, as in Plotinus, a concept of an intelligible *ousia* which grounds both the being and the concept of sensible *ousia*. The present discussion, devoted to Aristotle, has the same structure as the one preceding devoted to Plotinus: (1) Aristotle accepts the existence of an intelligible *ousia*; (2) this intelligible *ousia* is the principle of unity for the different *ousiai* which come after it; and (3) this intelligible *ousia*, unknowable in itself, is known to us by analogy with sensible *ousia*. Here is the portion of Dexippus' text that corresponds to the first two points:

> Now for this question, I will appeal to what is said in the *Metaphysics*. For there are two *ousiai* according to Aristotle, the intelligible *ousia* and the sensible *ousia*; intermediate between these two is physical *ousia*. The *ousia* which is composite is sensible *ousia*; the *ousia* reduced to matter and form is physical *ousia*; the *ousia* above these is intellective and incorporeal *ousia*, which Aristotle often calls 'unmoved' on the one hand, and 'motive' on the other hand, in so far as it is the cause of specifically living movement.
>
> This is in fact what Aristotle demonstrated in Book 12 of the *Metaphysics* concerning these *ousiai*. And in this treatise he brought together the several *ousiai* into the total *ousia*. For he arranged them in a single system and traced them back to a single principle. For otherwise what will participate in the One, if *ousia* itself – that which has its being in the One – is deprived •of the internal cohesion which is attributed to the One? (Dexippus, *in Cat.* 41,7-18)

Let us say straight away that this discussion appears to be the work of Porphyry, as did the preceding one. In fact, from parallels to be found in Simplicius (77,4ff), we can again confirm the distortion which Iamblichus has inflicted on Porphyry's text. Dexippus' source refers to Book 12 of the *Metaphysics* and tells us explicitly that what it reports concerning the Aristotelian doctrine of *ousia* originates from this treatise. In this book of the *Metaphysics* (1069a30ff and 1071b3), one does in fact find the classification of *ousiai* which Dexippus' source mentions: a distinction between an unmoved *ousia* and a sensible or physical *ousia*, and then a distinction within the latter, that is, between sensible, corruptible *ousia* and truly physical, eternal *ousia*. The two sensible *ousiai* are the subject of physics, whereas unmoved *ousia* is the subject of a higher science. Now, in Simplicius the Aristotelian classification of *ousiai* distinguishes an intelligible *ousia*, a mathematical or psychical *ousia*, and a sensible *ousia*. This is the first distortion: this division is not to be found in book 12, but in Books 6 (1026a6-19) and 11 (1064b1-3). This division, and especially the close association of mathematical *ousia* and psychical *ousia*, is particularly dear to Iamblichus, as P. Merlan has shown (*From Platonism to Neoplatonism*, the Hague 1960, 11-33). Indeed, it appears that Iamblichus might have considered it unworthy of a Platonist to accept a classification of *ousiai* which did not make a place for the soul and *mathematica*. Porphyry, on the contrary had probably retained the classification of *ousiai* into the sensible, the physical, and the intelligible, because, as can be seen from the text of Dexippus, it allowed the systematisation of the different kinds of *ousia* which Plotinus, following Aristotle, had distinguished: composite *ousia* corresponded to sensible, corruptible *ousia; ousia* reduced to matter or to form corresponded to physical, incorruptible *ousia*, since matter and form, being incorporeals, were incorruptible and since, as they composed sensible *ousia*, they were the subject *par excellence* of physical science. Finally, unmoved *ousia* corresponded to intelligible and intellective *ousia*, since Aristotle showed in Book 12 that this *ousia* at its highest level was the Thinking of Thinking. By substituting for the classification of Book 12 a classification which made room for mathematical *ousia*, Iamblichus was no longer able to perform the systematisation which has just been described: *ousia* considered as matter or as form could not be assimilated to mathematical *ousia*. Iamblichus found in Porphyry's commentary the systematisation which makes composite *ousia* correspond to sensible *ousia, ousia* as matter or form to physical *ousia*, and intelligible *ousia* to unmoved motive *ousia*. No longer able to present this systematisation as Aristotle's as Porphyry had done, Iamblichus (77,7) did not hesitate to attribute it to Archytas, who actually had spoken (cf. Simplicius, *in Cat.* 76,20) of a sensible *ousia* and a physical *ousia* (without, however, distinguishing one from the other), as well as of an *ousia* conceived by the mind, though not, it appears, having said anything about a motive *ousia*, and still less an unmoved *ousia*.[1] Here we see the second distortion which Iamblichus has inflicted on Porphyry's text, by attributing to Archytas what Porphyry had presented, not unjustly, as Aristotelian.

To repeat, the distortions Iamblichus inflicted on Porphyry's text cause Porphyry's argument to lose all its vigour. What Porphyry wanted to show was that the systematisation of *ousiai* in Book 12 was not incompatible with the Plotinian doctrine of *ousia*. For this project it was completely irrelevant to show that Archytas also traced *ousiai* back to a single principle: this has nothing to do with the problem in question.

We know from Simplicius (*in Cael.* 503,34 and 506,13) that Porphyry had commented on Book 12 of the *Metaphysics*. The several lines we have just read in Dexippus allow us to form a general idea of this commentary. We saw how Porphyry drew a systematic correlation between sensible *ousia* and composite *ousia*, physical *ousia* and matter and form, unmoved *ousia* and intelligible *ousia*. This represents a certain systematisation and transformation of Aristotle's doctrine. In fact, Aristotle does not speak explicitly of physical *ousia*, but distinguishes two degrees of sensible *ousia*: corruptible sensible *ousia* and incorruptible sensible *ousia*. The first actually corresponds to *ousiai* composed of matter and form – Aristotle himself gives as an example plants and animals (1069a31) – incorruptible, or eternal, sensible *ousia* corresponds to the *ousiai* of the celestial, superlunary world. In Porphyry, on the other hand, the first category remains unchanged, but the second is called 'physical *ousia*' and is considered as the subject *par excellence* of the *Physics*. The latter, however, is no longer a matter of astronomy, as it is in Aristotle, but of the ultimate principles of the physical world, that is, matter and

---

[1] Parallel texts of Simplicius, *in Cat.* 77, 7-10 and 76,17-22 and Dexippus, *in Cat.* 41,9-12.

form. This is why Porphyry no longer speaks in this regard of sensible *ousia*, but of physical *ousia*, for matter and form are not sensible. Yet they are incorruptible. On this point, Porphyry might have thought that there was a short treatise of physics in Book 12 itself (1069b-1070a), since in that passage Aristotle showed how composite sensible *ousiai* presuppose matter and form and that the matter and form are ungenerated (1069b35). Matter and form, since they are ungenerated and therefore incorruptible, could thus correspond to incorruptible *ousia*, which is the subject-matter of the highest part of physics. With regard to the unmoved *ousia* of which Aristotle speaks (1069a34 and 1071b4), Porphyry gives it several names: 'intelligible', 'intellective', 'incorporeal', 'unmoved' and 'motive'. This group of names can already be found in the description which Alexander of Aphrodisias gives of Aristotle's first cause (*Quaest.* 3,20-4,25). He therefore conforms to the Aristotelian tradition, and one actually re-encounters the description of Aristotle's Prime Mover in Book 12. None of these names poses difficulties for a Platonist except 'mover', which could apply to the soul, the principle of movement for the body, but applies only with difficulty to an intelligible *ousia* that is pure thought. Porphyry therefore tries to explain this phrase in a manner satisfactory to a Platonist by saying that intelligible *ousia* is motive to the degree that it is the cause of life, which is movement: 'insofar as it is the cause of movement specified as living'. This interpretation agrees with the definition of the Prime Mover as a perfect, eternal living being, whose life consists in its own acts of intellection (1072b26).

The last lines of the text of Dexippus we are commenting on reveal in an extremely interesting manner how Porphyry interpreted the whole of Book 12 from a Plotinian perspective. For a pupil of Plotinus, the intelligible, unmoved, motive *ousia* of Aristotle corresponds to the second hypostasis, that is, to Intellect. Beyond this first *ousia*, there was the One, the absolutely simple principle of *ousia*. In Porphyry's eyes, the Aristotelian doctrine of *ousia* presupposes and ultimately entails the Plotinian One. In fact, Book 12 of Aristotle's *Metaphysics* proposes a system of *ousiai*, a system whose unity and coherence are assured by a single and first principle, intelligible *ousia*. Now, according to a fundamental axiom of Neoplatonism, which can be found already in Plotinus (5.6.3.1-23; 6.6.13.17ff), every ordered multiplicity, every 'system', presupposes the transcendent One whose unity grounds the possibility of that order. Hence the system of *ousia* implies the transcendence of the One. There must be a system of *ousiai*, that is, different *ousiai* must form an ordered and unified multiplicity, since, as Porphyry tells us, *ousia* has its being in the One. The formula probably alludes to two Plotinian concepts. First of all, it recalls the Plotinian principle: 'All beings have their being from the One' (6.9.1.1; 5.1.7.15; 5.5.6.14ff). Secondly, it might be an allusion to the exegesis which Plotinus gives of *Timaeus* 37D6, when he says that eternity (here assimilated to intelligible *ousia*) remained 'within the One' (*en heni*). Porphyry (*Sent.* 44.21 and 45.2-3) will later use the expression again: in accordance with the One, within the One (*kath' hen, en heni*). Therefore, if the *ousia* which is so close to the One, since it has its being in the One, were not unified, were not coherent and did not form a system, what then would participate in the One? The whole would be completely scattered and rent. It may legitimately be supposed that Porphyry had attempted to redis-cover this Plotinian doctrine in Book 12 of the *Metaphysics*. The last chapter of Aristotle's book, in fact, permits the notion that in the nature of the whole the Good was both something separate, existing by itself and in itself, and the order of the whole (1074a11). A Plotinian might have been able to recognise in this Good, existing by itself and in itself, the One which is the principle of universal order and especially of the system of *ousia*. The last chapter of this book insisted precisely on the internal cohesiveness of *ousia*: 'Those who want mathematical number to be the first reality – and thus always accept one *ousia* after another and always different principles for each of these *ousiai* – render the *ousia* of the All incoherent (*epeisodiôdê*); for one substance in no way affects another by its existence or non-existence, and they accept a multiplicity of principles. Yet the beings do not wish to be badly governed: "Government by many is not good; One should be sovereign" ' (1075b38). We can discern this Aristotelian sentence behind Porphyry's discussion: 'He has ordered the *ousiai* into a single system and has traced them back to a single principle. For what then will participate in the One, if *ousia* itself – that which has its being in the One – is deprived of the internal cohesiveness which is attributed to the One?' Thus it can be shown by what reasoning it was possible for Porphyry to give a Plotinian interpretation of Book 12.

The last part of Dexippus' text (41,18-42,3) is devoted to the relation – whether homonymy, synonymy, or analogy – which unites the different *ousiai* and most especially to the manner in which we know intelligible *ousia*; this was the third point we distinguished above (p. 132):

> Most certainly intelligibles are ineffable: he therefore uses the term *ousia* in accordance with metaphor and analogy with things knowable through sensation.
>
> For all things which share the same name do so in three ways: homonymously, synonymously, and in accordance with the relation of the proper sense to the metaphorical sense–homonymously, as the foot of a tool stands in relation to the feet of other instruments; synonymously, as when one says that a sword is sharper than another sword and a voice is sharper than another voice (but not that a sword is sharper than a voice, since the quality 'sharp' is different in one and in the other); and by the relation 'proper-metaphorical', as for example with our foot and the foot of mountains.
>
> Intelligibles, thus, are ineffable: it is therefore metaphorically that Aristotle uses the word *ousia*, bringing us to know imperceptible things with the help of things that are sensible and perceived by us.
>
> In fact, just as *ousia* will be homonymous in relation to intelligible *ousia* (because it only means intelligible *ousia* by pure analogy), so too *ousia* will be synonymous in relation to physical *ousia*, because it means physical *ousia* in virtue of the fact that it is composite.

For, in the same way that Aristotle in the treatises of the *Physics* (or: *Metaphysics*?) calls a certain incorporeal *ousia* 'body' – calling it incorporeal because it proceeds from intellective *ousia*, but asserting further that it possesses the being of body since it is already in movement towards sensible *ousia* – so too, by saying that this *ousia* is synonymous in relation to physical *ousia*, though homonymous in relation to intelligible *ousia*, he makes the other *ousiai* known through sensible *ousia* and above all makes it known that the description which relates to sensible *ousia* – 'neither said of a subject nor in a subject' – can also apply to the other *ousiai*. (Dexippus, *in Cat.* 41,18-42,3)

This text develops, within the framework of the general interpretation previously given of Book 12, the doctrine of the analogy of the concept of *ousia*, which, we have seen, concluded the exposition of the Plotinian doctrine of *ousia*. Here and there, one re-encounters the claim: it is possible to extend the Aristotelian description of *ousia* ('not being in a subject, not being said of a subject') to all *ousiai*, even to intelligible *ousia*. This possibility is grounded precisely in the fact that the different *ousiai* are unified in intelligible *ousia*, which is their principle.

There are, therefore, the following relations between the different *ousiai*. Sensible or composite *ousia* is synonymous in relation to physical *ousia*, that is, *ousia* considered as matter or as form. Sensible or composite *ousia* is homonymous in relation to intelligible *ousia*, this homonymy not being complete, however, since it is compatible with an analogical relation. This doctrine is implicitly presented as Aristotelian. It can in fact be justified by the Aristotelian division of the sciences. The *Physics* has for its subject form, matter, and the composite of the two – thus, on the one hand, physical *ousia*, and on the other hand, composite or sensible *ousiai* (*Phys.* 194a12). First Philosophy, by contrast, has as its subject the 'separated' (*khôriston*), that is, intelligible *ousia* (*Phys.* 194b14). The synonymy of the *ousiai* that are the subject of the *Physics* is grounded in the concrete unity of *phusis*, the principle of movement and formal principle of natural *ousiai* (*Metaph.* 5.4, 1014b35; 12.3, 1070a5ff; *Cael.* 1.8, 276b1-6). On the contrary, the homonymy between sensible *ousia* and intelligible *ousia*, that is, between the subject of the *Physics* and the subject of First Philosophy, corresponds to the total difference of principles that exists between sensible *ousia* and intelligible *ousia*, (*Metaph.* 12.1, 1069b1; 4, 1070b15-20). That this homonymy is not absolute, but permits an analogical relation, results from the discussions of analogy contained in Book 12 (1070b30-1071b3). What grounds the analogy is the very fact that all the *ousiai* refer ultimately to intelligible *ousia*, from which they originate. The analogical relation thus tends to be confused with the relation 'from one and to one' (*aph' henos kai pros hen*), although this relation is not made explicit either in Aristotle or in Porphyry. In any case, in Porphyry's eyes, by affirming that there is an analogical relation between sensible *ousia* and intelligible *ousia*, Aristotle is in profound agreement with Plotinus, who writes in his treatise 'On the genera of being' (6.3.5.3): 'This is what must be said about *ousia* here below; does all this suit *ousia* in the higher world? Perhaps, but it is by analogy and homonymously (*kat' analogian kai homônumôs*)'.

We have just mentioned analogical relation. Dexippus' text seems to confuse this with metaphor, since, before telling us that composite *ousia* stands in analogical relation to intelligible *ousia*, he declares that Aristotle uses the term *ousia* 'in accordance with metaphor and analogy' in order to speak of intelligible substance. In fact, in his commentary in question and answer form on the *Categories* (66,34), Porphyry points out that Atticus classes analogy and metaphor together. He does not himself distinguish between the two either, but in the same commentary (67,4) he takes care to distinguish between metaphor and homonymy: homonymy occurs when a single term designates different things, without there being a distinct word to designate these things: for example, with the 'foot' of a bed and the 'foot' of a table; metaphor occurs when the same term designates different things, even though there is a distinct word to name them, as, for example, with the 'foot' of a mountain (since the word *hupôreia* designates this) and the 'foot' of a ship (since the term *pêdalion* designates this). As Simplicius remarks (*in Cat.* 33,11), Porphyry appears to have given up this kind of distinction between homonymy and metaphor in his greater commentary addressed to Gedalius, since in that work he gave the foot of the ship as an example of homonymy and the foot of the mountain as an example of metaphor. One can perhaps recognise the traces of the commentary to Gedalius in Dexippus' text, where the foot of the mountain is given as an example of metaphor and the feet of different machines or tools (probably with the foot of the ship contained in this category) as an example of homonymy. One might even think that Porphyry had been led to modify his theory of metaphor and homonymy because of the doctrine of *ousia*. If sensible *ousia* and intelligible *ousia* are homonyms, they are still not only that, for there also exists a relation of analogy and metaphor between them. In that case, if the definition of metaphor proposed in the question and answer commentary were applied, one could not say that there was a metaphorical relation between the two *ousiai*, since it would be necessary to assume that there was a distinct term for designating intelligible *ousia*. Now, the doctrine expounded in our text consists solely in the assertion that there is no name properly belonging to intelligibles: they are ineffable. It is necessary, therefore, to accept that a metaphor can apply to something which has no distinct name.

Intelligibles are ineffable precisely because they are imperceptible. All of our language originates from sensation (Porphyry *in Cat.* 91,8 and 20). The word '*ousia*', therefore, can only properly designate the sensible individual, and therefore composite *ousia*. In applying the term '*ousia*' to intelligible *ousia*, one is only using it as a metaphor.

This doctrine is never stated explicitly by Aristotle: the Greek terms corresponding to 'ineffable' and 'imperceptible' do not even belong to his vocabulary. At the very most, one can note that Aristotle time and again (*An. Post.* 1.2, 71b33; *Phys.* 1.1, 184a16; *Metaph.* 2.1, 993b9; 7.3,

1029b3-12) asserts that what is knowable in itself is, in relation to us, the most difficult to know, and that we must seek to attain it by beginning with that which is more easily knowable for us, that is, with that which can be grasped by sensation. The doctrine can nevertheless be developed from Aristotelian principles. Theophrastus comes very close to it in his *Metaphysics* (9a18): 'If there exist certain things that are only knowable in that they are unknowable, as some maintain, the manner of inquiry into them would be one peculiar to them, but needs some care to distinguish it from others; though perhaps, in cases where it is possible, it is more appropriate to describe them *by analogy* than by the very fact that they are unknown – as if one were to describe the invisible by the mere fact that it is invisible.' Traces of this doctrine are re-encountered in Albinus (*Didask.* 165,17 Hermann). Yet curiously it is in Porphyry himself that we again find the general system in which this doctrine is integrated most clearly expressed. For Porphyry, the incorporeals are defined only by a negative method (*Sent.* 19, 27, 35 and 38): their name is fixed by saying what they are not, without our being able to define what they are. One can equally define them by the method of attributing antithetical predicates ('everywhere – nowhere', for example). There is a complete reversal of perspective once we pass from the sensible to the intelligible or vice versa: the intelligible is nothing in relation to the sensible, the sensible is nothing in relation to the intelligible. It is therefore a genuine negative theology that is applied to the intelligible.[2] This is completely different from Plotinus, who restricts the methods of negative theology to knowledge of the One and never stretches the opposition between the intelligible and the sensible to the point of making each the negation of the other.

It remains then to explain Dexippus' curious allusion to a text of Aristotle's in which the latter might have called a certain incorporeal *ousia* a 'body'. Even the sense of the allusion is double. To begin with, in the immediate context, it illustrates the double relation of sensible *ousia* to physical *ousia* and to intelligible *ousia*. Sensible *ousia* is synonymous with physical *ousia*, but is homonymous to intelligible *ousia*, that is, the term '*ousia*' is transferred from sensible *ousia* (where it is employed in a proper manner) to intelligible *ousia*, because the latter is the principle of sensible *ousia*. In the same way, the incorporeal *ousia* of which Aristotle is said to speak could be called both 'body' and 'incorporeal': 'incorporeal' synonymously with intelligible *ousia*, from which it originated, but 'body' homonymously, since body and sensible *ousia* originate from it. The term 'body', when applied to this incorporeal *ousia*, would be metaphorical, just as '*ousia*' is when applied to intelligible reality. A second reason motivates this curious citation of Aristotle. Plotinus had objected to the Aristotelian doctrine of *ousia* that if sensible *ousia* and intelligible *ousia* had something in common, then the incorporeal would be body and body incorporeal as a result (cf. p. 126 above). Porphyry appears, therefore, to be

[2] cf. P. Hadot, *Porphyre et Victorinus*, Paris 1968, 110 and 420.

responding here to this objection by saying: it is possible to call the incorporeal 'body' – Aristotle himself has done it – but using 'body' homonymously and metaphorically; it is in precisely the same way that the word *'ousia'* is applied to the intelligible.

To which text of Aristotle's is Porphyry alluding? To judge by the explanation which Porphyry offers of the text, Aristotle spoke of a reality which was placed between intelligible, intellective *ousia* and sensible *ousia*. In Aristotle's system, this substance is very probably that of the Heavens, whose description in the *de Caelo* (1.9, 279a19ff) might cause a Neoplatonist to think that this was an incorporeal *ousia*.[3] Now this reality was quite clearly presented by Aristotle as a body (*Cael.* 1.9, 278b10ff). Yet according to Dexippus' text, Porphyry apparently alluded to a passage in the *Metaphysics*. In Book 12, there is a single passage (1074a30) where there is a question of 'divine bodies' carried in the heavens. It is not very likely that it was this passage to which Porphyry alluded: the relation of these bodies to an incorporeal *ousia* is hardly sugested by the context. One may ask, therefore, whether it might not be necessary to read 'in the *Physics*' in place of 'in the *Metaphysics*'. Note moreover that Dexippus always introduces a citation of the *Metaphysics* with *'en têi'* and a citation of the *Physics* with *'en tois'*. The expression *'en tois Phusikois'*, in Aristotelian usage could designate the *de Caelo* (*Metaph.* 1.8, 989a24), among other works. Porphyry might therefore be making an allusion to this treatise in which the first body presents the properties of a divine being, on which the being and life of each thing depends, and which moves itself endlessly in a circular motion (279a11-b3). One might even wonder whether Porphyry had a precise text of the *de Caelo* in mind, in which a textual error justified his interpretation. Note that in a discussion devoted to the first body, Aristotle uses the following formula: 'that there is naturally some corporeal *ousia* which is different from all the other structures here, and which is more divine and prior to all of these (*hoti pephuke tis ousia sômatos allê para tas entautha sustaseis, theiotera kai protera toutôn hapantôn)*' (269a30). Porphyry might have read: 'some incorporeal *ousia* (*tis ousia asômatos)*'. Whatever it was, here there is again a glimpse of a fascinating Neoplatonic exegesis of Aristotle's system. The first mobile (*Cael.* 288b1) proceeds from the incorporeal *ousia* and, by its movement, initiates the procession towards sensible *ousia*. It is in exactly the same situation as the soul in the Neoplatonic system.

Dexippus appears, therefore, to have preserved in his commentary on the *Categories* a precious testimony of the manner in which Porphyry was able to comment on Book 12 of the *Metaphysics*, while seeking to interpret Aristotle's philosophy in order to set it in harmony with

---

[3] Notably 279a19ff: 'Hence the upper things are by nature neither in a place nor caused by time to grow old, nor is there any change in anything beyond the outermost motion, but they spend their entire duration unchanged and unaffected, having the best and most self-sufficient life .... On them depend the rest – some more clearly, others dimly – for life and existence'.

Plotinus' philosophy. Certain indications permit a glimpse even of Porphyry's rediscovery of the doctrine of the transcendent One in Book 12 of the *Metaphysics*. If that is true, there is something of a paradox about a pupil of Plotinus rediscovering in Aristotle the very doctrine which Plotinus expressly reproaches Aristotle for having ignored.

CHAPTER SEVEN

Porphyry's legacy to logic: a reconstruction

Sten Ebbesen

1. Introduction

Porphyry's importance as an Aristotelian commentator has been a commonplace for a long time. He is generally recognised as the great sifter of the tradition, so that the history of the commentaries may be represented schematically as follows

ante-Porphyrian works

\\\ | / /

Porphyry

/ / | \\\

post-Porphyrian works

This means that whatever ante-Porphyrian materials are found in later commentaries came to them via Porphyry. Of course, this cannot be true without modifications, but it is obvious from a reading of the preserved commentaries on the *Organon* that the stemma works in a great many cases.

This much is fairly uncontroversial. The evaluation of Porphyry's activity as a scholastic logician is less so. One question which I find interesting is whether the works quarried by posterity were like much of their offspring in being jumbles of scholia containing tantalisingly

---

* In the footnotes, these special abbreviations are used:

CLCAG = Sten Ebbesen, *Commentators and Commentaries on Aristotle's Sophistici Elenchi*, 3 vols, Corpus Latinum Commentariorum in Aristotelem Graecorum 7.1-3, Leiden 1981.

Comm. 2 = a Byzantine commentary on Aristotle's *Sophistici Elenchi*, excerpts from which are edited in *CLCAG* 7, vol. 2.

ps.-Alex.-1 *in SE* = The final version of Michael of Ephesus' commentary on Arist. *SE*, published as *Alexandri quod fertur in Aristotelis Sophisticos Elenchos commentarium*, ed. Maximilianus Wallies, Commentaria in Aristotelem Graeca 2.3, Berlin 1898.

disconnected pieces of logico-semantical theory. The question has received little attention.[1] In my opinion, his major commentaries, like the great one on the *Categories* and the one on *de Interpretatione*, are likely to have differed from their offspring in this respect.

Now, suppose (1) that some of the most important and tantalising bits of doctrine found in later authors should be traced back to Porphyry's works. Suppose (2) that he had a coherent – if not entirely consistent – set of views on questions of logic. Suppose further (3), that his voluminous production contained not only more details than the less extensive works of later scholars, but also some better indications of the mutual dependence of the sundry pieces of logical theory. If all three suppositions are granted, it follows that such later scholars as had access to Porphyry's own writings would have known and presumably found acceptable the systematic context of the fragments of doctrine which they themselves chose to transmit to posterity. If only the two first suppositions are granted, it still follows that a systematic understanding of the fragments presupposes an understanding of Porphyry's theory – unless, indeed, the later authors managed to have an essentially different theory while still having a place for items that fitted into Porphyry's as well.

The nature of our sources makes it very difficult to produce convincing support of supposition (3). The greatest obstacle is the loss of all Porphyry's commentaries except for the concise *Introduction to the Categories* (the '*Isagoge*') and the equally concise minor commentary on the same work. But at least the preserved writings and the reports of the lost ones point to a high degree of consistency. This raises hope that we may successfully reconstruct some main outlines of his logical theory in accordance with supposition (2). I shall try to do so and to show that supposition (1) receives support from the fact that several important items of later commentaries do actually become intelligible when placed in a Porphyrian framework.

Since the purpose of this chapter is primarily to elucidate pieces of doctrine that have to do with fallacies, it is, of course, important to know whether Porphyry ever wrote a commentary on the *Elenchi*. There are signs that he did so;[2] but the problem is not quite as acute as it might seem, for the affiliation of the *Elenchi* scholia that I am going to discuss is generally such that if they do not stem from Porphyry's notes on that work, they certainly count scholia of his on other books of the *Organon* among their ancestors. One thing is known with certainty: Porphyry on several occasions stressed the role of concepts in the semantic process. He considered vocal discourse as a sign of mental discourse and the principal

---

[1] The best attempt to reconstruct a coherent Porphyry is by A.C. Lloyd, 'Neoplatonic and Aristotelian logic', *Phronesis* 1, 1956, 58-72 & 146-60. Porphyry's logic is also treated in Bent Dalsgaard-Larsen, *Jamblique de Chalcis: exégète et philosophe*, Diss., Århus 1972, ch. 5, but his approach is so fundamentally different from mine that it would make no sense to polemicise against details of his interpretation. I must leave it to the reader to judge whose reconstruction of Porphyry is the most convincing.

[2] See *CLCAG* 7, ch. 5.4.

terms (words) of a vocal proposition (sentence) as signs of terms (concepts) of the mental proposition. Words signify things only via the concepts. It is also clear that 'concepts' are somebody's concepts, not self-subsistent entities independent of their human possessors. I shall come back to the evidence for this later, but first some general considerations.

By stressing the role of concepts in the semantic process Porphyry shows that he had successfully resisted the temptation felt by many logicians to eliminate the human users of language. Can we use our knowledge of this fact as a clue to his logic? I think we can.

One natural consequence of saying that signification depends on concepts and that concepts are somebody's concepts is that an analysis of language is something distinct from an analysis of the nature of things. Studying the way language is used we study the ways in which concepts are expressed but not the structure of reality. We may reach an insight into the manner in which reality is conceptualised, and that will be reflected in language, but logic cannot get us nearer to reality than this. That is, logic does not comprise ontology.

Another consequence is this: vocal language must be public and it must be possible to identify concepts across the boundaries of individual minds. Otherwise communication would break down.

Further, and for the same reason, people must be assumed to have a tendency to link concepts in the same way, so that it is possible to cross-identify their conceptualised reality. But it must also be possible for some individual to link concepts in a way that does not correspond to reality as commonly conceptualised. If this were not the case, concepts would be an otiose element in the semantic model. But this being so, it is natural to hold that truth and falsity are primarily properties of mental propositions, wrongly linked concepts constituting false propositions, whereas vocal sentences are not strictly speaking true or false. They may be called so only in the sense that they are correct expressions, according to common usage, of true or false mental propositions.

On the other hand, we may expect a Porphyrian logician to hold that ambiguity is a property of words and sentences, not of mental language. Holding that a concept could be ambiguously related to things would imply a claim that we can know more about the things than our concepts give us. Within the framework of this kind of logic, the claim is hardly acceptable, whereas it is perfectly possible that one element of vocal language can express several elements of mental language.

Ambiguity, then, will be a property of expressions and dependent on a conventional use of one such expression to signify several concepts or combinations of concepts. – A conventional use, I say, because with signification depending on the way people understand expression, i.e. the way they relate them to their concepts, it is reasonable, though not strictly necessary, to consider vocal language as man-made and usage as a matter of convention. – But it is also reasonable to assume that many features of this conventional language can be explained genetically as resulting from the way in which the concepts it is designed to express are formed.

In the main, I think, the texts bear out the above expectations concerning Porphyry's views. I shall try to show that he considered Aristotelian logic as an instrument designed to deal with the language whose primary function is to describe the commonly conceptualised sensible world, and that he thought the instrument could be used for such purposes without clashing with Platonic ontology. I think his position can be compared to the way many modern people view Einsteinian and Newtonian physics. They accept the former as the comprehensive theory and the latter as a useful theory for limited purposes, which, however, happens to be of particular importance for normal life. And as long as the less comprehensive theory is applied within the proper confines, there is nothing wrong about accepting it. In the same way, I suggest, Porphyry assigned the little corner of the universe that interests most men as a sphere of operation for Aristotelian logic on the condition that it must not extend its field of operation to ontology proper which can be investigated only in Platonic terms.

Besides this, I shall try to show that Porphyry had consistent or at least interconnected theories to explain phenomena falling within the domain encompassed in his view by Aristotelian logic, and, in particular, that he had a theory concerning the rise of concepts which he connected with a genetic account of the rise of vocal language; that he considered ambiguity a property of expressions and truth as a property of mental propositions, primarily at least. Finally, I shall try to show how Porphyrian theory and the problems that interested him lived on – though more or less maimed – constituting an important factor in the shaping of the Greek scholastic tradition in many fields, and with important consequences for the treatment of fallacies as well.

If the picture of Porphyry that arises from the reconstruction should remind anybody of William of Ockham or John Buridan, that will hardly be fortuitous. I find that on many basic points the three philosophers agree so closely that in matters where our knowledge of the medieval thinkers surpasses what we know of their ancient predecessor we may use them as guides to the reconstruction of his thought. This is not to say that I have deliberately tried to model Porphyry in the likeness of Buridan or Ockham, but they have no doubt had an influence on my conception of what logic with such basic tenets must be like. If anybody should think it incredible that the so-called 'nominalism' was to any important degree a revival of Porphyrian thought, the reply is that this is not so very incredible: fourteenth-century philosophers were busy readers of such late pupils of Porphyry's as Ammonius, Simplicius and Boethius. Porphyrian logic was as accessible to late medieval men as it is to us, though they knew less about the provenance of what they read. There is nothing incredible in the idea that men with the flair for consistency that Buridan possessed should have picked up from the ancient sources exactly such materials as had belonged in the context of one coherent logic, namely Porphyry's.

2. The harmony of Plato and Aristotle

Porphyry's basically friendly attitude towards Aristotelian logic is beyond doubt. He wrote commentaries and companions to several parts of the *Organon*,[3] and the preserved part of his work shows that he was not polemical. That he thought Platonism and Aristotelism to be compatible, at least to a high degree, is demonstrated by the fact that he wrote a work in seven books to show that the two philosophical systems are really one and the same (*Peri tou mian einai tên Platônos kai Aristotelous hairesin*).[4] To be sure, he also wrote a treatise *On What Separates Plato from Aristotle (Peri diastaseôs Platônos kai Aristotelous)*,[5] but we have no reason to believe it was anti-Aristotelian. It was written for the benefit of the same Chrysaorius for whom he composed the *Introduction to the Categories*, so in all likelihood it was a short treatise designed to show that the two men's different approaches to philosophy did not amount to a radical disagreement.

Of course, Porphyry was not blind to the differences between Plato and Aristotle; he just did not think that the peculiarities of the latter's philosophy were such as to make his words worthless to the Platonist. A few passages from the *Isagoge* and the minor commentary on the *Categories* should suffice to delineate his attitude:

A Platonist need not disagree with Aristotle's claim that 'being' (*to on*) is equivocal. Plotinus did not, Pletho – much later – did.[6] But surely one does not expect a Platonist to mention the Aristotelian doctrine without any kind of comment. Yet, Porphyry quietly remarks:[7] 'As being is equivocal, in Aristotle's opinion, [...] therefore he talks first of equivocals' (i.e. therefore the *Categories* treat of equivocals before univocals).

Most Platonists have found it shocking that Aristotle ranks abstracts as secondary substances and sensible entities as primary substances.[8] Porphyry's remarks on the question reveal much, I think, about the way he viewed Aristotelian logic.

Of course, he says,[9] intelligible entities like the intelligible god and the intellect and the ideas – if in fact ideas exist (*eiper eisin ideai*) – are primary. But that is no real argument against Aristotle's terminology, which is quite justified in its context. The theme of the *Categories* is significative expressions and the classification of realities they indicate; but men started by giving names to the things they saw and felt; linguistic occupations with the entities that are naturally prior, but posterior with respect to the senses was a secondary event. So, in relation

---

[3] cf. Ebbesen, 'Anonymus Aurelianensis II, Aristotle, Alexander, Porphyry and Boethius. Ancient scholasticism and twelfth-century Western Europe', *Cahiers de l'Institut du moyen âge grec et latin (CIMAGL)*, University of Copenhagen, 16, 1976, 11.

[4] See J. Bidez, *Vie de Porphyre le philosophe néo-platonicien*, Gand-Leipzig 1913, 68*.

[5] ibid.

[6] Plotinus 6.1.1; Pletho *de Diff.* ch. 3 *PG* 160:893-6.

[7] Porph. *in Cat.* 61,10-12.

[8] Thus Plotinus 6.3.9; Pletho *de Diff.* ch. 4 *PG* 160:896-7.

[9] Porph. *in Cat.* 91,14ff.

to the significative expressions, individuals and sensible substances are the primary ones, even though the intelligible ones are so from the perspective of nature.

The main point in this passage is clear: the doctrine of the *Categories* does not have universal application, but within its own confines it is valid.

A little bit of extrapolation leads to the conclusion that Porphyry thought of the whole of Aristotelian logic in that way. There is evidence[10] that he (like many later commentators) considered the *Organon* as a systematic whole moving from simple expressions in the *Categories* to compound expressions (sentences/propositions/premisses) in the *de Interpretatione* and to compounds of sentences (syllogisms) in the *Prior Analytics*, and thence to the several kinds of syllogisms dealt with in the *Posterior Analytics*, the *Topics* and the *Sophistici Elenchi*.

So, the whole of logic is a study of the properties of extramental language considered as an instrument basically used to comment upon the world of experience.[11] This is why there cannot be a clash between Aristotelian logic and Platonic metaphysics as long as the logician works within the confines of his art.

The same attitude is manifest in the proem of the *Isagoge* where Porphyry says that although he is going to write about genus and species, he will not treat the difficult question of their mode of existence. He just wants to indicate what older philosophers, and in particular the Peripatetics, have said about them from a logical point of view.[12] The implication must be that as long as you do not confuse it with metaphysics, Aristotelian logic is both a useful discipline and one that does not clash with Platonism.

Again, talking about *differentiae*, Porphyry explains why a genus cannot have the differentiae of its subordinate species actually, but only potentially. He does not even mention that Platonists have another opinion. Only the presence of an unobtrusive 'as they [i.e. the Aristotelians] claim' hints at the possibility that their claim may not have universal validity.[13]

3. The rise of language and the formation of concepts

Concept-formation and the naming of concepts were closely related processes in Porphyry's view. We have rather good information on the question, but I must begin by mentioning one difficulty. It is this:

Whereas later reports and echoes of his logical writing state in an unequivocal way that he paid great attention to the role of concepts in the semantic process, the most important of his extant works for the present

---

[10] ibid. 56,23-p.57.

[11] cf. Simpl. *in Cat.* 9-13.

[12] Porph. *Isag.* 1,15 *logikôteron* [...] *dielabon*; I do not think Boethius' translation 'probabiliter [...] tractaverunt' hits the mark, though he argues well for it in his *in Isag.*[2] I, ch. 12 p. 168 (Brandt). Ammonius *in Isag.* 44-5 takes my view.

[13] Porph. *Isag.* 10,22-11,6. Cf. the judicious remarks in Ammonius *in Isag.* 101-5.

purpose does not even contain the word *noêma* ('concept'). Why is it that the minor commentary on the *Categories* generally treats of signification as a direct relation of expressions to things? Does it belong to some phase of his philosophical development other than the great commentaries on the *Categories* and *de Interpretatione*? Hardly so. A much simpler solution imposes itself. The preserved commentary on the *Categories* is of a decidedly compendious character. The author felt it was important that people – and in particular the individual for whose benefit the work was written – should not think that the *Categories* is a treatise 'On What There Is', because interpreted as metaphysics its doctrine cannot be reconciled with Platonism. But to drive home this point he had no need to expatiate on concepts as the immediate significates of expressions. To produce a compendium of a reasonable size he had to sacrifice something, and he chose to sacrifice the concepts. They do not occur under their own name in the book, though there are some passages in which they are hinted at. In exactly the same manner he does not introduce the technical term *akatataktos* (unranked) which he is known to have used in the lost major commentary. Furthermore, as there is hardly a place in which his argument would be spoilt if it were complicated by the insertion of concepts as a link between expressions and things, I feel convinced that we are entitled to take what he says in the concept-less commentary as part of the same theory that he defended in his other writings. The following reconstruction of Porphyrian semantics presupposes that all statements about words and things can, and should, be regarded as abbreviated statements about words, concepts and things.

I shall use the following conventions:

<dog>   = a thing which is a dog
/dog/   = a concept of a dog
[dog]   = the word 'dog'

Some central pieces of Porphyrian semantics are describable by means of a genetic model of the rise of concepts and language. I shall call the theory behind that model 'the theory of imposition'. Porphyry gives a short version of it in the minor commentary on the *Categories*.[14] It can be read as an historical account implying that at some definite time men introduced all the words that refer to sensible reality, and at some later time they resolved to introduce the vocabulary used to speak of the primary language. Some later commentators took this to be Porphyry's intention,[15] but they were surely wrong. What he meant was rather that there are certain natural steps in the development of our stock of concepts and words. Objects must be sensed and conceptualised before anybody can speak about them. The use of class-names presupposes a process of abstraction. A meta-language has no sense unless there is an

[14] Porph. *in Cat.* 57-8.
[15] See *CLCAG* 7, ch. 4.4.8.

object-language. Whether or not the historical development of the Greek language has any similarity to the process described in the model is really irrelevant.

On the following pages I shall reconstruct a fuller version of the theory of imposition than any that occurs in the sources. It will be a version that Porphyry perhaps never wrote, but not, I hope, one he would have rejected.[16]

The theory takes for granted that men have sense-perception of perceptible objects. If some more comprehensive metaphysical theory were to claim that the sensible world is not really real, it does not matter in this connection. For the present purpose the sensible world is supposed to be real and prior to our perception of it and to our conceptualising of the percepts. If the metaphysical theory were to claim that the sensible world is an illusion, the logician is entitled to say, 'All right, but for practical purposes we need a theory which treats the illusion as if it were a reality; and nothing, of course, prevents us from adding a qualification like "as it seems" whenever we say "real" '.

Suppose, then, that we have got a social group of some people. They come across an object. They perceive it and they straightaway get a concept of that individual object. They somehow establish the convention that when one wants to externalise his own concept and evoke the corresponding one in another member of the group, he just has to say [dog].

For the theory to work it must be supposed that it is possible to identify one man's concepts with another's. Porphyry actually made that assumption, as we shall see later.

It is now time to introduce some essentials of the terminology used by Porphyry and 'Porphyrian' philosophers in the context of the theory.[17]

---

[16] Porph. *Isag.* (in particular pp. 6-7); Porph. *in Cat.* (in particular pp. 57-8, 75, 81, 90-1); Porph. *in Cat. ad Gedalium* ap. Simplicium *in Cat.* 53 & 79 are the main sources for the following. Many details have been filled in with the help of Dexippus *in Cat.* (in particular pp. 7-16) and Simplicius *in Cat.* (in particular 10,20–13,18; I hold that Simplicius' interpretation of Porphyry is correct). By using Dexippus and Simplicius I run the risk of attributing to Porphyry views that were Iamblichus' and not his; but, on the whole, Iamblichus will not have deviated from Porphyry (cf. Simpl. *in Cat.* 2,9ff). On imposition, see Porph. *in Cat.* 57-8; Dexippus *in Cat.* 11-16; Ammonius *in Cat.* 11; Simplicius *in Cat.* 15; Boethius *in Cat.* PL 64:159. Sources for details will be given in subsequent notes.

[17] The following is a selection of passages containing semantic terms. More may be found via the indexes of *CAG*. As for terms for mental and oral discourse, see *CLCAG* 7, ch. 4.3.6. *dēloun* Porph. *in Cat.* 57,7-8, 20-2; 58,12-14; 60,16-19 [≈ Simpl. *in Cat.* 22,15ff]; Dexippus *in Cat.* 11,14-15; 11,28; 19,20-2. *ekpherô* Porph. *in Cat.* 107,35; 112,17-20; 115,31; Simplicius *in Cat.* 155,6; 160,1; ps.-Alex.-1 *in SE* 23,13. On the Stoic use of the word: Ammon. *in An. Pr.* 68,4-6 ≈ Philoponus *in An. Pr.* 243,1-4; cf. Dionysius Halicarnass., *de Compositione Verborum* ch. 8, secs 45-6, p. 32 (Usener-Radermacher). *ekphônein* Porph. *in Cat.* 115,25; Simplicius *in Cat.* 64,26; 132,9-12; ps.-Philoponus *in An. Post.* 421,3-4; ps.-Alex.-1 *in SE* 23,8; 28,27-8; 36,15. *(ex)angellein* Porph. *in Cat.* 58,23; Nemesius *de Natura Hominis* ch. 1, p. 43 (Matthaei); Ammonius *in Int.* 5,15; 18,31; Olympiodorus *in Cat.* 19,20-4 (in what purports to be a quotation of Alexander): Olympiodorus *in Phaedonem* 4, sec. 10, p. 85 (Westerink) = p. 27 (Norwin); Elias *in Cat.* 130,11-13; Stephanus *in Int.* 5,20-36; Psellus (?) *Schol. in Int.* ch. 1 MS Vat. Barb. gr. 164: 17rM; ps.-Alex.-1 *in SE* 11,27; Michael Ephesius &

That of which a *concept* (*noêma*) is a concept is a *thing* (*pragma*); as long as the conceptual and linguistic apparatus of men is not much more sophisticated than in the society at the stage we just considered, the only relevant 'things' are a primitive kind of sensible units which I shall call *objects* (roughly corresponding to 'spatio-temporal particulars'), though the Greeks just say 'things'. Concepts are elements of the *mental* (*en dianoiâi*) or *interior* or *dispositional* (*endiathetos, en diathesei*) *language* or *discourse* (*logos*). [dog] is an element of the *vocal* (*en phônêi*) or *'forthbringing'* (pronouncing) (*prophorikos, en prophorâi*) *language* or *discourse* (*logos*). Though this is not yet known to our primitive men, such elements of the vocal language may be considered from various points of view. In so far as they are sounds *'brought forth'* (pronounced) (*propheromena*), *'brought out'* (*ekpheromena*) or *'sounded out'* (*ekphônoumena*), they are rightly called *words* (*phônai*, also translatable as '(articulate) sounds'). Their role is to externalise elements of the interior language, and in that capacity they are *expressions* (*lexeis*, literally 'sayings' or 'callings'), whereas the concepts are *expressed* (*legomena*). As the theory under construction will only incidentally deal with [dog] and the like as mere words, we may perhaps forgive the old philosophers for not always observing the distinction between 'word' and 'expression'. Expressions may be compounds of several simple elements (words); a compound expression is often called a *compound word (sound)* (*sunthetos phônê*). The term 'expression' has to do with the externalising of concepts seen from the perspective of the speaker. Seen from the perspective of the person who hears the word [dog], it may be said to be a *sign* (*sêmeion*) of the presence of a certain concept in the speaker, and so it is said to *signify* or *signal* (*sêmainein*) the concept, which is the *signified* or *significatum* (*sêmainomenon*). To indicate more clearly the communicative function of words, Porphyry and others liken them to messengers (*angeloi*, in Latin: *nuntii*) and say that they 'bring forth messages about' or *enunciate*[18] (*exangellousi*) concepts.

Thus far the terminology is reasonably clear, though the reader may expect trouble to arise from the liberties taken in the use of 'word' and from the fact that the terminology does not allow for a distinction

---

Anon. Coislinianus *in Int.* (*CAG* 4.5, xlvi); Leo Magentinus *in Cat.*, prooemium, MS Vat. gr. 244: 32v. *hermêneuein* Ammonius *in Int.* 5; Boethius *in Int.*[2] pp. 10-11 (Meiser); Philoponus *in Cat.* 9,29-31. *legein* Dexippus *in Cat.* 7-10; *Comm. 2* in *SE* 166a1-6; ps.-Alex.-1 *in SE* 11,26. *mênuein* Porph. *in Cat.* 56,6; 57,27; 63,16; 125,18. *(kat)onomazein* Porph. *in Cat.* 57,21, 28; 60,15ff; 91,6, 22; Dexipp. *in Cat.* 6,14ff; 9,16-20. *paristanein* Porph. *in Cat.* 55,8-12 [≈ Dexipp. *in Cat.* 6,18-20]; 57,23; 58,3. *propherein* Porph. *in Cat.* 59,12; 71,5, 29-30; 104,27; 112,18; Dexippus *in Cat.* 8,28-9,1; 9,14; Philoponus *in An. Pr.* 273,4; *Comm. 2* in *SE* 166a1-6. *sêmainein* Porph. *de Abstinentia* 3,3; Porph. *in Cat.* 57,28; Dexipp. *in Cat.* 7-10; Ammonius *in An. Pr.* 1,8-9; Philoponus *in Cat.* 8-9; Simplicius *in Cat.* 9-13; Boethius *in Int.*[2] pp. 26-36 (Meiser); *Comm. 2* in *SE* 166a26-8. *(kata)tassein epi/kata* Porph. *in Cat.* 65,33; Dexippus *in Cat.* 20,3-4; Simplicius *in Cat.* 27. *tithenai* Porph. *in Cat.* 57,28-31.

[18] The Latin *enuntiare* seems to copy *exangellein*, but in extant literature it appears to represent *apophainesthai*; cf. Gabriel Nuchelmans, *Theories of the Proposition: ancient and medieval conceptions of the bearers of truth and falsity*, Amsterdam and London 1973, 107.

between word form token, word form type, and lexeme.[19] But this is nothing compared to the trouble that is created by an extended use of 'signify', 'enunciate' and 'express'.

In our simple language, at least, in which we have to consider only the word [dog], the concept of which it is a sign, and the object of which the concept is and which is the cause of the concept, it seems reasonable to say that just as [dog] is a sign of the presence of the concept in the speaker, so the concept is a sign of the presence of the object in sensible reality. But then it would seem that signification is a transitive relation. If one of our primitive men is a cave-dweller and says [dog], and the word signals the presence in his mind of a concept which signals the presence outside the cave of an object, is it not reasonable to say that [dog] is a sign of the presence of the object, or for short, that it signifies the object? Porphyry and his followers thought so and they would say 'the word signifies the thing' without hesitation except when they feared lest people forget that the concepts also play a role. Then they would say 'the word signifies primarily the concept and secondarily the thing' or 'the word signifies the thing via the concept'. They would also say 'the speaker signifies (by means of a word) ...' without sharply distinguishing this usage from the one in which the subject-term is 'the word'. With 'express' they seem in practice to have respected the stipulation that the subject must be a person, the proper objects being concepts, though secondary usage allowed for things or even words as the objects. 'Enunciate' was treated exactly like 'signify', as, probably, was 'inform of' (*mênuein*) which seems to mean exactly the same as 'enunciate'. Further, they would say that the speaker or words *interpret* (*hermêneuousi*) certain kinds of interior discourse (categorical propositions), *make present* (*paristanousi*) the things (to the collocutor), and that men *name* (*(kat)onomazousi*) things, by *calling* (*kalountes*) them something. When people first call a thing by a name, they *lay down* (*tithentai*) a name for it or *put* a name *on* it (*epitithenai*: in the following I shall translate this by *impone*) or *assign* a name *to* it (*katatattein epi*). 'Names' occur as elements both of the vocal and of the mental discourse,[20] but usually a 'name' is understood to be a word and to be a 'name of' (*onoma* + a noun in the genitive) a thing. Finally, 'to indicate' (*dêloun*) is used to cover almost any semantic relation, much like 'signify', though most often we find speakers or words 'indicating' things.

The invention of the art of writing further complicates the picture. Men write (*graphousi*) names or expressions (*onomata, lexeis*) which inform of, enunciate or signify the corresponding elements of vocal language, and thus ultimately of the things.

Hardly any ancient or medieval philosopher was quite consistent in his use of 'semantic' terms, and the locution 'concepts signify/enunciate things' was not commonly used because 'man and his words signify

19 On the distinction, cf. John Lyons, *Semantics*, vols 1-2, Cambridge 1977, 1.13ff.
20 cf. Porph. *in Int.* ap. Boethium *in Int.*[2] I, ch. 1, p. 30 (Meiser).

concepts which signify things' was normally represented by the telescoped locution 'man and his words signify things *via* the concepts'.[21]

With this terminology in mind we may return to our primitive society in which the word [dog] is used as uniquely signifying (the concept of) some particular object. Their concept of that object has an important peculiarity: it is structured. They may not know so and they have no words to describe the fact, but nevertheless it is a fact which is going to influence their behaviour.

Men of a more sophisticated age may say that something in the structure of the objects or in our perception and conceptualisation of them makes us have structured concepts of them. Each concept may be described as an ordered set of components, each component being a value of some feature for which we instinctively investigate the object. The concept of the first object called dog is likely to be analysable in something like the following way: +*corporeal*, +*animate*, +*sentient*, −*rational*, +*quadrupedal*, +*able to bark*, +*floppy-eared*.[22]

Armed with such a concept our primitive men come across more objects and form concepts of them. It so happens that each of the new concepts has exactly the same components as the original one with only one exception: some or all of the new concepts lack the component +*floppy-eared*. Without reflecting on it the primitive men decide in each case that the proper word to use as a sign of the concept is [dog].

To some extent, this is impractical, because it makes it difficult to refer unambiguously to one object. At some point in their mental development people will solve the problem by introducing real proper names like [Snuffy], [Rover] and so on.[23] Porphyry does not comment on this, but he does mention, though rather briefly, the important discovery which is a presupposition for the introduction of a separate class of proper names.[24]

The interesting discovery is this: people realise that they use the word [dog] to signal all such concepts as have the components + *corporeal*, +*animate*, +*sentient*, −*rational*, +*quadrupedal*, +*able to bark*, or, to put it differently, they realise that they use [dog] as a name of all such objects as are corporeal, sentient, irrational, quadrupedal and able to bark. (Observe once more that it does not matter whether the objects seen from the perspective of some metaphysical theory really exist and really *are* corporeal, etc. What matters is that they are sensible objects, i.e. the kind of objects whose existence must be taken for granted in the world of

[21] Variants of the formula *hai phônai sêmainousi ta pragmata dia mesôn noêmatôn* are ubiquitous. See, e.g., Ammonius *in An. Pr.* 1,8-9; Philoponus *in Cat.* 9,14-15; Simplicius *in Cat.* 42,5-6; *Comm. 2 in SE* 166a1-6; ps.-Alex.-1 11,25-7.

[22] My 'components' are *idiotêtes* in Greek; see Porph. *Isag.* 7 (e.g.). Concepts of individuals are rarely mentioned by the commentators (Aristotle's text did not invite them to do so); but see Dexippus *in Cat.* 10,20; Philoponus *in Cat.* 12,4-9; Boethius *in Int.*[2] 28,18ff. (Meiser); Simplicius *in Cat.* 69,15-16. It is possible that Porphyry would not use the word *noêma* but *ennoia* when speaking of concepts of individuals.

[23] 'Socrates' is a word of the first imposition according to Dexippus *in Cat.* 15,27.

[24] Porph. *in Cat.* 90-1.

experience, and that they are conceptualised as bodies that are sentient, irrational etc.)

The new discovery results in the acquisition of a concept of such an object. And the word people will use when they want to signal a mental discourse involving the new concept will be [dog].

This means that we are left with two uses of the word [dog]. One in which it is employed as a sign of a sensible and ostensively identifiable object, a 'this something' (*tode ti*) whose existence prior to perception and conceptualising must be assumed; another in which it is employed to signify a non-sensible and not ostensively identifiable 'such a thing' (*toionde ti*) whose 'existence', for all we know, is entirely a product of our concept of it. If it so happens that there really exists something matching our concept of 'such a thing', this is a contingent and irrelevant fact seen from the perspective of the present theory (logic), unless, indeed, it is argued that we could never recognise similarities[25] between sensible objects if there were no pre-existing intelligible objects possessing, in some particularly genuine way, all the features whose values we were able to identify across the boundaries of individual objects, thus being able to see the objects as similar and to name them identically. Porphyry certainly did not consider the question unimportant;[26] but as it was an intricate and much disputed one, he thought it need not bother the mind of the student of logic, at any rate not the incipient student, for whichever the solution to the problem, logic would not be invalidated: if the recognition of similarities turns out to be explainable in terms of the independent existence of intelligible objects, so much the better; if not, this will leave logic unimpaired – the only thing the logician needs to do is to postulate the ability to discover similarities.

But let us have another look at the two uses of [dog]. We have seen that only in the case of the very first bearer of the name – and that dog may have died and become irrelevant a long time ago – was the choice of the name [dog] really arbitrary (for all we know, though, considerations of no concern for logic might point to a not completely arbitrary choice).[27] All subsequent naming was systematic and the people of our primitive society have even realised this. It was based on an analysis of the objects in which features like 'floppy-eared' were consistently left out of consideration, though people certainly had concepts including all the components of a dog-concept plus a component like +*floppy-eared*. At this stage of development, at least, it is no longer possible to say that men signify the object a more sophisticated age would call 'Snuffy' via a solely individual-identifying concept when they speak of it by means of the word [dog]. The concept involved somehow does and does not include the individualising component.

[25] On similarity as an important factor in abstraction: Boethius *in Isag.*[2] I, ch. 11, p. 166 (Brandt) = *PL* 64:85B (Boethius may depend on Alexander of Aphrodisias – see p. 164 (Brandt) = 84B (Migne) – but Porphyry would hardly disagree); Simpl. *in Cat.* 103,7.

[26] See *CLCAG* 7, ch. 4.4.2.

[27] See ibid., ch. 4.4.8.

If we say it does not, then it has exactly the same components as the concept /common dog/, and the difference between /this particular dog/ and /common dog/ is rather syntactical than one of inner structure: /this particular dog/ is necessarily associated with a concept like /Snuffy/ – which is otherwise identical with it but includes an individualising component; /common dog/ is definitely not associated with any components later in the ordered series than +*able to bark*.

If you cannot quite make up your mind on the question, and I think Porphyry could not, /this particular dog/ has a strange intermediary status between /Snuffy/ and /common dog/. In a sense it is identical with the former, in a sense with the latter and in a sense, maybe, it is a compound of the two.

The terminology used by Porphyry and his followers is indicative of their hesitation. It reflects both a will to identification and a will to separation of concepts on different levels.

Let us repeat: Not all significata of concepts are accessible to direct inspection; only individual sensible objects, such as <Snuffy> are so, <common dog> is not. The components of /common dog/ are the initial segment of the series of components constituting /Snuffy/, but they are considered *qua* not having had a position assigned to them in any such series, and so /common dog/ may be called the concept of the 'un-ranked' (*akatataktos*). If we consider the same components *qua* having had a position assigned to them in a series that comprises 'lower' components too, we have a concept of a 'ranked' dog (*katatetagmenos*) which is in a sense identical with the unranked dog and in a sense identical with Snuffy.[28]

Unranked universals are created by lifting components out of their context; therefore they may be called *aposulêmata dianoias*,[29] i.e. the booty that the mind has carried off (from the sensible things); they are secondary to and come after the particulars (they are *epi tois pollois, husterogenê, post rem*)[30] and subsist only by virtue of a secondary conceptualisation.[31] Ranked universals have a kind of intermediary

[28] *katatassein, suntassein* and their derivatives are frequent in the commentaries, but usually in the Neoplatonist sense. See, e.g., Dexippus *in Cat.* 26,9; 45,22; 51,13; Simpl. *in Cat.* (see the index of *CAG* 8 s.v. *katatattein*); Philop. *in An. Post.* 133,24; Asclepius *in Metaph.* 189,27; 447,25; Syrianus *in Metaph.* 7,12; 20,9; 28,14; 30,28; 32,9-10; 36,28; 95,11; 98,34; 155,29; Elias *in Cat.* 154,17-19; ps.-Alex. *in Metaph.* 524,9-12; Damascius *in Phaedonem* I.502 & II.51 (Westerink); Damascius *in Philebum* sec. 80, p. 39 (Westerink) (further references in Westerink's index, p. 137); Iamblichus *in Timaeum* fr. 60 (Dillon); Proclus *in Parmenidem* col. 939 (Cousin) (and in many other places).

[29] This use of *aposulan, aposulêma* is apparently not attested before Ammonius. Cf. my 'Hoc aliquid – quale quid and the Signification of Appellatives', *Philosophia* 5-6, 1975-6, 382; add to the references: Leo Magentinus *in Cat.*, prooem., MS Vat. gr. 244: 32v. [I have now discovered a similar use of '*aposul-*' in Iamblichus' commentary on Nichomachus' *Arithmetic*, so Ammonius is not the earliest source.]

[30] This terminology is used by Ammonius *in Isag.* 41-2 and by several later authors.

[31] This formulation was used by Porphyry. See the index of *CAG* 4.1 s.vv. *epinoein, epinoia*. In Simplicius *in Cat.* 104,21-2 *katatakhthenta eidê* are distinguished from *ta kath' hauta epinooumena*; the passage is probably of Porphyrian origin.

status between the truly universal and the particular; they are the universal/common 'in' or 'as considered in' the particulars ((*theôroumenon*) *en tois pollois, in re*), and the dog in Snuffy may be described as the dog that is 'ranked with' or 'ranked in' (*sunkatatetagmenos, enkatatetagmenos*) Snuffy.

Unfortunately, the 'ranked/unranked' terminology was also used in another sense. In Neoplatonist terminology ranking was the deployment of an idea (or any supra-sensory entity) on even lower levels; each time we pass to a new level, some undifferentiated feature of the idea acquires a differentiated value to the exclusion of others: thus, in a way, the ranked is poorer than the unranked which contains the *differentiae* of all its subordinates in an undifferentiated way and is prior to them (*pro tôn pollôn, ante rem*).

I do not think Porphyry used 'unranked' in the sense of *ante rem* in his Aristotelian commentaries, but he did use the term, and to later commentators it may not have been obvious he had meant *post rem*. However, they are generally aware of the fact that Aristotelian universals are not *ante rem*; Ammonius and later scholastics sometimes say Aristotelian universals are *in re*, but in practice they often neglect the distinction between *in re* and *post rem* universals. Porphyry may also have neglected it sometimes, but at any rate both he and others were willing to distinguish between concepts on different levels and with different syntactical possibilities, so we may assume that they would admit that any particular man has a limited number of dog-concepts: one of the *post rem* dog and a finite number of concepts of the common dog in the particulars. But it is easily seen that in virtue of his having the concept of 'such a thing as a dog', any man is able, in principle, to enlarge indefinitely his set of concepts of particular dogs; only his death or shortage of dogs could stop the process. And what the individual man cannot do because he is mortal may be possible for his race. Suppose the sensible world is eternal and neither men nor dogs become extinct. Then the set of objects of which people will have particular dog-concepts is infinite. And suppose the abstraction of the concept of the absolutely common dog is not only conceived of as a unique historical event, but also as occuring in each individual man. It will then be true that seen from the perspective of history the basis of abstraction for common concepts are infinite sets.

No such reasoning is found in the writings of Porphyry, but a couple of statements of his seem to require it; for in the *Isagoge*[32] he says that the number of individuals are of the infinite order, and in the minor commentary on the *Categories*[33] he says that common concepts are

[32] Porphyry *Isag.* 6; cf. Porph. *in Cat.* 58,7-8, where it is said that both things and words are virtually (*skhedon*) infinitely many. It is uncertain if the restriction *skhedon* bears on both things and words or only on the latter. If Porphyry interpreted Arist. *SE* ch. 1 165a10-12 literally, he must have believed that in the Aristotelian system things are assumed to be infinitely many, but not words.

[33] Porph. *in Cat.* 90,32-4.

derived from *all* the particular things that bear the same name as the universal.

A related difficulty is this: Porphyry sometimes, in Aristotelian contexts, speaks of the common comprising (*periekhon*) all the particulars falling under it, and of the particulars as sharing or participating (*metekhonta*) in it.[34] If my account of Porphyry's way of thinking has been correct to any reasonable degree, he cannot have meant by 'participation' anything that presupposes *ante rem* universals, and he cannot have meant by 'comprising' that the significatum of a concept of something common *in abstracto* – and hence of the word signifying the concept – can be extensionally delimited. What he must have meant is this: as long, at any rate, as our language and our concepts are used for their primary purpose, both interior and exterior discourse ultimately referring to the sensible world, universal concepts have no function at all except by virtue of their having each an associated set of concepts of particulars. For an unranked concept to comprise ranked concepts and for the unranked universal to comprise the particulars is simply to have such an associated set.

This interpretation is supported by some carefully phrased passages of the *Isagoge* and the minor commentary on the *Categories*. In one place he explains that 'man' 'makes present' (*paristêsi*) two things at least: an essential quality and a community between the subordinate substances.[35]

Later commentators embroider the Porphyrian explanation and make generic and specific names 'signify a set and a quality' and 'indicate a gathering and collection of the particulars' (so Ammonius[36]), or 'indicate a set and community comprising several members, and a quality' (Philoponus[37]), or 'indicate a qualified set' (Commentator III[38]). I do not think Porphyry would have approved of those changes of his wording.

He does use such words as 'set' and 'collection' himself. But notice how careful he is. At the very beginning of the *Isagoge* he examines the meaning of *genos*.[39] The first use of the word, he says, was to designate the origin of each man's birth, and next it came to designate the set (*plêthos*) or collection (*athroisma*) of people sharing a common origin of birth. It is not in any of these senses, he continues, that we use the word when we speak of the *genos* to which the species are subordinate, but probably the logical use was established in imitation (*kath' homoiotêta*) of prior usage: for *in a sense* the genus of logic is the origin of its subordinate species, and it comprises, *as it were*, the whole subordiante set (*kai gar arkhê tis esti to toiouto genos tôn huph' heauto kai dokei kai to plêthos periekhein pan to huph' heauto*). As I understand the text, the purpose of

---

[34] cf. the index of *CAG* 4.1 s.vv. *metekhein, periekhein.*
[35] Porph. *in Cat.* 96,19-20.
[36] Ammon. *in Cat.* 49,6-11.
[37] Philoponus *in Cat.* 72.
[38] *Comm. 3* in *SE* 169a33 (sch. 12).
[39] Porph. *Isag.* 2.7-12; cf. Porph. *in Cat.* 77,27-30; 90,4-9.

writing *arkhê tis* and *dokei periekhein* instead of the plain *arkhê* and *periekhein* is to point out that the genera of logic are neither *ante rem* nor simply identical with a collection of extensional objects they 'comprise'. Similarly, for the particular objects to participate in the common thing and for the concepts of them to participate in the common concept, means for each of them to be a member of a set associated with the common thing or concept whose ranked form they display. They participate or 'share' the unranked by each of them displaying a ranked 'manifestation' associated with it.

It is now time to return to the concept- and language-forming men of the primitive model-society. We left them with concepts and names of nothing but dogs, but, of course, the same procedure that enabled them to think and speak of dogs will enable them to acquire other concepts on the same levels, like that of Socrates (components: +*corporeal*, +*animate*, +*sentient*, +*mortal*, + *x* (*x* is individualising)) and of man (same components less *x*) and to impone the relevant names. Using once more the same procedure, they acquire concepts of a higher level, such as that of an animate sentient body, and associate names with them, such as 'animal'.

The examples used so far might suggest that the conceptual field of the men in Porphyry's model is limited to substances. But this is not so. Porphyry is explicit on the point that they also acquire names (and, of course, concepts) of numbers, magnitudes, colours, and so on, in the same way.[40] In short, they create all the kinds of words necessary in order to be able to signify the things of the sensible world.These are the ten kinds of words dealt with by Aristotle in the *Categories*, words of the *first need* (*tês prôtes khreias*) and of the *first imposition* (*prôtês theseôs*).[41]

But men have more needs than the first. They do not only wish to signal single concepts of things. It is all right to be able to point out Snuffy and say [Snuffy] or [dog] or [animal] or [barking]. But mental discourse is more complicated than that. We do not just have concepts presenting themselves to consciousness in disconnected succession, each one alone. We have compounds (*suntheseis, sumplokai*) of concepts, such as /Snuffy + deep + hole + barking/. Such a compound is a mental proposition – atomic or molecular – and to be able to signal it in an intelligible way people must invent a new kind of words that will not each signal a concept but the structure of such compounds.

The new kind of words are connectives and include what the grammarians call conjunctions, articles, prepositions, plus certain adverbs and, probably, the copula. They are not in themselves significative – no particular concept being associable with each one of them – but taken together with significative words they help express complex concepts. Hence they are said to be *consignificative* (*sussêmanti-kai*). Porphyry in his lost commentaries on the *Categories* and *de*

---

[40] Porph. *in Cat.* 57.

[41] *prôtê thesis* Simplicius *in Cat.* 15,7-8, e.g.; *prôtê/deutera khreia* occurs several times in Dexippus *in Cat.* (see the index of *CAG* 4.2), but not in other authors, as far as I know.

Interpretatione no doubt used a time-honoured simile, comparing such connectives to glue and to the bolts and tar that hold the planks of a ship together.[42]

With connectives at their disposal men can frame such sentences as [Snuffy is barking in a deep hole], [Snuffy is barking near a deep hole] and [If Snuffy is barking, the hole is deep].

The notion of compounds of concepts has many obscure sides to it. I do not know whether Porphyry could give a satisfactory account of the general relations of such a compound to its constituents, to its and their significata, and to expressions. Only as regards essential predication do I think we can catch a glimpse of how his machinery was supposed to work.

Essential predication[43] or predication *hôs kath' hupokeimenou* 'as of a subject', occurs when the [P] of [S is P], without being either the name of an individual <S> or the expression of an individualising component, is the expression of one of the components constituting the concept /S/ or the expression of a concept constituted by a string of components which is identical with some initial part of the string of components constituting /S/. Examples are [Socrates is rational], [man is animate] and [Socrates is a man], [man is an animal].

To predicate, Porphyry says, is (1) to 'mention the things in respect of some significatum', or more generally (2) 'to say a significative expression of things'.[44]

If we say [Socrates is an animal], we mention <Socrates> but we invite people to use their concept /Socrates/ only to single out the thing that we talk about and then to consider him via the concept /animal/, i.e. to pay attention to those components of /Socrates/ that are also components of /animal/. [Socrates is an animal] evokes two concepts, that of <Socrates> and that of <animal>, and indicates a composite concept which is that of the particular ranked animal of which we also have the concept /Socrates/.

Description (2) simply says that we use the word [animal] and that we claim that it is one correct way of signifying the subject – which, in fact, it is, because one of the immediate *significata* of [animal] is the concept of the ranked animal which is Socrates.

Someone might object that on this account an essential predication is a mere tautology like 'Socrates is Socrates' or 'an animal is an animal'. Simplicius[45] informs us that some people actually did so and objected to

---

[42] On connectives: Dexippus *in Cat.* 32-3; ps.-Augustinus *Categoriae Decem* 2; Ammonius *in Int.* 12-13; Boethius *in Int.*[2] I, ch. 1, p. 6 (Meiser); Boethius *Syll. Cat.* I, *PL* 64: 796C-D; Simplicius *in Cat.* 64-5; they all certainly reflect Porphyry – who *in Cat.* 57,32 implies that articles have been introduced before the second imposition. The glue-and-bolt simile was known as Peripatetic to Apollonius Dyscolus (*Fragmenta* = *GG* 2.3, p. 31; cf. Priscianus *Inst.* 11.2.6) and in all probability to his source, the first-century BC grammarian Trypho as well. On 'is' as a connective, see Porphyry *in Int.* ap. Boethium *in Int.*[2] I, ch. 3, p. 77 (Meiser) (cf. Ammonius *in Int.* 55-7 and also Simplicius *in Cat.* 42,23-4).

[43] The term 'essential predication' may not be Porphyrian, but that is of no consequence here.

[44] Porph. *in Cat.* 58,16-18, cf. 56,8-13 and the quotation in Simpl. *in Cat.* 17,3-7.

[45] Simpl. *in Cat.* 53,4ff. Cf. Plotinus 6.3.5.

Aristotle's use of *heteron* ... *heteron* 'one (thing) ... another' in
Cat. 3 1b10-15: 'When one [thing] (*heteron*) is predicated of another (*kath'
heterou*) as of a subject, all [things] that can be said of the predicate can
also be said of the subject; for instance, man is predicated of the
particular man and animal of man; consequently animal may also be
predicated of the particular man.' Aristotle ought not, the objection ran,
to have said 'one of another', for animal is predicated of man *qua* animal
and colour of white *qua* colour. Porphyry's rejoinder, Simplicius says,
consisted in pointing out that the notion of animal is twofold (*dittê hê
epinoia tou zôiou*), viz. of the ranked and of the unranked. When animal is
predicated of man it is the unranked animal that is predicated of the
ranked, and thus it is correct to say that it is one (thing) that is predicated
of another.

The passage is important for an understanding of Porphyry's thought.
He cannot possibly have meant that the expression [unranked animal] is
predicated of the expression [ranked animal]. For one thing, this would
conflict with his explanation of what 'to predicate' means; and for
another, the actual words of the sentence are not [unranked animal is
predicated of ranked animal]. Nor does it make sense to impute to him
the theory that the significata of [man] and [animal] are [ranked animal]
and [unranked animal] respectively.

He cannot, either, have meant that the *ante rem* animal is predicated of
the *in re* animal.[46] If he had intended to say that, the word *epinoia* would
have been very infelicitous and he would have abandoned the position
that the universals we operate with in Aristotelian logic are not
self-subsisting entities, but just mental constructs, the products of
epinoia.

I do not think it is possible to make sense of Porphyry's statement
unless we assign some role to concepts, in spite of the fact that he does not
mention them explicitly.[47] What he can have meant is this: If we put the
pure concept of animal on top, as it were, of the concept of man, the result
will be a concept of man in which the components it shares with that
animal are emphasised. That is, the attention is directed to the ranked
animal in man. In a sense this is putting /animal/ on top of /animal/, but
only in a sense, for the predicate /animal/ is unranked, while the /animal/
which the predicate draws attention to in the subject is ranked.

The mental proposition signified by [man is an animal] is thus
describable as a concept of man with emphasis on its animal components,
as a concept of that particular ranked animal which is man, or as a
compound of the concepts of man and animal. To make the compound we
must have the concept of the unranked animal, but by using it in
connection with /man/ we rank it.

[46] As supposed by P. Hadot, 'La métaphysique de Porphyre', *Fondation Hardt*, Entretiens
12, *Porphyre*, 1966, 152.
[47] Ammonius does. On two occasions (*in Int*. 21,21ff and 51,20-2) he says that to be a
subject or predicate is not a property of things, but primarily of concepts and secondarily of
words.

It might be asked whether the concept /man/ is really /this ranked man/ or /this ranked man, that ranked man .../ or /man unranked/, but the answer is of no consequence, as /unranked animal/ can help us see /ranked animal/ in /man/ whether the *significatum* of /man/ is the mental construct <common man> or any or all of the individual men. The properties of /man/ which interest us in the present connection are not such as belong exclusively to /unranked man/. So in the context, the /man/ may be treated as delimiting a 'this something' (*tode ti*) that is co-extensional with <this ranked animal>.

Thus the *significatum* of the subject term is, in a sense, the same as the *significatum* of the whole proposition. In this sense the subject thing is ranked, and we draw attention to the fact by 'mentioning it in respect of' the concept /unranked animal/ – in short, we predicate animal of it.

It is unfortunate that we have so little left of Porphyry's disquisitions into the matter. But in spite of difficulties in interpreting the remains, it seems clear that the main point he wanted to make was that although even a very elementary form of discourse (mental and oral) cannot be explained except by assuming that people have and employ concepts of universals, this does not imply that their discourse is about universals as such.

We have no account of how Porphyry would verify or falsify 'man is an animal' or 'Socrates is a man'. But scattered information about statements of his and later echoes of his works give some foundation for a reconstruction.

It can be taken for granted that somehow truth and falsity were dependent on an *adaequatio rerum et intellectuum* and resided in a composition of concepts, i.e. in mental propositions. It is *a priori* likely that a *sine qua non* – and maybe sufficient – cause of the falsity of a mental proposition was the failure of such a thing as it signifies to exist.

But how can men have wrong compounds of concepts?

It might be assumed that a man can have incorrectly structured concepts and so be able to form in his mind compounds which would not be possible if his concepts were correctly structured. Probably Porphyry acknowledged such pseudo-concepts. Yet he would not even call them concepts (*noêmata*) because the man who holds them cannot properly be said to have conceived or understood (*nenoêkenai*) the objects. This argument occurs in a passage in Boethius which indubitably reproduces a Greek commentary; it can hardly be anyone's but Porphyry's.[48]

As Porphyry certainly believed in wrong compositions of genuine concepts, it must be assumed that he thought that we can have correctly structured concepts without, at first, being able to analyse them correctly, and that it is possible to form in the mind pseudo-compounds of concepts which are not really combinable.

Verification or falsification of a mental proposition of the essential-predication type then presumably takes place as follows: we perform a

---

[48] Boethius *in Int.*[2] ch.1, p. 41 (Meiser).

kind of checking of the subject concept to see if it can really be analysed in such a way as to reveal the predicate concept ranked in it. If doubt lingers because the structure of the subject concept remains opaque, the decisive check will consist in a confrontation with the sensible objects ultimately responsible for the formation of the concept in question. If they do, in fact, give rise to a concept which on close scrutiny and under elimination of various disturbing factors is seen to be of the desired structure, the proposition was true, otherwise false.

In practice, of course, one will usually have to be content with an epagogical (imperfectly inductive) procedure, no man being able to make a complete survey of the infinitude of objects underlying a universal concept.

A special case occurs if the objects of interest are all non-contemporaneous with the speaker and his collocutors.[49] Then other procedures, such as confrontation with the writings of earlier authors, must replace the direct confrontation with the objects.

If, finally, the objects held responsible for the formation of the concept turn out to be not there, as would be the case with centaurs or goat-stags, the concept is that of a fictitious entity and the proposition involving it is either neither true nor false, nothing enabling us to check how the concept is to be correctly analysed,[50] or the proposition is false if every positive statement about the non-being is false.[51]

Many questions, particularly about sentences in which the predicate is the name of an accident, remain to be solved. I shall not try to solve them. Only one thing seems certain: the theory of such statements must, as far as possible, be reconstructed so as to employ the same machinery as the theory of essential predication.

We have followed Porphyry's model men to a point where they are able to speak of all kinds of things that occur in the world of experience prior to their own conceptualising of it. They are also, presumably, able to judge the truth of propositions, though probably they cannot yet say [This is true] or [This is false]. Presumably they have to cast their judgment about 'Socrates is a man' in the form [Socrates is a man].

The 'invention of universals' was a major event in man's intellectual history. But still the possession of concepts of universals and of the words that signify them has only the function of letting us form handily short propositions and sentences ultimately concerned with the objects that we found in the sensible world when our own intellectual activity started.

The decisive turn which makes scientific man out of merely rational man occurs when he begins to reflect on products of his own intellectual activity: universals, concepts, names. He then becomes capable of forming concepts of non-ranked universals *qua* non-ranked and making statements about them. He can bar the gate to the descent to individuals and say [man is different from Coriscus] meaning 'the pure concept of

---

[49] Dexippus was aware of this problem (*in Cat.* 7-8,10).
[50] This was probably Dexippus' opinion. See his *in Cat.* 7-8.
[51] So Ammonius *in Int.* 52.

man, i.e., /man unranked/, has less components than the concept of Coriscus, and so the mental construct <man> and the sensible object <Coriscus> are not identical'. He can also make statements about names of universals or of individuals, saying, for instance, [man is monosyllabic]; – or about the 'syntactical' properties of names and concepts, saying, e.g., [man is a species], meaning 'the word [man] is such that there is a concept of unranked man with an associated set of several concepts of ranked man whose *significata* are individuals; /man unranked/ fits into any concept of a ranked man and any of the several possible sentences of the form [*x* is a man] expresses a true mental proposition if *x* is the name of one of those individuals.' In none of the three statements is it presumed that the predicate concept is one that could be arrived at by abstraction of the upper string of components of the concepts given us by inspection of each particular man. And to that extent such cases resemble accidental predication, as when we say [Socrates is white], more than they resemble the superficially similar proposition expressed by means of the words [man is an animal].[52]

The examples [man is monosyllabic] and [man is a species] are remarkable for the fact that they include words that can only be used when we talk about the products of our mental activity: they can never refer to the primary objects of sensation. Porphyry called the institution of such expressions the *second imposition* of expressions/names (*hê deutera thesis tôn lexeôn/onomatôn*).[53]

With the invention of metalanguage man has reached a sort of linguistic and intellectual maturity. He is now able to speak about the sensible world and he is even capable of speaking of his cognition of it. Of course, new concepts and new words may arise, but they will all be describable within the framework we have delineated.

The logician's task, then, consists in pointing out the conditions for vocal sentences expressing true reasoning, and for that purpose he will have a permanent need to refer to the genesis of expressions.

It might be objected that on this account we should not be able to speak about supra-sensory realities; and we should not be able to judge statements about them if such statements were nevertheless expressible. I think we can imagine what Porphyry would answer.[54] He would probably say that supra-sensory realities are neither conceptualisable in the same way as the objects of the sensible world, nor expressible (they are *arrêta*). Some sort of acquaintance with them is possible and the best we can do is to talk as if they were cognisable in the same way as objects of the sensible world, using our regular object- and meta-language, yet knowing that all such talk has the character of a simile. If such talk is to be at all intelligible it must obey some of the basic rules of the language in

[52] See Porph. *in Cat.* 81.

[53] In Porph. *in Cat.* onoma and *rhêma* are the only examples of words of the second imposition (57,32-3); Dexippus *in Cat.* 13-16 and 26 adds many more; I think Dexippus had understood Porph. correctly.

[54] cf. Dexippus *in Cat.* 41,18ff; Simpl. *in Cat.* 73-4.

which it is couched, but the rules of logic are not infallible guides in such questions. Suprasensory reality is outside the scope of Aristotelian logic.

But much is within its scope, and we shall now return to the consideration of fallacies and see how some of them are explainable in the Porphyrian framework. We shall also see how that very rough outline of the genesis of concepts and language can be refined.

4. Ambiguity and its bearers

In Porphyrian theory ambiguity must be a property of sentences, not of mental propositions; i.e., if a sentence is ambiguous, it must be capable of signifying at least two non-ambiguous mental propositions. A simple example of an ambiguous sentence would be one containing an equivocal expression – and in Porphyrian theory that must mean an expression that signifies two or more concepts.

The point is nicely made by Dexippus, a staunch supporter of what I style 'Porphyrian semantics'. He is very insistent on the importance of recognising that the primary significata of expressions are concepts, things only being signified in a secondary manner (*kata sumbebêkos*).[55] In support of the thesis he claims, *inter alia*, that sentences derive their truth or falsity from mental propositions and that the explanation of amphibology, equivocation, and all other fallacies dependent on expression is that one expression corresponds to several concepts so that the mind is directed now to one, now to another of them.[56]

This is in perfect harmony with a scholium of Porphyry's on *de Interpretatione* 1 related by Boethius, who informs us[57] that Herminus had raised a difficulty concerning the 'passions of the soul' or 'concepts'[58] which according to Aristotle are the significata of expressions. For how could they be the same to all when in the case of equivocation one and the same utterance has several significata (*unus idemque vocis modus plura significat*)? Porphyry solved it by saying that: (a) The speaker has in his mental discourse a certain concept that signifies one thing only. (b) When he talks he intends that one thing only. (c) The recipient of the message expects a message about one thing and interprets the message he gets in one sense; but it may be another than the one the speaker intended, i.e. the two relate the utterance to different concepts corresponding to different things (the ultimate significates). (d) When the difference in interpretation is discovered, the speaker must formulate his message in a clearer way; and then (e) the speaker and the recipient of the message will join in having the same concept. Consequently the fact that equivocation occurs is no objection to Aristotle's claim that people have identical concepts and of the same things.

[55] Dexippus *in Cat.* 7,1-2.
[56] ibid. 10,3-10.
[57] Boethius *in Int.*[2] I, ch. 1, pp. 39-40 (Meiser).
[58] Boethius says *intellectus*. There is no doubt possible that it renders *noêmata*: cf. Boethius *in Int.*[2] I, ch.1, p. 28 (Meiser), e.g., and Ammonius *in Int.* 24,29-30.

The main conclusion to be derived from this passage is that the concepts had by different individuals are cross-identifiable. Admittedly, Boethius does not say that Porphyry said that he himself believed so. He says that Porphyry thought Aristotle believed so and explained how such a belief could be defended. But here, as elsewhere, it must be assumed that Porphyry did not want to disagree with the Stagirite.

The passage further shows that he thought it possible to signify the same concept by means of an ambiguous and an unambiguous expression.

The man who, in good faith, has expressed his concept /x/ by means of expression [z] which happens to signify also concept /y/, can express /x/ by means of some expression [x] which does not signify any other concept. Boethius does not tell us how Porphyry thought expression [x] would look, but we are hardly off the mark if we suggest that he would consider the following an obvious example: /x/ = /Ajax, son of Telamon/; /y/ = /Ajax, son of Oileus/; [z] = [Ajax]; [x] = [Ajax, son of Telamon]. A passage in his preserved commentary on the *Categories* gives us the right to think so.[59] He is likely to have held other methods of disambiguation to be equally useful: some scholars have not hesitated to claim a Porphyrian origin for the four types listed in Boethius' *de Divisione*.[60] The claim has weak foundations, but even so it is extremely unlikely that Porphyry would have disagreed with Boethius on the point. In fact, neither he nor any of his successors among the Greek commentators seem to have thought there was any problem at all: they considered it a matter of course that the ambiguity of a term may be neutralised in various ways and that one way is to use the same term, but provided with some restricting addition. If the old scholastics saw any problem at all, it was rather the reverse: how is it possible for a term to signify ambiguously if to signify is to signify some thing? If the only way of signifying one of the supposed significata of [dog] is to say [dog that can bark] and the only way of signifying another of them is to say [dog that is a star], these are two unambiguous names and no role as a name is left for the supposedly 'common name' [dog].[61]

To the modern observer the possibility of disambiguation by means of restricting additions may also seem so obvious that there is no need to make a point of it. Yet, many western thirteenth-century philosophers saw a problem here, and they did so exactly because they had accepted one important part of Porphyry's logic, namely the theory of imposition of names. If, it was argued, a name has been imposed to express several significata, nothing can prevent it from doing so; and consequently 'Ajax, son of Telamon, duelled with Hector' is no less ambiguous than 'Ajax duelled with Hector'. The solutions they advanced are of no relevance here, but it is interesting to notice to whom the problem seemed one and

[59] Porph. *in Cat.* 64,9-17.

[60] See *CLCAG* 7, ch. 2.3.4 note 19.

[61] The problem was formulated by Nicostratus. We find discussions of it in Dexippus *in Cat.* 19 and Simplicius *in Cat.* 26-8. Porphyry must have discussed it too, for it seems that it was he who transmitted the Nicostratean problems to posterity (cf. Simpl. *in Cat.* 29-30).

to whom it became a non-problem. The Parisian masters of the late
thirteenth-century were generally much more favourable to 'hyposta-
sising' than the Porphyry I reconstruct, and much more interested in
relations like signification that could be assumed to have been fixed once
and for all than in such elusive relations as supposition (the
context-bound relation of a term to something else – concept or
extramental thing). For these Parisian masters there was a problem. For
people whose basic approach to logic was more like Porphyry's and more
like Buridan's the problem evaporated.[62]

A third conclusion to be drawn from Boethius' report of his great
predecessor's scholium is that Porphyry thought that the terms of vocal
language can have several senses whereas the terms of mental discourse
(the concepts) cannot.

It is only consistent that he should have held that sentences can be
ambiguous whereas mental propositions cannot. Once more Boethius
provides the evidence. Before Porphyry, he says,[63] nobody had succeeded
in producing a correct explanation of *de Interpretatione* 5, 17a15-17, 'for a
declarative *logos* to be one is either to indicate one [thing] or to be one by
conjunction – and to be many is either to indicate many [things] and not
one or to be unconjoined' (*esti de heis logos apophantikos ê ho hen dêlôn ê
ho sundesmôi heis, polloi de hoi polla kai mê hen ê hoi asundetoi*).

A comparison of Boethius' report of Porphyry's exposition with
Ammonius' scholium on the passage[64] shows that in the main the latter
can be used as a substitute for the Phoenician's lost text, and so I shall
borrow a few details from that source; but they are not essential for the
purpose. As far as the essentials go, Boethius' account is clear enough.

Porphyry, then, showed that the passage need not baffle commentators,
for every bit of it becomes intelligible when we remember that a *logos* has
not necessarily the same properties when we look at the expression and
when we look at the expressed; Aristotle speaks of the *logos* seen from
both points of view, and what he wants us to understand is that the
expression is no infallible guide when we ask about unity and plurality. If
we say [a rational mortal animal is walking], we get the impression of
something very complex, but there is just one *logos*, exactly as when we
say [a man is walking]. But if we say [Ajax duelled with Hector], there is
more than one *logos* in spite of surface simplicity, for unity and plurality
is considered on the level of *significata*, not on the level of expression, and
[Ajax] has two *significata*. The following may serve as a rule of thumb: the
number of *logoi* equals the number of the *significata* of the subject
expression(s) multiplied by the number of the *significata* of the predicate
expression(s).[65]

Porphyry added many niceties that need not detain us here. The
conclusion emerges clearly enough: ambiguity is a property of sentences

[62] See my 'The dead man is alive', *Synthese* 40, 1979, 43-70.
[63] Boethius *in Int.*[2] II, ch. 5, pp. 106ff (Meiser).
[64] Ammonius *in Int.* 72-5; cf. Dexippus *in Cat.* 9,14-15.
[65] cf. Ammonius *in Int.* 73,8-11; 126,11-14.

and the number of mental propositions signified by an ambiguous sentence is a function of the number of the significata of the terms of the sentence. I do not think there was anything new in this conception. As usual Porphyry's greatness consisted more in remembering in the right places what everybody was supposed to know than in introducing novelties.

His influence lasted till the end of scholasticism. People like Leo Magentinus did not have very clear conceptions of semantics, but still we find scholia such as the following:[66] 'or we may understand [*sc.* 17a15] as follows: you ought not to characterise a *logos* as one or many on the basis of the pronounced *logos* (*prophorikos logos*) but of the signified, for "(a/the) dog is walking" looks in the pronounced *logos* like one, but nevertheless it is several *logoi* because "dog" signifies many [things]; in fact, as many [things] as "dog" signifies, so many propositions have you said.' (*ê houtôs noêteon, hoti ouk opheileis kharaktêrizein ton hena logon kai tous pollous apo tou prophorikou logou, all' apo tou sêmainomenou; to gar 'kuôn peripatei' ei kai heis tôi prophorikôi logôi dokei, alla polloi logoi eisi, dioti to 'kuôn' polla sêmainei; hosa gar sêmainei to 'kuôn', tosautas kai protaseis eirêkas.*)

5. Truth and its bearers

If ambiguity is a property of some expressions, truth can hardly be a property of expressions, at least if it is held that (a) any categorical proposition must be either true or false and cannot be both; (b) 'p is true' $\leftrightarrow$ '$\sim p$ is false' and 'p is false' $\leftrightarrow$ '$\sim p$ is true'. For supposing that the 'propositions' which are the bearers of truth and falsity may be sentences (expressions), it is possible to construct examples that force us to admit that (1) p is both true and false; (2) p is true and $\sim p$ is also true; (3) p is false and $\sim p$ is also false.

Suppose the world once contained a pair of heroes, both bearing the name of Ajax, one of whom had Telamon for his father, while the other was the son of Oileus. Suppose that it is a fact that the son of Telamon once duelled with Hector, whereas the son of Oileus never did so. Suppose further that we, the members of a linguistic community, have just two concepts with which we associate the name 'Ajax', namely one concept of the son of Telamon and one of the son of Oileus. It is irrelevant whether the feature by which we can distinguish the two concepts is 'being the son of X and not Y': what matters is only that we have, in fact, distinct concepts. Let it be the criterion of truth of a declarative sentence that the concepts named by its subject and predicate terms are joined in the way it states and that there is a corresponding composition *in rebus*. Then consider the following pair of 'contradictory' sentences:

(1) Ajax duelled with Hector.
(2) Ajax did not duel with Hector.

---

[66] Leo Magentinus in *in Int.* 17a15, MS Vat. gr. 244: 104v, sch. *lê.*

We have concepts of two distinct persons called Ajax, and we know the relevant facts concerning duelling with Hector about each of them. To determine the truth-value of the sentences, we may try to replace the word 'Ajax' with expressions that signify our distinct concepts in an unambiguous way. For convenience I shall use 'Ajax, son of Telamon' as an expression that unambiguously signifies one of the concepts, and 'Ajax, son of Oileus' as an expression that unambiguously signifies the other of the concepts with which we associate the word 'Ajax'. The following rewritten pairs of sentences might be considered:

(I)   (1) Ajax, son of Telamon, duelled with Hector.
         (2) Ajax, son of Telamon, did not duel with Hector.
(II)   (1) Ajax, son of Oileus, duelled with Hector.
         (2) Ajax, son of Oileus, did not duel with Hector.
(III)   (1) Ajax, son of Telamon, duelled with Hector.
         (2) Ajax, son of Oileus, did not duel with Hector.
(IV)   (1) Ajax, son of Oileus, duelled with Hector.
         (2) Ajax, son of Telamon, did not duel with Hector.
(V)   (1) Ajax, son of Telamon, or Ajax, son of Oileus, duelled with Hector.
         (2) Ajax, son of Telamon, or Ajax, son of Oileus, did not duel with Hector.
(VI)   (1) Ajax, son of Telamon, and Ajax, son of Oileus, duelled with Hector.
         (2) Ajax, son of Telamon, and Ajax, son of Oileus, did not duel with Hector.
(VII)   (1) Ajax, not definitely the son of Telamon and not definitely the son of Oileus, duelled with Hector.
         (2) Ajax, not definitely the son of Telamon and not definitely the son of Oileus, did not duel with Hector.
(VIII)   (1) Ajax, both definitely the son of Telamon and definitely the son of Oileus, duelled with Hector.
         (2) Ajax, both definitely the son of Telamon and definitely the son of Oileus, did not duel with Hector.

(I-IV) are certainly permissible rewritings of the two sentences on the suppositions previously stated concerning our concepts. (V)-(VIII) are more dubious, but they might be tried to see if they could help to find a way of interpreting (1) and (2) so that they can be ascribed definite truth-values without elimination of the double signification of 'Ajax'. Now, the truth-values we will have to assign to the rewritten sentences are these:

	(1)	(2)
(I)	T	F
(II)	F	T
(III)	T	T
(IV)	F	F
(V)	T	T
(VI)	F	F
(VII)	~T&~F	~T&~F
(VIII)	~T&~F	~T&~F

If we consider (I)-(IV) only, it appears that the non-permissible combination TT occurs in (III) and the similarly non-permissible combination FF in (IV). In Greek terms, (1) and (2) *sunalêtheuousi* and *sumpseudontai* ('are true together, are false together'). Further, (I)-(II) show that (1) is both true and false – and (2) likewise.

The trick of substituting a disjunctive or a conjunctive phrase for 'Ajax' leads to the illicit combinations TT and FF in (V) and (VI).

The final, desperate attempts of (VII)-(VIII) probably lead to ~T&~F for both sentences, for we have no concept of an Ajax who is not definitely one or other of the two we know or definitely both, and so the sentences as phrased in (VII)-(VIII) are meaningless: it is not possible to find a pair of mental propositions and compare them to the facts of the world to see whether there is correspondence or not. We might expect a philosopher in the Porphyrian tradition to say that they are neither true nor false.

So, what must our philosopher do? He wants to save the principles of contradiction and excluded middle. He holds that sentences have mental propositions for their primary significate and that verification and falsification require comparison of the mental propositions with the extramental realities. The simple – and the only – way out of the difficulties is to say that the real bearers of truth and falsity are the mental propositions. If sentences can nevertheless be called 'true' or 'false', their truth values must be a function (the sum) of the truth values of the mental propositions they signify.

An inspection of the sources bears out our expectations. With a single exception we have not got any statements about the question with direct ascription to Porphyry, but the later commentators who are known to depend on him agree so well that it is inconceivable that he should have thought otherwise.

The one certainly Porphyrian statement unfortunately occurs in the concept-less minor commentary on the *Categories*. Yet, it is indicative of what we might expect from his less compendious works. In agreement with Aristotle he mentions[67] *logos* as an example of what falls under the category of quantity. For precision he adds that the *logos* in question is not the one in the mind but the one whose constituents are long and short syllables. A little later[68] he tells his pupil that a quantum has no opposite and shows this to be the case with lines, surfaces, etc. – 'Not even *logos*

[67] Porph. *in Cat.* 101,24ff.   [68] ibid. 106,11ff.

has an opposite, qua *logos*'. This elicits the question: 'How does it then come that one *logos* is called true and another false?' To which Porphyry answers: 'But it was not in so far as it is significative that it was taken to belong to the category of quantity: it was in so far as it is in pronunciation and is measurable in terms of long and short syllables'. Strictly speaking this passage does not prove that Porphyry thought truth and falsity do not at all reside in vocal sentences. What it proves for certain is that at least he would not say that sentences understood just as phonic stuff could be bearers of truth and falsity. But if we remember that Porphyry in this concise commentary speaks as little as possible about mental propositions, I think we may interpret the passage to the effect that he means: 'The true bearers of truth and falsity are the mental propositions. If sentences can be said to be true or false this, at least, is only in virtue of their signifying true or false mental propositions.'

That was how Dexippus saw the situation. He says[69] 'There could not possibly be a true or false *logos* if the *logos* did not receive its truth or falsity from the concepts, for the *logos* in the mind is prior, and it is probably after it that "saying" (*legein*) and the vocal *logos* are named.'

Boethius did not disagree.[70] 'In view of the fact that simple concepts do not yet share in truth or falsity it is obvious that the vocal expression (*prolatio*) of such a simple concept must also be beyond either. But when a composition or division involving 'to be' [*compositio secundum esse facta vel etiam divisio*] occurs in the concepts, – which is where truth and falsity are primarily engendered – then, since the words receive their meaning (*significatio*) from the concepts, they [i.e. the words] must also be true or false according to the quality [i.e. truth-value] of the concepts.' (The translation paraphrases slightly.)

Ammonius concurs;[71] 'And it will be established [*sc.* in *de Interpretatione*] that nouns and verbs are simple words, which signify neither truth nor falsity [...] but the true and the false belong to (*theôreitai peri*) the declarative *logos*, which results from the intertwining (*sumplokê*) of them; and that truth and falsity belong to the concepts before the words, as the concepts are the causes of the words. For concepts, too, are either simple or composite. The simple ones, which are signified by the simple words, cannot be bearers of any truth or falsity; but the composite ones, which are about composite things and are indicated by intertwined words, can be bearers of truth and falsity. But to the things as such no one could possibly ascribe such properties, not even to the composite ones.' (The translation paraphrases slightly.)

. We have no ancient discussion of the 'disambiguated' sentences (V-VII); (V-VI) were the object of discussion in Western medieval scholasticism, and we can only suppose that the Greeks would have declared that they do not solve the problem of equivocation for the same reasons as their

[69] Dexippus *in Cat.* 10,3-6.
[70] Boethius *in Int.*[2] p. 49 (Meiser).
[71] Ammonius *in Int.* 18,2-12; cf. 21,4ff.

Western colleagues did.[72] (VII) is hinted at by the same Western schoolmen. We have no discussion of it in Greek, but Dexippus, at least, seems to have held that sentences that contain words to which no significatum corresponds or whose significatum is a concept of a fictitious entity are neither true nor false.[73] (VIII) is dismissed as meaningless by Boethius.[74]

Examples like (I-IV) are discussed in all commentaries on *de Interpretatione*. Ammonius' comments on 17a15-17 and 17a35-7[75] give us fair compensation for the loss of Porphyry's *ipsissima verba*.

Having established the principle that counting of propositions must happen on the level of significates, Ammonius exemplifies as follows;[76] 'If we say "Ajax duelled with Hector" without determining which of the two Ajaxes we are making a statement about, no reasonable man would say that this is one proposition as we see it to be simultaneously true and false.'

Some pages later[77] he explains that 'Ajax duelled with Hector' and 'Ajax did not duel with Hector' may both be true and both be false although they appear to be constituted of the same terms; however, the identity between the proposition which may truly be affirmed and the one that may at the same time be truly negated is only an identity on the level of expression, not on that of the significata. To make it necessary for the affirmative and the negative propositions – and this time Ammonius ought to mean 'on the level of expression' – to have opposite truth-values, one must disambiguate the expression so that it is clear about which Ajax one is talking.

He returns to the question in a scholium[78] on 18a26-7, explaining that a pair like 'this [*or*: there] is a white cloak' and 'this [*or*: there] is not a white cloak' are exactly parallel to 'Ajax duelled with Hector' – 'Ajax did not duel with Hector', if a convention states that 'cloak' is a name that can be used as a substitute for 'horse' as well as for 'man'. In such cases, he says, the use of an equivocal expression makes it possible for the two sentences (*protaseis*) to be both true; both false; or one of them true, the other false.

The terminology in which *protasis, logos* etc. are used both of entities on the level of expression and of their significates creates many difficulties of interpretation, and certainly helped confuse the discussion already in antiquity. Intending, no doubt, to be faithful to Porphyry's way of thinking, Boethius on one occasion[79] explains that 'Alexander abducted Helen' will have different truth-values when intended as a statement about the son of Priam and when about the king of Macedonia. His wording strongly suggests that he considers 'Alexander abducted Helen'

[72] cf. my 'Can equivocation be eliminated?', *Studia Mediewistyczne* 18.2, 1977, 103-24.
[73] Dexippus *in Cat.* 7,30-8,1 in particular, and pp. 7-10 in general.
[74] Boethius *in Int.*² II, ch. 8, p. 182,17-20 (Meiser) (Boethius uses another example).
[75] Ammonius *in Int.* 72-5; 84-6.   [76] ibid. 73,11-14.
[77] ibid. 84,30-85,3.   [78] ibid. 128,3-14.
[79] Boethius *in Int.*¹ I, ch. 6, pp. 81-2 (Meiser).

to be one proposition that changes from true to false when compared to one of the two portions of reality signified by it rather than to the other, so that in this account the mental language has dropped out, vocal language being seen as having realities for its immediate significates.

Certain passages in Ammonius can be read in the same way. Thus in the scholium on 18a26-7 he says[80] that the reason why a proposition (*protasis*) with an equivocal subject and its negation need not have different truth-values is that nothing prevents one of the several things signified by the equivocal word from participating and another of those things from not participating in that which is predicated.

Yet, it is clear that the thought that underlies all of his discussion of ambiguity, and which is a Porphyrian thought, is that truth and falsity are strictly speaking properties of the propositions of mental language,[81] even if vocal sentences may be called true or false in a derivative sense. The principles of contradiction and excluded middle apply to the mental propositions only – but there they certainly apply.[82] Porphyry is known to have defended them,[83] and the context in which his defence is mentioned even suggests that he said something like, 'In spite of the counter-argument that may be derived from ambiguous sentences, the principles must be upheld.'

Porphyry's teaching was never quite forgotten as long as scholasticism lasted, and the discussion of 'Ajax duelled with Hector' was a standard item of commentaries on *de Interpretatione* and the *Sophistici Elenchi* till the end of the Middle Ages.[84] No one ever ventured a frontal attack on the great scholar's positions and consequently we find fragments of Porphyrian doctrine even in the works of Michael of Ephesus and Leo Magentinus. In fact, their works are scarcely intelligible if one forgets about the Porphyrian background. But it is also clear that few of his successors had his ability to remember trivialities in the right places. No one doubted the importance of mental language, but most commentators became like Michael of Ephesus who duly mentions it in his scholia on the initial chapters of *de Interpretatione*[85] and in one scholium on the *Elenchi*[86] – but who forgets about it in his comments on chapter 17 of the *Elenchi*,[87] where it is obvious that many difficulties disappear if one

---

[80] Ammonius *in Int.* 128,4-14.

[81] cf. Boethius *in Int.*[2] I, ch. 1, p. 28 (Meiser) (a Porphyrian passage: cf. p. 26,17 (Meiser)).

[82] Except, perhaps, if they are affirmative statements about fictitious entities, though Ammonius *in Int.* 62 says that any negative proposition about *ficta* is true and seems to hold that any affirmative proposition about them is false.

[83] Boethius *in Int.*[2] II, ch. 6, p. 134,20ff (Meiser).

[84] See, e.g., Psellus *Paraphrasis Int.*, MS Vat. Barb. gr. 164: 5v; Michael Ephesius (?) *Sch. in Int.*, MS Paris. gr. 1917: 24rM; Leo Magentinus in *in Int.* 17a34, MS Vat. gr. 244: 106r sch. *mb*' and MS Paris. gr. 1917: 25r; ps.-Magentinus *in Int.*, MS Paris. gr. 1928: 141r; Blemmydes *Logica*, *PG* 142: 900C (from Ammonius?); *Comm. 3* in *SE* 175b7, cod. 150: 200r. Related examples in ps.-Alex.-1 *in SE* 129,8-9; 141,6-7; 179,6ff.; *Comm. 3* in *SE* 176a3-4 (sch. 19).

[85] MS Paris. gr. 1917: 17r ff. Some extracts are printed in *CAG* 4.5, pp. xlv-xlvii.

[86] ps.-Alex.-1 11,23-8.

[87] ibid. 128,14ff.

remembers the distinction between non-ambiguous true or false mental propositions and surface sentences, which may contain ambiguities and hence be excepted from the principles of contradiction and excluded middle.

Quite generally, it may be said that the post-Porphyrian commentators tend all too often to regard complex concepts (mental propositions) and complex expressions (sentences) as equally suited to be the bearers of truth and falsity,[88] i.e. they tend to overlook the counter-argument derivable from the occurrence of ambiguous sentences. They also, reasonably enough against such a background, tend to disregard mental propositions altogether, leaving us with sentences and facts or things of the world as the only relevant elements in the semantic process. These tendencies are quite obvious in all extant collections of scholia on the *Elenchi.*

To some extent, Porphyry himself carries the responsibility for the fate of his logic. He was a man of compromises, at least as far as expression goes. Hardly a single piece of new terminology can be shown to be of his making, and hardly a single piece of theory can be demonstrated to originate with him. What he did was to accept what everybody accepted and give some pieces of doctrine a twist so as to fit into the rest. He was more consistent than most people in his dealings with the 'triangle of signification', but he probably never thought of eliminating the dangerous ambiguity of semantic terms like 'discourse' (mental or vocal) and '*significatum*' (mental or real). He tended to say: 'Primarily truth belongs to a *logos* viewed this way, and derivatively to a *logos* viewed that way', rather than: 'Sentences are neither true nor false; propositions are either true or false', just as he said: 'The notion of man is twofold', rather than: 'There are several concepts sharing a common origin and a common name, but which are distinct concepts'. What distinguishes Porphyry from his followers is that he treats the differences indicated by such locutions as 'qua this ... qua that' as important differences, so much that I think it is justifiable to translate his '*logos* qua this' as 'mental proposition' and his '*logos* qua that' as 'sentence' – whereas Ammonius and later commentators often seem to think that 'qua this' or 'qua that' does not make any important difference.

---

[88] cf., e.g., ps.-Magentinus *in Int.*, MS Paris. gr. 1917: 18v-19r; Stephanus *in Int.* 6,17-21; Michael Ephesius *in Int.*, MS Paris. gr. 1917: 18vM; Leo Magentinus *in Int.*, MS Vat. gr. 244: 94r sch. *ê.*

CHAPTER EIGHT

How did Syrianus regard Aristotle?*

H.D. Saffrey

The great inquiry which Paul Moraux initiated into the history of the
Aristotelian tradition will cover only the period from the first century BC
to the second century AD.[1] The results of this great work will obviously be
decisive for appreciating the use which first Plotinus[2] and then his
Neoplatonic successors made of Aristotle's treatises in order to develop
their own philosophy. Porphyry had been able to write that the *Enneads*
were a 'digest' of Aristotle's *Metaphysics*.[3] This observation expresses the
profound regard Porphyry had for Aristotle, and we shall see that this
regard remained as a matter of tradition in Athenian Neoplatonism. By
taking us to the very beginning of the fifth century AD, I would like to
offer to Paul Moraux, as a token of my esteem, some items for the record
by showing how Syrianus, the master of the Neoplatonic school in
Athens, regarded Aristotle.

Syrianus is the author of an extant commentary of Platonic inspiration
on books 3, 4, 13 and 14 of the *Metaphysics*[4] and of commentaries on the
Categories, the *de Interpretatione*, the *Prior Analytics*, the *de Caelo* and
the *de Anima*, which are lost and are known to us only from later authors.
The first document that I would like to submit for examination is the
prologue to the commentary on book 13 of the *Metaphysics*. As is well
known, the long prologues to the Neoplatonists' principal books have in

---

*Translated by Victor Caston.

[1] Paul Moraux, *Der Aristotelismus bei den Griechen von Andronikos bis Alexander von
Aphrodisias*. Bd. 1, *Die Renaissance des Aristotelismus im I Jh. v. Chr.* (Peripatoi 5), Berlin
1973. Bd. 2, *Der Aristotelismus im I und II Jh. n. Chr.* (Peripatoi 6), Berlin 1984. The third
volume, dealing with the doctrine of Alexander of Aphrodisias, will be published under the
direction of J. Wiesner.

[2] For a specific example of the influence of Alexander of Aphrodisias and Aristotle on
Plotinus, cf. Paul Henry, 'Une comparaison chez Aristote, Alexandre et Plotin' in *Les
Sources de Plotin*, Entretiens sur l'Antiquité classique, vol. 5, Vandoeuvres-Genève 1960,
427-49. As P. Henry notes in this article, it is Émile Brehier to whom we owe the finest
remarks on the influence of Aristotle and Aristotelianism on Plotinus. It is obvious that the
work of Paul Moraux will help to revive this important question. In the meantime, see T.A.
Szlezák, *Platon und Aristoteles in der Nuslehre Plotins*, Basel 1979, 135-43.

[3] cf. Porphyry, *Vita Plotini* 14,5-7.

[4] On this commentary generally, cf. Karl Praechter, 'Syrianos', 1, in *RE* IV A, cols
1769,56-1775,2.

general a programmatic value.[5] This prologue proves to be no exception:

Syrianus, *in Metaph*. 13 (*CAG* 6.1), pp. 80,4-81,14:

I do not count myself among those who systematically try to pick a quarrel
with Aristotle, nor indeed among those who make him their master with
regard to a small number of subjects or on trivial points. On the contrary, I
belong among those who admire in an ordinary manner his logical methods
and who appreciate his moral treatises and natural philosophy a great deal.
And – so as not to appear too lengthy in enumerating here all the very fine
and excellent doctrines which this great philosopher produced – who[6] would
not rightly admire, if he is endowed with good sense, whatever in this very
perfect treatise is said of relevance to the subject of forms united with
matter and to the definitions, or whatever is pointed out by means of
demonstrations appropriate to the subject of divine and immobile causes
which transcend the world entirely, although they are objects which
surpass all composite thought and all rigorous, discursive argumentation?
Indeed, who would not name the author of this work the benefactor of
humanity?
    For these reasons, we owe recognition no doubt as great as do those who
have sensed the sagacity of his spirit.[7] Yet since – for what reasons I do not
know – in other parts of his treatise on theology no doubt, but particularly
in the last two books, 13 and 14, Aristotle was moved to charge violently in
an assault on the first principles of Pythagoras and Plato, without saying
anything sound or adequate against them and even, if one must speak the
plain truth, without succeeding for the most part in touching them (because
in these attacks he puts forward his own presuppositions), it appeared
reasonable, in order to prevent the newest among my auditors, impressed
by the author's deserved reputation, from being borne away by the flood of
contempt for the divine realities and the Ancients' divinely inspired
philosophy, to submit the text to a critical and impartial examination using
the best of our abilities and to show that the doctrines concerning Plato's
and Pythagoras' first principles remain unrefuted and unshaken, and that
Aristotle's undertakings against these doctrines most often miss their
mark[8] and examine subjects which in no way concern these divine men,
whereas in a small number of cases they strive to say something no doubt
which holds against them and to criticise them, but without being able to
effect a refutation, whether great or small. And it had to be thus, since 'the

----

[5] On the prefaces of Proclus, for example, see H.D. Saffrey, 'Théologie et anthropologie
d'après quelques préfaces de Proclus', in *Images of Man in Ancient and Medieval Thought* (=
Studia Gerardo Verbeke...dicata), Leuven 1976, 199-212.
[6] I have adopted here Praechter's correction (in *Gött. gel. Anz.* 1903, 517; = *Kleine
Schriften*, Hildesheim 1973, 250); I read *tis ou* [*pas*] (80,9).
[7] *tês ankhinoias* (80,16). In his *in Tim.*, 1,24-2,1, Proclus says: 'That Plato, right down to
the finest detail in which he wrought the present instruction, was alone able to preserve
from beginning to end the traits which characterise Pythagoreanism in natural science –
this is what the most sagacious spirits must examine (*tous ankhinousterous*)' (from the
translation of Festugière). For Proclus, the sagacity of Aristotle did not reach quite that far.
[8] *para thuras apantôsas* (80,28). On this phrase, cf. L.G. Westerink's note on Damascius,
in Phaed. 1, §380,6 (207): ' "come to the wrong door", that is, answer the wrong question; or,
more vaguely, probably owing to a confusion with *apantan* "answer": give the wrong
answer, a number of times in Olympiodorus, *in Gorg.* (see index).'

truth can never be refuted', as this divine man says [Plato, *Gorgias* 473B10-11], and because the fathers of these treatises concerning first principles, by making them resemble the realities, founded them 'in durability and infallibility to the degree attainable by treatises' [*Timaeus* 29B6-8].

But enough of preambles. And since we have just stated the intention and plan of this work, it is time to engage in the combats[9] themselves. However that may be, whether we should be called a combatant because we answer charges brought against the finest and best of philosophies, or whether we should rather be called a judge who decides between the most simple and most intellective intuitions of the epoptic philosophy of Pythagoras' pupils and the aporias raised in a dialectical manner against them by one who in this field is the strongest of all that have ever been heard speak, Aristotle, we will not refuse to bear these titles; the only thing which matters is to conduct these battles with justice, intelligence and love of the truth.

This fine text begins with a declaration of intent. Syrianus intends to distinguish himself from his predecessors: he does not reject the authority of Aristotle purely and simply, and he does not have the hypocrisy to appeal to him only where his intervention is without importance and solely decorative. In the long dispute over the agreement between Aristotle and Plato, he maintains an equal distance from the two extremes, and strives to separate the Platonic and Aristotelian positions.[10] This is why he emphasises his admiration for Aristotle the logician, the moralist or natural philosopher, but withholds judgment when he exposes Aristotle's attacks concerning the Platonic first principles. Proclus, even more than his teacher, will note the divergences between Aristotle and Plato, since he will pass the same global judgment on the *Physics* that Syrianus passes on the *Metaphysics*, and will even go so far as to say: 'As for the great Aristotle, it is my opinion that he arranged as much as possible his treatise on nature in a spirit of rivalry with the teachings of Plato',[11] and his commentary on the *Timaeus* will at every opportunity establish the superiority of Plato over Aristotle.

That having been said, however, it is necessary to notice the wholly exceptional title which Syrianus gives to Aristotle when he proclaims him the 'benefactor of humanity (*euergetên tou tôn anthrôpôn biou*)'. In itself, the mere epithet of 'benefactor' is ordinary – all those to whom you owe some kindness are your 'benefactors': the cities used to declare their great

[9] It seems that *tôn agônôn* has its normal sense here, since in what follows Syrianus will claim in turn to be a combatant and a judge. Yet in rhetoric, the opposition of *agônes* to *prooimion* is known in the attenuated sense of the development of the treatise in contrast to the prologue, and this sense is known to Syrianus himself, cf. *in Herm.* 2 (Rabe), 111 and 170, and Olympiodorus, *in Alc.* 213,3-4.

[10] For the Neoplatonists' appreciation of Aristotle, see R.T. Wallis, *Neoplatonism*, London 1972, 24-5 and 143-4, and Fr. Romano, *Studi e richerche sul Neoplatonismo*, Naples 1983, ch. 3, 'Lo "sfruttamento" neoplatonico di Aristotele', 34-47. For the assimilation of Aristotelian logic, cf. A.C. Lloyd, 'Neoplatonic and Aristotelian logic', *Phronesis* I, 1955/56, 58-72 and 146-60, and his 'The assimilation of Aristotle's logic' in *The Cambridge History of Later Greek and Early Medieval Philosohy*, ed. A.H. Armstrong, Cambridge 1967, 319-22.

[11] Proclus, *in Tim.* 1,6,21-4 and its whole development until 7,16.

men the 'benefactors of the city', and a friend or parent who wished to honour a dead man to whom he owed much would often have engraved on the tomb that he was his benefactor.[12] To remain within Neoplatonic usage, one might compare what Proclus said of his teacher, Syrianus: 'If we had to repay the debt of gratitude, incurred by his kindnesses to us (*tôn euergesiôn*), not even the whole of time would suffice.' Thus, Proclus considered Syrianus as his benefactor. We shall come back to this. Ammonius, for his part, said the same thing of Proclus when he called him 'our teacher and benefactor (*euergetês*)'.[13] But the appellation 'benefactor of humanity' is much more significant. To my knowledge, it was more or less reserved for the emperor himself, who is often acclaimed with the formula 'Saviour and benefactor of the entire world', for the reason that his providence in fact exerted an influence over the whole of the empire.[14] Yet it is open to doubt whether Syrianus truly intended to compare Aristotle to the emperor. Looking elsewhere, it should be remembered that the Stoics had taught the Greeks to deify the first inventors of the sciences and crafts as the great benefactors of humanity, for the reason that their inventions were made for the benefit of all men.[15] Aristotle, for Syrianus, might be considered the inventor of theology, since his treatise, the *Metaphysics*, had 'Theological Treatise (*theologikê pragmateia*)' as its title, at least in Syrianus' day, which he even mentions in the text cited above when he speaks of certain 'parts of his treatise on theology'.[16] Did Syrianus think that Aristotle, in creating the first treatise of theology proper, had merited being called, on a level with the emperors, the 'benefactor of humanity'?

Whatever the reason, this benefactor of humanity will have to be contested by Syrianus in the name of the first principles of Pythagorean and Platonic philosophy, by which one must understand the philosophy of the One. This is why, in engaging in the commentary on book 13 of the *Metaphysics*, Syrianus tells us that he is in fact engaged in a combat in

[12] cf. B. Kötting, s.v. 'Euergetes' in *RAC* 6, cols 848-60, especially cols 858-9, 'Verwendung in nachkonstantinischer Zeit'.

[13] Proclus, *Theol. Plat.* (Saffrey-Westerink) 1.1,7,10; Ammonius, *in Int.*, CAG 4,5 (Busse) 181,30-1.

[14] cf. A.D. Nock, 'Soter and Euergetes' in *The Joy of Study, Papers... F.C. Grant*, New York 1951, 127-48, reprinted in *Essays on Religion and the Ancient World*, Oxford 1972, 720-35. On the emperor as *euergetês*, cf. K.M. Setton, *The Christian Attitude towards the Emperor in the Fourth Century*, New York 1941, 51.

[15] On this subject, see the arguments of Cicero in *de Nat. Deor.* 1.15.38, with Pease's note on the words 'a quibus...utilitas', and 2.24.62, with Pease's note on the words 'beneficiis excellentis viros'.

[16] *en allois men meresi tês theologikês pragmateias* (80,17); see also Elias, *Prolegomena Philosophiae*, CAG 18,1 (Busse), 20,19-20: 'for it is written in the theological treatise, the *Metaphysics* (*en gar têi Meta ta phusika pragmateiai theologikêi epigegramme̅ei...*)', a name based on the Aristotelian division, *Metaph.* 6.1, 1026a18-19: 'so that there would be three contemplative philosophies: mathematical, natural, and theological (*hôste treis an eien philosophiai theôrêtikai, mathêmatikê, phusikê, theologikê*)', with Ross's remark (ad loc.): 'The designation of metaphysics as *theologikê* is confined to this passage and the corresponding passage in 11,7, 1064b3'.

which he will be one of the participants and, in turn, the judge who will determine the victor. It is again as a judge between Plato and Aristotle that Syrianus is presented by Ammonius in his commentary on the *de Interpretatione*, when he says:

> The great Syrianus has *judged* this question in an excellent and very penetrating manner, by showing very clearly what is the nature of these realities (the contraries) and their mutual distinction, by emphasising the agreement of our common and innate notions with the words of the treatise, by examining each of Aristotle's arguments in themselves, and by teaching through an analysis of the wording of the treatise what in this text has been transmitted correctly, on the one hand, and, on the other, in a way no doubt probable but inexact.[17]

We see that here also Syrianus uses the same method, dividing the true from the false, the exact from the approximate, the argument which holds from the one which runs aground. We know, moreover, that at least once in the same commentary Syrianus dares to contradict Aristotle and show the falsity of his doctrine.[18]

In this sense, the great text of the commentary on book 13 of the *Metaphysics* ends with a second declaration of intent. Far from wanting to indulge in a base polemic with a philosopher whom he admires and respects, it is in the name of 'justice, thought and the love of the truth' that Syrianus will judge the debate which he initiates between the philosophy of Aristotle and that of Pythagoras and Plato.

These texts reveal to us Syrianus' philosophical qualities and bear testimony to a tradition that engendered great respect for Aristotle in the Neoplatonic school of Athens, even when one is committed to refuting him. It should no longer be surprising that the best commentaries on Aristotle, those of Simplicius, are the last productions of this Athenian Neoplatonic school, even after the closing of the school by Justinian in 529.

Yet another document confirms this favourable impression. Syrianus had been the teacher of Proclus, and we said that the latter celebrated Syrianus as his benefactor because of the perfect education which he had received from him. Now, the manner in which Syrianus proceeded in educating Proclus has been described by Marinus in his writing entitled *Proclus, or On Happiness*. For the first anniversary of the death of his teacher (485), Marinus composed a sort of funeral eulogy, whose theme is the happiness the philosopher acquires by practising the six degrees of virtue. To illustrate his subject, Marinus recounts numerous facts from Proclus' life, and in particular the education which he received from Syrianus. The division of this treatise into chapters was introduced in

---

[17] Ammonius, *in Int., CAG* 4,5 (Busse), 253,12-17.
[18] cf. L. Tarán, *Anonymous Commentary on Aristotle's De Interpretatione* (Beiträge zur klassischen Philologie, Heft 95), Meisenheim am Glan 1978, 120,13-14: *prôtos de Surianos ho philosophos anteipen kai apodeiknusin pseudos on.*

1700 by J.A. Fabricius and was followed afterwards by all the editors including J.F. Boissonade, the author of the last edition in 1814.[19] A summary of these texts follows.

(Proclus' Aristotelian education had in fact begun before his arrival in Athens, although, even in Alexandria, he attended the course of a professor named Olympiodorus, of whom we know practically nothing.[20])

1. Marinus, *Proclus* §9 (in Alexandria).

> He begins to attend the lectures of professors on the philosophy of place. For Aristotelian studies, he would frequent the school of the philosopher Olympiodorus, who had a great reputation. For mathematics ... Whenever he attended the lectures of Olympiodorus – who had a great facility in speaking and who, because of the rapidity of his elocution and the sublimity of his argumentation, was accessible only to a small number of his auditors – Proclus, after leaving the lecture, would repeat its entire content from memory before his fellow students in its original formulations even though there was a great deal of it ... Moreover, Proclus even understood the logical treatises of Aristotle easily, and this after a simple reading, although they are difficult for those who study them to understand.

2. Marinus, *Proclus* §12 (once in Athens, Syrianus puts the young student in the hands of the old Plutarch of Athens).

> Proclus thus read Aristotle's treatise *On the Soul* and Plato's *Phaedo* with Plutarch.

3. Marinus, *Proclus* §13 (after the death of Plutarch, Syrianus takes him into his own hands).

> In less than two complete years, Syrianus read all the treatises of Aristotle with him, the logical, ethical and political and those on the theological science (the *Metaphysics*) which surpassed them all. Then, once he had been well introduced by these words as if by certain preparatory sacrifices and small mysteries, he was led step by step to the mystagogy of Plato...

4. Marinus, *Proclus* §14.

> Proclus acquired the political virtues by reading Aristotle's *Politics* and Plato's *Laws* and *Republic*.

From these four texts, we can extract precious information on the education Proclus received as regards Aristotelian philosophy. We note that from an early age, Proclus learned Aristotelian logic, of which he had a thorough mastery; he knew by heart the treatises which he understood in a single reading (text 1). On the other hand, in the Neoplatonic school

[19] J.F. Boissonade, *Marini Vita Procli*, Leipzig 1814.
[20] cf. *PLRE*, s.v. 'Oympiodorus' 2.

at Athens, the complete study of Aristotle had always been considered as preparatory to the study of Plato:[21] the reading of the *de Anima* as preparation for the reading of the *Phaedo* (text 2), the study of logic, ethics, politics, physics, and metaphysics as preparation for Platonic 'mystagogy' (text 3); the reading of the *Politics* as preparation for the reading of the *Laws* and the *Republic* (text 4). One sees this: if the Neoplatonists held that assuredly Plato's philosophy surpassed Aristotle's in every respect[22] they did not for all that neglect extensive study of the Aristotelian treatises. It suffices to read their writings to collect the evidence of their genuine familiarity with Aristotelian philosophy.[23]

This regard for Aristotle in the Neoplatonic school of Athens and with Syrianus in particular must be interpreted within the context of the long debate on the problem of the agreement between Aristotle and Plato. In the period in which Aristotle was known perhaps solely through his exoteric works, the thesis of agreement could be easily invented by Antiochus of Ascalon and diffused by Cicero. But familiarity with the great Aristotelian philosophical treatises must have modified radically the idea that people had of the relation between Aristotle and Plato. The thesis of agreement, rejected first by Atticus and taken up again immediately by Alcinous in the form of the doctrine that the Ideas are the thoughts of God, could be maintained by putting Plato's intelligible realm within Aristotle's transcendent Intellect. With Plotinus, the correlation of the intelligible and the intellect came to entail a superior principle, beyond the Intellect and Being, the One. In this way, Neoplatonism's fundamental hierarchy of the three hypostases was established.

From this point, what Aristotle will come to be reproached with continually is precisely that he stopped at the Intellect in the doctrine of the first god, without ascending further to the One.[24] In the confines of the inferior hypostases a certain agreement between Aristotle and Plato will always be sought, but the superiority of Plato will always be loudly affirmed because of his doctrine of the first hypostasis, the One, the first god. This is the position which we have discovered in Syrianus, when in his commentary on books 13 and 14 of the *Metaphysics* he sets Pythagoras' and Plato's doctrine of first principles in opposition to Aristotle's. Syrianus taught this position to Proclus, and through him to all the philosophy of the Middle Ages and above all the Renaissance.[25]

---

[21] This is also Themistius' point of view, cf. *Orat.* (Downey-Norman) 20, vol. 2, 6,10-19; Aristotelianism serves as the *proteleia* to the *epoptia* which is Platonism.

[22] cf. L.G. Westerink, *Anonymous Prolegomena to Platonic Philosophy*, §9, 24-34.

[23] See, for example, the index of the different books of Proclus' *Theol. Plat.*

[24] See, for example, Proclus *Theol. Plat.* 2.4.

[25] cf. Joseph Moreau, 'De la concordance d'Aristote avec Platon' in *Platon et Aristote à la Renaissance* (De Pétrarque à Descartes XXXII), Paris 1976, 45-58.

CHAPTER NINE

Infinite power impressed: the transformation of Aristotle's physics and theology

Richard Sorabji

The focus of this chapter will be on an argument about infinite power, which was started by Aristotle, but which was subsequently connected with the idea of a Creator God.

In the thirteenth century, Bacon, Bonaventure and Thomas Aquinas all thought, in one sense or another, that Aristotle's God was a Creator and Sustainer of the universe.[1] Some thought that he was a Creator in the sense of being causally responsible for the beginningless existence of the universe, some in the sense of giving it a beginning. Any such belief in his causal role is hard to credit, for the main action of Aristotle's God in the world seems to be merely that of a *mover*. He moves the heavens, but he does not seem to give them *existence*. Admittedly, he has a certain indirect responsibility for the existence of *compound* bodies down below the heavens. For he unconsciously inspires the sun's motion, which by the obliquity of its angle in turn produces seasonal disturbances, and so makes earth, air, fire and water turn into each other, relocate themselves and mingle to form new compounds. But it is not obvious that he has even indirect responsibility for the existence of the main masses of earth, air, fire and water, or of the heavens themselves.

The contrary view of Aristotle's God as Creator or Sustainer was based partly on spurious works, several of them associated with the ninth century AD. A particularly important one, to which I shall shortly return, is the *Theology of Aristotle*. Others which mention a Creator or Sustainer God and which were wrongly attributed to Aristotle are the early *de Mundo* from around the beginning of our era, the *Liber de Causis* and the *Secretum Secretorum*. But I want to draw attention to a quite different kind of influence, that of the Neoplatonist commentator Ammonius (c. 435/45 – c. 517/26 AD). Ammonius maintained that Aristotle did indeed make God the efficient cause of the world, in the sense of making him

---

[1] For references, fuller detail and translations of the main passages discussed below, see Richard Sorabji, *Matter, Space and Motion*, London and Ithaca NY, 1988, ch. 15. The materials were first prepared for the Charles Schmitt Memorial Colloquium at the Warburg Institute, and presented there, as here, in abbreviated form.

causally responsible for its *beginningless* existence. His aim was to harmonise Aristotle with Plato, for Plato's God in the *Timaeus* was a Creator, and Ammonius took him to be a Creator in the same sense, of vouchsafing a *beginningless* existence. Plato makes his Creator explain that because the heavens are a composite entity, they can in principle be dismantled but that they will in fact be held together by his good will.[2] One later interpretation among others was that the heavens are a compound of Aristotelian matter and form. On this view, the prime matter might be expected to survive a process of dismantling, but the heavens, being a compound of prime matter with form, would not.

Ammonius was not the first to represent Aristotle's God as a Creator or Sustainer. Arius Didymus was Stoicising in the first century BC, when he made Aristotle's prime mover 'hold together' (*sunektikon*) the heavenly bodies.[3] In the fourth century AD, St Ambrose was reading or misreading an early dialogue, *On Philosophy*, from Aristotle's days in Plato's school, when he characterised Aristotle's efficient cause as the *operatorium* who brought things about merely by willing. This does not represent Aristotle's mature view and may represent only the view of an interlocutor in the now fragmentary work.[4] A desire to harmonise Platonism with Aristotle accounts for the Neoplatonist Dexippus, in the same century as Ambrose, understanding Aristotle's talk of dependency (*êrtêtai*) in *Metaphysics* 12 as meaning that substances owe their unity and at least in some cases their life and form to the supreme Neoplatonist deity, the One.[5] A still more extreme harmonisation is attempted by the fifth-century Neoplatonist Hierocles, when he ascribes to both Plato and Aristotle belief in divine Creation not out of any substratum. He further credits for the general thesis of harmony his teacher Plutarch of Athens, and an earlier Ammonius – Ammonius Saccas, who taught Plotinus in the third century AD.[6] But the interpretation of Aristotle's God as Creator or Sustainer did not yet stick. We shall see that Plutarch's other two pupils, Syrianus and Proclus, resisted it. So it was left to Ammonius to drive it home, and we are told that he wrote a whole book on the subject.[7]

Ammonius' influence on later Greek Neoplatonist commentators seems to have been decisive. His view of Aristotle's God was published by Asclepius and endorsed also by Philoponus, Simplicius, Olympiodorus, Elias and (if he is the author of the extant commentary on Aristotle's *de Anima*, Book 3) Stephanus. Even more important, Ammonius is cited,

[2] Plato *Timaeus* 41A-B.

[3] Arius Didymus, fr. 4, in *Dox. Gr.* 450,16.

[4] Ambrose *Hexaemeron* 1.1.1-2, p. 3, 10-13 (Schenkl). The imprint in mud of a papyrus recently found in Afghanistan may contain a further fragment of *On Philosophy*, assigning to God a different causal role, that of making things participate in Forms: P. Hadot, 'Les textes littéraires grecs de la trésorie d'aï Khanoum', *Bulletin de correspondence hellénique* 111, 1987, 225-66.

[5] Dexippus *in Cat.* 40,28-41,3; 41,7-18, with reference to Aristotle *Metaph.* 12.7, 1072b14.

[6] Hierocles ap. Photium *Bibliotheca* 171b33ff; 172a22ff (Bekker).

[7] Simplicius *in Phys.* 1363,8-12; cf. *in Cael.* 271, 18-21 and Farabi's *Harmony*, discussed below.

along with the spurious *Theology of Aristotle*, as an authority for the view of Aristotle's God as Creator by the Islamic philosopher Farabi (c. 873-950 AD), in his work *The Harmony of Plato and Aristotle*,[8] although Farabi diverges from Ammonius in denying that Aristotle's cosmos is eternal. I shall draw attention below to a neglected passage in which Avicenna (c. 980-1038) accepts that Aristotle's God is a Sustainer, and Maimonides (1135-1204) repeats that Aristotle's God is the efficient cause of the world's beginningless existence.[9] Farabi was read by Avicenna, Farabi and Avicenna were read by Maimonides, and Maimonides was read, in Latin translation, by our thirteenth-century authors. So there is a perfectly possible route by which Ammonius may have acted, alongside other influences, to shape the thirteenth-century misreadings of Aristotle's theology.

Tantalisingly, Farabi tells us that Ammonius' arguments are too well known to need repeating. But Simplicius (writing after 529 AD) gives a series of arguments drawn from Ammonius, the last of which is the argument about infinite power.[10]

The original argument on infinite power appears in *Physics* 8.10, where Aristotle maintains that what moves the heavens cannot be a spatially extended entity, nor a power lodged in a spatially extended entity. For what produces unending motion must be *infinite*, whereas any extended entity, and any power lodged in an extended entity, is finite. If the mover is neither a spatially extended entity, nor a power (or soul) lodged in one, this opens the way to the view made explicit in *Metaphysics* 12.7, where the argument is repeated (1073a5-11), that the mover is God: God can supply the required infinite power.

So far the argument concerns only the *motion* of the heavens. But it was changed to an argument about their *existence* by the work of four successive Neoplatonists who stand in a teacher-pupil relationship: Syrianus, Proclus, Ammonius and Philoponus. Syrianus (died c. 437 AD) protests that Aristotle should have admitted that the source of the heavens' infinite motion is also the source of their unending being. Aristotle would then have been in agreement with Plato, as Syrianus interprets him. Plato even implies at *Phaedrus* 245E, in Syrianus' view, that in giving motion to the heavens, God *thereby* gives them being.[11] The connecting link between motion and being is not explained, but one might be found in the view later propounded by Aristotle, that circular motion is

[8] Farabi, *Harmony of Plato and Aristotle*, with German translation, Dieterici (ed.), *Alfarabi's philosophische Abhandlungen*, Leiden 1892, 24,13-25,1 and 28,22-29,5.

[9] Maimonides *Guide for the Perplexed*, part 2, ch. 21 (translations by M. Friedländer, London 1904, and S. Pines, Chicago 1963). Maimonides' Aristotle believes, but does not think he can prove, the world to be beginningless, part 2, ch. 15.

[10] Simplicius *in Phys.* 1361,11-1363,12, esp. 1363,4-12.

[11] Syrianus *in Metaph.* 117,25-118,11. I am indebted for my account of Syrianus and Proclus especially to Carlos Steel, who was kind enough to show me an advance copy of his article, 'Proclus et Aristote sur la casualité efficiente de l'Intellect divin', in J. Pépin and H.D. Saffrey (eds), *Proclus – lecteur et interprète des Anciens*, Actes du Colloque Proclus, CNRS, Paris 1987.

the *defining* characteristic of the celestial body. That might well be taken to imply that the preservation of its motion guarantees its preservation as the celestial body. A connexion between motion and being such as that suggested by Syrianus was already hinted at by Aristotle's immediate successor Theophrastus[12] and is later found on one interpretation in Simplicius,[13] in the passage of Avicenna to be discussed below, and in Abravanel.[14]

But of more relevance is the argument suggested by Syrianus' pupil Proclus (c. 411-485 AD). For instead of moving *directly* from motion to being, Proclus suggests doing so indirectly, by means of reapplying the infinite power argument. The *same* infinite power argument, says Proclus, which excludes an infinite power of *moving* from a finite body will also exclude from it an infinite power of *existing*. So this power of existing must *equally* be derived by the cosmos from elsewhere, most plausibly from the same divine source:[15]

> In just the same way, everything shows that it [the cosmos] will obtain its infinite power of *existing* from there [from the Intellect], because of the argument which says that an infinite power never exists within a finite body....
>
> Something else, then, will give it the power of existing, and will give it not all at once, since it would not be capable of receiving it all at once. It will give it, then, in the amounts it can take, in a stream that flows and ever flows onto it. No wonder the cosmos is for ever *coming* into being and never *has* being.

Syrianus and Proclus were both deprecating Aristotle's failure to agree with Plato on the issue, although they thought he agreed on many others. But Proclus' pupil Ammonius takes the harmonisation of Plato and Aristotle further. The argument sketched by Proclus is what Aristotle actually *intended*: he meant us to re-apply the infinite power argument and conclude that God produced the being as well as the motion of the heavens. This is the last of the arguments drawn by Simplicius from Ammonius' book:[16]

---

[12] Theophrastus asks, *Metaph*. 6a5-13; 10a10-15, whether the heaven would stop existing as a heaven, if it lost its rotation.

[13] Simplicius *in Cael*. 301,4-7. So Robert W. Sharples, 'The unmoved mover and the motion of the heavens in Alexander of Aphrodisias', *Apeiron* 17, 1983, 62-6, at 63, but Simplicius might instead intend Proclus' re-application of the infinite power argument, since he endorses that elsewhere (*in Phys*. 1363,4-8).

[14] Isaac Abravanel, *The Deeds of God* 9.9.

[15] Proclus *in Tim*. (Diehl) 1,267,16-268,6 (quoted in part here) and in a work entitled *Examination of Aristotle's Objections to Plato's Timaeus*, ap. Philoponum *contra Proclum* 238,3-240,9; 297,21-300,2; 626,1-627,20.

[16] Simplicius *in Phys*. 1363,4-12. The best account of Ammonius' theology that I know is that of Koenraad Verrycken, *God en Wereld in de Wijsbegeerte van Ioannes Philoponus*, Ph.D. diss., Louvain 1985. The relevant section is summarised in Chapter 10 below.

And if, according to Aristotle, the power of any finite body is itself finite, clearly whether it be a power of moving or a power that produces being, then, just as it must get its eternal *motion* from the unmoved cause, so it must receive its eternal *being* as a body from the non-bodily cause. My teacher Ammonius wrote a whole book offering many proofs that Aristotle thought God was also an efficient cause of the whole cosmos, a book from which I have here taken over some items sufficient for present purposes. More complete instruction on the subject can be got from there.

Ammonius' pupil Philoponus (c. 490-570s AD) agrees that Aristotle makes God the efficient cause of the world's beginningless existence.[17] But he himself is a Christian, and accordingly he tries to rewrite the infinite power argument, to support the *Christian* belief that God created the universe in the more conventional sense of giving it a *beginning*. As a result, he makes the argument much more complex, and his version has been very variously interpreted.[18] But I believe it can be seen to have four stages.

First, Philoponus argues on behalf of Christianity that, since the world cannot contain infinite power, it must have a beginning and end.[19] But he knows that Proclus has an answer to this, and he records, as the second stage in the argument, Proclus' reply that the world can perfectly well be unending, provided that the infinite power needed for this result is not housed within the world.[20] He therefore has to reply to Proclus, and he

[17] Philoponus *in Phys.* 189,10-26; 240,18-19; *in GC* 136.33-137.3 (cf. 286,7); *in DA* 37,18-31; *in An. Post.* 242,26-243,25.

[18] The interpretation which seems to me right is that of Lindsay Judson, 'God or nature? Philoponus on generability or perishability', in Richard Sorabji (ed.), *Philoponus and the Rejection of Aristotelian Science*, London and Ithaca NY 1987. I shall be diverging in various ways from the interpretations of H.A. Wolfson, 'The Kalam arguments for creation in Saadia, Averroes, Maimonides and St. Thomas', *Saadia Anniversary Volume, American Academy for Jewish Research, Texts and Studies* 2, New York 1943 at 202 and 240; id., *The Philosophy of the Kalam*, Cambridge Mass. 1970, at 377-8 and 381; H.A. Davidson, 'John Philoponus as a source of medieval Islamic and Jewish proofs of creation', *Journal of the American Oriental Society* 89, 1969, at 362; id., 'The principle that a finite body can contain only finite power', in S. Stein and R. Loewe (eds), *Studies in Jewish Religious and Intellectual History Presented to Alexander Altmann*, Alabama 1979, at 80 and n. 37; Michael Wolff, *Fallgesetz und Massebegriff*, Berlin 1971, at 94-9; Carlos Steel, ' "Omnis corporis potentia est finita" ', in Jan P. Beckmann, Ludger Honnefelder, Gangolf Schrimpf, Georg Wieland (eds), *Philosophie im Mittelalter*, Hamburg 1987, 213-24.

[19] Philoponus *contra Proclum* 1.18-2,11; *contra Aristotelem* ap. Simplicium *in Cael.* 142,22-5; in an Arabic summary of a later lost work, translated into English by S. Pines, 'An Arabic summary of a lost work of John Philoponus', *Israel Oriental Studies* 2, 1972, 320-52, at 323-4 (reprinted in his *Collected Works*, vol. 2, Jerusalem and Leiden 1986), and into French by G. Troupeau, 'Un épitomé arabe du "de contingentia mundi" de Jean Philopon' in *Memorial A.J. Festugière = Cahiers d'Orientalisme* 10, Geneva 1984, 77-88, at 84; and in a work recorded by Simplicius *in Phys.* 1327,14-16; 1329,17-19. In his earlier *in Cat.* 50,28-51,12, Philoponus was content merely to expound Aristotle's version of the infinite power argument.

[20] Philoponus *contra Proclum* 238,3-240,9; 297,21-300,2; 626,1-627,20 quotes Proclus' *Examination of Aristotle's Objections to Plato's Timaeus*. The same argument is ascribed to Plato by Philoponus *contra Proclum* 235,4-19 and propounded without ascription, Philoponus *contra Proclum* 2,11-14; Arabic summary translated Pines 324, Troupeau 84.

does so in the third stage of his argument by reversing an idea about *nature* employed much earlier by Alexander of Aphrodisias.[21] Proclus claims to be following Plato, but he has failed to ask whether Plato's cosmos is imperishable 'in accordance with the *logos* of its own nature', or rather through God's *overriding* its nature. In fact, its nature as a *composite* entity means that it can in principle be dismantled, so if it is imperishable, this must be due to God's overriding its nature. Proclus has therefore misrepresented Plato, whose world must be *perishable* in accordance with the *logos* of its own nature. It ought therefore to follow, by a principle which Proclus himself accepts,[22] that the world is also *generable* in accordance with the *logos* of its own nature.[23]

This third stage of the argument is resisted by Simplicius, who says that the world is not really perishable by its own nature, because it is by nature fitted (*epitêdeios*) to receive the eternity that God gives it.[24] Proclus in one passage concedes Philoponus' point that his cosmos will have to be perishable by its own nature (*ek tês oikeias phuseôs*),[25] but in another insists that the heavens get their imperishability from their own consti- tution (*sustasis*), which belongs to their essence, even though they receive their constitution from God.[26] He adds that the cosmos 'by its very being and nature desires the Intellect' from which it gets its being.[27]

In the fourth stage of his argument, Philoponus tries to go further. He does not deny Proclus' claim that God might override the world's natural *perishability*, although he does not agree that God will in fact do so. But he seems to think it impossible even for God to override the world's natural *generability* and give it a beginningless existence after all. Hence he ascribes to Plato, and himself upholds, the view that the world is generable not just by nature, but without qualification, and that it was actually generated and had a beginning in time.[28] He does not, however, explain the asymmetry which allows God to override natural perishability and impose endless existence, but not to override natural generability and impose beginningless existence.

The four stages of Philoponus' argument stand out particularly clearly in the Arabic summary of a lost work of his which has been translated by Shlomo Pines. I will mark the stages (i) to (iv):

21 Alexander *Quaest.* 1.18,30,25-32,19; and fragment of the lost *in Cael.* preserved at Simplicius *in Cael.* 358,27-360,3, both translated by R.W. Sharples, in 'Alexander of Aphrodisias: problems about possibility 2', *Bulletin of the Institute of Classical Studies* 30, 1983, at 99-102, and discussed by him there and in 'The unmoved mover and the motion of the heavens in Alexander of Aphrodisias', *Apeiron* 17, 1983, 62-6.
22 Philoponus *contra Proclum* 119,14-120,14; cf. 549,7-550,24.
23 ibid. 225,14-226,19; 240,23-6; 241,26-7; 242,11-22; 304,4-9.
24 Simplicius *in Cael.* 143,17-29; *in Phys.* 1331,30-3; cf. 1358,29-30. Same point made against Alexander *in Cael.* 361,10-15, cf. 360,23-4.
25 Proclus *Examination of Aristotle's Objections to Plato's Timaeus,* ap. Philoponum *contra Proclum* 627,17-18; cf. 239,1. I am grateful to Andrew Smith for the Proclus references.
26 Proclus *in Tim.* 3.212,21-2 (Diehl).
27 Proclus *in Tim.* 1.267,10, just before the passage translated above.
28 Philoponus *contra Proclum* 237,7-15.

Then he said: (i) if the world is a finite body, as has been demonstrated by Aristotle in the first treatise of his book on the Heaven and (if) the forces of every finite body are finite, as has been likewise demonstrated by Aristotle at the end of the eighth treatise of the Book of Physics, (then) because of what we have, and of what Aristotle has demonstrated, the world must have been created in time (and) have come into existence after not having existed.

Supposing, however, that someone says: (ii) as Aristotle has explained and demonstrated, the body of the world is finite and it is impossible that a finite body should have an infinite force; however the force which has ensured the preservation of the essence of the world in the eternity *a parte ante* [and] which will ensure its permanent and perpetual preservation in the future, is the force of the Creator, may He be blessed, who causes the heaven to move in perpetual motion; we should answer:

(iii) The disagreement between us and him does not (concern) the (portion) of the Creator, may He be blessed and exalted, which is imparted to the world. The disagreement solely (concerns) your saying that the world is by nature eternal *a parte ante*. For if, as you say, it is eternal *a parte ante*, it does not need a force ensuring the preservation of its essence to be imparted to it. For it is a characteristic of a thing which is eternal *a parte ante* by nature that the force which ensures the preservation of its essence should be a force natural to it and not drawn by it from something else. [If however this force is drawn by it from something else] and received by it from a thing other than its essence (the thing in question) is not eternal *a parte ante* by nature, for it is not then... It is (106b) eternal *a parte ante* only because of a force (belonging) to some other (thing).

(iv) Its eternity *a parte ante* would have been abolished if there had not been this thing which gives it permanent (being) and ensures the preservation of its essence preventing the latter from perishing. Since the world is not by nature eternal *a parte ante*, as is asserted by the Eternalists, it must be by nature created in time, as is asserted by us. And it is impossible for what is by nature created in time to be eternal *a parte ante*. In this there is a refutation of the doctrine concerning the eternity *a parte ante* of the world adopted by the Eternalists.

The main points of the first treatise of the discourse of John the Grammarian are finished. Glory be to God always, for ever, eternally.[29]

Philoponus' argument was available in Arabic not only in the summary just presented, but also thanks to the translation of his *contra Proclum* and *contra Aristotelem*. The detective work of Islamic scholars has shown that various stages of the argument were known to the Jewish philosopher Saadia (died 942 AD), to Farabi's Christian pupil Yaḥya Ibn ʿAdî (892-1073) and in turn to his Christian pupil Ibn Suwâr (born 942). But what has not to my knowledge been discussed, nor translated, is a portion of commentary by *Avicenna* (c. 980-1038) on Aristotle's version of the infinite power argument, as it appears in his *Metaphysics*. I am grateful to Fritz Zimmermann for supplying me with an abstract. I

[29] 'Philoponus, an Arabic summary of a lost work', translated by S. Pines, *Israel Oriental Studies* 2, 1972, at 323-4, repr. in his *Collected Works* 2, 1986; French translation by Troupeau 84-5.

believe that Avicenna here does four things. First, he endorses, without
ascription, the view of Ammonius that Aristotle's God is the Sustainer, as
well as the Mover, of the heavens (sec. 6). Secondly, he distinguishes the
type of argument which we found in Syrianus which moves directly from
God's preservation of the heavens' *motion* to his preservation of their
existence (2b). Thirdly, he reapplies the infinite power argument, to make
Aristotle's God the Sustainer of the heavens, very much in the way we
saw Proclus doing, and Philoponus recording in the second stage of his
argument (2d). Finally, he adopts a position like that which Philoponus
forces on Proclus in the third stage of his argument: the existence of the
heavens is necessary (they are imperishable) because of God, not because
of their own nature (3,4). Averroes later describes Avicenna as following
Philoponus' point here – although he misidentifies it as Alexander's – and
it is he (Averroes) who puts Avicenna's point, as does Abravanel after
him, in terms of God versus *nature*.[30]

Avicenna's argument is hard to follow, because the commentary is
probably a reconstruction, whether by himself or by someone else, of part
of a larger production in twenty volumes, which he lost in the sack of
Isfahan three years before his death. It may be significant that in
announcing his hope of reconstructing the work, he mentions that he is
studying not only Alexander and Themistius, but also Philoponus.[31]

I need to show in more detail how the line of thought I have described
emerges from the passage. Avicenna is attacking (sec. 6) commentators
on Aristotle, especially (sec. 4) the Nestorian Christian Abu Bishr Matta
of Baghdad (died c. 940), who had translated Aristotle, Alexander and
Themistius into Arabic. Abu Bishr had said (2a) that the existence of the
celestial sphere was necessary in itself, so that (4) God's role was confined
to producing motion and to making motion perpetual. Avicenna objects
(3,4) that nothing other than God is intrinsically necessary; all other
necessity is owed to God, including that of the celestial sphere. This is the
view that Averroes later connects with the third stage of Philoponus'
argument, which he misidentifies as Alexander's. Avicenna goes on (6) to
accept the interpretation of Aristotle provided by Ammonius and his
followers including Philoponus, according to which Aristotle's God is the
Sustainer of the universe. On the other hand he thinks (1) that neither
the commentators he is attacking nor Aristotle himself supply an actual
argument for this conclusion. The only argument they supply for God

---

[30] Averroes *Middle Commentary on Aristotle's de Caelo*, translated from Hebrew version
into Latin by Paul Israelita, available as 'paraphrasis' in the Juntine edition of 1562-1574,
vol. 5, 293 v, a, H-I, partly translated into English from the Hebrew by H.A. Wolfson,
Crescas' Critique of Aristotle, Cambridge Mass. 1929, 681-2. Avicenna is here described as
the *companion* (*comes* in Latin) of 'Alexander', and the terminology of *nature* is associated
with Avicenna here and later by Abravanel *The Deeds of God* 2.3, 126, translated from the
Hebrew by H.A. Wolfson, op. cit., 597 and 682.

[31] Avicenna, *Letter to al-Kiyâ*, M. Badawi (ed.), *Aristû 'ind al-'Arab*, Cairo 1947 (repr.
Kuwait 1978), 120-2, second part translated into French by S. Pines, 'La "philosophie
orientale" d'Avicenne et sa polémique contre les Bagdadiens', *Archives d'histoire doctrinale
et littéraire du moyen âge* 19, 1952, 5-37, at 6-9. See esp. 9.

concerns the *motion*, not the *existence*, of the universe. In particular, they do not use the idea which we found in Theophrastus, Syrianus and possibly Simplicius (2b). Avicenna then refers to an argument which would do the trick (2d), and would show God to be the Sustainer of the universe. It is the infinite power argument used by Proclus and recorded *inter alios* by Philoponus. According to the misguided interpretation of certain commentators, the celestial sphere will be receptive (a concept found also in the Greek texts) of the motion imposed by God, and even *perpetually* receptive of it, despite the absurdity that no provision has been made for its *existence* to be perpetual. For its own power is finite, so that it has no *internal* source of perpetual existence. Its perpetual existence cannot then be assured, unless these commentators are wrong, and the divine source of its motion, which acts as a *final* cause filling it with desire, also acts as an *efficient* cause, that is, I take it, as an efficient cause of its *existence*. ('It will have to be receptive and perpetually in motion despite the fact that its power is finite – unless there is another cause and emanation on account of which the desired end becomes an *effective* principle'.) The following are the relevant sections of Avicenna, with key portions italicised:

Comments on *Metaph.* 12.6, 1071b5-31

(1) *He [Avicenna] criticises Aristotle and his commentators as follows. It is improper to argue to God from the fact of motion. For in that way they cannot show that the true One is the principle of all existence.* If the first principle is a principle of the *motion* of the sphere, it need not therefore be a principle of the *substance* of the sphere.

(2) He [Avicenna] says: Let us examine their belief that the motion of the sphere is necessary and without beginning or end. They do not show:
    (a) that the existence of the sphere is necessary in itself;
    (b) *that for it to exist is to be in motion, so that if it ceased to move it would cease to exist.*
    (c) Rather, they argue as follows: the sphere exists; it is in motion; therefore its motion must be beginningless. But that is a *non sequitur.* For suppose we knew it existed but not whether it had ever moved. From the fact of its existence we could not tell whether it moved, perpetually or otherwise. Neither could we proceed to tell that or how it, its matter and form, had been brought into being [by a creator].
    (d) *In a word, how is it supposed to be desirous, receptive, eternal? It will have to be receptive and perpetually in motion despite the fact that its power is finite – unless there is another cause and emanation on account of which the desired end becomes an effective principle.*

Comments on *Metaph.* 12.7, 1072b3

(3) If it sets things in motion by dint of being intrinsically desirable, and because the thing moved is fit so to be affected as to get moving, that motion is brought about jointly by conditions in both mover and moved. If so, act and effect follow necessarily, if only in faculties close to reason (Greek: *logos*). Act and effect will thus be necessary, and will constitute a sublime

necessity which has a noble existence, since the order of the whole universe flows from it. We do not mean to say that that necessity is one of compulsion or ineluctability. It is one where things could not conceivably be different. This passage (1072b3) does not mean that the heavenly motion is intrinsically necessary, in the sense that it could not be otherwise. It is necessary in the sense explained earlier. Nothing exists of necessity when considered in isolation from the First. Indeed, if the tie to the First could be broken, everything would reduce to nothing. In respect of itself, everything is vain and perishes, except the face of the First Truth.

(4) Some, failing to distinguish between 'conditionally necessary' and 'strictly necessary', have mistaken the necessity here at issue for an intrinsic necessity, arguing as follows, (lacuna). *Now I ask Abu Bishr: on the assumption that it is of necessity that things are as they are, what part is there for the first cause to play in relation to them? He answers: to maintain them in perpetual motion. But that is absurd. The part played by the First is that it is on its account that there is necessity, with no necessity accruing to anything else on account of itself.* A sign of the folly of that (Baghdadian) position is that it makes necessity *intrinsic* to things, perpetuity *extrinsic*: that intrinsic necessity of theirs is not supposed to entail perpetuity; perpetuity is to be furnished from outside. But if perpetuity is bestowed on motion, does that not also make it necessary? If it were necessary by itself, would not that make it independent of its mover?

(5) The truth is that motion, its existence, the necessity of its existence while it exists, and the perpetuity of its existence, all depend on the causes of motion. God is too lofty to be made a cause only of motion. It is He that furnishes the existence of every substance. It is through Him that everything else must be and acquires the necessity consequent upon the relation there must be between Him and it.

Comments on *Metaph*. 12.7, 1072b13-14

(6) '*Thus upon such a principle does the heaven depend*'. The principle in question is primary, single, simple, intrinsically intelligible, absolutely good, the object of desire for the whole universe. It is from it that necessity emanates to things. Besides it, no importance can be attached to non-existence [as a possible source of existence]. It either excludes non-existence altogether or extends a power to exist to things in the measure in which they are fit to be affected. '*Depends*': Aristotle means to *say that the universe itself is sustained by that principle. It is wrong to confine its blessings to the lowly gift of motion, as do those commentators.*[32]

That the infinite power arguments recur in Averroes (c. 1126-1198) has been well brought out in some very interesting work by modern Arabists. What I think can now be clarified is the relationship of Averroes' texts to the preceding ones of Avicenna, Philoponus and others. Perhaps the most important point is that the first three stages of Philoponus' argument

---

[32] Avicenna, Notes on *Metaphysics* 12 from his *Kitâb al-Inṣaf*, Badawi (ed.), *Aristû 'ind al-'Arab*, 23-6 (whole text 22-33), abstract by Fritz Zimmermann.

recur in Averroes, but modern scholarship has not been aware of this, because Averroes was not aware himself. He correctly identifies the first stage as coming from Philoponus, but by a signal error ascribes the second and third stage to *Alexander*, and his ascription is taken at face value by Thomas Aquinas and by more recent commentators.[33]

It is clear that the second-stage argument for God as Sustainer, which Philoponus takes from Proclus, should not be ascribed to Alexander. For Alexander argues on the other side that, if the world escapes destruction, this cannot be due to an external cause, such as God.[34] And a passage of Simplicius informs us that he goes only as far as making his Aristotelian God an efficient, as well as a final, cause of the world's *motion*, not a cause in any way of its *existence*.[35] It is equally wrong to ascribe to Alexander the idea from the third stage of Philoponus' argument, that the world is destructible by nature, but preserved by God. That is another thing that Alexander argues to be impossible.[36]

Averroes addresses the subject in five of his commentaries on Aristotle and in his *de Substantia Orbis*. The three most informative commentaries are the *Long Commentary on Physics 8*, the *Middle Commentary on de Caelo* and the *Long Commentary on Metaphysics 12*.[37] I will mark separately the first three stages of Philoponus' argument, as it appears in some of Averroes' fullest formulations, along with a relevant part of Averroes' reply, and his assimilation of Avicenna to Philoponus (misidentified as Alexander). But I shall slightly alter Genequand's translation of the *Long Commentary on Metaphysics 12*, 1628, to distinguish Philoponus' argument from Averroes' reply by making the quotation from Philoponus end earlier.

[33] H.A. Wolfson, *The Philosophy of the Kalam*, Cambridge, Mass. 1976, 381; H.A. Davidson, 'John Philoponus as a source of medieval Islamic and Jewish proofs of creation', *Journal of the American Oriental Society* 89, 1969, 361, n. 41; S. Feldman, 'The end of the universe in medieval Jewish philosophy', *Association for Jewish Studies Review* 1986, 76.

[34] ap. Simplicium *in Cael.* 301,3; 359,14.

[35] Simplicius *in Phys.* 1361,31-3; 1362,11-15. On this particular point I diverge from C. Genequand's valuable discussion *Ibn Rushd's Metaphysics*, Leiden 1984, 36.

[36] Alexander *Quaest.* 1.18,30,25-32,19; fragment of lost *in Cael.* ap. Simplicium *in Cael.* 358,27-360,3.

[37] (i) Averroes *Long Commentary on Physics 8*, comm. 79 (available in the thirteenth-century Latin translation by Michael Scot, in the Juntine edition of 1562-1574, vol. 4, reprinted Frankfurt 1962, 425 verso, col. a, sec H – 427 recto, a, B); (ii) *Middle Commentary on de Caelo* translated from Hebrew version into Latin by Paul Israelita (available as 'paraphrasis', Juntine edition, vol. 5, 293, v. a, G – 293 v. b, K; 294 r. b, D – 295 r. a, B), also translated in part directly from the Hebrew version by H.A. Wolfson, *Crescas' Critique of Aristotle* 596-7; 681-2; (iii) *Long Commentary on Metaphysics 12*, comm. to text 41, 1626-38, translated from Arabic by C. Genequand, op. cit., 162-8. Below I use the the translations from Hebrew and Arabic by Wolfson and Genequand and otherwise translate from the Latin. Other works are: (iv) *Long Commentary on de Caelo 2*, comm. 71, Latin translation by Michael Scot, in Juntine Edition, vol. 5; (v) *de Substantia Orbis 3*; and (vi) a work inaccessible to me, the Hebrew MS version of the *Middle Commentary on Metaphysics 12* (Casanatense Heb. MS no. 3083, 140(141)b – 141(142)a). This reference is given, along with the others, by H.A. Davidson 'The principle that a finite body can contain only finite power', in S. Stein and R. Loewe (eds), *Studies in Jewish Religious and Intellectual History Presented to A. Altmann*, Alabama 1979, 75-92, at notes 53, 58, 61, 64.

Averroes' *Long Commentary on Metaphysics 12*, 1628, translated from Arabic by Genequand.

> Stage (i): John the Grammarian [Philoponus] raised strong objections against the Peripatetics concerning this problem. He says: 'if every body has a finite power and the heaven is a body, then it will have a finite power; but everything finite is necessarily corruptible, so that the heaven is corruptible.'
>
> Stage (ii): If it is said that it acquires incorruptibility from the eternal separate power,
>
> Averroes' reply: there will be something destructible but eternal. But this has been shown to be impossible at the end of the first book of the *de Caelo et Mundo*.

Averroes' *Long Commentary on Physics 8*, 79, Juntine vol. 4, 426v, a, l-L.

> Now in the proposition here assumed, according to which the power of any body is finite, it can be doubted whether it applies to the celestial body or not. If it does, then the power of the celestial body will be finite, but what has finite power is destructible.... This first question at least is very difficult and full of snags.
>
> Stage (ii): And Alexander answers in some of his treatises, and says that the celestial body receives (*adeptus fuisse*) eternity from its mover, who is not enmattered.
>
> Averroes' reply: But this would make it something that can be destroyed, yet never will be destroyed. This is Plato's opinion too, that is, that there is something eternal which can be destroyed. But Aristotle proved at the end of the first book of the *de Caelo et Mundo* [1.12] that there could not be anything eternal that contained a potentiality for destruction.
>
> Stage (i): Now John the Grammarian [Philoponus] maintained his own opinion [reading *opinionem* with the Latin of the 1489 edition] against the Peripatetics, in that he thinks that the world is destructible and generable. And this is the strongest of all the doubts that can befall us on this, especially because Aristotle says expressly in the second book of the *de Caelo et Mundo* [2.12, 293, a, 10-11] that the power of the heaven is finite.

Averroes' *Middle Commentary on de Caelo 1*, translated from Hebrew version by Wolfson (Latin translation from Hebrew in Juntine vol. 5, 293v, a, G and 294v, b, M).

> Stage (iii): The inference must therefore be that while the sphere by its own nature has the possibility of being corrupted, it must be free of corruption on account of the infinite immaterial force, outside the sphere, which causes its motion. That this is so is maintained by Alexander in a treatise of his, and he is followed by Avicenna....

Averroes' reply: On this account, i.e. by virtue of its being simple, the celestial body has no substratum and no contrary. Hence Aristotle maintains that it is ungenerated and incorruptible.

Averroes' reply reveals his relation to a number of further thinkers. It includes a point which modern scholars have understood as coming from Philoponus, and indeed as forming the nub of Philoponus' argument, but in fact I believe that he does not use it here.[38] The point is that the pseudo-Alexandrian view violates Aristotle's conclusion in *Cael.* 1.12, that an eternal thing cannot have a potentiality for destruction.[39] Averroes concludes that the view must be rejected. He prefers to return to the idea which we found in Abu Bishr, that the heavens' existence is necessary *of itself*. One reason why the celestial body endures by its own essence is that Averroes thinks it is not a composite of matter and form.[40] Another reason is that it lacks a contrary, and so has no potentiality for destruction. Motion differs, according to Averroes, because it does have a contrary, rest, and so it gets its perpetual motion, unlike its necessary existence, from elsewhere.[41] In thus separating motion from existence, Averroes distances himself from the type of argument found in Syrianus, according to which preserving the celestial body's motion is the *same thing* as preserving its existence. For this departure he was later rebuked by Abravanel.[42] Had he but known it, Averroes should have claimed Alexander as an ally, not an opponent. For the true Alexander would have agreed that the heaven's existence is necessary of itself.

Averroes' treatment of the subject is important because of its extensive influence on subsequent Christian and Jewish discussions. Of the three commentaries of Averroes from which I have quoted, two were translated into Latin from Arabic in the thirteenth century by Michael Scot, namely the long commentaries on the *Physics* and *Metaphysics*. Consequently, Averroes' discussion was known to such thirteenth-century scholars as Robert Grosseteste and Roger Bacon in Oxford and Bonaventure and

[38] I am persuaded here by Lindsay Judson, op. cit. I do not think that Philoponus is represented as using the point at Simplicius *in Phys.* 1333,28-30; 1334,37-9. This passage rather concedes for the sake of argument the position of Plato and Proclus that the potentiality for destruction will remain for ever unactualised. The contrary interpretation is that of Wolfson (1943 at 202 and 240; 1976 at 377-8 and 381) and Davidson (1969 at 362 and 1979 at 80 and n. 37) cited above. But Davidson expresses some misgivings as to how it fits, in 'The principle that a finite body can contain only finite power' (1979) at n. 37. Averroes' type of point is to be found elsewhere in Philoponus, but in a different context, at *contra Proclum* 131,26-132,28.

[39] Averroes *Long in Phys.* 8, 426v, b, K; *Middle in Cael.* 293v, a, I; 294r, a, F; *Long in Metaph.* 12, 1628.

[40] Averroes *Middle in Cael.* 294r, b, D – 295r, a, B. Its non-compositeness does not seem to be used for the same purpose at *Long in Phys.* 8, 426v, b, M – 427r, a, B, nor (*pace* Genequand, 46) at *Long in Metaph.* 12, 1634.

[41] Averroes *Long in Metaph.* 12, 1631; *Middle in Cael.* 294v, b, M.

[42] Isaac Abravanel, *The Deeds of God* 9.9, cited by S. Feldman, 'The end of the universe in medieval Jewish philosophy', *Association for Jewish Studies Review* 1986, at 76.

Thomas Aquinas in Paris, to name them in rough chronological order.[43] Grosseteste, surprisingly, takes a view like that of Averroes.[44] Bacon sides with what I have called Philoponus' opening move,[45] while Bonaventure reverses Philoponus' view. According to him, God does indeed give the world a beginning, but in doing so overrides, rather than follows, its nature.[46]

The most thoughtful discussion is that of Thomas Aquinas.[47] He refers to Averroes' long commentaries on *Physics* and *Metaphysics* 12 and to his *de Substantia Orbis*, and he reports the controversy in Averroes' own terms as being between Averroes and *Alexander*. The belief that *Alexander* made God a Sustainer eternally overriding the world's natural tendency to finite duration takes on a new significance in Thomas. For it will have confirmed him in his view that this was also the opinion of Alexander's master, Aristotle.

Thomas does not side with Philoponus' opening move, because unlike Philoponus, he accepts that, though the world had a beginning, it will have no end.[48] He therefore favours the view, wrongly ascribed to Alexander, that the celestial body receives its eternity not from any infinite power of its own, but from the infinite power of the divine mover. He does so, even though the so-called 'Alexander' goes beyond him, by treating the celestial body as not only endless, but also beginningless in time. He defends 'Alexander' from Averroes' reply by insisting that the celestial body does not have a potentiality for non-being, but is indestructible. So Alexander is immune to the objection that he violates the ban in Aristotle *Cael*. 1.12 on an eternal thing being destructible.[49] This is not to deny that the celestial body receives its perpetual existence from God, since necessary things can perfectly well have a cause of their necessity. It has been found puzzling that the celestial body can be necessary both by its own nature and because of God.[50] But this is very close to the position that we found in Proclus, who argued that it gets its

[43] Richard Dales tells me he finds arguments against infinite power also in the relatively early Vatican MS Latin 185.

[44] Robert Grosseteste *de Motu Supercaelestium*, in L. Baur (ed.), *Die philosophischen Werke Grossetestes*, 96,29-99, 4.

[45] Roger Bacon *Opus Maius*, part 7, Moral Philosophy, part 4, ch. 1 (in *Opus Maius*, J.H. Bridges (ed.), vol. 2, Oxford 1897).

[46] Bonaventure, *Commentary on Lombard's Sentences* 2, d.1, par. 1, a.1, q. 2, conclusion (translated by Paul Byrne, in Cyril Vollert, Lottie Kendzierski, Paul Byrne, *St. Thomas Aquinas, Siger of Brabant, St. Bonaventure, On the Eternity of the World*, Milwaukee, Wisconsin 1964, 105-13, at 109-10); and *in Hexaemeron* Collatio 6, n. 5 and Collatio 7, n. 2.

[47] Thomas Aquinas, *Commentary on Aristotle's Physics* 8, *lectio* 21, 1147, 1152, 1154. There is an English translation of the Commentary by Richard J. Blackwell, Richard J. Spath and W. Edmund Thirlkel, London 1963.

[48] Thomas Aquinas, *Commentary on Aristotle's Physics* 8, *lectio* 21, 1147 and *Summa Theologiae* 1,104, a.4, ad 1 and 2.

[49] See the excellent account in Carlos Steel, ' "Omnis corporis potentia est finita" ', in Jan P. Beckmann, Ludger Honnefelder, Gangolf Schrimpf, Georg Wieland (eds), *Philosophie im Mittelalter*, Hamburg 1987, 213-24.

[50] Carlos Steel, op. cit.

nature from God, and in Simplicius, who maintained that it is by nature fitted (*epitêdeios*) to receive the indestructibility God gives it:

> Even with his intention granted, however, Averroes cannot draw a conclusion against Alexander. For the latter did not posit that the celestial body acquires eternity from another on the understanding that of itself (*de se*) it has potentiality for being and non-being, but on the understanding that its being does not come from itself (*ex se*)... Now the only being it has from him is perpetual being. So it has its perpetuity from another. And Aristotle's words are also consonant with this, when he says in *Metaphysics* 5 and above at the beginning of this eighth book that some necessary things have a cause of their necessity.[51]

Elsewhere Thomas tries out other arguments.[52] He also rules out the type of move found in Syrianus, according to which the heavens would have a potentiality for acquiring existence from their motion.[53]

Averroes' influence did not stop with Thomas, but extended to the Jewish thinkers Gersonides (1288-1344), Crescas (1340-1410) and Abravanel (1437-1509), the first two of whom attacked the foundations of the infinite power arguments, with results of considerable interest for dynamics.[54] It is with some of the implications of the infinite power arguments for dynamics that I want to finish.

I believe there are several implications. First, I have argued elsewhere that Philoponus must be regarded as the originator of impetus theory, if an impetus is viewed not merely as an internal force, but as an internal force impressed from without (*vis impressa*).[55] But this claim must now be qualified, for we have seen that it is an impressed force (*dunamis*) which Proclus, before Philoponus, imagines God as implanting in the heavens.[56] I doubt, however, if the qualification is very significant. For

---

[51] Thomas Aquinas *Commentary on Aristotle's Physics* 8, *lectio* 21, 1154.

[52] Thomas denies that the heavens have a finite potentiality for being, on the grounds that their only potentiality is for motion, not for being (*Commentary on Lombard's Sentences* 2, d.1, a.1, q.5, ad contra 8). But that solution clashes with *Physics Commentary* 1153 and *Summa contra Gentiles* 1.20, obj.3, which allow a potentiality for being. Consequently, the latter passage offers a different solution. The heaven has the power of changeless being, but that need not be an *infinite* power, because changeless being has no quantitative extension and is not touched by time, whether the heaven endures for an instant, or for infinite time.

[53] Thomas Aquinas, *Commentary on Lombard's Sentences* 2, d.1, a.1, q. 5 ad contra 8.

[54] On Crescas, see *The Light of the Lord*, translated in part by H.A. Wolfson, *Crescas' Critique of Aristotle*, Cambridge Mass. 1929, proposition 12, part 2, 271, with Wolfson's notes; and H.A. Davidson, 'The principle that a finite body can contain only finite power', in S. Stein and R. Loewe (eds), *Studies in Jewish Religious and Intellectual History Presented to A. Altmann*, Alabama 1979, 75-92, at 85-9. For Gersonides *Ways of the Lord* 5.3.6; 6.1.3; 6.1.14, see the account of C. Touati, *La pensée philosophique et théologique de Gersonide*, Paris 1973, 308-15; and for Abravanel *Deeds of God* 9.9, see S. Feldman, 'The end of the universe in Jewish medieval philosophy', *Association for Jewish Studies Review* 1986, 53-77, at 74-6.

[55] Richard Sorabji, 'John Philoponus', in Sorabji (ed.), *Philoponus and the Rejection of Aristotelian Science*, London and Ithaca NY 1987.

[56] There is no reference to impressed force in the much earlier pseudo-Aristotelian *de Mundo* 398b20, where God is said to transmit the power (*didôsi dunamin*) which moves the

one thing, Proclus does not extend the idea of impressed force to the most interesting case of projectiles. For another, he seems not to have influenced Philoponus in this regard, even though Philoponus quoted some of the relevant passages cited above from Proclus. For Philoponus started by applying the idea of impressed force to projectiles. He did so in his commentary on Aristotle's *Physics*,[57] of which the first edition can be dated to 517. It was only some thirty or forty years later in the *de Opificio Mundi* of 546-9, or even 557-60, that he first thought of making God implant an impetus in the heavens.[58] And even then he was not following Proclus, because Proclus' argument for God's impressing a force depended on a belief which Philoponus rejected, the belief in the infinite duration of the heavens.

The infinite power arguments carry a second implication for dynamics. Why should an infinite force be needed to keep the celestial spheres rotating for ever? In his attack on motion in a vacuum, Aristotle includes two pertinent difficulties. If there were motion in a vacuum would not the speed be infinite in the absence of resistance,[59] and where would the motion ever stop, if no stopping place in a vacuum differs from any other?[60] Avicenna endorses the second objection in his own person, and argues in detail that projectile motion in a vacuum would not stop.[61] Is there not, then, we may ask, a worry about the rotation of the celestial spheres? Although Aristotle surrounds them not with a vacuum, but with nothing at all, the question retains its force: why should they stop at one position or time rather than another? And this in turn creates a clash with the demand for infinite power. For no infinite power is needed to spin a finite body, and once it is spinning without differentiation in its surroundings, why, if Aristotle's argument is acceptable, should it stop? Conversely, if we take seriously the demand for infinite power, we presuppose that a finite power would be *exhausted*. But then we can answer Aristotle's question why something should stop after three miles, rather than four miles, of travel in a vacuum.

An analogous difficulty was noticed by Philoponus about Aristotle's *other* suggestion, that speed in a vacuum would be infinite, not because of the lack of differentiation but because of the lack of resistance. Rotation, he pointed out, and in particular the rotation of the heavens, encounters no resistance, but is none the less finite in speed.[62] The point is repeated by Ibn Bajja or Avempace (died 1138).[63]

inner celestial spheres from the outermost one. For the simile of *endosis* used here is not that of impressing a force, but of striking a key note.

[57] Philoponus *in Phys.* 641,13-642,20; cf. 384,29-385,11.
[58] Philoponus *Opif.* 28,20-29,9.
[59] Aristotle *Phys.* 4.8,215b22-216a4.
[60] ibid. 215a19-20.
[61] Avicenna, *Shifâ* 1, p. 154f, translated into French and discussed by S. Pines, 'Études sur Awḥad al-Zamân Abu' l-Barakât al-Baghdâdî', *Revue des Études Juives* n.s. 3, 1938, repr. in his *Collected Works* 1, Leiden 1979, 52-6.
[62] Philoponus *in Phys.* 690,34-691,5.
[63] Avempace is reported by Averroes, *Long Commentary on Physics* 4, text 71, Latin in

Averroes and Thomas Aquinas both try to rescue Aristotle, Averroes by arguing that it is the heavenly spheres themselves, and not any surrounding medium, which provide the resistance to motion.[64] Thomas suggests that Aristotle's connexion of lack of resistance with infinite speed is a merely dialectical move against opponents who postulate vacuum as the *sole* cause of motion,[65] but I have to say that I see no sign that Aristotle's opponents are as extreme as that.

One way or another, it looks as if something in Aristotle's dynamical theory must give. Or does he have a way out of the difficulties? As regards the lack of differentiation, someone might plead that we will find differences, if we look beneath the heavens, rather than beyond them. At some stage in the celestial rotation, the most prominent heavenly body, the sun, will be directly over the highest mountain. So it cannot be said that there are *no* differences between different possible stopping points for the celestial rotation. But it may still be wondered if these differences would provide a *good* reason for the celestial rotation to stop at one point rather than another. As regards the lack of resistance to celestial motion, an attempt might be made to find sources of friction by pointing out that some of the celestial spheres draw round with them (*sumperiagein*) the lower belts of fire and air, creating heat by inducing friction there (*parektribesthai*).[66] But whether they suffer friction in return is not said.

There is another reason for wondering why infinite power should be needed for everlasting celestial rotation.[67] In an earlier treatment of celestial motion in *On the Heavens*, we find no integral and undisputed reference to the role of God. Instead, Aristotle combines two ideas, that the heavens are made of an indestructible fifth element which can undergo no change but motion, and that circular motion is natural to that element. If it can undergo no other change, what reason could there be for its natural motion to cease? It cannot tire, or grow bored, or perish, for these would be changes. Nor does circular motion have a terminal destination. It looks, then, as if in his earlier work Aristotle allowed for a motion that was eternal not because of any infinite power, but because of immunity to further change in something to which circular motion was natural.

There is a final corollary. For the question whether finite power would be *exhausted* has implications for the definition of impetus. It has been

---

Juntine edition 1562, repr. Frankfurt 1912, 160r, b, E-F, translated in E.A. Moody, 'Galileo and Avempace, the dynamics of the leaning tower experiment', *Journal of the History of Ideas* 12, 1951, at 226-7. Thomas Aquinas gives the argument in his *Commentary on the Physics* 4, *lectio* 12,534, translated by R.J. Blackwell, R.J. Spath, W.E. Thirlkel, London 1963.

[64] Averroes, *Long Commentary on Physics* 4, text 71; Thomas Aquinas gives the argument in his *Commentary on the Physics* 4, *lectio* 12, 535.

[65] Thomas Aquinas, *Commentary on Physics* 4, *lectio* 12, 536. On the other hand, Thomas does not discount as dialectical Aristotle's 'why stop here?' question, *lectio* 11, 526.

[66] Aristotle *Meteor*. 1.3, 341a17-22; 1.7, 344a11-13; *Cael*. 2.7, 289a20-35.

[67] I owe the point to John Cleary.

suggested that impetus is by definition something that gets exhausted,[68] and indeed Philoponus does say that it would be. This is his answer to Aristotle's question why motion in a vacuum would stop here rather than there: the force impressed in a projectile would be exhausted (*exasthenêsêi*), as Aristotle himself admits in regard to the different force which he postulates in the pockets of air behind a projectile.[69] However, it seems dangerous to elevate exhaustibility into a defining characteristic of *all* impetus, since Avicenna maintains in the passage just discussed that only resistance exhausts the force in a projectile, and that in a vacuum the force would *not* be exhausted.[70] Similarly Buridan insists[71] that the impetus by which God sets the heavens moving at the time of Creation will never run out.

I shall conclude by drawing attention to the role played by the Neoplatonist commentators on Aristotle, not only in dynamics, but also in the earlier issue of Creation. What started in Ammonius as an attempt to harmonise Aristotle's God with Plato's Creator ended up by helping (only helping, of course) to harmonise Aristotle with *Christianity*. And what began in the Christian Philoponus as an effort to argue for the *beginning* of the universe, finished in Thomas Aquinas as an argument ascribed to Alexander against its ending. The Aristotelian philosophy that was handed on to the Middle Ages was not just that of Aristotle, but a far richer compilation transformed by the preoccupations of the intervening commentators.[72]

---

[68] Michael Wolff, 'Philoponus and the rise of preclassical dynamics', in Richard Sorabji (ed.), *Philoponus and the Rejection of Aristotelian Science*, at 84-5. For his reply to the doubt about Avicenna, see p. 85.

[69] Philoponus *in Phys.* 644,16-22.

[70] Avicenna *Shifā* 1, p. 154f.

[71] Buridan *in Phys.* 8.12, fol. 120, translated into French and discussed by P. Duhem, *Études sur Léonard de Vinci* 3, Paris 1913, 40-2; also discussed by G. Sarton, *Introduction to the History of Science* 3, part 1, Baltimore 1947, 543; M. de Gandillac, *Le mouvement doctrinale du XIe au XIVe siècles*, Paris 1951, 459; C. Touati, *La pensée philosophique et théologique de Gersonide*, Paris 1973, 312-13; Marshal Claggett, *The Science of Mechanics in the Middle Ages*, Madison, Wisconsin 1959, 510-15.

[72] I am very grateful for help to David Barlow, John Cleary, John Dillon, Jill Kraye, Ian Mueller, Tom Settle, Robert Sharples, Andrew Smith and above all Fritz Zimmermann. This chapter is a revised version of a paper originally written for the Charles Schmitt Memorial Symposium held at the Warburg Institute in 1987. The original version was published in Sarah Hutton and John Henry (eds), *New Perspectives in Renaissance Thought: Essays in the History of Science, Education and Philosophy: Studies in Intellectual History in Memory of Charles B. Schmitt*, London 1989, and presented in a more detailed version in my *Matter, Space and Motion*, London and Ithaca NY 1988.

CHAPTER TEN

The metaphysics of Ammonius son of Hermeias

Koenraad Verrycken

It is no overstatement to say that the latest period of Alexandrian philosophy (starting from Ammonius) is virgin territory for the greatest part. Up to now students of ancient philosophy seem to have had rather strong feelings of disinterest, discouragement and even aversion to all those cheerless volumes of Greek. As a result, an area of considerable importance has remained largely unknown for too long. This situation has allowed several rather serious misconceptions on the subject of the Ammonian school to persist. In this chapter I shall try to prove that the prevailing view of Ammonius' philosophy is incorrect, and that a better understanding of its true nature may contribute towards a more adequate definition of the 'problem of Alexandrian Neoplatonism'.

In what follows, I shall refer to the three levels (or hypostases) of orthodox Neoplatonic theology: (1) the One, the Good, the highest or first principle, the First, the first cause; (2) the Demiurge of Plato's *Timaeus*, the Platonic Creator, the Intellect, Mind, *Nous*, the second principle; (3) the world soul, the third principle. The scheme treats each level as the efficient cause that produces the level below, while each lower level is said to proceed by a procession from the higher. The level which the world soul produces is the still lower level of the sensible world. The supreme producer, however, which is directly or indirectly responsible for all levels, and especially for the level of matter, is the One. The Intellect is said to exist in the realm of intelligible and intellective entities. Being and non-discursive thought are associated with it. The One, by contrast, is *above* being and thought and other characteristics, so that it can be described either not at all, or only negatively, while the world soul engages only in a lower kind of thinking – discursive thought. The Platonic Demiurge produces lower levels (directly or indirectly) by containing the Platonic Ideas as creative *logoi* within itself. Aristotle's God had usually been understood before Ammonius differently from the Platonic Demiurge, not as an efficient cause of existence, but only as a final cause or goal which inspires the heavens to move.

At the beginning of this century Karl Praechter initiated the view that Alexandrian Neoplatonism was clearly distinct from Athenian Neo-platonism. According to Praechter there were four different types of

Neoplatonic philosophy: (1) Plotinus and Porphyry, the founders of the
system. (2) The speculative branch, which developed metaphysical
thinking to the utmost. It is to be divided into (a) the Syrian school
(Iamblichus, etc.) and (b) the Athenian school (Plutarch of Athens,
Syrianus, Proclus, Damascius, Simplicius, etc.). (3) The religious-
theurgic branch, i.e. the school of Pergamon (Maximus of Ephesus, Julian
the Apostate, etc.). (4) The 'learned' branch: (a) the Alexandrians
(Hypatia, Hierocles, Hermeias, Ammonius, Olympiodorus, Philoponus,
Elias, David, etc.) and (b) the Western Neoplatonists (Macrobius,
Calcidius, Boethius).

Simplicius' work, according to Praechter, stands midway between the
Athenian school and the Alexandrians.[1] Typical of Alexandrian
philosophy, Praechter believed, was its being influenced by two local
traditions, namely the interest in the (exact) sciences (which made it tend
to turn away from metaphysics) and the study of Christian theology.[2]
Christian influence, according to Praechter, was already to be found in
the philosophy of Hierocles, a pagan who was active in the first half of the
fifth century.[3] Praechter was convinced that Hierocles' metaphysics was
considerably simplified in comparison with Athenian Neoplatonism, and
that this simplification was characteristic of Alexandrian Neoplatonism,
or rather Alexandrian Platonism, in general. This philosophy was
influenced, of course, by the style of the great speculative systems
(Iamblichus-Proclus). At the same time, however, the 'theology' of the
Alexandrians was of a more elementary character, and their exegesis of
Plato and Aristotle was comparatively sober.[4] Praechter held that
Hierocles regarded the Platonic Creator, the Demiurge, as the highest
principle; there was no One. Accordingly, he did not hesitate to call the
system 'theistic',[5] meaning that it accepted a single supreme God, though
with the proviso that this theism was inspired, not so much by
Christianity, but rather by pre-Plotinian Platonism.[6] On the other hand,

[1] K. Praechter, 'Richtungen und Schulen im Neuplatonismus', *Genethliakon C. Robert*,
Berlin 1910, 155-6. Praechter's classification was meant to improve on that on which E.
Zeller, *Die Philosophie der Griechen in ihrer geschichtlichen Entwicklung* III 2 had based
his treatment of Neoplatonism. Zeller had classed most of the Alexandrians under 'The
Athenian School', some of them (Hypatia, Synesius and others) under 'Iamblichus and the
Syrian School'.

[2] K. Praechter, op. cit., 151; id., 'Christlich-neuplatonische Beziehungen', *Byzantinische
Zeitschrift* 21, 1912, 2-3.

[3] K. Praechter, 'Christlich-neuplatonische Beziehungen', 3-27; id., 'Hierokles 18', in G.
Wissowa and W. Kroll (eds), *Realencyclopädie der klassischen Altertumswissenschaft* VIII,
2, 1913, col. 1482.

[4] K. Praechter, 'Hierokles', col. 1481.

[5] K. Praechter, 'Christlich-neuplatonische Beziehungen', 3-4: 'His (i.e. Hierocles')
supreme entity is the Demiurge. He is conceived in an absolutely theistic way as the creator,
the organiser, the legislator and the leader of the world. He is simply "god *(ho theos)*".
Beyond him there neither is the One nor any other hypostasis, He is the only
supra-mundane being, the "God of gods *(theos theôn)*", the "supreme and best God *(theos
hupatos kai aristos)*". Immediately after Him come the intra-mundane gods *(enkosmioi
theoi)*, the astral gods.'

[6] K. Praechter, 'Christlich-neuplatonische Beziehungen', 4-5. In his article on Simplicius

Hierocles' Demiurge is said to create the world from eternity out of nothing by his mere will. In Praechter's view this doctrine clearly has its origin in Christian theology.[7] The manner in which Hierocles solves the problem of the relation between human free will and divine providence was believed to be influenced by Christianity likewise.[8] It is important that Praechter extended the characteristics of what he called Alexandrian Neoplatonism to Ammonius, Philoponus and further. Ammonius, he believed, increasingly had to take into account the presence of Christians among his hearers (e.g. Philoponus): he had to make concessions, and he was no longer free to engage in metaphysical speculation in the style of Proclus, because of its connexions with Hellenic polytheism. The young Christians in the philosophical school were not looking for the highest truth, which they possessed already in their religion. What they were looking for was the knowledge of Plato and Aristotle. According to Praechter, Ammonius concentrated on Aristotle, in particular on his logical writing, the Organon, which was neutral matter. As a consequence the Alexandrian school more and more lost its positively Platonic character and became 'an institute for general philosophical education'. This was exactly what enabled it to survive after 529, when the Athenian school was closed.[9] Praechter supposed a continued effect of pre-Plotinian theism on the Alexandrian school after Hierocles. Meanwhile, this theism clearly had the function of diminishing the distance between Platonism and Christianity. On the other hand Praechter was convinced that the Alexandrian variant of Neoplatonism is also to be found in Simplicius' *Commentary on Epictetus' Enchiridion*,[10] which, he thought, was written at the time Simplicius was still a pupil of Ammonius in Alexandria and not yet influenced by the Athenian Neoplatonism of Damascius.[11] The theism of Ammonius, according to Praechter, is documented in the *Commentary on the Isagoge*,[12] if not in

Praechter refers to Origen the pagan and Longinus (K. Praechter, 'Simplikios', in G. Wissowa and W. Kroll (eds), *Realencyclopädie der klassischen Altertumswissenschaft* IIIA, 1, 1927, col. 208).

[7] K. Praechter, 'Christlich-neuplatonische Beziehungen', 5-9; id., 'Hierokles', col. 1482.

[8] id., 'Christlich-neuplatonische Beziehungen', 12-21.

[9] id., 'Richtungen und Schulen', 151-4.

[10] id., 'Simplikios', col. 207: 'It is the simpler doctrine of principles of the Alexandrian school, known to us in its more elementary character from Hierocles .... It is only little influenced by Plotinus and the Neoplatonism based on Plotinus, and essentially links up with the older evolution of Platonic doctrine. The most important point of difference is the identification of "the principle of principles (*arkhê arkhôn*)" with the Demiurge who creates and governs the world. This identification implies the absence of the One, the principle which transcends the whole intelligible world and which is characteristic of the doctrine of Plotinus and his followers.'

[11] ibid., col. 206.

[12] id., 'Christlich-neuplatonische Beziehungen', 5 n. 5: 'I shall only indicate here that other Alexandrian Neoplatonists, just like Hierocles, know only one supra-mundane God. Ammonius for instance (*in Isag.* 3,9ff; 9,16f; 9,21; 11,11 etc.) talks about "God (*ho theos*)", his properties and activity completely in the traditional way, without betraying any knowledge of the complicated theological system elaborated by non-Alexandrian Neoplatonism.'

the *in Metaphysica* of his pupil Asclepius.[13]

Up to now Praechter's picture of the philosophy of Ammonius has remained largely unchallenged. Eminent scholars like P. Merlan and L.G. Westerink have agreed with it. I quote Westerink first: '...we are very incompletely informed about his (Ammonius') metaphysics. Yet one essential point is clear: from the testimonies...we learn that to Ammonius the Aristotelian Intelligence is both the final and the efficient cause; as this Intelligence is identified with the Creative Mind of the *Timaeus*, it follows that the Creator is also the Supreme God. Accordingly, the Alexandrian School has the characteristic habit of referring to God as "the Demiurge", a practice continued later by the Christian Olympiodoreans. The reason for the identification was no doubt partly to bring Plato into harmony with Aristotle, but the ultimate motive (as already in Hierocles) was to adapt both to Christian monotheism. As a result, the complicated metaphysical superstructure of Athenian Platonism had to be discarded, or at least had lost its interest...'[14] Here we find the main reason why Praechter's view on Ammonius is regarded as correct to the present day: Ammonius' interpretation of Aristotle's God is believed to be theistic in character. Everyone concluded that this could not mean anything other than that Ammonius himself considered the divine Intellect or Demiurge as the highest principle, and that he consequently rejected the Neoplatonic distinction of a higher God, the One.

Merlan adduces a further argument, which is taken from the so-called *Ammonius* or *de Mundi Opificio*. This dialogue was written by Zacharias Scholasticus, a Christian who attended the lectures of Ammonius for a while in Alexandria. It makes no mention at all of any difference, in Ammonius' philosophy, between the highest principle of reality and the Demiurge, a fact that brought Merlan to the following conclusion: 'If we rely on Zacharias, we shall have to admit that Ammonius either did not profess the doctrine of a god above the Demiurge, i.e. Plotinus' One, or at least gave it scant attention. As to the nature of God there seems to be no difference at all between Ammonius and Zacharias. ...It is this un-Plotinian idea of God as creator and omniscient provider which Boethius shares with Ammonius. We should not forget that according to Ammonius, Aristotle's god was also efficient cause – in other words, Ammonius tried to reconcile the Platonic concept of the Demiurge with the Aristotelian concept of the Unmoved Mover.'[15]

The first to oppose Praechter's theory about Alexandrian Platonism was A.C. Lloyd. He pointed out that Simplicius' *Commentary on the*

[13] id., 'Simplikios', col. 208: '... his (i.e. Ammonius') *Commentary on the Metaphysics* too, recorded by Asclepius, in comparison with Syrianus shows a more elementary construction of the highest levels of reality.'

[14] L.G. Westerink, *The Greek Commentaries on Plato's Phaedo*, vol. 1: *Olympiodorus*, Amsterdam, Oxford, New York 1976, 24.

[15] P. Merlan, 'Ammonius Hermiae, Zacharias Scholasticus and Boethius', *Greek, Roman and Byzantine Studies* 9, 1968, 200-1; cf. id., 'Ammonius, son of Hermias', in C.C. Gillispie (ed.), *Dictionary of Scientific Biography*, vol. 1, New York 1970, 137: 'Its (i.e. the Alexandrian school's) Platonism was in many respects pre-Plotinian ...'

Enchiridion does not regard the Demiurge as the highest principle, and that Asclepius' *Commentary on the Metaphysics* does not confirm Praechter's view either.[16] Unfortunately, Lloyd did not specify his own opinion about the nature of Ammonius' metaphysics. But his criticism of Praechter was taken up and extended by I. Hadot. On the basis of a thorough study of Hierocles' philosophy and Simplicius' *in Enchiridion Epicteti*, Mme. Hadot concluded that Praechter's position[17] was untenable. As to Hierocles first, she showed convincingly that his views on matter, the Demiurge, soul and providence represented a type of Neoplatonism which, via Plutarch of Athens, went back to Iamblichus.[18] Consequently, there is no reason to suppose that he was influenced by Christianity. The fact that Hierocles nowhere refers to a principle above the Demiurge does not imply that his philosophy was theistic. With regard to the *de Providentia* the *argumentum e silentio* is very weak, given the limited length of Photius' summaries. With regard to the *Commentary on the Carmen Aureum*, where no god transcends the level of *Nous*, Mme. Hadot emphasised that Hierocles was addressing himself to beginners in philosophy. Hence a full development of the Neoplatonic theological system in all its complexity would have been out of place.[19] As to Simplicius' *in Enchiridion Epicteti*, the second support of Praechter's theory: Mme. Hadot was convinced that it was not possible in any way either to date the commentary (even relatively) or to determine its place of composition.[20] Moreover, Simplicius' theology in this commentary is not pre-Plotinian and theistic at all. On the contrary, it is identical with the theology of Simplicius' other commentaries, namely the metaphysical system of Damascius.[21] But one should not forget that in this case also

[16] A.C. Lloyd, 'The later Neoplatonists', in A.H. Armstrong (ed.), *The Cambridge History of Later Greek and Early Medieval Philosophy*, Cambridge 1970, 316.

[17] As late as 1976 Praechter's theory was defended by T. Kobusch, *Studien zur Philosophie des Hierokles von Alexandrien. Untersuchungen zum christlichen Neuplatonismus*, Munich 1976.

[18] I. Hadot, *Le problème du néoplatonisme alexandrin. Hiéroclès et Simplicius*, Paris 1978, 143. Recently N. Aujoulat, *Le néo-platonisme alexandrin. Hiéroclès d'Alexandrie. Filiations intellectuelles et spirituelles d'un néo-platonicien du Ve siècle*, Leiden 1986, has made a renewed attempt to show that Hierocles' Neoplatonism was different from Roman and Athenian Neoplatonism. Hierocles is believed to represent a typically Alexandrian Neoplatonism, which originated with Ammonius Saccas and Origen the pagan. In assuming a link between Hierocles and Ammonius Saccas Aujoulat follows Heinemann, Langerbeck and Theiler. One distinctive feature of Alexandrian Neoplatonism, according to Aujoulat (55-65), is the fact that the Demiurge was considered the highest principle of reality. Although Aujoulat is convinced that Hierocles was influenced in this by Christianity, his general approach to Hierocles does more justice to the Neoplatonic character of his philosophy than Praechter's did. Nevertheless, his case for a theistic interpretation of Hierocles is unconvincing.

[19] I. Hadot, op. cit., 115-16.

[20] ibid. 33-43. Mme. Hadot has changed her mind, and now thinks it was written at Ḥarrân: 'La vie et l'oeuvre de Simplicius d'après les sources grecques et arabes', in I. Hadot (ed.), *Simplicius, sa vie, son oeuvre, sa survie*, Berlin 1987, 18.

[21] ibid. 47-65. Cf. also I. Hadot, 'Le système théologique de Simplicius dans son commentaire sur le Manuel d'Epictète', in P. Hadot (ed.), *Le néoplatonisme*, Paris 1971, 265-79.

considerations of a pedagogic and pragmatic nature lead to a simplification or rather fragmentation of Neoplatonic metaphysics.[22]

So far Mme. Hadot did not extend her investigations to the school of Ammonius. It is clear that her conclusions lead to the following question: if Praechter's theory is invalid with regard to Hierocles and Simplicius, what are we to think of its validity with regard to the other Alexandrians? Isn't it possible that they too are *Neo*-platonists rather than Platonists in Praechter's sense? And, secondly, if their philosophy proves to be Neoplatonic, what exactly are the differences – if any – between Alexandrian and Athenian Neoplatonism? In this chapter I shall focus these questions on Ammonius. First I shall try to outline Ammonius' metaphysics as it appears in Asclepius' *in Metaphysica*. Then I shall offer some remarks on the *Ammonius* of Zacharias Scholasticus and the Ammonian commentaries on the Organon. Thirdly, I shall briefly discuss Ammonius' interpretation of the Aristotelian concept of God. Finally, I shall deal with the problem of a possible difference between Ammonian and Athenian Neoplatonism.[23]

Ammonius' metaphysics in Asclepius' *in Metaphysica*

Asclepius' *in Metaphysica* was written 'from the voice of Ammonius (*apo phônês Ammôniou tou Hermeiou*)', that is, as an edition of his lectures.[24] The frequency and docility of the pupil's references to his 'hero' and 'master'[25] assure us that, apart from the insertion of excerpts from Alexander,[26] we may consider him a faithful witness to Ammonius' philosophy,[27] and assume that the statements in the first person plural[28] render Ammonius' viewpoint. Nowhere is there any trace of divergence of opinion between the pupil and his master. This implies that, whatever information about Ammonius we get from other sources (Ammonius' other commentaries, Zacharias, Philoponus, Simplicius), we should try to harmonise it with what Asclepius tells us.

The text of Asclepius gives us at least some idea of the Neoplatonic character of Ammonius' metaphysics. On three points we have sufficient

---

[22] I. Hadot, *Le problème du néoplatonisme alexandrin*, 189-91.

[23] The studies which K. Kremer devoted to the school of Ammonius, 'Die Anschauung der Ammonius (Hermeiou)-Schule über den Wirklichkeitscharakter des Intelligiblen. Ueber einen Beitrag der Spätantike zur platonisch-aristotelischen Metaphysik', *Philosophisches Jahrbuch* 69, 1961-2, 46-63; id., *Der Metaphysikbegriff in den Aristoteles-Kommentaren der Ammonius-Schule*, Münster 1961, are for several reasons hardly relevant to the present purpose. Their main defect is that they take little account of the Neoplatonic character of the Ammonian school.

[24] Asclepius *in Metaph*. 1,2-3; 113,1-2; 137,2-3; 222,2-3.

[25] ibid. 92,29-30.

[26] cf. M. Hayduck, Praefatio, *CAG* 6.2, pp. v-vi.

[27] L.G. Westerink, *Anonymous Prolegomena to Platonic Philosophy*, Amsterdam 1962, p. xi; L. Tarán, 'Asclepius of Tralles, Commentary to Nicomachus' Introduction to Arithmetic', *Transactions of the American Philosophical Society*, n.s. 59, 1969, 8.

[28] e.g. Asclepius *in Metaph*. 102,17; 106,33-4; 140,15-16; 141,22; 145,15; 146,5; 147,28; 148,24; 151,1; 159,16; 163,11; 168,31; 181,32; 189,12; 190,5; 191,7; 194,13 ....

evidence to venture a somewhat more detailed reconstruction. These three points are: the concept of the highest principle, the doctrine of the divine Intellect, and Ammonius' view of the nature of the creative process.

(a) The highest principle

I do not think one can any longer doubt that Ammonius' view of the highest principle is Neoplatonic. To start with, let us consider what Asclepius says about the first cause[29] of reality. It is the principle (*arkhê*) of everything,[30] the First,[31] the Divine.[32] It is the Good, the final cause of the universe.[33] At the same time it is the productive principle from which everything originates.[34] The final cause of reality is identical with its efficient cause.[35] The Good is the One.[36] The unity of the One transcends not only difference (*heterotês*) but identity (*tautotês*) as well.[37] Accordingly, even the self-identity of Intellect (or Mind) is transcended by the One. The unity of the One is neither numerical nor specific: numerical unity cannot occur without matter, whereas the One, as the origin of matter, is immaterial;[38] specific unity is impossible as well, since the One transcends all species and all universals.[39]

[29] 'The very first and transcendent cause (*hê prôtistê kai exêirêmenê aitia*)': Asclepius *in Metaph.* 38,18-19; 'the first cause': (*hê prôtê aitia*): 56,24; (*to prôton aition*): 23,3; 35,10-11; 35,15; 39,17; 52,7; 115,37; (120,10-11 Alexander); 121,7-8; 147,4; 301,15.
[30] '(The)(only) principle of the totality ((*Hê*)(*mia*) *arkhê* (*tôn*) *pantôn*)': Asclepius *in Metaph.* 17,7; 19,34-5; 48,5-6; 60,23-4; 99,5; 105,31-2; 148,10-11; 183,22-3; 186,2; 194,14; 'properly the principle of all beings (*hê kuriôs arkhê pantôn tôn ontôn*)': 195,26; 'the very first (of all) principle(s) (*hê arkhê* (*hê*) *prôtistê pasôn*)': 147,29-30; 148,33; 'the only principle properly (*hê mia kuriôs arkhê*)': 56,20; 'the first principle (*hê prôtê arkhê*)': 147,7; 148,27-8; 191,8.
[31] *to prôton*: Asclepius *in Metaph.* 42,14; 52,1-2; 144,28; 146,6; 151,29; 158,18; 198,30; 225,16.
[32] *to theion*: ibid. 439,26-7.
[33] ibid. 15,8; (17,29-18,1 Alexander); 47,9; 52,1-2 ('... all things have turned themselves towards the First'); 106,33-107,4 ('... the first henad, ... towards which all beings have turned themselves'); 108,25; 123,16-17; (128,21-2 Alexander); 151,22-32; 450,25-7.
[34] The productivity of the One is often referred to by the terms *paragein-paraktikos* (Asclepius *in Metaph.* 26,6; 28,6; 35,15-16; 52,7; 56,20-1; 106,23; 146,7-8; 147 *passim*; 148,27; 191,12-13; 194,13-17; 202,12; 217,3-5; 227,37) and *proagein-proaktikos-proagôgos* (105,32; 107,12; 123,16; 147,8-9; 151,19; 151,25; 176,12; 201,9-10; 201,26; 206,19; 216,23; 217,2-4; 226,13). The first principle is said to possess a 'generative potency (*gonimos dunamis*)' (202,11; 202,19; 206,18-19; 208,21-2; 217,3-4; 225,16; 226 *passim*; 227,37); cf. 20,27-8; 123,15. The One is the 'source' of goodness (21,19) and truth (115,37): everything is produced through its 'gushing power' (249,3-4). The genesis of intelligible and sensible reality is a 'procession' (*proodos*: e.g. 223,35), a 'proceeding' (*proienai*: e.g. 196,6-7; 202,22; 225,15-17; 226,7; 230,4).
[35] ibid. 108,23-5; 151,24-7.
[36] *to hen*: Asclepius *in Metaph.* 33,34-5; 54,25-6; 249,3; 'that which is essentially One (*to hen to kat' ousian*)': 151,18-19.
[37] ibid. 144,28-30. Cf. 148,13-5. The identity of efficient and final causality in the One exists only *for us* (151,26-7).
[38] Asclepius *in Metaph.* 144,30-2; 148,24-7; 191,7-11; 217,4-5.
[39] ibid. 191,11-13; 217,2-4; 148,28-32.

Not only is Ammonius' view of the highest principle Neoplatonic, we can add that his Neoplatonism must at least to some extent have been in keeping with that of Syrianus and Proclus. This is obvious from his theory of henad, monad and dyad. In the metaphysics of Syrianus, monad and dyad as a pair of principles transcending all being come immediately after the One. They also reappear at every level of being.[40] The supreme monad is the principle of unity, rest and identity,[41] the supreme dyad is the principle of plurality, procession and difference.[42] In Proclus the supreme monad and dyad are called 'the first limit' (*to prôton peras, autoperas*) and 'the first infinity' (*hê prôtê apeiria, autoapeiria*) respectively.[43] Proclus thus uses the terms from the *Philebus*.[44] On the other hand, he often calls the One itself 'the henad'.[45] In Asclepius we find a combination of Syrianus' and Proclus' terminology: monad and dyad derive from the henad. The One is the henad,[46] the supraidentical origin of identity and non-identity. This 'definition' of the highest principle as the henad is the starting point for a comprehensive derivation of the rest of reality. Without being diminished itself,[47] the henad gives rise to the monad and the dyad. The monad is the principle of union, likeness, formative power, identity, and, in short, of all coherence. The dyad is the principle of difference, division and unlikeness. The henad is the first cause, which transcends both the monad and the dyad.[48] These two subordinate principles together are 'intelligible number',[49] i.e. pure unity and twoness. They generate definiteness (*peras*) and indefiniteness (*apeiria*).[50] The duality of unity and twoness is the basis of arithmetic: odd numbers are definite, even numbers indefinite.[51] The duality of definiteness and indefiniteness is the basic structure of the whole of reality. Due to its indivisibility and priority, the monad is identified with the Intellect (*nous*), which is stable (*monimos*).[52] The dyad is identical with Soul (*psukhê*), the moment of procession and discursive

---

[40] Syrianus *in Metaph*. 112,14-17. For my account of monad and dyad in Syrianus and Proclus I rely on A.D.R. Sheppard, 'Monad and dyad as cosmic principles in Syrianus', in H.J. Blumenthal and A.C. Lloyd (eds), *Soul and the Structure of Being in Late Neoplatonism. Syrianus, Proclus and Simplicius*, Liverpool 1982, 1-5.

[41] e.g. Syrianus *in Metaph*. 113,15-16.

[42] e.g. ibid. 112,35-6.

[43] e.g. Proclus *El. Theol.* prop. 90. See Dodds's commentary, 246-8.

[44] Plato *Phil*. 16C.

[45] References in Proclus *Theol. Plat*. III, H.D. Saffrey and L.G. Westerink (eds), Paris 1978, p. xv.

[46] Asclepius *in Metaph*. 35 *passim*; 38,18; 48,5; 52,6; 99,5-6; 100,3; 106,22; 107,12; 178,1; 201,9; 201,25-6; 202 *passim*; 208,21; 216,23; 223,36. Cf. Proclus *Theol. Plat*. III Saffrey-Westerink, p. lxxvi.

[47] Asclepius *in Metaph*. 202,11-12; 202,19-22; 206,18-20. The One is 'infinite in potency' (*apeirodunamon*: 121,8-9), it possesses a 'superfluity of potency' (*periousia dunameôs*: 194,14-15), a 'superpotent potency' (*dunamis huperdunamos*: 439,26-7).

[48] ibid. 35,2-16 (for the ascription to the Pythagoreans cf. n. 68 below); 147,4-6.

[49] ibid. 201,23; 202,22-3; 207,18-19.

[50] ibid. 38,13-16; 38,21-4; 39,7-9.

[51] ibid. 38,21-9.

[52] ibid. 36,22: *monimos-monas*.

thought.[53] Thus the production of the hypostases Intellect and Soul from the One is understood as the origination of a monad and a dyad from a henad. The same process is repeated, at a lower level, as the origination of form (monad) and matter (dyad) respectively from 'productive Nature (*phusis proagôgos*)'.[54] Form is a limit (*peras*) which defines and limits matter. Matter is indefinite and infinitely divisible.[55]

The transcendence of the One[56] excludes not only describing it affirmatively (affirmative theology), but, strictly speaking, even the possibility of a negative theology. 'Concerning the First,' Asclepius writes, 'there is room neither for affirmation nor for negation, since it transcends both being and every human concept and in a word all intellective activity. For, even if Plato says that I do not know what it is, but know what it is not, negation cannot therefore really comprehend it (i.e. the First). No, negation (in this case) just indicates that there is no grasping. But the First cannot be grasped..., since it is beyond every concept.'[57] Asclepius especially emphasises the transcendence of the One in relation to the next level down, intelligible reality or being, and for this he relies on Plato[58] and Plotinus.[59] It is true that the henad is sometimes called 'being in the proper sense (*kuriôs on*)',[60] 'being absolutely (*haplôs on*)',[61] 'being really (*ontôs on*)',[62] 'substance absolutely (*haplôs ousia*)'[63] or 'the very first substance (*prôtistê ousia*)'.[64] However, these formulas are concentrated at the beginning of the commentary on *Metaphysica* 4. One gets the impression that they are just intended to interpret Aristotle's definition of metaphysics as the theory of being qua being and to give it a theological sense, i.e. to understand his being qua being as the Good or the One, and the being of the remaining beings as a participation in the goodness of the One.[65] On the other hand, the One does not seem to lose

[53] ibid. 34,28-30; 38,13-14; 198,26-7; 202,8-9. In 201,40-202,9 monad and dyad are identified with Empedocles' Love (*philia*) and Strife (*neikos*) respectively. Cf. Syrianus *in Metaph*. 43,6-23 (A.D.R. Sheppard, 'Monad and dyad as cosmic principles in Syrianus', 8-9).
[54] Asclepius *in Metaph*. 38,11-13. In 202,23-5; 207,19-20; 207,23-7 and 208,18-22, on the other hand, Asclepius calls nature (*phusis*) the (sensible) monad, not a henad. Hence the *henadic* function continues to rest with the One directly.
[55] Asclepius *in Metaph*. 38,22-4; 39,8-9.
[56] ibid. 33,34-5.
[57] ibid. 158,18-23.
[58] ibid. 42,14-15.
[59] ibid. 309,15-18.
[60] ibid. 223,35-6; 225,15-17; 225,22; 225,34-226,3; 226,6-8; 230,4.
[61] ibid. 226,6; 226,16-17; 227,2; 227,12.
[62] ibid. 238,5; it is the subject matter of the 'very first philosophy (*prôtistê philosophia*)'.
[63] ibid. 226,17-18.
[64] ibid. 232,9-10; 'first substance (*prôtê ousia*)': 309,14-15.
[65] ibid. 226,3 ('... granting being to all things'); 227,3-4 ('it grants being to all things'). Cf. G. Verbeke, 'Aristotle's *Metaphysics* viewed by the Ancient Greek commentators', in D.J. O'Meara (ed.), *Studies in Aristotle*, Washington DC 1981, 122, 124. It is also characteristic of this theological approach to ontology that it gives a theological interpretation to Aristotle's resolution of ambiguities in different uses of the predicate being. When Aristotle says that the different uses are all related to one thing (*aph' henos*, or *pros hen*, cf. e.g. Philoponus *in Cat*. 17,2-10), the reference to 'one thing' is taken to imply a variety of ways of being

its supra-intelligible quality in this context.[66] I think that the connexion of the definition of metaphysics in *Metaphysica* 4 with the highest principle is to be considered as a Neoplatonic interpretation of Aristotle rather than as an Aristotelian contamination of Neoplatonism. For elsewhere in Asclepius' *Commentary* it is repeatedly affirmed that the Good transcends being and actuality.[67] The One (*autoen*) and Being (*autoon*) are different hypostases. The One can be predicated of being, but not vice versa. The henad is above being, because being is a form (*eidos*), and the henad transcends all form, for it produces the forms.[68] The One not only transcends all being as its origin and final goal, it also supports being, for in its ultimate emanation it takes on the guise of Matter and in that guise receives the intelligible form of beings. Matter still participates in the One, but, just like the highest principle itself, it is being and non-being at the same time.[69]

(b) The second principle: the demiurgic Intellect

The Good is the source, the ground and the final goal (*telos*) of all existence. The second divine principle is the Intellect. Ammonius seems to have accepted the division of the Intellect into Being, Life and Thought.[70] Did he also accept Proclus' setting of Plato's Creator, the Demiurge, at the level of intellective being (the *noeron*)?[71] Not necessarily. As a matter of fact Asclepius does not define more exactly or more explicitly the relation of the Demiurge to the Intellect as a whole. However, the overall impression is that he simply identifies the two. The Demiurge produces the sensible world on the basis of the demiurgic

---

dependent on, or oriented towards, the One. Cf. Asclepius *in Metaph.* 223,33-6; 227,2-4; 232,18-25.

[66] ibid. 226,2-4; cf. 439,26.

[67] ibid. 77,16-17; 148,33-4; 202,31-2.

[68] ibid. 201,4-12. Asclepius ascribes the theory to 'the Pythagoreans and Plato' (201,4), but at 201,11-12 he accepts it as correct.

[69] ibid. 233,29-31; cf. Ammonius *in Int.* 213,8-10.

[70] Asclepius *in Metaph.* 202,27-32: 'That the henad precedes everything is clear from what follows. Life is above Intellect. For whatever participates in Intellect also participates in Life, whereas not everything that participates in Life also participates in Intellect. Again, Being is at all events above Life. For whatever participates in Life also participates in Being, whereas not everything that participates in Being also participates in Life. The henad, however, is even above Being, since it is above existence.' Cf. e.g. Proclus *El. Theol.* prop. 101 and Dodds's commentary 252-3; for further references W. Beierwaltes, *Proklos. Grundzüge seiner Metaphysik*, Frankfurt a.M. 1979, 2nd edition, 106 n. 69.

[71] cf. e.g. R. Beutler, 'Proklos 4', in G. Wissowa and W. Kroll (eds), *Realencyclopädie der klassischen Altertumswissenschaft* XXIII, 1, 1957, col. 228.

logoi,[72] universal ideas[73] which flow from the henad.[74] So far, the picture is clearly Neoplatonic. On the other hand, the use of the term 'God' (*ho theos*) might seem to suggest the theistic view that the Intellect is after all to be identified with the One as the supreme God.[75] How are we to reconcile these apparently incompatible doctrines? I think a text like Asclepius *in Metaphysica* 148,30-4 might contain the core of the solution: 'But it is God (*ho theos*) who sows those universal *logoi* in souls and nature; hence He even transcends universality, and with him nothing is potential, but He is actuality without potentiality in the case of the Intellect, whereas the very first principle even transcends actuality.'[76] The quotation shows that the use of the term *ho theos* is perfectly compatible with a distinction between the divine Intellect (*Nous*) and 'the very first principle (*hê prôtistê arkhê*)'. This ambiguity makes it possible to indicate, by the single term *ho theos*, either the highest principle alone[77] or the Demiurge,[78] or, as we have just seen, both together.[79] Now, this possibility of either unfolding or telescoping, as it were, the concept of God according to the needs of the context, seems to be one of the basic features of Ammonius' metaphysics. Hence even an apparently plainly theistic terminology does not mean that Ammonius identified the supreme God and the Demiurge. It only means that it is not always necessary to draw a distinction between the two principles. I shall return to this point later. But it may already be relevant to refer to a similar practice in Christian theology: one can consider the Christian God either as a simple principle (namely *ad extra*, in His relation to the world) or as a complex principle (namely *ad intra*, in so far as the relation between the persons of divine Trinity is concerned).

(c) Divine causality

In the third place, the Commentary of Asclepius gives us some information about Ammonius' conception of divine causality. This causality is of a double nature: it is both efficient and final.[80] To take the final aspect first: everything is directed towards the One as its goal or final cause.[81] But the Demiurge too is said to move the universe as a final

[72] Ammonius-Asclepius not only ascribe the doctrine of the demiurgic *logoi* to Plato and Aristotle; it is an essential part of Ammonius' own system as well. Cf. e.g. Asclepius *in Metaph*. 48,5-7; 70,2-4; 73,21-3; 75,32-3; 76 *passim*; 80,30-1; 81,2-4; 88,4-7; 89,21-2; 142,38-143,1; 145,17-18; 165,35-166,1; 166,29-31; 167,32; 168,34-5; 173,22-3; 173,31-3; 175,16-18; 209,35-7; 216,24-6; 218,3-5. The term is also to be found in Zacharias, *Ammonius* ll.371; 388; 511-12; 766-7; 871-2 Colonna.

[73] Asclepius *in Metaph*. 173,22; 175,16; 183,21-3.

[74] ibid. 48,5-6; 52,6-7; cf. 54,25-6.

[75] cf. Praechter, nn. 5 and 12 above.

[76] Asclepius *in Metaph*. 148,30-4: ... *energeia aneu dunameôs epi tou nou, hê de prôtistê arkhê kai huper energeian estin*.

[77] e.g. ibid. 20,25-6; 28,6; 41,31-3; 108,24; 144,30-1; 195,26-7; 309,12-13.

[78] e.g. ibid. 81,2-4.

[79] e.g. ibid. 77,8-17; 122,25-6; 147,32; 148,30-4; 158,27-8.

[80] cf. n. 35 above.

[81] cf. n. 33 above.

cause or good: the circular movement of heavenly bodies is the sensible imitation of the reflexive thought of the divine Intellect.[82] As to efficient causality: it is conceived as a stratified process. The Good produces, from the abundance of its power, what are called 'intelligible forces',[83] 'intellective forces',[84] angels and souls.[85] The articulation of this intelligible world remains very vague. Rather, the main emphasis is on its absolute dependence on the highest principle. Divine creativity is an eternal process; to 'give being'[86] is the essence of the Good. God's simplicity makes His goodness absolutely necessary.[87] At the same time this necessity is absolute freedom: only God is free, because he does not need anything outside Himself, whereas everything else needs Him.[88] This means that Ammonius, just like the other Neoplatonists, cannot avoid the aporetic conclusion that on the one hand the Good is not dependent on anything outside itself, but on the other hand it *necessarily* gives existence to other things. But this is one of the mysterious truths which can only be apprehended in a mystical way.[89] Its mythical expression is the duality of ambrosia and nectar. In God, Asclepius writes, there are two perfections. The first one (absolute freedom) pertains to His essence, to what He is in Himself: it is symbolised by the solidity of ambrosia. The second perfection is symbolised by the fluidity of the nectar: it is necessary emanation.[90] At the level of the demiurgic Intellect divine goodness becomes conscious (though not deliberate) creation. Because the ideas are immanent in it (*dêmiourgikoi logoi*),[91] the divine Intellect eternally contemplates itself. Hence, at this level, the creation of the material world is the product of the creative Intellect's reflection on itself.[92] But Asclepius does not answer the question how divine causality can break out of this self-sufficient self-consciousness. This means that the relation between the Intellect's reflexive thinking and its creativity is just as problematic as the relation between the freedom and the emanation of the Good.

The *Ammonius* of Zacharias Scholasticus and the Ammonian commentaries on the Organon

(a) Zacharias

Zacharias, who later became the Bishop of Mytilene, was a student of

[82] Asclepius *in Metaph.* 151, 8-12.
[83] ibid. 11,35-6; cf. 147,6-11.
[84] ibid. 57,9; 119,33-4 (*noerai ousiai*).
[85] ibid. 57,8; 226,3. See further M. Hayduck, Index verborum, *CAG* 6, 2 s.v. *angelos* (p. 455).
[86] ibid. 226,2-3; 227,3-4: *to einai kharizesthai*.
[87] ibid. 309,10-15; 309,24-6; 368,13-15.
[88] ibid. 20,25-8.
[89] ibid. 309,15-18.
[90] ibid. 195,37-196,10.
[91] ibid. 88,4-7.
[92] ibid. 151,9-11; cf. 70,26-9.

Ammonius in Alexandria c. 485-7.[93] The teaching of Ammonius and the contradiction between his belief in the eternity of the world and Christian doctrine prompted Zacharias to write, perhaps during his stay in Beirut (487-91), a polemical dialogue called *Ammonius* or *de Mundi Opificio*.[94] The main part of the work has four sub-divisions. The first section (ll.92-350 Colonna) is introduced as the account of a discussion between Ammonius and Zacharias (referred to as *Khristianos*) about the eternity of the world *a parte ante* and *a parte post*.[95] The second section (ll.351-937) reports a dispute on the same subject between Zacharias and the medical specialist (iatrosophist) Ges(s)ius, a pagan student of Ammonius. In the third section (ll.938-1093) Zacharias discusses, with Ammonius again, the co-eternity of the world with God. In the last section, which is very short (ll.1094-1136), the same interlocutors deal with the problem of the divine Trinity.

At first sight there seems to be no difference between Zacharias' theistic concept of God and the one ascribed to Ammonius.[96] But one should not forget that both Zacharias' and Ammonius' arguments are focused on the problem of the eternity of the sensible world. Hence the articulation *ad intra* of the divine creative principle is not the point at issue here. The fact that the discussion does not enter into the Neoplatonic distinction between the One and divine Intellect does not imply that Ammonius believed in a supreme personal God, any more than Zacharias' reference to the Creator excludes his belief in the doctrine of divine Trinity, expounded ll.1094-1136. The main discussion between Zacharias and his master is about the relation of the sensible cosmos to its closest creative principle, the Demiurge. This problem is first of all

---

[93] G. Bardy, 'Zacharie le Rhéteur', *Dictionnaire de Théologie Catholique*, vol. 15, Paris 1950, col. 3677; K. Wegenast, 'Zacharias Scholasticus', in G. Wissowa and W. Kroll (eds), *Realencyclopädie der klassischen Altertumswissenschaft* IXA, 2, 1967, col. 2212; M. Minniti Colonna, *Zacaria Scolastico, Ammonio*, Naples 1973, 23.

[94] The dating of the *Ammonius* in 487-91(92) is accepted by G. Bardy, op. cit, col. 3679 and M. Wacht, *Aeneas von Gaza als Apologet. Seine Kosmologie im Verhältnis zum Platonismus*, Bonn 1969, 18 n. 17; it is regarded as likely by K. Wegenast, op. cit., col. 2215. Originally, Mrs Minniti Colonna was of the opinion that Zacharias wrote his dialogue at least 10 or 20 years after 480-90, when Aeneas of Gaza composed his *Theophrastus* ('Zacaria Scolastico, il suo Ammonio e il Teofrasto di Enea di Gaza', *Università di Napoli. Annali della Facoltà di Lettere e Filosofia* 6, 1956, 117 n. 9). In her edition of the Ammonius (p. 30) Mrs Minniti Colonna thinks that Zacharias probably wrote his dialogue in Constantinople (where he settled in 491: ibid. p. 25), more specifically after his definitive renunciation of monophysism (which, maybe, must be set in 512: ibid. p. 26), maybe even after the death of Aeneas of Gaza (c. 518) (ibid. p. 44). Regardless of whether one prefers the earlier or a later dating of the *Ammonius*, this much is certain, that the introduction of the dialogue, the talk between Zacharias and his friend, is set at the time of Zacharias' stay in Beirut. Accordingly, the 'now' in Ammonius l.22 Colonna refers to the period 487-91.

[95] According to P. Courcelle, 'Boèce et l'école d'Alexandrie', *Mélanges d'Archéologie et d'Histoire de l'Ecole française de Rome* 52, 1935, 216, this discussion really took place during the summer of 486 (or perhaps 487). Cf. M. Minniti Colonna, *Zacaria Scolastico, Ammonio*, 39.

[96] Zacharias *Ammonius* ll.108 ('... the Father and Maker of this universe'); 122 ('... the Demiurge ...') etc. God simply is *ho theos* (ll.117; 123; 126 etc.).

what one might call a problem of natural philosophy, whereas the subordination of the divine Intellect to the highest principle pertains to metaphysics.[97] The situation of Ammonius here is comparable to that of his master Proclus in his *de Aeternitate Mundi* (which survives in the *de Aeternitate Mundi contra Proclum* of John Philoponus). Nowhere in that work does Proclus speak about the place of the Demiurge in the world of intelligible reality, because it is sufficient in an argument about the eternity of the sensible world simply to accept a transcendent creative principle. And no one would call Proclus' theology theistic because of his not offering in his *de Aeternitate Mundi* a derivation of the demiurgic principle from higher intelligible reality.

(b) Ammonius' in de Interpretatione

The foregoing may have shown that Zacharias' dialogue yields no decisive indications in support of Merlan's theistic interpretation of Ammonius' theology.[98] Conversely, it is not possible either to find much in it to prove positively the Neoplatonic character of Ammonius' teaching on God and creation. Anyway, the discussions between Ammonius and Zacharias are chronologically close to Ammonius' *in de Interpretatione*, which, as we shall see, contains clearly Neoplatonic elements. This commentary indeed must be dated to the early period of Ammonius' philosophical activity,[99] and Zacharias is referring to the beginning of Ammonius' Alexandrian professorship.[100] It is not very likely that Ammonius temporarily gave up Neoplatonism in or about 486 (the time at which Zacharias was his student) and afterwards, e.g. in his *Commentary on the Metaphysics* (recorded by Asclepius), returned to it.[101] As to *in de Interpretatione*, I would like to show (1) that the influence of Proclus is found in this commentary, and (2) that it contains some evidence of the possibility of treating intelligible reality in two different ways, each of which is valid at its own level.

There can hardly be any doubt that *in de Interpretatione*, in spite of the sporadic use of terms like 'God (*ho theos*)'[102] or 'the Demiurge (*ho dêmiourgos*)',[103] has a basically Neoplatonic context. Aristotle's distinction of spoken sound (*phônê*), psychological state (*pathêma tês psukhês*) and objective reality (*pragma*)[104] is interpreted as corresponding to the

[97] cf. below.
[98] cf. above.
[99] cf. L.G. Westerink, *The Greek Commentaries on Plato's Phaedo*, vol. 1: *Olympiodorus*, 19.
[100] Zacharias *Ammonius* ll.19-24.
[101] It seems legitimate to suppose that Asclepius' *in Metaphysica*, written 'from the voice of Ammonius', is posterior to Ammonius' *in de Interpretatione*, written by Ammonius himself (cf. for this L.G. Westerink, *Anonymous Prolegomena*, xi; L. Tarán, 'Asclepius of Tralles', 14).
[102] Ammonius *in Int.* 1,11; 217,28-9; 240,10-11.
[103] ibid. 250,12-19.
[104] Aristotle *Int.* 16a3-8.

three Neoplatonic hypostases: Soul, Intellect, God.[105] Intellect is not the highest level of reality: it is transcended by 'non-being', in the sense of that which is above being and form, and which produces both form and matter.[106] The highest principle is just as formless as matter.[107] Moreover, I think it is possible to find, in Ammonius' *in de Interpretatione*, traces of the divine henads which Proclus tries to accommodate at the level of the One. At one place Ammonius refers to 'divine ranks (*theiai diakosmêseis*)' which are produced by the unique principle of reality, and each of which possesses its own 'specific character (*idiotês*)'.[108] This recalls Proclus' terminology for the henads,[109] as well as his theory that each henad, because of its specific character, is one particular 'excellence (*agathotês*)'.[110] Further allusions to the henads are perhaps to be found at *in Int.* 132,14-16,[111] 243,2-4[112] and 249,17.[113] In the digression on contingency and determinism (*in Int.* 130,27-138,10), on the other hand, Ammonius had the opportunity of being somewhat more explicit on the role of the henads, which, according to Proclus, are the primary locus of providence, of *pro-noia*, understood as 'that which precedes the *Nous*'.[114] In fact, Ammonius appears here to consider the gods as belonging not to the first level of reality, but to the second, that of *being* and of intelligible entities,[115] although his characterisation of divine knowledge resembles that by Proclus,[116] whose henads are at the first level. An example of Ammonius even completely neglecting the

---

[105] Ammonius *in Int.* 24,24-9: '... since there are three originative orders above physical substances, namely the divine, the intellective and moreover the psychic order, we say that things (*pragmata*) are created by the divine, thoughts (*noêmata*) are brought about by intellects, and words (*phônai*) are produced by those souls which are characterised by reason and have an essence separated from all body.'

[106] ibid. 213,1-5.

[107] ibid. 213,8-10.

[108] ibid. 135,28-32.

[109] Proclus *El. Theol.* prop. 132, p. 116,30 Dodds ('the ranks of the gods ...'); prop. 151, p. 132,27 ('the divine ranks').

[110] ibid. prop. 133, p. 118,8-14.

[111] Ammonius *in Int.* 132,14-16: '... or rather (if I have to say it more accurately) having established their own true existence even above intellective particularity itself.'

[112] ibid. 243,2-4: '... Aristotle thinks fit to call the gods "intellects", and perhaps he indicates that they possess a nature which is even more august than intellect.'

[113] ibid. 249,17: '... the intelligible gods and the secret causes above them ....'

[114] Proclus *El. Theol.* prop. 120, p. 104,32; '... the primary providence resides in the gods' (Dodds).

[115] cf. Ammonius *in Int.* 133,19-23 ('things which really have being ...'); 136,20-4.

[116] Compare e.g. Ammonius *in Int.* 136,15-17 ('It is necessary indeed that the gods have an undivided and unextended knowledge of things divided, a unitary knowledge of things plurified, an eternal knowledge (*aiôniôs*) of things temporal, and an ungenerated knowledge of things generable') with Proclus *El. Theol.* prop. 124, p. 110, 10-13 ('Every god has an undivided knowledge of things divided and a timeless knowledge of things temporal; he knows the contingent without contingency, the mutable immutably ...') (Dodds). For Proclus, however, it would be impossible to use Ammonius' term 'eternally (*aiôniôs*)', which is appropriate to the second level of reality: the henads transcend eternal being (Proclus *Theol. Plat.* I,99,6-7 Saffrey-Westerink). I have not been able to see L. Obertello, 'Proclus, Ammonius and Boethius on Divine knowledge', *Dionysius* 5, 1981, 127-64.

henads is *in Int.* 248,7-249,26.[117] However, I do not think that Ammonius rules out the existence of henads here. Rather, I have the impression that, generally speaking, he accepts the distinction between the henads at the higher level and the intelligible gods at the lower. But the theory of henads arises only when one goes into a kind of detail (*akribeia*)[118] that is not indispensable in all circumstances. Hence the references to the henads have only a supplementary or even redundant character, either especially emphasising the distance between the material world and the highest region of reality,[119] or adding a further rung for the ascent of our intellect.[120] They are introduced only occasionally when the context makes it necessary to introduce them from below. For it is not the task of the *in de Interpretatione* to deduce the metaphysical system in full completeness from the highest principle. The commentator merely has to refer to this principle from time to time, to explain the conditions of the possibility of the sensible world. I think it is legitimate to consider this economical type of metaphysics as a Neoplatonic version of Aristotle's 'theology from the standpoint of natural philosophy (*phusikôs theologein*)'.[121] In principle, there is no need for this 'minimal' metaphysics to meet the same requirements of detail (*akribeia*) as a complete and systematic metaphysics. Obviously, the theory of henads is an item for the latter rather than for the former. Hence, even Ammonius' account of the relation between contingency and determinism can virtually do without the henads: in the non-metaphysical context of *in de Interpretatione* it is sufficient to set providence at a level where, in Proclus' system, it is only secondary, namely at the second level, that of the intelligible gods.[122]

Consequently, the way in which Ammonius, in his early *in de Interpretatione*, deals with the henads is closely related to what we have already observed in Asclepius' *in Metaphysica* and in Zacharias' *Ammonius*, namely the possibility of unfolding or telescoping the concept of God. In Asclepius' *in Metaphysica* the henads have disappeared. This has rightly been noticed by Saffrey and Westerink. They explain it as follows: 'Despite the close links that existed between the schools of Athens and of Alexandria, there was at Alexandria a more strictly monotheist tradition than at Athens, and that excluded *a priori* the possibility of teaching the theory of divine henads there with approval.'[123] However, I think *in de*

---

[117] The gods (*ontôs theoi*: Ammonius *in Int.* 248,31) are 'pure acts' (*autoenergeiai*: 248,18; 248,28); further 248,17-18: '... the very first and supreme among beings, that is to say the intelligible and divine ones ....'

[118] ibid. 132,15: *ei khrê to akribesteron phanai*; cf. n. 111 above.

[119] ibid. 132,14-16; 243,2-4.

[120] ibid. 135,28-32.

[121] The commentators often oppose Aristotle's 'theology from the standpoint of natural philosophy (*phusiologikôs theologein*)' to Plato's 'natural philosophy from the standpoint of theology (*theologikôs phusiologein*)' (cf. K. Kremer, *Der Metaphysikbegriff*, 189-95): e.g. Elias *in Cat.* 120,30-121,3; 124,21-3; Philoponus *in Phys.* 5,21-5.

[122] cf. Proclus *El. Theol.* prop. 134, p. 118,20: 'Every divine intelligence exercises intellection *qua* intelligence, but providence *qua* god' (Dodds).

[123] Proclus *Theol. Plat.* III, H.D. Saffrey and L.G. Westerink (eds), p. lxxxvi.

Interpretatione shows that Ammonius at the beginning of his career still accepted the doctrine of henads. Later he seems to have given it up. But this should not, in my opinion, be interpreted as a consequence of any theistic tradition. Rather, it is one element of Ammonius' eventual simplification of Neoplatonism in comparison with Proclus.

(c) Ammonius' in Isagogen, in Categorias *and* in Analytica Priora

Like *in de Interpretatione*, the other logical commentaries contain only a few indications concerning Ammonius' theological views. Yet they are sufficient to confirm what we have found so far. The *Prooemium* of the *in Isagogen* has some references to a substantial, omniscient and provident God which sound very theistic.[124] However, since this prooemium is probably not authentic,[125] the fact does not demand particular attention. Things become recognisable again in the opening words of the corpus of the commentary, where it is stated that the Good is the principle of all reality.[126] We also find the classical Neoplatonic doctrine of the presence of paradigms in the demiurgic Intellect.[127] The definition which Ammonius gives of the goal *(telos)* of Aristotle's philosophy in the *Prooemium* of his *in Categorias*[128] is characteristic of his Neoplatonic exegesis. The highest principle is said to be the subject of negative theology.[129] I think a formula like 'there is nothing above the first beings *(huper de ta prôta ouden)*'[130] should be understood, not as a denial of the existence of the One,[131] but merely as a statement that there are no higher genera beyond the first substances,[132] i.e. the intelligible gods.[133] Finally, Ammonius may have identified the absolute Good with absolute Beauty.[134]

Ammonius' interpretation of Aristotle's concept of God

I have so far spoken of Ammonius' *own* theology, but now we arrive at

---

[124] Ammonius *in Isag.* 3,9-15; 4,7-8; 11,11-13; cf. 9,16-17. See n. 12 (Praechter).

[125] A. Busse, Praefatio, *CAG* 4.3, vi n. 4.

[126] Ammonius *in Isag.* 24,2-5: 'All beings by their very nature long for the Good, since there is one principle of all beings, the Good. Therefore all things tend upwards to the Good as their own good, and every being is perfected by participating in the Good in accordance with its own limitations.'

[127] ibid. 41,20-42,26; 63,14-16.

[128] Ammonius *in Cat.* 6,10-12: '... to raise oneself up to the common principle of all things, and to come to know that it is unique, incorporeal, without parts, not to be comprehended, undefinable and of infinite potency: absolute goodness ... *autoagathotês:*' cf. e.g. Proclus *El. Theol.* prop. 127, p. 112,33; Elias *Proleg.* 17,2.

[129] Ammonius *in Cat.* 36,25-6.

[130] Ammonius *in An. Pr.* 25,20.

[131] This is the opinion of K. Kremer, *Der Metaphysikbegriff*, p. 39: 'The noetic things do not have a ground any more to found their *logos* and existence on.'

[132] Ammonius *in An. Pr.* 25,11-20.

[133] Ammonius *in Cat.* 26,2-3; 35,20-1; 37,1-10.

[134] cf. Ammonius *in An. Pr.* 5,19-22.

what is undoubtedly the most famous, not to say the only tenet in Ammonius' philosophy that is generally known: his doctrine of the nature of *Aristotle's* God. So far, an erroneous interpretation of this doctrine has been the main source for the conviction that Ammonius adopted the Christian identification of the supreme God and the demiurgic Intellect. I do not pretend to be able to propose a complete solution of the problem at the present stage of my research. For this would require further investigations into its history before Ammonius and e.g. into Simplicius' ideas concerning the relation between physics and metaphysics. But a first step can already be taken: I think it is possible to reconcile Asclepius' and Simplicius' apparently incompatible accounts of the theory of Ammonius.

(a) Simplicius

At both *in Cael.* 271,13-21 and *in Phys.* 1360,24-1363,24, Simplicius tells us that to Ammonius the Aristotelian God is not only the final but also the efficient cause of the universe:[135] he mentions a monograph by Ammonius completely devoted to this question. As late as the tenth century al-Farabi refers to this monograph as the source of his own interpretation of Aristotle.[136] Simplicius notes that it was the purpose of the theory to harmonise Aristotle with Plato,[137] and that it was opposed to orthodox Peripatetic exegesis, including Alexander's.[138] We may add that it was opposed to Proclus' exegesis as well: Aristotle's conception of God, Proclus writes, contains only half of the truth.[139] Ammonius by contrast is credited by Simplicius[140] with five instances to prove that Aristotle considered God as an efficient cause:[141] *Phys.* 2.3, 194b29-31;

[135] Most scholars discuss the issue just on the basis of Simplicius' texts, without referring to Asclepius at all: e.g. P. Tannery, 'Sur la période finale de la philosophie grecque', in P. Tannery, *Mémoires scientifiques*, vol. 7, Toulouse and Paris 1925, 226-7; E. Zeller, *Die Philosophie der Griechen* III, 2, 894 n. 1; K. Praechter, 'Simplikios', col. 211; R. Vancourt, *Les derniers commentateurs alexandrins d'Aristote: l'école d'Olympiodore, Etienne d'Alexandrie*, Lille 1941, 18-21; M. Wolff, *Fallgesetz und Massebegriff. Zwei wissenschaftshistorische Untersuchungen zur Kosmologie des Johannes Philoponus*, Berlin 1971, 129 n. 32; id., 'Philoponus and the rise of preclassical dynamics', in R. Sorabji (ed.), *Philoponus and the Rejection of Aristotelian Science*, London and Ithaca NY 1987, 108.

[136] E. Behler, *Die Ewigkeit der Welt. Problemgeschichtliche Untersuchungen zu den Kontroversen um Weltanfang und Weltunendlichkeit im Mittelalter*, vol. 1, Munich, Paderborn, Vienna 1965, 74-5, 128, 137; M. Mahdi, 'Alfarabi against Philoponus', *Journal of Near Eastern Studies* 26, 1967, 236-7 n. 9.

[137] Simplicius *in Phys.* 1360,28-31. The point was rightly emphasised by H.D. Saffrey, 'Le chrétien Jean Philopon et la survivance de l'école d'Alexandrie au VIe siècle', *Revue des études grecques* 67, 1954, 400 n. 3. Cf. n. 184 below.

[138] Simplicius *in Cael.* 271,13-14; *in Phys.* 1362,11-15.

[139] Proclus *in Tim.* I, 266,28-267,12 (cf. L.G. Westerink, *Anonymous Prolegomena*, 19); *in Parm.* 842,26-35; cf. further *in Parm.* 788, 12-28 (cf. A.J. Festugière, *Proclus, Commentaire sur le Timée* II, Paris, 1967, 108, n. 4.); Philoponus *Aet.* 31,7-32,10. Probably the term 'some men' (*tines*) in Simplicius *in Phys.* 1360,24 includes Proclus; cf. 258,14.

[140] Simplicius *in Phys.* 1363,8-12. The entire passage 1361,11-1362,12, is translated in Richard Sorabji, *Matter, Space and Motion*, London and Ithaca NY, 1988, 275-7.

[141] Simplicius *in Phys.* 1361,12-1362,10.

Cael. 1.4, 271a33; *Cael.* 1.9, 279a27-30;[142] *GC* 1.3, 318a1-5;[143] *Metaph.* 1.4, 984b15-22. However, a further question is this: of what exactly is Aristotle's God the efficient cause? No one would deny that He is the efficient cause of sublunary movement, albeit indirectly, by directly moving the heavens.[144] According to Simplicius Alexander even accepted that to Aristotle God was the efficient cause of heavenly movement.[145] At the same time, however, Alexander denied that the unmoved Mover was the efficient cause of heavenly substance.[146] Ammonius, on the other hand, was convinced that Aristotle's God was the efficient cause of the whole universe (*tou pantos kosmou*),[147] which seems to mean: both of its movement (heavenly and sublunary) and of its existence as a substance (heavenly and sublunary). Therefore Simplicius, who agrees with Ammonius, adduces two arguments against Alexander's limitation of efficient causality to movement.[148] The first argument is this. That which receives its movement from elsewhere, also receives its existence from elsewhere.[149] Heaven receives its movement directly from the Unmoved Mover as efficient cause.[150] Therefore, it receives its corporeal substance from the incorporeal Unmoved Mover as well.[151] The second argument is that at *Phys.* 2.6, 198a5-13 where Aristotle says Intellect and nature are the causes of 'this universe (*tou ouranou toude; toude tou pantos)*'.[152] Accordingly, Ammonius' ascription of an efficient causality to the Unmoved Mover represents a major alteration, not only of Aristotle's concept of God, but also of his concept of efficient causality: God is the efficient cause of the universe, not only as the principle of its movement (*hothen hê arkhê tês kinêseôs*),[153] but also as the principle which produces its very existence (*hupostasis*) as a substance (*ousia*).[154] Moreover, the efficient causality at issue is an eternal relation. This is the reason, Simplicius adds, why Aristotle was less explicit in calling God the efficient cause of the world than he was in calling Him its final cause: the idea of efficient causality is

---

[142] cf. n. 191 below.

[143] cf. Philoponus *in GC* 50,1-5. Cf. n. 189 below.

[144] Simplicius *in Phys.* 1362,17-20.

[145] ibid. 1361,31-3; cf. 258,13-25.

[146] ibid. 1362,11-15. R. Vancourt, *Les derniers commentateurs*, 20-1 writes: 'Simplicius devotes a special paragraph to refuting Alexander's interpretation, according to which God is the final cause and not the efficient cause of heavenly movement, which is itself ungenerated and eternal.' I do not think this is what Simplicius' text says. The sentence ascribed to Alexander is this: 'The first mover is the efficient cause of the movement of the divine body, which is ungenerated (*to goun prôton kinoun tês tou theiou sômatos kinêseôs aition esti poiêtikon ontos agenêtou)*', Simplicius *in Phys.* 1361,32-3. Vancourt erroneously takes *ontos agenêtou* to refer to *kinêseôs*; if that were correct we would have *ousês agenêtou*.

[147] Simplicius *in Phys.* 1363,9-10; cf. 1360,30-1.

[148] ibid. 1362,11-1363,8.

[149] ibid. 1363,2-4.

[150] ibid. 1362,17-19.

[151] ibid. 1363,4-8.

[152] ibid. 1362,20-1363,2.

[153] Aristotle *Phys.* 2.6,198a3.

[154] Simplicius *in Phys.* 1363,2-8.

too readily associated with the idea of a temporal beginning of the effect.[155]

The foregoing already suggests that the background of Ammonius' theory is Neoplatonic. Aristotle is said to conceive the relation between God and the world as a double process: on the one hand, the world is produced by God as its 'efficient' cause (this is its procession – *proodos*), on the other hand it is directed towards God as its final cause (this is its reversion – *epistrophê*). Yet, there is no trace, in Simplicius' account, of any corresponding 'Neoplatonisation' of Aristotle's concept of God itself.[156] According to Simplicius, Ammonius simply considered Aristotle's God as the divine Intellect.[157]

(b) Asclepius[158]

In Asclepius the picture is different: Ammonius is said to have identified Aristotle's God with the highest principle of Neoplatonism, not with divine Intellect. This interpretation is influenced, of course, by the fact that Aristotle himself calls God the 'first principle (*arkhê*)' of the entire cosmos,[159] and that, as everyone agreed,[160] he considers God the *final* cause,[161] that is, the final cause of being. He even calls Him 'the Good (*to agathon*)'.[162] To Ammonius, if we rely on Asclepius, Aristotle's God is 'the

[155] ibid. 1363,12-24.

[156] 'Neoplatonisation' is meant here as the 'distinction between the Good and the Intellect'. Simplicius does not say anything here about the fact that Ammonius' reinterpretation implies that Aristotle's God is no longer self-thinking Thought, but a demiurgic Intellect in the Neoplatonic sense, which includes the Ideas in itself. Obviously, however, he is aware of this, and he himself is convinced that for Aristotle also the ideas are immanent in the demiurgic Intellect (*in Cael*. 87,3-11).

[157] e.g. Simplicius *in Phys*. 1360,25; 1362,7-8; 1362,16-17; 1362,32. It is true that Simplicius *in Cael*. 271,21-7 calls Aristotle's God 'the One (*to hen*)'. However, this predicate here concerns only the uniqueness of the first Unmoved Mover, and as only 'the object of desire (*monôs epheton*)' at that. Neither does the fact that Aristotle's God at *in Phys*. 257,13-16 is said to be both 'intellect (*nous*)' and 'good (*agathos*)' mean that Simplicius here identifies the Good and the divine Intellect. Rather, the term *agathos* here refers to the final causality of the Intellect with regard to the world. Simplicius understands the goodness (*agathotês*) of the *Platonic* Demiurge (*Tim*. 29E1) as final causality (e.g. *in Phys*. 7,17-19; 26,15-18; 43,6), and he puts Aristotle's divine Intellect at the same level as Plato's Demiurge (cf. *in Phys*. 1360,28-34). For Simplicius' own real view on Aristotle's God cf. n. 182 below.

[158] According to L.G. Westerink, *Anonymous Prolegomena*, 19; *The Greek Commentaries on Plato's Phaedo*, vol. 1: *Olympiodorus*, 24, Ammonius' interpretation of Aristotle's concept of God is also to be found in Philoponus (= Stephanus), *in DA* 571,1-5. However, it should be noted that the beginning of that passage is not about the object of appetency (*orekton*) (a final cause of movement, like the Unmoved Mover; cf. Proclus *in Tim*. I, 267,9) but about the *orektikon*, i.e. the impulsive faculty of the soul. It is this faculty that is said to act as an efficient cause. At the end of the passage the intellect is called 'an efficient, not a final cause (*poiêtikos kai ou telikos*)', which does not recall Ammonius' view on Aristotle's theology either. I think that the text is purely psychological, and that Stephanus does not allude here to the Aristotelian divine Intellect.

[159] Aristotle *Metaph*. 12.7, 1072b13-14.

[160] cf. Simplicius *in Phys*. 1361,11-12.

[161] Aristotle *Metaph*. 12.7, 1072b1-3.

[162] ibid. 12.10, 1075a11-12.

Good, which everything is longing for':[163] it is the Neoplatonic first cause.[164] This God is said to be not only the final cause, but also the absolute origin of all reality.[165] Terming the latter aspect an *'efficient causality*'[166] is to speak rather loosely: Aristotle conceived efficient causality only as an activity exerted upon an already existing substance.[167]

But what are we to do about the fact that Aristotle describes God as an Intellect? In principle, Asclepius' identification of Aristotle's God with the Neoplatonic first cause suggests the possibility that Aristotle's God contains *both* a supreme principle and, distinct from it, an Intellect. As far as I know, Asclepius does not say anything like that explicitly. But an indirect indication of Ammonius applying that distinction to Aristotle might be found in the following argument. We are told by Asclepius[168] that Ammonius ascribed to Aristotle the distinction between Being and the One with regard to the lowest level of the ontological hierarchy, namely matter. Aristotle's matter is both being and non-being.[169] It is being, one is to understand, in so far as it is not nothing, and it is non-being in so far as it is not anything in particular. This means, according to Asclepius, that for Ammonius Aristotle himself accepted the transcendence of the One compared to Being – 'The One surmounts being (*huperbebêke to hen to on*)': matter, as it is non-being but not nothing, *is* the One, below all being. Now, the analogy of the status of matter to that of the One is obvious. I refer to a text written by Ammonius himself, where the different modes of non-being are enumerated: matter, Ammonius writes, is non-being because of the absence of forms, and this implies a similarity accompanied by dissimilarity (*anomoios homoiotês*) between matter and the first principle.[170] As a consequence, it is not too far-fetched, I think, to infer from Asclepius' text on matter that Ammonius interpreted Aristotle's God in an analogous way, as containing both being and a principle above being. Moreover, in the case of Aristotelian matter, that which transcends Being is called by Asclepius *the One*. Accordingly, Aristotle's highest principle also is *One*. This means a fortiori that it cannot be identical with the divine Intellect, since for Ammonius Aristotle's Intellect is not just a unitary self-thinking thought, but contains within itself the *plurality* of Platonic Ideas.

[163] Aristotle *EN* 1.1, 1094a3, quoted by Asclepius, *in Metaph.* 28,26-7. Cf. Proclus *El. Theol.* prop. 12, p. 14,18.

[164] Asclepius *in Metaph.* 28,31-2 (*prôton aition*).

[165] ibid. 148,10-11; 225,15-17; cf. 105,30-2 (where Ammonius is mentioned as 'the philosopher'). According to L.G. Westerink, *Anonymous Prolegomena*, p. 19, Ammonius' interpretation of the Aristotelian God is also reflected in Asclepius *in Metaph.* 151,15-32. I have the impression that this text is not primarily concerned with Ammonius' view on Aristotle's God, but rather expounds Ammonius' own theology.

[166] Asclepius *in Metaph.* 28,20-2; 103,3-4.

[167] cf. Aristotle *Phys.* 2.3., 194b29-32.

[168] Asclepius *in Metaph.* 233,25-31.

[169] cf. n. 69 above.

[170] Ammonius *in Int.* 213,8-10; cf. Simplicius *in Phys.* 205, 8-15; Philoponus *in Phys.* 162,12-20.

In this last reference to Plato's Ideas, it is again Ammonius' intention to harmonise Aristotle with Plato.[171] Aristotle's opposition to the theory of Ideas is said to be directed, not against the existence of Ideas, but against those interpreters of Plato who wrongly think that the Platonic Ideas are entities subsistent outside the demiurgic Intellect. In Ammonius' view both Plato and Aristotle hold that the Ideas exist as demiurgic *logoi* within the divine Intellect.[172] Asclepius mentions four arguments in favour of this Neoplatonic interpretation of Aristotle. In the first place he refers to *Metaph.* 12.10, 1075a12-17, where the immanence and the transcendence of the Good in relation to the cosmos is compared with the presence of the order of an army both in the general and in the army itself.[173] Secondly, at *DA* 3.4, 429a27-8 Aristotle calls the soul 'the place of forms (*topos eidôn*)'.[174] At first sight it is not very clear how this text can be made relevant to the ontological status of Ideas. In my opinion the argument is this: universal Ideas (the *logoi*) are present in God, in nature, and in the rational soul. In God this presence is both cognitive and creative, in nature it is only creative, in soul it is only cognitive.[175] Now, if at the level of soul the *logoi* are already contained within the unity of a 'place', this is true a fortiori for the divine *logoi*. The third argument is Aristotle's statement at *DA* 3.5, 430a19-20 (cf. 3.7, 431a1-2) that 'the intellect in act is things' (i.e. is identical with the objects of its thought).[176] Finally, Asclepius says, according to *DA* 3.5, 430a14-15 'the intellect in potency is active, but the intellect in act is productive' (sic).[177] This interpretation of Aristotle's divine Intellect seems hardly compatible with the view that Aristotle's God is the Neoplatonic One, unless one accepts that Ammonius implicitly ascribes to Aristotle the doctrine that the Intellect is subordinate to the highest principle.

(c) The compatibility of Simplicius' and Asclepius' accounts

The hypothesis just mentioned (subordination of the Intellect to the One) is necessary, I think, in order to prevent Asclepius from contradicting himself on Ammonius' interpretation of Aristotle's theology. On the other hand there is nothing in Simplicius' texts on Ammonius to confirm it: if we rely on Simplicius, Aristotle's God for Ammonius simply was the divine Intellect. Therefore, the conclusion that the two commentators contradict each other seems at first sight inevitable. If we try to explain

---

[171] Ammonius' diligence in harmonising Plato and Aristotle on the subject of the doctrine of Ideas is also mentioned by Zacharias *Ammonius* 1.952.

[172] Asclepius *in Metaph.* 44,32-7 (cf. K. Kremer, *Der Metaphysikbegriff*, 168); 69,17-27 (cf. Kremer, ibid. 185-6); 75,27-8; 167,14-34; 183,14-16; 233,38-40; 363,1-5; 393,34-394,2; 441,27-31; 442,1-2; cf. K. Praechter, 'Simplikios', col. 211. To Proclus *in Tim.* I, 267,1 the Aristotelian God is still an 'intellect without plurality (*nous aplêthuntos*)'.

[173] Asclepius *in Metaph.* 44,35-7.

[174] ibid. 69,19-20; 167,29-31.

[175] ibid. 81,2-4; 148,29-31.

[176] ibid. 69,20; 167,31. M. Hayduck ad 69,20 also refers to *DA* 3.8, 431b21.

[177] ibid. 69,20-1.

the contradiction, at least three possibilities may be considered.

First of all, one might suppose that there was a difference between Ammonius' esoteric exegesis of Aristotle within the school (represented by Asclepius) and the monograph he published for a wider public (referred to by Simplicius). On this hypothesis some influence of Christianity on the published work might seem to be possible. However, one should not forget that Simplicius completely agrees with the purport of Ammonius' book, and, moreover, that he clearly indicates the Neoplatonic character of Ammonius' view on the causal relation between Aristotle's God and the world. This suggests that Simplicius regarded Ammonius' interpretation as fully in line with Neoplatonism, which would have been impossible if there were any influence of Christian theism in it.

Did Ammonius' monograph perhaps represent his later position, a position facilitating a convergence between Aristotelianism and Christianity by changing in a theistic direction the original, Neoplatonically inspired interpretation of Aristotle's theology? I think that the objections just raised against the first possibility hold against this one also.

The third possibility is that both Asclepius and Simplicius give an incomplete account of the theory of Ammonius. If that is correct, the contradiction is only apparent, and the two versions should be considered as two complementary variants of the same theory. Both in Asclepius and in Simplicius, one might suppose, Aristotle's identification of the first principle and the Intellect is replaced by an *implicit* subordination of the Intellect to the highest principle. In Asclepius, as we have seen, this implication is rather obvious. In Simplicius it is not, but this should not necessarily mean that it is not present at all. In my opinion the difference between the two versions is indeed a matter of different emphasis. In *Asclepius*, Ammonius' ascription of a double causality to Aristotle's God is primarily related to the level of the supreme cause, the One. Consequently, Asclepius neglects to mention explicitly that the same double causality belongs likewise to the demiurgic Intellect. Moreover, it means that divine efficient causality is styled as a process *beyond* thought and consciousness. In *Simplicius*, on the other hand, Ammonius' interpretation of Aristotle's God is primarily related to the level of divine Intellect. Hence Simplicius omits the fact that final and efficient causality for Aristotle also belong to the supreme cause. I assume that the difference between Asclepius and Simplicius is nothing but a shift of emphasis.

Maybe this shift itself can be explained. Asclepius is speaking as a commentator of the *Metaphysics*, Simplicius as a commentator of the *Physics*. The distinction between these two disciplines seems to offer, in the Alexandrian tradition, the possibility of giving different emphases to Aristotle's concept of God. In this respect we have a very important piece of evidence in Elias' *in Categorias*. Why, Elias wonders, does Aristotle in his *Metaphysics* call the Intellect the very first principle (*hê prôtistê arkhê*) and not, like Plato, the Good (*to agathon*)? The answer is this: the *Metaphysics* is a theological treatise, but it immediately follows the physical treatises.[178] This explains why Aristotle does not ascend from the Intellect to the Good in his *Metaphysics*: the Intellect is the more physical of the two principles (*hê phusikôtera arkhê*). But the fact that in the *Metaphysics* the Intellect is regarded as the ultimate principle does not mean that Aristotle was not aware of the transcendence of the Good compared to the Intellect. The beginning of the *Nicomachean Ethics*, a treatise which is further removed from natural philosophy, shows that he was. In general, however, one can characterise, according to Elias, Aristotle's way of theological thinking as 'theology from the standpoint of natural philosophy (*theologôn phusiologei*)'.[179]

But how does this remark of Elias help us to understand the difference between Asclepius and Simplicius? Would one not anticipate, relying simply on Elias, that Asclepius, as a commentator of the *Metaphysics*, held the view that the Intellect is the highest principle, rather than introducing the Good? Asclepius' commentary proves that this conclusion would be erroneous. Therefore we should concentrate on the following points in Elias' account: (1) Aristotle knew the difference between the Intellect and the Good; (2) he kept silent about the Good in the *Metaphysics* all the same; (3) he could do so (a) because his metaphysics (or theology) is limited to indicating the immediate transcendent cause(s) of the *physical* world, and (b) because the divine Intellect is closer to the physical world than the Good. The text of Elias shows that the Alexandrian school conceived of Aristotle's God as consisting of two 'hypostases', the Good and the Intellect. Aristotle is said to have telescoped his concept of God in the *Metaphysics*. This means that one can consider Aristotle's God, according to one's point of view, either as the Neoplatonic Good or as the Neoplatonic divine Intellect. When we apply this principle to the relation between Asclepius' and Simplicius' versions of the Ammonian interpretation of Aristotle's concept of God, the result is as follows. At the *metaphysical* level (Asclepius) the Unmoved Mover is primarily understood in its ultimate depth as the Good, the first origin and the final cause of all reality. At the level of *natural philosophy* (Simplicius) the Aristotelian God is primarily conceived as the demiurgic Intellect, which at the same time is the final cause of cosmic movement. In this perspective the apparent contrast between Asclepius and Simplicius gives no ground for the hypothesis of a synchronic and/or diachronic duality in Ammonius' interpretation of Aristotle's theology.

However, it remains somewhat curious that, in reporting Ammonius' view on Aristotle's God, Simplicius does not say anything about the two 'hypostases'. I assume that this has to do with the fact that *in Physica* and *in de Caelo* belong to natural philosophy. Simplicius was aware of the limits imposed on theological speculation in natural philosophy.[180] And

[178] *ta phusiologika*, broader than just the *Physics*.
[179] Elias *in Cat*. 120,23-30.
[180] e.g. Simplicius *in Phys*. 148,22-4.

in the very lines of *in Physica* where he refers to Ammonius' monograph he draws attention to the incompleteness of his account.[181] More clarity – if any – should come from a complete study of Simplicius' own statements about Aristotle's theology, scattered throughout his commentaries. But I want to state right now that Simplicius too, speaking on his own authority, credits Aristotle with the distinction between the divine Intellect and the supreme principle, just like Elias.[182] I think this fact considerably increases the plausibility of my hypothesis that Ammonius already ascribed the Neoplatonic distinction between the first two hypostases to Aristotle, despite Simplicius' silence about the distinction in his texts on Ammonius.

(d) Philoponus

The way in which both Simplicius and Asclepius deal with Ammonius' ascription of final and efficient causality to Aristotle's God should have made clear (1) that Ammonius' theory has nothing to do with any attempt to 'Christianise' Aristotle and (2) that it did not imply a theistic concept of God either. Since it was launched by P. Tannery,[183] the 'Christian' hypothesis has been accepted by several scholars.[184] However, a number considerations should have raised suspicions about its correctness. First, Simplicius would never have agreed with any theory that tried to Christianise Aristotle. Secondly, Simplicius says clearly that the purpose of the theory (in Ammonius' mind also, we may add) was to harmonise Aristotle with *Plato*.[185] And this harmonisation was indisputably a concern of pagan Neoplatonism, not of Christian philosophy.[186] Thirdly,

[181] ibid. 1363,10-12.

[182] Simplicius *in Cael.* 485,19-22: 'That Aristotle has the notion of something even above Intellect and being is shown by his saying clearly, near the end of his book "On Prayer", that God is either Intellect or something even beyond Intellect' (= Aristotle fr. 49 Rose; I adapt Ross's translation).

[183] P. Tannery, 'Sur la période finale', 226-7.

[184] The 'Christian interpretation' has been accepted by L.G. Westerink, *The Greek Commentaries on Plato's Phaedo*, vol. 1: *Olympiodorus,* 24; M. Mahdi, 'Alfarabi against Philoponus', 237, n. 9; G. Verbeke, 'Some later Neoplatonic views on divine creation and the eternity of the world', in D.J. O'Meara (ed.), *Neoplatonism and Christian Thought*, Albany 1982, 46. It is also implied in a remark by E. Ducci ('Il to eon parmenideo nell' interpretazione di Filopono', *Rassegna di Scienze Filosofiche* 17, 1964, 272), who detects the Christian conviction of the author in the statement 'God is the *efficient* cause of all things (*Deus causa efficiens omnium est)*' in ps.-Philoponus *in Metaph.* fol. 2rA (Patrizzi). The opposite position is that Ammonius' theory intended to harmonise Plato and Aristotle; it was taken by H.D. Saffrey, 'Le chretien Jean Philopon', 400 n. 3; P. Merlan, 'Ammonius Hermiae, Zacharias Scholasticus and Boethius', 201; A.C. Lloyd, 'The Later Neoplatonists', 317. R. Vancourt, *Les derniers commentateurs*, 19, and É. Évrard, *L'école d'Olympiodore et la composition du 'Commentaire à la Physique' de Jean Philopon*, diss., Liège 1957, 208-9 (and Westerink; cf. the quotation p. 202) are of the opinion that the two positions are compatible.

[185] cf. n. 137 above.

[186] cf. e.g. A.C. Lloyd, 'The later Neoplatonists', 275; H.J. Blumenthal, 'Neoplatonic elements in the *de Anima* commentaries', *Phronesis* 21, 1976, 65-7 (= Chapter 13 in this volume, pp. 306-8); I. Hadot, *Le problème du néoplatonisme alexandrin*, 68, 73-6. In 529 AD

it should be remembered that Ammonius does not question Aristotle's belief in the eternity of the world. Hence, even in the revised interpretation there remains a considerable distance between divine causality in Aristotle and Christian creationism (although some Christians, irrespective of Ammonius' intentions, may have felt that an eternally 'creating' Aristotelian God was less un-Christian than the Mover usually ascribed to Aristotle which is only a final cause). Finally – and in my opinion this is conclusive – the fate of Ammonius' theory in the philosophy of Philoponus proves that it was regarded as closely related to pagan Neoplatonism.

One of the discontinuities between Philoponus' earlier and later work, which leads me to speak [187] of Philoponus 1 and Philoponus 2, is precisely his about-turn with regard to the interpretation of both Platonic and Aristotelian theology. I must limit myself to a few essentials here. Philoponus 1, without mentioning his master in this respect, accepts Ammonius' view that, for Aristotle, God is both the final and the efficient cause of the universe. He uses two types of arguments. On the one hand, there are two passages in *in de Generatione et Corruptione* where it is stated that Aristotle *implicitly* ascribes efficient causality to 'God'.[188] On the other hand, Philoponus also finds *explicit* evidence in *de Generatione et Corruptione*.[189] As a result, it is a matter of course to Philoponus 1 that Aristotle's God is also the efficient cause of the universe.[190] The way in which Philoponus understands this is very similar to what we found in Asclepius: Aristotle's God is the source of all reality, including matter,[191] i.e. He is the One. Just like Asclepius and Simplicius, Philoponus 1 believes that, for Aristotle, the Platonic Ideas are *logoi* immanent in the demiurgic Intellect.[192] His first piece of evidence is *Metaph.* 12.10,

---

Philoponus indirectly claims that the theory that Aristotle's God is an efficient cause as well (a theory which is implied in the harmonising ascription of the doctrine of Ideas to Aristotle) is due to the fact that some recent philosophers were ashamed about the disagreement between Plato and Aristotle (Philoponus *Aet.* 29,2-8; cf. 32,10-13). (K. Praechter names the recent philosophers in question as 'Ammonius Hermiae and his circle', 'Simplikios', col. 211, but it escapes his attention that Philoponus 1 had been advocating Ammonius' view himself). The underlying idea is this: the Neoplatonists try to harmonise Aristotle with Plato out of shame over the discord within Greek philosophy compared to the consensus in Christian doctrine. However, according to Elias *in Cat.* 123,2-3 Iamblichus was already of the opinion that Aristotle and Plato did not contradict each other with regard to the doctrine of Ideas (cf. H.J. Blumenthal, 'Neoplatonic elements', 66 (= p. 307 below)).

[187] See Chapter 11 below.

[188] Philoponus *in GC* 136,33-137,3; 152,23-153,2. According to E. Evrard, 'Les convictions religieuses', p. 354, the first passage is redundant in its context: Philoponus, Evrard believes, goes especially out of his way to expound his Christian view of Aristotle. I cannot enter into this any further now; the mere reference to *in GC* 152,23-153,2 is sufficient, I think, to refute Evrard's view.

[189] *GC* 1.3, 318a1-5 (Philoponus *in GC* 50,1-5; cf. n. 143 above); *GC* 2.10, 336b31-4 (Philoponus *in GC* 297,15-24).

[190] Philoponus *in Phys.* 298,6-10; 304,5-10.

[191] ibid. 189,13-17, referring to *Cael.* 1.9, 279a27-30 (cf. p. 205 above) and *Metaph.* 12.7, 1072b13-14.

[192] Philoponus *in DA* 37, 19-31.

1075a12-17, as in Simplicius and Asclepius.[193] Two further arguments (*DA* 3.4, 429a27-8 and 3.5, 430a19-20) are common to Asclepius and Philoponus.[194] Whereas Asclepius finds his fourth argument in *DA* 3.5, 430a14-15, Philoponus may be referring to *Metaph.* 12.9, 1074b33-4, where Aristotle, he says, identifies the divine Intellect's self-contemplation (*heauton horôn*) with its contemplation of reality (*ta pragmata horâi*).[195] All this means that the picture in Philoponus 1 is very much the same as in Asclepius. It is most significant that Philoponus 2, wanting to dissociate himself publicly from Alexandrian Neoplatonism and to present himself as a Christian philosopher, immediately drops his master's interpretation of Aristotle's God. Both in his *de Aeternitate Mundi contra Proclum* and in his *in Analytica Posteriora* Philoponus argues that Aristotle *rejected* Plato's theory of Ideas itself, not just an erroneous interpretation which regarded the Ideas as substances outside the demiurgic Intellect.[196] If Aristotle only intended to criticise those Platonists who hypostatised the Ideas outside the Demiurge, and not the very existence of the Ideas, he would have made this clear, and he would have indicated which interpretation of the theory of Ideas is the correct one.[197] Instead, he calls the Ideas mere 'twittering (*teretismata*)'.[198] Moreover, it is recorded that Aristotle was already strongly opposing the doctrine of Ideas when Plato was still alive.[199] Philoponus 2 no longer accepts the evidential value of the Aristotelian texts that are adduced by those who try to harmonise Aristotle with Plato.[200] The important thing in all this is that Philoponus 2, by denying that Aristotle agreed with the doctrine of Ideas, at the same time denies that Aristotle's God is also the *efficient* cause of the universe. Indeed, if Aristotle rejected the existence of Ideas *ante res*, then his God cannot be anything but pure self-thinking thought. This means that the divine Intellect to Aristotle is no longer a *creative* Intellect: an Intellect without Ideas cannot be creative, it is merely the final cause of the universe.

In this way we arrive at an unexpected conclusion. Ammonius' interpretation of Aristotle's concept of God is not only free of Christian influence, but is even regarded as an anti-Christian attempt to make pagan philosophy more harmonious than it was. Philoponus 2 implicitly returns to the view that Aristotle's God is merely the final cause of the

[193] ibid. 37,20-6.

[194] ibid. 37,26-8.

[195] ibid. 37,28-31. Needless to say, Aristotle claims that God is pure self-consciousness.

[196] Philoponus *Aet.* 26,24-32,13; *in An. Post.* 242,14-243,25.

[197] Philoponus *Aet.* 29,8-30,6.

[198] ibid. 30,8-12. The reference is to Aristotle *An. Post.* 1.22, 83a32-3, which is part of the lemma of Philoponus *in An. Post.* 242,14-243,25.

[199] Philoponus *in An. Post.* 243,20-1. This may be another hint by Philoponus at his own relation to Ammonius as he wanted it to be interpreted after 529. Cf. Chapter 11 n. 181 below.

[200] Philoponus *in An. Post.* 242,26-243,13. Three of the texts referred to are the same as in *in DA* 37,19-31: *Metaph.* 12,10, 1075a12-17; 12.9,1074b33-4 (?); *DA* 3.4, 429a27-8. The remaining reference (*in An. Post.* 243,7) is perhaps to *DA* 3.8, 432a2 (intellect = form of forms).

universe. This is a Christian reaction which denies the harmony of Plato and Aristotle and rejects the idea of an eternal 'creation' implied in the interpretation of Ammonius and Philoponus 1. Both to Ammonius and to Philoponus 1 that idea was so obviously correct that they ascribed it to Aristotle as well. To Philoponus 2, by contrast, 'eternal creation' has become something inconceivable, a contradiction in terms. Consequently, Philoponus 2 can no longer consider Aristotle's eternal world to be created by the divine Intellect, just as, conversely, he can no longer regard Plato's created universe eternal *a parte ante*.

Ammonius and the problem of Alexandrian Neoplatonism

What does my analysis of the metaphysics of Ammonius contribute to the discussion of 'the problem of Alexandrian Neoplatonism'? Obviously, the result of Mme. Hadot's investigations on Hierocles and Simplicius are confirmed by my findings on Ammonius, in so far as the Neoplatonic and non-Christian character of Alexandrian philosophy is concerned. I do not think that Ammonius' theology was essentially influenced by Christianity, nor that his interpretation of Aristotle's theology was inspired by Christian motives. His philosophy is no return to pre-Plotinian Platonism either: it is clearly *Neo*-Platonism.

More delicate, however, is the question to what extent Ammonius remained faithful in his mature years to the Neoplatonism of his master Proclus. Asclepius' *Commentary on the Metaphysics* displays some characteristics which might suggest that Ammonius tended to simplify the system: the henads disappear; the Demiurge seems to be simply identified with the divine Intellect; there is not much left of Proclus' construction of innumerable triads; the articulation of the intelligible world at levels between the divine Intellect and the sensible world has been blurred. Moreover, Ammonius is inclined to remodel the hierarchy of ontological levels into a dichotomy between the creative and the created. As a result, the Intellect and the One are frequently taken together in the notion 'God (*ho theos*)'. Soul, on the other hand, which is actually intermediate between intelligible (creative) and sensible (created) reality,[201] is sometimes decoupled from the first two levels of reality and considered as 'caused by God'.[202] All this seems to mean that, with the appropriate qualifications, Praechter was not completely wrong in ascribing to Ammonius 'a tendency to retrogression'.[203]

But at this point another question arises: isn't it possible that this simplification is characteristic of Ammonius' exegesis of Aristotle only, and that in his lost commentaries on Plato he practised metaphysical speculation in a more Athenian style? We know that in Athenian Neoplatonism the reading of Aristotle was considered propaedeutic to the

[201] Asclepius *in Metaph*. 98,5-15; Ammonius *in Cat*. 37,17-18.
[202] Asclepius *in Metaph*. 147,31-2.
[203] K. Praechter, 'Richtungen und Schulen', 145-6.

study of Plato.[204] And we know also that Ammonius, at some stage of his career, commented on the *Gorgias* and the *Theaetetus*.[205] Consequently, one cannot rule out *a priori* the possibility that he reserved a fuller exposition of his Neoplatonic metaphysics for his commentaries on Plato. If this is true, then the status of metaphysics in Ammonius' commentaries on Aristotle[206] would seem comparable with the status of metaphysics in Hierocles' *in Carmen Aureum* and Simplicius' *in Epicteti Enchiridion*. In all cases, one might argue, the system is simplified and/or fragmented because of the preparatory level of the texts and commentaries at issue.[207] I think there can be little doubt that this holds true for Ammonius' commentaries on the Organon, regardless of whether or not there was any fundamental difference between Ammonius' metaphysics in Asclepius' commentary and in his commentaries on Plato. Hence we must concentrate on Asclepius' *in Metaphysica*: is what we have there Ammonius' last word in metaphysics? Or do we have solid reasons to suppose that Asclepius too offers only a reduced version of Ammonius' metaphysics? Obviously, any answer to this question must remain highly speculative: one cannot compare existing with non-existing commentaries. But in my opinion this does not necessarily mean that we are completely in the dark.

Let us first try to see what arguments can be adduced for affirming that Ammonius' Neoplatonism was not essentially different from contemporary Athenian Neoplatonism. (1) The fact that Ammonius was a pupil of Proclus is not sufficient in itself for supposing that he never departed from his master's system. Ammonius' interpretation of Aristotle's theology was different from Proclus'; the doctrine of henads has disappeared from Asclepius' *in Metaphysica*. These examples show that Ammonius did not recoil from some originality. (2) A better argument is, of course, the propaedeutic character of the study of Aristotle. In principle the hypothesis that Ammonius may have expounded a fuller 'Athenian' system in his commentaries on Plato covers two possibilities. Either one thinks of the Platonic commentaries as contemporary with or posterior to the 'Asclepian' version of Ammonius' metaphysics, or one considers them

---

[204] Marinus, *Vita Procli* XIII; cf. I. Hadot, *Le problème du néoplatonisme alexandrin*, 149.

[205] L.G. Westerink, *Anonymous Prolegomena*, p. xi. According to Westerink, *The Greek Commentaries on Plato's Phaedo*, vol. I: *Olympiodorus*, 83, Philoponus at *in An. Post.* 215,4-5 refers to a commentary of Ammonius on the *Phaedo*. H.D. Saffrey, 'Le chrétien Jean Philopon', 406 n. 1, thinks the reference is to the currently used school commentary; cf. W. Haase, 'Ein vermeintliches Aristoteles-Fragment bei Johannes Philoponos', *Synusia. Festgabe für W. Schadewaldt*, Pfullingen 1965, 350 n. 47. Others believe that Philoponus refers to a lost *in Phaedonem* of his own, e.g. A. Gudeman, 'Ioannes Philoponus', in G. Wissowa and W. Kroll (eds), *Realencyclopädie der klassischen Altertumswissenschaft* IX, 2, 1916, col. 1772 and C.M.K. MacLeod in G. Verbeke, *Jean Philopon, Commentaire sur le De Anima d'Aristote. Traduction de Guillaume de Moerbeke*, Louvain and Paris 1966, xviii.

[206] I think A.C. Lloyd, 'The later Neoplatonists', 315 is exaggerating somewhat when he says: 'But when the simplicity and hard-headedness of the Alexandrians' Neoplatonism is contrasted with the elaboration and "speculative" character of Athenian metaphysics, a simple but hard fact must be remembered. We have not got their metaphysics.'

[207] cf. above.

as earlier. On the latter alternative Ammonius gave up the study of Plato in order to concentrate on Aristotle. This would rather suggest that he moved away, to some extent, from his Athenian background. However, Ammonius must have been commenting on Plato until the end of his career, given the fact that Olympiodorus, who was born probably after 495[208] says he attended a lecture of Ammonius on the *Gorgias*.[209] But it is important to note that there is no mention of Ammonius commenting on the *Timaeus* or the *Parmenides*. He is only known to have lectured on more 'elementary' dialogues.[210] It remains to be seen how far it is possible to infer something more definite about the contents of Ammonius' lectures on Plato on the basis of Olympiodorus' commentaries. Meanwhile, one cannot rule out *a priori* the possibility of a more elaborate system in these Platonic commentaries. (3) A third argument is that in Asclepius' *in Metaphysica* the different 'forces' in the intelligible world are only referred to in a very vague way,[211] which might imply that it is in principle possible to give a more detailed account of the structure of intelligible reality.

On the other hand there are several arguments for the assumption that Ammonius' later philosophy did indeed represent an intrinsic simplification of Neoplatonism, in other words, that Asclepius gives a more or less complete account of Ammonius' system.

(1) The study of Aristotle's *Metaphysics* is the final stage in the study of Aristotelian philosophy.[212] The goal (*telos*) of this philosophy is defined as raising oneself up to the highest principle, Goodness-itself.[213] The *Commentary on the Metaphysics* contains a theology which derives everything from this principle and does not limit itself to a metaphysical reference to the Intellect. Hence, one might argue, the *Commentary on the Metaphysics* no longer represents a preparatory level of thinking. On the contrary, it seems to aim at a radical and ultimate explanation of reality. In his non-metaphysical commentaries, on the other hand, Ammonius sporadically practises the so-called physical type of metaphysics. In this perspective, *Neoplatonic* theology (in a reduced form) may be supposed to have its (or an) appropriate locus in the *Commentary on the Metaphysics*. Consequently, there need not be a fundamental difference between the metaphysical standpoints of this commentary and of the Platonic commentaries respectively. Maybe, therefore, Ammonius had not much more to say about metaphysics than what we read in Asclepius.

(2) A second argument for this conclusion might be that there is no great

---

[208] L.G. Westerink, *Anonymous Prolegomena*, p. xiii.

[209] Olympiodorus *in Gorg.* 199,8 Westerink; cf. L.G. Westerink, *Anonymous Prolegomena*, p. xi.

[210] For the order of study of the Platonic dialogues cf. L.G. Westerink, op. cit., pp. xxxvii-xl; A.J. Festugière, 'L'ordre de lecture des dialogues de Platon aux Ve/VIe siècles', *Museum Helveticum* 26, 1969, 281-96 (= A.J. Festugière, *Études de philosophie grecque*, Paris 1971, 535-50).

[211] cf. above.

[212] Ammonius *in Cat.* 6,17-20; cf. Philoponus *in Cat.* 6,3-16; Olympiodorus *in Cat.* 9,31-10,2; Elias *in Cat.* 121,5-19; Simplicius *in Cat.* 6,15-18.

[213] Ammonius *in Cat.* 6,10-16; cf. above n. 128.

difference, in Asclepius' *in Metaphysica*, between the ways in which Ammonius treats Plato's and Aristotle's theology respectively. Nothing indicates that, for Ammonius, Plato is the metaphysician proper and that Aristotle's metaphysics is only preparatory. On the contrary, the attempt to 'Neoplatonise' Aristotle's theology rather points to an *upgrading of Aristotle* compared to Plato. The result of this effort to bring both philosophers closer together is, so far as Plato's theology is concerned, a picture which is largely the same as that of Aristotle's. Plato's Ideas too are *logoi* in the demiurgic Intellect.[214] The Platonic Demiurge is both the efficient and final cause of the cosmos: his goodness generates the cosmos[215] and is its goal (*telos*) as well.[216] None the less, he is not the supreme principle of reality. The Platonic Ideas are produced by the One,[217] and, for Plato, the One transcends being and form.[218] Ammonius' obvious desire to make Plato's and Aristotle's theology converge does not suggest that he considered Plato as the real thing and Aristotle merely as a propaedeutic.

(3) So far I have not said anything about one of the standard items in any treatment of Ammonius, namely Damascius' remark on Ammonius' deal with the Alexandrian bishop, to the effect that Ammonius made concessions in exchange for financial compensation.[219] H.D. Saffrey supposed, on the basis of this remark, that Ammonius gave up teaching Platonic philosophy.[220] However, both Asclepius and Olympiodorus refer to Ammonius commenting on Plato.[221] Therefore the agreement with the Church probably did not affect the teaching of Plato. Moreover, the ecclesiastical authorities can hardly have had much greater sympathy for

[214] Asclepius *in Metaph.* 44,32-5; 166,31-4; 167,24-6.
[215] ibid. 21,18-21.
[216] ibid. 52,21-4; cf. 55,25-6; 103,9-12.
[217] ibid. 54,25-6.
[218] ibid. 42,14-5.
[219] Damascius *Vita Isidori* fr. 316, p. 251 Zintzen. According to L.G. Westerink, *Anonymous Prolegomena*, pp. xii-xiii, Ammonius 'even went through the formality of being baptised'. This 'conversion' was also accepted by P. Merlan, 'Ammonius Hermiae, Zacharias Scholasticus and Boethius', 203 and apparently not excluded by A. Cameron, 'The last days of the Academy at Athens', *Proceedings of the Cambridge Philological Society* 195 n.s. 15, 1969, 14-15. It is rejected e.g. by É. Évrard, 'Jean Philopon, son commentaire sur Nicomaque et ses rapports avec Ammonius', *Revue des études grecques* 78, 1965, 597-8; M. Mahdi, 'Alfarabi against Philoponus', 235 n. 6; L. Tarán, *Asclepius of Tralles*, 10, n. 48; G.A. Lucchetta, 'Aristotelismo e cristianesimo in Giovanni Filopono', *Studia Patavina* 25, 1978, 582. It is very unlikely indeed that the patriarch succeeded in altering anything about the traditional paganism of the leading academic milieu in Alexandria. Cf. for this R. Rémondon, 'L'Egypte et la suprême résistance au christianisme (Ve-VIIe siècle)', *Bulletin de l'Institut français d'archéologie orientale* 51, 1952, 63-6.
[220] H.D. Saffrey, 'Le chrétien Jean Philopon', 400-1; likewise W. Wolska, *La Topographie Chrétienne de Cosmas Indicopleustès*, Paris 1962, 149; M. Mahdi, 'Alfarabi against Philoponus', 234 n. 3; more prudently I.P. Sheldon-Williams, 'The Greek Christian Platonist tradition from the Cappadocians to Maximus and Eriugena', in A.H. Armstrong (ed.), *The Cambridge History of Later Greek and Early Medieval Philosophy*, Cambridge 1970, 478.
[221] cf. L.G. Westerink, *Anonymous Prolegomena*, p. xi; É. Évrard, *L'école d'Olympiodore*, 207-8.

Aristotle than they had for Plato.[222] On the other hand, there is a text of Simplicius implying that there was no more teaching of Plato in Alexandria at the time Philoponus studied with Ammonius.[223] Simplicius must be exaggerating somewhat here, the message being probably that there was nothing in Alexandria to compare with the Athenian exegesis of Plato's great dialogues. 'If nothing has survived of his (Ammonius') interpretation of Plato, the reason is no doubt that the work of the Athenian school was felt to be more important; just as, on the other hand, Proclus' commentaries on Aristotle have left hardly any traces.'[224] But why, one may ask, was Ammonius' exegesis of Plato considered inferior to that of the Athenians? The only possible answer seems to be that his approach must have been more sober, less fantastic and less sophisticated than Proclus' or Damascius'. I think that this relative decrease of interest in Plato is the other side of an increasing concentration on Aristotle. It remains uncertain whether or not all this had anything to do with the agreement between Ammonius and the Church; I feel rather sceptical about that. Probably Ammonius was just not the type of the true Platonic hierophant by Athenian standards. Instead, he developed a Neoplatonising exegesis of Aristotle.

(4) A further argument for the thesis that Ammonius' metaphysics, compared with Athenian Neoplatonism, underwent an intrinsic simplification, is that the Neoplatonisation of Aristotle's metaphysics is met by a corresponding 'Aristotelianisation', if you will pardon the expression, of the Neoplatonic system. Ammonius' metaphysical system has a cosmological orientation. The criteria according to which the ontological hierarchy is constructed pertain largely to the Aristotelian concepts of matter and form.[225] Once the principle is accepted that the hierarchy of substances must primarily be conceived as a gradation involving both matter and form,[226] there is little room left for a differentiation of intelligible reality at the level of pure form. Whereas in Proclus' system the sensible world is only the modest foothill of an impressive intelligible superstructure, the centre of gravity in Ammonius' system lies in cosmic reality. Obviously this shift of interest constitutes a major difference between Alexandrian and Athenian Neoplatonism. This need not mean that Ammonius came to reject a great part of Proclus' system. The few vague allusions in Asclepius to the possibility of a more detailed elaboration of the picture of intelligible reality rather seem to indicate that Ammonius was prepared in principle to unfold some more elements of the 'Athenian' metaphysics if necessary, but that he felt no particular inclination to do so. His preference for the study of Aristotle is in line with this tendency.

[222] S. Pines, 'An Arabic summary of a lost work of John Philoponus', *Israel Oriental Studies* 2, 1972, 338 n. 266.
[223] Simplicius *in Cael.* 84,11-13; cf. Chapter 11 below.
[224] L.G. Westerink, *Anonymous Prolegomena*, pp. xi-xii.
[225] cf. Chapter 11 below.
[226] cf. Ammonius *in Cat.* 35,18-36,4.

(5) Finally, one should not forget that Philoponus 1, whose philosophy in all probability is very close to that of his master, also fails to suggest that, for Ammonius, the study of Aristotle's metaphysics was just propaedeutic to the study of Plato's. It is generally accepted that the substance of the Aristotelian commentaries of Philoponus (Philoponus 1) is based on Ammonius' lectures, even if the formula 'from the lectures of Ammonius, son of Hermeias (*ek tôn sunousiôn Ammôniou tou Hermeiou*)' does not appear in all titles.[227] Ammonius' legacy was primarily Aristotelian and consisted of three main parts: logic, natural philosophy (including psychology) and metaphysics (Asclepius). I cannot enter here into a detailed comparison of the pictures of Plato's philosophy in Philoponus 1 and Asclepius respectively. Roughly speaking, there is a great similarity in their approaches to the relation between Plato and Aristotle. In Philoponus 1 too there are a few excursions into Platonic-Pythagorean philosophy,[228] but as in Asclepius they do not suggest that Ammonius was much interested in a large-scale multiplication of entities in the manner of Proclus.

The conclusion from all this has to be, in my opinion, that with Ammonius something like a specifically Alexandrian Neoplatonism emerges, characterised by a tendency to simplify the complicated system of Proclus. Due to the loss of Ammonius' Platonic exegesis we cannot know to what extent this simplification is only a feature of his exegesis of Aristotle. Yet the Aristotelian commentaries themselves point rather in the opposite direction. Regardless of whether or not what we have contains the essence of Ammonius' metaphysics, this much is clear, that the study of Aristotle became more important than the study of Plato: the 'Neoplatonisation' of Aristotle was Ammonius' main achievement. Platonic exegesis in the Athenian manner became less relevant to this purpose. Or the other way around: Ammonius may have felt that it was useless to rival Proclus in Platonic exegesis, and instead preferred to develop his Neoplatonic and harmonising exegesis of Aristotle. This 'Ammonian' Neoplatonism is to be found in Asclepius, of course, and also in Philoponus 1. Further investigation should teach us how far Ammonian Neoplatonism survives in the philosophy of Olympiodorus and, beyond, in the commentaries of Elias, David and Stephanus. It is only if it does that we shall be fully entitled to call it 'Alexandrian' Neoplatonism.[229]

---

[227] There is no mention of Ammonius in the titles of *in Categorias, in Physica* and *in Meteorologica*.

[228] e.g. Philoponus *in DA* 116,1-121,10 (on Plato's psychogony).

[229] I thank H.J. Blumenthal, A.C. Lloyd and R.R.K. Sorabji for their helpful and stimulating comments on earlier versions of this chapter.

CHAPTER ELEVEN

The development of Philoponus' thought and its chronology*

Koenraad Verrycken

Since the end of the nineteenth and the beginning of the twentieth century, when the Berlin corpus of Greek commentaries on Aristotle was published, historians of ancient philosophy have had at their disposal the materials for studying not only the commentators' exegetical merits, but also their own philosophical views. But the availability of the texts has not yet resulted in research to match their volume and historical importance.[1] In particular, the commentaries from the late fifth and sixth centuries AD have not (Simplicius' writings apart) received anything like the attention they deserve. Two main factors are responsible for this situation. In the first place, the commentaries are usually not read as a whole: they are consulted in connection with certain passages of Aristotle or in relation to a special problem. Consequently, scholars are generally less interested in their autonomous philosophical background, a background which clearly shows that the commentaries have their roots in late Neoplatonism. In the second place few historians who study late Neoplatonism for its own sake pay much attention to the Aristotelian commentators, although they make an exception for Syrianus and Simplicius, who both belong to the tradition of Athenian Neoplatonism. For this Athenian philosophy based mainly on Platonic exegesis is, at least as a metaphysics, much more important than the philosophy of Alexandria. Because of this neglect, the study of late fifth- and sixth-century commentaries on Aristotle, taken as a whole, is one of the areas where the task is not simply one of adding to existing interpretations.

The foundations of Alexandrian Aristotelian exegesis were established by a pupil of Proclus, Ammonius son of Hermeias. Among Ammonius' own

---

* This chapter summarises some historical and philological conclusions drawn from the presence of two different systems in the philosophical works ascribed to Philoponus. I am preparing further publications on the subject.

[1] Richard Sorabji's translation project, The Ancient Commentators on Aristotle, will remedy this.

pupils were Asclepius, Philoponus and Olympiodorus. Olympiodorus himself is considered the originator of the last group of Alexandrian commentaries: those of Elias, David and Stephanus. What is noteworthy about Philoponus is that besides his commentaries he wrote autonomous philosophical treatises of a clearly Christian tendency as well as a great number of dogmatic works of theology. This poses our main problem about Philoponus in its most elementary form: what is the relation between the commentaries attributed to the author and his Christian writings? The first attempt at a global solution was undertaken in 1916 by A. Gudeman.[2] According to Gudeman, Philoponus was not a Christian by birth (so, originally, his name was not John). As a pagan, 'John' became a pupil of Ammonius. In the first period of his creative career the author, still a pagan, wrote his grammatical works, his commentaries on Aristotle and most of his other non-theological works. About 520 AD, according to Gudeman, our philosopher was converted to Christianity, and from then onwards his writings, including the more philosophical ones, clearly show the Christian conviction of the author. This picture of Philoponus' career was and still is accepted by several scholars.[3] In 1953, however, É. Évrard argued convincingly that Philoponus' *in Meteorologica* (at least in its present form) is posterior to the *de Aeternitate Mundi contra Proclum*.[4] Moreover, Évrard believes, the presence of several passages in the *in Physica*, arguing against the eternity of the world, proves that by 517 AD Philoponus was already a Christian.[5] All this means that Gudeman's thesis, according to which Philoponus' Aristotelian commentaries were written by a non-Christian author, has

[2] A. Gudeman, 'Ioannes Philoponus', in G. Wissowa and W. Kroll (eds), *Realencyclopädie der klassischen Altertumswissenschaft* IX, 2, 1916, cols. 1769-72.

[3] See W. von Christ, W. Schmid and O. Staehlin, *Geschichte der griechischen Literatur* II, 2 (*Handbuch der Altertumswissenschaft* VII, 2, 2), 6th ed. Munich 1924, 1067; M. Meyerhof, 'Joannes Grammatikos (Philoponus) von Alexandrien und die arabische Medizin', *Mitteilungen des deutschen Instituts für ägyptische Altertumskunde in Kairo* 2, 1931, 2-3; id., 'La fin de l'école d'Alexandrie d'après quelques auteurs arabes', *Archeion* 15, 1933, 3; B. Tatakis, *La philosophie byzantine*, Paris 1949, 39-40; O. Perler, *Patristische Philosophie* (I.M. Bochenski (ed.), *Bibliographische Einführungen in das Studium der Philosophie* no.18), Bern 1950, 36; L. Bréhier, *La civilisation byzantine*, Paris 1950, 357; M.V. Anastos, 'Aristotle and Cosmas Indicopleustes on the Void. A note on theology and science in the sixth century', *Hellênika* 4, 1953 (repr. in his *Studies in Byzantine Intellectual History*, London 1979), 48; K. Axelos, 'Les lignes de force de la spiritualité byzantine', *Bulletin de l'Association Guillaum⌐ Budé*, 1957, 4; A. Abel, 'La légende de Jean Philopon chez les Arabes', *Acta Orientalia Belgica* (*Collection Correspondance d'Orient* no. 10), Brussels 1966, 252; H. Dörrie, *Platonica Minora*, Munich 1976, 187, n. 64; G. Reale, *Storia della filosofia antica*, vol. 4, Milan 1978, 694. The thesis that Philoponus was a convert was already advanced by G. Cave, *Scriptorum ecclesiasticorum historia literaria a Christo nato usque ad Saeculum XIV*, vol. 1, Oxford 1740, art. Johannes Philoponus, 567. I have not been able to see E.G.T. Booth, 'John Philoponos: Christian and Aristotelian conversion', *Studia Patristica* vol. 17, part 1, 1983, 407-11.

[4] É. Évrard, 'Les convictions religieuses de Jean Philopon et la date de son Commentaire aux "Météorologiques"', *Bulletin de l'Académie royale de Belgique, Classe des lettres, sciences morales et politiques*, Série 5, 39, 1953, 303, 339, 345.

[5] ibid., 352-4.

to be rejected: Philoponus is not a convert, he was always a Christian.[6] Since Évrard's and Saffrey's[7] articles this 'unitarian' approach to Philoponus' philosophical works has become predominant.[8] Nevertheless, Évrard was aware of some of the problems arising from his views: for instance, what are we to think about Philoponus' affirmation of the pre-existence of the human rational soul?[9] And how are we to reconcile, within the limits of one and the same commentary (*in Physica*), arguments against the eternity of the world and the acceptance of Aristotle's fifth essence and, consequently, of the eternity of heaven?[10] Évrard's solutions to such problems are basically of two types. On the one hand, doctrines such as that of a rational soul which is eternal *a parte ante* are said not to be necessarily incompatible with Christianity (Évrard, rather arbitrarily, suggests that Philoponus may have been influenced in this matter by Origen).[11] On the other hand, passages which imply an affirmation of the eternity of the world are supposed to have only an exegetical significance: Philoponus could not always expound or even indicate his own point of view[12] when expounding Aristotle's.

[6] ibid., 345-7, 356-7.

[7] H.D. Saffrey, 'Le chrétien Jean Philopon et la survivance de l'école d'Alexandrie au VIe siècle', *Revue des études grecques* 67, 1954, 402, 408.

[8] See P. Joannou, 'Christliche Metaphysik in Byzanz, Johannes Philoponos (VI. Jh.)', *Wissenschaftliche Zeitschrift der Martin-Luther-Universität Halle-Wittenberg* 10, 1961, 1389; id., 'Le premier essai chrétien d'une philosophie systématique, Jean Philopon', *Studia Patristica* vol. 5, 1962, 508; L.G. Westerink, *Anonymous Prolegomena to Platonic Philosophy*, Amsterdam 1962, p. xii (modified); C.M.K. MacLeod, *'Jean Philopon', Commentaire au De Intellectu. Traduction latine de Guillaume de Moerbeke*, diss. Louvain 1964, vol. 1, 15-16; J.L. Kraemer, 'A lost passage from Philoponus' *Contra Aristotelem* in Arabic translation', *Journal of the American Oriental Society* 85, 1965, 323; G.A. Lucchetta, 'Aristotelismo e cristianesimo in Giovanni Filopono', *Studia Patavina* 25, 1978, 583-4; R. Sorabji, 'John Philoponus', in R. Sorabji (ed.), *Philoponus and the Rejection of Aristotelian Science*, London and Ithaca NY 1987, 4-5. According to some authors the issue of a possible conversion remains open: W. Wieland, 'Die Ewigkeit der Welt (Der Streit zwischen Joannes Philoponus und Simplicius)', in D. Heinrich, W. Schulz and K.H. Volkmann-Schluck (eds), *Die Gegenwart der Griechen im neueren Denken. Festschrift H.G. Gadamer*, Tübingen 1960, 294; S. Sambursky, *The Physical World of Late Antiquity*, London 1962, 155 (but in his article 'Philoponus, John', in P. Edwards (ed.), *The Encyclopedia of Philosophy*, vol. 6, New York and London 1967, 156, Sambursky thinks that Philoponus is likely to have been a Christian by birth); W. Böhm, *Johannes Philoponos, Grammatikos von Alexandrien. Christliche Naturwissenschaft im Ausklang der Antike, Vorläufer der modernen Physik, Wissenschaft und Bibel. Ausgewählte Schriften*, Munich, Paderborn, Vienna 1967, 27; 'The Greek Christian Platonist Tradition from the Cappadocians to Maximus and Eriugena', in A.H. Armstrong (ed.), *The Cambridge History of Later Greek and Early Mediaeval Philosophy*, Cambridge 1970, 478-9.

[9] É. Évrard, 'Les convictions religieuses', 349-50; e.g. Philoponus, *in DA* 16,10-26; *in Phys.* 128,22-31 (soul versus *hê genêtê kai phthartê ousia*).

[10] É. Évrard, op. cit., 324-5 gives the following instances of Philoponus' acceptance of Aristotle's theory of aether in the *in Physica*: *in Phys.* 9,23-10,2; 219,19-22; 220,20-5; 340,31. One can add: *in Phys.* 15,29-30; 16,2; 16,8; 156,10-12; 438,9-10. See further n. 60 below (eternity of heaven).

[11] É. Évrard, op. cit., 350.

[12] ibid., 355, n. 3: 'The brief allusions which we find in the commentaries to the eternity of

The position I should like to defend is to some extent intermediate between that of Gudeman and that of Évrard. I think Évrard is right in rejecting the hypothesis of Philoponus' conversion. But I also think Gudeman was right in assuming – more or less conjecturally – a duality in Philoponus' philosophical work. Both Gudeman and Évrard, however, pose the problem wrongly in terms of 'religious conviction' only. If Philoponus did not develop a Christian philosophy in his first philosophical period, that does not show that he must have been a pagan at that time. And if he was born a Christian, that does not establish that his philosophy must always have been Christian in character. Philosophy is one thing, religion another. In my opinion, the problem should first be posed on the purely philosophical level: what does the author say? Only afterwards can one try to 'project' the results of the philosophical analysis onto the levels of biography and psychology. This is the method I employ. To start with, I shall outline very briefly the main characteristics of the philosophical systems of 'Philoponus 1' and 'Philoponus 2', as I shall call them. Then I shall try to piece together something of what can reasonably be said about Philoponus' biography. Thirdly, I shall propose the first sketch of a new solution to the problem of the chronology of the author's Aristotelian commentaries. I shall finish with some remarks on the development of Philoponus 2.

Philoponus 1 and Philoponus 2

The philosophical system of Philoponus 1 (i.e. of Philoponus before 529 AD) can be labelled an 'Alexandrian Neoplatonism'. In theory it does not accept a personal God as supreme, but is instead Neoplatonic in character, and like orthodox Neoplatonism, it postulates above the divine Intellect a still higher principle of reality, called the One, or the Good.[13] Creation is a necessary, not a deliberate, process.[14] Typical of the Alexandrian form of Neoplatonism (Ammonius, Asclepius, Philoponus) is the thesis that Aristotle's God is the cause, both final and efficient, of the existence of the universe,[15] not merely the final cause of its motion and order. Aristotle's efficient causation is supposed to have worked through the presence of Platonic Ideas as creative *logoi* in the demiurgic Intellect.[16] In the ontology of the early Philoponus being consists of a

---

the world should not give us pause. A commentator is inevitably led to repeat some theses of the author he is expounding, without being able to criticise them every time. What clearly proves that they have scarcely any importance is that they are found in the *Physics* commentary (e.g. 490,14), a work which, as already seen, *attacks* the thesis of the eternity of time, of movement and of the world.'

[13] e.g. Philoponus *in Phys.* 22,13-15; 163,2-12; 187,6-9; *in GC* 296,19-21; *in DA* 119,22-4.

[14] Philoponus *in Cat.* 145,8-11.

[15] Philoponus *in GC* 136,33-137,3; 152,23-153,2. See Chapter 10 above.

[16] Philoponus *in DA* 37,19-31.

hierarchy of substances (*ousiai*).[17] Substances are ranked according to a list of properties: proximity to pure form, degree of actuality, activity, unity, and identity. The basic relations among the members of this ontological hierarchy are participation, imitation and mediation. All this results in the following structure of being: the One (above being); the demiurgic Intellect; transcendent intellects;[18] undescended rational soul; the heavens (the celestial spheres have rational souls);[19] sublunary life (rational, irrational, vegetative); the four elements; three-dimensionally extended substance; form (*eidos*); matter (below being). Evidently this structure had no beginning in time, but is eternal: the sensible world, with its different levels, has being to a lesser degree than pure form, but has never lacked being. It is a necessary part of the totality. All levels of this totality possess different degrees of substantiality, and imitate with decreasing perfection the fullness of being which exists in the demiurgic Intellect.

The system of Philoponus 2 (after 529) is no longer Neoplatonic. First of all, it clearly has the concept of a supreme personal God: the creative Intellect is the highest, not the second highest, principle. Creation is no longer a necessary process: it is the result of God's free decision.[20] Aristotle is said now to have rejected Plato's theory of Ideas.[21] This means that the Aristotelian God is again considered merely as the final cause of the world's motion and order. The ontology of the later Philoponus has become dualistic instead of hierarchical: God is independent of the world, the world is no longer divine. This 'secularisation' of the world applies to intellects and souls as well as to sensible reality. Philoponus 2 argues at length against the eternity of movement, time and the world, and against Aristotle's theory of the eternal fifth element as the matter of the heavens. He even goes so far as to deny the possibility of an eternal matter.[22]

The philosophical career of John Philoponus

There seems no reason to doubt that our philosopher had the Christian name 'John' right from his birth, and that he was born in Alexandria. That the name 'Philoponus' refers to his (temporary) membership of a group of *philoponoi* (some kind of militant Christian brotherhood) is not

---

[17] Philoponus *in Cat.* 49,23-51,21 (cf. Ammonius *in Cat.* 35,18-36,4); 67,7-10; *in de Intell.* 22,21-5 (=Sophonias *in DA* 126,17-19).

[18] Philoponus *in DA* 35,1-2; *in de Intell.* 84,63-9; cf. Ammonius *in Int.* 248,17-31; 250,34-251,1.

[19] Philoponus *in DA* 260,18-25.

[20] Philoponus *Aet.* 78,11-17; 566,4-10.

[21] Philoponus *Aet.* 26,20-32,13; *in An. Post* 242,14-243,25.

[22] Philoponus *Aet.* 458,5-7; 469,6-10.

238 *Koenraad Verrycken*

impossible, but by no means certain.[23] Probably he was born about 490,[24] perhaps a few years earlier. He studied 'philology' first, and turned to the study of philosophy only afterwards. That could be the reason why Simplicius calls him a late learner (*opsimathês*) in philosophical matters.[25] When did this transition to philosophy take place? Saffrey's proposal (c. 510) is quite likely.[26]

What exactly was Philoponus' relation with his teacher Ammonius? According to Saffrey, Philoponus became an 'assistant' of Ammonius: his function was that of an 'official editor' of the master's commentaries. For fear of the ecclesiastical authorities in Alexandria, Saffrey thinks, Ammonius used his Christian assistant to cover him, not daring to publish his commentaries under his own name.[27] There are, however, some objections to this view. First of all, nothing proves that Philoponus' project to edit a series of Ammonius' commentaries was inspired or even supervised by Ammonius himself. In the case of the *Commentary on Nicomachus' Introductio Arithmetica*, Philoponus seems to have based his version not on notes he had made himself from the voice of Ammonius (*apo phônês Ammôniou*), but on Asclepius' redaction of Ammonius' lectures.[28] And one cannot rule out the possibility of a similar situation for (some of) the commentaries on Aristotle. The *in Categorias* and the *in Analytica Priora* ascribed by the modern editors to Ammonius are in fact students' redactions comparable to Asclepius' *in Nicomachi Introductionem Arithmeticam* and *in Metaphysica*.[29] So Philoponus may have made his own versions of *in Categorias* and *in Analytica Priora* in the same way as he probably wrote his *in Nicomachi Introductionem Arithmeticam*. All this points in a direction other than Saffrey's

[23] The suggestion was first made by S. Pétridès, 'Spoudaei et Philopones', *Echos d'Orient* 7, 1904, 343-4; still hesitating: J. Maspéro, *Histoire des patriarches d'Alexandrie depuis la mort de l'empereur Anastase jusqu'à la réconciliation des églises jacobites (518-616)*, Paris 1923, 197-8, n. 4 and M. Meyerhof, 'Joannes Grammatikos', 2-3; affirmative: e.g. II.D. Saffrey, 'Le chrétien Jean Philopon', 403-4; P. Joannou, 'Christliche Metaphysik', 1389; id., 'Le premier essai chrétien', 508; G.A. Lucchetta, 'Aristotelismo e cristianesimo', 584; M. Wolff, *Geschichte der Impetustheorie. Untersuchungen zum Ursprung der klassischen Mechanik*, Frankfurt a. M. 1978, 104-13; prudent: e.g. C.M.K. MacLeod, *Jean Philopon*, vol. I, 13-14; W. Böhm, *Johannes Philoponos*, 26-7; sceptical: A. Segonds, *'Jean Philopon, Traité de l'astrolabe*, Paris 1981, 10-11; H.J. Blumenthal, 'John Philoponus: Alexandrian Platonist?', *Hermes* 114, 1986, 317-18.
[24] H.D. Saffrey, 'Le chrétien Jean Philopon', 403.
[25] Simplicius *in Cael.* 159,3; 159,7; *in Phys.* 1133,10; cf. *in Cael.* 29,7-8; 140,5.
[26] H.D. Saffrey, 'Le chrétien Jean Philopon', 403.
[27] ibid., 408; cf. M. Mahdi, 'Alfarabi against Philoponus', *Journal of Near Eastern Studies* 26, 1967, 234-5.
[28] L.G. Westerink, 'Deux commentaires sur Nicomaque: Asclépius et Jean Philopon', *Revue des études grecques* 77, 1964, 530 (reprinted in his *Texts and Studies in Neoplatonism and Byzantine Literature. Collected Papers*, Amsterdam 1980, 108); L. Tarán, *Asclepius of Tralles, Commentary to Nicomachus' Introduction to Arithmetic, Transactions of the American Philosophical Society*, n.s. 59, 4, Philadelphia 1969, 10-13.
[29] The *in de Interpretatione* was written by Ammonius himself; cf. L.G. Westerink, *Anonymous Prolegomena*, p. xi; id., *The Greek Commentaries on Plato's Phaedo*, vol. 1: *Olympiodorus*, Amsterdam, Oxford, New York 1976, 19; L. Tarán, *Asclepius of Tralles*, 14.

hypothesis. One rather gets the impression that it was not Philoponus, but pupils like Asclepius who first received or took over the task of 'officially editing' Ammonius' lectures. But from a certain moment onwards (when? how?) Philoponus, though only a philologist (*grammatikos*), got himself recognised, or appointed himself as the main philosophical heir to Ammonius, and started the publication project all over again, beginning with his lost **in Isagogen*. None of this is to deny that Philoponus was a pupil of Ammonius, and that he could rely on his own notes for (some of) his Aristotelian commentaries. A second reason for doubting Saffrey's view on the relation between Philoponus and his master is that in the *in Physica* Philoponus openly criticises the doctrine of the eternity of the world, a doctrine which we know Ammonius adhered to without any hesitation.[30] He even goes so far as to reject tenets which he explicitly ascribes to Ammonius.[31] This is not exactly the type of behaviour Ammonius would have expected from a mere editor of his commentaries.[32] In the third place, one wonders why Ammonius, who had agreed with the Alexandrian bishop, according to Saffrey, to teach only Aristotle, not Plato,[33] would still have needed to hide behind a Christian collaborator when publishing precisely his Aristotelian commentaries.

In my opinion Philoponus, after studying for some years under Ammonius, somehow came to be the leading figure *de facto* of the Ammonian school, without, however, at first teaching philosophy himself.[34] The only absolute chronological indication concerning this period is the date to be found in the *in Physica*: 10 May 517.[35] We do not know whether Ammonius was still active or even alive at that time. Given that he was born between 435 and 445,[36] he would have been at least 72 years old in 517. It is not very likely that his active career lasted a long time after that date. And it is quite possible that by then others already controlled things in the Alexandrian school. Consequently, the

---

[30] Ammonius' eternalism is the main subject of Zacharias Scholasticus' dialogue *Ammonius*.

[31] In the relevant passages Ammonius is called *ho philosophos*: Philoponus *in An. Post.* 47,24-48,11; 158,7-11; 177,19-29; 258,26-30; 260,29-261,8; *in Phys.* 583,13-585,4 (*Coroll. de loco*).

[32] cf. E. Evrard, *L'école d'Olympiodore et la composition du 'Commentaire à la Physique' de Jean Philopon*, diss. Liège 1957, 213-14. I thank É. Évrard for allowing me to read his unpublished works *Philopon, Contre Aristote. Livre premier*, Liège 1943, and *L'école d'Olympiodore*.

[33] H.D. Saffrey, 'Le chrétien Jean Philopon', 400-1.

[34] According to A. Gudeman, 'Ioannes Philoponus', col. 1769, Philoponus stopped teaching after 529. As we shall see, exactly the opposite may have been the case. After Ammonius died or retired, the mathematician Eutocius seems to have held the chair of philosophy *de iure*; cf. L.G. Westerink, 'Elias on the Prior Analytics', *Mnemosyne*, Series IV, 14, 1961, 129, 131 (=Collected Papers 62, 64); id., *Anonymous Prolegomena*, p. xiii; A. Cameron, 'The last days of the Academy at Athens', *Proceedings of the Cambridge Philological Society* 195, n.s. 15, 1969, 26.

[35] Philoponus *in Phys.* 703,16-17.

[36] L.G. Westerink, *Anonymous Prolegomena*, p. x.

date in the *in Physica* probably refers to Philoponus' own redaction of this
commentary (the first redaction, as we shall see), rather than to lectures
of Ammonius at that time. On the other hand *in Physica* was not
Philoponus' first commentary: at least **in Isagogen* and *in Categorias*
were written earlier.[37] Hence we can assume that in 517 our philosopher
had been involved in the publication project for some time. However, is it
not a contradiction to say that Philoponus was a *Christian* by birth and at
the same time that he became the most important public spokesman of
what proves to be Ammonius' *Neoplatonic* system? I do not think so. It
seems quite conceivable that under the influence of Ammonius the
Christian John himself became a Neoplatonic philosopher, and that his
faith was more or less superseded by Neoplatonism. After all, would this
be the only case of a young adult losing or changing his conviction?
Moreover, Zacharias of Mytilene tells us that Ammonius had just such a
reputation of dislodging young Christians from their faith.[38] If it is true
that Philoponus drifted away from his Christian background (which
should not mean that there are absolutely no traces of Christianity in his
early philosophical works), then it is also true that his later transition to
Christian philosophy was not the result of a conversion, but rather a
return (on the level of doctrine) to Christianity.[39]

Towards the end of the 520s there is a radical change, a rupture in
Philoponus' thought. One has only to compare *in de Anima* with *de
Aeternitate Mundi contra Proclum*, written in 529,[40] to realise the depth
of the gap between Philoponus 1 and Philoponus 2. Why is this? By his
editions of Ammonius' commentaries Philoponus had declared himself
the new coryphaeus of the Alexandrian school. Why, then, did he
dissociate himself radically from pagan philosophy in 529? According to
Saffrey it was the author's intention to save the Alexandrian school by
means of a Christian manifesto from being closed down like the Athenian
school.[41] But this is not very likely. First of all, one should not forget that

[37] cf. nn. 104-105 below.
[38] Zacharias *Ammonius* ll.27-32 Colonna: 'Well then, tell me: how is his (=Ammonius')
school (*phrontistêrion*) and the assembly of his hearers? Is the school still being frequented
by honourable youths, pure in spirit? Indeed, "I am stricken with mortal fear": I am anxious
that he is filling the youths with his nonsense. For he is clever in ruining their souls by
removing them from God and the truth (*deinos gar ho anêr diaphtheirai neôn psukhas,
aphistôn theou te kai tês alêtheias)'*. In the 'Hypothesis' of the dialogue (p. 93 ll.1-2 Colonna)
Zacharias likewise refers to Ammonius' skill in 'converting' young Christians to 'Hellenism':
*Phoitêtês tis Ammôniou, tou dêthen philosophou, genomenos kai êrema pros Hellênismon
apoklinas....* This 'slight inclination' to Hellenic philosophy was to become considerably
stronger in Philoponus' case.
[39] According to Zacharias, *Ammonius* ll.998-1002, Ammonius prevented some of the
youths he had 'converted' from hearing the arguments of the Christians: they might be
seduced to become Christians again (*...hôs an...mê...khristianizein authis anapeistheien)*! I
must dissent here from Mrs Minniti Colonna, who translates: 'for fear...that they...might
let themselves be convinced to profess Christianity thereafter' (p. 177). I think *authis* has its
full value here ('again'). This is made clear by ll.999-1000: the students at issue are
'Hellenised' Christians (cf. the formula 'fill with his nonsense', repeated from l.30).
[40] Philoponus *Aet.* 579,14-15.
[41] H.D. Saffrey, 'Le chrétien Jean Philopon', 408-9; followed e.g. by A. Tuilier, 'La

the Alexandrian school as such was not really 'Christianised'. Olympiodorus undoubtedly was a pagan scholarch.[42] And the so-called 'Christian' members of the Olympiodorus school (Elias, David, Stephanus) did not oppose the traditional doctrine of the eternity of the world.[43] Moreover, at the end of the 530s Philoponus disappeared from the philosophical scene, a rather strange fate for the 'saviour' of the Alexandrian philosophical school. Everything suggests that within the school Philoponus' recantation on the eternity of the world was essentially a one-man affair. What were his motives? Roughly speaking, there are two possibilities. The first is that the Christian Philoponus became conscious of the true philosophical implications of the faith of his youth. On this hypothesis our author renounced his philosophical past out of honest conviction. The second is that he acted against his own conviction, out of opportunism. I feel more inclined to the latter than to the former of these interpretations, although the evidence may not seem to be entirely conclusive. Probably we would be in a better position if we still had the beginning (and end) of *de Aeternitate Mundi contra Proclum*. The issue is not in itself crucial to my analysis, since whatever biographical interpretation one prefers to give to the rupture in Philoponus' philosophical thought, that duality itself just remains what it is. So I shall postpone further discussion until later on.

It is not unlikely that from 529 onwards Philoponus taught philosophy *de facto* for some time, although *de iure* he was only a *grammatikos*, i.e. a professor of philology.[44] In this period he may have made the revised version of the *in Physica* as well as the present redaction of the *in Analytica Posteriora* and the *in Meteorologica*. But here again evidence is very scanty. Gudeman indicates only two passages which might prove that the texts at issue belong to an oral exposition.[45] However, it is striking that both passages occur in the *in Meteorologica*, a work which

tradition aristotélicienne à Byzance des origines au VIIe siècle. La formation de la scolastique byzantine', *Association Guillaume Budé. Actes du Congrès de Lyon 8-13 Septembre 1958*, Paris 1960, 190-1; W. Wieland, 'Die Ewigkeit der Welt', 315 n. 24; C.M.K. MacLeod, *Jean Philopon*, vol. 1, 38; J.L. Kraemer, 'A lost passage', 322; M. Mahdi, 'Alfarabi against Philoponus', 235; M.V. Anastos, 'Byzantine philosophy', in P. Edwards (ed.), *The Encyclopedia of Philosophy*, vol. 1, 437; P. Lemerle, *Le premier humanisme byzantin. Notes et remarques sur enseignement et culture à Byzance des origines au Xe siècle*, Paris 1971, 24; G.A. Lucchetta, 'Aristotelismo e cristianesimo', 582-3.

[42] L.G. Westerink, *Anonymous Prolegomena*, pp. xiii-xx; A Cameron, 'The end of the ancient universities', *Cahiers d'histoire mondiale* 10, 1966, 671; id., 'The last days of the Academy', 9, 26-7.

[43] L.G. Westerink, *Anonymous Prolegomena*, pp. xx-xxiv; A. Cameron, 'The last days of the Academy', 27; G. Verbeke, 'Some later Neoplatonic views on divine creation and the eternity of the world', in D.J. O'Meara (ed.), *Neoplatonism and Christian Thought*, Albany 1982, 46.

[44] For this meaning of the term *grammatikos* (against M. Wolff, *Geschichte der Impetustheorie*, 108-9) see L.G. Westerink, *Anonymous Prolegomena*, p. xiii; A. Segonds, *Jean Philopon, Traité de l'astrolabe*, 10; cf. already P. Tannery, 'Sur la période finale de la philosophie grecque', in P. Tannery, *Mémoires Scientifiques*, vol. 7, Toulouse and Paris, 1925, 227 n. 2.

[45] A. Gudeman, 'Ioannes Philoponus', col. 1766: Philoponus *in Meteor.* 53,26-7 and 71,3-4.

everyone now dates after 529. Moreover, it is possible to complete
Gudeman's data.[46] Characteristic of many passages in the *in
Meteorologica* are the strong self-consciousness of its author and the
frequency of references to his own points of view and writings.[47] These
characteristics are also present in the texts I take to represent the second
redaction of the *in Physica*,[48] whereas they are far less prominent in e.g.
in de Anima or *in de Generatione et Corruptione*. I am inclined to believe
that both the present version of the *in Meteorologica* and the texts which
Philoponus 2 inserted in the original redaction of the *in Physica* were
composed in connection with the actual teaching activity of their author
after 529. As to the chronological limits of this activity, it seems to have
started with the publication of *de Aeternitate Mundi contra Proclum*.
First of all, this treatise is clearly the programmatic work by which
Philoponus 2 announces himself as a Christian philosopher. Besides, not
only the *in Meteorologica* but probably also the second redaction of the *in
Physica* was written after *de Aeternitate Mundi contra Proclum*.[49] There
are reasons to suppose that towards the end of the 530s Philoponus
stopped teaching philosophy. With the publication of a third,
non-polemical work about the creation of the world (probably between
535 and 540)[50] we seem to have reached the end of the 'philosophy of
Philoponus 2' strictly speaking, or at least of its exposition in autonomous
treatises.[51] On the other hand, Olympiodorus' appointment to the chair of
Philosophy in succession to Ammonius and Eutocius has to be set in the
same period at the latest, if not earlier.[52] So we can affirm, without great
risk, that Philoponus' second philosophical period ends after Olympiodorus' appointment as a scholarch. We do not know whether it was a long
time afterwards. But it is reasonable to suppose that the transition to an
anti-eternalist doctrine of creation had isolated Philoponus within the
Alexandrian school. At a certain moment Eutocius, perhaps a rather

[46] See Philoponus *in Meteor.* 63,8-9: 'we shall hear the philosopher saying...'; and
probably also 118,25-6: 'and that is why we too should terminate this discussion here and
move on to the next issue, making a new start.'

[47] For these references to his other writings see M. Hayduck, Index nominum, *CAG* 14.1
s.v. 'Philoponos' (153-4) and É. Évrard, 'Les convictions religieuses', 339-45. Self-confident
utterances occur in the first person singular (e.g. *in Meteor.* 8,13; 9,8; 15,23; 22,8; 43,7;
75,30; 79,31; 110,13...) and in the first person plural (e.g. *in Meteor.* 23,22; 43,37; 47,30;
48,14; 61,16; 77,23; 78,31; 82,17; 86,18-19; 96,22...).

[48] cf. below. The frequent criticism of Ammonius in the *in Analytica Posteriora* (cf. n. 31
above) is probably another striking example of the self-confidence of Philoponus 2.

[49] cf. below.

[50] cf. below.

[51] Philoponus *Opif.* 1,6-17; H.D. Saffrey, 'Le chrétien Jean Philopon', 408: 'After the 530s
our John appears to follow a theological rather than a philosophical career. He does not
seem to play any further role in the university.'

[52] On Olympiodorus' start as a scholarch: L.G. Westerink, 'Elias on the *Prior Analytics*',
128, 131 (*Collected Papers*, 61, 64), where it is stated that Olympiodorus must still have
been relatively young; id., *Anonymous Prolegomena*, p. xiii: 'His appointment to the chair of
philosophy took place a good many years before 541, if it is true that Elias was his pupil...'.
According to Westerink, Olympiodorus was born between 495 and 505. Cf. also id., *The
Greek Commentaries on Plato's Phaedo*, vol. 1: *Olympiodorus*, 20.

neutral figure, was succeeded by Olympiodorus, overtly a pagan. This indicates that, maybe from as early as the beginning of the 530s onwards, opportunities for pagan philosophy must have opened up again, and that Philoponus' Christian alternative was soon threatened or superseded by a new impulse of the Ammonian tradition. Undoubtedly, under Eutocius also, the Alexandrian school remained essentially true as an institute to the spirit of Ammonius. Hellenic tradition in Alexandria recovered its full rights in the person of Olympiodorus. I assume that this meant, in one way or another, the end of Philoponus' philosophical role: the 'traditionalists' eventually succeeded in eliminating him as a philosopher. Philoponus retired from 'academic philosophy',[53] which does not necessarily mean that he gave up his chair of philology. The rest of his life was to be devoted to dogmatical theology.

The chronology of Philoponus' commentaries on Aristotle

So far hardly anything has been said on the order of writing of the commentaries. But everybody now accepts two basic facts: that 'the' *in Physica* was written in or about 517, and that 'the' *in Meteorologica* is posterior to 529. The solution I propose consists in dividing the surviving commentaries into two groups. The first group embraces *in Categorias, in Analytica Priora, in de Generatione et Corruptione*, and *in de Anima-in de Intellectu*. These writings imply the philosophical system of Philoponus 1, without capital contradictions. For the moment it is of only secondary importance to know their order of composition. The second group embraces *in Analytica Posteriora, in Physica*, and *in Meteorologica*. These commentaries contain passages which are obviously incompatible with the system of Philoponus 1. However – and this seems to be the key to the whole problem – the *in Physica* clearly has elements of both Philoponus 1 and Philoponus 2. Hence my hypothesis that the commentaries of the second group were originally composed by Philoponus 1, but were revised by Philoponus 2. But why, one may ask, did Philoponus 2 limit himself in the *in Physica* to a revision which left the earlier version intact, so as to produce plain contradictions? The answer might be that he needed a commentary (for didactic purposes), but had neither the time nor the desire to make a completely new one. The sporadic insertion of elements from his new system would have had the effect of making the old text seem to have a purely exegetical purpose, when it was no longer consistent with his views, while the small number of insertions publicised the author's own ideas on critical issues. Why was there no revision of the first group of commentaries? We do not know. But this problem as such is

---

[53] cf. the term 'solemn philosophy (*semnê philosophia*)' at Philoponus *Opif.* 1,9. That Philoponus did indeed take his leave of philosophy seems indicated also by the opening sentence of a later treatise, the *Tractatus de totalitate et partibus ad Sergium presbyterum*, where he speaks of his return, just for once, to philosophical discussion (*...rursus ad rationalia certamina nos incitat...*) (A. Sanda, *Opuscula Monophysitica Ioannis Philoponi*, Beirut 1930, 126).

no greater than the problems that arise from a unitarian approach, e.g.: Why does Philoponus criticise eternalism in the *in Physica*, but not in *in de Generatione et Corruptione* and *in de Anima-in de Intellectu*, especially since the latter two commentaries were composed 'with certain observations of his own (*meta tinôn idiôn epistaseôn)'*?[54] I fully realise that my hypothesis creates some new problems, and that a large amount of philological work remains to be done. But I also think that it is less problematic than the solutions advanced hitherto; maybe it can serve as a first basis for further investigation.

(a) The date of the in Physica

Most scholars regard the year 517 as the date of 'the' redaction of the *Commentary on the Physics*.[55] Others, somewhat more prudently, consider 517 as the date at which Philoponus was working on the redaction of his commentary.[56] But one most significant fact has not yet been sufficiently taken into account: Philoponus refers three times in the surviving part of the work to his lost critical commentary on *Physica 8* as to an already existing text.[57] This can be explained in two different ways. The first possibility is that the anteriority of **in Physica 8* was just a matter of succession within one and the same redaction: Philoponus then must have written Book 8 before he wrote Books 1-4.[58] But why should he have done so? And if he did, why didn't he simply refer to it in the future tense? Therefore, it seems better to think of a discontinuous anteriority. On the other hand, it is impossible to consider the fragments of *in Physica 8* edited by H. Vitelli as belonging to the anti-eternalist **in Physica 8*,

---

[54] Philoponus *in GC* 1,3; *in DA* 1,3. The formula occurs also in the title of *in Analytica Posteriora* (1,3).

[55] e.g. M. Wallies, *Berliner Philologische Wochenschrift* 36, 1916, col. 587; É. Évrard, 'Les convictions religieuses', 299; S. Sambursky, *The Physical World of Late Antiquity*, 154; W. Wolska, *La topographie chrétienne de Cosmas Indicopleustès*, Paris 1962, 149; C.M.K. MacLeod, *Jean Philopon*, vol. 1, 19, 22; W. Böhm, *Johannes Philoponos*, 28, 31.

[56] H.D. Saffrey, 'Le chrétien Jean Philopon', 401; I. Hadot, *Le problème du néoplatonisme alexandrin*, 25; cf. W. Haase, 'Ein vermeintliches Aristoteles-Fragment bei Johannes Philoponos', *Synusia. Festgabe für W. Schadewaldt*, Pfullingen 1965, 345, n. 1. 'About 517': A. Gudeman, 'Ioannes Philoponus', col. 1779; M. Wolff, *Fallgesetz und Massebegriff. Zwei wissenschaftshistorische Untersuchungen zur Kosmologie des Johannes Philoponus*, Berlin 1971, 110; id., *Geschichte der Impetustheorie*, 67, n. 2.

[57] Philoponus *in Phys.* 458,30-1; 639,7-9; 762,7-9. Cf. H. Vitelli, Index nominum, *CAG* 17 s.v. 'Philoponos', 995.

[58] This seems to be the opinion of É. Évrard, 'Les convictions religieuses', 353.

since some of them clearly accept the eternity of the world.[59] This points in the direction of two different versions of *in Physica 8*: a first one in which the author had not yet challenged Aristotelian eternalism, and a later, separate one in which he criticised Aristotle's arguments for the eternity of movement. Moreover, those passages where Philoponus refers to his anti-eternalist **in Physica 8* must be still later again than this separate commentary. Consequently, we should distinguish at least three successive stages in Philoponus' work on the *Physics*. The distinction between the second *(*in Physica 8)* and the third stage (*in Physica²*: the second redaction of at least *in Physica 1-4*) is clear. But what exactly are my reasons for distinguishing a first stage (*in Physica¹*) from the second and the third?

In the introduction to this chapter I mentioned an indication of a doctrinal duality in the *in Physica*, namely the inconsistency with regard to the eternity of the world. Similar inconsistencies can be found in Philoponus' accounts of place and void. I think that a brief survey of the contradictions which occur on these three subjects will be sufficient to show that, in the present text of *in Physica*, there are at least two strata, representing the systems of Philoponus 1 and Philoponus 2 respectively.

It is well known that the *Commentary on the Physics* contains several passages in which Philoponus challenges the doctrine of the eternity of the world: *in Phys.* 54,8-55,26; 191,9-192,2; 428,23-430,10; 456,17-458,31; 467,1-468,4; 762,2-9. On the other hand the commentator affirms the eternity of heavenly substance,[60] of the sublunary cosmos,[61] of movement[62] and of time.[63] The excerpts from Books 5-8 are eternalist as well: heavenly bodies are eternal;[64] sublunary substances possess an eternity by way of creation and destruction (*aidiotês kata genesin kai phthoran*);[65] the earth is said to be eternally immobile;[66] the eternity of

---

[59] cf. below.

[60] cf. n. 10 above (fifth element) and Philoponus *in Phys.* 1,17; 1,23-4; 15,30; 152,5-7, 'Some things, though natural, are ungenerated, I mean celestial things'; 362,21-5 and 497, 8-9 (only local movement); 601,12-13 (implicitly); 777,11-12 (implicitly).

[61] Philoponus *in Phys.* 236,29-237,4; 303,18-25 (read, ll.24-5 ...*aidia einai kata arithmon, têi diadokhêi*...) 405,3-7; 484,15-19.

[62] Philoponus *in Phys.* 298,6-12; 303,1-5; 438,5-6; 747,1-3.

[63] ibid., 410,21-4.

[64] ibid., 898,2-4.

[65] ibid., 838,14-15; 893,6-28.

[66] ibid., 859,30.

movement is repeatedly affirmed;[67] time is without beginning or end.[68]

In his *Corollarium de loco* (*in Phys.* 557,8-585,4) Philoponus rejects Aristotle's definition of place as the first immobile limit of [a thing's] surroundings (*to tou periekhontos peras akinêton prôton*),[69] which had still been accepted by Ammonius.[70] In his subsequent commentary on *Phys.* 4.4, 212a7ff Philoponus likewise disagrees with the Aristotelian definition.[71] To him, the place of physical bodies is their empty, incorporeal, three-dimensional extension. From this definition, according to Philoponus, there follow none of the absurdities which Aristotle, *Phys.* 4.4, 211b14-29 alleges.[72] In his exegesis of *Physica 3* and *Physica 4,1-4* (down to 212a7), on the other hand, Philoponus does *not* identify place

[67] ibid., 812,22-3; 820,30-821,4; 824,22-5; 870,3-8; 894,8-10; 897,23-7; 898,15-16; 905,19-21; 906,38-40 (eternity of heavenly circular movement); 832,17-18, '[the motion] must be eternal as proved at the beginning (...*anankê aidion einai [sc. tên kinêsin] hôs dedeiktai en arkhêi*)'; 838,20-1; 838,28-33; 873,1-2 (eternity of movement). According to M. Wolff, *Fallgesetz und Massebegriff*, 94-5, Philoponus at *in Phys.* 797,23-6 rejects the necessity of the eternity of movement. However, the passage only concerns the finite power of intra-mundane generated substances, not of the cosmos as a whole. Moreover, in Aristotle's eternalist view the principle that no finite substance has infinite power is valid even for the cosmos as a whole: the cosmos is not *naturally* eternal (cf. *Phys.* 8.10, 266a24-b6). In the fragments of the commentary on *Phys.* 8.6-8 Philoponus explicitly associates himself with Aristotle's argument, e.g. *in Phys.* 889,17-23, 'we proceeded for the rest to prove that there are some ever-moving things...'; 893,6-9, 'For above he established the eternal mover from the fact that there is something eternally in motion, whereas here he infers something eternally in motion from the eternal mover. But this was not unreasonable.' He affirms the correctness of Aristotle's demonstration, e.g. *in Phys.* 894,26; 897,15-17, 'There must always be motion, for he established this at the beginning of this book (...*anankê aei kinêsin einai (touto gar en arkhais tou bibliou toutou kateskeuasen...*)'; 906,38-9, 'But if motion must be eternal, as he proved (*ei d'anankê aidion einai kinêsin, hôs edeixe...*)'. I do not see any reason to suppose that the commentator dissociates himself from Aristotle. And it is most unlikely that *in Phys.* 890,7 'As was said there (...*hôs en ekeinois elegeto*)' refers to the anti-eternalist **in Physica 8*, as H. Vitelli, Index nominum, *CAG* 17 s.v. 'Philoponos' (995) suggests. The formula just takes up 890,2-3 'He reminded us of the problem (*aporia*) raised at the beginning of this book (...*anemnêsen hêmas tês en arkhêi tou bibliou toutou aporias...*)', which is a reference to *Phys.* 8.2, 253a7-21 (and not, as Vitelli ad loc. thinks, to 8.1, 250b11). At *Phys.* 8.2, 253a7-21 Aristotle himself refers to a later passage, namely 8.6, 259b1-20, which is exactly the text Philoponus is commenting on here. According to G.A. Lucchetta, finally, *in Phys.* 891,33-892,24 must be connected with *Opif.* 28,20-29,9, where God is said to have given an initial impetus to the heavenly bodies (G.A. Lucchetta, 'Ipotesi per l'applicazione dell' "impetus" ai cieli in Giovanni Filopono', *Atti e Memorie dell' Accademia Patavina di Scienze, Lettere ed Arti* 87, 1974-5, 341-7; id., 'Aristotelismo e cristianesimo', 588; *Una fisica senza matematica: Democrito, Aristotele, Filopono*, Trento 1978, 137-50). This would mean that the anti-eternalist doctrine of creation of Philoponus 2 is already to be found at *in Phys.* 891,33-892,24. It would lead me too far afield to refute in detail Lucchetta's analysis here. Suffice it for the moment to say that he wrongly takes 'kinetic power' (*kinêtikê dunamis, in Phys.* 891,35), 'unmoved causes' (*akinêtoi aitiai*, 892,7) and 'lives' (*hai zôai*, 892,18) to refer to impetus. But what Philoponus is talking about is not an external impetus, but a principle of movement that is immanent in heavenly bodies: soul.

[68] Philoponus *in Phys.* 812,23; 820,30-2; 823,16-20; 870,2-9.

[69] Aristotle *Phys.* 4.4, 212a20-1.

[70] Ammonius *in Cat.* 58,16-17. Cf. ibid., 29,9-10; Ammonius *in Isag.* 41,1-2; 110,22.

[71] e.g. Philoponus *in Phys.* 592,16-32.

[72] ibid., 563,20-5; cf. 567,29-33.

and extension, but accepts the Aristotelian definition without criticism. He himself defines place as the limit of the surroundings (*peras tou periekhontos*);[73] having a place is being limited.[74] He uses the Aristotelian concept of place without any reserve,[75] and even appears positively to agree with it.[76] It is erroneous, we are told, to identify place with three-dimensional extension.[77] Such a concept of place entails absurdities which do not follow from Aristotle's definition of place as the limit of the surroundings.[78]

In *Physics* 4,6-9 Aristotle denies the existence of void as a place deprived of body:[79] there is no void, either outside or in bodies.[80] Philoponus begins by commenting on Aristotle's text down to *Phys.* 4.9, 217a21,[81] not without some critical interventions.[82] The *Corollarium de inani* (*in Phys.* 675,12-695,8) expounds Philoponus' own theory on void. In the first part (677,9-689,25) the commentator attacks Aristotle's refutation of the existence of external void. In the second part (689,26-694,27) he argues that local movement is possible in the void, and that it is even impossible without a void. This does not mean, however, that Philoponus considers real void as something existing on its own, without corporeal filling; it is always a filled void.[83] The *Corollary* is followed by the exegesis of the rest of *Phys.* 4.9.[84] But the author does not defend the doctrine of the *Corollary* in the entire commentary. Although one should not, of course, put every statement down to the commentator's personal conviction, there are a few texts which show that Philoponus must originally have shared Aristotle's view on the existence of void. At *in Phys.* 440,16-17 he writes: '...that there is no void among the things there are, he (Aristotle) will prove in the next Book.'[85] Elsewhere

---

[73] ibid., 454,23-4; 536,6-7; 539,5-6; 555,25-7.

[74] ibid., 447,18-20; 448,20-1.

[75] ibid., 444,5-6; 463,3-4; 499,26-7; 542,17-18; 543,1-4; 546,16-17.

[76] ibid., 499,26, 'we will say (*eroumen*)'; 536,6, 'I mean (*legô dê*)'; 542,18, 'I mean (*legô dê*)'; 542,36, 'so I say (*phêmi oun*)'.

[77] ibid., 526,20-3: '...Once this has been shown, I mean what place is, we have the solution of all the aporias which made it seem that there is no place, and especially of those which arose from erroneous conceptions of what place is, like the aporias which assume that place is three-dimensionally extended.'

[78] ibid., 555,25-7: 'Hence none of the absurdities that result for those who hold that place is extension follow for those who say that place is the limit of the surrounding (body).' One can hardly imagine a sharper contradiction than that between *in Phys.* 555,25-7 and 563,22-5: 'The argument has sufficiently proved, I think, that for those who hold that place is extension which is empty according to its own definition and different from the bodies that enter it, none of the so-called absurdities mentioned by Aristotle follows.'

[79] cf. Aristotle *Phys.* 4.7, 214a16-17.

[80] cf. ibid., 4.9, 217b20-1.

[81] Philoponus *in Phys.* 606,25-675,11.

[82] ibid., 632,4-634,2; 639,3-643,8.

[83] ibid., 675,21-9.

[84] ibid., 695,9-702,9.

[85] *...kenon de hoti ouk estin en tois ousin, deixei en tôi ephexês bibliôi.* Cf. *in Phys.* 2,25-7: 'Aristotle proves (*deiknusin*) in the fourth book of this work that there cannot be void anywhere (*all' hoti men oudamou dunatai einai to kenon deiknusin en tôi tetartôi tês prokeimenês pragmateias ho Aristotelês...*)'. There can be no doubt that Philoponus was

Philoponus seems to dissociate himself clearly from 'certain physicists' according to whom movement takes place through the void,[86] which is precisely the view he will himself defend in the *Corollarium de inani*.[87] In this respect, there is even a contradiction, at least verbally, between the *Corollary*[88] and its immediate exegetical sequel.[89] Outside the *Corollary* the idea of a necessary concomitance of body and void[90] is rather emphatically ascribed to 'some physicists'.[91] And a reserve with regard to the reality of void may also be implied in the frequent attribution to others of the definition of void as a place deprived of body.[92]

The only explanation I can see for the inconsistencies just mentioned is that *in Physica* was originally written by Philoponus 1 and later revised. The *Corollaries*, although they are not necessarily contemporaneous with the anti-eternalist passages, do not in my opinion belong to the first redaction.[93] The year 517 may very well have been the time at which

---

aware of the full significance of (*deiknunai*): cf. *in Phys*. 762,8-9: 'He tries to prove in the eighth book of this work that there is always motion, but in fact proves anything but this (*Hoti de hê kinêsis aei estin, en tôi ogdoôi tautês tês pragmateias peiratai men deiknunai, pan de mallon deiknusin ê touto...*)'. Cf. also 584,14.

[86] Philoponus *in Phys*. 340,7-9; 619,1-4; 661,9-12; cf. 346,8-9.

[87] ibid., 677,9-686,29; 689,26-694,27.

[88] ibid., 693,30: 'that it is altogether impossible for there to be motion, if there is no void.'

[89] ibid., 697,26: 'And it is very obvious that there will be motion, even if there is no void.'

[90] ibid., 689,4-16.

[91] ibid., 2,21-2; 347,9-11.

[92] Philoponus *in Phys*. 340,12-13; 347,10-11; 405,28-9; 408,14-15; 500,28-9; 611,16.

[93] The question whether or not the *Corollaries* fit perfectly with the system of Philoponus 2 requires further investigation. For the moment I shall discuss only one relevant point. According to M. Wolff, *Fallgesetz und Massebegriff*, 136, n. 42, Philoponus *in Phys*. 686,16-17 'for things unlike in kind cannot be compared (*ou gar sumblêta ta anomoiogenê...*)' distinguishes the fifth element which makes up the heavens from the sublunary elements down here. If this were correct, it would mean that at least one feature of Philoponus 1 survives in the *Corollarium de inani*. I do not exclude that, on detailed analysis, other texts might prove the presence or persistence of Philoponus 1 in the *Corollaries*, but I do not think *in Phys*. 686,16-17 proves that Philoponus still accepted the Aristotelian theory of the fifth element when he wrote this text. It seems to me that the author is not talking here about a heterogeneity between the heavenly and the sublunary *body*. The passage concerns the question of a possible proportionality between movements, the times they need, and the media in which they take place. It does not follow, Philoponus says, if there is a certain ratio between the time during which a body moves in a straight line and the time of the revolution of the lunar sphere, that there should be a proportionate ratio between the respective 'media'. Times are always mutually comparable magnitudes, but the same does not necessarily hold true for movements and their media. Movements not comparable to each other are, e.g., qualitative and quantitative change, or understanding and local movement. Media of movement not comparable to each other are, e.g., intellect and body, body and void, and body and surface (*in Phys*. 685,23-686,29). In other words, the heterogeneity between the sublunary world and the lunar sphere is not, in this case, a matter of different substance. In my opinion, it simply means that the medium of rectilinear movement is a *body*, the 'medium' of heavenly movement, however, a spherical *surface*. This seems to be the appropriate way to understand *in Phys*. 686,12-17: '...nor, again, I presume, if the duration of every rectilinear movement *through a body* has a certain ratio to the duration of the movement of the lunar sphere, is it necessary on that account that the "media" of the respective movements, e.g. the air (i.e. a body) and *the surface* surrounding the (sphere of the) moon, should also have the same ratio to each other, or should be

Philoponus was writing this first version, as a part of the project of editing Ammonius' lectures on Aristotle. It is possible that this text was a complete commentary on *Physica* 1-8.[94] Later on Philoponus expounded his changed view about the eternity of movement and the nature of artificial movement[95] in a separate **in Physica 8*. Eventually he reworked at least Books 1-4 to their present form. Apart from the contents, there are also formal indications of the digressive and supplementary character of the anti-Aristotelian passages in the *in Physica*. In the case of the Corollaries textual autonomy is evident. But in addition the closing words of some of these personal arguments show their excursive nature. For Philoponus twice refers in closing to his **in Physica 8*,[96] once to a work of his which he does not identify,[97] and once to a future, separate account of the problem of the infinity of time.[98] Finally there is a hidden reference to another work or other works in the statement that the complete argument about the origin of matter is too long to be incorporated in the commentary on *Phys.* 1.9, 192a25-33.[99] This striking frequency of references to other writings in the anti-eternalist passages seems to suggest that the author was in somewhat of a hurry, an impression reinforced by his emphasis on the limitations imposed by the context[100] and on the greater completeness of other demonstrations.[101] Apparently he was aware of the perplexity he caused his readers by contradicting himself on the eternity of the world. The references to other works are intended to assure the reader that anti-eternalism is indeed the position of the author, notwithstanding the eternalism of *in Physica¹*.

In my opinion, the following texts at least do not belong to the first redaction of *in Physica*: *in Phys.* 54,8-55,26; 191,9-192,2; 428,23-430,10; 456,17-459,1; 467,1-468,7; 557,8-585,4 (*Corollarium de loco*); 592,16-32; 619,10-13; 632,4-634,2; 639,3-643,8;[102] 675,12-695,8 (*Corollarium de inani*); 761,34-762,9.

Let us return once again to the date of 517. If we were to accept the *communis opinio* that the whole text as it now stands was written in or about 517, this would mean that by an early age Philoponus would already have written quite a lot of works (which, of course, is not impossible in

---

comparable at all; for things of different kind are not comparable (to each other)....'

[94] This can be inferred, of course, from the remaining fragments of the commentary on *Physica* 5-8. See also J.L. Kraemer, 'A lost passage', 318-19.

[95] cf. Philoponus *in Phys.* 639,7-10.

[96] ibid., 458,30-1 and 762,8-9.

[97] ibid., 55,24-6; cf. below.

[98] ibid., 430,9-10.

[99] ibid., 191,34-192,2.

[100] ibid., 55,25; 191,34-192,1; 458,15-6.

[101] ibid., 55,26; 191,1-2; 430,9-10.

[102] In this passage Philoponus develops his theory of impetus. It contains a reference to **in Physica 8* (639,7-9) and a typical remark concerning the limits imposed by the context (640,23-5).

itself): grammatical treatises,[103] and certainly also *in Isagogen*,[104] *in Categorias*,[105] the **Summikta Theôrêmata*[106] and **in Physica 8*. On the other hand, as we shall see, neither *in de Generatione et Corruptione* nor *in de Anima-in de Intellectu* show any trace of the progressive ideas Philoponus develops at several places in the *in Physica*. So we would have to locate these two commentaries too before 517, thereby implying a radical change in the author's thought before 517 (cf. **in Physica 8*). And for the period 517-529 there would remain at most: *in Analytica Priora*, **in Topica*[107] and *in Analytica Posteriora*. If, however, we are right in connecting the date of 517 with the first, 'Ammonian' redaction of *in Physica*, these difficulties disappear: **in Physica 8* can be put after *in de Generatione en Corruptione* and *in de Anima-in de Intellectu* without any problem; we will no longer need to set these two commentaries before 517; and *in Physica¹* becomes a member of a group of early commentaries representing the philosophy of Philoponus 1.

If this solution to the chronological problem contains some truth, it is perhaps possible to say something about the date of Philoponus' later revision of *in Physica* 1-4 as well. First: when did he write the anti-eternalist **in Physica 8*, whether or not this was a separate book? Maybe there are reasons to suppose that this happened *after* the publication of *de Aeternitate Mundi contra Proclum* in 529. On two occasions indeed *de Aeternitate Mundi contra Proclum* refers to the future *contra Aristotelem*, where we should expect a reference to **in Physica 8* if in 529 that work existed at all.

(1) First, there is a brief argument on the impossibility of the eternity of movement in *Aet.* 7,6.[108] Philoponus does not say anything about his **in Physica 8* here. Everyone will agree that it would be rather strange if the author completely forgot here a book he mentions three times in his *in Physica*. For even if one takes account of the possibility that **in Physica 8* only criticised Aristotle's arguments for the eternity of movement, without proving that this eternity is impossible, the relevance of its contents to *Aet.* 257,4-259,6 is clear. No kind of movement, Philoponus argues, can be eternal: substantial change necessarily has a beginning and an end, and so do qualitative and quantitative changes. The only form of movement to remain is local movement. Rectilinear movement cannot be eternal. This, says Philoponus, has been proved by Aristotle.[109] For the circular movement of heavenly bodies the author refers to the

---

[103] Philoponus was a late starter in philosophy (cf. n. 25 above). Since, according to Simplicius *in Cael.* 26,21-3, he studied philology first, it is reasonable to set his grammatical writings at the beginning of his career.

[104] Philoponus *in Phys.* 250,28. Cf. H. Vitelli, Index nominum, *CAG* 17 s.v. 'Philoponos', 995.

[105] Philoponus *in Phys.* 414,21-2; 705,21-2. Cf. H. Vitelli, loc. cit.

[106] cf. below.

[107] That Philoponus was the author of a lost *in Topica* may perhaps be inferred from Philoponus *in An. Post.* 3,2-4.

[108] Philoponus *Aet.* 257,4-259,6.

[109] Aristotle *Phys.* 8.8, 261b31-262b8.

contra Aristotelem. Now, a statement about the value of Aristotle's arguments for the eternity of circular movement (*Phys.* 8.8-9) would exactly parallel the mention of Aristotle with regard to rectilinear movement. But there is no such statement. What would have been more natural here than a reference to **in Physica 8*, like that at *in Phys.* 762,7-9? It is difficult to imagine that Philoponus would not have referred to his **in Physica 8* (as he did in the ultimate version of *in Physica*) if this work already existed in 529. Instead, he promises to refute the eternity of circular movement in *contra Aristotelem.* He must indeed have done so in *contra Aristotelem* Book 6.[110] At the same time he promises the publication of the third, non-polemical work on the creation of the world.[111] And the very words he uses might imply that **in Physica 8* also lay in the future: '...when we have got rid of the annoyance resulting from all the aporias.'[112] The task of refuting all eternalist arguments in 529 is still ahead in part, namely in so far as Aristotle is concerned. Apart from indicating that the *de Aeternitate Mundi contra Proclum* is probably Philoponus' first anti-eternalist work, the quoted passage reveals the logic of the author's enterprise. First he wants to refute the arguments of the eternalists (*de Aeternitate Mundi contra Proclum, contra Aristotelem*), i.e. to preserve the possibility that the world is not eternal *a parte ante*; afterwards he will prove that this possibility is a *necessity*. But already in the first two treatises there are arguments which should strictly speaking have been reserved for the third work.[113] Whether or not the lost *in Physica 8* tried to prove the actual necessity of the non-eternity of movement, we can say that it is, together with the *contra Aristotelem*, intermediate in Philoponus' project between the *de Aeternitate Mundi contra Proclum* and the non-polemical work.

(2) A second text to prove, or at least to make it very likely, that **in Physica 8* was not yet written in 529, nor even planned, is *Aet.* 10,6 (397,25-400,3). This chapter is also, like part of 7,6, about the eternity of circular movement. Whereas in 7,6 Philoponus postponed the subject to *contra Aristotelem*, in 10,6 he argues against the eternity of circular movement, without, however, going any further than denying the necessity of this eternity. At the end of the chapter the author writes:

> But if, relying on the attempted proofs of Aristotle, they say that circular movement has no beginning or end, we shall see whether any of those reasonings is cogent when, with God's help, we arrive there. For there is no need to debate those matters now, since the philosopher [Proclus] in his own arguments has not put forward anything like that. Let us see also whether

---

[110] Simplicius *in Cael.* 201,3-4. 'Since he (Philoponus) tries also to refute the arguments in the eighth book of the *Physics* which prove the circular movement to be eternal.' Cf. É. Évrard, *Philopon, Contre Aristote*, 87-9.

[111] Philoponus *Aet.* 259,3-5.

[112] cf. ibid., 9,22-6: *...pasas tas peri tou aidion einai ton kosmon aporias elenxantes...*

[113] Impossibility of eternal movement: Philoponus *Aet.* 257,4-259,6; *contra Aristotelem* 6 (Simplicius *in Phys.* 1178,7-1179,26). Impossibility of infinite time: *Aet.* 619,3-620,7. Impossibility of an eternal cosmos: *Aet.* 9,1-11,23.

there are any arguments by means of which we can show that it is impossible
for circular movement to be eternal. For the moment we have only set
ourselves to object to Proclus' attempted proofs. [Hence] we have adduced
only, to the best of our ability, what is germane to refuting his arguments.[114]

Why would Philoponus only refer to a *future* refutation of Aristotle's
arguments for the eternity of circular movement, if such a refutation
were *already* contained in his **in Physica 8*? Reference to an existing
work would better have served the purpose of assuring the reader that
the author of *de Aeternitate Mundi contra Proclum* was able to cope with
Aristotelian eternalism than a promise not yet fulfilled.

I think it is difficult to avoid the conclusion that Philoponus in 529 did
not even have the intention of composing an anti-eternalist *in Physica 8*
distinct from *contra Aristotelem 6*. On the other hand, *contra Aristotelem
6* did contain, so far as we can gather from Simplicius, a number of
arguments against the eternity of movement. Some of these arguments
refuted Aristotle, others even tried to prove that eternal movement is
impossible. Thus at least the first group of arguments is identical with
what we surely know to have been (part of) the content of **in Physica 8*.
As already mentioned, we no longer possess the refutation of Aristotle's
proofs of the eternity of circular movement (*Phys.* 8.8-9).[115] But we do
have Philoponus' arguments against *Phys.* 8.1, where Aristotle proves the
eternity of movement as such: against *Phys.* 8.1, 251a8-b10. Philoponus
defends the possibility of a first movement;[116] against *Phys.* 8.1,
251b10-28, he argues that the concept of time does not imply the eternity
of movement;[117] and against *Phys.* 8.1, 251b28-252a5, he defends the
possibility of a last movement.[118] It appears that **in Physica 8*, so far as
Philoponus' personal views are concerned, must have been very close in
content to *contra Aristotelem 6*. One might even be tempted simply to
identify the two books. But the threefold recurrence of the term *skholai*
with regard to **in Physica 8* seems to leave no other possibility but that
this text was a real commentary. It must have anticipated, paralleled, or
repeated in exegetical form (part of) the content of *contra Aristotelem 6*.
Maybe its composition had to do with Philoponus' teaching activities in
those years.

If **in Physica 8* was indeed written after 529, the same holds true for
the revised redaction of *in Physica 1-4*, in which Philoponus mentions his
separate Commentary on Book 8. In my opinion it is not unlikely that *in
Phys.* 55,24-6 refers to the *de Aeternitate Mundi contra Proclum*:

> Let this for the present purpose be a sufficient reply (*eirêsthô* Diels) from us
> also to (the proposition) that being did not originate, since we have

[114] Philoponus *Aet.* 399,20-400,3. Unlike 258,22-6, this text does not mention the title of
the *contra Aristotelem*.
[115] cf. above.
[116] Simplicius *in Phys.* 1130,7-1131,7; 1133,17-1135,15; 1147,10-1149,4.
[117] ibid., 1157,6-1159,4; 1164,11-30; 1166,37-1167,16.
[118] ibid., 1171,30-1175,26 (with insertions by Simplicius).

discussed that kind of proposition adequately elsewhere (*en allois hêmin gegumnasmenôn hikanôs tôn toioutôn theôrêmatôn*).

A. Gudeman considered this passage to be a reference to a lost *in de Caelo* of Philoponus,[119] a view which was sufficiently refuted by É. Évrard.[120] Évrard himself is convinced that Philoponus here refers to his **Summikta Theôrêmata*, and he was followed in this by M. Wolff. To Évrard first: the only argument in favour of his supposition is the occurrence of the term *theôrêma* at *in Phys.* 55,26.[121] But this is not very conclusive. Évrard is not entirely consistent indeed in his understanding of *theôrêma*: he first takes it to mean 'thèse', and further understands it as 'discussion'. Apparently, however, the *theôrêmata* at issue are 'propositions', not of Philoponus, but of his opponents.[122] By the formula 'that kind of proposition' the author probably means views 'of the same kind' as the theory that being is without beginning, views which constitute the subject matter of at least one of his former works. It is only through a shift of meaning (from 'thèse' to 'discussion') that Évrard can take the term *theôrêma* to refer to the title of the **Summikta Theôrêmata.* Wolff [123] adduces another argument, namely the thematical connection he supposes to exist between the question of the immutability of the three-dimensional second substrate (according to *in Phys.* 156,16-17, the **Summikta Theôrêmata* dealt with that question) and the problem of the eternity of the world. This leads Wolff to the conclusion that the **Summikta Theôrêmata* most probably expounded *in extenso* the point of view of *in Physica* with regard to the eternity of the world. I cannot enter here into a discussion of Wolff's construction of a 'theory of substance of 517'. I do not believe that the *in Physica* contains a single point of view on matter at all. But even apart from that, why should a work whose title already makes clear that its subject matter is heterogeneous ('*Miscellaneous Theôrêmata*') have developed a coherent theme? We only know that it dealt with an optical[124] and a geometrical[125] subject, and with extension as a substrate of bodies.[126] One gets the impression of a real diversity of subjects, as we might expect on the basis of the title. Consequently, if the work referred to at *in Phys.* 55,24-6 is not the **Summikta Theôrêmata*, we have to look for other possibilities. In principle there are three: *de Aeternitate Mundi contra Proclum*, *Contra Aristotelem* (*de Aeternitate Mundi contra Proclum*), or the third, non-polemical work (+ *de Aeternitate Mundi contra Proclum* + *contra*

[119] A. Gudeman, 'Ioannes Philoponus', col. 1779.

[120] É. Évrard, 'Les convictions religieuses', 340, n. 3.   [121] ibid.

[122] cf. e.g. Philoponus *in Phys.* 639,7-9: 'Against this *theôrêma* I have spoken in due measure in the comments on the eighth book of this work (*Kai eirêtai men moi pros touto to theôrêma metria en tais skholais tou ogdoou tautês tês pragmateias*)'; *Aet.* 399,24-6: 'For there is no need to rehearse those arguments now (*oudemia gar nun ekeina gumnazein anankê...*)'.

[123] M. Wolff, *Fallgesetz und Massebegriff*, 121-2, n. 27, 133.

[124] Philoponus *in An. Post.* 179,10-11.   [125] ibid., 265,5-6.

[126] Philoponus *in Phys.* 156,16-17. It is to be noted that in these three cases the title *Summikta Theôrêmata* is explicitly mentioned.

Aristotelem). To start with the last one, the final redaction of *in Physica* is not likely to be posterior to the third treatise. There is indeed a good chance that *in Phys*. 430,9-10 refers to the third work as still to be written: *Ton de peri toutôn entelesteron logon idiâi episkepsômetha*. This promise concludes an argument on the impossibility of infinite time, based on the impossibility of an eternal world (*in Phys*. 428,23-430,10). It parallels the announcements of the third treatise in *Aet*. 9,20-7 (*...en heterôi men proïontes...entelesteron deixomen*), 11,14-17 and 259,3-5 (*hôsper oun kai entelesteron idiâi deikhthêsetai...*).[127] And we know that the third work tried to prove not only the impossibility of the eternity of the *world*,[128] but also, separately, the impossibility of the infinity of *time*.[129] I am therefore inclined to believe that *in Phys*. 430,9-10 also announces the non-polemical treatise, and, consequently, that the final redaction of *in Physica* is anterior to this treatise. Is it possible that *in Phys*. 55,24-6 refers to *contra Aristotelem* (or rather both to *contra Aristotelem* and *de Aeternitate Mundi contra Proclum*)? I do not think that this can be ruled out (that is, at the present stage of investigation). After all, **in Physica 8* (written before *in Physica²*) was very close in content to *contra Aristotelem 6*. But even if *in Phys*. 55,24-6 was written after the *contra Aristotelem*, it refers primarily to the *de Aeternitate Mundi contra Proclum*. For *contra Aristotelem 1-5* was mainly devoted to a refutation of the theory of aether, *contra Aristotelem 6* mainly to a refutation of the eternity of movement. Problems *like* that of the eternity *a parte ante* of being are actually dealt with in *de Aeternitate Mundi contra Proclum*.[130]

As a result of my analysis I advance the hypothesis that *in Physica* was first written about 517, that a separate **in Physica 8* was composed after 529, and that the *Commentary* took its present form (through the insertion of at least the anti-eternalist texts) after 529 as well, either before or after *contra Aristotelem*,[131] almost certainly before the composition of the third treatise.[132]

(b) The date of in de Generatione et Corruptione and in de Anima-in de Intellectu

The inconsistencies which allowed us to distinguish earlier and later texts in the *in Physica* concerned the eternity of the world, the definition

[127] For these references see É. Évrard, *Philopon, Contre Aristote*, 16-19.

[128] cf. S. Pines, 'An Arabic summary of a lost work of John Philoponus', *Israel Oriental Studies* 2, 1972, 330-6.

[129] ibid., 325-30; Philoponus *Aet*. 117,20-1: 'We will show elsewhere that time has a beginning.'

[130] Such problems are: 'Whether body has been generated or not, whether the world has been generated or not, and, if it has, whether from things that are, or from things that are not', Philoponus *in Phys*. 55,20-2. In *Aet*. 9,8-10 (338,21-344,26) Philoponus argues that it is possible that the world has come into existence from absolute non-being.

[131] The *terminus ante quem* for the *contra Aristotelem* is the date of Simplicius' *in de Caelo*.

[132] The *terminus ante quem* for the third treatise is the date of Simplicius' *in Physica*.

of place and the existence of void. It soon emerges that, on the first of these subjects, *in de Generatione et Corruptione* and *in de Anima-in de Intellectu* agree with *in Physica*[1].

There can be no doubt that in *in de Generatione et Corruptione* and *in de Anima-in de Intellectu* Philoponus still accepts the eternity of movement, time and the world. As to *in de Generatione et Corruptione*: sublunary substantial change is a perpetual process of generation (*aeigenesia*), the efficient cause of which is the perpetual motion (*aeikinêsia*) of the heavenly bodies.[133] Movement as a whole is eternal,[134] change of place is eternal in so far as it is circular.[135] In Philoponus' exegesis of *de Generatione et Corruptione* 2.11, where Aristotle argues that an absolutely necessary, eternal movement can only be cyclical, nothing betrays even the slightest doubt about the correctness of Aristotle's doctrine.[136] Time is infinite.[137] Heavenly bodies are 'numerically' eternal,[138] sublunary living substances are 'specifically' eternal.[139] And of course, *in de Generatione et Corruptione* agrees with Aristotle's theory of the fifth element.[140] *In de Anima* also views movement as eternal[141] and time as infinite.[142] Heavenly bodies are eternal,[143] and so are sublunary species.[144] Here again the fifth element is evidently accepted.[145] In *in de Intellectu*, finally, Philoponus likewise appears to believe in the eternity of heavenly bodies[146] and mankind,[147] as well as in the theory of aether.[148]

Compared with the statements about the eternity of the world, Philoponus' position with regard to the definition of place and the existence of void in *in de Generatione et Corruptione* and *in de Anima-in*

---

[133] Philoponus *in GC* 49,12-13; 49,23; 288,19-289,22; 290,12-13; 290,24-5; 291,21-3; 296,14-17; 299,18-19.

[134] ibid., 299,22; 299,25; 300,1-3; 300,7-8.

[135] ibid., 312,17-18: 'It has been demonstrated in the eighth book of the *Physics* that only circular motion is eternal.'

[136] cf. R.B. Todd, 'Some concepts in physical theory in John Philoponus' Aristotelian commentaries', *Archiv für Begriffsgeschichte* 24, 1980, 159, n. 34: 'The commentary on the *GC* was probably an early work, since in discussing 2.10 and 11 Philoponus does not question Aristotle's theory that the movement of the heavenly bodies was eternal; such criticism…was to come later.'

[137] Philoponus *in GC* 45,5-6.

[138] ibid., 1,9-12; 3,1-4; 134,4-5; 206,2-4.

[139] ibid., 296,14-298,8.

[140] e.g. ibid., 129,6-14; 135,1-2; 135,23-4; 139,20-1; 144,21-2; 147,19-25; 199,4-6; 282,23-7; 283,1-10.

[141] Philoponus *in DA* 21,1-2; 132,32-133,3.

[142] ibid., 133,1-2.

[143] ibid., 18,27; 24,27-9; 141,2-4; 259,9-10; 324,15-16.

[144] ibid., 7,12-19; 228,16-17; 265,30-4; 268,6-9; 268,37-269,1; 269,26-7; 270,2-4; 270,29-30; 272,31-2; 279,11-12; 286,19-21; 286,32-4.

[145] ibid., 9,6-7; 9,14-15; 56,2-4.

[146] Philoponus *in de Intell.* 78,2-4.

[147] ibid., 52,21-3; 59,21-4.

[148] e.g. ibid., 32,67-8; 36,57-9.

de Intellectu is not so evident. However, what is clear is that the author has not yet developed in these commentaries the views he defends in the *Corollaries* of *in Physica*. Let us first examine the concept of place, beginning with *in de Generatione et Corruptione*. It is true that some passages in this work are somewhat ambiguous, because they try to define place on the basis of a connection between the concepts of a limit (*peras*) and an extension (*diastêma*).[149] But nowhere does one find the categorical opposition to the Aristotelian doctrine of place which is characteristic of part of the *in Physica*. On the contrary, the general impression is that Philoponus seems to agree with Aristotle, e.g. with *GC* 1.6, 322b33-323a1 ('position' belongs to those things which also have a 'place', tr. Forster):[150] on this occasion he recalls explicitly the Aristotelian concept of place.[151] Elsewhere place is defined as a boundary (*horos*),[152] as a relation of the surrounding to the surrounded.[153] In *in de Anima* the Aristotelian concept of place is not contested.[154] And in *in de Intellectu* there is a passage which implies that the non-Aristotelian definitions of place are false.[155]

The existence of void is rejected more than once in *in de Generatione et Corruptione*.[156] And one passage in *in de Anima* denies the possibility of movement through the void.[157]

I think that the materials gathered here are sufficient for us to affirm that *in de Generatione et Corruptione* and *in de Anima-in de Intellectu* were composed by Philoponus 1. As I have already said, it is less important for the moment whether these commentaries are earlier or later than *in Physica¹*. What is essential is that they allow us to complete the system we find in *in Physica¹*, without the risk, which is in principle present in my analysis of *in Physica*, of taking texts with a purely exegetical intention to contain Philoponus' personal views. The fact that e.g. the doctrine of the eternity of the world in *in de Generatione et*

---

[149] Philoponus *in GC* 73,28-30; 157,5-6.

[150] ibid., 132,12-13; 132,19.

[151] ibid., 134,1-4. The formula 'according to the argument on place handed down by Aristotle' does not seem to imply any reserve; rather it indicates the consistency of Aristotle's argument.

[152] ibid., 280,21-4.

[153] ibid., 301,28-9.

[154] Philoponus *in DA* 100,6-16.

[155] Philoponus *in de Intell.* 42,91-6: 'It is said in the fourth Book of the *Physics*, since there was doubt among the ancients about place, that it is necessary to give such an account of place that all the characteristics which it possesses according to its very concept are entailed in it, the doubts which are raised about it are solved, and the reason why the ancients went astray on the subject is revealed to us (*Dictum est autem in quarto De Naturali auditu, quoniam apud antiquos de loco ideo dubitabatur, quod oportet talem assignare de loco rationem, cui omnia quae secundum propriam intelligentiam insunt assequuntur, et dubitationes quae feruntur circa ipsum solvantur, et causam nobis manifestam faciat propter quam antiqui de ipso erraverunt)*'.

[156] Philoponus *in GC* 4,17; 73,8; 156,20-5; 178,21-2. 'For it was proved in the *Physics* that it is absolutely impossible for there to be void.'

[157] Philoponus *in DA* 359,10.

Corruptione and *in de Anima-in de Intellectu* is not only not contested, but even accepted by Philoponus in his own person, entitles us to consider the eternalist elements in *in Physica* as not merely exegetical, but representative of an *in Physica[1]* written according to the principles of Alexandrian Neoplatonism.

(c) The date of the Commentaries on the Organon

I have already mentioned that *in Analytica Posteriora* belongs to the same group as *in Physica* and *in Meteorologica*. With regard to the eternity of the world, it fits in with the commentaries of Philoponus 1.[158] However, at *in An. Post.* 242,14-243,25 Philoponus rejects the thesis that Aristotle accepted Plato's theory of Ideas. This means that he agrees here with *de Aeternitate Mundi contra Proclum*.[159] Hence *in An. Post.* 242,14-243,25[160] was written by Philoponus 2. According to Philoponus 1, on the contrary, Aristotle did accept the existence of transcendent Ideas as *logoi* in the demiurgic Intellect.[161] So we have to conclude that *in Analytica Posteriora*, just like *in Physica*, contains elements of both Philoponus 1 and 2, and that it received its present form at least partially around or after 529. This particular *volte-face* is set in a wider context in my chapter on Ammonius.

As far as I can see at present, *in Categorias* and *in Analytica Priora* do not contain anything which clearly belongs to the system of Philoponus 2. In the *in Categorias* Philoponus refers approvingly to *Physica 8* and explains the eternity of movement by reference to the infinite power of the first unmoved cause.[162] The world is eternal in its present structure; God creates it by necessity,[163] from all eternity.[164] At the time Philoponus wrote his *in Categorias* he had not yet changed his mind on the definition of place. More than once he refers explicitly to Aristotle's definition,[165] he alludes to it[166] or uses it.[167] And at least one text shows that the author had not yet developed the doctrine of the *Corollarium de inani* on the possibility of movement through the void.[168]

(d) The date of in Meteorologica

É. Évrard has proved that *in Meteorologica* in its present form has to be

[158] Philoponus *in An. Post.* 67,17-18 (implicitly); 110,14-15; 135,11-15.
[159] cf. nn. 16, 21 above.
[160] See also Philoponus *in An. Post.* 133,30-134,2.
[161] cf. n. 16 above.
[162] Philoponus *in Cat.* 50,23-31.
[163] ibid., 145,10-146,2.
[164] cf. Philoponus *in An. Post.* 243,17-24; 244,18-25.
[165] Philoponus *in Cat.* 33,22-6; 87,7-10, 'As we said before, place is the boundary of the surroundings insofar as it surrounds what is surrounded'; 165,1-2.
[166] ibid., 32,20-2.
[167] ibid., 99,29-30.
[168] ibid., 86,23-7.

set after *de Aeternitate Mundi contra Proclum*.[169] However, I have the impression that the text shows traces of an earlier version, that it is the result of a later revision which, just as in the *in Physica*, has produced some inconsistencies. At present I have to limit myself to one provisional remark, which poses the problem rather than solving it. It is well known that in his *in Meteorologica* Philoponus vigorously rejects Aristotle's theory of the fifth element.[170] On the other hand, there are a few passages where the author still seems to accept a fundamental difference between heavenly and sublunary reality (which is typical of the system of Philoponus 1). At *in Meteor.* 11,24-37 the heaven is considered as intermediate between intelligible and perishable being. At *in Meteor.* 12,24-32 also, heaven is ranked on a higher ontological level than the sublunary world.[171] Closer investigation is needed to answer the question whether the commentary presents still other anomalies which might reinforce the supposition that it is a revision by Philoponus 2 of an older version.

The motives for Philoponus' *volte-face*

I return now to the motives for Philoponus' *volte-face*. In Arabic philosophy there is a tradition that he 'deceived' his public. Let us start with the important findings of J.L. Kraemer on this subject.[172] The section on Philoponus in the *Ṣiwân al-Ḥikma* of as-Sijistânî (tenth century) deals with the Alexandrian's intentions when writing his *de Aeternitate Mundi contra Proclum* and *contra Aristotelem*. According to one of as-Sijistânî's sources, Philoponus undertook his refutations of both pagan philosophers (I quote Kraemer) 'in order to pacify the wrath of his fellow Christians, aroused by his preoccupation with the exegesis of Aristotle's works, and to protect himself against their threats of diverse forms of duress'.[173] According to another source he received money from

[169] cf. n. 4 above. Évrard is convinced that *in Meteorologica* was written between *de Aeternitate Mundi contra Proclum* and *contra Aristotelem*. According to C. Wildberg, 'Prolegomena to the Study of Philoponus' *contra Aristotelem*', in R. Sorabji (ed.), *Philoponus and the Rejection of Aristotelian Science*, 202-8, the *in Meteorologica* is later than *contra Aristotelem*.

[170] See É. Évrard, 'Les convictions religieuses', 328-34.

[171] Philoponus *in Meteor.* 12,30-1: 'And that (the heaven) by its essence transcends the bodies it encircles and governs everything by its activities.'

[172] J.L. Kraemer, 'A lost passage', 321-5.

[173] ibid., 322. There is a certain parallel here with what Philoponus himself says in the Preface of *de Opificio Mundi*. This work too appears to have been solicited by other Christians. The author begins by recalling that he has already devoted several books to the problem of creation, in order both to refute the pagan eternalists and to prove positively that the world had a beginning (1,6-14). Yet since then people have been continually putting a gentle pressure upon him (*sunekhôs hêmin ênôkhloun êrema pôs*), blaming him a little (*hupôneidizon*) for limiting himself to the refutation of philosophical arguments and not having done anything yet to defend the Mosaic creation story against its detractors (1,14-2,4). The person who urged Philoponus most of all was Sergius, the patriarch of Antioch, 2,4-8: 'You pressed on me heavily, urging me and almost even forcing me to contribute my best efforts to the cause (*...polus epekeiso protrepôn, mononoukhi kai*

the Christians for writing both treatises.[174] 'Both reports have in common', Kraemer writes, 'the view that Philoponus did not express his true convictions in the *contra Aristotelem* and in the *contra Proclum* but acted, according to the first, in the interest of self-protection or, according to the second, in the interest of material gain. Are these stories unfounded or do they contain a grain of truth? There are grounds for preferring the second alternative.'[175] Kraemer's references to other Arabic texts show that this view was not uncommon. Even Avicenna was convinced that Philoponus had deceived the Christians by trying to give the impression that he disagreed with Aristotle. And Avicenna adds the simple but invaluable remark that whoever studies Philoponus' other works, e.g. his *in de Generatione et Corruptione*, will not fail to notice his *agreement* with Aristotle.[176]

Thanks to the work of M. Mahdi we know that al-Farabi, in his *Against John the Grammarian*, likewise held that Philoponus' *contra Aristotelem* did not express the Alexandrian's real conviction. I quote, in Mahdi's translation, the end of al-Farabi's Introduction to his treatise:

> Then, in many of his objections and in many of [the things] by means of which he (Philoponus) seeks to free himself from the doubts that he raises against himself [or his own position], he makes use of the opinions [or doctrines] laid down [or legislated] in [various] religions [or religious communities] and whatever consequences follow from them [that is, from these religious opinions]. It is unlikely that he did not understand how far removed these opinions are from the nature of things. Therefore one may suspect that his intention from what he does in refuting Aristotle is either to defend the opinions laid down in his own religion about the world, or to remove from himself [the suspicion] that he disagrees with the position held by the people of his religion and approved by their rulers, so as not to suffer the same fate as Socrates.[177]

Maybe – but this is just a prudent suggestion – a glimpse of the same accusation is to be found in Simplicius. As we shall see,[178] there are reasons for suspecting that Simplicius knows more about Philoponus than he claims. If this is correct, at least one of his sneers at Philoponus might be taken to allude to the insincerity of his adversary. 'No one,' he

---

biazomenos, ta eis emên suneispherein tôi pragmati dunamin)'. At the moment he wrote these words (546-9 G. Reichardt, W. Wolska or 557-60 É. Évrard, H.D. Saffrey) Philoponus' anti-eternalist treatises and commentaries had already been published for some time. If the Christians were not yet completely satisfied with *de Aeternitate Mundi contra Proclum, contra Aristotelem* etc., it is not difficult to imagine what their attitude must have been about 529, when Philoponus had produced mainly Aristotelian-Neoplatonic philosophical writings, without any contribution to the Christian cause.

[174] J.L. Kraemer, 'A lost passage', 323, draws attention to the resemblance between this allegation and Damascius' famous remark about the agreement of Ammonius with the ecclesiastical authorities.

[175] J.L. Kraemer, op. cit., 322.

[176] ibid., 323-4.

[177] M. Mahdi, 'Alfarabi against Philoponus', 256-7.

[178] cf. p. 263 below.

says, 'aimed in such an unserious way, because of the prevailing worthless conceptions about the demiurge of the world, only at *seeming to* oppose those who demonstrate the eternity of the world.'[179]

Obviously, some elements of the Arabic tradition concerning Philoponus' deception of the Christians (e.g. Avicenna's remark on *in de Generatione et Corruptione*) are nothing more than the result of an interpretation of the doctrinal duality in his philosophy. But one cannot for that reason reject the tradition in its entirety. After all, the facts are that Philoponus started his philosophical career as an adherent of Ammonius and that in 529 he wrote *de Aeternitate Mundi contra Proclum*, a book in which he radically abjured his philosophical past. For it is impossible to conceive the relation between the basic tenets of e.g. *in de Anima* and *in de Generatione et Corruptione* on the one hand, and those of *de Aeternitate Mundi contra Proclum* on the other as a gradual process of moving away from Alexandrian Neoplatonism. There *is* an evolution (in the proper sense) from *de Aeternitate Mundi contra Proclum* via *contra Aristotelem* through *de Opificio Mundi*.[180] But 529 is a clear rupture with the past, and for this rupture we have to find an explanation. There can be little doubt that it had something to do with the hostile attitude of Justinian towards the teaching of pagan philosophy. In 529 at the latest Philoponus must have felt the necessity of publicly renouncing his earlier philosophy. Maybe, as the Arabic tradition suggests, the Christians, in one way or another, were powerful enough to force him to do so. On this hypothesis (which covers several possibilities: serious threats, moral pressure, promise of remuneration etc.), the Christians put pressure on Philoponus because he must have been a famous philosopher by then, and because they had never ceased to claim him as a Christian and/or because he himself continued to play that role (notwithstanding his adherence to the philosophy of Ammonius). Or else they considered him a renegade to whom, for lack of a better protagonist, they offered another chance. Anyway, Philoponus was cooperative. This may have been due to fear, but it is not impossible either that there was something more. As we have seen, there is some evidence that Philoponus (continued or) started *teaching* philosophy after 529. Apparently, he wished to remain active as a philosopher, and considered his *volte-face* as the beginning of a new period in his *philosophical* career. Perhaps his fellow Christians and he himself tried to use the new situation in order to establish Christian philosophy at the Alexandrian school. Launching an attack on *Proclus* for Philoponus had a double advantage. First, it associated him with the spirit of Justinian's action against Athenian philosophy. Secondly, it offered him the possibility of attacking Ammonius only indirectly, of diverting the

---

[179] Simplicius *in Cael.* 59,13-15: *...oudeis mentoi kakoskholôs houtôs eis monon apeblepsen to antitetakhthai dokein tois aidion ton kosmon apodeiknusi dia tas kratousas euteleis ennoias peri tou ton kosmon dêmiourgêsantos.* On the meaning of formulas like *hai kratousai ennoiai* cf. below.

[180] cf. below.

public's attention from the fact that he was a former adherent of Ammonius.[181] Moreover, it is reasonable to suppose that, in the lost Introduction to *de Aeternitate Mundi contra Proclum*, Philoponus justified his sudden change of position in one way or another. Even in the remaining corpus of the treatise there are a few allusions which may offer an indication of the manner in which the author wanted his audience to understand his transition from Neoplatonic to Christian philosophy. It appears that he turned things upside down, and that he was trying to convince his readers that his Neoplatonic works (up to 529) did not express his personal views, but were produced under some kind of external pressure. This seems to be implied in Philoponus' references to Plato's fear of the masses. In order not to suffer the same fate as Socrates (one should remember what al-Farabi says about Philoponus himself) Plato often conformed to popular mythology and was silent about his real conviction: *...phoboi polla tôn deontôn aposesigêken.*[182] In the same way, Philoponus wants to imply, I myself, going along like Plato with the

[181] It is noteworthy that Ammonius is not mentioned by name in *de Aeternitate Mundi contra Proclum* (at least not in the surviving text). By contrast, *in Analytica Posteriora* and *in Physica* contain passages overtly polemicising against *ho philosophos* (cf. n. 31 above), and in the *in Meteorologica* Ammonius is mentioned as *ho hêmeteros didaskalos* (91,3) and *ho hêmeteros didaskalos Ammônios Hermeiou* (106,9). A possible explanation of this difference might be that Philoponus wrote the commentaries just mentioned in connection with a teaching activity of his (within the school there would have been no sense in trying to conceal his philosophical past). *De Aeternitate Mundi contra Proclum*, on the other hand, was written for a larger audience, and Philoponus may have been prudent enough not to draw special attention to his relation with the pagan scholarch Ammonius. I think there is a text in *de Aeternitate Mundi contra Proclum* that might substantiate this view. In *Aet.* 9,11 (344,27-365,11) the author argues that the *eidos* of material beings comes to be out of and perishes into absolute non-being. In order to reach this conclusion he rules out, one by one, seven other possibilities (cf. 316,3-14). The last of these alternative solutions is introduced by the following sentence: 'Driven into a corner by these and similar arguments of ours, and trying, not clumsily at all, to rescue his own opinion, he invented an argument like this' (359,14-17). This text suggests that Philoponus is referring here to an oral discussion (whether fictitious or not), a discussion which, of course, he cannot remember literally. After the 'quotation' he writes: 'Such was *his* (*ekeinou*) argument, and we refuted the plausible element in the argument (*Ta men oun par'ekeinou toiauta. Kai hêmeis de tou logou toutou to pithanon apelenkhontes*)', 360,8-11. Who is 'he (*ekeinos*)'? Obviously it is not Proclus. This might also be inferred from the fact that Philoponus, when he quotes Proclus, habitually indicates the work from which the quotation comes (cf. in the present context *Aet.* 364,5-6). In my opinion *ekeinos* might very well be Ammonius. It has to be someone on the 'Hellenic' side. Moreover, it has to be someone whom Philoponus' readers in 529 know or can assume to have had personal contact with Philoponus. Finally, it must be someone who both is very well known (otherwise there would be no sense in using *ekeinos*) and whose name Philoponus, apparently by some *damnatio memoriae*, does not want to mention publicly. This interpretation, if correct, implies that in 529 Philoponus tried to assure his readers that he had already been opposing eternalism at the time he was still a pupil of Ammonius.

[182] Philoponus *Aet.* 331,17-332,23, quoting (332,1-11) Plato *Epist.* 5, 322A-B. The reference to silence out of fear, combined with the opposition 'secret belief in a personal god versus apparent agreement with paganism' seems to leave no room for the possibility that Philoponus' allusion is to his being threatened by the Christians himself. Yet, there is no fundamental objection either, I think, to crediting Philoponus' story about Plato with a double basis.

prevailing opinion (*têi tote kratousêi doxêi hepomenos*),[183] and in order not
to become a victim of pagan fanaticism,[184] have been expounding a
philosophy with which I did not agree. Most significant in this respect is
what Philoponus, *contra Proclum* 2,2 (26,20-33,5) writes about Aristotle's
criticism of Plato's theory of Ideas, although the suggested excuse is less
strong here. Quoting *EN* 1.6, 1096a11-17,[185] Philoponus implicitly
parallels Aristotle's relationship to Plato with his own relationship to
Ammonius: Plato (Ammonius) is a friend, a greater friend the truth
(*amicus Plato (Ammonius), magis amica veritas*). And when he refers to
Aristotle's 'respect for his teacher' (*hê aidôs hê pros ton didaskalon*) he
may first of all have in mind the effect of this formula on the way his
readers will appreciate his own 'emancipation' from Ammonius. The
philosopher, we are told, must be prepared, not only to correct the errors
of others for the sake of truth, but also to revise his own suppositions if
these prove to be incorrect.[186] Philoponus is no longer implying here (as
he is when talking about Plato's fear of the masses) that he has been
forced to hide his real conviction. Rather, he seems to concede that he has
been erring himself, and he is prepared to abjure his earlier philosophy
(*elenkhein tas oikeias hupotheseis*). Doesn't all this sound like an attempt
to create the impression that he feels guilty about his past? I think the
frequency of announcements of the anti-eternalist books still to be
written, announcements that culminated in the lost *proanaphônêsis tôn
hexês*[187] at the end of the work, points in the same direction. What is the
reason for this strongly marked concern to remove all possible doubt
about his position? Doesn't it seem as if the author feels the need to
compensate? Promise is debt, but isn't the reverse true as well? In my
view all these announcements are to be explained by the fact that the *de
Aeternitate Mundi contra Proclum* was a very surprising publication to
the Alexandrian public, and that no one expected such a book from

---

[183] Philoponus *Aet.* 635,22-3. Similar formulas are often used by pagan authors to refer to
the dominant position of Christianity. A. Cameron, 'The last days of the Academy', 18 gives
four instances from Damascius' *Vita Isidori* (including the fragment on Ammonius: fr. 316,
251 Zintzen). The term 'the present (*ta paronta*)' is used in a similar sense by Proclus ('the
present time, *ho parôn khronos*'), Damascius, Simplicius and Olympiodorus (A. Cameron,
op. cit., 15). On the other hand such formulas also occur in Christian authors: cf. I. Hadot,
'Le problème du néoplatonisme alexandrin', 23-4, n. 31.

[184] Philoponus may have hoped that the allusion reminded his readers of the fact that in a
not too distant past Christian students were not always accepted in Alexandrian academic
life. Zacharias, *Vita Severi*, 22-7 Kugener tells the story (c. 485-7 AD) of an
aspirant-Christian, Paralios, beaten up by his pagan fellow-students with the Grammarian
Horapollo the Younger; cf. H.I. Marrou, 'Synesius of Cyrene and Alexandrian
Neoplatonism', in A. Momigliano (ed.), *The Conflict between Paganism and Christianity in
the Fourth Century*, Oxford 1963, 136-7.

[185] Philoponus *Aet.* 30,25-31,7. On *Aet.* 2,2 in its entirety cf. L. Tarán, 'Amicus Plato sed
magis amica veritas. From Plato and Aristotle to Cervantes', *Antike und Abendland*, 30,
1984, 112-14.

[186] Philoponus *Aet.* 30,15-25: ...*kai dikaion...*, *philosophous ontas, mê monon tas allôn
hupotheseis epi sôtêriâi tês alêtheias elenkhein alla kai tas oikeias hekaston, ei mê têi
alêtheiâi sumphônoi heuretheien*.

[187] ibid., 611,25-6.

Philoponus. Consequently, the author had a great interest in presenting his new theories as part of a larger programme, a new cosmology with which he wanted to be identified in the future. He, or those who commissioned the book, must have felt that the *de Aeternitate Mundi contra Proclum* alone did not justify forgetting and forgiving the entire 'Ammonian' production of Philoponus. That is, I think, why he tried to diminish the incredulous amazement of the people who knew him as a philosopher. By promising the publication of the *contra Aristotelem* and of the third, non-polemical work about the creation of the world, he obviously wanted to get credit for the future. The fact that Philoponus offered a programme for a new philosophy and his assurance of personal reliability and predictability might both point to an attempt at establishing Christian philosophical *teaching* in Alexandria.

Simplicius' acquaintance with Philoponus

Simplicius' contention that he never met the Grammarian (*in Cael.* 26,18-19) is mostly believed to be sincere.[188] Consequently, an explanation is sought for this 'fact'.[189] However, one cannot rule out the possibility that Simplicius is indulging here in a haughty lie: that newcomer in philosophy (*nearos: in Cael.* 42,17), that philologist, professional philosophers did not even take notice of him. It might be significant that Simplicius does not write 'whom I have never even seen (*hon oude etheasamên pôpote*)'. For there may have been, at the time he published his *in de Caelo*, enough former pupils of Ammonius among the philosophical public to know that this statement (and, at the same time, Simplicius' 'depersonalisation' of the controversy) was a lie (if it was a lie indeed). He writes: 'whom I am not conscious of ever having even seen (*hon oude ('not even') theasamenos oida pôpote*)' which, I presume, is not the same as 'whom I know I never saw (*hon oudepôpote theasamenos oida*)'. This might imply the following calculation: maybe there are readers who know for sure that Simplicius and Philoponus were in Ammonius' school at about the same time. Well, in that case they certainly will get the message, namely that for real philosophers the Grammarian was simply negligible. The sincerity of Simplicius' claim not to know Philoponus has recently been questioned again by H.J. Blumenthal.[190] On the other hand one should not go so far as to suppose that Simplicius' hostility towards Philoponus was *primarily* inspired by a personal grudge, for instance about the succession to Ammonius. In this I

---

[188] cf. recently P. Hoffmann, 'Simplicius' polemics: some aspects of Simplicius' polemical writings against John Philoponus: from invective to a reaffirmation of the transcendency of the heavens', in R. Sorabji (ed.), *Philoponus and the Rejection of Aristotelian Science*, 68.

[189] cf. e.g. H.D. Saffrey, 'Le chrétien Jean Philopon', 402, n. 4: 'It would be explicable that Simplicius did not meet Philoponus at Alexandria, if he was a philosophy student, when Philoponus was still a philology student.'

[190] H.J. Blumenthal, '529 and its sequel: what happened to the Academy?', *Byzantion* 48, 1978, 379-80, and 'John Philoponus: Alexandrian Platonist?', 318.

agree with K. Praechter against Gudeman and Wieland.[191] Yet there are enough elements to venture the hypothesis that Simplicius *did* know Philoponus. The mere fact that he claims three times not to know his opponent (*in Cael.* 26,19; 49,24-5; 90,12) is already sufficient in itself to raise suspicion. Further, if Simplicius does not know Philoponus, where did he get his information about him? It is true that much of what Simplicius says about Philoponus' lack of philosophical education is based just on what Philoponus wrote. Some of it even could be taken to be deduced *a priori* from the title 'Grammarian' (*in Cael.* 119,7: *houtos ho Grammatikon heauton epigraphôn*). But how does Simplicius know that Philoponus never had a teacher in Platonic philosophy? At *in Cael.* 84,11-13 he writes: 'But since – I don't know how – Plato's views seem to please this individual (Philoponus), although he had no teachers in that matter, as they say (*hôs phasi*), and although he has not investigated himself with (real) love of knowledge the true meaning of (what) Plato (said) either...'. The formula *hôs phasi* might very well be a rather transparent attempt to hide the truth. Or is the statement that Philoponus had no teachers in Platonic philosophy just an inference from the fact (which, one might argue, could be verified in the libraries) that the Grammarian never seriously devoted himself to Platonic exegesis, if that is the meaning of 'neither having himself examined Plato's intention with any care (*mête auton philomathôs ezêtêkota ton tou Platônos noun*)'? Regardless of whether or not Simplicius is completely sincere here, the text seems relevant to a possible limitation of Ammonius' teaching to Aristotelian philosophy (cf. Chapter 10 above).

The evolution of Philoponus 2

I shall sum up my chronological conclusions briefly. The publication of the *de Aeternitate Mundi contra Proclum* in 529 marks a decisive break in Philoponus' philosophical production. Before that date the author was what we might call an 'Alexandrian Neoplatonist'. On the basis of the teaching of Ammonius he edited several commentaries which display the philosophical system that I have called 'Philoponus 1'. Among the surviving texts the following belong to this first group: *in Categorias*, *in Analytica Priora*, *in de Generatione et Corruptione* and *in de Anima-in de Intellectu*. To these one should add *in Physica¹*, probably the earlier stratum of *in Analytica Posteriora*, and maybe some older parts of *in Meteorologica*. The *de Aeternitate Mundi contra Proclum* was probably Philoponus' first anti-eternalist work. It was followed by the *contra Aristotelem* and by at least one other work on the creation of the world. At the same time Philoponus 2, probably for teaching purposes, revised some of the earlier exegetical material. The most obvious case of revision is the *in Physica*. There were at least two successive stages in this revision.

---

[191] K. Praechter, 'Simplikios', in G. Wissowa and W. Kroll (eds), *Realencyclopädie der klassischen Altertumswissenschaft* III A, 1, 1927, col. 204; A. Gudeman, 'Ioannes Philoponus', cols 1766-7; W. Wieland, 'Die Ewigkeit der Welt', 301.

Philoponus first wrote an anti-eternalist commentary on *Physica 8* (**in Physica 8*). Afterwards he inserted, in the original text (*in Physica¹*), a number of anti-eternalist passages (*in Physica²*). I assume that both **in Physica 8* and *in Physica²* are later than the *de Aeternitate Mundi contra Proclum* and earlier than the third, non-polemical treatise. *In Analytica Posteriora* has a passage on the doctrine of Ideas which is clearly Philoponus 2. *In Meteorologica* in its present form is Philoponus 2 as well. I have limited myself in this chapter to the problem of distinguishing Philoponus 1 from Philoponus 2. My chronology involves only one new element for relative dating within one group, namely the posteriority of *in Physica²* to the *de Aeternitate Mundi contra Proclum*. The relative chronology of *in Categorias, in Analytica Priora, in de Generatione et Corruptione* and *in de Anima-in de Intellectu* awaits further investigation.

Obviously, there are many problems left. On p. 243 I indicated two of them, and proposed an answer to the first: the failure to rewrite *in Physica* completely. As to the second, the failure to revise the other early commentaries, we can only speculate. The non-revised commentaries pertain to logic (*in Categorias, in Analytica Priora*), natural philosophy (*in de Generatione et Corruptione*) and psychology (*in de Anima-in de Intellectu*). We just don't know why *in Categorias* (one might plausibly argue that *in Analytica Priora* hardly needed any revision) was not revised, whereas *in Analytica Posteriora* was, nor why Philoponus 2 rewrote *in Physica* and *in Meteorologica*, but not *in de Generatione et Corruptione*. Only with regard to *in de Anima-in de Intellectu* could one reasonably propose an explanation. The *Neoplatonic* inspiration of this commentary, one might say, was so dominant that in this case a dichotomy between mere exegesis of Aristotle and criticism of him (such as is found in the *in Physica*) was not possible. Moreover, the ontological place of the human rational soul was a major difficulty for Philoponus 2, as I shall explain below. If it is true that Philoponus 2 made his revisions for teaching purposes, then it is legitimate, I think, to suppose that his lectures must have been primarily about natural philosophy. After all, the philosophy of Philoponus 2 was primarily a cosmology.

The difference between the systems of Philoponus 1 and Philoponus 2 cannot be explained by supposing a gradual evolution from Alexandrian Neoplatonism to the Christian doctrine of creation to be found in the *de Aeternitate Mundi contra Proclum* etc. In the first section of this chapter I summarised the main discontinuities between Philoponus 1 and Philoponus 2. One can assume an evolution only when there is room for some intermediate stage. But what could possibly serve as the middle term between Philoponus 1 and 2 on such questions as the eternity of the world, divine freedom, the harmony of Plato and Aristotle, the principle 'nothing comes from nothing', etc.? One of the most striking examples of Philoponus' *volte-face* is the radical change in his interpretation of Plato's psychogony (*Tim.* 34-6).[192]

---

[192] This is clear from a comparison between *in DA* 115,22-121,10 and *Aet.* 6,24

By contrast, there certainly is an evolution properly so-called from the *de Aeternitate Mundi contra Proclum* via the *contra Aristotelem* through to the *de Opificio Mundi*. For, although this last (a commentary on the *Hexaemeron*) is a theological work, it represents in certain respects the final stage of Philoponus' *philosophical* thinking. I shall briefly indicate a few points to substantiate my thesis. It is not unlikely that the *de Aeternitate Mundi contra Proclum* was written rather quickly: the situation no doubt required prompt action. As a result, the book is not free from inconsistencies and concealed aporias.

(1) For instance, there is some hesitation with regard to the problem of the unity of divine will: is it a simple, unique will,[193] or is it rather to be conceived as invariance through successive acts of will?[194] In principle Philoponus affirms the former alternative, but actually he is forced to use the latter.

(2) A similar ambiguity is to be found in his concept of God's intellective activity. In principle divine thinking is conceived as a static 'thinking all things at once *(panta hama noein)*';[195] on the other hand, it is said not to exclude a succession of 'earlier *(proteron)*' and 'later *(husteron)*',[196] if that succession is not understood as a temporal one.[197]

(3) A major aporia in *de Aeternitate Mundi contra Proclum* – I come to the evolution of Philoponus 2 now – is the place of angels (transcendent intellects) in the order of creation. There is no doubt, Philoponus says, that they have been created by God:[198] God is the efficient cause of intelligible substances.[199] On the other hand, one important new principle on which Philoponus 2 bases his system is the principle of the posteriority of the effect to its (efficient) cause. This means that an eternal being cannot have a cause. A being is either eternal or created: eternal creation is impossible.[200] Only God has no cause.[201] The aporia is clear: angels have been created; hence they cannot be eternal *a parte ante*. But in Philoponus 1 the eternity of transcendent intellects had been

---

(195,7-200,3). I shall expound the results of this comparison in a separate paper. There is no doubt that the opposition Philoponus 1-Philoponus 2 appears likewise in the interpretation (eternalist versus literal) of Plato's cosmogony. I must reserve this matter too for later. But it has to be mentioned here that Philoponus in his *in Nicomachi Introductionem Arithmeticam* gives up silently Ammonius' (and his own earlier) eternalist understanding of Plato's cosmogony. This was established by L. Tarán, *Asclepius of Tralles*, 10-12, 74 on the basis of a comparison between Asclepius *in Nicom.* I, 3, 68-9 and Philoponus *in Nicom.* I, 3, 54-8. On the other hand, there are elements in Philoponus' *Commentary on Nicomachus* that recall 'Philoponus 1' rather than 'Philoponus 2'. This could mean that in this case too there was a later revision and adaptation of an earlier text.

193 e.g. Philoponus *Aet.* 81,12-25; 568,6-16; 573,13-574,12.

194 e.g. ibid., 80,26-7; 574,13-578,9; 583,23-584,3.

195 e.g. ibid., 575,21-2; cf. 568,21-8; 570,18-571,2. Philoponus 1 uses the formula to characterise the activity of the demiurgic Intellect: *in DA* 126,26-7; 132,30-1.

196 Philoponus *Aet.* 583,12-23; cf. 114,19-116,1.

197 cf. ibid., 584,11-18.

198 ibid., 110,3-4; 575,13-14.

199 cf. ibid., 171,4-6.

200 ibid., 14,14-20; cf. 23,20-1; 473,23-5.

201 Philoponus ap. Simplicium *in Phys.* 1141,19.

so obvious[202] that in 529 he does not yet dare to deny their eternity outright. However, he no longer explicitly calls them eternal either.[203] It seems that in the *de Aeternitate Mundi contra Proclum* he deliberately avoids deciding. In the *contra Aristotelem* his position may have become clearer.[204] In the *de Opificio Mundi*, he finally solves the problem by siding with Basil's view that creation is divided into two stages: a purely angelic phase precedes the creation of the sensible world.[205] Accordingly, angels are not eternal *a parte ante*. God creates them at a certain 'moment' before the creation of the sensible world;[206] their coming into existence is a 'supramundane coming into being *(huperkosmios genesis)*'.[207]

(4) Obviously, the problem with eternal created beings returns at the level of rational soul in the broad sense of the term. I will first give some brief indications concerning *celestial* souls. Philoponus 1 was convinced that in the case of heavenly bodies (as opposed to sublunary bodies, both simple and composite) there is an identity of natural and psychogenic movement. This theory had the function of harmonising Plato and Aristotle, and Philoponus 1 ascribed it to Aristotle himself.[208] Actually he gave two different versions of it in the *de Anima*.[209] The first variant, taken from Alexander of Aphrodisias,[210] was this: heavenly soul just *is* the nature of heavenly bodies *(phusis estin hê psukhê)*, i.e. it is the only moving principle in the realm of the fifth element and it moves automatically. The second variant was this: heavenly bodies have both a bodily nature and a soul which differs from it: accordingly they possess a double movement, one caused by their nature and another caused by their soul; however, the two movements are identical, they coincide in a single, circular, movement.[211] In the first case the identity natural movement-psychogenic movement[212] is only 'subjective', i.e. it is we who say that the soul of the

---

[202] Intelligible substances are *autoenergeiai*, i.e. pure acts. Cf. e.g. Philoponus *in DA* 35,1-2; 63,12-14; 94,18; 216,33-5; 297,10-11; *in de Intell.* 84,63-9 *(autoactus, autoenergia)*; Ammonius *in Int.* 248,17-31; 250,34-251,1.

[203] Philoponus *Aet.* 576,19-21: 'It is possible, or rather necessary, that intellective substances should exist, even when the world does not', strictly speaking affirms only the pre-existence of intellective substances compared to the material world, not their eternity. But the latter is, of course, implied.

[204] Simplicius *in Phys.* 1159,18-19: 'The eternity which he (Philoponus) thinks fitting only to God (*...tês aidiotêtos, hên houtos [i.e. Philoponus] monôi tôi theôi prosêkein oietai...)*'.

[205] Philoponus *Opif.* 16,19-17,3, quoting Basil *Hom. in Hexaemeron* PG 29, 13C. Philoponus defines Basil's position as follows: 'That there was some condition of reality older than the creation of the world, suited to the intellective powers above the cosmos', 16,20-2.

[206] Philoponus *Opif.* 26,21-27,6; 34,21-35,10; cf. 33,6-25; 45,10-12.

[207] ibid., 25,22-3.

[208] Philoponus *in DA* 138,21-3.

[209] ibid., 101,34-102,31.

[210] ibid., 102,1; cf. e.g. Alexander ap. Simplicium, *in Phys.* 1219,3-5; H.A. Wolfson, 'The problem of the souls of the spheres from the Byzantine commentaries on Aristotle through the Arabs and St Thomas to Kepler', *Dumbarton Oaks Papers* 16, 1962, 69, 72-5.

[211] Roughly speaking this was the view of Simplicius; cf. e.g. *in Cael.* 387,12-19; H.A. Wolfson, op. cit., 75-6.

[212] Philoponus *in DA* 102,17.

heavenly body is its nature or principle of movement: there is no principle of movement other than soul, and consequently no movement other than psychogenic movement either. In the second case the identity natural movement-psychogenic movement is objective: the heavenly body has two different principles of movement, nature and soul, which together produce a single movement. Philoponus 1 does not seem to have a clear preference for either of these versions. This preference is only a matter of secondary importance for him in comparison with what is common to both versionŝ, namely the conviction that the heavenly body and heavenly soul are inseparably united.

In *de Aeternitate Mundi contra Proclum* the author maintains the existence of heavenly soul(s). However, his view on the relation heavenly body-heavenly soul is not the same anymore in this treatise as in *in de Anima*.[213] The second version of *in de Anima* has disappeared. Philoponus' rejection of Aristotle's theory of aether[214] made it impossible for him at this stage to consider the circular movement of heaven as an effect of the peculiar nature of the heavenly body itself any longer. On the other hand, the first version of *in de Anima*, paradoxical as this may seem, could be maintained. Already in the earlier work it was said (first version) that circular *movement* is natural for the heavens, while at the same time the *principle* of this movement, namely soul, is a force superior to the heavenly body itself (*kreittôn dunamis*).[215] Hence heavenly movement is natural (*kata phusin*), but not caused by nature (*oukh hupo phuseôs, mê phusei*).[216] This view was still usable in 529. It is argued now that circular movement is natural for the heavens, not in so far as it is a body, but in so far as it is a living being, animated by soul.[217] As a body, the heaven is motionless;[218] it has no principle of movement on its own. It is moved only by soul, a force superior to body (*kreittôn dunamis*).[219] Although the principle of circular movement is supernatural for the body of the heaven (*huper tên tou sômatos autou phusin*),[220] the movement itself is natural for the heaven as a living being.[221] This view, which in *in de Anima* had nothing to do with any doubt about the eternity of celestial movement, in *de Aeternitate Mundi contra Proclum* unexpectedly offered the opportunity both for affirming and for denying the eternity of heavenly soul, as I shall immediately explain. The second version of *in de Anima* is deliberately cut out: in 529 Philoponus had not yet reached the point where he could conceive a nature of the heavenly body itself which

---

[213] I thank Richard Sorabji for helping me to clarify my argument. cf. his *Matter, Space and Motion*, London and Ithaca NY 1988, 241, 246.

[214] Philoponus *Aet.* 492,5-493,24; 517,7-519,17.

[215] Philoponus *in DA* 102,2.

[216] ibid., 102,1; 102,18.

[217] Philoponus *Aet.* 485,5-10 (Plato and Philoponus); 487,17-20; cf. 489,28-490,1.

[218] ibid., 489,24-490,1.

[219] ibid., 492,26-7

[220] ibid., 492,27-493,1. For the whole argument in *Aet.* cf. É. Évrard, *Les convictions religieuses*, 309-14.

[221] cf. n. 217 above.

was (1) different from heavenly soul, (2) responsible on its own for the circular movement of the heaven, (3) yet different from the nature of Aristotle's fifth element. Only in *contra Aristotelem* will he be able again to regard the circular movement of the heaven as the effect, not only of the presence of heavenly soul, but also of the bodily nature of the heaven. In 529, by contrast, he is still of the opinion that the elements in their natural places are motionless by themselves.[222]

In *contra Aristotelem* Philoponus still holds to the theory of heavenly soul, a fact that provokes Simplicius' surprise.[223] As I have already indicated, he can fall back now on the second view of his *in de Anima*: heavenly movement is caused both by the nature of the heavenly body and by heavenly soul;[224] there is an identity between the natural inclination (*phusikê rhopê*) of the body and the impulse caused by the soul (*hê tês psukhês hormê*), as in the case of a bird flying straight down.[225] In contrast to *in de Anima*, however, *contra Aristotelem* finds that Aristotle is contradicting himself on the subject.[226] In contrast to *de Aeternitate Mundi contra Proclum*, on the other hand, Philoponus has now succeeded in conceiving the nature of the heavenly body as something which is different from heavenly soul, which is responsible on its own for the circular movement of the heaven, and yet is different from the nature of Aristotle's fifth element. Apart from being caused by the soul, the circular movement of heaven is also the effect of the very nature of its body. In this last respect there is no difference between heavenly movement and the circular movement of the sphere of fire and of the upper air, a movement which is natural for those elements as totalities, in their natural place.[227]

In the *de Opificio Mundi*, finally, Philoponus completely gives up the doctrine of celestial soul. What is the moving principle of heavenly bodies? It is impossible, he argues, to say that they are moved by angels. For how could bodies of that size continue to be moved over such distances by an unnatural (*para phusin*) moving force? Why would it be impossible for God, who created heavenly bodies, at the same time to put in them a natural force to make them move in a circle, a force similar to the heaviness and lightness in bodies that move in a straight line?[228] *De Opificio Mundi* 6,2 is largely devoted to the refutation of the presence of souls in heavenly bodies.[229]

The evolution of the later Philoponus with regard to the problem of heavenly soul is clear: *de Aeternitate Mundi contra Proclum* accepts its

[222] cf. É. Évrard, loc. cit.
[223] Simplicius *in Cael.* 91,17-19.
[224] ibid., 78,17-21.
[225] ibid., 79,8-13.
[226] ibid., 78,21-79,8; 79,13-14.
[227] ibid., 34,5-11; cf. E. Evrard, op. cit., 318-20.
[228] Philoponus *Opif.* 28,20-29,9. Movement is either natural or unnatural (29,5-7). Both movement by immanent souls (formerly 'supernatural') and movement by external intellects (angels) are considered now 'contrary to nature (*para phusin*)'.
[229] Philoponus *Opif.* 231, 3-233,17.

existence, but does not identify it with the nature of the heavenly body itself; *contra Aristotelem* both accepts the existence of heavenly soul and identifies the effect of its activity with the movement caused by the nature of the corresponding body itself; *de Opificio Mundi* rejects the existence of heavenly soul and reduces the capacity for circular movement to an inanimate nature.

Now, what has all this to do with the question of the *eternity* of celestial souls? I think that the evolution just outlined is relevant to this problem as well. *De Aeternitate Mundi contra Proclum*, first, in considering heavenly soul as a principle which is supernatural to the heavenly body, clearly uncouples the question of the eternity of the former from that of the eternity of the latter. This uncoupling creates the opportunity of denying the eternity *a parte ante* of the heaven without necessarily denying the eternity *a parte ante* of heavenly soul. I cannot enter here in detail into Philoponus' position with regard to the eternity of world soul and heavenly souls in 529. It may be sufficient at present to point out that the main problem in this respect is to determine how far Philoponus' interpretation of Plato's cosmogony and psychogony can be taken to reflect his own views. There is some ambiguity. On the one hand Philoponus assumes that for Plato the world soul is eternal *a parte ante*, which implies that it existed as a pure intellect before it became the animating principle of the material world.[230] This is the view which is predominant in *de Aeternitate Mundi contra Proclum*; it is the guiding principle of the interpretation Philoponus 2 gives of the psychogony of the *Timaeus*. On the other hand there is at least one text that creates the impression that Philoponus does not exclude a possible coming into existence of the Platonic world soul.[231] Does this exegetical hesitation reflect indecision on the part of Philoponus himself? I think it does. Anyhow, the uncoupling of heavenly soul and heavenly body fortunately leaves room both for the eternity and for the non-eternity of heavenly souls. Obviously, Philoponus' problem in this case was the same as in the case of transcendent intellects (angels). The revised concept of efficient causality excluded the eternity of heavenly souls. But in the *de Aeternitate Mundi contra Proclum* Philoponus still seems to have recoiled from drawing this conclusion at once. In the *contra Aristotelem*, by contrast, he may have cut the knot. The psychogenic movement of heaven is again identified here with the natural movement of the heavenly body. Obviously this movement cannot be eternal *a parte ante*. But what about the eternity of heavenly soul itself? Strictly speaking the soul might be eternal without animating the body from eternity. Yet the union between body and soul is closer now than it was in *de Aeternitate Mundi contra Proclum*. The reintroduction of the nature of the heavenly body as the co-principle of its movement clearly tends to make heavenly soul super-fluous,[232] to reduce it to a redundant inheritance from the past. This

---

[230] Philoponus *Aet.* 195,13-196,19.

[231] ibid., 267,16-268,10.

[232] In the system of Philoponus 1, the function of heavenly souls was both kinetic and hierarchical.

depreciation must have affected its ontological status as well, including its eternity, if we can rely on Simplicius' remark that Philoponus reserved eternity for God.[233] From here it was only one step to the final solution in *de Opificio Mundi*: it is just the nature of the heavenly body, a nature created by God, which is the principle of its movement.

(5) Only with regard to the *human* rational soul does Philoponus venture to draw the inevitable conclusion in 529: it cannot be eternal *a parte ante*. The reason referred to is that it is subject to evil (*kakia*),[234] i.e. that it has the capacity for turning to a state contrary to its nature,[235] that it is characterised by natural weakness.[236] Everything that is capable of evil is perishable, and therefore it must have come into existence.[237] This means, of course, a decisive break with the Neoplatonic psychology of Philoponus 1: just like the sensible world, the soul has been created by God *ex nihilo*. However, another important question remains unanswered in the *de Aeternitate Mundi contra Proclum*: if the soul is generated, does it come to be together with or after the body, or is it pre-existent to it? The author discusses the subject in *de Opificio Mundi* 1,10, in connection with the generation of angels. The human soul is certainly created after the creation of the world.[238] It does not come to be together with the body.[239] But is it created after the conception of the body or is it pre-existent to it? Philoponus' view on this point is not clear, as the text seems to contain arguments for both interpretations.

(6) Another issue on which Philoponus 2 later evolved a view different from that of *de Aeternitate Mundi contra Proclum* is the end of the world. In the *de Aeternitate Mundi contra Proclum* he seems to draw no distinction yet between the end of the cosmos *sensu stricto* (i.e. of the present formal structure of the sensible world) and the end of the world *sensu lato* (i.e. form *and* matter): the world will perish.[240] How does he

---

[233] cf. n. 204 above.

[234] Philoponus *Aet.* 468,26-469,5: 'First it is unclear – to say only this much now – whether each of the things mentioned (i.e. matter and soul) did not have a beginning of its existence. For, as far as I know, there is no argument necessitating (the assumption) that they had no beginning. In another Book (i.e. Book 9: cf. 336,1-337,13) we have sufficiently discussed the fact that no being which by its nature is capable of deficiency, such as our soul, can have a beginningless existence.'

[235] ibid., 302,25-303,2; 336,5-8.

[236] ibid., 302,25-303,25 *passim*; 336,1-337,13 *passim*.

[237] ibid., 336,1-337,13. Philoponus does not enter into the obvious problem of how to save, on these premises, the immortality of the rational soul.

[238] Philoponus *Opif.* 26,23-4.

[239] ibid., 25,6-9; 26,5-6.

[240] Philoponus *Aet.* 312,7-16: 'So we acknowledge both that the world was generated and that it will perish, having Plato's vote as well as the truth in support of its having been generated, but in support of saying that having been generated it will perish, come what may, and will not be undissolved and immortal, as Plato thinks... (*Hôste hêmeis kai gegonenai ton kosmon kai palin phtheiresthai homologountes, hoti men gegonen, sumpsêphon ekhomen meta tês alêtheias kai Platôna, hoti de genomenos pantôs phtharêsetai kai oukh, hôs Platôni dokei, alutos estai kai athanatos...)'. There is no doubt that *kosmos* here refers to the world *sensu lato*, since the term *gegonenai* obviously means 'generation *ex nihilo*'.

account for this statement? The ultimate ground for it is not cosmological. In spite of Simplicius' contention,[241] Philoponus does not infer the necessity for the world to perish *on the basis of* its intrinsic finiteness, neither in the *de Aeternitate Mundi contra Proclum* nor in the third, non-polemical work. To Philoponus this finiteness only proves that the world *may* perish, it does not prove that it will.[242] *De Aeternitate Mundi contra Proclum* has indeed a few passages which, merely hypothetically, envisage the possibility that the world will not perish for a *supernatural* reason, namely the will of the Creator.[243] This hypothesis is to be found in the third treatise as well.[244] Yet Philoponus is convinced that the world *must* perish, not on cosmological, but on theological grounds. If the Creator, he writes, is able to dissolve the world without ever actually dissolving it, he will always be in potentiality in this respect, never in actuality. This means that in this respect he will always be imperfect, which is impossible. An eternal being cannot forever remain in potentiality. Consequently, God *must* dissolve the world.[245] The cosmological version of this theological argument would be: the world contains in itself the potentiality for being dissolved, and this potentiality has to actualise itself. But Philoponus nowhere defends this proposition. Cosmology cannot prove that the world will never perish,[246] nor that it must perish either. On Philoponus' premises, the necessity for God to dissolve the world at some time should apply to matter as well.[247] In the *contra Aristotelem*, on the other hand, Philoponus was convinced that the end of the present cosmos would not be the end of the world: it would only be the transition to a more perfect, a more divine sensible world.[248] We are left to conclude that the view of *contra Aristotelem* is different from that of *de Aeternitate Mundi contra Proclum*, namely that the sensible world (form and matter) will necessarily perish. The present cosmos, the

[241] Simplicius *in Phys.* 1327,15-16: 'He (Philoponus) thought that what has finite power is at once shown to be perishable.'

[242] [For a different analysis of Philoponus, see Chapter 9 – Ed.]

[243] Philoponus *Aet.* 300,17-21 (at 300,20 read *athanasian* for *astheneian* Rabe; cf. 300,11; 301,1); 312,21-6; 630,12-17. W. Wolska, *La Topographie Chrétienne*, 186 from *Aet.* 312,21-6 erroneously infers: 'In the final analysis, Philoponus falls in with his Greek opponents and acknowledges the indestructibility of the world, with qualifications...He infers the indestructibility of the heavens, but attributes it to the intervention of a *force majeure*, the will of God.' It is true that Philoponus holds in the *contra Aristotelem* that the world is unperishable. But he is talking then about another 'cosmos', not about this one, as the Hellenes do.

[244] Philoponus ap. Simplicium *in Phys.* 1333,23-7.

[245] Philoponus *Aet.* 131,26-132,28.

[246] Philoponus ap. Simplicium *in Phys.* 1333,27-30: *phthoras de ekhonta logon ouk estin apeirodunama. Pothen gar hoti ho logos tês phthoras houtos...oukh hêxei pote kai eis energeian?* I think we have to alter Diels's punctuation, here as well as in 1334,37-9, in order to avoid ambiguity. In Diels's reading (*Pothen gar? Hoti ho logos...*) the *hoti*-sentence seems to give the answer to the question *pothen gar* ('whence?'), which would give an absurd meaning. If we read *Pothen gar hoti...* the *hoti*-sentence is clearly a subject clause. 'Whence is it that that principle of passing away will never come to actuality?', i.e. 'Why...not?'

[247] cf. Philoponus ap. Simplicium, *in Phys.* 1177,22-6.

[248] Simplicius *in Phys.* 1177,38-1178,5. See now also C. Wildberg, 'Prolegomena', 198-200.

components of which are all perishable by nature, will be replaced, it is said, by a new order of matter. This fits in with what we know to have been the doctrine of Philoponus' *de Resurrectione*: God will create new, imperishable bodies, and there will be a new world.[249]

These examples are sufficient, I think, to show that in the *de Aeternitate Mundi contra Proclum* the system of Philoponus 2 was not yet finished. The book was conceived starting from one idea: anti-eternalism. It is remarkable to see how this tenet really had to make its way through Philoponus' Alexandrian Neoplatonic heritage, turning the whole system upside down. The result shows that this was not attainable at once. By 529 our author was not yet completely in line with Christian doctrine,[250] nor did he know the Bible as well as he did in the *de Opificio Mundi*.[251] Apparently it was not so easy for him to Christianise his original world view. Some Christians must have felt that he was not entirely successful, even in his *de Opificio Mundi*. To Cosmas Indicopleustes he remained a pseudo-Christian, someone whose ideas were too 'Hellenic'.[252] In *de Aeternitate Mundi contra Proclum* the theological elaboration of anti-eternalism clearly runs behind cosmology. The cosmological system itself was not complete at once either. This is shown by such later developments as that concerning the cause of the movement of the heaven and elemental fire. Moreover, there might be a connection between Philoponus' new theory on matter in the *de Aeternitate Mundi contra Proclum* (which is related to the idea of a creation *ex nihilo*) and his new theory on void in the *in Physica*. This remains to be investigated.

Finally, let us return briefly to the duality Philoponus 1-Philoponus 2. This duality does not, of course, exclude there being a lot of continuity between the two systems, not only in respect of vocabulary and stylistics,[253] but also on a number of minor issues, for instance of natural philosophy. Further, it is important to realise that the distinction between Philoponus 1 and Philoponus 2 at the level of doctrine is independent of my chronology. In other words: even if the proposed chronology should prove to be false, the duality of doctrine in Philoponus' writings remains what it is. One would then only have to look for a better explanation. We have to take both systems seriously: up to now students of Philoponus have not only overlooked the Alexandrian Neoplatonism of Philoponus 1, but also identified the philosophy of Philoponus 2 too easily with his dogmatic theology. I think that we first have to study both philosophies just as they present themselves, irrespective of the fact that

[249] cf. R. Sorabji, 'John Philoponus', 32-3.

[250] It is noteworthy that in *de Aeternitate Mundi contra Proclum* Philoponus seems not yet to accept the Christian view that creation took some time ('six days'): cf. 367,9-18. In *contra Aristotelem*, by contrast, he seems to have understood creation in the sense of the biblical Hexaemeron: cf. Simplicius *in Phys.* 1174,22-5.

[251] cf. Philoponus *Aet.* 75,19-20: 'As the Holy Scriptures say somewhere' (*hôs pou ta hiera phêsin logia*).

[252] cf. W. Wolska, *La Topographie Chrétienne*, 150.

[253] I merely draw attention to the close similarity between e.g. Philoponus *in DA* 116,1-21 and *Aet.* 196,25-197,15, and *in DA* 297,1-10 and *Aet.* 65,11-22.

Philoponus 1 is more Ammonius than Philoponus, irrespective also of the motives of Philoponus 2. For a philosophy is not just a subject's product; it is a figure of Thought as well.[254]

---

[254] I am particularly indebted to Richard Sorabji for his suggestions for improving my text.

CHAPTER TWELVE

The life and work of Simplicius
in Greek and Arabic sources*

Ilsetraut Hadot

In this attempt to make an inventory of research on the life and works of
Simplicius, I am conscious of the fact (and even rejoice in it) that some
fifteen years hence this inventory will be obsolete, at least in part. For the
time has finally arrived when we are studying Simplicius' commentaries
for themselves, rather than restricting ourselves to several citations of
the Presocratics and to his *Corollary on Time*. Several years ago, Philippe
Hoffmann undertook a new critical edition of Simplicius' commentary on
Aristotle's *de Caelo* with an annotated French translation; Leonardo
Tarán is undertaking a new critical edition of the commentary on the
Physics with an English translation; and I myself expect to finish, in the
very near future, my own critical edition of the commentary on Epictetus'
Encheiridion with an annotated French translation. Henry Blumenthal
has devoted himself to an interpretation of Simplicius' commentary on
the *de Anima* and will publish an English translation of it within the
framework of the great enterprise directed by Richard Sorabji, which has
as its goal the translation into English of a large part of the commentaries
on Aristotle edited in the Berlin Academy's *Commentaria in Aristotelem
Graeca*. Concetta Luna, under the direction of Professor F. del Punta, has
already finished a translation of Simplicius' commentary on the
Categories into Italian, and a French annotated translation of the same
commentary has been undertaken by Philippe Hoffmann, Pierre Hadot,
and myself.[1] Sylvia Donati (Books 1-2) and Cecilia Trifolgi (Books 3-8) of
the University of Pisa are in the process of translating Simplicius'
commentary on the *Physics* into Italian.

I have no doubt that the sum of this research, by making us genuinely
familiar with the thought of Simplicius and the other Neoplatonic
commentators on Aristotle, will considerably modify the accepted image
that K. Praechter first constructed concerning Simplicius' relations with
the so-called Athenian and Alexandrian schools, and will especially

---

* Translated by Victor Caston, in the light of minor revisions by the author.
[1] *Simplicius, Commentaire sur les Catégories, traduction commentée*, fascicles 1 and 3,
Brill, Leiden, forthcoming 1989.

modify the received opinions on the Alexandrians. Praechter claimed, of course, that the Alexandrian school studied Aristotle for his own sake, interpreting him in his true sense, whereas the Athenian school applied a Neoplatonic interpretation to the few works of Aristotle in which they were interested.[2] These ideas have been accepted not only by philologists of classical languages and historians, but also by Arabists and Orientalists. Nevertheless, a cursory glance at the commentaries on the *Metaphysics* written in part by Syrianus (of the Athenian school) and in part by Ammonius-Asclepius (of the Alexandrian school), ought to have convinced K. Praechter of the contrary, since the tendency in the two commentaries is appreciably the same, and Ammonius-Asclepius' commentary even borrows a complete portion of Syrianus' refutation of Aristotle.[3] It is evidence that the critique of the Pythagorean doctrines on numbers and of Plato's doctrine on the Ideas, which Aristotle carries out in several places in the *Metaphysics*, could not as such be accepted by any Neoplatonist, whether he taught at Athens or at Alexandria, whereas there was no insurmountable difficulty concerning Aristotle's logical and physical teaching.[4] To cite Syrianus himself: 'I am not one of those who are hostile to Aristotle, nor one of those who claim the authority of Aristotle's teaching on details or trivial matters, but one who thoroughly admires his lessons on logic and who enthusiastically approves of his ethical and physical treatises'.[5] In fact, the whole of Aristotle's logical, ethical, and physical treatises had been definitively incorporated into Neoplatonic teaching[6] at the latest with Syrianus-Proclus, though probably already with Porphyry, who had himself commented, at least partially, on Aristotle's logical works, *Physics, de Anima*, Book 12 of the *Metaphysics*, and on one ethical treatise.[7] More than any other works, the different commentaries on the *Categories* will probably furnish the crucial material which will best allow revision of Praechter's global views,

---

[2] cf. F. Überweg, *Grundriss der Geschichte der Philosophie*, Part I: K. Praechter, *Die Philosophie des Altertums*, 12th edition, Berlin 1926, p. 638: 'Iamblichus referred to the *noera theôria* [intellective theory] everywhere in his commentary on the *Categories*, and Simplicius, who informs us on this matter (*in Cat.* 2,13), did the same as he. In contrast, the Alexandrian commentators on Aristotle's logical works restricted themselves to a sober explanation of the text in accordance with its natural sense.' Cf. also K. Praechter, 'Richtungen und Schulen im Neoplatonismus', in *Genethliakon für Carl Robert*, Berlin 1910, pp. 105-56.

[3] Asclepius *in Metaph.* 432,29-436,8. This citation shows that Syrianus must have commented on Aristotle's *Metaphysics* in its entirety, since it corresponds to Book 7, for which Syrianus' commentary no longer exists.

[4] For a more ample discussion of this matter, cf. I. Hadot, *Le problème du néoplatonisme Alexandrin: Hiéroclès et Simplicius*, Paris 1978, pp. 195ff.

[5] Syrianus *in Metaph.* 80,4-7.

[6] For Porphyry, cf. F. Romano, *Porfirio e la fisica aristotelica* (= *Symbolon*, Studi e testi di filosofia antica e medievale III), Catania 1985, the chapters 'L'interesse di Porfirio verso Aristotele' and 'I commentari aristotelici di Porfirio'.

[7] cf. I. Hadot, 'Les introductions aux commentaires exégétiques chez les auteurs néoplatoniciens et les auteurs chrétiens', in M. Tardieu (ed.), *Exégèse et philosophie*, Paris 1987, pp. 99-122. For the importance of Porphyry as a commentator of Aristotle, cf. F. Romano, op. cit. in n. 6.

since we have the opportunity to compare Simplicius' commentary with six other Greek commentaries, namely those of Porphyry, Dexippus, Ammonius, Philoponus, Olympiodorus, and David[8] and still further with Boethius' Latin commentary. Furthermore, Simplicius' commentary introduces us to large parts of the lost commentaries on the *Categories*, namely, Porphyry's (addressed to Gedalius) and Iamblichus', as well as to several not insignificant remarks from the lost commentary on the *Categories* by Syrianus, Proclus' teacher. Of these commentaries, four – by Ammonius, Philoponus, Olympiodorus and David – belong, according to Praechter's views, to the rational and sober interpretation of the Alexandrian school, whereas Simplicius' commentary followed the Athenian tendency of Syrianus and Proclus, who themselves were inspired by Iamblichus. Having worked through the first forty pages of Simplicius' commentary by comparing them with the four so-called 'Alexandrian' commentaries, Philippe Hoffman, Pierre Hadot and I did not encounter a single piece of evidence which favoured Praechter's thesis, that is, we were unable to establish any difference concerning the interpretative tendency of Simplicius' commentary, on the one hand, and the commentaries of Ammonius, Philoponus, Olympiodorus and David, on the other. Similarly, A. Sheppard,[9] in pointing out parallels between Proclus' commentary on the *Cratylus* and Ammonius' commentary on the *de Interpretatione*, concludes that all these parallels between Proclus and Ammonius show how close the connections between Athenian Neoplatonism and Alexandrian Neoplatonism are, to the extent that she doubts the justice of the view that there is a significant difference between the Athenian and Alexandrian attitude towards Aristotle. In her opinion, the tone of the later Neoplatonic commentaries is determined more by the text to be commented on than by the 'school' to which the commentator belonged. Let us cite Ammonius himself, who considered his commentary on Aristotle's *de Interpretatione* to be merely the fruit of his teacher Proclus' instruction on the same subject: 'In the eyes of the wise, Aristotle's *de Interpretatione* is a work of great importance and has no little honour thanks both to the density of theories expounded in it and the difficulty encountered in its literal explanation (*lexis*). This is why many exegetes have written many reflections on the subject of this work.

---

[8] A. Busse (*Eliae in Porphyrii Isag....*, CAG 18.1, pp. viiff), who was followed by Y. Manandean (*L'école hellénisante ...*, Vienna 1928, in Armenian, pp. 25 and 39), claimed to show that, despite the unanimous Greek and Armenian manuscript tradition, the author of the commentary on the *Categories* could not have been the author of the commentary on the *Isagoge*, but must have been the philosopher Elias. This thesis has been refuted point by point by S.S. Arevšatjan in his article, 'L'héritage de David l'Invincible sous une lumière nouvelle', in *Banber Matenadarani* IX, 1969, 7-22 (in Armenian with a French abstract). The expert on Armenian literature, J.-P. Mahé, who had the kindness to bring these works to my attention, considers this refutation decisive. Cf. J.-P. Mahé, 'David l'Invincible dans la tradition arménienne', forthcoming in *Simplicius, Commentaire sur les Catégories, traduction commentée*, Appendix II, Brill, Leiden, 1989.

[9] cf. A. Sheppard, 'Proclus' philosophical method of exegesis: the use of Aristotle and the Stoics in the Commentary on the *Cratylus*', in J. Pépin and H.D. Saffrey (eds), *Proclus – lecteur et interprète des Anciens*, colloques internationaux du CNRS, Paris 1987, pp. 137-51.

If we should be able to contribute anything to the elucidation of this book ourselves while recalling the exegeses of our divine teacher Proclus, the Platonic Diadochus, who practised to the heights that human nature can attain both the ability to explain the views of the ancients and to distinguish scientifically the nature of things, we would greatly thank the God of language.'[10] Thus, until the contrary is proven, I will reaffirm the conclusions expressed in my book, *Le problème du néoplatonisme Alexandrin: Hiéroclès et Simplicius*, namely, that there was no Neoplatonic school in Alexandria whose doctrinal tendencies differed from those of the school at Athens.[11] This uniformity of tendency does not imply a uniformity of system in all its details: there is no uniformity of system between Plotinus and his pupil Porphyry, between Porphyry and his pupil Theodore of Asine, between Iamblichus and Proclus, or between Damascius and his pupil Simplicius, but rather a uniformity of tendencies, and it is this same uniformity of tendencies which in my opinion ties the schools of Athens and of Alexandria closely together. The doctrinal differences which may appear do not result from divergences between schools, but from the divergences between persons.

If I am now speaking about the life and works of Simplicius again after having devoted a chapter of my book *Le problème du néoplatonisme Alexandrin* to this subject eight years ago, it is because in the intervening period new research has been conducted which seems to me capable of enriching our knowledge considerably on this subject. In fact, whatever I was then able to say about Simplicius' life was very slight: according to the statements of Agathias,[12] Simplicius, a native of Cilicia in Asia Minor, attended the course of Ammonius, the son of Hermeias, in Alexandria. This information is given to us by Simplicius himself.[13] Now, Ammonius taught in Alexandria between approximately 475 and 526. Simplicius also speaks of Damascius as his professor,[14] but he specifies neither the date nor the place of his studies under Damascius. Nevertheless, both teacher and pupil are mentioned together by the historian Agathias,[15] who states that, 'Damascius the Syrian, Simplicius the Cilician, Eulamius (or Eulalius) the Phrygian, Priscianus the Lydian, Hermias and Diogenes both from Phoenicia, Isidore of Gaza, the most noble flower ... of our time,' had fled the Byzantine empire because of the

---

[10] Ammonius, *in Int.* 1,3-11. Ammonius also follows Proclus' interpretations in his commentary on the *Prior Analytics*, which is only partially extant (apart from an edition of his lectures made by Philoponus): cf. *CAG* 4, 40,16ff, where he cites Proclus who had given him a course on the *Prior Analytics* following the commentary of Iamblichus quite strictly, and 43,30f, where he cites the *skholikon hupomnêma* on the first book of the *Prior Analytics*.

[11] Paris 1978. In the same book, on pp. 9ff, I likewise explained the sense that must be given to the phrases 'the School at Athens' and 'the School at Alexandria', if the use of these names is to continue.

[12] Agathias, *Hist.* 2.30.3 (Keydell, p. 80.7).

[13] Simplicius, *in Cael.* 462,20.

[14] For references, cf. the Index nominum of Diels' edition of Simplicius, *in Phys.* under the name, 'Damaskios'.

[15] Agathias, *Hist.* 2.30.3ff (Keydell, p. 80.7ff).

persecution of pagans and had made their way to the court of the Persian king, Chosroes. The latter, again according to Agathias, permitted them to return to their homeland and to live out the rest of their lives there without fear and without being required to abjure their philosophical convictions, by having a special clause included in the peace treaty about to be concluded with Justinian in AD 532. A turn of phrase used in the text of the treaty (as reported by Agathias) raises several difficulties. Here is the clause in question: '... *dein ekeinous tous andras es ta sphetera êthê kationtas bioteuein adeôs to loipon eph' heautois ...*'[16] In this clause, *eph' heautois* cannot do double duty with *eis ta sphetera êthê kationtes* (returning to their homeland) and cannot therefore mean 'in their homeland'. Referring to this clause, Westerink[17] claims, 'The ban on teaching activities, it should be noted, was maintained formally: ... *bioteuein adeôs to loipon eph' heautois,*' apparently because he understands *eph' heautois* in the sense of 'in undisturbed privacy' and as indicating that all teaching activity remained forbidden to philosophers. Formerly, I accepted this view of Westerink's.[18] Today, in light of research summarised below, I would rather translate *eph' heautois* as 'according to their wishes', that is to say, 'these men, in returning to their homeland, must be able to live there according to their wishes without fear for the rest of their lives, without being compelled to think anything which might be in contradiction with their views or to change the beliefs of their ancestors'. Neither Agathias nor any other Greek source tells us from which city in the Byzantine empire they came nor if they lived together before their stay in Persia. There is, however, a strong probability, though no certainty, that they came from Athens – the reference is probably to the last successor in the private Platonic school in Athens, Damascius and his students. Agathias paints on the whole a rather malicious picture of these pagan philosophers by attributing naïve, utopian, and quickly disappointed ideas about Persia to them.[19] In reality, the decision taken by our pagan philosophers to emigrate to Persia was not at all a matter of a utopian dream, but on the contrary had a very realistic basis. For quite some time, they had before them the example of Nisibis, a Nestorian university formerly established at Edessa in Syria. Already before 532, it enjoyed considerable freedom of thought under the Persian kings, which contrasted favourably with Byzantine intolerance, from which the theological school had had to flee to Persia. This heterodox Christian school was a bastion of Greek culture mediated by the Aramaic language, which was spoken on both sides of the border. It may be supposed that Damascius, Hermias, Diogenes and Isidore knew this language, since they were natives of Syria, and probably also

[16] Agathias, *Hist.* 2.31.4ff (Keydell, p. 81.17).

[17] L.G. Westerink, *Anonymous Prolegomena to Platonic Philosophy*, Amsterdam 1962, p. xv = Chapter 14 below, p. 331.

[18] In *Le problème du néoplatonisme Alexandrin*, p. 24 and n. 32.

[19] Agathias, *Hist.* 2.30.3-31.2 (Keydell, pp. 80.5-81.12); cf. I. Hadot, *Le problème du néoplatonisme Alexandrin*, p. 24.

Simplicius at least, who originated from a country bordering on Syria. Persia thus for a time combined all the favourable conditions to which our philosophers could aspire: tolerance in religious matters and provision of a centre of Greek culture.

Agathias tells us nothing further about the place where the philosophers made their way after their stay with Chosroes. He only informs us that they undertook the return journey together, at least as far as the Byzantine frontier.[20] It must also be noted that Agathias apparently had knowledge of the manner in which they lived afterwards, since he says in this regard[21] – and one senses a bit of envy piercing through his summary – '... they took advantage of their exile, not in a small and negligible way, but so as to spend the rest of their lives in the most agreeable and pleasant manner.' Such an expression does not suggest that our philosophers were forced to live in ideological isolation, merely tolerated by a hostile environment. I have discussed elsewhere[22] the reasons which impelled me to reject the hypothesis that Simplicius, if not the other philosophers, might have returned to Athens or Alexandria. Rather, I then envisaged the possibility that he had retired to a city of Asia Minor situated perhaps in Cilicia, his homeland. Yet with all these hypotheses, one cannot imagine by what miracle these philosophers could even have safeguarded their lives far away from the protection of the Persian king, let alone led the type of joyous life of which Agathias speaks. For, in reality, what does a clause of a treaty mean against an omnipotent Christian church which could always organise lynchings, as in the case of the philosopher Hypatia? Could our philosophers have been reckless and naïve enough to trust a piece of paper fated to become worthless far from the armed forces capable of guaranteeing it? An answer to these questions has recently been provided, not by a philologist of classical languages, nor by a pure historian, but by a specialist on gnosticism in the person of Michel Tardieu: working from Arabic texts and interpreting them in light of Greek philosophical literature as well as the history of Manicheanism, he arrived at the conclusion that, in all probability, our Neoplatonic philosophers made their way after their stay in Persia to Ḥarrân (Carrhae), a Byzantine city of Greco-Aramaic tongue where 'Hellenism' had remained powerful and active, situated quite close to the Persian border, 30 kilometres SSE of Edessa. Tardieu discussed his arguments in 1984 at the 6th International Congress on Gnosticism, which was held at the University of Oklahoma, and also in an article entitled 'Ṣâbiens coraniques et "Ṣâbiens" de Ḥarrân', in the *Journal Asiatique*. In what follows, I will attempt to give a summary of it.[23]

---

[20] Agathias, *Hist.* 2.31.5ff (Keydell, pp. 81.21ff).

[21] ibid. 2.31.3 (Keydell, pp. 81.13ff).

[22] *Le problème du néoplatonisme Alexandrin*, p. 26ff.

[23] M. Tardieu's article has appeared since this chapter was written (*Journal Asiatique* 274, 1986, 1-44), but nevertheless I believe it useful to retain the summary of it which I gave at the colloquium on Simplicius. For scholars and students of classical languages and ancient history or philosophy, the *Journal Asiatique* is only rarely to hand. Furthermore,

The city of Ḥarrân, or Carrhae, is known to Latinists and Hellenists mainly for two incidents: the Roman army was defeated by the Parthians in 53 BC in the vicinity of Carrhae, and its commander, the Proconsul of the province of Syria, L. Licinius Crassus, retreated into the city with the rest of his troops and was assassinated. In this same city the emperor Julian in the year 363 AD offered sacrifices in accordance with local rituals in the famous temple of the Moon, before being defeated and killed some months later by the Persians. In the eyes of the Christian Theodoret of Cyrrhus, the visit to the pagan city of Ḥarrân was an intentional affront on Julian's part to the neighbouring Christian city of Edessa. For Orientalists, Ḥarrân is the city *par excellence* of the Ṣâbians (not to be confused with the Sabaeans) known to the Arabic sources. Who were the Ṣâbians of Ḥarrân? I cannot enter into all the details of Tardieu's extensive and judicious argument, but must limit myself to the selection of a few points which are of particular interest to historians of Neoplatonism. For convenience, I will begin at the ending, that is, at the destruction of the last pagan temple in Ḥarrân in 1081, a date after which there is no longer any mention of Ṣâbian activity in this town. Yet in the tenth century Ṣâbianism is still alive in Ḥarrân, since the Caliph ᶜAbd al-Karîm confirms by letter to the Ṣâbians of Ḥarrân, Raqqa and Diyâr Muḍar their right to worship and education. And it was in the tenth century, in 943, that the Arab author al-Masᶜûdî made his way to this town. He recounted his impressions later on in his book *Kitâb murûǧ al-ḍahab wa-maᶜâdin al ǧauhar*. al-Masᶜûdî's account contains an essential detail which modern, contemporary criticism had not raised before Tardieu. The following is the text in question (from the French translation of C. Pellat): 'I have seen in Ḥarrân, on the door knocker of the Ṣâbians' meeting place, an inscription in Syriac characters, taken from Plato; it was explained to me by Mâlik b. ᶜUqbûn and other persons of the same sect: "Whoever knows his nature becomes a god." It is also Plato who said, "Man is a celestial plant. Indeed, man resembles an upside-down tree, whose roots are turned towards the heavens and whose branches [plunge] into the earth".[24] Chwolsohn, the author of a book entitled *Die Ssabier und der Ssabismus* (St. Petersburg 1856, vol. 2, p. 826) had mentioned a correction by Fleischer of the translation of the inscription found on the door knocker, a correction whose import had passed totally unnoticed: 'Who knows his own essence (who knows

---

the summary which I offer of Tardieu's article concentrates on facts which, in the text and in the notes, relate to Simplicius and to the Neoplatonic school in Ḥarrân, leaving aside an important portion bearing on gnosticism and the Ṣâbians of the Koran.

If the hypothesis that the Greek philosophers Damascius, Simplicius, and the others mentioned by Agathias remained in Ḥarrân after their stay in Persia is already rendered more than probable by Tardieu's article, then another discovery by the same author renders it almost certain. See his 'Les calendriers en usage à Ḥarrân d'après les sources arabes et le commentaire de Simplicius à la *Physique* d'Aristote', in I. Hadot (ed.), *Simplicius – sa vie, son oeuvre, sa survie*, Actes du colloque international de Paris, Berlin and New York 1987, pp. 40-57.

[24] M. Tardieu, 'Ṣâbiens coraniques', p. 13.

himself) becomes divine, resembling God.' No one before Tardieu had
identified these two citations, of which one can be found in the *Timaeus*
(90A7-B2) and the other is obviously an allusion to the *Alcibiades I* 133C.
In another book, the *Kitâb al-tanbîh wa-l-išrâf*, al-Mas͏ᶜûdî returns once
more to this axiom in these words: 'And we have stated what they [= the
Ṣâbians of Ḥarrân] think of Plato's saying: "Whoever knows himself in
truth becomes a god", and this other saying of the author of the *Logic*:
"Whoever knows himself knows all things." ' As Tardieu tells us, 'in
Arabic this small text does not include a main clause. It is part of a long
enumeration ... of the different matters treated by the author in two of
his previous works, no longer extant today, but for which al-Mas͏ᶜûdî
provides the titles. One was entitled *Book of Tenets on the Principles of
Religions*; the other concerned *The Treasures of Religion and the Secret of
Worlds*.'[25] Thus, in sum, al-Mas͏ᶜûdî spoke of the Platonic axiom of the
Alcibiades in at least four of his books. 'If he returned to it rather
frequently, it is because he had grasped perfectly that this axiom was
fundamental to his Ḥarrânian interlocutors and just by itself
summarised their entire philosophy.'[26] According to the summary of the
two lost books that al-Mas͏ᶜûdî gives in the *Kitâb al-tanbîh*, 'it appears
that the context of the citation from Plato in these two works concerned
reports relating to the "Greek Ṣâbians". The ideas which the author
attributed to them show that this denomination, encompassing that of
the "Ḥarrânian Ṣâbians", is to be taken here in a strictly philosophical
sense, as designating "the Platonists". Not only is Porphyry's name cited,
but also that of his correspondent, "the Egyptian priest Anâbû [Anebo]".
The doctrinal differences between Porphyry and Anâbû have been
recorded, al-Mas͏ᶜûdî claims, in epistles "known to whoever is interested
in the ancient sciences".'[27]

'In the immediate context of the citation of the Platonic axiom in the
al-Tanbîh, another citation appears which is attributed by al-Mas͏ᶜûdî to
"the author of the *Logic*". This expression, as is so often the case with
Arabic authors, does not designate Aristotle himself, but one of his
Alexandrian commentators. In fact, the axiom: "Whoever knows himself
knows all things", of which al-Mas͏ᶜûdî gives the Arabic version, is
Neoplatonic. It occurs word for word in two Alexandrians, namely, in
Hermeias' *in Phaedrum*: "Who understands himself knows everything
(*ho heauton gnous ta panta oiden*)" and in Olympiodorus' *in Alcibiadem*:
"Who knows himself knows all things (*ho eidôs heauton ta onta panta
oiden*)", which in both cases are juxtaposed with the Delphic precept. The
association of the two axioms in the *al-Tanbîh* is in line with the
traditional interpretations of "Know Thyself (*gnôthi sauton*)" given by the
Neoplatonists when commenting on the *Alcibiades*. The "Ṣâbians of
Ḥarrân", who explained to al-Mas͏ᶜûdî the Syriac inscription engraved on
the knocker of their front door and who considered themselves to be

[25] ibid., p. 15.
[26] ibid.
[27] ibid., pp. 15-16.

"Greek Ṣābians", are nothing other than "Platonists" in the strict sense',[28] or rather, Neoplatonists.

According to the direct testimony of al-Mas^cûdî, the building whose front door knocker bore the central axiom of *Alcibiades I* engraved in Syriac was called 'maǧma^c' in Arabic. This was, therefore, where the philosophers of Ḥarrân met. 'al-Mas^cûdî grouped the Ḥarrânians into two categories: the philosophers ... "of a low and vulgar level", partisans of the pagan religion of the city, and the "sages in the strict sense", the heirs of the Greek philosophers. "By associating them with the philosophers," the author further specifies, "we have thought not of their wisdom, but of their shared origin, for they are Greeks". To give an example of the upper echelon of these "Greek sages" in Ḥarrân, al-Mas^cûdî at this point recounts what he read on the entrance door of their maǧma^c; then, in conclusion, he launches into a technical exposition of Greek philosophy. In such a context, maǧma^c cannot mean anything other than a meeting place for intellectuals.'[29]

'al-Mas^cûdî distinguishes the cult sites or "temples" of the popular religion perfectly from the maǧma^c where the "Greek philosophers" met. As regards the former, he recognises at the time', when he gives his summary of the two lost books, which we mentioned above, that is, in 947, 'that there remained only one, "the temple called Maǧlitiyâ; it is located in the city of Ḥarrân, near the Raqqa gate." The second centre, still thriving, of Ḥarrânian paganism was the institution of the "Greek Ṣābians", that is, the Platonists.'[30] Here, therefore, 'maǧma^c' means their school, a sort of academy. The building whose door knocker was decorated with the Syriac inscription which al-Mas^cûdî took care to have explained was the Platonic school of Ḥarrân. 'Those who accompanied al-Mas^cûdî on the course of his visit were members of this Academy, and Mâlik b. ^cUqbûn, cited as the interpreter of the inscription, was in all probability the head of this Academy. al-Mas^cûdî equally claims to have consulted him on technical and historical questions of Greek philosophy. During this consultation, he learned from Mâlik b. ^cUqbûn and the other members of the group, that is, from the other Greek philosophers of the school, that they categorically rejected the sacrificial and divinatory practices of the Ḥarrânians as well as the "secret and mysterious" rites. al-Mas^cûdî therefore distinguishes perfectly between the ordinary pagans of Ḥarrân and the Ḥarrânian philosophers. If he made the effort to give an account of his interview with Mâlik b. ^cUqbûn, it is because the latter had rank and authority in the school.[31]

'The school of Ḥarrân, in line with Plato's ancient Academy (or rather with reports of it), bore a maxim, not on the pediment of its portal, but on its door knocker, which invited anyone who crossed the threshhold to the philosophic life (*bios philosophikos*). At the time of al-Mas^cûdî's visit in

[28] ibid., p. 16.
[29] ibid., p. 18.
[30] ibid.
[31] ibid., pp. 18-19.

943, Ḥarrânian paganism possessed two centres of activity: the temple called Maġlitiyâ and the Platonic school. The critical thoughts he heard from those who attended the school show that the two institutions of Ḥarrânian paganism answered different aims and for this reason were rivals.'[32]

Tardieu has therefore demonstrated that the Ṣâbians of Ḥarrân were not Gnostics and that, contrary to Chwolsohn's now commonly held opinion – according to which all intellectual activity ceased after Ṭâbit b. Qurra left Ḥarrân in order to live in Baghdad and to found the famous school of Baghdad there – the Platonic school of Ḥarrân still remained a vital organism in the tenth century. His departure for Baghdad was not the result of a 'schism', according to Tardieu. Rather, it would appear that Ṭâbit b. Qurra was attracted by the Caliph's subsidies and had chosen Baghdad 'for social and political reasons, as the Abbasid capital at that time offered greater possibilities for influence than Ḥarrân, the capital of Diyâr Muḍar. Yet his departure for Baghdad meant neither the closure nor the end of the school in Ḥarrân, which was to endure, since it still had members and a head when al-Masᶜûdî visited it in 943, more than seventy years after Ṭâbit b. Qurra's move to Baghdad. Mâlik b. ᶜUqbûn ensured the continuation in Ḥarrân of a prestigious and centuries-old institution.'[33]

Tardieu also demonstrates convincingly that the argument of Max Meyerhof's famous article, 'Von Alexandrien nach Bagdad. Ein Beitrag zur Geschichte des philosophischen und medizinischen Unterrichts bei den Arabern', written in 1930 and authoritative since then, does not survive critical examination.[34] According to Tardieu, Meyerhof was mistaken in accepting to the letter the testimony of the Arabic sources concerning a relocation of the Neoplatonic school from Athens to Alexandria, from there to Antioch, from Antioch to Ḥarrân, and finally from Ḥarrân to Baghdad, for which the chronology is in every way erroneous. The Arabic accounts must be understood not as a 'chronology of institutional relocations, but as a confirmation of the intellectual vitality of Antioch (the city and its outskirts) as much as Ḥarrân (the city and its outskirts)' around 700 AD (the end of the first century of the Hegira), 'each of the two centres laying claim at that time to the title and the honour of being the repository of the Alexandrian heritage'.[35]

'Under the Ummayyads ... the two intellectual centres which were the melting-pot for the transmission of Greek science to the Arab world were Syrian: Greco-Syriac in Christian Antioch and Greco-Arabic-Syriac in pagan Ḥarrân, which was to become the capital of the Empire with the accession of Marwan b. Muḥammad to the Caliphate in 744. The Christians who came from the Alexandrian school settled quite naturally in Antioch and in the peripheral monasteries, and from there they

[32] ibid., p. 19.
[33] ibid.
[34] ibid., pp. 19-22.
[35] ibid., p. 21.

launched the intellectual conquest of Ḥarrân.'[36] With the help of another Arabic source, Tardieu shows that intellectual traffic had always existed between Antioch and Ḥarrân, but that it was due to the Christians alone. The testimony of al-Masᶜûdî on the relocation of Greek science from Antioch to Ḥarrân must be taken, according to Tardieu, 'with great caution, since it comes from a Christian source anxious to lay claim to Alexandrian authenticity of its intellectual heritage for its own credit versus the rival school of the "Greek Ṣâbians", that is, of the true Platonists. Thus, there had not, properly speaking, been a relocation of the old institution of Ammonius, where Simplicius had taken courses at the beginning of the sixth century, either to Antioch or to Ḥarrân ..., but a double claim to a single heritage, mediated by Antioch in the case of the Christian Ḥarrânians, direct and more ancient for those whom the Arabs would call "Greek Ṣâbians".'[37]

Tardieu has led us through the existence of a Neoplatonic school from the end of the seventh to the tenth century AD. 'Now,' he concludes,[38] 'as the school of Ḥarrân did not simply fall from the sky in the first century of the Hegira (thus between 622 and 722), it is not implausible to suppose that it is there, in Byzantine territory (but in proximity to the Iranian border), that the exiles from Athens, the last battalion of Greek resistance to Christianisation, found refuge and settled, among Platonists who had attended Ammonius' school. This would explain the insistence with which the Christian authors, in both Syriac and Arabic, ridicule the school of the "Hellenes" in Ḥarrân, a sort of rival to the neighbouring school of the "Persians" established in Nisibis, the one pagan, secular, and philosophic, the other Nestorian, ecclesiastical, and theological, but both under the protection of the King of kings.' As regards this protection, Tardieu cites a text of Procopius (*Bella* 2. 13.7) which specifies that Chosroes in 549 had exempted the inhabitants of Ḥarrân from paying tribute because they had preserved the old religion.[39] This testimony shows clearly that the Persian king favoured any ideology opposed to the ideology of the Christian church adopted by the Byzantine state; he therefore favoured paganism *tout court*, the philosophical paganism of the Neoplatonists and the heterodox Christianity of the Nestorians.

'Olympiodorus compares the *Alcibiades* to a propylaeum whose adytum is the *Parmenides*. It is the same in Ḥarrân. The *Alcibiades* is at the entrance, the *Parmenides* in the centre. In fact, according to the testimony of al-Kindî, whom Ibn al-Nadîm cites from al-Saraḥsî, the core of the metaphysical thought of the "Ḥarrânian Ṣâbians" was summarised in the claim that "in the world there is a cause which has never ceased: a monad, not a plurality, which does not take on the attributes of anything caused whatsoever." '[40] D. Chwolsohn, followed by W. Scott, thought this doctrine

[36] ibid., pp. 24-5.
[37] ibid., p. 26.
[38] ibid., p. 23.
[39] ibid.
[40] ibid., p. 27.

to belong to the Hermetica. But Tardieu has had no trouble in showing that its origin is purely Neoplatonic. Yet al-Kindî's account not only confirms that the philosophy of the 'Ṣâbians' of Ḥarrân belonged to Neoplatonism, and what is more, to a Neoplatonism of the most refined sort; it equally reveals, Tardieu tells us, 'the other side of this philosophy. These Ḥarrânian intellectuals had their public festivals, their prayers, their fasts and their dietary customs. Such observances – difficult in the Athens of Proclus and Damascius and in the Alexandria of Ammonius and Olympiodorus, as well as in the Abbasid Baghdad where Ṭâbit b. Qurra went to live – could be performed very freely in Ḥarrân, at the heart of a social group where paganism was still alive, in proximity to a temple (that of the Moon goddess), whose activity had never ceased since the Hurrian era. Living communally in their school, these Platonists could without hindrance devote themselves to the theurgic practices which their philosophy required.'[41] I would only add, for my part, that such a life seems to agree thoroughly with Agathias' remark, namely, that the Greek philosophers, after their departure from the court of Chosroes, 'were able to spend the rest of their lives in the most agreeable and pleasant manner'.[42] 'The error of perspective on the part of the Arabic authors – and, consequently, on the part of Western orientalism', Tardieu continues[43] – 'is to have placed together in the same category of "Ṣâbian" the observances of these philosophers and that of their compatriots who attended the temples, the doctrine of the one and the religion of the others. The only two authors who did not make this amalgamation were a philosopher and a tourist: al-Kindî and al-Masᶜûdî, both Mesopotamians. The philosopher's information is drawn from a good source, since his informant and student, al-Saraḥsî, was a correspondent of Ṭâbit b. Qurra. The tourist's information has incomparable value, since it is the direct echo of what was still the Platonic school of Ḥarrân during the tenth century.'

According to Tardieu, it is also in all probability in Ḥarrân that Simplicius wrote his commentary on Epictetus' *Encheiridion*.[44] Recall that it was once believed, thanks to K. Praechter's theories, that this commentary had been written in Alexandria before Simplicius' stay in Persia and that it contained doctrinal elements characteristic of the school of Alexandria and opposed to the school of Athens. I have refuted Praechter's views in my book *Le problème du néoplatonisme Alexandrin*, where among other things I arrived at the conclusion that the commentary on Epictetus' *Encheiridion* offered no precise evidence that would allow for even a relative dating. In the same book,[45] I also refuted in detail A. Cameron's hypothesis, namely, that the same commentary had been written in Athens in the same period as the other great

[41] ibid., p. 28.
[42] cf. p. 280 above.
[43] M. Tardieu, 'Ṣâbiens coraniques', pp. 28-9.
[44] ibid., p. 24, n. 105.
[45] pp. 33-40.

commentaries of Simplicius, after the stay in Persia. My criticism of Cameron's two articles must have gone completely unnoticed, for her theses have been repeated since as if they were established facts. It is with regard to the date and location of composition of Simplicius' commentary on Epictetus' *Encheiridion* that Tardieu enters as a specialist of Manicheanism. In fact, in my analysis of the long discussion in Simplicius' commentary devoted to the refutation of Manicheanism, I had drawn attention to the fact that, according to the text of my new critical edition of this commentary, Simplicius personally spoke with a Manichean sage.[46] I therefore asked, without being able to answer this question, where Simplicius could have had the opportunity to speak with a Manichean. According to Tardieu, at this period, that is, after 533, 'there were only two cities in the Byzantine empire where there were *certainly* Manicheans: Constantinople, where they hid, and Ḥarrân, where they had settled since the end of the third century and where, thanks to the local socio-political conditions, they survived for several centuries. The zeal shown against them by the Bishop of Ḥarrân, Theodore Abû Qurra, around 764-5 according to the *Chronicle* of Pseudo-Dionysius of Tell-Mahrê, confirms that they were still significant in the religious landscape of Ḥarrân in the eighth century.'[47] Tardieu also states that if Simplicius wrote this detailed refutation of Manicheanism, 'it is because there was urgency and external pressure. One fact about anti-Gnostic and anti-Manichean controversies in the schools of Platonic philosophy deserves to be repeated unceasingly: Plotinus refutes the Gnostics because the Gnostics frequented his school. Alexander, the head of the Platonic school of Lycopolis, refutes the Manicheans because the Manicheans attended his courses. Why, then, did Simplicius set his heart on refuting the doctrine of the Manicheans himself, if they were not present where he worked on the edition of his commentary and if they did not disturb the serenity of his rationalism through their intrusiveness and inopportune questions? The only place where the direct contact would have been possible and lasting, from a perspective which is at once historical, sociological, linguistic and scholarly, is Ḥarrân.'[48]

In favour of the thesis that Simplicius did not write his commentary in either Athens or Alexandria, I would further add an argument of textual criticism.[49] It has been remarked on by several scholars that the text of the fragments from Parmenides' poem which Proclus, Ammonius, Asclepius, Olympiodorus and Simplicius provide cannot come from the same

---

[46] I. Hadot, 'Die Widerlegung des Manichäismus im Epiktetkommentar des Simplikios', *Archiv der Geschichte der Philosophie* 50, 1969, p. 46. The text of my new edition is actually the following: 'but as one of the wise men among them revealed to me (*all' hôs emoi tis tôn par' autois sophôn exephêne*)' instead of 71.48 Dübner: 'but as a certain wise man among them said they were (*all' hopoias tis tôn par' autois sophôn exephênen*)'.

[47] M. Tardieu, 'Ṣâbiens coraniques', p. 24, n. 105.

[48] ibid.

[49] Yet see above all Tardieu's article, 'Les calendriers en usage à Ḥarrân d'après les sources arabes et le commentaire de Simplicius à la *Physique* d'Aristote.'

source.[50] The manuscript of the poem on which Simplicius relies coincides neither with the copy used by Proclus which must have been in the library of the Neoplatonist school at Athens, nor with that of Ammonius, Asclepius and Olympiodorus at Alexandria. According to J. Whittaker and K. Deichgräber,[51] Simplicius had at his disposal a manuscript which had been badly copied from an exemplar which contained scholia. Concerning Proclus' text, C. Guérard recently expressed the opinion that Proclus substituted several Neoplatonic retouchings for the text of the poem with the intention of making the contents of the poem coincide with those of Plato's dialogue the *Parmenides*.[52]

In this context, evidence contained in the short entry the Arabic writer Ibn al-Qiftî devotes to Simplicius might also be interesting. As H. Gätje explains in his article, 'Simplikios in der arabischen Überlieferung',[53] Simplicius appears here in an alphabetical list of scholars as a celebrated mathematician, who had composed, among other widely read writings, a commentary on Euclid and who had assembled around himself students and successors who took their name from their professor. The statement that Simplicius, like all the Neoplatonists, was a mathematician, has recently been entirely confirmed, notably by A.I. Sabra's article, 'Simplicius' proof of Euclid's parallel postulate'.[54] We will return to this later in the second part of the chapter. The evidence that Simplicius taught must therefore be taken more seriously as well. Yet where could he have done this, except in a city like Ḥarrân?

One might object, however, that Simplicius could not have written his commentaries without the aid of a very ample library, and that such a library could not be found except in Athens or Alexandria. I believe this is a prejudice which will not survive historical criticism. We can leave Alexandria aside, since Simplicius could not have gone there after his stay in Persia without having encountered Philoponus. He claims never to have known Philoponus personally.[55] As regards the famous libraries of Athens, the wealth accumulated during the Hellenistic era had been transported by Sulla to Rome following his military conquest of the city in 86 BC. It is very likely that under the Roman emperors and above all in the period of the Antonines libraries of value were reconstituted in Athens, but it is very nearly certain that these were destroyed in the year 267 AD during the sack of the city by the Heruls. This is at any rate the

[50] cf., for example, H. Diels, *Parmenides' Lehrgedicht*, Berlin 1897, p. 26; J. Whittaker, 'God, time, being', *Symbolae Osloenses*, Suppl. 23, 1971, pp. 19ff.

[51] K. Deichgräber, 'Xenophanes' *Peri Phuseôs*', *Rheinisches Museum* 87, 1938, p. 3.

[52] C. Guérard, 'Parménide d'Elée selon les néoplatoniciens', in *Études sur Parménide*, ed. P. Aubenque, vol. 2, Paris 1987, pp. 294-313.

[53] H. Gätje, 'Simplikios in der arabischen Überlieferung', *Der Islam* 59, 1982, p. 16.

[54] *Journal of the Warburg and Courtauld Institutes* 32, 1969, 1-24. In this context, cf. P. Hoffmann, 'Sur quelques aspects de la polémique de Simplicius contre Jean Philopon...', in I. Hadot (ed.), *Simplicius – sa vie, son oeuvre, sa survie*, Berlin and New York 1987, p. 192 and n. 42, who speaks about the public to which Simplicius' commentary on the *de Caelo* is addressed.

[55] Simplicius, *in Cael*. 26,17-24.

opinion of H.A. Thompson, who in his article 'Athenian twilight: AD 267-600' gives a summary of the results of excavations dating from before 1959.[56] According to this article, the city of Athens never recovered from its almost total destruction by the Heruls. The intrusion of the Goths in Attica in 396, even if it spared the city itself, which at that time was very reduced in extent, nevertheless caused economic suffering through the devastation of its hinterland. The Neoplatonist Synesius, when he visited the city around 400, compared it to the skin of a dismembered victim, the only remaining evidence of what was a living animal not long before.[57] Even though some activity of reconstruction is manifest from the beginning of the fifth century, this remained modest, and the economic importance of Athens never redeveloped in any manner comparable to that of a number of Greek or Greco-Syriac cities in Asia Minor. The least that one can say in taking account of the collection of facts and evidence that Thompson presents is that the circumstances were hardly favourable to the reconstitution of libraries comparable to the ones which had existed before the conquest of Sulla and the sack of the Heruls. On the contrary, everything suggests that a certain number of cities on the Asiatic continent had come to surpass Athens as regards the wealth of their libraries by far.

In considering the group of arguments I have just presented and in taking account of those I have discussed elsewhere, I am now more than ever persuaded that it is completely necessary to reject the hypothesis that Simplicius returned to Athens or Alexandria after his stay in Persia. There is a strong presumption and, after the publication of Tardieu's article on calendars,[58] even a near certitude of the correctness of the thesis that, in the company of his teacher Damascius and his fellow students, Simplicius turned towards the city of Ḥarrân, where he was welcomed along with the other philosophers into the heart of a pre-existing Neoplatonic school where all the philosophers continued to live, work and teach together.

*

Let us proceed to Simplicius' work. As H. Gätje stated in the article cited above, the Arabic literature preserves characteristics of Simplicius' scholarly personality which would have remained unknown to us, had we only taken into consideration the Greek works which the accidents of manuscript transmission have preserved for us. Let us begin with the latter. I believe that it is unanimously agreed that all of Simplicius' great commentaries on Aristotle which we still read today were written after the stay in Persia, thus after 532. Simplicius' cross-references allow us to establish a relative chronological order for three commentaries whose

---

[56] *Journal of Roman Studies* 49, 1959, pp. 61-72.

[57] Synesius, *Epist.*, 136.

[58] M. Tardieu, 'Les calendriers en usage à Harrân d'après les sources arabes et le commentaire de Simplicius à la *Physique* d'Aristote'.

authenticity is not contested, namely, the following: the commentary on the *de Caelo*, the commentary on the *Physics*, the commentary on the *Categories*. In the commentary on the *de Caelo*, Simplicius twice mentions Philoponus' treatise *de Aeternitate Mundi contra Proclum*, which was written in 529. On the other hand, from a report of an observation made close to the river Aboras (Chaboras) in Mesopotamia, a report which is also to be found in the commentary on the *de Caelo*,[59] it was concluded that this observation was made during his journey to Persia and that the commentary on the *de Caelo* must therefore have been written either in Persia at the court of Chosroes or somewhat after the stay in Persia. Today we know that the observation in question could more probably have been made later, after Simplicius had settled at Ḥarrân, as this river, a tributary of the Euphrates, passes to the east of Ḥarrân at a distance of about 40 kilometres.[60] As regards the commentary on the *Physics*, Simplicius speaks there of his master as someone no longer living. This commentary must, therefore, have been written at least after 532, the date at which Damascius was still alive according to Agathias, though probably only after 538. The latter date is based on an epigram for a deceased slave, contained in the *Palatine Anthology* and attributed to Damascius the philosopher.[61] In this regard, I must mention a correction Tardieu[62] has made of my book *Le problème du néoplatonisme Alexandrin*. There I wrote that the original source of this epigram, that is to say the funeral stele, had been found in Emesa (Ḥimṣ) in Syria. But in fact, it is merely preserved in the museum of that city, while its provenance is unknown. By following P. Waltz, I was once more mistaken concerning the date of the stele. It is not dated 537, but 538. If we assume the philosopher Damascius of this epigram to be identical with the Neoplatonist Damascius, the teacher of Simplicius, the year 538 is obtained as a *terminus post quem* for the composition of the commentaries on the *Physics* and on the *Categories*.

As regards the fourth Aristotelian commentary preserved under Simplicius' name, the commentary on the *de Anima*, its authenticity was already put in question at the beginning of the seventeenth century by Franciscus Piccolomini[63] and more recently by F. Bossier and C. Steel in an article entitled, 'Priscianus Lydus en de "In de anima" van Pseudo(?)-Simplicius'.[64] Piccolomini already considered Priscianus Lydus to be the author of this commentary, the same Priscianus who, according to Agathias, was present with Damascius and Simplicius at the court of Chosroes and whose *Solutiones eorum de quibus dubitavit Chosroes*

[59] Simplicius, *in Cael*. 525,13.

[60] cf. M. Tardieu, *Coutumes nautiques mésopotamiennes chez Simplicius*, in preparation.

[61] *Anthol. Palat.*, VII,553; vol. 5, 90 (Waltz).

[62] M. Tardieu, 'Ṣâbiens coraniques', p. 22ff and n. 103.

[63] cf. *Francisci Piccolominei Senensis commentarii in libros Aristotelis De caelo, ortu et interitu; adjuncta lucidissima expositione, in tres libros eiusdem de anima, nunc recens in lucem prodeunt*, Moguntiae 1608, p. 1001f.

[64] In *Tijdschrift voor Filosofie* 34, 1972, pp. 761-822.

Persarum rex we possess in a Latin version, a work that was probably also written in Ḥarrân. But while Piccolomini took it for granted that there was no doctrinal difference between Priscian and Simplicius, Bossier and Steel base part of their argument on the alleged existence of such differences, differences which H.J. Blumenthal and I deny. In this regard, I continue to maintain all I said in my review of their article in an appendix to my book *Le problème du néoplatonisme Alexandrin*[65] and in my article, 'La doctrine de Simplicius sur l'âme raisonnable humaine dans le commentaire sur le Manuel d'Epictète'.[66] At the time when I wrote this review, I was nevertheless seduced by the arguments of Bossier and Steel concerning the textual parallels between the commentary on the *de Anima* and Priscian's *Metaphrasis in Theophrastum*, so that I believed it probable that the commentary on the *de Anima* was Priscian's. I must say that today these textual parallels impress me much less, since I have encountered a large number of such parallels while comparing Simplicius' commentary on the *Categories* with those of Ammonius, Olympiodorus et al., parallels which are essentially due to a scholarly tradition that had become firmly settled in its manner of commenting on the *Categories* and due also to dependence on the same text for comment. Similarly, I think today that the absence of long discussions of the doctrines of previous philosophers, which had so astonished a number of scholars including myself, can be easily explained. Aristotle speaks in a more or less detailed manner of the opinions of the Presocratics and Plato's school at the beginning of the *Physics*, in several books of the *Metaphysics*, and also in the treatise *de Anima*. His Neoplatonic commentators thus had the opportunity to discuss this subject in three different commentaries. Yet for a Neoplatonist like Simplicius, who had already commented on the *Physics* and the *Metaphysics* – since I am convinced that he actually did write a commentary on the *Metaphysics* which is lost today[67] – it would have been overly fastidious to repeat himself endlessly. I thus think that the reason Simplicius gives for the absence of discussions on the Presocratics and the Platonists in his commentary on the *de Anima* is completely plausible. It is in effect: 'I have analysed the thought of these men in a sufficiently clear manner in the commentaries I have written on the books of the *Metaphysics*. For the present, we shall speak of them only to the degree that is necessary in order to explain the text on which we are commenting.' For all for these reasons, therefore, I have today many more reservations than before concerning the hypothesis of this commentary's inauthenticity, although I do not regard discussion of this issue as closed.

In the commentary on the *de Anima*, Simplicius refers twice to his commentary on the *Metaphysics*, three times to his commentary on the

[65] pp. 193-202.
[66] In H.J. Blumenthal and A.C. Lloyd (eds), *Soul and the Structure of Being in Late Neoplatonism*, Liverpool 1982, pp. 46-70.
[67] cf. my article 'Recherches sur les fragments du commentaire de Simplicius sur la Métaphysique d'Aristote' in *Simplicius – sa vie, son oeuvre, sa survie*, pp. 224-45.

Physics, and once to his epitome on Theophrastus' *Physics*, works which are all lost. The commentary on the *de Anima*, if it is authentic, is therefore situated chronologically after the commentary on the *Physics*, but its chronological relation to the commentary on the *Categories* cannot be determined. Of the commentary on the *Metaphysics* and the epitome on Theophrastus' *Physics*, we only know that they were written before the commentary on the *de Anima*.

The Arabic tradition also attributes a commentary on the *de Anima* to Simplicius. Here is the English translation of an entry in the *Fihrist* concerning the treatise *de Anima*, in the translation given by F.E. Peters in his book *Aristoteles Arabus*:[68] 'Liber animae: It has three books, Hunayn translated it into Syriac in its entirety; Ishâq translated all but a small part of it, then Ishâq made another version, emending it in the process. Themistius commented on this work in its entirety: the first book in two books, the second in two books, and the third in three books. And there is a (add. Al-Qifti: good) Syriac commentary by Olympiodorus and I read this in the handwriting of Yaḥyâ ibn ʿAdi. And indeed there is extant in Syriac a good commentary which is attributed to Simplicius, and he made this for Athâwâlîs. And indeed there is extant in Arabic an Alexandrine epitome of this work, about a hundred leaves. And there is Ibn al-Biṭrîq's compendium of this work. Ishâq said: I translated this work into Arabic from a corrupt copy, and after thirty years, I found an excellent copy, and I collated this with the first version, and this is the commentary of Themistius.' This text can be interpreted in different ways because it does not contain punctuation.[69] According to H. Gätje in his article, 'Simplikios in der arabischen Überlieferung', this passage was understood by Steinschneider, Dodge, and Ǧabr in the sense that Simplicius had written a commentary on the *de Anima* that was dedicated to a person named Athâwâlîs and that this commentary existed in a Syriac and an Arabic version.[70] For Peters, on the contrary – as his commentary demonstrates[71] – this text only signifies that there existed a Syriac translation of Simplicius' commentary. H. Gätje himself, when commenting again on the same passage in his book *Studien zur Überlieferung der aristotelischen Pyschologie im Islam* three years after Peters,[72] followed the views of Steinschneider, Dodge, and Ǧabr on this point. Unfortunately, orientalists have so far not recovered any trace of either a Syriac version or an Arabic version. Concerning Simplicius' dedication of his commentary on the *de Anima* to a certain Athâwâlîs, we are in the most complete ignorance as regards the identity of this person, who was not necessarily a Greek. For, if we can take the view that the

[68] Leyden 1968, p. 40f.

[69] cf. H. Gätje, *Studien zur Überlieferung der aristotelischen Psychologie im Islam* (= Annales Universitatis Saraviensis, Reihe Philosophische Fakultät, vol. 11), Heidelberg 1971, p. 20.

[70] In *Der Islam* 59, 1982, p. 11.

[71] F.E. Peters, op. cit., p. 42f.

[72] op. cit. (in n. 6), p. 26.

commentary was written in Ḥarrân, it might be that Simplicius wished to dedicate his work to a Syrian,[73] just as Priscian had addressed his *Quaestiones et Solutiones* to the Persian king Chosroes (in a Pahlavî or Syriac version?). Al-Qiftî, when rereading this text some three hundred years later, transformed the sentence 'he made this for Athâwâlîs' into 'Athâwâlîs likewise did this'. I have the impression that Arabists prefer the *Fihrist's* version, probably on account of its antiquity. Whichever version is followed, one cannot argue from the existence of this dedication, attested by the *Fihrist*, to the rejection of the authenticity of the commentary with which we are familiar today under Simplicius' name on the pretext that it does not contain the dedication in question. Nevertheless, in order to refute this argument, it will not suffice to say, as H. Gätje does[74] (following Steinschneider), that all the Greek manuscripts preserve this commentary without its opening, that is to say, its preface, and that for this reason we cannot know whether the dedication was originally there or not. This would not be entirely correct, for we have to distinguish between preface and dedication. In fact, among the Greek manuscripts which Hayduck mentions in the preface to his critical edition of this commentary, there is, besides two manuscripts which contain the preface in the form of a scholion, one manuscript, Matritensis Biblioth. Nat. 54, dated by Hayduck as being from the fourteenth century, which possesses the preface and the opening of the commentary up to page 31,19 of Hayduck's edition. According to the editor, this manuscript represents an independent manuscript tradition which is often better than that of the other manuscripts, all of which appear to belong to a single branch of the tradition. A new critical edition of this commentary, which is absolutely necessary in my opinion, will certainly bring further clarifications concerning the transmission of the text of the preface, though probably nothing on the subject of the dedication. Dedications, which were often presented in the form of a

---

[73] Tardieu has had the kindness to send me the following note concerning the name 'Athâwâlîs': 'This patronym,' he says, 'is in my opinion a case of a double Greco-Semitic name, associating the name of the male Arabo-Syrian god 'Itâᶜ, known from inscriptions CIS V/1, no. 3944 and 2595 (another spelling: Yatiᶜ, in CIS V/1, no. 218, 2288, 2636, a Greek transcription attested by the inscription of H. Waddington, IGLS no. 2209: *Ethaos*), with the Latin name Valens (in Greek: *Oualês*, Arabic and Syriac: Wâlîs with normal iotacisation of the Greek eta). From this combination we get *Etha-Oualês*, 'Eτâwâlîs or 'Iţâwâlîs. It is therefore an apotheosising name meaning: "Valens is 'Iţâᶜ". The occurrences of double Greek-Semitic names are frequent in the inscriptions of cities with a strong indigenous population: for Palmyra, see CIS II/3, no. 4566: Šalman Marcellus; no. 4402: Apollodôros Elabêlos; for Bostra, IGLS XIII/1, no. 9300: Severus Abdisar; no. 9274: Asados Priscus; no. 9415: Onemos Maximos. The Arabic transcription attested by Ibn al-Nadîm is explained by having been translated from the Greek, and not the Syriac (in which case the Arabic would have preserved the ᶜayn of 'Iţâᶜ). Consequently, the commentary on the *de Anima* attributed to Simplicius, of which Ibn al-Nadîm speaks, was not composed in Syriac. The expression "suryânî" ("in Syriac"), in the text of the *Fihrist* concerns the language of the testimony on which the Arabic version of the *in de Anima* was made, and not that of the original itself, which was in Greek.'

[74] cf. H. Gätje, *Studien zur Überlieferung*, p. 26.

detached letter, hardly interested the Byzantine scholars who were responsible for the transmission of texts, above all if they were lengthy. It is for this reason that while Simplicius in the sixth century still read[75] the dedication that Arrian, the compiler of Epictetus' *Encheiridion*, had addressed to a certain Messalinus when sending him the *Encheiridion*, this dedication has not been preserved for us despite the enormous quantity of manuscripts containing the *Encheiridion* that still exist today. Thus, if Simplicius' dedication to Athâwâlîs, as attested by *Fihrist*, is no longer extant today in any of the manuscripts containing the commentary which we read under Simplicius' name, this cannot be an argument in favour of its inauthenticity.

Regarding Simplicius' commentary on Epictetus' *Encheiridion*, K. Praechter used it in addition to Hierocles' commentary on the Pythagorean *Carmen Aureum* to support his thesis that there existed a fundamental difference between the doctrines of the Neoplatonic school at Athens and of that at Alexandria. An essential element of his thesis was the dating of this commentary: according to Praechter, it must have been composed at a time when Simplicius still adhered to the Alexandrian school while attending Ammonius' course and therefore his departure for Athens, where he would fall under the influence of that school, an influence with which all his commentaries on Aristotle were marked. I wrote *Le problème du néoplatonisme Alexandrin: Hiéroclès et Simplicius*[76] as an introduction to my critical edition of Simplicius' commentary to Epictetus' *Encheiridion*. There I refuted Praechter's hypotheses in detail and showed that there were not such doctrinal differences either between the schools of Athens and Alexandria, or between Simplicius' commentary on the *Encheiridion* and his other commentaries, and that this commentary reveals, as do all of his commentaries, Damascius' influence. In that book, I had not put forward any hypothesis regarding the date of this commentary, as I was not able to take advantage of Simplicius' statement that he had personally spoken about the doctrines of the Manicheans with an initiate of that sect. Today, I subscribe to Tardieu's arguments concerning the dating and the location of the writing of this commentary, which I have summarised above: it must have been written in Ḥarrân after 532.

I am profoundly sorry that H. Dörrie, in his article 'Simplikios' in the *Kleine Pauly*, did not indicate the sources on which he based the following claims: 'Preserved in the manuscripts, but not yet edited (!) are a commentary on the art [*tekhnê*] of Hermogenes and another on Iamblichus' treatise *On the Pythagorean Sect* [*Peri tês Puthagorou haireseôs*].' I have carried out some research on library catalogues, but I have not found anything of the sort so far. Certainly my investigations have not been exhaustive, but I none the less believe that H. Dörrie was the victim of an over-hasty reading of Praechter's article 'Simplikios' in

---

[75] cf. Simplicius, *in Ench. Epict.*, 1,13ff (Dübner).
[76] Paris 1978.

Pauly-Wissowa. There Praechter in fact states: 'As for the other unedited works, supposedly preserved in the manuscripts (Scholia on Hermogenes' *Tekhnê*, commentary on Iamblichus' three books *On the Pythagorean sect*, treatise on the syllogism), see Fabricius-Harles, *Bibliotheca Graeca* V.770 and IX.567.'[77] Is it possible that H. Dörrie did not see the word 'supposedly'?

When the text of the *Bibliotheca Graeca* of Fabricius-Harles that Praechter mentions is examined, it is apparent that Fabricius refers, regarding Simplicius' commentary on Iamblichus' treatise *On the Pythagorean Sect*, to an entry of Petrus Ioannes Nunnesius, who in turn had relied on Gesner's *Bibliotheca*; and when Gesner's text is appealed to, it becomes clear that he reproduces a statement by Raphael of Volterra, according to whom such a commentary by Simplicius, comprising three volumes, had existed in the Vatican library. Raffaello Maffei of Volterra's book *Commentariorum urbanorum octo et triginta libri* appeared for the first time in 1506 in Rome.[78] The modern printed catalogues of the Vatican do not make mention of such a manuscript and, as far as I know, neither does the manuscript catalogue. For my own part, I do not have a great deal of confidence that the manuscript which Raphael mentions will ever be found.

Yet, as F. Bossier has very clearly demonstrated,[79] a manuscript of this commentary certainly still existed in the sixteenth century. For in a lending record of the Bibliotheca Marciana, published by H. Omont,[80] we find the following remark: 'The above named gentleman Master Sebastiano Erizzo, on the instructions of the Riformatori, on the 7th day of November 1553, took out a work, namely, the three books of Iamblichus of Chalcedon on the Pythagorean Sect, with the commentary of Simplicius; and I took as security a little diamond set in a gold ring. On the said day, he returned the above named book, which he said was not what he wanted, and took a second copy, said to be the fourth book of Iamblichus on the Sect, with a commentary of the same on the letters of Porphyry, and also Hierocles' introduction to Pythagoras' *Carmina Aurea*, 7. Δ no. 526; and the security remained in my possession'. Bossier notes that the second codex was identified by Sicherl as the extant Taurinensis gr. 146: it is a manuscript which belonged to Cardinal Bessarion. Yet what was the first manuscript which Erizzo had returned and which contained Simplicius' commentary? Bossier takes the

---

[77] 'Simplikios', *Paulys Realencyclopädie*, vol. III A.1 (second series), 1927, col. 205.

[78] cf. F. Bossier, *Filologisch-historische navorsingen over de middeleeuwse en humanistische Latijnse vertalingen van de Commentaren van Simplicius*, part 1 (thesis from the Catholic University in Louvain, 1975, though unfortunately not yet published), p. 16.011, n. 2: there Bossier cites the following remark from book 18, f.189 (verso) of the 1511 edition: 'On his sect, Iamblichus wrote three books, which are still extant. Simplicius wrote a work on those commentaries, which is to be found in the Vatican library'.

[79] F. Bossier, op. cit., 16.011-16.014.

[80] H. Omont, *Deux registres de prêts de manuscrits de la Bibliothèque de Saint-Marc à Venise (1545-1559)*, Paris 1888, p. 40. [I thank Jill Kraye for help with the interpretation of this entry. – Ed.]

reasonable view that this manuscript must also have belonged to Bessarion's library bequeathed to Venice, although we have not found any trace of it in any of the old and new catalogues of Bessarion's donation and of the Bibliotheca Marciana. Yet the two pieces of evidence (one from Raphael of Volterra, the other from the lending record of the Bibliotheca Marciana) concerning the existence of a commentary by Simplicius on Iamblichus' *De secta Pythagorica*, one in 1506 in Rome, the other in 1553 in Venice, exclude the possibility that it was pure invention.[81]

Bossier's very rich thesis also contains a discussion[82] of a piece of evidence found in C. Gesner's enlarged edition of the *Bibliotheca universalis*,[83] which mentions a *Commentariolus de syllogismis* by Simplicius. It might be that the fact that a *Tractatus brevis de syllogismis* by an anonymous author follows the great commentary of Simplicius on the *Categories* in several manuscripts suggested the notion that this short treatise came from the same author as the commentary on the *Categories*. According to Bossier, thorough inquiry into this short treatise, of which there exist Christian and non-Christian versions, might eventually bring some clarification to the question of its provenance.

Bossier[84] also argues against the claim which H.D. Saffrey and L.G. Westerink make[85] that Simplicius possessed a copy of Proclus' commentary on the *Timaeus*, a copy which contained glosses. Here is the scholion in question, which occurs in the Paris. Coisl. 322 and which actually presents a distich as Simplicius' gloss on Proclus' commentary on the *Timaeus*:

> By Simplicius on the words, 'But may the divine Iamblichus be well disposed to us':
>
> Here is the work of Simplicius. O Iamblichus, dispenser of all goods,
> Forgive me if I have vanquished you, since it is by your own words!
>
> (*Simplikiou eis to 'all' ho men theios Iamblikhos eumenês estô'*:
>
> *Simplikiou ponos houtos; Iamblikhe dôter eaôn*
> *hilathi nikêtheis, all' hupo sôn epeôn.*)

By citing numerous examples of Hellenistic epigrams, Bossier demonstrates that, to begin with, the phrase 'Here is the work of Simplicius' does not mean that Simplicius designates himself as the author of the distich, as Saffrey-Westerink thought (p. cliii), but that the

---

[81] F. Bossier thinks that an exhaustive investigation of the collection of scholia of Iamblichus' treatise, *On the Pythagorean Sect*, which are contained in the Laurent, gr. 86.3, might eventually provide an answer to this enigma.

[82] op. cit. 16.004-16.006.

[83] cf. C. Gesner, J. Simler, J. Frisius, *Bibliotheca instituta et collecta, primim a C. Gesnero. Deinde in Epitomen redacta, et novorum librorum accessione locupletata, tertio recognita, et in duplum post priores editiones aucta, per I. Simlerum. Iam vero postremo aliquot mille, cum priorum tum novorum authorum opusculis ex instructissima Viennensi Austriae Imperatoria Bibliotheca amplificata per I.J. Frisium* ... Zurich 1583, p. 759, col. 1.

[84] op. cit. 16.006-16.008.

[85] In *Proclus, Théologie platonicienne*, vol. 1, Paris 1968, pp. clii-cliii.

distich is an epigram in the etymological sense, that is, an inscription which, in our case, occurred at the beginning of a book by Simplicius and indicated its content in a concise and pregnant manner. 'Here is the work of Simplicius' must therefore be understood as follows: 'The work which follows the distich is by Simplicius', or 'the commentary which follows is by Simplicius'. Bossier then shows that the distich in question has a greater chance of referring to Simplicius' commentary on the *Categories* than to one of his other works: it is probably not an accident that the same epigram appears three times in a manuscript of Simplicius' commentary on the *Categories*, specifically in the cod. Ambros. 306 (E 99 sup.), folios Ir, IIr, IIIr. Moreover, Simplicius, according to his own words in the preface to his commentary on the *Categories*, is largely relying in this commentary on Iamblichus' commentary. Bossier thinks that a certain scholiast glossing Proclus' commentary on the *Timaeus*, on coming to the words *eumenês estô* in the text of Proclus, recalled the similar phrase *hilathi nikêtheis* in the distich introducing Simplicius' commentary on the *Categories*, which led him to reproduce this distich in the margin. Another scholiast, when reading the distich in the margin, made the mistake of thinking that the distich had been composed by Simplicius himself concerning the words *eumenês estô*.

Bossier also corrected[86] A. Wartelle's faulty entries in his *Inventaire des manuscrits grecs d'Aristote et de ses commentateurs*,[87] according to which several Greek manuscripts contain a commentary by Simplicius on the *Sophistici Elenchi*, by showing that there is nothing of the sort.

*

As regards Simplicius' commentary on Hermogenes' *Tekhnê*, Harles[88] refers to a manuscript in Vienna, cod. 137, that is, Vindob. Phil. gr. 15. The description of this manuscript by Lambeck-Kollar for folios 49r-173v mentions a 'Compilation of the Introductions of Various Authors to Hermogenes' Rhetorical Art, namely from: Longinus, Iamblichus, Syrianus, and Simplicius, who were pagans; and John the Sicilian, John the Geometer, Gregory the Metropolitan of Corinth, John Doxopatres, and George Diairetes, who were Christians'.[89] I have not seen this manuscript and therefore do not know the corresponding Greek title. H. Hunger, in his study devoted to John Chortasmenos (= Ignatius of Selymbria) which contains among other things an almost complete edition of those of his works contained in Vindob. Suppl. gr. 75 (Chortasmenos' autograph), makes mention of a 'Collection of the Most

---

[86] op. cit. 16.010-16.011.

[87] Paris 1963, pp. 97 and 196.

[88] J.A. Fabricius – G.C. Harles, *Bibliotheca graeca sive notitia scriptorum veterum graecorum quorumcumque monumenta integra aut fragmenta edita exstant tum plerorumque e mss. ac deperditis, editio quarta*, Hamburg 1790-1809, vol. 5, p. 770.

[89] cf. P. Lambeck, *Commentariorum de Augustissima Bibliotheca Caesarea Vindobonensi liber septimus, editio altera studio et opera A.F. Kollarii*, Vienna 1781, cols. 550-3.

Essential Commentators on Rhetoric, etc.'[90] which is to be found on folios 97r-112v and of which he unfortunately does not give the complete title. It deserves mention that this very long title names not less than ten authors, pagans and Christians, as sources for this collection of extracts from introductions to rhetoric: from the Christians, the philosopher John the Sicilian, John Didaskalos the geometer, Gregory the Metropolitan of Corinth, John Doxopatres, George called the Diairetes; and from the Greeks, Simplicius, Longinus, Syrianus and Iamblichus. In the text itself none of these names appears again. H. Hunger thinks that this compilation was probably made by Chortasmenos himself.[91]

Could the title of this compilation be the same as that of Vindob. Phil. gr. 15 and as that of an anonymous work mentioned by L. Allatius in his *Diatriba de Georgiis*, a title which was reproduced by C. Walz in vol. 6 of his *Rhetores Graeci*[92] as follows: 'Collection of the Most Essential Commentaries on Rhetoric as Explained by Christian Commentators and by Greeks, of whom the Christians are John the Great Philosopher and Most Orthodox Sicilian, a different John Didaskalos the Geometer, Gregory the Metropolitan of Corinth, a different Metropolitan of Sardes Doxopatres named John, George called the Diairetes; the Greeks are Simplicius, Longinus, Syrianus, and Iamblichus'?

The same title, with a few slight modifications, is found again in another manuscript, Londin. Harleianus 5697 on folio 104r: 'Introduction to Fire Breathing Rhetoric from the Explanations of the Commentaries on this, by Christian and Greek Commentators, of whom the Christians are John the Great Philosopher and Most Orthodox Sicilian, a different John Didaskalos the Geometer, Gregory the Metropolitan of Corinth, another Metropolitan of Sardes the Doxopatres named John, George called the "Diairetes"; the Greeks are Simplicius, Longinus, Syrianus, Iamblichus'.

This manuscript contains the following works: <John Chortasmenos'> commentaries (with paraphrases and extracts) on the Organon of Aristotle and on Hermogenes; Proclus' *Elements of Physics (Stoikheiôsis phusikê)*. The writing which occupies the greatest part of our manuscript, including the *Prolegomena to Rhetoric*, has been identified by J. Wiesner[93] as that of Chortasmenos. The manuscript belonged to Cardinal Bessarion, a student of Chortasmenos, and was integrated much later into the collection of Greek manuscripts of the Palazzo Farnese.[94] E. Harley bought it ⌐n 18 January 1723/24. H. Hunger, in his study on Chortasmenos cited above, speaks neither of this manuscript nor of

[90] cf. H. Hunger, *Johannes Chortasmenos (c. 1370-c. 1436/37): Briefe, Gedichte und Kleine Schriften, Einleitung, Regesten, Prosographie, Text* (= Wiener Byzantinische Studien, vol. 7), Vienna 1969, p. 29.

[91] H. Hunger, op. cit., pp. 29ff.

[92] cf. C. Walz, *Rhetores Graeci*, vol. 6, Stuttgart, Tübingen, London and Paris 1834, p. vi.

[93] J. Wiesner, in P. Moraux, *Aristoteles Graecus: Die griechischen Manuskripte des Aristoteles* I, Peripatoi 8, Berlin and New York 1976, pp. 432ff.

[94] cf. L. Pernot, 'Nouveaux manuscrits grecs Farnésiens', in *Mélanges de l'École Française de Rome* 93, 1981, p. 706.

Vindob. Phil. gr. 15, so that the relationship between the three *Prolegomena to Rhetoric* and, if possible, that of Allatius' manuscript, has yet to be determined. A thorough investigation will perhaps reveal that this collection of extracts is not the work of Chortasmenos, but is older.

H. Hunger says the following of the collection from Vindob. Suppl. gr. 75.[95] It consists of two parts. The first, from folio 97r to 104v, essentially comprises extracts taken from the rhetorical works of John Doxopatres, of Maximus Planudes, and of Troilus. The second part (folios 104v-111v) contains discussions on concepts like 'truth-itself' (*autoalêtheia*), 'paradoxes' (*paradoxa*), and 'received opinions' (*endoxa*), on the 'dialectical premise' (*protasis dialektikê*), 'dialectical and logical problems' (*problêmata dialektika kai logika*), on the 'first principles of the sciences' (*prôtai arkhai tôn epistêmôn*), and on the difference between 'premise' (*protasis*) and 'problem' (*problêma*). Hunger remarks that these discussions are based in large part on Aristotelian definitions, taken above all from the *Topics*, and he adds that he was unable to determine whether Chortasmenos or his source used one of the already edited commentaries on Aristotle.[96] However that may be, the very word 'truth-itself' (*autoalêtheia*) reveals the Neoplatonic tenor of the second part, but nothing indicates that it came from a commentary of Simplicius. As regards the first part, it may be assumed that Chortasmenos knew at least the rhetorical work of Doxopatres and of Maximus Planudes. Now, these two authors themselves used ancient and above all Neoplatonic sources, sometimes naming them, sometimes not. Thus, one of the texts used by Chortasmenos which H. Hunger had correctly identified as belonging to Maximus Planudes, has parallels in a *Prolegomenon* attested as belonging to Syrianus in Paris. gr. 1983, a manuscript used moreover by Planudes.[97] As for Doxopatres, he cites for example Porphyry's *Isagoge*[98] and one of Porphyry's two commentaries on the *Categories*,[99] an unnamed work of David,[100] an unnamed work of Simplicius which I believe to be his commentary on the *Categories*,[101] and Plato's *Gorgias*.[102] He also cites Dionysius Thrax, the rhetorical commentaries of four Neoplatonic philosophers, to wit, Marcellinus, Sopatros, Eustathius, and Syrianus,[103] and among Christians a certain George and a geometer who are probably respectively the George the

[95] H. Hunger, op. cit., pp. 30ff.

[96] ibid., p. 30.

[97] On the use of Paris. gr. 1983, dated to tenth/eleventh century, and of Maximus Planudes' Prolegomenon 13, cf. H. Rabe, *Prolegomenon Sylloge*, Leipzig 1935, pp. xlv and lx. The Prolegomenon 13 was attributed in Paris. gr. 1983 to Syrianus by a later hand: cf. R. Rabe, ibid., p. 183.10 (critical apparatus). Cf. Prolegomenon 7 (Maximus Planudes), p. 64.11-12 and 15-19 (Rabe) and Prolegomenon 13, p.190.6-7 and 18-25 (Rabe).

[98] cf. C.Walz, *Rhetores Graeci*, vol. 2, 1832, 95,6ff.

[99] ibid., 157.4ff; cf. Porphyry, *in Cat.* 60,17f; 153,30-154,2.

[100] ibid., vol. 2, 154,3 (cf. David, *Prol. Philos.* 12,23).

[101] ibid., vol. 2, 153.30-154.2; cf. Simplicius, *in Cat.* 55,24-9.

[102] cf. C. Walz, *Rhetores Graeci*, vol. 2, 104,18ff.

[103] Concerning the Neoplatonists Marcellinus, Sopatros, Eustathius and Syrianus, cf. most recently G.A. Kennedy, *Greek Rhetoric under Christian Emperors*, Princeton 1983.

so-called Diairetes and the John Didaskalos the geometer mentioned by
Chortasmenos in his *Collection*. It could very well be that Chortasmenos or
his source knew a commentary by Simplicius on Hermogenes' *Tekhnê*,
even if he knew it only through the mediation of other Byzantine
commentaries rather than by a direct reading. This is not improbable,
since as we shall see in regard to Simplicius' lost commentary on the
Metaphysics,[104] the Byzantines of the eleventh to thirteenth centuries
clearly possessed more information than we do on Simplicius' works. If one
is very suspicious, one might clearly imagine that Chortasmenos had
taken Doxopatres' mere mention of Simplicius' name as testimony of the
existence of a rhetorical commentary by Simplicius, mention which would
probably refer to the commentary on the *Categories*.[105] For my part, I do
not believe this to be the case, and I base my opinion on a series of three
epigrams in honour of Simplicius, published in E. Cougny's *Anthologiae
Graecae appendices*, which I reproduced in the biographical chapter of my
book *Le problème du néoplatonisme Alexandrin*.[106] One of these three
epigrams is addressed to Simplicius as the author of the commentary on
the *Categories*, the second makes allusion to his commentary on the *de
Caelo*, and the third glorifies him in his dual capacity as orator and
philosopher. Here it is:[107]

To Simplicius:
Is Simplicius an orator or a philosopher?
Both, it seems to me, and by my word, the best.

(Eis Simplikion
Rhetor ho Simplikios, ê philosophos;
Amphô dokei moi, kai, ma tous logous, akros.)

(Utrum rhetor Simplicius, an philosophus?
Utrumque videtur mihi, et per litteras, summum.)

That a Neoplatonic philosopher should preoccupy himself with rhetoric
should not, moreover, be surprising. I described in my book *Arts libéraux
et philosophie dans la pensée antique* the slow evolution within the
Platonic school, which led, beginning with a hostile attitude towards
rhetoric in Plato's life, to the inclusion of rhetoric in the plan of studies for
the future Platonic philosopher and to the conviction that the abilities of
the orator were indispensable to a philosopher if he wished to address
others for persuasion.[108] We know, moreover, with certainty that
Porphyry had written a commentary on Minucianus and other rhetorical

[104] cf. I. Hadot, 'Recherches sur les fragments du commentaire de Simplicius sur la
Métaphysique d'Aristote', in *Simplicius – sa vie, son oeuvre, sa survie*, pp. 225-45.
[105] cf. n. 101.
[106] op. cit., p. 31.
[107] E. Cougny, *Anthol. Graecae appendices*, Paris 1890, vol. 3, ch. 3, p. 321, no. 180.
[108] *Études Augustiniennes*, Paris 1984, pp. 50, 76-7, 83, 91-4, 107, 228, 279.

works,[109] that Iamblichus had written a rhetorical work cited by Syrianus,[110] and similarly for Iamblichus' students Sopatros and Eustathius. Marcellinus and Syrianus, also Neoplatonists, had composed commentaries on Hermogenes.[111] Damascius, Simplicius' teacher, perhaps did not write a commentary, but he himself says that he had taught rhetoric for nine years.[112] For all these reasons, I believe it probable that Simplicius wrote a commentary on Hermogenes' *Tekhnê*, of which one can perhaps find traces when systematically exploiting the enormous mass of manuscript material that still exists in the form of anonymous scholia concerning rhetoric.

To come finally to the Arabic tradition as regards Simplicius, H. Gätje's article, 'Simplikios in der arabischen Überlieferung',[113] attempts to provide an inventory. The same *Fihrist* of Al-Nadîm, of which we have already spoken in connexion with the remark on Simplicius' commentary on the *de Anima*,[114] also attests the existence of a commentary on the *Categories*[115] as Al-Qiftî does much later, who as a general rule produces the material found in Al-Nadîm with some additions, omissions and alterations. Yet regarding Simplicius' other commentaries on Aristotle, the Arabic bibliographic sources are silent. Conversely, in these two Arabic authors, Simplicius is named in the capacity of mathematician and astronomer, and as having written a commentary on the first book of Euclid's *Elements*. Al-Qiftî adds in this regard, as already mentioned above,[116] that Simplicius had founded a school and that he had students who were named after him. A.I. Sabra in his article, 'Simplicius' proof of Euclid's parallel postulate',[117] has collected besides the extracts of this commentary cited by al-Nayrîzî[118] in Arabic in his own commentary on Euclid's *Elements*, an extract contained in a letter of ᶜAlam al-Dîn Qayṣar ibn Abi 'l-Qâsim to Naṣîr al-Dîn al-Ṭûsî, and beyond that a text contained in an Arabic manuscript, Bodleianus Thurston 3, fol. 148r.[119] al-Nayrîzî's commentary was known in the West through the Latin translation of Gerard of Cremona. Simplicius is cited there under the name of 'Sambelichos'. The Greek tradition only allows us to conclude indirectly

---

[109] cf. R. Beutler, 'Porphyrios', in *Realencyclopädie der klassischen Altertumswissenschaft*, vol. 22, 43. Halbband, 1953, col. 300.

[110] Syrianus *in Hermogenem* I, 9.10ff (Rabe), Leipzig 1892.

[111] On all of these Neoplatonists, cf. St. Gloeckner, *Quaestiones rhetoricae. Historiae artis rhetoricae qualis fuerit aevo Imperatorio capita selecta*, Breslauer Philol. Abhandlungen, vol. 8, no. 2, Breslau 1901, and most recently G.A. Kennedy, op. cit. in n. 103.

[112] cf. Photius *Biblioth.*, cod. 181, vol. 2, p. 192 (Henry).

[113] In *Der Islam* 59, 1982, 6-31.

[114] See above, p. 292.

[115] cf. also F.E. Peters, *Arisoteles Arabus*, Leyden 1968, p. 7.

[116] See above, p. 288.

[117] The article cited in n. 54.

[118] G. Freudenthal has been kind enough to tell me that E. Wart of the Library of the Hebrew University, Jerusalem, has discovered in an MS from the Yemen some pages containing in Arabic translation new fragments of the commentary of Simplicius on the first book of Euclid's *Elements*.

[119] A mathematician living in the ninth century AD.

about Simplicius' capacities as a mathematician: his commentary on the *Physics* actually contains discussions on the theory of the quadrature of half lunes by Hippocrates of Chios, a mathematician who lived before Aristotle. Yet there is no need of indirect testimony in order to be convinced of the identity of Simplicius the commentator of Aristotle, Epictetus, and Hermogenes with Simplicius the mathematician. To begin with, the *Fihrist* clearly connects the philosopher and the mathematician, and further we know that every Neoplatonist philosopher was also a mathematician in so far as he was a philosopher. Generally speaking, as I have shown in *Arts libéraux et philosophie dans la pensée antique*,[120] it was the schools of philosophy, Platonic or Stoic, which in the Hellenistic or Imperial period gave instruction in mathematics and in astronomy to youth desiring to gain knowledge in these matters within the framework of the acquisition of general culture. The instruction of surveyors and engineers in geometry was only directed by professionals to future professionals.

At this point, let us add a further interesting detail. In one of the textual fragments of Simplicius' commentary on the first book of Euclid's *Elements* reported by al-Nayrîzî, Simplicius speaks of his 'ṣâḥib' named 'Aghânîs' or 'Aġânîs' and cites a mathematical demonstration from him.[121] What might the corresponding Greek term be? A.I. Sabra translates this by 'our associate', which might possibly make one think of a professional associate in the school which, according to al-Nadîm, Simplicius directed.[122] It might also be a matter of an Arabic translation of the Greek term *hetairos* which, in the manner that Neoplatonists use it, designates a fellow student who has been admitted to the inner circle of true adherents of Neoplatonic philosophy. As regards his name, until recently only a Greek or Latin name was sought beneath this Arabic form, as for example 'Geminus' (the mathematician) or 'Agapius'.[123] Yet it might be more simple to take the name 'Aġânîs' as such and recognise in it, with Tardieu, a patronym attested in Egypt.[124] In this case, the 'Aġânîs' cited in the fragment of al-Nayrîzî is not a corrupted form of some Greek or Latin name at all, but the real name of Simplicius' 'ṣaḥib', who is probably an Egyptian.

[120] *Études Augustiniennes*, Paris 1984, 252-61.
[121] cf. A.I. Sabra, op. cit., p. 6 in English translation.
[122] cf. above, pp. 288 and 301.
[123] cf. the summary of interpretations made until recently in A.I. Sabra's article, 'Thâbit Ibn Qurra on Euclid's Parallel Postulate', *Journal of the Warburg and Courtauld Institutes* 31, 1968, p. 13, n. 6.
[124] I am indebted to Michel Tardieu's kindness for the following points: the patronym 'Aġânîs' is formed from a masculine common noun which means, in Semitic and in Egyptian, 'cup', 'jug', 'vase'. This patronym is attested as such only in Egypt: (a) in the form *Agânis*, *Agenis* in the Greek documents (cf. F. Preisigke, *Namenbuch*, Heidelberg 1922, p. 6); (b) in the form '*Agan* in the Aramaic documents of Elephantine (cf. E. Sachau, *Aramäische Papyri und Oustraka aus einer Militär-Kolonie zu Elephantine*, Leipzig 1911, Ostracon 75/2: French translation by P. Grelot, *Documents araméens d'Egypte*, Paris 1972, no. 12b/15, p. 105; cf. H. Ranke, *Die ägyptischen Personennamen*, 2 vols, Glückstadt-Hamburg 1935-52, vol. 2, p. 186).

Finally, a doctor named Simplicius also appears in the Arabic biographical and bibliographical tradition. Must this or these doctors named Simplicius (it seems that al-Nadîm probably spoke of two different doctors named Simplicius) be identified with our Simplicius? It is a fact that apart from al-Nadîm, the Arabic doctor ar-Razi (who died in 925) attributed to an author the form of whose name could be translated by Simplicius a commentary on the Hippocratic treatise, *On Bone Fractures*.[125] The dating of this Simplicius causes problems. According to al-Nadîm, he lived after Aristotle and Euclid, but before Galen. Yet the remark 'before Galen' does not necessarily have to be taken strictly, as Gätje claims. In any case, the latter is certainly wrong in thinking, on the grounds that there were two different doctors named Simplicius, that the first Simplicius could have been a contemporary of Hippocrates.[126] This hypothesis is impossible because of the name 'Simplicius' alone, which, for a Greek, can only be late. Anyway, I believe that, given the present state of research, it is more prudent to pronounce a *non liquet* concerning the hypothesis that our Neoplatonist philosopher Simplicius could have written a commentary on a Hippocratic treatise.

Here, therefore, are the conclusions to which one might be led as regards Simplicius' works. We have extant: the commentaries on Epictetus' *Encheiridion*, on Aristotle's *de Caelo, Physics, Categories*, and probably on his *de Anima*. Lost, though attested in a more or less certain fashion: a commentary on the first book of Euclid's *Elements*, a commentary on Aristotle's *Metaphysics*,[127] a commentary on Iamblichus' work devoted to the Pythagorean sect, an epitome of Theophrastus' *Physics* (if the commentary on the *de Anima*, where one finds a reference to this work, is authentic), and perhaps a commentary on Hermogenes' *Tekhnê*.

---

[125] cf. H. Gätje, 'Simplikios in der arabischen Überlieferung', *Der Islam* 59, 1982, pp. 12f and 18f.

[126] H. Gätje, op. cit., p. 13.

[127] cf. I. Hadot, op. cit. in n. 67, pp. 225-45.

CHAPTER THIRTEEN

Neoplatonic elements in the
de Anima commentaries[1]

Henry J. Blumenthal

Most scholars who refer to the Greek commentators for help in the understanding of difficult Aristotelian texts seem to expect straight-forward scholarly treatment of their problems.[2] Not infrequently they are disappointed and complain about the irrelevance of the commentary they read, or inveigh against the incompetence of the commentators.[3] Only Alexander is generally exempt from such censure, and that in itself is significant. For he is the only major commentator whose work survives in any considerable quantity who wrote before Neoplatonism. Shortly after Alexander the kind of thought that is conveniently described by this label came to dominate Greek philosophy, and nearly all pagan philosophy and philosophical scholarship was pursued under its influence, if not by its active adherents. It is the purpose of this paper to argue that these facts are not trivial items of background interest, but are fundamental to a proper assessment of the later commentators' opinions on points of Aristotelian scholarship. It is necessary to take account of the ideas and purpose of these commentators if one is to make any serious critical use of their work, and this cannot be done if one merely dips into their voluminous works in the hope of occasional enlightenment.

That these men were swayed by their own opinions and preconceptions is perhaps obvious once stated. Even Simplicius, notwithstanding his reputation for careful scholarship, is no exception. Simplicius may have done us a great service by preserving fragments of the pre-Socratics, but

---

[1] A paper read to the Southern Association for Greek Philosophy at Cambridge, Sept. 1973. A much abbreviated form of some of this material was included in a communication to the 14th International Congress of Byzantine Studies. *Note*: References to the commentators are by page and line of the Berlin Academy edition. All unspecified references are to their *de Anima* commentaries.

[2] For this attitude cf. K.O. Brink, 'Peripatos', *RE* supp. vol. 7, 1940, 947; W.K.C. Guthrie, *History of Greek Philosophy* I, Cambridge 1962, 367, writing on the pre-Socratics: 'Simplicius ... was a learned and careful commentator ...'; E.R. Dodds, s.v. 'Simplicius', *Oxford Class. Dictionary*[2], Oxford 1970, speaks of his 'learned and sober commentaries'.

[3] cf. W.D. Ross, Aristotle. *De Anima*, Oxford 1961, 43; W. Theiler, *Aristoteles, Über die Seele*, Berlin 1959, 82f.

he was nevertheless a man who entertained ideas which were not likely to lead to the correct interpretation of Aristotle, as Hicks for one saw[4] – Ross it seems did not.[5] In fact one might go so far as to say that Simplicius was less well fitted than some of the other commentators to give a good account of his subject. Those whose immediate reaction to such a statement is that it is grossly unfair to so fine a scholar might be disturbed by some of the material in the preface to Simplicius' *de Anima* commentary – as they would by that in Philoponus' as well – material which often escapes notice for the simple reason that one normally refers to these works for help with specific passages and does not read them as a whole. This is not to say that there are no obvious signs of what is going on in the body of the commentaries, for there certainly are. A case in point is Simplicius' claim in the *de Caelo* commentary (640,27-32) that Aristotle's criticisms of Plato are directed not against Plato himself, but against those who failed to grasp Plato's real meaning. In the preface to the commentary on the *Categories* Simplicius goes further and says that in dealing with Aristotle's attacks on Plato one should not consider only the philosophers' language and complain about their discord, but rather one should concentrate on their thought and seek out their accord on most matters (*in Cat.* 7,29-32). Here we have two expressions of the normal Neoplatonic view that Plato and Aristotle were usually trying to say the same thing. This view can of course be traced back to the revival of positive teaching in the New Academy.[6] This is not to say that no Neoplatonist was aware of the differences, and certain Aristotelian doctrines remained unacceptable. In the passage we have just mentioned Simplicius talks about accord in *most* matters (*hê en tois pleistois sumphônia*, and elsewhere he shows that he is alive to differences (e.g. *in Cael.* 454,23ff), even if he does regard Aristotle as Plato's truest pupil (ib. 378,20f)[7] or his best interpreter (*in DA* 245,12). Philoponus, moreover, actually protested against the view that Aristotle's attacks on Plato's ideas were not directed at Plato himself, a view that seems to have had

[4] Aristotle, *De Anima*, Cambridge 1907, lxv. Cf. also P. Wilpert, 'Die Ausgestaltung der aristotelischen Lehre vom Intellectus agens bei den griechischen Kommentaren und in der Scholastik des 13 Jahrhunderts', in Festschrift M. Grabmann, *Beitr. zur Gesch. der Phil. und Theol. des Mittelalters* supp. vol. 3.i, 1935, 451 and n. 20; O. Hamelin, *La Théorie de l'intellect d'après Aristote et ses commentateurs*, Paris 1953, 44-7. This long posthumous publication provides the fullest treatment yet of Simplicius on *nous*, but is marred by the now outdated view that the Neoplatonists constituted a more or less unified 'école d'Alexandrie', cf. esp. 44 and 56. Though Hamelin makes certain distinctions between Plotinus, Iamblichus and Simplicius, he takes no account of such differences as would have obtruded themselves had he considered Ps.-Philop. on 3.5, and in particular he seems unaware of the typically Athenian elements in Simplicius.

[5] cf. his remarks on the interpretation of 3.5, loc. cit.

[6] cf. e.g. Cicero *Acad.* 1.4.17: 'But on Plato's authority there was instituted a form of philosophy which was unitary and harmonious under two names, those of Academics and Peripatetics, and they agreed materially while differing in designation.' For the Neoplatonic period cf. K. Praechter, s.v. 'Simplikios', *RE* III a i, 1927, 210f. and the collection of texts in I. Düring, *Aristotle in the Ancient Biographical Tradition*, Göteborg 1957, 334-6.

[7] An accolade elsewhere bestowed on Xenocrates, *in Phys.* 1165,34.

some currency (cf. *Aet.* 3.2 = 29.2-8 Rabe).[8] None the less ever since Plotinus, whose adoption of much Aristotelian thought would be clear enough without Porphyry's explicit statement on the point (*Vita Plot.* 14.4ff), the new Platonism had been more or less Aristotelianised: the controversies about whether or not Aristotelian views could be accepted by Platonists which had been current in the middle Platonic period were no longer live. By the time Simplicius and Philoponus composed their commentaries,[9] Aristotle's philosophy had been used as the standard introduction to Plato for at least two centuries.[10] The tendency among certain modern scholars to see Aristotle simply as a Platonist has a precedent in the activities of the Neoplatonists: in both cases it depends on a somewhat special understanding of Plato.

Let us now look at some of the information about his bias that Simplicius himself provides at the start of the preface to his *de Anima* commentary (1,3-21). His purpose is best understood in terms of the word *sumphônia*, which appears almost as a slogan. Next to the truth the chief object of study is an understanding of the views of those who have reached the summit of knowledge, and therefore we must deal with Aristotle's work on the soul. Plato has produced many inspired speculations about it, but these have been adequately and consistently (*sumphônos allêlois*) expounded by the commentators on Plato – we might envy them their success. But in the case of Aristotle there is much inconsistency among the interpreters, not only as to the meaning of his language, but also as to the actual content. In other words, one of the usual Neoplatonic methods of dealing with inconsistency, to argue that it is merely a matter of different terminology applied to the same truth,[11] is not available. Therefore, says Simplicius, he decided to seek and set out Aristotle's consistency – *sumphônia* again – both with himself and the truth. That statement in itself might give rise to doubts about the objectivity of Simplicius' interpretation, doubts which are heavily reinforced by what follows. For Simplicius goes on to say that he will try as far as possible to stick to the truth of things in accordance with the exposition of Iamblichus in his own writings on the soul. This, he claims, is the same task as the exposition of Aristotle in terms of Aristotle's own philosophy. Here we are faced with the basic methodological defect of all Neoplatonic commentary, the conviction that Plato, Aristotle and the

---

[8] Thus Elias *in Cat.* 123,1-3, tells us that Iamblichus claimed that Aristotle was not opposing Plato on the theory of Ideas. In this at least he was not followed by Proclus, cf. Philop. *in Cat.* 31,7 ff [and for Philoponus, see Koenraad Verrycken, chapter 11 above – Ed.]

[9] In Philoponus' case we should perhaps rather say published, since his commentary is basically the publication of Ammonius' work, as the title proclaims, 1.1 f. On the relation of Philoponus' commentaries to Ammonius' courses cf. my paper 'Did Iamblichus write a commentary on the *De Anima*?', *Hermes* 102, 1974, 553 n. 56 and the references given there.

[10] For one roughly contemporary attitude cf. Marinus *Vita Procli* 13, who likens Aristotle's works to minor preliminary mysteries. A more sober view, perhaps characteristic of the Alexandrian school, is indicated by Elias *in Cat.* 123,10f, who merely says they are an introduction.

[11] See e.g. the passage from Simpl. *in Cat.* cited above and *in Phys.* 1336,35ff.

Neoplatonists themselves were all expressing the same truth. Sometimes of course this conviction was shaken, but as we shall see such doubts often sprang from differences among the Neoplatonists themselves as to what that truth was. That Iamblichus should be presented as a witness to it is at least alarming, notwithstanding recent and perhaps overenthusiastic attempts to rehabilitate Iamblichus, and rescue him from the reputation of a mere superstitious mystery-monger.[12] And it is not simply a matter of lip service to a figure revered by Athenian Neoplatonists – the Alexandrian attitude may have been different[13] – paid at the beginning of a work and then forgotten, for Simplicius refers to Iamblichus as an authority on several occasions in the body of the commentary.[14] Had Iamblichus himself written a *de Anima* commentary, which he probably did not,[15] it is likely that he would have figured more prominently in that of Simplicius, for in his *Categories* commentary Simplicius refers to Iamblichus with great frequency throughout.[16] For a similar attention to Iamblichus' views we must go to Proclus' commentary on the *Timaeus*,[17] and Proclus is not usually reckoned among Aristotelian scholars, though he did write commentaries on some of the logical treatises.[18] If we ask how close attention to the views of Iamblichus would affect an Aristotle commentary, the answer is that it would characteristically tend to produce explanations by the multiplication of entities, for Iamblichus seems to have been at least in part responsible for the complex mediations and triadic schemes of that Neoplatonism which is attested in the work of Proclus, where the relation between any two terms is likely to be explained in terms of a third which has some but not all the characteristics of each.[19] Hence a tendency to deal with certain problems about the soul by splitting it into components in a way that Aristotle did not, and returning to a position in some ways more like Plato's, though informed by a somewhat different view of the relations between the parts. Thus some sort of compromise was possible between Aristotle's view that body and soul were inseparable and Plato's that they were not. The latter was the basic position of the Neoplatonists, though they thought in terms

[12] So R.T. Wallis, *Neoplatonism*, London 1972, ch. 4; J.M. Dillon, *Iamblichi Chalcidensis in Platonis Dialogos Commentariorum Fragmenta*, Leiden 1973, ch. 2. Cf. also A.C. Lloyd in A.H. Armstrong (ed.) *Cambridge History of Later Greek and Early Medieval Philosophy*, Cambridge 1967, 296f.

[13] cf. Ammonius *in An. Pr.* 38,40-39,2 and n. 58 to the article cited in n.9.

[14] cf. e.g. 89,33-5, 187,36f and esp. 313,6f.

[15] On this see the article cited in n. 9.

[16] Roughly once in 2½ pages.

[17] The relevant passages are now conveniently assembled by Dillon, op. cit. 106-205.

[18] References to these are listed by L.G. Westerink, *Anonymous Prolegomena to Platonic Philosophy*, Amsterdam 1962, xii n.22.

[19] cf. now Wallis, op. cit. (n.12) 125ff, who may, however, exaggerate Proclus' dependence on Iamblichus. That Iamblichus invented at least the henads has now been shown by Dillon, 'Iamblichus and the origin of the doctrine of henads', *Phronesis* 17, 1972, 102-6. [Dillon now qualifies his view in response to Saffrey and Westerink in his 'Iamblichus of Chalcis' in W. Haase (ed.), *Aufstieg and Niedergang der römischen Welt*, 36.2, Berlin 1987, 862-909, at 883-4. – Ed.]

of degrees of separability, a matter which we must consider further in relation to their comments on Aristotle's definition of the soul.[20] For the moment it will suffice to say that Neoplatonists saw the individual soul as a descending succession of forms or as a series of reflections from, or images of, its highest part.[21] Thus for instance the sensitive soul was a reflection of the rational soul, the vegetative of the sensitive and sometimes a further sub-vegetative phase was distinguished whose function was to inform matter,[22] so producing body, which derived life only from the layer above.[23] At times, however, this information of matter was seen as a function of the world soul:[24] in the last resort individual souls were identical both with the world soul and with each other.[25] As one descends down the series the soul becomes more closely tied to body. Hence it is possible to talk in terms of information and to see the body: soul relation as one between matter and form, at least at the lowest level, in spite of the fact that soul was strictly separate from body, and even at this lowest level was regarded as illuminating or irradiating matter rather than being its form in any Aristotelian sense.[26] This is probably at least part of the reason for an apparent ambivalence about the body:soul relation which we find at various points in the commentaries. As for terms, either the sub-vegetative irradiation, or the vegetative soul, or both together, could be described as *phusis* (nature), while *psukhê* (soul) might be used not only as a term for soul in general, but also more specifically to describe the soul above the level of *phusis*.[27] Thus in his preface Simplicius makes a distinction between *phusis*, which is the informing cause (*eidêtikê aitia*), which makes the thing informed capable of the movement characteristic of what is alive, and another cause which is responsible for the movement: that is *psukhê* (4,14ff).

Several degrees of separability, as opposed to the two which might legitimately if arguably be found in the text of Aristotle, appear also in the preface to Philoponus' commentary. This preface too provides us with clear indications that what we are about to read is not necessarily straightforward exposition of Aristotle. For a start, we are confronted with a series of appeals to Plato (pp. 1-3). Further on we are told that psychology is important because it affects our whole life: *allôs te ti*

---

[20] See below, pp. 321-2.

[21] Terms like image, illumination, appearance (*eidôlon, ellampsis, indalma*) are frequently found to express this relation, cf. Plot. 1.1.11, 5.9.6.15-19, 6.5.8., Philop. 195, 2ff, 202,22ff, Simpl. 85,18.

[22] For these distinctions in the lower sections of the soul cf. Plot. 4.4.17-21 *passim.*, Simpl. 51,28ff.

[23] cf. e.g. Plot. 6.4.15.8ff.

[24] Plot. 4.3.7.25-8.

[25] Hence Plotinus at least felt no contradiction between statements that the lowest level of soul comes from the individual soul and others that it comes from the world soul, cf. my *Plotinus' Psychology*, The Hague 1971, 27ff.

[26] The *Timaeus* rather than the middle books of the *Metaphysics* would probably be seen as the appropriate authority on the relation of form to matter, though the relevant section of that dialogue, 50Bff, is not, as far as I know, referred to in discussions about body and soul.

[27] This usage is often found in Plotinus, cf. e.g. 4.4.18.1ff.

oikeioteron hêmin tês hêmôn autôn gnôseôs (12,14f).

That was a slogan of the time, and one of the reasons why the *First Alcibiades* came at the start of the Plato course, a practice that we learn from Proclus went back at least as far as Iamblichus.[28] Having said that, Philoponus announces his intention of showing (1) that all soul is incorporeal, (2) that only the rational soul is separable from all body, (3) that the irrational soul is separable from the gross body (*tou men pakheos toutou* sc. *sômatos*) but inseparable from the *pneuma*, particularly if there is a pneumatic body, (4) that the irrational soul survives for a time after its departure from the body, (5) that the vegetative soul (*phutikê psukhê*) has its being in the gross body and perishes with it (12,15-22). Here we have a number of un-Aristotelian notions which were part of the general body of Neoplatonic thought. First there is the gradation of degrees of union between body and soul parallel to that which we have already noticed in Simplicius, whose description of nature (*phusis*) as informing cause (*eidêtikê aitia*) implies, if it does not actually state, that the survival of that level of soul is closely linked with that of the body. And we certainly have the same distinction between an irrational soul (*alogos psukhê*) and a lowest level, as opposed to that simple dichotomy into a rational and an irrational part which may sometimes be found in Aristotle.[29] Thus irrational (*alogos*) in Philoponus and Simplicius has a special sense, namely the part between reason on the one side and the vegetative soul on the other. Most striking is the appearance of the *pneuma*. The slight hesitation implied by 'again if this pneumatic body exists at all (*eti ei holôs estin auto touto to pneumatikon sôma*)' suggests that Philoponus may have had doubts as to whether that part of the soul was simply closely bound up with that connate (*sumphuton*) *pneuma* which appears in some of Aristotle's works, but never in the *de Anima*, or whether it was actually attached to the full-scale pneumatic body which the later Neoplatonists used as an intermediate entity to explain how immaterial soul could be associated with material body, a belief of which there are already hints in Plotinus,[30] but which did not become a fixed and important part of Neoplatonic thought until some time afterwards.[31] Other passages in Philoponus' commentary can show that he did in fact accept the usual formulation.[32] Simplicius too believed in such an entity.

[28] *in Alc*. 11. Proclus gives us the reasons for it in the first 7 chapters of this commentary. Ch. 11 need not, as Dillon thinks, op. cit. (n. 12) 264, show that Iamblichus himself established this order of reading the dialogues: it could simply indicate that Proclus is giving Iamblichus as an authority for the system. Albinus had already prescribed *Alc*. I as a start for suitably disposed individuals, *Eisagoge* 149.31ff. H, and H.-R. Schwyzer, 'Plotin und Platons "Philebos" ', *Rev. Int. Philos*. 24, 1970, 185, points out that the twelve dialogues in Iamblichus' canon, with the addition of *Rep., Laws* and the *Letters*, provide nearly all the references to Plato in Plotinus. On the order in which the dialogues were studied cf. Westerink, op. cit. (n. 18) xxxviiff and A.J. Festugière, 'L'ordre de lecture des dialogues de Platon aux Ve/VIe siècles', *Mus. Helv*. 26, 1969, 281ff.

[29] e.g. *EN* 1102a27-32, *Pol*. 1260a6f.

[30] So at 2.2.2.21f, 4.3.9.3-9: on the significance of these cf. *Plotinus' Psychology* 139.

[31] cf. Dodds, Proclus. *Elements of Theology*[2], Oxford 1963, app. II.

[32] e.g. 17,19-23, 164,11-13.

Discussing why fire cannot be a living thing in spite of its association with a soul higher than ours (73,25ff), he simply assumes the need for a vehicle (*okhêma*) – the standard technical term for the pneumatic body – which joins soul to the body. With this one might compare Proclus' statement that the beginning of mortal life comes when the demiurge provides soul with its vehicle (*in Tim.* III 234,3-5D).[33] It may by Simplicius' time have become generally accepted that the doctrine was Aristotelian, for Proclus had already spoken of Aristotle assuming a pneumatic vehicle (ib. 238,20f).[34]

What cannot easily be read into Aristotle is a further elaborated version of this theory which appears in Proclus (e.g. *in Tim.* III 238,2ff) and also Philoponus (18,22-33), namely that there was not one such vehicle for the soul but two, one immortal and one perishable, the second being that which Proclus finds in Aristotle. In any case neither Proclus, Philoponus nor Simplicius bothered to mention that the *de Anima* says nothing about connate *pneuma*, and that in the *de Generatione Animalium* it is part of the body's mechanisms.[35] They were however being true to the aim of making Aristotle self-consistent through a knowledge of the whole of his philosophy.[36] They were also using the late Neoplatonic method of explaining the connection between two entities by interposing a third. Apart from having a semi-material body between body and soul we have also a part of soul which is separable – from the material body – and inseparable – from the pneumatic body – between the separable higher soul and the inseparable lower soul.

Such then are some of the presuppositions with which the commentators approached Aristotle. They are stated plainly and openly enough: the only thing that is not stated is the fact that the ideas were not Aristotle's, and that is not stated for the simple reason that the commentators were no longer sufficiently aware of the difference. This unawareness of the differences between their own views and a legitimate interpretation of Aristotle, which we may call a first stage of confusion, led, not surprisingly, to a second, where a philosopher's view on a subject treated by Aristotle could be seen as commentary on Aristotle's treatment. Both can be seen in the discussion of *de Anima* 3.5 which appears in what we have as Book 3 of Philoponus' commentary, but which is clearly the work of another commentator. This was Stephanus of Alexandria, who was trained in the school of philosophy there, and then held an official academic post at Constantinople in the early seventh century.[37] The spirit and orientation of this pseudo-Philoponus

---

[33] Interestingly both Simplicius and Proclus use the term 'of mortal type' (*thnêtoeidês*), though Simplicius applies it to the body, Proclus to the moral life.

[34] Proclus of course found it in the *Timaeus*, 41Cff, cf. *in Tim.* III 233,23ff.

[35] On connate *pneuma* here cf. A.L. Peck's Loeb edition of *GA*, App. B.

[36] Stated explicitly by Elias *in Cat.* 123,7-9.

[37] On the authorship of Bk. 3, cf. M. Hayduck on p.v. of his edition, *CAG* 15, 1897. Though Hayduck did not claim certainty, Stephanus' authorship is now generally accepted. Cf., however, M. de Corte, *Le Commentaire de Jean Philopon sur le troisième livre du "Traité de l'Ame" d'Aristote*, Bibl. de la Fac. de Phil. et Lett. de l'Univ. de Liège, Paris 1934, xf. This

commentary are, however, sufficiently similar to the fifth- and
sixth-century commentaries for the time lapse to be of no great
significance.

Stephanus' discussion of 3.5 gives a doxography presenting the views
on the meaning of active intellect (*nous energeiâi*) of Alexander, Plotinus,
Plutarch of Athens and Marinus, Proclus' pupil, biographer and
successor. These opinions are presented as the various solutions of
commentators to a problem of interpretation: 'the commentators resorted
to many different roads (*hoi exêgêtai epi pollas kai diaphorous hodous
etrapêsan*).' They were accepted as such by Ross, who complained, not
unreasonably on that premise, about their inadequacy.[38] Fortunately
there is no need for the present discussion to lose itself in the labyrinth of
what Aristotle meant by his distinction between the active and passive
intellects – or functions of intellect. No one who has consulted them on
this question would expect the commentators to help him play Theseus.
The point is that an examination of what they do say can show that their
remarks are virtually irrelevant to the solution, and one might go so far
as to say that if any of those whom Stephanus cites – Alexander excepted
– had given us Aristotle's meaning, whatever it was, that would have
been more or less fortuitous. This assertion clearly requires justification,
but such justification is not difficult to produce.

Let us start with Plotinus, for Alexander's opinion that the active
intellect was the highest unmoved mover is irrelevant to our present
purpose. Stephanus tells us that Plotinus thought the active intellect was
the human intellect, but held that some part of it was always active:
*Plôtinus de energeiâi noun enoêse ton anthrôpinon noun, ton men aei
energounta, ton de pote energounta* (535,8-10). This report is at first sight
puzzling, and is in fact inconsistent with what we read a few lines later,
where we are told that Plotinus says that by active intellect Aristotle
means the human intellect which is always in act: *phêsin oun ho Plôtinos
hoti energeiâi noun legei ton anthrôpinon noun ton aei energounta* (ib.
12f). Now we know that, in so far as the distinction between active and
passive intellect can be applied to Plotinus' views on *nous*, it is the second
of these two statements that fits rather than the first. The first can,
however, be explained in terms of what Plotinus does say in the *Enneads*.
The second represents what is simply Plotinus' view about the human
intellect, namely that it is a part, or rather a faculty or phase, of the
human soul which does not descend to be present to the body – that being
how Plotinus will strictly describe the body: soul relation (4.3.22.1ff) – but
remains in the intelligible world above. Being thus wholly a part of the

edition of the partial Latin translation which is all that survives of Philoponus' commentary
on Bk. 3 has now been superseded by G. Verbeke, *Jean Philopon. Commentaire sur le de
Anima d'Aristote. Traduction de Guillaume de Moerbeke*, Louvain/Paris 1966. Though
longer, this commentary pays less attention to doxographical detail than our Greek Bk. 3.
For the purpose of making comparisons it has seemed best to stick to the Greek texts in the
first place.
[38] loc. cit. (n. 3).

intelligible rather than the sensible world, it is necessarily always active, since eternal activity is a feature of that world. Plotinus explains our intermittent use of intellect by saying that we think noetically, as opposed to discursively, when we so to speak switch on to this highest part of our soul; that is when we focus our attention on it we then become assimilated to it and participate in the intellection which is always taking place (cf. 1.2.4.25-7, 4.3.30.11-15). As for Aristotle, the only similarity is that Plotinus adopts Aristotle's view of intellection as a process of total assimilation parallel to that involved in vision (cf. 5.1.5.18f).

From the standpoint of the Platonists, Plotinus' view was unusual, and Plotinus himself frankly presents it as heterodox. At 4.8.8.1-3 he introduces it with the words 'if one must dare to state one's view more clearly, in opposition to the opinion of others, not all of our soul descends, but some of it is always, in the intelligible [realm]'. The status of the human intellect, and in particular Plotinus' view that it did not descend, remained a controversial issue throughout the history of Neoplatonism. Most Neoplatonists rejected Plotinus' view on the grounds that he offered no adequate explanation of why we are not always engaged in *noêsis*, but Damascius, the last head of the Academy, a colleague of Simplicius and a contemporary of Philoponus, accepted Plotinus' view, arguing that an unchangeable substance must have its being and existence in the intelligible (*de Princ.* II 254.3-7 (Ruelle)). And he was expounding Plato. It is the contention of this paper that the views which Stephanus gives us are in the first place a contribution to this Neoplatonic discussion and were only secondarily, if at all, produced as Aristotelian exegesis, notwithstanding the way they are here introduced.

The reservation must of course be made that these two aims were liable to confusion. But in the case of Plotinus we can say with some confidence that the view here produced as his opinion on the meaning of Aristotle's text was not offered as such. In his case we have, unusually, a complete record of his works given us by Porphyry (*Vita Plot.* 24-6), who was Plotinus' editor as well as biographer, and the works contained in that list are available to us in Porphyry's edition, namely the *Enneads*. On one subject, the categories, we have a whole treatise, 6.1-3, part of which, 6.1, is devoted to a discussion and refutation of the Aristotelian categories. And we do know that some of the Peripatetic commentaries were studied in Plotinus' classes.[39] But *ex professo* commentary on the *de Anima* did not exist, and Plotinus cannot properly be described as an *exêgêtês* (exegete).[40] This rules out one of the possible explanations of the inconsistent reports in Stephanus, namely that Stephanus, or his source, has simply juxtaposed a piece of Plotinus' own philosophy and a piece of his interpretation of Aristotle, an explanation suggested by the way Alexander's own *de Anima* is sometimes confused with his lost commentary on Aristotle's *de Anima* even today. There is of course a

[39] cf. Porphyry *Vita Plot.* 14,10-14.

[40] He did of course claim that his three hypostases were merely exegesis of ideas not fully expressed by Plato, 5.1.8.10-14.

theoretical possibility that there was a tradition of Plotinian Aristotle exegesis which was preserved by his pupils but does not appear in the *Enneads*,[41] but it is probably true that there was no serious body of unwritten Plotinian philosophy, and it is fairly safe to assume that any form of commentary on the *de Anima* would have been recorded, though certainty is of course impossible.

Another explanation of our text is, however, possible, and in terms of Plotinus' own works it is a simple one. Plotinus, like Aristotle, uses *nous* in two different senses, either, strictly, to refer to the intuitive intellect as opposed to the discursive reason, or sometimes loosely, to refer to the latter. Confusion rarely arises, and when necessary, Plotinus will carefully and explicitly distinguish between them (e.g. 5.9.8.21f). The report that Plotinus thought the intellect consisted of a permanently and an intermittently active part may be a confused conflation of what for Plotinus were two distinct levels of soul. Some modern interpreters have also thought that Plotinus' intuitive intellect (*nous*) and discursive reason (*dianoia*)[42] could be equated with Aristotle's active and passive intellect, an equation which, as I have argued elsewhere, is illegitimate.[43] The correct representation of Plotinus' view about *nous* in the strict sense is that in Stephanus' second report. But that it was originally offered as interpretation of Aristotle is almost certainly not the case. Apart from several occasions where he quotes what had become a tag about knowledge of immaterial objects being the same as the objects, which may or may not be in place in 3.5,[44] there is no clear reference in the *Enneads* to this chapter of the *de Anima*.[45] A sentence at 5.9.2.21f which distinguishes between an intellect which always thinks and is the true one, and another which thinks intermittently, is clearly parallel to other passages where Plotinus distinguishes between intellect and discursive reason (e.g. 6.9.5.7ff.). Thus it is not discussing two elements in the operation of intuitive thought, though it is perhaps the text which could

[41] A thesis argued by P. Henry, who maintains that a considerable quantity of Plotinian material in Dexippus' and Simplicius' commentaries on the *Categories* is not based on the *Enneads*, first in 'Vers la reconstruction de l'enseignement oral de Plotin', *Bull. de l'Ac. R. de Belgique* ser. 5.23, 1937, 316-20, and most recently in 'Trois apories orales de Plotin sur les Catégories d'Aristote', in *Zetesis*, Festschr. E. de Strijcker, Antwerp/Utrecht 1973, 234-65; *contra* Schwyzer, 'Nachlese zur indirekten Überlieferung des Plotin-Textes', *Mus. Helv.* 26, 1969, 261ff.

[42] Recent work on the so-called Arabic Plotiniana, which had sometimes been taken as dependent on Plotinus' lectures, so Henry, 'Vers la reconstruction ...' 320ff, indicates that differences from the *Enneads* are probably due to Porphyry. For the *status quaestionis* see my 'Plotinus in the light of twenty years' scholarship, 1951-71' in W. Haase and H. Temporini (eds.), *Aufstieg und Niedergang der römischen Welt*, vol. II.36.1, Berlin/New York 1987, 536-41.

[43] So P. Merlan, *Monopsychism, Mysticism, Metaconsciousness*, The Hague 1963, 10; cf. *Plotinus' Psychology* 104 n. 10.

[44] On this see Ross ad loc.

[45] References to an intellect that is or may be separate (5.3.3.42, 5.9.3.7), or the statement that the first intelligible is separate, need not be to this chapter, since that is hardly the only place in Aristotle, or elsewhere, where immaterial entities are spoken of as separate.

most easily have been the ultimate source for Stephanus' statement. Be that as it may, we can conclude that when Stephanus says that Plotinus says that by active intellect Aristotle means the constantly thinking human *nous*, he is in fact producing as interpretation of Aristotle a view that was not so intended, but was merely part of Plotinus' own psychology.[46]

Since then we can show that this was the status of the Plotinus view in our list, we must at least consider the possibility that the same may be true of the others. Plutarch of Athens, we are told, thinks that we have a simple rather than a double *nous*, and that it thinks intermittently, a view of which Stephanus himself approves (13-15).[47] This view, however, happens to be that of the anti-Plotinian side of the Neoplatonic controversy about the undescended intellect. The formulation, 'Plutarch does not say that it always thinks, but that it sometimes thinks', recalls the last proposition, 211, of Proclus' *Elements of Theology*, a work which has never been suspected of being Aristotelian commentary. Proclus there argues that the undescended intellect would always think, and so according to him would not be part of a soul at all: uninterrupted intellection would be characteristic of intellect rather than soul. This is probably the distinction that Plutarch is making in different words, when he says that active intellect is the human intellect which sometimes thinks (535,15f). Stephanus himself thought that in so far as actualisation is caused by another intellect, that is some other human intellect (539,1ff).[48] At 536,2-5 we are told that Plutarch justified his view by saying that Aristotle's work was about soul. This type of argument is characteristic of Neoplatonic exegesis after Iamblichus, who either devised or canonised the system of assigning a single purpose (*skopos*) to each of the works of Plato, and extended it to Aristotle's as well.[49] Their contents were then interpreted in such a way as to make them fit with the stated aim. The results can be imagined if we consider the likely consequences of taking the *Sophist* as a theological dialogue, as Iamblichus apparently did.[50] That Plutarch is reported as solving the active intellect problem in terms of the treatise's overall aim does suggest commentary, and we do have evidence, apart from the references in Stephanus' commentary on Book 3, that Plutarch did produce a commentary on at least part of the *de Anima*, if perhaps not the whole.[51] But we know that Plutarch read the *de Anima* with Proclus who was his

[46] All this is not to deny that Aristotle's distinction between active and passive intellect may have had something to do with Plotinus' distinction between intellect and discursive reason.

[47] As did Philoponus himself ad loc., 45,53-9V.

[48] So too Philoponus, 55,4-7V.

[49] On Iamblichus' methods cf. Praechter, 'Richtungen und Schulen im Neuplatonismus', in *Genethliakon C. Robert*, Berlin 1910, 138ff.

[50] According to the *scholium vetus*, printed in the Teubner Plato, VI.249,26f, Iamblichus said it was about the sublunary demiurge.

[51] Commentary is indicated, if not proved, by such references as Simpl. 21,35ff, 186,26ff, and Priscian *Metaphr. in Theophrastum* 34,7f.

pupil,[52] and so is likely to have followed his master's teaching on many points.[53] Now Proclus, as we know from the *Elements*, took the same view as Plutarch on the status of the intellect. Proclus makes no suggestion there, or in other passages when he discusses the matter,[54] that he is himself interpreting Aristotle, and so we may justifiably suspect that what we have before us is a view on the human intellect shared by both Plutarch and Proclus which was imposed by Plutarch on his reading of the *de Anima*. The usual motivation, seeing Aristotle's philosophy as a manifestation of Neoplatonic truth, will have played its part.[55] Further, there is still the possibility that Plutarch's view as here presented was originally no more a part of a *de Anima* commentary than was that of Plotinus which we have just considered, and against which both Plutarch and Proclus were arguing.[56] But since in Plutarch's case we know that he did comment on at least some of the *de Anima*, whereas in Plotinus' we know that he did not, we should perhaps accept that Plutarch did express this view in the course of a commentary.

That it was possible to do so we may see from Simplicius. He states his adherence to the same side in the controversy when he is talking about his own views on the soul in the preface to his *de Anima* commentary, and he proceeds to introduce it into his discussion of 3.5. In the preface Simplicius writes that he will not follow Plotinus in maintaining that some part of the soul remains constantly pure and unchanged and does not proceed: it descends as a whole though it does not lose its nature in its inclination to the sensible. This position, he says, will be shown by the whole account to be the opinion of Aristotle, set out more clearly by Iamblichus (6,12-16). The reference to Iamblichus, apart from what it tells us about Simplicius' approach, is puzzling, since the reports we have of his position in this controversy are not entirely consistent. Proclus agrees in reporting that he opposed the undescended intellect theory (*in Tim*. III.334,3f), but another text from Simplicius, this time from the *Categories* commentary, tends to suggest the opposite, for there we read: 'whether in us too there is some such (sc. knowing) which always remains above, as Plotinus and Iamblichus think' (191,9f). The close connection between Aristotle exegesis and Plato interpretation which appears in the similarities we have already noted between Proclus and the other participants in the controversy, is further evidenced by the fact that Damascius' approval of Plotinus' position is expressed in the course of what is a commentary on the

[52] Marinus *Vita Procli* 12.

[53] It might be argued that Plutarch's influence will not have been great, as he died two years after Proclus came to him, Marinus ib. 12. But he had also taught Syrianus, to whose care he entrusted Proclus, ib.

[54] cf. *in Parm*. 948,18f (Cousin)², *in Tim*. III 333,28ff.

[55] Plutarch should, however, have been aware of the hazards, for Philoponus tells us that he had accused Alexander of presenting his own philosophy dressed up as commentary (21,20-3).

[56] *in Tim*. 333,29f is directed specifically at Plotinus and Theodore of Asine: 'preserving in us something impassive and always thinking'.

Parmenides,[57] and that Hermeias' *Phaedrus* commentary provides another example of the opposite view (160.1-4 (Couvreur)). Its appearance in Hermeias is interesting from the historical point of view, for it points to Plutarch – if not Iamblichus, who would be the obvious candidate were it not for the difficulty just mentioned – as the man who may have been responsible for the adoption of this position by all those we have mentioned. For Plutarch taught Syrianus[58] and Proclus,[59] Syrianus taught Proclus[60] and also Hermeias,[61] the father and teacher of Ammonius, whose lectures are represented by Philoponus' *de Anima* commentary (cf. 1,1f) and were attended by Simplicius,[62] while the tradition of Ammonius and Philoponus is probably represented by Ps.-Philoponus on Book 3 of the *de Anima*.[63] Ammonius himself had studied under Proclus.[64] Nevertheless it should perhaps be said that shared opinions do not necessarily follow from common discipleship. Simplicius and Damascius[65] were both pupils of Ammonius but remained capable of disagreement.

To return to Simplicius. He fulfils his promise to demonstrate his view about intellect in his discussion of 3.5 (240,1ff). Though Simplicius' Aristotelian scholarship is typical of the Alexandrian milieu where he went to Ammonius' courses, rather than the Athenian where he was Damascius' pupil and later colleague,[66] his treatment of 3.5, as of many other topics, is set out in language that one would normally associate with the Athenians. That a piece of commentary should be written in Neoplatonic technical language does not of course mean that it cannot provide a useful interpretation of Aristotle's thought, though Aristotle's own discussions of pre-Aristotelian ideas should serve as ample warning of the risks. There is even a passage elsewhere in the *de Anima* commentary where Simplicius indicates that he is aware of language differences between Aristotle and himself (102,12ff). Yet it is probably fair to say that one could read a large part of this discussion without realising that it is about Aristotle's philosophy at all. The main point at issue in the first part is the level of soul that is being discussed. And in the vocabulary of the Athenian school the fully descended human intellect is not *nous* at all but *psukhê* (soul). It is, as we have seen, such a fully descended intellect in which Simplicius himself believed. Unlike Plutarch and Stephanus he accepted that our *nous* is double (240,8), a

---

[57] See p. 313 above.
[58] Procl. *in Remp.* II 64,6f (Kroll).
[59] Procl. ib. and Marinus *Vita Pr.* 12.
[60] Marinus ib. 12, 13.
[61] Damascius *Vita Isid.* fr. 120 (Zintzen).
[62] cf. *in Cael.* 271,19, 462,20.
[63] The exact relation between Philoponus' and Stephanus' commentaries on Bk. 3 is not yet clear. A possible intermediary might be the lost *de Anima* commentary by Olympiodorus.
[64] Damascius *Vita Isid.* fr. 127.
[65] ib. fr. 119.
[66] cf. *in Phys.* 774,28f, Agathias 2.30.

part proceeding and another not (244,37-9), a view that may be seen as a
symptom of his greater preference for solving problems by multiplying
entities.[67] But like Plutarch (Philop. *in DA* 536,2-5), he produces as an
argument for the meaning of the particular text under discussion the
overall purpose of the treatise as he saw it, not methodologically the best
possible approach. Simplicius begins by arguing that Aristotle is talking
about the rational soul since soul is the subject of the treatise. He does
however back up this contention by drawing attention to the words 'in the
soul' (240,4f). This for him means that the active intellect is not
transcendent, as it could still be on the Plotinian type view which
regarded a transcendent intellect as part of the human soul, a situation
well expressed in Plotinus' paradoxical remark at the end of *Enn.* 1.1: 'for
this too is part of us and we ascend to it.'

   In Simplicius' terms the discussion is not about the intellect
participated by soul, or the one above that (240,2f, 247,41f). The one
above that would be what others called divine intellect.[68] Simplicius calls
it unparticipated intellect (244,40f), as Proclus often does.[69] Here we have
the standard set of three terms, pure A, pure B, and between them A
participated by B, the series in this case being unparticipated intellect,
soul and participated intellect.[70] At 244,39ff these two levels of intellect
are distinguished from the intellect which has its existence in the highest
part of the soul, and which Simplicius himself would not normally call
intellect without qualification. At 245,37 it is called the soul's intellect:
shortly before we read that intellect without qualification (*haplôs*) is that
above the level where the highest part of the soul's knowledge is
simultaneous intellection and knowledge (ib. 13-15). In accordance with
such distinctions Simplicius is also able to find a difference of levels
between intellect described as separate (*khôristos*) and separated
(*khôristheis*) (*DA* 430a16,22): the latter is not in substance activity in the
same way as the former (245,21f). There is in our intellect when
separated a less perfect degree of unity. In Neoplatonic thought higher
degrees of unity correspond of course with higher degrees of being, and
the possibility of distinguishing between intellect, its object and its act
was for them sufficient reason to refuse to recognise Aristotle's unmoved
mover as the supreme principle.[71]

   Faced with this series of Neoplatonic terms and ontological
distinctions, one must exercise some care in differentiating Simplicius'
own views from the piece of Aristotelian doctrine he is professedly

[67] See below. It should be noted that when Simplicius talks about our *nous* being double
he is not simply reproducing Aristotle's distinction. For Simplicius' passive intellect is
sometimes equated with imagination (*phantasia*), cf. 17,2-5, 248,2ff; cf. also Philop.
490,18ff.
[68] That is other Neoplatonists, cf. e.g. Syrianus *in Metaph.* 142,19. Procl. *El. Th.* 181ff: the
meaning is not of course the same as Alexander's divine intellect, *de An. Mant.* 112,19ff
which is the supreme principle; cf. also Philop. 37,28f, 165,8-13.
[69] Proclus uses the two terms as equivalent, *El. Th.* 163.
[70] For this series cf. e.g. Proclus, ib. 166.
[71] cf. e.g. Plot. 5.3.13.9ff.

elucidating. But this does not mean that the two are always inextricably confused: they can be disentangled in places by a process of translation. Thus for him, as we have seen, rational soul does not mean discursive reason but intellect, as it did for Philoponus too (165,5-9). Its attributes, however, tend to be determined by the conceptual structure within which Simplicius himself operated.

It is in terms of this structure that one can make some sense of the views of Marinus reported by Stephanus, for Marinus was Proclus' pupil and successor as head of the Academy. Marinus, we are told, held that the active intellect was not that which is principle of all things, but some demonic or angelic intellect (535,5f). At first sight this might suggest medieval interpretations rather than the *de Anima*. Once again what we have is straight Neoplatonism. Marinus too is working with a series of highly, not to say excessively, differentiated entities: the angelic intellect is neither ours, nor that of the principle of all things. Though he has located our intellect at a different level from that chosen by Simplicius, the layers involved are the same. We can see from Proclus' *Timaeus* commentary (III 165,7-25) that the kind of intellect or being described as angelic is an intermediary between the divine intellect (*theios nous*), what Simplicius called unparticipated intellect, and the level of soul in which our world is located and which both Simplicius and Proclus call the secondary (*ta deutera*). In fact it is angelic in the sense of being a messenger and interpreter: it interprets and translates the divine intellect for the secondary. It proceeds in accordance with intellectual life (*kata tên noeran zôên*) and intellectual intellect (*nous noeros*) is the middle participated term below divine intellect (*theios nous*) in another of Proclus' series (cf. *El. Th.* 175 and 183). The same passage of Proclus' *Timaeus* commentary also tells us why Marinus, having proposed demonic or angelic intellect as alternatives, chose the latter: it is the angelic intellect which performs the function of messenger and interpreter in accordance with the intellectual capacity of *nous* rather than its demiurgic capacity, in accordance with which the demonic intellect orders nature and the cosmos (ib. 25-7). The third member of the triad, the heroic (*to hêrôikon*) does not concern us here. The point of placing Marinus' view in Proclus' triadic schemes is simply to show that in Marinus' case too the opinion about active intellect consists of no more than locating it at some point in his own intelligible universe. It could be salvaged as a piece of Aristotelian exegesis if it could be shown that Marinus tried to argue that Aristotle's active *nous* should be identified with some entity between man and the first unmoved mover, but we have no evidence that he did. Though it can perhaps be shown that the Arabic commentators' interpretation of the active intellect as an 'intelligence' stems from Marinus' opinion, that would not in itself show that Marinus was in fact engaged in the interpretation of Aristotle. Though Marinus will doubtless have given lectures on Aristotle, for no other reason than that he taught philosophy, it may be to the point that he is not normally cited as an authority on Aristotle and that, though Stephanus is quite generous with citations of earlier authorities, Marinus' name is not mentioned outside the page on 3.5. His status as an Aristotelian is therefore not very different from that of Plotinus.

Much more could be said about the details of these Neoplatonic theories on *nous* and the upper soul: as we have already seen there are important differences. But such details belong to the study of Neoplatonism as such. For the present purpose the type of thought involved is more important, and for the moment it should be sufficiently clear just what the 'interpretations' we have been considering in fact are, that is personal positions in a live philosophical debate.

Simplicius' commentary is perhaps more thoroughly pervaded by Neoplatonism than were others. This is a factor that should be taken into account in looking at the commentators' views on other questions, though it will be safer to make one initial reservation. That is that the status of our intellect was clearly a more important question to these men than were, at the other extreme, details of the soul's operations. In this area Neoplatonic doctrine was fairly thoroughly Aristotelianised in any case. But on questions falling between these extremes the extent to which the commentators read their own views into Aristotle could, in principle, be less marked.

A totally different approach may be seen in Themistius, who was not involved in this debate and was, moreover, still trying to be an Aristotelian. The aims he states at the start of his *de Anima paraphrasis* are to follow Aristotle, to clarify and if necessary expand him (1,2-5): there is no mention of the truth, no appeal to Plato or to figures in the Platonic tradition. Themistius was of course writing some two centuries before Simplicius and three before Stephanus but Neoplatonism was already the dominant philosophy: Plotinus, Porphyry, and Iamblichus were all dead before Themistius' career had begun.[72] That does not mean that he excluded Platonic or Platonist ideas.[73] That was no longer possible for an Aristotelian, any more than it was possible for a Platonist to refuse to accept any of Aristotle's notions. But his orientation was certainly different from that of the Neoplatonists. His attitude to Plato was independent: he followed him occasionally if he thought fit. Simplicius remarks on this in his *de Caelo* commentary: 'although Themistius offers the views of the Peripatos in most things, in this he seemed to favour those of Plato' (69,9f). A fairly cursory examination of Themistius' comments on *de Anima* 3.5 will make the point clearly enough. That Themistius appears to be puzzled, and offers little help, is not to the present point.[74] But what

[72] Iamblichus died in 325 or 6, cf. J. Bidez, 'Le philosophe Jamblique et son école', *REG* 32, 1919, 32. Themistius was born about 320.

[73] Thus he accepted the Platonist concept of philosophy as assimilation to God as far as possible (*homoiôsis tô theôi kata to dunaton*) and followed Plato on divine benevolence, cf. *Or.* 2,32d-33a = 39,4-20 (Dindorf). That he expresses more enthusiasm for Plato in the speeches than in the commentaries may be a function of the genre, cf. Düring, op. cit. (n. 6) 333.

[74] On the difficulties in this account cf. Merlan, op. cit. (n. 43) 50 and n. 3.

he does is, basically, to say what Aristotle says, if at much greater length, with some attention to the opinions of Theophrastus (98,12-109,3). The vocabulary is Peripatetic, and the thought shows no signs of the Neoplatonic multiplication of entities: there are no participated and unparticipated transcendent intellects, no distinctions between intelligible and intellectual life, no members of triads. Whether or not it would still have been possible to write this kind of paraphrase in the sixth century is another matter.[75]

Having now established that the late commentators' own views were likely to have been the determining factor in their interpretation of 3.5 let us look at their comments on some other sections of the treatise. It should not now be surprising if they turn out to be somewhat over-Platonic. Perhaps the most obvious test case is Aristotle's definition of the soul as the form and first actuality of a natural body that has life potentially and has organs (*organikou*). A simple scholarly explanation should perhaps concern itself with explaining how soul could be the form of the body and why it is first actuality. On this basis Simplicius' relatively brief comments (90,29-91,4) would be puzzling. His main concern is with *organikou* which might seem to be the part of the definition which requires the least comment. For him *organikou* (with organs) is not a description of the matter in the compound of matter and form which is the living being. It is rather a term implying that the soul uses the body as an *organon* (instrument), as well as causing it to be one in the first place. The idea of soul using body as an instrument is of course straight Platonism. Simplicius manages to make it compatible with what Aristotle says by using another piece of Neoplatonic doctrine, namely the notion that the soul is a series of layers.[76] Thus he exploits the idea of a double entelechy by explaining it in terms of levels, and finds two separate components in what Aristotle presents as a single definition: having life potentially and being equipped with organs (*organikou*). Though, he argues, the two come together in so far as what potentially possesses life is an *organon* (instrument) of the soul, and the instrument of the soul potentially possesses life, they are not the same. One refers only to the lowest form of life by which the body is informed and made a living body, the other to that which uses and moves it. What we have here is that Neoplatonic distinction to which we have already referred, between a layer of soul which imparts form to the body, and a higher layer or series of layers which control the already informed body, a distinction Simplicius had initially made in his preface. One might compare the way Plotinus treats the concept of entelechy (actuality) as if it deals with how soul informs an already ensouled body (4.7.8[7]), and Philoponus' remarks about body and each section of soul being related to that above it as matter to form (198,22-9). Lest there be any doubt about Simplicius' intentions, the final sentence of the present section shows us what he thinks a definition of the

---

[75] To do so might well have been seen as a sign of perversity, cf. Damascius on Isidore's conversion of Dorus, Suda s.v. 'Doros' = *Vita Isid.* fr. 338.

[76] On this see above, p. 309f and n. 22.

soul should tell us: 'and that is why you need both for the complete definition of the soul, so that it can be made clear that it uses the body as an instrument'. All Aristotle's care to show that body and soul form a single entity has gone for nothing.

That could be described as blatant misrepresentation. With Philoponus the case is different. Perhaps it would be as well to recall that Philoponus' commentary on Book 2 is not the same work as Ps.-Philoponus' commentary on Book 3, and therefore we should be prepared for a different approach. As it is, Philoponus does not comment directly on Aristotle's revised definition of soul in its full form, but he gives us a few lines to elucidate the words 'and any body with organs is of that sort' (217,9-15). From these it is immediately clear that he does not take 'with organs' (*organikon*) as an indication that the body is subordinate to the soul. He explains that organs are that in virtue of which activities involving life take place, and therefore that in virtue of which a body has life as its first actuality, as opposed to being merely a natural body like fire, whose first actuality is the power of heating and not soul. Here Philoponus has avoided importing Neoplatonic views of the kind which his preface shows that he held,[77] and his preceding comments on 412a16ff (215,4-216,26) show that he is quite prepared to explain Aristotle's concept of soul as actuality in the sense in which it was intended.

Philoponus' account of 'with organs' seems to be on the same lines as Themistius' rather less concise exposition (42,15ff). Interestingly Themistius says quite specifically that 'with organs' should be taken as an explanation of 'having life potentially' and not as signifying something different (42,35-7). It looks as if he is objecting to the interpretation later offered by Simplicius, or something very like it, which both shows that such an interpretation had long been current, and helps to confirm that Themistius' position was a matter of personal conviction rather than mere chronology.

Similar differences appear when the commentators tackle the crux at the end of the same chapter where Aristotle, having argued that the form is the inseparable form of the body, ends the discussion by saying that it is not clear whether it is separable (413a8f).[78] Once again Simplicius gives a Platonist solution (96,3-15) – which might have some merit if Aristotle's remark were a piece of Platonism which somehow survived revision, an explanation that was not of course available in antiquity. Simplicius is disturbed by 'it is not clear' because for him it not only makes sense, but is actually correct, to think of soul as a separable entelechy. He solves the problem in terms of two layers or aspects which he finds within that phase of soul which we have already met as the one which uses the body as an instrument: this, he says, in inseparable in the sense that it always uses the body, and separable in the sense that it uses it in a transcendent fashion (*exêirêmenôs*), as a subordinate instrument.

[77] See above, p. 310f.

[78] The reading *psukhê* <*ê*> does not help, since the second of the alternatives it produces is no easier to explain than the sentence as it stands.

In accordance with this distinction he takes the comparison with a sailor in a ship as an indication that the actuality both uses the body and does not use it at all: in the latter case it is separable.[79] According to Simplicius 'not clear' does not apply to the intellect *theôrêtikê* because that does not even use the body as an instrument, that is, it is separable beyond any possibility of doubt. What is unclear, he thinks, is the status of the irrational faculties, and this will be clarified by investigation of each of these. Once again we have a set of three terms with two extremes being bridged by a middle term sharing characteristics of each: soul altogether separate, elsewhere called rational soul, the inseparable life which in discussing the definition he speaks of as informing body, and the actuality which uses the body which is both separate and inseparable.

Simplicius may be given credit for an acute piece of misrepresentation. Philoponus' comments (224,10-225,31) are less incisive, but once again show him trying to understand Aristotle in terms of the *de Anima* itself, in spite of his own convictions. The result, not surprisingly, is that he is unable to offer a clear-cut solution. His attempts to find an explanation show the same kind of vacillation which appears to be present in Aristotle's text, and he is even prepared to entertain the idea that the rational soul itself is inseparable in some sense (224,28ff). But in the end he refused to follow Alexander's suggestion that Aristotle himself was in doubt, and refers the point to the as yet unresolved status of the lower faculties.[80] To do this, however, he has to say that one can have an actuality like the steersman in a ship (225,20-31), which of course makes nonsense of Aristotle's previous discussion. In contrast to Simplicius, Philoponus' discussion is complicated by his attempts to find an explanation which does not simply jettison Aristotle's concept of the soul as the form of the body.

Themistius, on the other hand, is not distracted by hesitations about the relation between the soul below intellect and the body. He is forced to explain 'not clear' as referring to the status of intellect only and like Philoponus, who may of course have taken the idea from him, has to deal with actuality by suggesting that the helmsman is a separate actuality. He may have been aware that this is unsatisfactory, for he ends by exploiting Aristotle's 'let this be a sketch' (413a9f): he suggests that some of what has been said is not accurate and remains to be cleared up when all the soul's faculties have been discussed. But he does make it clear that as far as he is concerned the uncertainty affects only the possibility that some part of the soul is separable (43,25-34).

The passages we have inspected should suffice to show that the personal standpoint of the commentators was liable to be a major factor in determining their interpretations. Clearly this will be most apparent

---

[79] At. 4,18-20 Simplicius uses the comparison for the soul which moves rather than informs the body: the former is the same layer as that which uses it as an instrument.

[80] cf. his comments on 408b29, 'Perhaps intellect is something impassive and more divine', where he takes 'perhaps' (*isôs*) to refer not to doubt but merely to the as yet incomplete state of the discussion, 165,4ff.

when they were confronted with texts that related, or could be taken to relate, to crucial points in their own philosophy. But it is not unfair to say that, notwithstanding differences between commentators, the late Greek commentaries are pervaded by Neoplatonism. Perhaps enough has been said to show how this affected details of their interpretation and not just the broad outlines: the effects of this influence may be found on almost every page of these long and painstaking commentaries.

Addendum: March 1988

Though the *de Anima* commentary ascribed to Simplicius is not written in the same way as Simplicius' others, it was accepted as his by everyone, with the exception of F. Piccolomini, *Commentarii in libros Aristotelis de Coelo, orto et interitu ... de anima*, Mainz 1608, 1001, until 1972 when F. Bossier and C. Steel wrote a long and important article in which they maintained that both the language and doctrine of the *de Anima* commentary were different from the other commentaries and closer to that of Priscian, to whom it should be attributed: 'Priscianus Lydus en de "In De anima" van Pseudo(?) Simplicius', *Tijdsch. voor Filosofie* 34, 1972, 761-822. Their thesis was critically discussed by I. Hadot in an appendix to her *Le problème du néoplatonisme Alexandrin: Hiéroclès et Simplicius*, Paris 1978, 193-202, where she argues that the doctrines are the same, but thinks that language and authorship are an open question. In Chapter 12 she expresses further doubts about the Bossier-Steel view, and in particular questions the significance of verbal parallels with Priscian, but regards the matter as not yet settled. I have tried to show that there are no doctrinal differences in 'The psychology of (?) Simplicius' commentary on the *de Anima*', in H.J. Blumenthal and A.C. Lloyd (eds), *Soul and the Structure of Being in Late Neoplatonism*, Liverpool 1982, 73-93. During 1985 I had the opportunity to discuss the question with Bossier and Steel on separate occasions: both assure me that they are if anything more strongly convinced that Simplicius could not have been the author of this commentary.

CHAPTER FOURTEEN

The Alexandrian commentators and the introductions to their commentaries

L.G. Westerink

I shall pass in review the known representatives of the Alexandrian school since Proclus: Hermeias, Ammonius, Eutocius, Olympiodorus, Elias, David, Stephanus.[1] Biographical details are scarce; it is possible, however, in some cases to gain more exact data than those given in the handbooks. Besides the question which of them taught Platonic Philosophy, their attitude towards Christianity is also a relevant point.

1. The Alexandrian School from Hermeias

Hermeias, the first Alexandrian professor to be considered, was also the first to introduce the doctrine of the Athenian School at Alexandria. At least, we may suppose so, since he was a pupil of Syrianus, but in fact nothing is known of his own teaching, for the commentary on the *Phaedrus* that we possess is only a set of unrevised notes of Syrianus' lectures on the dialogue.[2] Damascius describes him as industrious and kind-hearted, but limited.[3] His wife, Aedesia, was a relative of Syrianus, who had originally destined her for Proclus, until a divine warning prevented the match. Hermeias and Aedesia had at least three sons, but the eldest died at the age of seven; then came Ammonius and Heliodorus.[4]

As Proclus came to Athens only in 432, the earliest possible date for the birth of Ammonius is about 435; several years later seems much more probable, of course, but on the other hand Syrianus may well have been in a hurry to see his beautiful and accomplished charge settled, for Aedesia

---

[1] cf. my introduction to Elias *On the Prior Analytics, Mnemosyne* Series 4, vol. 14, 1961, 126-39. (= *Texts and Studies in Neoplatonian and Byzantine Literature*, Amsterdam 1980, 59-79).

[2] K. Praechter, *Byzant. Zeitschr.* 18, 1909, 524, n. 4. The suggestion of A. Bielmeier (*Die neuplatonische Phaidrosinterpretation*, Paderborn 1930, 33-5) that Hermeias inserted extracts from Iamblichus, requires further proof.

[3] *Vita Isidori*, Zintzen (ed.), Hildesheim 42, 1907, p. 100,9-12.

[4] 106,1-108,8; 109,7-9.

was then no longer a young woman, certainly not by the standard of those days. She was an 'old lady' somewhere between 470 and 475, when precocious young Damascius made her acquaintance at Alexandria and soon afterwards recited some of his own poetry at her funeral. This makes the year 445 the *terminus ante quem* for Ammonius' birth. Tannery[5] has advanced arguments to show that he was probably alive as late as 517, when Philoponus published the course on Aristotle's *Physics*. They are confirmed by the fact that Olympiodorus, whose own commentary on the *Meteorologica* is later than 565, cannot very well have attended the lectures on the *Gorgias* much before 515. If Asmus[6] is right in surmising that Ammonius was no longer alive when Damascius wrote his *Life of Isidorus*, we must place his death between 517 and 526.

The only book from Ammonius' own hand that has survived is his commentary on the *de Interpretatione*: it seems to be also the only large work he ever wrote, though he occasionally used the convenient form of the *monobiblos* to set down his ideas on some special question, as Proclus had done before him and Damascius did after him. To this kind belong the treatise on *Phaedo* 69D, defending Plato against the charge of scepticism,[7] another on hypothetical syllogisms,[8] and, probably, a work on the Aristotelian Idea of God, cited by Simplicius.[9] On the whole, however, M. Richard[10] is right in saying that Ammonius did not like writing and preferred to leave the publication of his lectures to his students. Three of these editions bear Ammonius' own name (*Isagoge, Categories, Prior Analytics*), one that of Asclepius (*Metaphysics*), eight more that of Philoponus (*Categories, Prior* and *Posterior Analytics, Physics, de Generatione et Corruptione, Meteorologica, de Anima, de Generatione Animalium*.) Philoponus wrote up his (or perhaps a fellow-student's) notes and added 'some observations of his own', as the titles of his editions usually state; Asclepius, having nothing of his own to add, mixed his lecture notes with extracts from Alexander, but only as far as the fourth book, 5, 6 and 7 being apparently pure Ammonius.

The reputation of Ammonius as a commentator rests entirely on his Aristotelian studies. Damascius already says that Aristotle was his speciality;[11] besides personal preference, caution also may have played a part in this, but there is no evidence to show that it went so far as to cause a break in the Platonic tradition at Alexandria. At some time between 475 and 485 Damascius had attended a course on Platonic philosophy by Ammonius,[12] and about forty years later Olympiodorus heard the old man

[5] 'Sur la période finale de la philosophie grecque', *Revue philosophique* 42, 1896, 274-5.
[6] *Das leben des Philosophen Isidoros von Damaskios aus Damaskos*, Leipzig 1911, 186 (note on 110,22.)
[7] Ol. *in Phaedo*. 8 §17, 6-7.
[8] Amm. *in An. Pr*. 67,32-69,28.
[9] *in Cael*. 271,13-21; *in Phys*. 1363,8-12.
[10] '*Apo Phônês*', *Byzantion* 20, 1950, 192.
[11] op. cit. 110,1-2.
[12] ibid. 111,10-11.

lecture on the *Gorgias*.[13] Asclepius refers to lectures on Platonic philosophy in general[14] and to a discussion of the *Theaetetus* in particular.[15] This leaves little room for the hypothesis[16] that the pact he made with the patriarch Athanasius II (c. 489-496)[17] obliged him to confine himself to Aristotle. If nothing has survived of his interpretation of Plato, the reason is no doubt that the work of the Athenian school was felt to be more important; just as, on the other hand, Proclus' commentaries on Aristotle have left hardly any traces.[18]

Whatever the concessions Ammonius made, they must have been considerable enough to make him a renegade in the eyes of Damascius, who refers to the episode in terms of bitter contempt. The most likely explanation is that Ammonius pledged himself to silence on certain essential doctrines contrary to the Christian faith (especially the eternity and divinity of the world).[19] A casual remark in Philoponus' *de Anima* commentary from the voice of Ammonius points the same way: 'Though it (the soul) may be forced by tyrants to profess an impious doctrine, it can never be forced to inner assent and to belief,'[20] an unheroic view, which seems to be rather a personal utterance than a stock phrase. As long, of course, as no systematic effort has been made to detach Philoponus' 'own observations' from the strictly reporting parts of the commentaries, it remains risky to use Philoponus as a source for Ammonius' teaching. There is, no doubt, an occasional phrase that has a Christian ring,[21] in one case belief in a God who works miracles is expressed,[22] and more importantly, in the commentary on the *Meteorologica* there is a consistent attempt to eliminate the fifth element and with it, by implication, the eternity of the heavens. As a rule, however, Philoponus repeats objectively and without any comment Ammonius' hard line position on such matters as the eternity of the world, the world soul, the pre-existence and reincarnation of the human soul. All these points, then the main issues between Christianity and Hellenism, are mentioned in

[13] Ol. *in Gorg.* 199,8-10.

[14] 77,4.

[15] 70,31.

[16] H.D. Saffrey, 'Le chrétien Jean Philopon et la survivance de l'école d'Alexandrie', in *Revue des ét. gr.* 67, 1954, 400-1.

[17] Damascius *Vita Isidori*, 250,2 and 251,12-14, two extracts from Photius, one of which names the patriarch. Since the context seems to be the persecution of the philosophers during the rebellion of Illus (484-488), Asmus (*Byz. Zeitschr.* 18, 1909, 469-70) concluded that this must be an error for Peter III Mongus (482-489); accordingly, Zintzen deletes the name of Athanasius. However, the name must come from Damascius, and the digressive character of his work makes inferences based on supposed context extremely precarious; it is to be noted especially that the alleged motive of Ammonius was not fear, but greed.

[18] Proclus on the *Isagoge*: Asclep. 142,36-7; introduction to the *Cat.*: Elias 107,24-6; lectures on the *de Int.*: Amm. *in Int.* 1,6-11; cf. 181,30-2; Steph. *in Int.* 46,25-47,12; on the *Prior Analytics*: Philop. *in An. Pr.* 40,30-1, cf. 31,24; 29,2; on the *Posterior Analytics*: Philop. *in An. Post.* 111,31-112,36.

[19] For other views see Koenraad Verrycken, Chapter 10 above, and also Chapter 1.

[20] 104,21-3.

[21] *in Cat.* 126,29-31.

[22] ibid. 169,19 (cf. Elias 242,11); not in Ammon. *in Cat.*

the lectures on the *Metaphysics* also, but Asclepius, either from conviction or from caution, always makes it clear that he is merely reporting Ammonius.[23] As regards Ammonius himself, it is evident that his treaty with the patriarch, whatever its terms, cannot have had any lasting influence on his teaching; twenty years later he continued to lecture on Plato and continued to express his unorthodox opinions even in his courses on Aristotle, which must have been given to a larger and more mixed audience than those on Plato. Zacharias of Mytilene's dialogue *Ammonius* reflects the reaction of at least one Christian student to his persistent belief in the eternity of the world. This seems to indicate that the position of the Hellenes had become easier towards 520 than it was a quarter of a century before.

Olympiodorus calls Ammonius ancestor (*progonos*) and, though it is perhaps worthwhile calling attention to the possibility that he may mean simply grandfather or great-grandfather, the usual explanation that there was another professor between them is the more obvious one.[24] It seems likely now that Ammonius' direct successor was the mathematician Eutocius, who gave a course on the *Organon* according to Elias *On the Prior Analytics* p. 134.[25] No further particulars are known. Philoponus never held the chair, for he is always given the title of *grammatikos* (professor of philology), never that of *philosophos*. H.D. Saffrey,[26] who pointed out the probable connection between the closing of the Athenian school in 529 and the publication of Philoponus' book *Against Proclus on the Eternity of the World* in the same year, thinks that he may have had a semi-official position in the school as editor of Ammonius' lectures. In that case the object of his book would have been to reassure the authorities as regards the religious views of the school. It is equally possible, however, that he wrote it on his own behalf only, to renounce his former allegiance to the school, which subsequently, under Olympiodorus, confessed its paganism more openly than it had ventured to do under Ammonius.

The birth of Olympiodorus must be dated before 505, or he could not have heard Ammonius, and after (or at least not much before) 495, since he was still teaching in 565. Of his three commentaries on Plato

[23] 89,4-5: if, *as they say*, the world is eternal. 90,27-8: *as our philosophy professor said*, the reference is to the world soul. 171,9-11: there is also an art of medicine on the intelligible level, the reason-principle in the demiurge, *he says*, by virtue of which principle the world is free from disease and ageing. 186,1-2: thus the sky is perishable in its essence, but it continues to exist, *he says*, owing to an inflow from the one principle of all things, as long as this inflow lasts. 194,23-6: ... through the heavenly bodies, which, *he says*, are also eternal, but their eternity is no longer of the same kind. As regards their substance, *he says*, the heavenly bodies are eternal, but not as regards their action. 226,12-15: for if, *he says*, the demiurge produces all things by his generative power and needs no time, but does so without change, why should we say, *he says*, that he began to produce at a certain point in time? Their contention is wrong, as (*he says*) we have shown elsewhere.

[24] Ol. *in Meteor.* 153,7 etc.; cf. *propatôr*, Proclus *in Parm.* 1058,22; Marinus *Vita Procli* 29.

[25] Article cited above, n. 1; cf. ibid. 129. His commentary on the *Isagoge* (20,10-11 Busse) is cited in Arethas' scholia on the *Isagoge*, Vat. Urb. Gr. 35, f. 4r, line 9.

[26] op. cit.

(*Alcibiades, Gorgias, Phaedo*) and two on Aristotle (*Categories* and *Meteorologica*) that on *Meteorologica* can be dated with certainty after 565;[27] an anonymous commentary on Paul of Alexandria (Ps.-Heliodorus), written down in 564, very probably also represents a course taught by Olympiodorus.[28] The evidence in the lectures on the *Alcibiades* is contradictory. Creuzer[29] thought that they were given before 529 on the ground of the famous passage on the estate of the Academy: 'Perhaps Plato made a point of refusing fees because he was a well-to-do man; that is why the endowment funds have lasted until the present time, in spite of the many confiscations that are taking place.'[30] I can make no sense of Zeller's objection[31] that *diadokhika* (the successor's, or head of the school's, endowment) can mean the salary of a professor or philosophy in any town. The remark is pointless unless applied to the wealth of the Athenian school. Olympiodorus' argument had been put forward before and had been answered by Damascius,[32] who explains that, contrary to current opinion, the estate of the Academy did not come from Plato's private fortune, but from the legacies of its friends and benefactors in the course of the centuries. The discussion throws a curious sidelight on the relations between the school of Athens, proud of its financial independence, and the Alexandrian university, whose professors were dependent on the salary of the city and the fees of students;[33] it also provides a background to the unkind comments of Damascius on Ammonius' alleged avarice.

Zeller's motive in advocating a later date was apparently the space of nearly forty years that would have to be assumed between the commentaries on the *Alcibiades* and the *Meteorologica*. This is not a valid objection, for Olympiodorus may well have come into the professorate before 530, but there are other chronological difficulties. In the biography of Plato that forms the beginning of the commentary on the *Alcibiades*, Olympiodorus tells a story about the welcome given to Hephaestus as

[27] *in Meteor.* 51,30-53,2.

[28] J. Warn, 'Le commentaire attribué à Héliodore sur les *eisagôgika* de Paul d'Alexandrie', *Recherches de Philol. et de Ling.*, 1967, 197-217; L.G. Westerink, 'Ein astrologisches Kolleg aus dem Jahre 564', *Byz. Zeitschr.* 64, 1971, 6-21 (= *Texts and Studies in Neoplatonism and Byzantine Literature*, Amsterdam 1980, 279-94).

[29] In his ed. of Ol. *in Alc.*, Frankfurt 1821 xiv. On the question in general there are three papers by A. Cameron: 'The end of the ancient universities', *Cahiers d'histoire mondiale* 10, 1967, 653-73, 'The last days of the Academy at Athens', *Proceedings of the Cambridge Philological Society*, 195, 1969, 7-29; 'Le fin de l'Académie', in *Le néoplatonisme*, Actes du colloque de Royaumont, CNRS, Paris 1971, 281-90.

[30] 141,1-3.

[31] *Philos. d. Gr.* III 2⁴, 917-19.

[32] *Vita Isidori* 212,1-5 = 213,8-14. It is to be noted that Damascius identifies the Academy with the Athenian School of the sixth century, as does Cameron. I. Hadot (*Le problème du néoplatonisme Alexandrin*, Paris 1978, 33) has pointed out that this is an error archaeologically, i.e. as regards the site. Nevertheless, the institution was considered as being the same, and this is how Damascius understood his title of Platonic successor (*diadokhos Platônikos*).

[33] cf. Ol. *in Gorg.* 224,20-4; 225,19-21; 226,24-6.

governor of Alexandria by a grammarian, one Anatolius. He is clearly alluding to an event that had happened several years before: *'a certain Anatolius, a grammarian, once* won considerable success by quoting this line in honour of Hephaestus, when he made his entry as governor of the city.'[34] Both Hephaestus and Anatolius are mentioned by other contemporaries. Hephaestus is depicted by Procopius in the *Anecdota*[35] as a hateful creature of Justinian, who had started his career as a barrister (*rhêtôr*) and then, as augustalis of Egypt, was responsible for the corn monopoly and for the confiscation of the poor fund started by Diocletian. John Lydus[36] knew him as *praefectus praetorii* in Constantinople and was addressed by him when he left the service in 551. He also provides the interesting detail that Hephaestus was from a noble Egyptian family and derived his descent from the first of the Pharaohs, the Hephaestus mentioned by Diodorus 1,13,3. An Alexandrian grammarian Anatolius occurs in the *Christian Cosmography* of Cosmas Indicopleustes: it was at his request that Cosmas added a seventh book on the eternity of the heavens not long after 547.[37] But for the possibility of a close relationship his identity with the one in Olympiodorus' story is practically certain. If Olympiodorus gave his lectures before 529, the episode of the welcoming speech can hardly have taken place later than the early twenties. This is impossible if Hephaestus owed his appointment to Justinian (as Procopius seems to imply though he does not say so expressly); it is highly improbable in any case, as it would make both the new governor and the official orator of the city very young men.

The use of the present participle 'that are taking place (*ginomenôn*)' by Olympiodorus shows that the expropriation of the Academy's estate took place only gradually. This leaves room for two explanations: either confiscations had been going on for some time and the edict of 529 was only the finishing stroke, or the action was started in 529 and completed in slow stages; all the slower, one imagines, because the local authorities cannot have co-operated whole-heartedly. If we take it that they succeeded in dragging the matter out till 532, it becomes possible to fit in Tannery's hypothesis that Chosroes in the peace-treaty of that year obtained the restitution of (a part of) the revenues for his *protégés* from the Academy.[38] The treaty itself, as reported by Agathias II 31, only stipulated that 'those men were to be free to return to their country and live quietly by themselves (*eph' heautois*) without being compelled to accept any belief against their conviction or to renounce the creed of their

[34] 2,80-2.

[35] 26,35-44. Cf. L. Cantarelli, *La Serie dei Prefetti di Egitto* III, Atti della R. Accademia dei Lincei, classe di sc. mor., stor. e filol., vol. 14, Roma 1909, 413-14. The *terminus a quo* is c. 520 (Licinius), the *terminus ad quem* 535 (Dioscorus).

[36] *de Magistr.* III,30.

[37] VII 385 C.

[38] op. cit. 286. On the hypothesis of a return to Athens and the meaning of *eph' heautois*, cf. I. Hadot, Chapter 12 above.

fathers, but if we decide for the late dating of the commentary on the *Alcibiades* some arrangement of the kind must have been made. The ban on teaching activities, it should be noted, was maintained formally,[39] and the remainder of the endowment can have served only to afford Simplicius and his group the leisure for literary work.

The case for the later dating is strengthened by some characteristic features of the *in Gorgiam* which point to a period at the beginning of Olympiodorus' career. It abounds in reminiscences and anecdotes about Ammonius, while the actual substance is of the poorest. It looks as if, besides Proclus' commentary on the myth, Olympiodorus had only his own notes of the lectures of Ammonius to draw upon. In the two other commentaries on Plato he shows himself better equipped: the most significant difference is the attention paid to Damascius.

The erroneous identification of Olympiodorus with his namesake the deacon and exegete by Anastasius Sinaita (PG 89,936 C 9-11; 1189 A12-13), together with the questionable testimony of an alchemical treatise, have given rise to the persistent belief that he was a Christian,[40] in spite of his own unequivocal statements to the contrary, some of which have already been brought forward by Skowronski and Norvin.[41] R. Vancourt, in his study *Les derniers commentateurs Alexandrins d'Aristote* (p. 24) still wrote: 'At all events, it is certain that at the time of Olympiodorus instruction in opposition to (Christian) dogma would not have been tolerated at Alexandria.' As the point affects the present question and is of great interest for the religious situation in the reign of Justinian, I shall quote the principal passages to show what *was* tolerated at Alexandria in the time of Olympiodorus.

A most illuminating one is *in Gorgiam* pp. 32-3, where Olympiodorus declares himself a monotheist, but at the same time distinguishes himself expressly from his (Christian) audience. After explaining Hera allegorically as air or rational soul he continues: 'You should not, therefore, put so superficial an interpretation on doctrines expressed in the form of a myth: *we, too,* know that there is only one First Cause, God, because there cannot be a plurality of first causes. This First Cause has not even a name, for names denote certain attributes, and if God transcends all attributes there can be no name either to call Him by.' In support of this negative theology Olympiodorus quotes the great hymn 'O thou that art beyond all things (*Ô pantôn epekeina*)',[42] then concludes

[39] ... live henceforth in undisturbed privacy.

[40] Tannery, op. cit. 277; K. Praechter, 'Richtungen und Schulen im Neuplatonismus', in *Genethliakon Carl Robert*, Berlin 1910. On Olympiodorus the alchemist, see Ol. *in Phaed.*, introd. 22-3.

[41] L. Skowronski, *De auctoris Heerenii et Olympiodori Alexandrini scholis cum universis tum iis singulis quae ad vitam Platonis spectant capita selecta*, Diss. Breslau 1884. W. Norvin, *Olympiodoros fra Alexandria*, Copenhagen 1915, 319.

[42] Printed in the editions of Gregory of Nazianzus, but claimed for Proclus by A. Jahn, *Eclogae e Proclo de philosophia Chaldaica*, Halle 1981, 62ff. Recently M. Sicherl, on the basis of an exhaustive survey of the MS tradition, has presented a strong case for the authorship of Ps.-Dionysius, to whom the hymn is explicitly attributed in Vat. Pal. gr. 39

that there must be certain intermediate entities between the First Cause
and its lowest creatures.

The passage is supplemented by a parallel one towards the end of the
same commentary:[43]

> You must know that *the philosophers* hold that there is one principle of all
> things and one primary supramundane cause from which all things have
> sprung, and to which they have not even given a name. [Here the same
> hymn is quoted.] They say, then, that the principle of all things is one, but
> that it does not produce the world here below directly; for that would be
> contrary to the natural order of things, if our world were created
> immediately by the First Cause ... It was therefore necessary that other,
> greater powers should be created by the First Cause and then, by these,
> ourselves, who are the dregs of the universe, since we had to be, or the world
> would be imperfect. There are, then, other, greater powers, which the poets
> call the Golden Cord because of their unbroken continuity. First there is the
> intellectual power, then the vivifying power and the healing power, and so
> forth; when they want to express them in words, they give them symbolic
> names. So do not be confused by mere words, when you hear of Kronian and
> Zeusian powers, and so on, but think of the reality for which they stand,
> think that we try to express something else by those words. *If you like*, you
> may take it that these powers have no being of their own and no separate
> existence, but that they are implicit in the First Cause, to which you can
> ascribe intellectual and vivifying faculties. And therefore, when we say
> Kronos, do not be shocked by the word, but ask yourself what I mean:
> Kronos is *koros nous*, i.e. pure intelligence.

These texts are open to one explanation only: the 'philosophers' are the
pagan Neoplatonists, and Olympiodorus reckons himself among them, as
the use of the first person proves. It should be stressed that the context
does not permit one to understand the 'we' as 'we Christians'.

At first sight there is a certain likeness between Olympiodorus'
reasoning and the theology of Hierocles, who also interpreted the Gods as
created (in the sense of caused) beings which we must postulate to bridge
the infinite chasm between the Supreme God and His lowest creatures.
But whereas Hierocles claimed divinity in the strict sense of the word
only for the Supreme God, Olympiodorus does not make any real
concession and is only trying to make his Pantheon acceptable for his
Christian students. It is merely on their behalf, to soothe their Christian
consciences, that he suggests they regard the lower orders of deities as
functions or attributes of God. It is, in fact, a deliberate invitation to talk
at cross-purposes, professor and students each attaching a meaning of
their own to the terms used.

Olympiodorus even ventures to end with a few words in defence of the
cult of images: 'And please do not think that the *philosophers* pay divine

---

('Ein neuplatonischer Hymnus unter den Gedichten Gregors von Nazianz', *Gonimos*,
Buffalo 1988, 61-83).
	[43] 243,16-244,17.

honours to stones and idols (*eidôla*). It is rather like this: since we live in a world of sense-perception and are therefore unable to attain the level of the incorporeal and immaterial powers, idols have been invented to remind us of them in order that by beholding and *worshipping* these, we may be put in mind of the incorporeal and immaterial powers.'[44] One wonders whether the student whose notes we possess translated *agalmata* (statues) by the Christian term *eidôla* (idols) or whether Olympiodorus did it for him.

Afterwards, Olympiodorus may have grown more cautious, but his opinions underwent no change. On the cardinal issue of the eternity of the world, on which Aeneas and Zacharias had attacked Ammonius and which Philoponus had chosen to emphasise his adherence to Christian dogma, there is no trace of a compromise even in the commentary on the *Meteorologica*.[45] The inevitable complement of this doctrine is the belief in reincarnation; for otherwise, if the world has existed from eternity, either there must be an infinite number of surviving souls (an inference contrary to the fundamental truth that form is finite) or the soul must be mortal, and for this very reason Aristotle is supposed to have taken the consequence of denying individual immortality.[46]

Olympiodorus is no less emphatic on the point of eternal punishment, which had been rejected by Neoplatonists ever since Plotinus: 'But we are not punished forever; for it is better to deny the immortality of the soul than to believe this.' What Plato calls *aiônion* (eternal) is a cosmic year.[47] (There is an indignant note by the scholiast: 'Note how this man explains away the unquestionable truth of eternal punishment.') The commentary on the *Phaedo*[48] takes the same view: the punishment for souls that have sinned consists in returning to life, but even the souls of the theurgists, i.e. of those who have attained highest perfection, cannot always stay in the intelligible world. The fullest discussion is found in *in Meteorologica* pp. 141-50, a digression on the myth of the *Phaedo*. What Plato calls Tartarus is simply genesis, either viewed from the physical side as the world of perpetual change, or from the moral side as the place where souls are purified. For punishment is not inflicted because of the wrath of God; when every sin has been expiated the soul is set free. The *Phaedo* commentary pictures a hereafter widely different from the Christian conception: whether we shall meet our loved ones is doubtful, because each soul returns to the sphere to which it naturally belongs.[49]

Olympiodorus' attitude towards suicide also conflicts with Christian ethics. After citing the arguments *contra* and *pro* at great length he

---

[44] 246,7-12.

[45] 115,11-13; 118,5-119,8; 120,13-14; 20-1; 153,19-21; *in Gorg.* 65,24-66,4.

[46] *in Phaedo* 10, §1,2-10; 12 §2, 14-18. (The passage 9 §6 is misreported or corrupted; its object, as 10 §5,1-6 shows, was to prove that irrational soul too is reincarnated). *in Gorg.* 97,5-9; 97,24-98,2; 109,18-22; *in Alc.* 27,10-16; 213,20-3; *in Meteor.* 147,24-148,6.

[47] *in Gorg.* 263,17-264,26.

[48] 10 §14.

[49] 7 §4, 1-12.

concludes that suicide can sometimes be justified, when a greater spiritual good can be attained by it, an opinion that must have been very shocking to Christian sentiment.[50]

A few chance phrases show that he shared with Proclus and Damascius their contempt of the Christian establishment: 'They [the poets of old] did not know that there would be a corrupted society which values only appearances and does not search at all for the hidden depth of the myth.'[51] Elsewhere he says: 'Formerly free men were distinguished from slaves by their names and by the way they wore their hair, slaves having such names as Geta, Davus or Phryx; but in our days, confusion prevails in these things too.'[52] Otherwise the tone in this work is discreet and even, in a way, conciliatory. A curious example is the comment on *Alc.* 111A-C, where Socrates makes mutual agreement a criterion of true knowledge. Proclus had observed that agreement is not necessarily evidence of truth, citing the Christians as an instance, who are agreed in denying the existence of the Gods, but only through ignorance.[53] Olympiodorus repeats this remark, but substitutes the Democriteans and their doctrine of the vacuum for the Christians.[54] He makes no secret of the motive for this attitude. After a lengthy discussion of traditional opinions on the subject of demonology, he concludes:[55] 'And this is what the commentators have to say about genii and guardian spirits; we, however, shall try to give an interpretation adapted to the prevailing circumstances.'[56] For Socrates, too, was condemned to the poison-cup for propagating new deities among young people and believing in Gods that the state did not recognise. Our view must be, then, that the guardian spirit (*eilêkhôs daimôn*) is conscience, which is the purest essence of the soul and the only part of us that is free from sin and a merciless judge and an unimpeachable witness of what has happened here below when we appear before Minos and Rhadamanthys.' The word *daimôn* (spirit, demon) was of course a dangerous one because of its pejorative development in Jewish and Christian usage, and Olympiodorus clearly did not want to be decried as a devil-worshipper. In the rest of the commentary he therefore avoids the word pretty consistently; twice he actually substitutes the word conscience where Proclus had compared Socrates to the Guiding Spirit or Good Spirit (*ephestôs*, or *agathos daimôn*).[57] Before mentioning this solution, however, he had already drawn the more obvious parallel between guardian spirits and guardian

[50] *in Phaed.* 1§2-9; cf. 3 §11,7-8.
[51] *in Gorg.* 238,16-19.
[52] 149,3. The phrase 'in our days confusion prevails in these things too', is Olympiodorus' own. Cf. *in Gorg.* 34,18. cf. Palladas, *Anth. Gr.* X 90,7: 'For today everything is turned upside down' (Paton).
[53] *in Alc.* 294,3-6.
[54] ibid. 92,6-7.
[55] ibid. 22,14-23,4.
[56] Damascius, too, uses *ta paronta* ('the present circumstances') in the meaning of 'the supremacy of Christianity', *Vita Isidori* 64,1.
[57] Proclus 199,9-14/ Ol. 68,24. Proclus 229,20-2/ Ol. 87,19.

angels:[58] 'But since we have mentioned guardian spirits, it should be observed that they are known also in common usage, though not by the same name. For instead of "demon" they speak of the "angel" of each of us; thus you can hear them say "by your angel", a phrase used of those who lead the life that is most pleasing to God.' The last clause is not quite clear; Olympiodorus may mean that the phrase was usually addressed to monks.[59] He goes on to say that whereas Plato speaks of demons only, the Chaldean Oracles distinguish between angels, heroes and demons. Angels had, of course, been incorporated into the Neoplatonic system long before.[60]

More interesting is the particular way in which *sunêtheia* (usage, custom) is used here. If there were only this passage to go by, it could be given its normal linguistic meaning; but it can only mean 'popular religion' in the preceding paragraph, where Olympiodorus, following Proclus, discusses the peculiarities of the *daimonion* (genius) of Socrates. It impressed him as a voice, Proclus explains,[61] not because the genius actually spoke, but because illumination came to Socrates in a form that affected the acoustic organs. Olympiodorus[62] adds an observation of his own: 'In the same way we can see it happen now in the common religious practice (*sunêtheia*) that those who follow the hieratic way of life suddenly become aware of a sweet smell and say that it is the presence of an angel, illumination affecting, in their case, the organs of smell.' Here there can be no doubt that monks are meant and the addition 'in the common religious practice' mainly serves to distinguish them from those who practise the native Egyptian religion, for whom the same expression 'who follow the hieratic way of life (*hieratikôs zôntes*)' is used.[63] But this very fact proves a more positive attitude towards the religious experiences and practices of the Christians; Olympiodorus seems to have accepted Christianity at least as a creed for the uneducated, a course already suggested, more than two centuries before, by his fellow-countryman Alexander of Lycopolis.[64] Two passages in which Olympiodorus alludes to confession and charity may be mentioned for completeness' sake.[65]

The fact that nothing of Ammonius' lectures and writings on Plato survives makes it difficult to draw a comparison between him and Olympiodorus as regards their relations with the Church. Platonic philosophy raised more controversial points, and the lecturer could count on a more select and more loyal audience. Yet the impression remains that Olympiodorus enjoyed a little more freedom in religious matters.

[58] 21,15-18.
[59] The ninth-century scholion paraphrases: 'May your angel be disposed in such and such a way (towards you), if you do this.'
[60] Porphyry *Letter to Anebo*: Iamblichus *de Myst.* 2,3-4.
[61] *in Alc.* 79,16-80,18.
[62] ibid. 21,9-14.
[63] ibid. 18,14.
[64] *Contra Manichaeos* 3,1-18 Brinkmann, Leipzig 1895.
[65] *in Gorg.* 139,11-18 and 125,25-6.

One reason may have been the Monophysite schism, which partly paralysed even the political power of Constantinople in Egypt. Then there was the failure to build up a continuous tradition in Christian philosophy; to those classes of society which used to provide the students for the philosophical schools the word philosopher must have meant what Olympiodorus implies it does, a pagan thinker. Even the Christians who continued the work of Olympiodorus did little to change this essentially pagan outlook.

In spite of the scarcity of biographical facts, it is likely for reasons to be mentioned below, that Elias[66] was the first of these. The heading of the incomplete commentary on the *Prior Analytics* identifies him as philosopher and *apo eparkhôn*. While the first of these two titles may safely be taken to designate a professor of philosophy, the second is more problematic. In his article on the subject,[67] R. Guilland says of it: 'The title *apo eparkhôn* – former eparch – lends itself to confusion, when it is not qualified by the expression *tês poleôs* (eparch of the city), or *tôn praitôriôn* (eparch of the praetorians), or less commonly *tou praitôriou* (of the praetorium). For it can designate either a former eparch of the city, or a former prefect-eparch, or an honorific title apoeparch.' The practice of bestowing the title on (e.g.) men of letters, comparable to the knighting of authors, actors and musicians in Great Britain, and formerly in Germany, is at least as old as the sixth century. Guilland cites as examples the historians Evagrius Scholasticus, John of Epiphania and Theophylact (this last of the seventh century), as well as Tiberius II's court physician Zacharias. It is much more probable that Elias the philosopher belonged to this category than that he is identical with Elias prefect of Illyricum to whom Justinian addressed his Novella CLIII in Dec. 541.[68] What has remained of his lectures relates to the Aristotelian Organon only: prolegomena to philosophy and commentary on the *Isagoge*; prolegomena to Aristotle and commentary on the *Categories*; some scholia on the *de Interpretatione*;[69] and the beginning of the commentary on the *Prior Analytics*. Yet there is no reason to doubt his express statement that he taught Aristotelian philosophy as a preliminary to Plato.[70] A reference in the commentary on the *Isagoge* proves that he also lectured on Galen's *de Sectis*.[71]

The usual view that Elias was a pupil of Olympiodorus is merely a deduction from the numerous parallels in the work of the two. But they are striking enough to justify the supposition. I shall cite the more important ones *in extenso*.

[66] cf. my paper cited above, n. 1; its biographical conclusions are open to doubt.

[67] '*Études sur l'histoire administrative de l'Empire Byzantin* III, L'apoéparque', *Byzantinoslavica* 43, 1982, 30-44 (30).

[68] ibid. 38; Westerink, op. cit. in n. 1, 127-8 (60-1).

[69] In *CAG* 4.5 xxvi-xxviii.

[70] 123,9-11. Cf. 110,28-30. – At Constantinople, Platonic philosophy was taught at least as late as 511, by Agapius, a pupil of Proclus (Lydus, *de Magistr*. III 26).

[71] *in Isag*. 6,7-9.

Elias 3,17-20: Or, again as Aristotle says in the work entitled *Protreptic* ... 'If we must philosophise, we must philosophise, and if we must not philosophise, we must philosophise; therefore we must philosophise in any case' (cf. David 9, 2-5).

Ol. *in Alc*. 144,15-17; And Aristotle said in the *Protreptic*; 'Whether we must philosophise, we must philosophise, or whether we must not philosophise, we must philosophise, but in any case we must philosophise.'

El. 16,20-5: The poets characterise the divine in three ways, by goodness, power and knowledge, as shown in 'the Gods givers of good gifts', 'but the Gods can do anything', 'the Gods know everything' (cf. Ammon. *Isag*. 3,9-15; David 17,2-9).

Ol. *in Gorg*. 65,20-4; In brief, you must know that the Demiurge possesses these three: goodness, as witness the poets, who say: 'the Gods givers of good gifts', knowledge, for which reason it is said, 'but the Gods know everything', and power, because 'the Gods can do anything'.

El. 22,19-23: Thus a man wounded in war while protecting a friend said: 'I have saved myself, what does that shield matter to me? Away with it!' calling his soul himself and his body a shield (cf. Ps.-Elias 12,19).

Ol. *in Gorg*. 140,28-141,2; Let us then think of saving our souls, knowing that possessions and the body make no difference; let us do as that man said: 'I have saved myself, what does that shield matter to me? Away with it!'

El. 22,25-6: And this: 'Pound, pound the bag of Anaxarchus, for you will never pound Anaxarchus himself' (cf. Ps.-Elias 12,18).

Ol. *in Gorg*. 185,20-2; This is what Anaxarchus said: 'Pound, pound the bag of Anaxarchus, for you will never pound Anaxarchus himself' (cf. *Alc*. 105,5).

El. 27,16: ... that from childhood on we love stories (cf. Ps.-Elias 18,14).

Ol. *in Gorg*. 237,22-3; since then, from our earliest childhood on we have been brought up with stories ...

El. 31,11-13: To show that music heals the passions of the soul: they say that at one time Pythagoras, when he saw a young boy following a flute-playing girl, ordered her to turn the flute around, and by spoiling the tune he put an end to his infatuation (cf. Ammon. *Isag*. 13, 24-7).

Ol. *in Gorg*.41,7-13: Thus Pythagoras, when he found a young man in the company of a cither-playing girl, knew as a physiognomist that the young man was naturally gifted and could be helped; so, out of pity, he ordered the girl to turn her flute or cither around and play it in that way, thus producing a tune that immediately cured the young man of his infatuation.

El. 39,12-14: ... when Porphyry himself had travelled to Sicily to see the craters of fire of Mt. Etna, since the philosopher should be curious to contemplate the works of nature.

Ol. *in Alc*. 2,94-6: And since the philosopher should be curious to contemplate the works of nature, he (Plato) also travelled to Sicily to see the craters of fire on Mt. Etna (cf. Philop. *de Opif*. 182,10: the craters of fire on Mt. Etna).

El. 109,10-14: He (Zeno) was called double-tongued, not because he was a dialectician, as Zeno of Citium, and argued against and for the same points, but because he was a dialectician in his way of life, saying one thing and thinking another. Once, when asked by a tyrant who were the most dangerous plotters against his rule, he denounced the bodyguards. The tyrant, believing him, killed them and was murdered.

Ol. *in Alc*. 140,12-16: For such was Zeno, a great dissembler, and this was why he was called double-tongued, not because he would defend both of two contrary propositions, but because he dissembled. Thus when a certain tyrant asked him who were the ones that had plotted with Zeno against his rule, he denounced the bodyguards. The tyrant killed them and was promptly murdered.

El. 110,18-20: And in the *Phaedo*, that we must go to Hades with this adamantine faith in the immortality of the soul (Pl. *Rep.* 10 619A: with an adamantine faith in this we must go to Hades).

Ol. *in Phaed.* 6 § 14: He himself says that we must go down to Hades with an adamantine faith in this (cf. 8 § 17,7-10, *Gorg.* 237,26-7).

El. 130,28: For philosophers are lovers of the universal.

Ol. *in Alc.* 160,16: because of the philosopher's love of the universal. (*Meteor.* 2,11-12; 55,9).

El. 236,6: For the *a-* is privative.

Ol. *in Alc.* 171,8: For the *ma-* is privative.

These examples are practically all from the introductions to the *Isagoge* (pp. 1-39) and to the *Categories* (pp. 107-134), not from the commentaries proper. This is a common phenomenon: in the introductory part the lecturer follows a narrow traditional scheme, in dealing with the text he is more apt to extemporise and to arrange the subject-matter according to circumstances. Still, if the correspondences were the result of a general familiarity with Olympiodorus' phraseology and ideas, one would expect them also in the commentary. A more probable explanation is therefore direct borrowing. If that is the cause, Elias cannot have used the extant version of the prolegomena to the *Categories*, in which there is nothing that answers to the extracts quoted from Elias (I have purposely omitted all direct correspondences found in the same context). Olympiodorus' commentary on the *Isagoge* is lost, but the most natural way to account for a word-for-word correspondence such as that between El. 39,12-14 and Ol. *in Alc.* 2,94-6 is that Olympiodorus expressed himself in almost identical words in the introduction to Porphyry. This literary dependence does not exclude a personal relation, of course; if Elias followed Olympiodorus rather than e.g. Philoponus (whom he also knew), the most obvious reason is that he was his pupil.

Both from his name and from his social status it appears that Elias must have been a Christian. As a rule, however, he does not allow his Christianity to interfere with his philosophy, though he does admit the possibility of miracles understood as direct acts of Providence, a point on which he follows Philoponus.[72] Such phrases as *Kata tas Hellênôn phêmi pseudeis doxas* (that is, according to the false opinions of the Greeks),[73] confidently deleted by Busse, are certainly a little suspect because they are in flat contradiction with the importance attached in the context to these 'false doctrines' and 'lying myths'. They may therefore be regarded as insertions by the *reportator*, but it is at least as likely that Elias himself used these convenient formulas to shield himself against possible attacks. In the crucial matter of the eternity of the world he is clearly unwilling to abandon the old belief.[74] This personal freedom of thought coupled with the outward conformist attitude must have been common enough among the intelligentsia of Justinian's reign. Its most outstanding representative is of course Procopius of Caesarea.[75]

David is even less known than Elias. The detailed biographical data preserved in Armenian sources[76] relate to a theologian of the fifth century, whereas the 'most pious and devout philosopher' whose commentary on the *Isagoge* we possess, was admittedly a late Olympiodorean of the second half of the sixth century or even the beginning of the seventh; the Armenian text[77] is a translation from the Greek, not conversely. The David of Armenian tradition is therefore either the result of a confusion between two, or more, different persons or a fictitious character named for the Greek commentator, whose translated works soon became classics of Armenian literature.

It is unlikely that David lectured on Plato as well as on Aristotle. Quotations are pretty frequent, but they are hardly at first hand. Of his own lectures he only mentions those on the *Organon* and on (Aristotelian) physics.[78]

Closely related to David's commentary, though not derived from it, is the text published as Pseudo-Elias (Pseudo-David), *Lectures on Porphyry's Isagoge*, Amsterdam 1967. Since the beginning is lost, the ascription to David has no authority; long extracts under the name of Elias may come from a complete copy, but the work is altogether too different from the genuine Elias to pass for an alternative version. The lecturer shows himself familiar with medical literature, and he may have taught medicine also, or even in the first place. As far as can be inferred

[72] p. 327, n. 22 above.
[73] 7,3; 12,1; 69,22.
[74] 120,16-17; 187,6-7.
[75] *de Bellis* V 3,5-9.
[76] cf. C. Neumann, 'Mémoire sur la vie et les ouvrages de David, philosophe arménien du Ve siècle de notre ère', *Nouveau Journal Asiatique* 3, 1829; M. Khostikian, *David der Philosoph*, Bern 1907. A.K. Sanjian (ed.), *David Anhaghtʿ, the 'Invincible' Philosopher*, Atlanta, GA, 1986 (9 papers and a full bibliography).
[77] David the Invincible, *The Definitions of Philosophy*, Armenian text and Russian translation by S.S. Arefshatian, Erevan 1960 (= introductory part of David *in Isagogen*); *Commentary on Aristotle's Analytics*, Armenian text and Russian translation, by S.S. Arefshatian, Erevan 1967; *Commentary on Porphyry's Isagoge*, id., Erevan 1976.
[78] See Busse's *index nominum* s.v. 'Dabid'.

from a few incidental utterances, the religious views of David and Ps.-Elias are much the same as those of Elias. Without strictly committing themselves one way or the other, they refer to the doctrines of the eternity of matter[79] and of the divinity of the celestial bodies,[80] to the irrational avenging spirits[81] and the long-living nymphs of Neoplatonic demonology.[82] The remark that God first made the elements, then man,[83] sounds like a citation from the Bible,[84] but it may also be a free adaptation of the *Timaeus*. On the whole, their main concern seems to be to keep philosophy and dogma as far apart as possible.

It should be repeated, however, that it is difficult to judge of these matters merely from a logical treatise, in which fundamental questions are rarely touched upon. In the case of Stephanus we are in a better position, because we have his commentary on the third book of the *de Anima*,[85] in which a number of crucial points could not possibly be avoided. His way of dealing with them is confused. On the one hand he accepts unquestioningly the authority of Christian dogma[86] and of the Bible.[87] On the other hand there is no attempt at a wholesale revision of the traditional material from the Christian point of view. All the old tenets continue to reappear: the eternity of the world ('according to Aristotle')[88] and of the fifth substance ('according to some'),[89] the pre-existence of the human soul[90] and the rationality of the heavenly bodies[91] (both without any attempt at refutation or reconciliation). We miss the clearness and consistency with which Philoponus handles controversies between philosophy and dogma in his work against Proclus and, in the exegetical sphere, in the *de Opificio Mundi*. Philoponus, however, had the advantage of being an outsider, who could in turn play the part of an opponent or of an impartial judge, while Stephanus was handicapped by being the official representative of classical philosophy,

---

[79] Ps.-Elias 42,20.

[80] ibid. 34,27: 'This question about the sky, whether it is animate or inanimate, is controversial to the present day'. Curiously enough, the sentence returns almost word for word in Theophilus, *in Hippocr. Aphor.* 247,35-248,2 Dietz (ed.), *Scholia in Hippocr. et Gal.* vol. 2, Königsberg 1834): 'For even now philosophers are engaged in controversy regarding the sky, whether it is a body or incorporeal, and whether limited or unlimited.' The link may be Stephanus, although the sentence is not found in the (slightly abridged) text of this author (*CMG* XI 40,6-9).

[81] Ps.-Elias 41,29-31.

[82] *CAG* 18.2 15,21-6; 24,11-12; 14-15. cf. Ol. *in Meteor.* 301,18-19.

[83] *CAG* 129,8-10.

[84] Some biblical phrases: Ps.-Elias 15,4, 'King of Kings' (*in Tim.* 6, 19; also in Elias 21,4); 13,26, 'is crowned by the Creator with the prize of victory.' (I Cor. 9:24)

[85] Published in the third book of Philoponus' *in de Anima*, *CAG* 15, 446-607. See Hayduck's preface and R. Vancourt, *Les derniers commentateurs Alexandrins d'Aristote*, Lille 1941, 43-8.

[86] 527,29-32.

[87] 547,11-14.

[88] 540,27.

[89] 448,6-7.

[90] 541,20-542,5.

[91] 595,33-598,7. Cf. above, n. 80, and Philop. *de Opif.* VI,2.

long before the purely historical point of view had developed.

That he had this function already at Alexandria before he was called to Constantinople is not certain, but probable. Soon after the accession of Heraclius (in 610) he was nominated *oikoumenikos didaskalos*, i.e. professor at the newly founded or restored Imperial academy.[92] According to the author of an astrological forgery written under his name about 170 years later, he taught Platonic and Aristotelian philosophy, the quadrivium, alchemy and astrology.[93] As far as we can check him, the falsifier was not badly informed; commentaries on the *de Interpretatione* and *de Anima* Book 3 are extant, a course in arithmetic is mentioned by Stephanus himself,[94] an astronomical work has been published (partly) by Usener,[95] and treatises on alchemy also circulated, rightly or wrongly, under his name. This, together with a note of not much more authority in an alchemical opusculum,[96] is the only formal confirmation of the presumption (in itself not an unlikely one) that Platonic philosophy was taught as late as the seventh century.[97]

2. Prolegomena to Aristotle and Porphyry

Most of the philosophers discussed above are represented in the *Commentaria in Aristotelem Graeca* by an introduction to philosophy in general and to Porphyry's *Isagoge* or by one to Aristotle and the

[92] H. Usener, *De Stephano Alexandrino*, Bonn 1879, 3-5. On the life and works of Stephanus in general see Vancourt, op. cit. 26-42; Lemerle, *Le premier humanisme byzantin*, Paris 1971, 79-81. The question of his identity with the professor of medicine Stephanus of Athens needs further investigation. His commentaries on Hippocrates and Galen are to be found partly in Dietz, *Scholia in Hippocratem et Galenum*, Königsberg 1834; new editions are in the course of publication in the *Corpus Medicorum Graecorum: Prognostic*, J.M. Duffy (ed.), Berlin 1983; *Aphorisms* vol. 1, L.G. Westerink (ed.), 1985, vols. 2 and 3 in preparation; *Ad Glauconem*, K.M. Dickson (ed.), in preparation. The author of the medical texts taught at Alexandria (I 335,5 Dietz); he is called *philosophos* (I 51; 233; II 237) and shows himself more familiar with current philosophical ideas than most of his colleagues; his lectures are edited on the pattern usual in the school of Ol. The fact that in the title of the *Aphorisms* commentary he is called Stephanus of Athens is no obstacle: cf. H. Rabe, *Prolegomenon sylloge*, Leipzig 1931, lviii n. 1: 'How many philologists were classified as "Alexandrian" by Suidas! No one believes they were all born in Alexandria.' On the other hand, the philosophical and astronomical information is often superficial or confused (though, of course, it is always possible to hold the notetaker, a medical student, responsible for this); further, if the author knew the iatrosophist Gessius personally, as the anecdote at *Aphor.* I 256,3-8 suggests, he cannot possibly have survived until the reign of Heraclius. The early sixth-century Latin commentary on the *Aphorisms* which P. Courcelle (*Les lettres grecques en occident*, Paris 1943, 387-8) attributes to Stephanus, cannot serve as proof, because the grounds for the attribution are too weak.

[93] H. Usener, *Stephani Alexandrini opusculum apotelesmaticum*, Bonn 1879, 17.

[94] *in de Anima* 457, 24-5.

[95] *De Stephano Alexandrino commentatio altera*, Bonn 1880.

[96] Vindob. Med. Gr. 14, f. 53r.

[97] The anonymous sequel to Proclus' commentary on the *Parmenides* (*Procli. Opera*, Cousin (ed.), 1864, 1237-1312), is the work of George Pachymeres (thirteenth century), and can therefore be left out of consideration. [For a different chronology, which puts pseudo-Elias and David back in Alexandria after Stephanus' move to Constantinople, see

Categories, or by both. These parallel texts offer valuable material for comparison.[98] Besides some individual features a survey of them will bring out, above all, the common characteristic of extreme conservatism. The family likeness is so strong that a comparison is most easily given in synoptic form. This is more especially true of the introductions to Aristotle.

The five commentaries on the *Categories*, of which they form the introductory part, are the following: Ammonius (*CAG* 4.4). Philoponus (13.1), Olympiodorus (12.1), Elias (18.1), and Simplicius (8). With the sole exception of Simplicius, they are all in the form of lecture notes. The contents are these:

I. Introduction to Aristotle in ten sections

The order of the sections varies slightly: Amm. 1-6,8-10,7; Ol. and El.1-10; Philop. 1-5, 8-9, 6-7, 10; Simpl. 1-5, 8-9, 7, 6, 10.

(1) Origin of the names of the various philosophical schools. They may be derived from: (a) the founder's name; (b) his native city or country; (c) the locality where he taught; (d) a particular style of life (Cynics); (e) its belief (Sceptics: Plato's arguments against them); (f) accidental circumstances (Peripatos); (g) its view as to the aim to philosophy (Hedonists).

Arrangement as above in Amm. and Ol.; Philop. and El. have (a)(b)(c)(e)(d)(g)(f), Simpl. (a)(b)(c)(f)(e)(g)(d). Both Ol. and El. add a diaeresis to show that this list exhausts the possibilities. Simpl. is very brief, omitting the digressions, El. is more explicit than even Ol.

(2) Classification of Aristotle's writings: (i) particular (*merika*), e.g. Letters; (ii) intermediate, e.g. the *Constitutions*; (iii) universal (*katholou*), subdivided into (a) notebooks (*hupomnêmatika*) (notes for personal use, either specialised (*monoeidê*) or various (*poikila*)) and (b) treatises (*suntagmatika*) consisting of (a) dialogues (*exôterika*) and (b) non-dialogical works (*akroamatika*). The last group includes (1) theoretical philosophy (true or false): theology, mathematics, physics; (2) practical philosophy (good or evil): ethics, economics, politics; (3) the Organon: its elements (*Cat., Int., An. Pr.*), the method itself (*An. Post.*), accessories (*Top., Soph. El.*).

Amm. omits the subdivision of (iii)(a). Ol. and El. discuss the difference between (iii)(b)(*a*) and (*b*) and Alexander's opinion on it. Only Elias gives a further classification of the physical works. In (iii)(b)(*b*)(3) Ol. distinguishes the method, contributing additions, clarifying additions, El. and Simpl. preliminaries, the method itself, substitutes for the method.

(3) The starting point: courses should begin with logic, ethics coming first only in the sense of practical morals.

Philop. and especially El. give a fuller doxography; Boethus (physics), Andronicus (logic), Platonists (ethics or mathematics), Amm. and Ol. also

Mossman Roueché's suggestion recorded in Chapter 1 – Ed.]

[98] The whole subject was treated as long ago as 1949 in a wider context (grammar, rhetoric and philosophy) by Marian Plezia, *De commentariis isagogicis*, Kraków 1949 (Archiwum Filologiczne 23). Unfortunately this book did not come to my attention until quite recently.

outline the rest of the course, as in section 5.

(4) The final goal: knowledge of God, the First Principle.

Ol., El. and Simpl. cite Hom. B204 (Arist. *Metaph.* 12.10 end).

(5) The way to the end: ethics, physics, mathematics, theology.

(6) Qualifications for the student.

Wording varies very much. Ol. and El. cite Pl., *Alc.* 114E. El. and Simpl. Arist. *Top.* 1.11.

(7) Qualifications for the exegete: critical attitude required.

El. and Simpl. mention the necessity of familiarity with the whole *corpus Aristotelicum* as well as with Platonic philosophy, in order to show their essential agreement.

(8) Aristotle's style: varies with the kind of writing.

Ol. and El. both characterise the epistolary style as *koinos hama kai idios*, destined for the general reader and yet personal (Hermogenes). Simplicius deals with the nature of Aristotle's works in general.

(9) The purpose of his obscurity: to exclude the unworthy (comparable to the function of curtains in temples).

Elaborate series of analogies in Ol. and especially El.

(10) Preliminaries to each separate work: (a) subject (b) usefulness (c) order of treatment (d) title (e) authenticity (f) disposition

Philop. lists these points in the order (a)(b)(d)(c)(f)(e), next (in Part II) discusses them in the order (a)(b)(d)(c)(e)(f); in Ol. this is (a)(b)(c)(d)(e)(f), resp. (a)(b)(d)(e)(c)(f); in El. (a)(b)(d)(e)(c)(f), resp. (a)(b)(c)(d)(e)(f); in Simpl. (a)(b)(d)(c)(e)(f), resp. (a)(b)(c)(d)(e)(f). Philop., Ol., El. and Simpl. dwell on the question of authenticity in general, listing the possible motives for forgery in slightly different ways.

Between I and II Ol. inserts, as an introduction to logic, a treatise on the question whether logic is a part of philosophy or merely its instrument. The subject is usually reserved for the introduction to the *Prior Analytics*.

II. Introduction to the Categories

(a) The subject: neither 'words' nor 'things' nor 'thoughts', but 'words denoting things by way of thoughts' (Iamblichus), with the further restriction 'simple' and 'as assigned in the first instance' (in contradistinction from propositions and syllogisms).

Doxographical details vary: Philop. ascribes the rejected definitions respectively to Alexander, Eustathius, Porphyry; Ol. to Porphyry, Herminus, Alexander; El. (combining Ol. and Philop.) to Alexander and Eustathius. Herminus, Porphyry. Only Simpl., who has consulted the sources, gives reliable details. Philop. adds a digression on the principle 'the beginning of action is the end of consideration', which reappears under (b) in Simpl. and under (c) in Ol.

(b) Usefulness: way to proof.

(c) Order of treatment; beginning of logic.
(d) Title.

> Amm. and Philop. explain only the word Categories, Ol. discusses two
> alternative titles, El. and Simpl. several more.

(e) Authenticity: the old libraries possessed two versions of the *Cat.*, of which one
has stood the test of criticism. Criteria.

> Amm., Philop. and Ol. compare the 40 (El. 42) books of the *Analytics*, of
> which four are left. Only Ol. mentions specific arguments against the
> authenticity of the *Cat.*

(f) Disposition: (i) preliminary notions, ch. 1; (ii) categories, chs. 2-9: (iii)
explanation of some terms, chs. 10-15. Part i deals with entirely new notions, part
iii gives a technical meaning to familiar words.

In the introductions to Porphyry, and especially in the general
prolegomena to philosophy that precede them, there is considerably more
variation. As time goes on, they tend to become more prolix and more
schematic. Ammonius (*CAG* 4.3), who may have introduced the *Isagoge* at
Alexandria, started on a moderate scale with a 24 page treatise on the
definition and subdivision of philosophy. Olympiodorus' introduction is
not extant, but that of Elias (*CAG* 18.1) ought to give a reasonably correct
idea of it. Elias devotes 15 lectures (39 pages) to this introductory matter;
two and a half lectures are needed to discuss definition in general, and
five more are taken up by lengthy commentaries on the six definitions of
philosophy chosen by Ammonius. In David and Ps.-Elias, the length of
the prolegomena is again nearly doubled: David's version (*CAG* 18.2)
consists of 28 lectures (94 pages), its counterpart in Ps.-Elias of 27
lectures, of which 7 are lost.

Because of these differences it is more convenient to analyse at least
Ammonius' prolegomena separately.

Ammonius' prolegomena

I. Introduction to philosophy

(A) Definition of philosophy. – What is a definition? – Any art can be defined either
from its matter or from its aim. Out of the numerous definitions of philosophy
Amm. chooses 'five or a few more'.

(1) 'Knowledge of reality as such';

(2) 'Knowledge of things human and divine';

(3) 'Assimilation to God as far as attainable for man, both in theory and in
practice; the restriction 'as far as attainable', because God and man are
essentially different;

(4) 'Training for death' (but not suicide: *Phaedo* 62B); 'natural' and 'voluntary'
death;

(5) 'Art of arts and science of sciences' (Arist. *Metaph.* 1.2); difference between
art and science; all derive their principles from philosophy;

(6) 'Love of wisdom' (Pythagoras); loose usage of *sophos* in older times
(Archilochus, Hom. *Il.* 23.712; 15.412), limited to God by Pythagoras.

(B) Subdivision of philosophy. – What is division, alternative division, subdivision?

(I) Theoretical philosophy: (1) theology (2) mathematics (3) physics (objects: the immaterial, the intermediate, the material; mathematics as a transitional phase). Mathematics is subdivided into (a) geometry (b) astronomy (c) music (d) arithmetic (ethical influence of music), i.e. continuous quantity, immovable (a) and eternally moving (b); discrete quantity, related (c) and absolute (d).

(II) Practical philosophy: (1) ethics (2) economics (3) politics. Amm. rejects the view that the three are identical. Each can be subdivided into (a) legislation (b) jurisdiction.

·II. Introduction to the Isagoge

The notion of a category; development of the category of essence and, very summarily, of the others. – The 'five words' are used by Arist. in *Cat.*, Porphyry explains them. Subject and title of the book. The usual prolegomena or technical preliminaries:

(1) The subject of the book: what is genus, species, differentia, property, accident?

(2) Its usefulness.

(3) Authenticity.

(4) Order of treatment: before *Cat.*

(5) Title.

(6) Disposition: preface, then (i) the five words separately, (ii) in pairs, (iii) together.

(7) Section of philosophy to which it belongs (logic).

Busse observes that the 'usual prolegomena' partly repeat what has already been said and thinks that they were interpolated in accordance with the later practice.[99] It is true that the text of Amm. has been treated with scant respect by scholars and scribes and the repetition is undeniable. On the other hand, there is no question of a 'later practice', for the same points are discussed in Ammonius' introductions to the *Cat.* and the *Prior Analytics*, and the fact that Boethius, too, deals with them in his commentary on Porphyry[100] is independent confirmation that Amm. himself must have done so already. Whether the passage in our text was added as an afterthought by Amm., or by some one else, makes no difference.

The most elaborate form of these prolegomena, David's version, can serve as a basis for a synopsis of the remaining three.

David's prolegomena

I. Introduction to philosophy

Planned on Arist. *An. Post.* 2.1: (i) if it is, (ii) what it is, (iii) of what kind it is, (iv) why it is.

[99] Note on p. 21,5 of his edition, and preface p. v n. 4.

[100] 4,17-5,10 Brandt. Another passage deleted by Busse (20,25-21,4) is proved genuine by Boethius 10,19-22.

Dav. only.

(i) *Does philosophy exist?* Four arguments of sceptics are answered: (1) *to on* (being) is homonymous, therefore undefinable, therefore unknowable; (2) all things are in perpetual flux; (3) all knowledge derives from the senses; (4) philosophy is general knowledge, which cannot exist in a particular subject. Positive proof of its existence is derived from the belief in providence. The argumentation of Pl. *Theaet.* 170C-171C, and Arist. *Protr.* fr. 51.

El. disposes of the whole point in a few lines, with only the last argument.

(ii) *What is philosophy?* As a unity, it is known through definition (A), as a complex, through subdivision (B).

(A) Definition of philosophy. Nine preliminary questions:
(1) What is definition?
(2) In what way does it differ from description, *horos* (term, definition), and descriptive definition?
(3) Origin of the word.
(4) From what are the definitions of philosophy derived? From its matter (= reality) or its aim (= becoming like God).
(5) Perfect and deficient definitions.
(6) The six definitions of philosophy (as given by Amm.).
(7) Why are these the only possible ones? Proof by diaeresis and from arithmetic (six is the first perfect number).
(8) (a) The order of the six definitions. – (b) Two additional ones are proved superfluous.
(9) Their origin: 1,2 and 6 come from Pythagoras, 3 and 4 from Plato, 5 from Aristotle.

El. deals with much the same matter, though a little less schematically, in the order (1)-(4), (8a), (6),(9),(7),(8b) – Ps.-El. begins at (7), to which he adds a long treatise on the qualities of the numbers from one to ten; he leaves out (8b).

The definitions explained separately:
(1) 'Knowledge of reality as such'.
(2) 'Knowledge of things human and divine'.
(3) 'Training for death'; four arguments against suicide. 'Natural' and 'voluntary' life and death. The five possible reasons for suicide according to the Stoa.

El. gives essentially the same matter in a somewhat different disposition.

(4) 'Assimilation to God as far as attainable for man'. Four meanings of *homoios*. Essential difference between God and man. The virtues of *Theaet.* 176A-B.

El. does not discuss the notion of *homoios*.

(5) 'Art of arts and science of sciences'; in the same way a king is called ruler of rulers and God King of kings. The other arts derive their principles from philosophy and are corrected by it. The definition does not imply that philosophy is an art. Art and science defined; the difference between the two.

The digression on art and science not in El.

(6) 'Love of wisdom'; the old general sense of wisdom (Hom. *Il.* 23,712) restricted

by Pythagoras. The degrees of knowledge: sense-perception, imagination, opinion (irrational and rational), discursive thought, intellection. – The four groups of definitions (1-2 from matter, 3-4 from aim, 5 from rank, 6 from etymology); significance of the number four.

Dav. adds the treatise on the properties of the numbers from one to ten which precedes the discussion of the separate definitions in Ps.-El. El. leaves out the digression on degrees of knowledge but adds one on perfect numbers.

(B) Subdivision of philosophy. – What is division, alternative division, subdivision? (I) Theoretical philosophy, (II) practical philosophy. Grounds for this division. While (I) has a wider range, (II) has a wider aim (the Good).

(I) Plato: (1) physics (2) theology (with mathematics as propaedeutics); Aristotle: (1) physics (2) mathematics (3) theology (1 material, 2 immaterial, 3 material in substance, immaterial in idea). Function of mathematics: *Epinomis* 992A; Plot. 1.3.3; meaning of the name. – Mathematics is subdivided into: (a) arithmetic (b) music (c) geometry (d) astronomy (in the order named), i.e. discrete quantity, absolute (a) and related (b), continuous quantity, immovable (c) or moving (d). Invented by Phoenicians (a), Thracians (b), Egyptians (c), Chaldeans (d). Practical counterparts of these theoretical sciences. Ethical influence of music.

Ps.-El. omits the paragraphs on music, but adds one on the individual 'inventors' of the *quadrivium*.

A long disquisition follows on the modes of divisions: what is the principle of division in the case of philosophy, of theoretical philosophy, of mathematics?

Only in Dav. and Ps.-El.

(II) Aristotle subdivides practical philosophy into (1) ethics, (2) economics (3) politics (his books on these subjects). The Platonists object that politics includes the other two, and divide into (1) legislation and (2) jurisdiction, for which the other three provide the material conditions.

Both El. and Ps.-El. try to prove that Pl. and Arist. really agree, but in entirely different ways.

(iii) *The nature of philosophy*: on the strength of the definitions it can be described as contemplative, directive, purificatory, social.

(iv) *The aim of philosophy: Tim.* 47B. Both the cognitive and the vital faculties of the soul are guided by it.

Headings (iii) and (iv) are absent from El.

II. Introduction to the Isagoge

(1) The subject: genus, species, differentia, property, accident. Diaeresis showing that all words can be reduced to these.

(2) Usefulness: the *phônai* contain the elements of (a) Aristotle's *Categories*, (b) all philosophy, (c) the dialectical methods (division, definition, demonstration, analysis).

(3) Title.

(4) Authenticity.

(5) Order of treatment: before *Cat.*
(6) Disposition; (i) the five words separately, (ii) correspondences and differences.

Dav. and Ps.-El. reject the division into three parts as given by Amm. and El.

(7) The method of instruction used (as under (2c)).
(8) Section of philosophy to which it belongs.

The order of these points is, in El., (1)(2)(5)(3)(4)(6)-(8); in Ps.-El. (1)(2)(5)(3)(4)(6)(8)(7) with a final paragraph on Porphyry's style.

In spite of successive additions, the main scheme has remained the same for a century; but not only the outline is traditional, a great many details, arguments, illustrative citations and anecdotes, too, have been passed on from generation to generation. For example the same lines from Homer are cited in proof of the omnipotence and omniscience of the Gods in Amm. (3,9-15), El. (16,20-5, and Dav. (17,2-9); another line (*Il.* 5,442) serves to emphasise the difference between Gods and men (Amm. 3,22-3, El. 17,7-8, Dav. 34,21-2, Ps.-El. 14,27.) In the discussion of voluntary death the epigram on Cleombrotus' suicide is obligatory (Amm. 4,22-5, El.14,4-7, Dav. 32,30-3, Ps.-El. 12,5). The same rare variant of Homer *Il.* 23,712 illustrates the use of *sophos* before Pythagoras (Amm. 9,8-15, El. 23,34-24,3, Dav. 45,7-9, Ps.-El. 17,5). Plotinus 1.3,3, on the function of mathematics in education, is referred to by Amm. 12,25-7, Dav. 59,17-19, Ps.-El. 18,29. The story of Pythagoras converting a young man by music is told by Amm. 13,24-7, El. 31,11-13 (cf. Ol. *in Gorg.* 41,7-13). Philosophy is characterised as *theia kai ephetê* with reference to *Tim.* 47B by Amm. 16,17-19, El. 1,19-2,2, Dav. 78,28-79,1. In Amm. 15,17-16,3, El. 34,10-21, Ps.-El. 22,20-1, the *Carmen aureum* is quoted for examples of the *dikastikon* (jurisdiction) in individual morals. This list could be made considerably longer, and a similar one can be drawn up for the introductions to Aristotle. In each of them only a fraction of the contents is the lecturer's own contribution, and the same may safely be inferred with regard to the prolegomena to Plato, lost or extant.

CHAPTER FIFTEEN

Boethius' commentaries on Aristotle

James Shiel

I

It is recognised that Aristotelian logic, which was to become an integral part of medieval scholasticism, was first transmitted to Latin Christianity through the work of Boethius. But the way in which he set about his self-imposed task has never been determined in detail.[1] We know that he promised to translate and comment upon 'every single work of Aristotle I can lay hands on (*omne Aristotelis opus quodcumque in manus venerit)*'.[2] 'To form the idea was a silent judgment on the learning of his day; to realise it was more than one man could accomplish; but Boethius accomplished much. He translated the *Isagoge* (Introduction to logic) of Porphyry and the whole of Aristotle's Organon. He wrote a double commentary on the *Isagoge* and commentaries on the *Categories* and *de Interpretatione* of Aristotle and on the *Topica* of Cicero. He also composed original[3] treatises on the categorical and hypothetical syllogism, on Division and on Topical Differences.'[4]

The genuine texts of Boethius' versions of Aristotle (except that of the *Posterior Analytics*) have now been identified among the manuscripts and his distinctive method of translation firmly identified.[5] The present article therefore proposes to examine the other extant results of Boethius' promise, the commentaries and treatises. Are they really original or are they too translated from Greek?

---

[1] M. Cappuyns, 'Boèce', in *Dict. d'hist. et géog. ecclés.* 9, Paris 1939, 367: 'The exact role of Boethius in the transmission of Aristotle's works is hard to disentangle at present.' This statement prompted the present enquiry. Dom Cappuyns' article is the best introduction to the subject. [Now however see the prefaces of *Aristoteles Latinus*, vols 1-6, and the supporting essays in L. Minio-Paluello, *Opuscula: the Latin Aristotle*, Amsterdam 1972.]

[2] *in Int.* II 79,16 Meiser.

[3] An adjective that is here disputed.

[4] H.F. Stewart and E.K. Rand, *Boethius: Tractates and Consolation*, Loeb ed. 1926, ix.

[5] L. Minio-Paluello, 'The genuine text of Boethius' translation of Aristotle's *Categories*', in *Mediaeval and Renaissance Studies (MRS)*, 1942, 151-77 (=*Opuscula*, 1-27) and 'The text of the *Categoriae*: the Latin tradition' in *Class. Quart.* 39, 1945, 63-74 (= *Opuscula*, 28-39).

1. *In Categorias*[6]

This work invites our first probings, for here we have an explicit indication of source from Boethius himself (160a): 'This comment is meant for the introductory stage, the stage of simple explanation. In composing it I have followed Porphyry because he seemed to be easier and clearer than others (*haec est tempori introductionis et simplicis expositionis apta sententia quam nos nunc Porphyrium sequentes quod videbatur expeditior esse planiorque digessimus*)'. And in fact detailed comparison shows a marked similarity between Boethius' work and the extant short commentary on the *Categories* by Porphyry by question and answer (*kata peusin kai apokrisin*).[7] We immediately notice the very same kind of phrase, detail, or concrete example being used by both authors: '...as in geometry the terms are explained first...'; '...there emerge then four relations between these terms'; '...for example, "I embrace – I am embraced" '; '...if a bushel is full of grain...'; '...Herminus says that "above" and "below" represent not place but position'; '...this kind of definition is considered Platonic'. And so on.

Practically every section of Boethius' commentary exhibits this sort of dependence on the corresponding part of the *Kata peusin*. Often the very questions of Porphyry's catechism are reproduced:

> If the treatise is about words that signify objects why does he here discuss objects rather than words?... Why if he here divides speech into ten categories does he in *On Interpretation* divide it into just two parts?... Why does he here treat the category of quantity before that of quality?... Why does he a little further on describe virtue and vice as qualities?

The final part of Porphyry's commentary (on *Cat*. 11b17-15b32, a sort of appendix, the so-called *postpraedicamenta*) is missing from the single extant Greek manuscript. But numerous parallels in other Greek commentaries show that the corresponding part of Boethius, Book 4, is still following *some* Greek work. There are dozens of parallel expressions in the Greek of Simplicius: 'This question has been raised by many, including Andronicus'; '...the single mean between heat and cold'; '...for example, puppies and children'; '...Aristotle here uses induction to strengthen his case'; 'We call Pythagoras "older" with reference to Socrates'. And in Ammonius: 'This will be explained in the book *On Interpretation*.' And in Philoponus: 'Aristotle here urges us on to deeper inquiry.'

And since Busse makes it clear that Porphyry did go on to comment on the *postpraedicamenta*[8] it is reasonable to assume that Boethius' fourth book still follows him. Some details support this assumption. At 264c

---

[6] *PL* 64, 159-294.

[7] *Porphyrii in Aristotelis Categorias Expositio per interrogationem et responsum*, A. Busse (ed.), *CAG* 4.1, Berlin 1887. [The Latin and Greek parallel passages are set out with their references in the earlier printings of this paper.]

[8] cf. Porph. *in Cat*. Busse, li, n. 2.

Boethius mentions the disparate views of Stoics and Peripatetics. Such discussion of Stoic views is a common thing with Porphyry, as Simplicius remarks.[9] At 264d 'those of better judgement' prove to be the same as 'certain of the Peripatetics' mentioned by Simplicius at 381,2, where he is certainly following Porphyry because a little later (381,20) he presents Iamblichus with a different view. At 283c Boethius says, 'these matters come under the heading of quality' and Simplicius says (414,34) that this point was discussed by 'the followers of Porphyry'. As the main pillars of Simplicius' commentary are Iamblichus and Porphyry, and Boethius' fourth book offers no parallels for the Iamblichus passages, it appears that for this as for the previous three books his main dependence is on Porphyry.

Thus far we have merely been independently testing and corroborating a suggestion already made by Bidez – that Boethius' commentary was taken almost completely from the *Kata peusin*.[10] But Bidez did not notice that there are important differences between Boethius and Porphyry. First, Boethius omits many of Porphyry's explanations, even some useful ones: Porph. 56,14: explanation of the word *katêgoriai*; 59,10: reference to Athenodorus, Cornutus, Herminus, Boethus; 64,30: explanation of *logos*; 78,35: explanation of 'chiasmic arrangement', and others.[11] Had these been in his Greek source he would surely have included some of them. Again, Boethius' topics are not always in the same order as Porphyry's, or even as Aristotle's.[12] Also, many of his explanations are simpler than Porphyry's: some of them add hardly anything to Aristotle's own words. The comment on *dispositiones* at 216d, a long explanation, not found in Porphyry, adds little or nothing to *Cat.* 6a32ff. And at 228b, the 'father-son' exemplification is from Porph. 118,8, but Boethius enlarges it with an extra note about the 'double-half' of *Cat.* 6b1.

Even where dependence on Porphyry is apparent, the verbal similarities are seldom exact. For instance, in the passage quoted above (p. 350) where Porphyry has 'four relations' Boethius has 'four differences'. And there is a telling difference between the two explanations of the Aristotelian phrase 'of a subject' (*Cat.* 1b10): Porphyry says it means 'univocally'; Boethius says it means 'in essence', 'in very substance'. In such cases Boethius' Greek is certainly not Porphyry's.

As a matter of fact, Bidez[13] seems to have overlooked at least seventy

---

[9] Simpl. *in Cat.* 2,8 Kalbfleisch.

[10] J. Bidez, 'Boèce et Porphyre', *Revue belge de philol. et d'hist.* 2, 1923, 189ff. This close adherence to Bidez seemed important to me before the appearance of the *Aristoteles Latinus* editions of Boethius. Had these editions been available I could have chosen rather to emphasise from the start the disparity of word-usage which rules out any idea of direct translation from Porphyry.

[11] Porph. 81,7; 81,16; 82,23; 98,34; 101,33; 132,4.

[12] Contrast Boeth. 184a, 190a, 192c with Porph. 88,14; 93,31; 94,20.

[13] Bidez, op. cit., 194: 'Apart from the references to Themistius and to Iamblichus (224c) cited above, I have discovered nothing in Boethius' commentary which is not a reproduction of, or which could not be considered as the development of, the parallel passage of the *Kata*

passages or phrases from all points of Boethius' work where
non-Porphyrian Greek parallels come to hand. Here are a few: '...the
Categories comes first in the order of school reading'; '...the work is also
useful for the study of moral philosophy'; '...without it Aristotle's work
would look truncated and unfinished'; '...there is another work by
Aristotle about categories, much the same in content but different in
style'; 'Archytas too wrote a work in two books called *On Universals*. He
was a Pythagorean from Tarentum and lived for a while with Plato'; 'As I
said before, this work is not about the genera of things, nor about the
things themselves, but about words'; 'Aristotle mentions only three of
these descriptions and two of them he unites into one'; '...where there is a
single concept and a single word to express it the expression is called by
him "incomposite" '; '...as milk, for example, hardens into cheese'. For all
those expressions, and a host of others, there are Greek parallels in
Simplicius. 'A strong indication that Aristotle is here thinking of words
and not of things is given in his phrase, "among forms of speech" ' (*Cat.*
1a16): that comment is matched in Olympiodorus. ' "Skindapsus" is a
meaningless utterance' is found also in Elias (*skindapsos*).

Even where we find no extant parallel *ad locum* we can still at times
sense the presence of the Greek source. Even the more casual and
personal phrases of Boethius and his very manner of introducing
Porphyry have a Greek touch: 'But someone may say...': this is a common
opening in Greek Aristotelian texts; '...the prolixity of the discussion
must be curtailed': Iamblichus in Greek similarly curtails the prolixity of
Porphyry's comments; 'many thinkers, including Andronicus, say... but
Porphyry's view is': this antithesis is found in Greek; 'I follow Porphyry
because his comment is simpler': so does Simplicius; 'As I have already
said (*ut docuimus*)': this looks at first like a personal statement by
Boethius, but it turns out to be merely the Greek scholiast's *eirêtai kai
proteron*. All this indicates that Boethius was not simply following an
exact or complete or first-hand copy of the *Kata peusin*.[14] But his Greek
document obviously reproduced a good deal of it, though not verbatim.

To proceed let us briefly compare his work with all the other known
commentaries on the *Categories*.

(1) Pre-Porphyrian commentaries (Herminus, Alexander, Andronicus,
the Stoics). Boethius knew these through the medium of Porphyry, for all

---

peusin'.

[14] This argument, written before the appearance of the *Aristoteles Latinus*, receives a
totally new emphasis from the work of Minio-Paluello, dramatically portraying the
psychology of Boethius as a translator. For instance, it is now abundantly clear that in the
examples here quoted, to go no further, Boethius could never have translated *skheseis* as
diversitates, *andrapodisamenos* as *complector*, *topon* as *loca*, *hupographê* as *definitio*,
prothesis as *intentio*. He was simply not translating Porphyry's Greek, but that of a later
work, 'a Greek Neoplatonist commentary which had used both commentaries by Porphyry
on the *Categories*, but which was not that of Ammonius' (I. Hadot, 105). As for Ebbesen's
suggestion (1987, 292ff) that 'Boethius turned to Porphyry ... in ... concern for pedagogy',
both the preference expressed for Porphyry and the concern for pedagogy are already plain
to be seen in the Greek commentators.

his quotations from them are found in the *Kata peusin*.

(2) Porphyry (died 309 AD) *Pros Gedaleion*. It seems that Boethius cannot have followed this larger and more profound commentary on the *Categories*, now lost. For in Boethius' first three books we find hardly any parallels for the numerous fragments of the *Pros Gedaleion* preserved by Simplicius, and usually the elementary *Kata peusin* accounts for all the subject-matter. And in Boethius' fourth book several whole sections are merely a spun-out repetition of Aristotle's text with no external material:[15] in these sections the Greek which Boethius followed cannot have been very voluminous or profound.

But there are in Boethius two explicit quotations from Porphyry not found in the *Kata peusin*. These must therefore, as Bidez admitted, come from the larger commentary.[16] But we must observe that in both cases the Greek manner of ushering them in and out shows that Boethius is not quoting at first hand: 'Certain commentators, among them Porphyry himself, argue as follows...: that is what Porphyry says'; the very same kind of post-Porphyrian phrasing occurs in Simplicius (379,8). Boethius shows no acquaintance with the numerous other passages of the *Pros Gedaleion* preserved in Simplicius. These two pieces are obviously detached fragments which he found in his Greek document: immediately after they end, the *Kata peusin* reappears.

(3) Iamblichus (died c. 325 AD). Boethius mentions Iamblichus by name twice. And there are traces of his lost commentary at other points,[17] for Simplicius in the parallel passages is expressly following Iamblichus. But Boethius' two explicit references to Iamblichus are obviously second-hand; at 162a he knows him through Themistius' criticism, and at 224c-225b he seems to be drawing upon a similar Greek criticism: 'in this matter we yield to the authority of Iamblichus' (paralleled in Simplicius). This latter passage is again a detached fragment, for it is awkwardly wedged into another comment on the art of composing names, which begins at 224c and is resumed at 225b.[18]

(4) Dexippus (died c. 330 AD). This commentator deals extensively with the Plotinian 'problems' (*aporiai*) of Iamblichus. The extant part of his commentary has hardly anything closely similar to Boethius.

(5) Themistius (died 384 or 385 AD). The few fragments of Themistius' commentary one can discover[19] have no parallels in Boethius.

(6) Syrianus (died c. 437 AD). The fragment of Syrianus preserved by Simplicius *in Cat.* 164,4 is not in Boethius.[20] But there are some affinities between the two commentators. Boethius at 168c notes that Aristotle

---

[15] e.g. 264b, 266abc, 270ab, 277d-278d, 280bcd, 288d.

[16] Attention should also be paid to the extract edited by P. Hadot.

[17] 180c, 181d, 184ab, 206d, 208b, 224c, 230c.

[18] Such awkward combination of detached scholia is noticeable elsewhere in Boethius' works. See Wiesner, *Aristoteles* II, 328.

[19] Themist. *in Phys.* 4,24; Olympiod. *in Cat.* 35,4; 48,14 [cf. *AL* I 5: *Anonymi Paraphrasis Themistiana*].

[20] The addition of the cognomen 'Philoxenus', at Boeth. *in Int.* II 87 Meiser, indicates quotation in Greek by someone later than Syrianus, not Syrianus himself (Pattin).

decided not to discuss multivocal and diversivocal words in his opening chapter; this, according to Simplicius (*in Cat.* 23,13), is a view of Syrianus. Syrianus was interested in the *pythagorica scientia* mentioned by Boethius in his *prooemium* (160b). The Athenian school of Syrianus was interested in rhetoric, and Syrianus himself wrote a commentary on Hermogenes; Boethius wrote two short rhetorical treatises.

(7) Proclus (died 485 AD). Though no *written* commentary by Proclus is mentioned by Simplicius in his list of commentators (*in Cat.* 1), his oral teaching on the *Categories* continued the tradition of Syrianus, and his school was flourishing in Boethius' time.

Here it is opportune to examine Boethius' *prooemium* (159a-163c). In it he goes through the *didascalica* or *kephalaia* (lecturer's headings), the traditional items dealt with in the *prooemia* of philosophical and rhetorical treatises. E.A. Quain has tabulated the number and order of these headings as they appear in various ancient treatises.[21] He shows that the early Aristotelian commentators have only two or three such headings (Porphyry's *Kata peusin* has only two);[22] but the commentators later than Proclus have an elaborate arrangement of from six to eight headings. Now we find Boethius with a complete set of six as follows:[23]

160a: *intentio* = *ho skopos* (the aim of the work).
161b: *utilitas* = *to khrêsimon* or *hê khreia* (its utility).
161c: *ordo* = *hê taxis* (its order of topics).
161c: *ad quam partem philosophiae* = *hupo poion meros* (which part of philosophy it belongs to).
161d: *Aristotelis liber* = *to gnêsion* (its authenticity).
162a: *inscriptio* = *hê epigraphê* (its correct title).

The late commentator Elias remarks that the organiser of these *didascalica* was Proclus (Elias *in Cat.* 107,24): 'Proclus said that students beginning to read in class the Aristotelian treatises should first go through all these headings, but he did not give a reason; so let us now add the reason as we distinguish them'. A briefer gloss intruded into Elias' text says, 'this is a Proclan arrangement'. Hence Boethius' fully-fledged system

[21] E.A. Quain, 'The Mediaeval Accessus ad Auctores' in *Traditio* 3, 1945, 243-56. Now there is the important work of I. Hadot, 'Les introductions aux commentaires exégétiques chez les auteurs néoplatoniciens et les auteurs chrétiens', in M. Tardieu (ed.), *Les règles de l'interprétation*, Paris 1987, as well as of L.G. Westerink in Chapter 14 above.

[22] Only *title* (*epigraphê*) and *purpose* (*prothesis*) receive formal and full treatment, but *en passant* there is informal reference to *order* and to *utility* (only of preliminaries and appendices to the main text, not of the whole treatise). For the references see I. Hadot, 127, nn. 45-8. Whether Porphyry, 'the cause of all good things for us' (Simpl. 2,6), had a longer and more formal list in his larger commentary we have no way of telling for certain. Certainly Proclus did not invent these headings; he simply 'arranged' them, as Elias says.

[23] Quain has overlooked two of Boethius' headings in his table: *Inscriptio* and *Aristotelis neque ullius alterius liber est*. The difference in number, vocabulary, and order, and the lack of technical terms, clearly rule out Porphyry as Boethius' immediate source.

of headings seems to have come from some source contemporary with or later than Proclus.[24]

(8) Ammonius and his school (c. 490 onwards AD). It is immediately clear from Quain's table that Boethius' *prooemium* is not modelled on Ammonius, who omits the heading *ad quam partem* but gives another instead, 'its division into chapters' (*hê eis ta kephalaia diairesis*) (*in Cat.* 8,6). This division into chapters displays in fact the whole arrangement of Ammonius' commentary – which never influences Boethius at all. Courcelle is not justified in concluding that because Boethius has *some* of his *didascalica* corresponding to those of Ammonius he is therefore following him.[25] These stereotyped headings were traditional; Ammonius is certainly following the scheme arranged by his master Proclus.[26] Dependence on the same source would explain the similarities in Boethius.

Courcelle argues that the rest of Boethius' commentary, too, is dependent on Ammonius as well as on Porphyry. But the only parallels he adduces between them are a pair of similar diagrams (Boeth. 175b; 291bc: Ammon. 25,12; 106). This, allowing for the possibility of a common source, is not enough to prove dependence. I find that detailed comparison produces about half a dozen other parallel passages in Ammonius, but all these turn up in Simplicius as well – which is in favour of an Athenian source for Boethius. Such comparison also reveals several very definite discrepancies between Boethius and Ammonius. For instance, the passages in Boethius which show the ultimate influence of Iamblichus have no parallels in Ammonius. Bidez has observed that Ammonius shows hardly any acquaintance with Iamblichus, for he often reproduces comments of Porphyry that had been improved upon by Iamblichus.[27] Neither he nor his pupils, Philoponus and Olympiodorus, in commenting on the *Categories*, give a single quotation from Iamblichus or Syrianus. Obviously their mentality differs from that of the Athenian School.[28]

[24] I. Hadot (103) rightly points out that Elias, and therefore presumably Proclus in his oral classwork (*sunanagnôsis*), gives a wider list of *ten* general questions and that these six *kephalaia* would come only as answer to the tenth question: 'For each treatise of Aristotle how many introductory points should be considered, and what are their names?' Boethius, working from fragmentary material, knows only about the details under this tenth heading which, dealing specifically with the treatise under consideration and not like the other nine about Aristotle's philosophy generally, easily got copied as a separate scholion and is found so detached in the margins of some Greek manuscripts. The six Boethian *kephalaia* therefore – if Elias is to be trusted – may still derive from the teaching of Proclus: they are found fully, though in varying order, only in the commentaries posterior to Proclus, that is, the 'Athenian' Simplicius and the four 'Alexandrians'. The fact that Boethius is inconsistent about the total number in his other commentaries is a good sign that he was working from fragmentary and discrepant Greek materials.

[25] P. Courcelle, *Les lettres grecques en Occident de Macrobe à Cassiodore*, Paris 1944, 273.

[26] Amm. *in Int.* 1,6; 181,30 Busse.

[27] J. Bidez, 'Unpublished papers on Porphyry' (use of which I owe to the kindness of E.R. Dodds and B.S. Page), cahier 16, 71.

[28] Minio-Paluello from an early stage of his research into Boethian word-usage rejected

(9) Simplicius (after 532 AD). Nearly all the Greek parallels we have found for Boethius occur in the Athenian commentator Simplicius. He preserves the school tradition of his predecessors Proclus and Syrianus, and, unlike Ammonius, he makes full use of Iamblichus. His commentary is too profound, too long, and apparently too late to have been Boethius' source. But the numerous parallels between them indicate a common origin – the oral teaching of Proclus.

That, then, seems to be Boethius' point of contact in the line of Greek commentaries on the *Categories*.

To sum up: (a) Boethius does not give us an integral copy of Porphyry's *Kata peusin*. He seems rather to depend on a later Greek work in which the order of Porphyry's commentary had been changed, the catechetical form dropped, and in which headings had been added. (b) The non-Porphyrian elements in his work are not substantial enough to prove that he had a second complete commentary in Greek. They are brief, and some of them appear to be detached insertions. (c) Boethius does not distinguish the Porphyrian material from the non-Porphyrian. For him it must all have been in the same hand. Apparently he can name a source only where his Greek material has done so. (d) In several passages he does not use the *Kata peusin* at all, but constructs his commentary out of brief non-Porphyrian glosses or repetition of Aristotle's text. (e) Some of the non-Porphyrian elements are Proclan.

These threads will tie together as follows: Boethius' Greek copy of the *Categories* contained brief marginal explanations. Most of these were passages of the *Kata peusin* copied verbatim;[29] the rest were additions from later sources, including Iamblichus. They all seem to derive from the school of Proclus.

2. *In librum de Interpretatione*
(two commentaries, *editio prima* and *editio secunda*)[30]

Here the only useful Greek material for comparison is the commentary of Ammonius.[31] But the parallels between them are sufficiently numerous to indicate that at all points in his work Boethius is translating from Greek. I have notes of ninety instances of Greek parallels.

These parallels, however, prove no more than that Boethius is

---

with finality the idea that Boethius depended on Ammonius. Yet it is Courcelle's view which is still being retained by many scholars, in spite of the fact that Courcelle himself eventually published in a gracious review (see Bieler, xix, n. 24) his final palinode deferring to Minio-Paluello's unrivalled insight into the habits of the Aristotelian translators.

[29] cf. Simpl. *in Cat.* 2,10. This, I now fear, was overstated out of youthful reverence for Bidez's Porphyrian scholarship. The similarities are only sporadically 'verbatim'. Nor were the comments always 'brief'. Some of them were evidently substantial, and all of them called for concentration and skill in their translator: it is far from being a case of 'one source, no thinking' (Ebbesen), as any modern Aristotelian translator (e.g. Barnes, 77) will agree.

[30] *Boethii commentarii in librum Aristotelis peri Hermeneias*, Meiser, Teubner, 1877-1880.

[31] The later commentary of Stephanus offers hardly any additional parallels.

everywhere using Greek. They do not prove Courcelle's thesis that he is following Ammonius.[32] In the case of the Aristotelian commentaries textual parallels must be treated carefully. One will often find the same words repeated through a whole series of commentaries. What one finds, for instance, in Ammonius will almost certainly reappear in Philoponus, Elias, or Olympiodorus. Therefore the parallel passages given by Courcelle do not prove Boethius' dependence on Ammonius. In one such passage (361,9) Courcelle's emendation, *sicut Ammonius docet* (Meiser: *sicut Eudemus docet*; MSS: *sicut audivimus docet*), is unconvincing because Boethius here does not in fact say the same thing as Ammonius: the latter does not distinguish two kinds of 'investigative question (*erôtêsis pusmatikê*)'; also, there is no palaeographical justification for the change.[33]

In general structure the two commentaries are completely different. For instance, Ammonius' comment on Aristotle's first chapter begins with the standard treatment of five *didascalica* or headings. The last of these, the division (7.15), marks off Aristotle's work, excluding ch. 14, into four sections. There follows a series of paragraphs, each dealing with a special problem arising out of the text. All these points are missing from Boethius, whose division is into six books. Vice versa, all the main points made by Boethius about the first chapter are missing from Ammonius.[34] It is the same through the rest of the two works. Ammonius often quotes Plato and insists on the harmony of Plato and Aristotle; Boethius merely quotes in turn Alexander, Aspasius, Herminus and Porphyry, and sometimes adds a snippet from the Stoics or Syrianus. In ch. 14 the difference is very marked: Ammonius goes through Syrianus' six 'contentions (*epikheirêmata*)' against the authenticity of this chapter; of these Boethius says not a word, but gives instead a very simple and thin commentary on it. Finally, certain of Boethius' phrases and examples that are obviously taken from Greek, because we can find Greek parallels, are not found at all in Ammonius. To take just a few:

...the *intentio* of the Categories is to deal with words that signify things through the medium of thoughts (*noêmata*). [The Greek parallel for this is found in Philoponus; Ammonius (like Porphyry) omits the mention of *nous/noêmata* as the medium.]

Interjections, pronouns and adverbs come under Aristotle's heading of 'noun' (*onoma*), for they can be treated as indeclinable one-case nouns (*monoptota*). [Porph. *in Cat.* 62,1]

... 'sword', 'blade', 'dagger', can all be referred to a single substrate. [Simpl. *in Cat.* 38,26]

[32] Courcelle, op. cit., 274-8.

[33] See my further note in *Vivarium* 12, 1974, 14-17: Meiser's emendation is brilliantly correct.

[34] This rejection of Ammonius, and of Courcelle's emendation, is supported to the letter by Tarán.

... having dealt with the preliminaries let us go on to the comments on Aristotle himself [*praedicenda* is the literal Boethian translation of Greek *prolegomena*].

The concept and nature of the heavenly bodies is such that they are not receptive of opposites [paralleled in Simplicius].

Here the philosopher wanted to exercise our intelligence [paralleled in Philoponus].

A proof that these expressions are 'by convention (*secundum placitum*)' is that their parts, verbs and nouns, are also 'by convention'.

If just one syllable of the word 'human' is added to it that will not produce a proposition. [For these last two instances parallel is found in the Syriac commentary by Probus (which too is evidently translated from Greek), but not in Ammonius.]

It therefore seems clear that Boethius' commentary on the *de Interpretatione* was not derived from Ammonius. Courcelle, in dwelling upon certain resemblances, did not allow for the much greater divergences. These seem too great to allow even his plea that Boethius may have followed a redaction of Ammonius' lectures differing from that now known to us. The various redactions would not differ any more widely, say, than the commentary of Philoponus on the *Categories* differs from that of his master Ammonius. But in the case of Boethius and Ammonius the whole structure and nature of the commentaries differ radically. Nothing indicates that one copied the other.[35]

There is one basic certainty. As in the commentary on the *Categories*, most of Boethius' material comes from Porphyry: ed. sec. 7,4: 'I have translated into Latin this elucidation, mainly from Porphyry but also from the others (*expositionem...quam maxime a Porphyrio, quamquam etiam a ceteris transferentes, Latina oratione digessimus*)'. Did Boethius know these 'others (*ceteri*)' – obviously Alexander, Aspasius, Herminus and the Stoics – as well as Porphyry? Bidez thought that he had direct access to the commentary of Alexander,[36] but the passages he adduces (87,15-16; 143-4) do not adequately prove this. Courcelle rightly argues from 293,27 that Boethius took from Porphyry all his information about the earlier commentators; this argument is supported by the fact that when Boethius quotes them he habitually adds Porphyry's criticism of them. Several passages in Boethius which do not thus mention Porphyry have parallels in Ammonius which do.[37] It is therefore safe to conclude that the main bulk of Boethius' work comes ultimately from Porphyry.

[35] As noted earlier regarding Porphyry on the *Categories* this argument could now be made more succinct and decisive by use of the *Aristoteles Latinus* editions to illustrate the divergent vocabularies of Boethius and Ammonius.

[36] Bidez, 'Unpublished papers', cahier 16, 535-6.

[37] Compare: Boethius: 65,20; 66,18; 66,31; 68,18; 75,10; 105,15; 143,1
                     Ammonius: 44,11; 32,4; 47,26; 50,10; 56,16; 70,4;   94,29

But Porphyry does not account for everything in Boethius. There are four quotations from Syrianus. They are obviously adventitious fragments: 'At this point there is a question by Syrianus'; '...let us add to this an extract from Syrianus' (18,26, *Syrianus hoc loco quaerit*; 321,20, *nos quoque a Syriano transferamus*). Boethius shows no acquaintance with the other Syrianus extracts preserved by Ammonius. But the four insertions mentioned are enough to show his contact with a post-Porphyrian source. And at times his very manner of quoting Porphyry betrays a later Greek medium: 160,5, 'Porphyry has given a fine explanation of when signified objects can be contraries'; the same compliment is paid to Porphyry in the Greek of Ammonius. Besides, Boethius' sixth book is not from Porphyry because, according to Ammonius (259,9), Porphyry did not comment on this section of Aristotle (ch. 14); and nowhere in this last book does Boethius give us his usual Porphyrian criticism of Alexander, Aspasius and Herminus.

In general, it seems evident that Boethius was not following an exact or complete copy of Porphyry's work. The latter was lengthy (Stephanus *in lib. de Int.* 63,9). But Boethius' commentary is built from scanty Porphyrian material, which he first translates and then applies to Aristotle's text. In the case of some *lemmata* the Porphyrian comment at his disposal was very small, and so he expanded it considerably by comparing it with each phrase of the text.

It is the same in the non-Porphyrian parts. For instance, the long Syrianus calculation at 321,20ff could all be constructed from a simple Greek diagram. In fact, such a diagram is extant in the Syriac commentary (fifth century) of Probus of Antioch,[38] whose work, just like that of Boethius, has all the signs of being a translation from Greek. Boethius' method is particularly evident in his last book where he had very little Greek and no Porphyry. The Greek comment in each case was a brief 'meaning' of the *lemma*, a *sententia*. This he first translated and then applied. For example:

428,12: That is the meaning; but the sequence of Aristotle's words is as follows (*sensus ergo huiusmodi est; talis vero est ordo sermonum*)

430,24: The comment fits the text as follows... (*quare quod dicitur* [i.e. the *sententia*] *hoc modo est* [as applied to the text])

438,10: That is the entire comment; but the order of the text is like this (*omnis quidem sententia talis est, ordo autem sermonum huiusmodi est*)

446,11: And if one goes on to connect the order of my comment to Aristotle's words... (*quod si quis Aristotelis verbis seriem nostrae expositionis annectat*)

449,14: Now I must turn to explain the order of the text (*nunc quis sermonum ordo sit explicetur*)

[38] J.G.E. Hoffmann, *De Hermeneuticis apud Syros Aristotelis*, Leipzig 1869, 111.

Boethius' material, then, consisted of brief notes in Greek, most of them, but not all, based on Porphyry.

Examination reveals that both *editio prima* and *editio secunda* come from the same Greek. The smaller is merely a shortened form of the larger: it displays the same language and is divided under the same headings. In the first work Boethius extracted simple and lucid points from among his Greek *sententiae* and in the second he translated them entirely: 251,1, 'What I omitted in the first edition because of its depth or subtlety I must fill in as clearly as possible in the second (*...quam pote planissime quod in prima editione altitudinis et subtilitatis omiseram secunda commentatione complerem)'*. Where his Greek materials are scanty this means repetition: 479,6, 'Although I explained all this as fully as possible in the second book of my first commentary, nevertheless to ensure that the explanation of the work should not seem curtailed I shall go over it here again (*licet haec omnia in primae editionis secundo commentario diligentissime explicuerimus ne tamen curta expositio huius libri esse videatur hic quoque repetentes explicabimus)'*. In the two *prooemia* we get a very clear proof of how both commentaries use the same Greek material. The first *editio* gives a few points about the *kephalaion* of *intentio*: 32,7, 'A brief clarification of its *intentio* must be given (*quae sit intentio breviter demonstrandum est)'*. To these the second adds other details, without repeating anything previously said – not even the word *intentio* – and then goes on to give the remaining three *kephalaia*: 'title', 'authenticity', 'utility' (*titulus, iudicium libri, utilitas*). All four were certainly together in the Greek. The first edition therefore gives us a small selection of that Greek and the second gives the rest of it.

Furthermore, the two editions between them give us *all* the Greek material. If Boethius in the *editio secunda* omits to translate any point he tells us so. 201,2, 'But Porphyry here inserts certain details about Stoic logic. These are foreign to Latin ears and therefore the point at issue would remain unclear. So I shall omit them (*Porphyrius tamen quaedam de Stoica dialectica permiscet: quae cum Latinis auribus nota non sit, nec hoc ipsum quod in quaestionem venit agnoscitur atque ideo illa studio praetermittemus)'*. In the smaller commentary Boethius does not mention the views of Alexander, Aspasius and the others, but only admits enough of his Greek source to give a simple explanation of the argument and text: 32,3, 'The reader should now expect of me only enough for him to grasp small details one by one following the order of the text, so that he may discover what lurks in its brevity (*nunc a me tantum lector exspectet quantum pedetemptim minutatimque secundum orationis ordinem textumque sermonis id quod angustia brevitatis latet intelligat)'*. But in the larger work he claims to give us all the Greek he had previously omitted: 251,1, '*quod in prima editione...omiseram secunda commentatione complerem*'. This plan of splitting up the Greek comments is his own idea:[39] 186,2, 'The best plan for me was to open up the closely argued

[39] But it was probably suggested by the lay-out of his Greek manuscript.

meanings of Aristotle through a double sequence of commentary (*quare recte mihi consilium fuit subtilissimas Aristotelis sententias gemino ordine commentationis aperire*)'.

And so we reach the same conclusion as in the case of the *in Categorias*: Boethius is translating marginal notes, the explanatory *sententiae* that he encountered in his Greek Aristotle: 250,20, 'The textual sequence is obscure and it is supplemented by extremely obscure scholia (*est quidem libri huius...obscura orationis series, obscurissimis adiecta sententiis*)'.[40] With the *de Interpretatione* he found a great mass of these marginalia and it took him a long time to decipher them: 421,3, 'For there are scholia of numerous points heaped up all together and so I have spent almost two years in a constant sweat of writing comments (*nam et plurimorum sunt in unum coacervatae sententiae et duorum ferme annorum spatium continuo commentandi sudore consumpsimus*)'.[41] These comments were (7,5) 'mostly from Porphyry (*quam maxime a Porphyrio*)', but Boethius faithfully 'translates all the other notes (*quamquam etiam a ceteris transferentes*)'. Sometimes these are under a commentator's name (18,26: *Syrianus hoc loco...*) but sometimes they are anonymous: 19,20, 'This too is in the margin (*illud quoque est additum*)'. The translation of these various marginalia and the arrangement of them into a continuous commentary according to the order of Aristotle's words would seem to be Boethius' only title to originality.[42]

---

[40] 'An obscure course of argument with highly obscure notes added to it', the translation rejected by Ebbesen (290, n. 2), is not mine but that of Barnes (79). But it is correct. Ebbesen adds: 'as far as I can see, the passage means "the doctrines of the book are very obscure, and on top of that the manner of presentation is obscure".' But, surely, *orationis series* (= *hē taxis tou logou*) is not just 'doctrines of the book'. Also, *adiecta* agreeing with *series* does not mean 'and on top of that' (= *et praeterea*): the real (post-classical) meaning of the word is clarified by Boethius a few lines later: 'where Aristotle in his brevity is obscure, I, by making some additions (*aliquibus additis*), may render the sequence easier through that annexation (*adiectione*).' And *sententiae* is not the 'manner of presentation': the correct sense, 'notes added', is warranted by other Boethian passages and is the same as that clearly seen in Isidore's chapter-heading *de notis sententiarum* ('on reference signs for locating marginal comments'). See *Scriptorium* 38, 1984, 340.

[41] This statement is meant to spell out the one just before it announcing that the sixth book will conclude the long commentary composed 'with great labour' (*magno labore*) and 'delay' (*temporis mora*): the reason for the great labour is the large 'pile' of *sententiae* going with the text, and the delay is explained as 'two years'. One should not translate *coacervatae sunt* (were heaped up together) as if it were *coacervavimus* (I have heaped together) matching the first-person *consumpsimus* as Chadwick (129) does: 'Boethius ... compressed into a single book'. The sweat (*sudor*), moreover, did not in my view 'consist in the deciphering of the tiny handwriting' (Chadwick, 129); the ancient scholia were not simply carelessly 'scribbled in the margins' (Barnes, 80); and I did not understand *coacervatae* to imply 'compressions' (Chadwick, 129), but rather the very opposite, 'heaps'.

[42] Even this may be an overstatement if we allow for ancient editorial activity. Such

3. *In Isagogen Porphyrii*[43]

Although Boethius in the *editio prima* of this work retained Victorinus' translation of the *Isagoge* he can hardly have used a commentary by Victorinus: the list in Cassiodorus' *Institutiones* II 18 (p. 128 Mynors) mentions only the translation by Victorinus but no commentary by him; and apparently Victorinus' work was nothing more than a concise one-book paraphrase (*de Definitione* 897a: *iam uno libro de bis quinque rebus plenissime disputavimus*). Anyway, Boethius reveals that even in this first commentary he is doing pioneer translation from Greek: 8,11 Brandt: '*noêta* I have never found in Latin translation; so I have coined a new word for it, "intellectibilia" (*quoniam Latino sermone numquam repperi, "intellectibilia" egomet mea verbi compositione vocavi*)'. He shows too that even for the *editio prima* he had ready at hand the Greek text of the *Isagoge*, for on occasion he is able to correct Victorinus' version: 23,17, 'Porphyry therefore promises to explain these five terms briefly and in proper measure – but this is omitted by Victorinus' (*haec igitur Porphyrius, non enim Victorinus, breviter mediocriterque promittit exponere*)'; 34,12, 'But Victorinus reduces those two genera to one (*Victorinus vero duo superiora genera in unum redigit*)'. Brandt gives a list of 17 parallels, covering both editions, between Boethius and the Greek of Ammonius;[44] and I find that detailed examination would multiply the number.

All this makes it quite clear that in composing *both* editions Boethius had at hand (a) a Greek text of the *Isagôgê* and (b) a Greek commentary.

Which commentary? Brandt noted that although there was a strong resemblance between Boethius and Ammonius there were also notable divergences:[45] 'It would be a mistake to think that there are no discrepancies in the general consensus of idea and word between Ammonius and Boethius. There are, and they are serious (*minime sane in universa quae inter Ammonium et Boethium est sententiarum atque etiam verborum congruentia differentiae eaeque graviores desunt*)'. Consequently, though he was inclined to believe that Boethius followed Ammonius, he was also ready to admit that both might have followed a

---

activity is very visible at *in Cat.* 263b, where it has corrupted all the extant manuscripts through Latin ignorance of a Greek title familiar to Boethius (Shiel 1957). In the case of the Boethian *Isagoge* editorial effort is again detectable at work on an original text laden with glosses (Shiel 1987). It will be the same elsewhere. 'To render *Organon* he feels obliged to use a hendiadys, *ferramentum et quodammodo supellex* ("instrument or perhaps implement")': Ebbesen 1987, 187. This duplication is not normal Boethian procedure, and it is anyway a poor specimen of hendiadys: it looks much more like an editor's attempt to cope with a variant gloss: *supellex/ferramentum*.

[43] Boeth. *in Isagogen Commenta* S. Brandt, CSEL, Vienna 1906.
[44] Boeth. *in Isag.* Brandt, xxiv-xxvi.
[45] ibid., xxiv.

common authority: 'This proviso should be added: if one feels that Boethius had for his source not Ammonius himself but rather Ammonius' own source, that conclusion should not hastily be dismissed (*verumtamen is modus iudicio imponendus est, ut si quis Boethium non Ammonium ipsum, sed eum quem Ammonius ducem habuisse velit, ea sententia non prorsus improbanda sit)*'. On our argument this seems the correct view. The divergences between Boethius and Ammonius are much greater even than Brandt supposed. The main plan and headings of Ammonius' commentary, which he sets out at the beginning,[46] and his frequent references to Plato, are unknown to Boethius. The similarities, on the other hand, are explained by their common source.

As in the case of the commentaries on the *de Interpretatione*, so here too Boethius seems to have used the same Greek material for both editions. For example, the prooemium of the *editio prima* (3,1-16,10) gives the enumeration and explanation of the six *didascalica*. The *editio secunda* does not repeat these but gives four other introductory points: (a) the division of powers in the soul and the consequent 'methods of dialectic'; (b) the origin of logic; (c) is logic a part or only an instrument of philosophy?; (d) the subject matter of the *Isagoge*. In the Greek commentaries these points are always found in the *prooemia* along with the *didascalica*.[47] Again, in the second edition (140,13ff) there occurs a division of philosophy which differs from that given in the *editio prima* (8,1); but both were together in the Greek material, for Boethius was able to say in the *editio prima* (9,21): 'there are other subdivisions of these which I must omit for the present (*sunt earum etiam aliae subdivisiones quas nunc persequi supersedendum est)*'.

Other passages likewise indicate that for the first work Boethius picked from the Greek only such items as he thought necessary for beginners. Brandt[48] gives a list of the points that are not repeated in the second work. They are mainly detached definitions of terms, e.g. of 'descriptive explanations (*hupographoi logoi)*' at 42,14. Brandt also observes that the subject-matter of the second edition seems to him to be really as elementary as that of the first; that Boethius keeps calling the second work, too, an introduction for beginners; and that there is no real discrepancy between the first and the second. All this is explained by the assumption that Boethius constructed both from the same Greek material. Twin offspring, therefore, of the same Greek parent, the two editions are aptly called by Boethius a *gemina expositio*.

The Greek source was obviously post-Porphyrian: 12,20, 'all beginners in logic following Porphyry (*omnes post Porphyrium ingredientes ad logicam...)*'. Also it was brief. The latter part of Ammonius' Greek commentary consists mainly of brief glosses on words of the text. But

[46] Amm. *in Isag.* 23,12 Busse.

[47] Similar displacement elsewhere (cf. Wiesner 318-19) indicates that Boethius, or his ancient editor, was unfamiliar with the full traditional order of introductory headings in a major, continuous Greek commentary. For this order now see I. Hadot, 120.

[48] Boeth. *in Isag.* xxi.

Boethius, by comparison, has even less to go on. What might have been a one-word gloss, or a diagram, in Greek, he expands into a paragraph by repetition of Porphyry's text. For example, his long explanation of *logikôteron* at 168,11 could all have been built on a one-word gloss like *endoxos*; and 319,15-325,7 could all be taken from a diagram. From the preface to Busse's edition of the *Isagoge* one can see that the oldest extant manuscripts of the *Isagoge* (ninth century) have comments of this sort in the margins, the comments being thickest on the opening pages of the text. It must surely have been the same in Boethius' time. His Greek document would have been a text of the *Isagoge* with brief marginal scholia. With the aid of some of these scholia he sets out in the first edition to elucidate the version of Victorinus, which he allows to stand in order not to confuse beginners by the strange terms of a new translation. But in the second edition his aim is to give them everything in his Greek text and marginalia: 135,7, 'I shall evidently have done good service if by providing philosophic books in Latin written with all the lucidity of total translation I shall have no further need to look for them in Greek (*multum profecisse videbor si philosophiae libris Latina oratione compositis per integerrimae translationis sinceritatem nihil in Graecorum litteris amplius desideretur)'.[49]

4. The treatises on the syllogism
(Introductio ad Syllogismos Categoricos; de Syllogismo Categorico libri III; de Syllogismo Hypothetico libri III)[50]

Comparison of the main points dealt with in the *Introductio*[51] and in the first book of the *de Syllogismo Categorico* makes it clear that both are translations – and both from the same Greek material: 794c, '... the commentaries from which I have taken these points (*eos commentarios de quibus haec nos protulimus)'*. That material is mainly a summary of the *de Interpretatione*, but the final part of it is obviously a simple Greek diagram of 'propositions (*protaseis)'* of which Boethius makes a double elaboration (*Introd.* 769c-792c; *de Syll. Cat.* I 798c-807a).

This double summary is apparently the summary (*breviarium*) which Boethius promised during his commentary on the *de Interpretatione*.[52]

---

[49] This passage refers not simply to 'a complete and unadulterated translation of Porphyry's *Isagoge* (and other basic texts), not of scholia' (Ebbesen 1987, 290, n. 3); for it immediately introduces Greek commentary material, not found in the *Isagoge* itself, about the triple powers of the soul. When Boethius opened his Greek *philosophiae libri* his eye fell at once on scholia as well as text.

[50] *PL* 64, 761,876. This paper, devoted to the commentaries proper, paid too scanty attention to the treatises. But I cannot regard these, however impressive their contents, as simply 'Boethius' own work' (Stump). They are versions of more substantial scholia (*prolegomena, eisagogai*) set between the works of the Organon. That some Greek scholia were of monograph length and sometimes complete with titles can be seen from the *Aristoteles Graecus*.

[51] cf. Cappuyns, op. cit., 370: 'According to Bidez's opinion as reported by A. van de Vyver, *Les étapes*, 443-6, it would represent a second redaction of *de Syll. Cat.* I.'

[52] *in Int.* ed. 2a 251,8.

Usener, in fact, has already argued[53] that the *Introductio* seemed to him to be the promised summary, but Brandt,[54] followed by Cappuyns,[55] rejected this view on the grounds that (a) three whole chapters of the *de Interpretatione* are omitted in the *Introductio*, and (b) Boethius' *de Syllogismo Categorico* – and therefore the *Introductio*, which is so similar – was written before the commentary on the *de Interpretatione*. But against this: (a) Boethius did not promise to make the *breviarium* adhere to all Aristotle's chapters but only 'in some, nearly all' of them (*in quibusdam et fere in omnibus*); (b) Brandt's method of establishing the chronology of Boethius' works by their cross-references is excluded by our argument that these references are not always Boethius' own, but based upon his Greek scholia.

Boethius' *Introductio* and *de Syll. Cat.* I are twin translations of a Greek *breviarium*, a summary of the *de Interpretatione* doctrine of categoric propositions, serving as an introduction to the *Analytics*. Porphyry himself seems to have written such an introduction,[56] and we even find him duly listing the *de Interpretatione* under the title of 'Categoric Propositions' (*Kata peusin* 56,25: 'Topics,...Analytics,... Categoric Propositions...Categories').

Indeed it seems that through all the three works on the syllogism, as in the previous commentaries, Porphyry is the main authority in Boethius' material. We find here, as before, the views of the ancients (Theophrastus and Eudemus) followed by Porphyry's criticism: *de Syll. Cat.* 813c, '... others add one other mode (in the third figure), as Porphyry himself does, following those predecessors (*addunt etiam alii unum sicut ipse Porphyrius, superiores scilicet sequens*)'. And, as before, Boethius apparently found this Porphyrian material in scholia added to the *Analytics* as *prolegomena*: 831c, 'I found this in very few of the Greeks, expressed sketchily and confusedly, and never in Latin (*...apud scriptores quidem Graecos perquam rarissimos strictim atque confuse, apud Latinos vero nullos repperi*)'. 829d, 'This is what I had to say as introduction to Categorical Syllogisms – all that the brevity of an introduction would permit (*haec de categoricorum syllogismorum introductione quantum parcitas introducendi permisit expressi*)'.

Only these three introductory treatises are extant, but apparently Boethius' text had other marginalia from which he hoped to compose a complete commentary on the *Analytics*:[57] 829d, '... if any points are

[53] H. Usener, *Deutsche Litteraturzeitung*, 1880, col. 369.

[54] S. Brandt, 'Entstehungszeit und zeitliche Folge der Werke von Boethius', *Philologus* 62, 1903, 258.

[55] Cappuyns, op. cit., 369.

[56] J. Bidez, *Vie de Porphyre*, Gand 1913, 66.

[57] An MS 'Latin commentary on the Analytics', discovered by Dr L. Minio-Paluello, seemed to him to be by Boethius: *Journal of Hellenic Studies* 77, part 1, 1957, 93-102. See my corroboration of his view in *Vivarium* 20, 1982, 128-41. I have since examined the language of these 'Scholia Anonyma Graeca a Boethio Translata' in close association with Dr Minio-Paluello, who approved my textual corrections, and the ascription to Boethius, for inclusion as an appendix in the next printing of *AL* iii. With the kind permission of the

missing we shall deal with them more insistently in our Analytics (*si qua vero desint in Analyticis nostris calcatius exprimemus*)'.

The way Porphyry is mentioned at 813c, 'as Porphyry himself says (*sicut ipse Porphyrius*)' and at 814c, 'Porphyry, an author of the highest standing (*Porphyrius gravissimae vir auctoritatis*)' suggests a Greek scholiast later than Porphyry. And Dürr's argument[58] that the logical doctrine of the *de Syllogismo Hypothetico* is different from that contained in Ammonius' work of the same title suggests somebody earlier than Ammonius. Once again we find ourselves thinking of the school of Proclus.

5. *De Divisione*[59]

This too is a translation of a Greek Introduction: 877a, 'So, as with my other works, I have translated it fully into Latin as an Introduction (*ego quoque id sicut pleraque omnia Romanis auribus tradens introductionis modo...perscripsi*)'.

6. *Commentaria in Topica Ciceronis*[60]

In this work Boethius undertook to complete Victorinus' commentary, which, though occupying four books, covered only a fraction of Cicero's text.[61] Boethius constantly shows off his possession of the Greek text of Aristotle's *Topics*, which neither Cicero nor Victorinus knew.[62]

---

present general editor of *AL*, and after meticulous editing by Dr J. Brams, this supplement has meanwhile been made public in *Bull. phil. méd.* 26. A chart of the word-usage (in the same journal) will, I believe, confirm further that the initial guess about Boethian authorship was a good one; it will also rule out *en passant* the conjecture (Ebbesen 1981, 9) that the translator might have been James of Venice – or any of the other translators so far edited in *AL*.

The Florentine scholia cannot be convincingly regarded as mediaeval 'excerpts from a whole commentary that was available in Latin' (Ebbesen 1981, 3; 1987, 291, n. 15). All the indications are that the Aristotelian text, *and* its marginal scholia, *and* their reference signs, were taken all at once from Greek by the same translator, and, as Minio-Paluello pointed out to me, the Florentine codex was specially ruled to accommodate both text and marginalia, all copied in the same hand as if carefully following an exemplar that was similarly arranged. The contention that the excerpting had already been done in Greek could be further supported, I believe, from internal evidence in the scholia themselves. So if we are to have a label for the lost Greek source it is not a '*commentum Graecum*' but – to borrow a plural from Boethius himself – *commenta Graeca*.

It does not help much to call the second book of the Philoponus Greek commentary 'a Byzantine collection' (Ebbesen 1981, 10). Minio-Paluello in his edition of the Boethian scholia in *AL* iii refers to it, following Wallies, as 'pseudo-Philoponus', but that does not mean that either he or Wallies considered its contents mediaeval. As in the case of the second half of Alexander's commentary on the *Topics* Wallies thought the second book different in style and authorship from the first. But there is nothing in it by way of either allusion or vocabulary to suggest that it is not ancient in content.

[58] K. Dürr, *The Propositional Logic of Boethius*, Amsterdam 1951, 13ff.
[59] *PL* 64, 875-92.
[60] ibid., 1039-74.
[61] cf. Boeth. *in Top. Cic.* 1041d.
[62] ibid., 1051b; 1052b; 1054b; 1091cd; 1098b; 1119b; 1145d.

Boethius has a quotation from the *Physics*,[63] but he had found it in his Greek notes: 1152c, 'But if anyone is interested in looking at my commentaries he should know that I have taken over this point from the second book of Aristotle's *Physics (sed si cui commentarios nostros inspicere vacuum fuerit, sciat haec nos ex Aristotelis secundo Physicorum volumine advertisse)'*. In fact he seems to be referring back to his commentary on the *de Interpretatione* (ed. 2a. 190,12ff), where he used the same Greek material.

7. *De Differentiis Topicis*[64]

Boethius tells us that he takes his *differentiae* from (a) Greek works and (b) Cicero's *Topics*: 1173c, 'There are two traditions to be presented, one extracted from Greek books and the other from the *Topics* of Cicero *(duplex est tradenda traditio, una quidem ex Graecis voluminibus eruta, altera vero ex M. Tullii Topicis sumpta)'*. But the *Graeca volumina* turn out to be (1133c) 'the eight books of my Latin translation of Aristotle's *Topics (octo voluminibus...quibus Aristotelis Topica in latinam vertimus orationem)'*.

Boethius also refers three times to a commentary of his own on Aristotle's *Topics*.[65] Hence – exactly as in the case of the *Analytics* – either he had translated from scholia a commentary which is now lost or else he was thinking of scholia which he was on the point of translating.

All the *dialecticae rationes* used in the *de Differentiis Topicis* by Boethius, including the long discussion of *magis, minus* etc., are elaborated from the simple Themistian diagram given in contrast to Cicero's at 1202c-d. Boethius' other references to Themistius (1214a, 1215a) are obviously based also on that diagram.[66] The diagram came from Themistius' commentary on the *Topics*, now lost.[67] And since it is precisely for this Themistian material that Boethius refers to his own commentary on the *Topics*, I take it for certain that the diagram was a scholion in his *Graeca volumina* of the *Topics*.

II

Before drawing our general conclusion about all these commentaries and treatises, a final doubt remains to be dispelled – the possibility of Latin intermediaries, the philosophic group of Macrobius and Victorinus. The

---

[63] The quotation from the *Physics* at 1152c is 196b 10-11 (and the mode of quotation suggests that Boethius took it from a commentary rather than the original text): omission of reference noted by Stump.

[64] *PL* 64, 1173-216.

[65] 1191a, 1209c, 1216d.

[66] I did not, however, mean to suggest that this diagram was the only scholion in the book (Stump) but that its data were repeated, in the common repetitive manner of detached Greek scholia.

[67] cf. Themist. *in An. Post.* 18,26 Wallies. I follow the *CAG* and Wallies rather than Stump in seeing here a reference to Themistius' own commentary (or paraphrase) on the *Topics*.

Macrobius circle devoutly studied Porphyry and Themistius.[68] The circle included the logicians Vettius Praetextatus and Albinus, as well as Symmachus, grandfather of Boethius' father-in-law. In this circle may have been produced the pseudo-Augustinian *Categoriae Decem*.[69] But Boethius makes it clear that this school did not help him: he shows no acquaintance with the *Categoriae Decem*; he says that he searched for Albinus' works but could not find them; he did have Praetextatus' *Analytics* but on reading them could easily detect that they were really translated from Themistius and not from Aristotle, whereas he himself has the genuine Aristotelian text.[70] He could find in Latin no commentaries on the syllogism either.[71] He openly displays the few items of Latin he did have, the *Isagoge, de Definitione* and *in Topica Ciceronis* of Victorinus – but their inadequacy only emphasises the superiority of his own Greek material and his duty of translating it. Hence the starkly Greek idiom of his language and his severe lack of reference to Latin models.

III

The general impression produced by this study is that Boethius in composing his commentaries on the Organon translated Greek notes which he found added to his text of Aristotle. If this is true, it gives us new insight into the way Boethius worked.

From the beginning it is evident that he considered the works of the Organon, including Porphyry's *Isagoge* (which Neoplatonic schoolwork put on a par with Aristotle), as a united whole. He begins, in fact, by listing the order of its contents, and his aim is to translate and comment on it all as one series: *in lib. de Int.* 343,7, 'In an attempt to transmit and explain its entire content, I have compiled a continuous sequence of commentary (...*totius prodere adgressos atque expedire doctrinam. itaque rectam commentationis seriem conteximus*)'. And the homogeneous character we have noted in his Porphyrian material is another indication that he found everything together in Greek.

The task he set himself was to put all this Greek, both text and scholia, into Latin: *in lib. de Int.* ed. 2a, 79, 16, 'I shall translate into Latin every work of Aristotle I can lay hands on, fully translating all their scholia as well (*ego omne Aristotelis opus quodcumque in manus venerit in Romanum stylum vertens eorum omnium commenta Latina oratione perscribam*)'. But the *commenta* were rather troublesome. Given the primary labour of translating the Aristotelian text, he could not deal with all these scholia at once: he therefore picked some for an elementary first *editio* and postponed the others to a second. So, in the case of the *Isagoge*

[68] Courcelle, op. cit., 32-5.
[69] Now edited as *Paraphrasis Themistiana*, in *AL* I; L. Minio-Paluello, 'The Text of the Categoriae', 67-8.
[70] *in Int.* ed 2a. 4,4; 3,7.
[71] *de Syll. Hyp.* 831c.

he began in the first *editio* with a selection of scholia which he elaborated into a dialogue. But the dialogue style proved cumbrous for all these technical notes, and in the second *editio* he abandoned it in favour of unadorned literal translation, allowing himself to lapse into the 'fault of the faithful translator *(fidi interpretis culpa)*'.[72] For the *Categories* we possess only one commentary, but the manuscripts call it too an *editio prima*, and in it Boethius expressly postpones some Greek notes to a second work.[73] However, his Greek material for it seems to have been more scanty than for the *de Interpretatione*, where it took him two whole years of labour to pack the last of the scholia into his second *editio*. With the *Analytics* and *Topics* he apparently managed to translate only the lengthy introductory scholia *(eisagôgai, prolegomena)*.

All his Greek text and scholia would fit comfortably into one codex. In fact a good example of the kind of book he had before him would be our oldest Greek manuscript of the Organon (Urbinas 35).[74] Written in Byzantium in the ninth century, during the renaissance that followed a three-century decline of Aristotelian learning, its format probably resembles that of its sixth-century predecessors. It has been shown that the Byzantine editors did not venture to interfere with the order of books in the Organon;[75] very likely, then, they copied out marginalia as they found them.

Some of Boethius' scholia, as we have seen, show a connection with the school of Proclus in Athens. His whole codex may well have had its origins there.[76]

---

[72] *in Isag.* 135,7.

[73] *in Cat.* 160b.

[74] But not just this one manuscript. The general Aristotelian manuscript tradition was one of annotation. The chapter headings in the *Aristoteles Latinus* editions of Boethius' translations are one ancient sign of this, but there are many others. The habit of systematic marginal annotation was well established in the Greek scriptoria before the time of Isidore. This is confirmed in recent work by papyrologists such as Turner and Wilson. See my references in *Scriptorium* 38.

The idea that it could have been a single codex, rather than several, containing the Organon treatises is palaeographically feasible but remains unsupported. But now combined study of the *Aristoteles Latinus* and the new *Aristoteles Graecus* would be illuminating on this point.

[75] F. Solmsen, 'Boethius and the history of the Organon', *Amer. J. Philol.* 65, 1944, 71.

[76] There were several Aristotelian schools and a connection with Proclus is difficult to substantiate because his teaching on the *Categories* was oral, and so there are no quotations from him in Simplicius. But the general expressions of indebtedness to 'the successor of Plato' in Simplicius and Ammonius in other works mean that we cannot ignore him. Nor can we ignore the explicit assertion of Elias about his elaboration of the *Kephalaia* into the scheme known to Boethius. On the other hand we cannot force the evidence. 'If God exists whence evils, and if he does not whence good things? *(Si deus est unde mala? Bona vero unde si non est?'* [*Consol.* I 4.30]) 'can be securely identified as a verbatim quotation from Proclus *in Parm.* 1056,10-16', according to Chadwick (129). But Boethius (in 12 words) is speaking about God *(deus)*, and Proclus (in 46 words) is speaking about Providence *(pronoia)*, a rather different topic in Greek philosophy. *Unde mala?*, incidentally, *is* a verbatim translation of the question reported by Plotinus at *Enn.* I 8:1,1 – a tiny reminder that the arguments of the *Consolatio* are built up, only more elaborately, from the very same kind of Greek School material as the Organon commentaries, as Sulowski has so well indicated (see Bieler, xxv,

Our view of Boethius the translator of scholia is not quite in harmony with all that scholars have written about him. It dulls the praise of his vast scholarship; for where he mentions works of Aristotle other than the logic, he is just translating references among his Greek scholia,[77] so that all his knowledge of Aristotle seems to derive from this one codex of the Organon. Again, an attempt has been made to fix the chronology of his works by their cross-references;[78] this, of course, will not work if similar references were already in his Greek. And scholars have been disappointed because Boethius in one place made a great promise which he never fulfilled – to harmonise all the doctrines of Plato and Aristotle;[79] but the promise is probably based on words of Porphyrian Greek – Porphyry in fact did write a book called *On the Unity of Doctrine in Plato and Aristotle*.[80] It has also been argued that, because of his similarity to his contemporary Ammonius, he cannot just have worked in a Roman philosophic school or in the solitude of his library: he must have been to Alexandria and heard the latest lectures of Ammonius there.[81] But we have explained his similarity to Ammonius by their common source, the Athenian school of Proclus (*Atheniensium scholas*);[82] and, given his acquaintance with previous Latin writers on logic and the fact that he was 'an accomplished master of both languages (*utraque lingua peritissimus*)', there was nothing to hinder him from translating an annotated Organon in his beloved *bibliotheca* far removed (*longe positus*) from either Alexandria or Athens.

This work of translation[83] does not diminish his real greatness. It is

---

no. 146).

[77] At *in Int* ed. 2a 27,14; 28,1 he carefully transcribes the Greek of two fragments of the *de Anima* and *de Iustitia*.

[78] Brandt, op. cit.

[79] *in Int*. II 79,16ff; cf. E.K. Rand, *Founders of the Middle Ages*, Cambridge Mass. 1928, 215ff; A. Kappelmacher, 'Der schriftstellerische Plan des Boethius', *Wiener Studien* 46, 1928, 215ff.

[80] J. Bidez, *Vie de Porphyre*, 68.

[81] Courcelle, op. cit., 300.

[82] This does not necessarily mean that his actual Greek copy (*volumina*) of the Organon came to him directly from Athens and not from one of the other imperial scriptoria. Courcelle in concentrating on Alexandria overlooked the fact that details in many of his other pages carried his readers' attention rather to Constantinople as the cultural capital to which Symmachus and Boethius turned for their inspiration and 'programme des études'.

[83] Even Boethius' first-person words are in some instances clear translations, in others arguably so. 'I shall re-read Theocritus today' (*in Int*. II 234,10-13) is no real clue to Boethius' own poetic tastes (Magee) but rather an intrinsic part of Philo's Greek explanation of 'possibility' by definition *with example*, just as in the companion comment (235,6-8) from Diodorus, 'drowning at sea' is the similar Greek example. When meeting with the same example in a more anonymous context (207,21; 240,10) Boethius, characteristically, changes the Greek poet's name to Virgil. And the words he uses to describe his work (*scribo, conscribo, perscribo, exprimo, edo, dissero, compono, digero*, etc.) do not imply the modern notion of 'creative writing'. Admittedly his *transfero* stands unequivocally for 'translate'. But likewise, *perscribo*, for instance, at *in Int*. II 79,16 (*latina oratione perscribam*) and *de Div*. 877a (*romanis auribus tradens ... perscripsi*) only amounts to 'translate fully'.

Boethius' work contains his own prolix expansions and connections and re-arrangements (or those of his early editor), Latin names substituted for Greek, personal prefatory

precisely the ground on which his friend Cassiodorus rhetorically praises him (*Variae* I 45): 'Though living at a distance you were able to enter the Athenian classrooms, mingling your Roman toga with the chorus of Greeks clad in pallium, and so you have turned the Greek *dogmata* into Roman *doctrina* (*sic enim Atheniensium scholas longe positus introisti, sic palliatorum choris miscuisti togam, ut Graecorum dogmata doctrinam feceris esse Romanam)*'. And there is a patriotic nobility about his motives. As consul he thinks it his duty 'to instruct my citizens in the studies I have laboured over (*elucubratae rei doctrina cives instruere)*' (*in Cat.* 201b) in conscious imitation of Cicero who as senator felt obliged to write his philosophic 'transcripts (*apographa)*'. In time of sorrow such concentrated study was Cicero's 'consolation (*levatio)*', likewise for Boethius it is a 'life's supreme consolation (*summum vitae solamen)*'. Cicero retired to his Tusculan study, Boethius to his 'study walls adorned with ivory and glass (*bibliothecae comptos ebore ac vitro parietes)*'. Our study of him as a translator emphasises anew his remarkable role of transmission: through him Aristotelian logic, the equipment of Neoplatonic paganism, is carried into the Christian Church to be eventually part of its armour of faith.[84]

Bibliography

Aristoteles Latinus I 6 xiv n. 3; II 1 ix n. 2.

J. Barnes, 'Boethius and the study of logic', in M.T. Gibson (ed.), *Boethius*, Oxford 1981, 79-80, 88 n. 16.

L. Bieler (ed.), *Boethii Consolatio, editio secunda,* Turnholti 1984, Praefatio.

M. Cappuyns, review of Shiel (1958), in *Bulletin de théologie ancienne et médiévale* 8, 1958-1961, no. 604.

H. Chadwick, *Boethius*, Oxford 1981, 129-31, 153, 299 n. 42, 300 n. 53.

H.D. Dauphin, review of Shiel (1958), in *Rev. d'hist. eccl.* 54, 1959, 1120.

J. Dillon, review of Chadwick (1981), in *Classical Review*, n.s. 33, 1983, 118.

S. Ebbesen, 'Fragments of "Alexander's" commentary on the Post. Analytics', in *CIMAGL* 16, 1976, 89-98; 'Analysing syllogisms', in *CIMAGL* 37, 1981, 1-20; 'Boethius as an Aristotelian scholar', in J. Wiesner (ed.), *Aristoteles: Werk und Wirkung* II, Berlin 1987, 286-311 (= Chapter 16 below).

I. Hadot, 'Les introductions aux commentaires exégétiques chez les auteurs néoplatoniciens et les auteurs chrétiens', in M. Tardieu (ed.), *Les règles de l'interprétation*, Paris 1987, 99-122.

P. Hadot, '*Un fragment du commentaire perdu de Boèce sur les Catégories*', in *Arch. d'hist. doctr. et litt. du moyen âge* 26, 1959, 27 n. 74.

W. & M. Kneale, *The Development of Logic*, Oxford 1962, 189.

J.C. Magee, 'The Boethian wheels of fortune and fate', in *Mediaeval Studies* 49, 1987, 525 n. 7.

---

remarks, an attempt at dialogue style, recourse to Latin writers, especially Cicero. To interpret me as thinking that 'every line and every word of Boethius' commentaries was a translation of Greek notes' (De Vogel) is, I fear, *più romano che il papa.*

[84] This illustrates a seasoned historian's judgment that 'ancient philosophies, rediscovered, are found to possess a disturbing vitality, even in modern times' (Hugh Trevor-Roper, *Catholics, Anglicans and Puritans*, 1987, vii).

J. Marenbon, *Early Mediaeval Philosophy*, London 1983, 29.

L. Minio-Paluello, 'Boezio: opere logiche', in *Diz. biogr. degli italiani*, Roma 1970; 'Boethius', in *Dict. of Scient. Biogr.*, New York 1970.

C. Mohrmann, introd. *Boezio Consolazione*, tr. O. Dallera, Milan 1976, 16.

P. Moraux, *Der Aristotelismus* I, Berlin 1973, 100 n. 12.

L. Obertello, *Severino Boezio*, Genoa 1974.

A. Pattin (ed.), *Simplicius in Praedicamenta, tr. Moerbeke*, Louvain 1971, xi.

L.M. de Rijk, 'On the chronology of Boethius' works on logic', in *Vivarium* 2, 1964, 1-49, 125-62.

R.W. Sharples, 'Alexander of Aphrodisias *De Fato*: some parallels', in *Classical Quarterly* 28, 1978, 258 n. 158.

J. Shiel, 'Boethius and Andronicus of Rhodes', in *Vigiliae Christianae* 11, 1957, 179-85; 'Boethius' commentaries on Aristotle', *MRS* 4, 1958, 217-44, reprinted with postscript in M. Fuhrmann and J. Gruber (eds), *Boethius*, Darmstadt 1984, 155-83, and extensively revised in this chapter; 'Boethius and Eudemus', in *Vivarium* 12, 1974, 14-17; 'A recent discovery: Boethius' notes on the *Prior Analytics*', in *Vivarium* 20, 1982, 128-41; 'A set of Greek reference signs', in *Scriptorium* 38, 1984; review of Chadwick (1981) in *Cathol. Hist. Rev.* 70, 1984, 117-18; 'Aristoteles Latinus III: supplementa', in *Bull. phil. médiév.* 26, 1984, 119-26; 'The Greek copy of Porphyry's *Isagoge* used by Boethius', in J. Wiesner (ed.), *Aristoteles: Werk und Wirkung* II, Berlin 1987, 312-40.

E. Stump, 'Boethius' works on the Topics', in *Vivarium* 12, 1974, 77-93.

L. Tarán, *Anon. Comm. on Arist. De Interp.*, Meisenheim 1978, viii n. 10.

C.J. de Vogel, 'Boethiana', in *Vivarium* 9, 1971, 49-66.

CHAPTER SIXTEEN

Boethius as an Aristotelian commentator*

Sten Ebbesen

By the end of the fifth century AD Greek philosophy had for centuries been dominated by Aristotelo-Platonic scholasticism.[1] The scholastic attitude is well expressed by Ammonius, who says that it is with good reason that earlier philosophers have established the tradition of introducing the reading of an authoritative text with an inquiry into its aim (*skopos*), utility and authenticity; for (1) if you do not know the aim, you are likely to drop the book before reaching the end of it; (2) if you do not know what it is useful for, you are not likely to embark with enthusiasm on the reading; and (3) even after having been told what it is good for, 'we are apt to doubt the utility of a book until we are assured that it is a genuine work of a classical author known to be generally esteemed, like Aristotle and Plato – for as far as they are concerned, we assume that whatever they have said is useful.'[2] In periods when the scholastic attitude to the *auctores* prevails, the exegesis of the classics of philosophy acquires great importance. By the year 500 a considerable number of commentaries and auxiliary treatises relating to the works of Aristotle and Plato had been written in Greek. Quite a few would be available to anyone with the will and the financial means to obtain them.

---

* Editions of Boethius' works are as follows. *Inst. Arith.*: *Anicii Manlii Torquati Severini Boetii De institutione arithmetica ...* (G. Friedlein) Leipzig 1867. *in Isag.*[1] (= ed. prima) and *in Isag.*[2]: *Anicii Manlii Severini Boethii In Isagogen Porphyrii commenta ...* (S. Brandt) (= *CSEL* 48), Vienna and Leipzig 1906. *in Cat.*: *Patrologia Latina* (Migne) 64. *in Int.*: *Anicii Manlii Severini Boetii commentarii in librum Aristotelis* PERI HERMÊNEIAS (C. Meiser), Leipzig 1877-80 (1 = ed. prima in vol. 1; 2 in vol. 2). *Introductio ad Syllogismos Categoricos, de Syllogismo Categorico, de Divisione, in Topica Ciceronis, de Differentiis Topicis: Patrologia Latina* 64. *Hyp. Syll.*: A.M. Severino Boezio, *de Hypotheticis Syllogismis*, L. Obertello (ed.) (= Istituto di filosofia dell' Università di Parma, Logicalia 1), Brescia 1969. Translations of Porphyry and Aristotle: *Aristoteles Latinus* 1-6. As a supplement to Migne's editions of *in Cat.* and *Syll. Cat.* I have used MS Thott 166-168, 2⁰, Royal Library, Copenhagen (tenth century).

[1] On ancient scholasticism, see S. Ebbesen, *Commentators and Commentaries on Aristotle's Sophistici Elenchi*, Leiden 1981, 1.52ff (= *Corpus Latinum Commentariorum in Aristotelem Graecorum (CLCAG)*, 7. 1; id., 'Ancient scholastic logic as the source of medieval scholastic logic', in *The Cambridge History of Later Medieval Philosophy*, N. Kretzmann. A. Kenny and J. Pinborg (eds) Cambridge 1982, 101ff.

[2] Amm. *in Isag.* 21.

But in spite of an attempt in the fourth century to produce a Latin scholastic library,[3] philosophy had not come to Latium. It had to wait for Boethius. How little his predecessors had achieved may be gauged from the fact that he has no standard Latin equivalents for several elementary Greek terms. To render *organon* (instrument) he feels obliged to use a hendiadys, *ferramentum et quodammodo supellex*.[4] For *phantasia* he uses *visum*. The term had been coined by Cicero five hundred years earlier, but Boethius introduces it in a way which shows that he expects his readers to be as unfamiliar with it as were Cicero's contemporaries.[5] To benefit from Plato's and Aristotle's useful writings a mastery of Greek was still required.

Boethius came to see it as his mission to bring Latin philosophical literature up to contemporary Greek standards. After an initial attempt to build on the foundations laid in the fourth century,[6] he decided he had to start from scratch, translating the *auctores* and then adding the necessary auxiliary works. At its most ambitious, his plan seems to have comprised:[7]

(a) a complete set of basic texts, viz. Porphyry's *Isagoge*, the whole of Aristotle, Cicero's *Topics* (which, of course, need not be translated), the whole of Plato;

(b) elementary commentaries on each of the basic texts;

(c) in some cases, at least, also a more comprehensive commentary;

(d) in at least one case, also a paraphrase;[8]

(e) supplementary monographs, including one demonstrating the compatibility of Aristotelian and Platonic philosophy.

Death prevented him from fulfilling his plan, but he managed to translate the whole *Organon* (with the possible exception of the *Posterior Analytics*) and to produce several commentaries and monographs. Most of

---

[3] Texts relating to the *Organon: Isagoge* (free translation) + commentary + monograph on definition, all by Victorinus; paraphrase of *Cat.* (= ps.-Augustine, *Categoriae Decem*); paraphrases of *An. Pr.* and *An. Post.* by Themistius, translated by Praetextatus; monograph on hypothetical syllogisms by Victorinus. It is very doubtful whether there was a translation or paraphrase of *Int.*; possibly Apuleius' *Peri Herm.* was used. Instead of Aristotle's *Topics*, Cicero's was read; Victorinus composed a commentary on it. Cf. on these matters, P. Hadot, *Marius Victorinus*, Paris 1971.

[4] Boeth. *in Isag.*[1] 10; cf. *in Isag.*[2] 93.

[5] Boeth. *in Isag.*[2] 25: the Greeks call them *phantasiai*, we may call them *visa*. Cicero *Acad.* 1 40: which they call *phantasia* we may call it *visum*.

[6] *in Isag.* ed. prima is keyed to Victorinus' version of the *Isagoge*.

[7] The basic source is Boethius *in Int.*[2] 79-80. See further L.M. de Rijk, 'On the chronology of Boethius' works on Logic', *Vivarium* 2, 1964, 1-49 and 125-62; L. Obertello, *Severino Boezio*, Genova 1974 (= Accademia Ligure di Scienze e Lettere, Collana di monografie I), I, 157ff.

[8] Boeth. *in Int.*[2] 251: 'After these twin commentaries we make [sic! one expects: shall make] a sort of compendium of this book, in such a way that we sometimes, indeed most times, use Aristotle's own words, except that when he obscures a matter by brevity of diction, we employ additions to make the presentation more lucid, so that our style strikes a balance between the brevity of the text and the diffuseness of a commentary by compressing

these works are still extant.[9]

The translations of the basic texts are extremely faithful to the originals which are rendered word by word and morpheme by morpheme[10] with a supreme contempt for normal Latin sentence structure.[11] The choice of this procedure was very deliberate. Boethius was a consummate master of Latin prose, but he wanted his readers to see the real thing.[12] The auxiliary works would provide the necessary amount of comment and paraphrase. His competence as a translator grew with time, but he never relinquished the principle of strict fidelity to the *auctor*. For this reason the translations tell us very little about his interpretation of Aristotle.

The commentaries and monographs are more informative, though it is difficult to evaluate their testimony because almost everything in them comes from a Greek source. Boethius himself makes no secret of the fact, which can also be established by means of comparisons with extant Greek works. Consequently, a mere recitation of Boethius' words is no sufficient answer to the question, 'What did Boethius think about problem *x*?' It must also be shown that his use of just those words reflects a choice, i.e. that several sources were available to him or that he sometimes chose to modify his source instead of copying it without change. Thus the fact that he repeatedly stresses that each word has its meaning thanks to a human decision and not by nature[13] cannot be taken to show that this is a problem he has given personal thought to unless we can assume that he could have presented another view. If all his sources are lost, we can never establish such a thing. And this is exactly what has been argued in recent times. It has been suggested that the only material at Boethius' disposal was a copy of the *Organon* with marginal scholia, and that this collection of scholia is no longer extant.[14] We may often be able to ascertain the remoter origin of one of the scholia Boethius knew, but we

the diffusely phrased and expanding the too compressedly written – but that is for later.' To me this looks like a description of a paraphrase, but there have been other suggestions. See De Rijk, op. cit., 37-8.

[9] See n* above. Surveys in *The Cambridge History of Later Medieval Philosophy*, Cambridge 1982, 53f, 74ff, 105. Fundamental studies in L. Minio-Paluello, *Opuscula*, Amsterdam 1972.

[10] Thus *proba-re* = *axioun*, *proba-mentum* = *axioma*, see *Aristoteles Latinus* 6.1-3, Leiden and Brussels 1975, 121.

[11] Thus the genitive absolute *khrêsimês ousês tês toutôn theôrias* (Porph. *Isag.* 1,6) becomes an ablative absolute without participle: *utili hac istarum rerum speculatione* (*Aristoteles latinus* 1.6-7: 5,5-6). Also in the commentaries there are occasional clumsy renditions of Greek phrases, as in *Int*[2] 13: *quae sint negationes cum modo propositionum ... considerator poterit diligenter agnoscere*; 'cum modo propositiones' renders *hai meta tropou protaseis* (cf. Amm. *in Int.* 8,19; 14,11; 213,33f.).

[12] cf. Boeth. *in Isag.*[2] 135.

[13] Thus *in Int.*[2] 23; 54-6; 92-4; *Intr. Syll. Cat.* 763A; *Syll. Cat.* 795A; *Divis.* 886C. cf. S. Ebbesen, *CLCAG* 1,177.

[14] J. Shiel, 'Boethius' Commentaries on Aristotle': *Medieval and Renaissance Studies* 4, 1958, 217-44, extensively revised in Chapter 15; id., 'Boethius and Eudemus', *Vivarium* 12, 1974, 14-17; id., 'A recent discovery: Boethius' notes on the *Prior Analytics*', *Vivarium* 20, 1982, 128-41.

shall never know whether he deviated from his direct source in any way and the standard answer to the question 'Why does Boethius say this?' can only be, 'Because it was in his only source.'

The 'one source – no thinking' theory has the support of eminent scholars and it cannot be refuted by any means that I can think of. But neither can it be proved by any conceivable means short of finding the supposed manuscript of the *Organon* with the marginal scholia. To my mind, the circumstantial evidence in favour of this theory, though not negligible, is less than convincing.[15] The observable facts are quite as easily explained on the assumption that Boethius had access to several

---

[15] The case for the marginalia and against Boethius' using Porphyry's commentary on the *Categories* rests on the following assumptions and arguments:

(1) Boethius' Greek copy of the *Organon* is likely to have looked much like Arethas' from c. 900 (Vat. Urb. 35), which contains rather ample marginalia. This is a doubtful assumption. Marginal scholia were known in late antiquity, but papyrological evidence does not suggest that a format like that of Urb. 35 was common then. By contrast, pillaging ancient sources to compose marginal scholia was no unusual occupation for Arethas and his contemporaries.

(2) Boethius himself says that he uses marginalia. For the meaning of *in Int.*[2] 250,20-3 '*est quidem libri huius ... obscura orationis series, obscurissimis adiecta sententiis*' is that the book has 'an obscure course of arguments with highly obscure notes added to it'. As far as I can see, the passage means 'the doctrines of this book are very obscure, and on top of that the manner of presentation is obscure'.

(3) Boethius used one book only for his source. His commentary on the *Categories* contains a lot of Porphyrian, but also some un-Porphyrian material. Therefore he used one book consisting for the most part of extracts from Porphyry but with some additions from later sources. I see no compelling reason to grant the first premise, though I admit that he is unlikely to have consulted a vast literature before writing his commentaries. It may be mentioned that Shiel's guess that all Boethius knew of Themistius' paraphrase of the *Topics* was a diagram has been disproved by E. Stump, 'Boethius' works on the *Topics*', *Vivarium* 12, 1974, 77-93; cf. S. Ebbesen, *CLCAG* 7.1,118f.

(4) Boethius was omnivorous. Yet he does not reproduce all of Porphyry's comments on the *Categories*. Ergo he did not possess a complete copy of that work. The passages which Shiel adduces in support of the first premise (in 'Boethius' Commentaries ...', 233 and 237, see n. 14 above) cannot bear the weight of proof. The crucial one is *in Isag.*[2] 135: 'Therefore I think I have accomplished a great deal if thanks to my rendering the books of philosophy in Latin in a complete and unadulterated translation, nothing from the Greek writings is felt to be wanting.' When seen on the background of the preceding lines it becomes clear that in this place Boethius is speaking about a complete and unadulterated translation of Porphyry's *Isagoge* (and other basic texts), not of scholia.

(5) One medieval Latin manuscript contains *An. Pr.* with scholia, both translated from the Greek by Boethius. This MS may be taken to mirror Boethius' Greek MS. There are strong stylistic reasons for attributing the translation of the scholia to Boethius, but also some arguments against doing so. See S. Ebbesen, 'Analyzing syllogisms, or Anonymus Aurelianensis III – the (presumably) earliest extant Latin commentary on the *Prior Analytics*, and its Greek model', *Cahiers de l'Institut du Moyen-Age Grec et Latin (CIMAGL)* 37, University of Copenhagen 1981, 1-10. Yet, even granted that the translator of the scholia was Boethius, it does not follow that the medieval manuscript is a mirror image of one produced by Boethius which again was a mirror image of his Greek manuscript. In fact, there is good reason to believe that the scholia in the medieval MS are just excerpts from a larger collection of scholia, possibly a whole commentary, which had been translated from the Greek and was available to some learned men in the twelfth century. See Ebbesen, op. cit. (this note, above). So, while the scholia may be remnants of material which Boethius gathered with a view to composing a commentary on *An. Pr.*, they cannot tell us how much Greek exegetic material relevant to the text Boethius had access to.

Greek monographs and commentaries and that he followed the common practice of using for each work one main source while also exploiting secondary sources. It is an old discovery that this hypothesis works well in the case of the extant short commentary on the *Categories*, the only case in which we still have what may be the main source. Boethius acknowledges a debt to Porphyry[16] and actually keeps so close to the latter's extant minor commentary on the *Categories* (*CAG* 4, 1) that it is simpler to assume that he had direct access to a complete copy of it than to assume second-hand acquaintance by way of a book which also contained the post-Porphyrian material detectable in Boethius' commentary.

Granted that Boethius' main source was Porphyry's extant work, we can begin to examine the way he used it. As it turns out, he follows his predecessor to the extent of reproducing most of the questions he raised and the answers he gave, but not to the extent of reproducing long segments of his text in direct translation. Boethius expanded arguments which he found too compressed while curtailing or suppressing other passages.[17] In fact, he followed the procedure which his own remarks in this and other works indicate[18] – and that procedure involved making choices. It looks as if it might be worth while to speculate about his possible motives for choosing as he did.

First of all: why Porphyry? It seems that Boethius turned to Porphyry not only when composing the commentary on the *Categories* but whenever there was a work of his to turn to.[19] If Boethius' choice was not determined by unavailability of other books, on what was it grounded? I suggest that it was grounded on the concern for pedagogy to which he often gives expression[20] – a concern which he shared with Porphyry.

---

[16] Boeth. *in Cat.* 160A; see n. 20 below.

[17] Expansion: e.g. Boeth. *in Cat.* 201D-202B vs. Porph. *in Cat.* 100,12-16; Boeth. 240C-D vs. Porph. 128,13-15. Curtailment: e.g. Boeth. 180C vs. Porph. 86,20-32. Suppression: e.g. Porph. 55,3-56,13; 100,23-7. Cf. J. Shiel, 'Boethius' Commentaries ...' (n. 14 above). For the work as a whole, expansion more than neutralises contraction. *PL* 64, cols 159-26, which correspond to *CAG* 4.1, pp. 55-142, would require some 125 *CAG* pages. Boethius' *in Cat.* is comparable in bulk to Philoponus' comm. *in Cat.*, and Boethius' *in Int.*[2] to Ammonius' *in Int.*

[18] e.g. Boeth. *in Cat.* 159A; *Syll. Cat.* 793C; *Introd. Syll. Cat.* 761C. Boethius uses conventional phraseology when saying that he will clarify, expand and abbreviate. Cf., e.g., Apollonius Dyscolus *de Pronomine* (= *GG* 2.1.1) 3; Themistius *in An. Post.* 1-2. But this does not imply that he does not mean what he says.

[19] Porphyry was certainly used for the commentaries on *Int.*, almost certainly for *Syll. Cat.* (and hence for *Intr. Cat. Syll.*) and *Divis.*; probably also for *Hyp. Syll.* The planned work on the concord between Plato and Aristotle presumably was to draw on Porphyry's book on the same subject. For the *Topics*, Boethius turned to Themistius. But then there is no evidence that Porphyry ever commented on that work. For the *Isagoge*, Boethius obviously had to turn to a non-Porphyrian commentary; hence the many un-Porphyrian features of his *in Isag.*[1] and *in Isag.*[2]

[20] Thus *in Isag.*[2]; 161 and 167; *in Cat.* 159A, 160A-B (see text in n. 53), 250C, 289C; *Syll. Cat.* 793C-794C (for better text than Migne's, see De Rijk, op. cit (n. 7) 30 and n. 57 below); *Intr. Syll. Cat.* 761C-762C; *Divis.* 877A. Notice the motives for following Porphyry that Boethius himself gives: *in Cat.* 160A: 'This is a suitable interpretation for purposes of introduction and simple exposition: and for now, at least, this is the one we have decided to

It was the general belief of the scholastics that Aristotle himself was consciously pedagogical and that this is apparent from the structure of the *Organon*.[21] The books about demonstrative (and, some would add, dialectic) reasoning, i.e. *An. Post.* (and *Top.*), form the core of Aristotle's work. But pedagogical considerations motivated him to introduce these books with a treatise on syllogistic reasoning as such (*An. Pr.*); and this again with a book on the proximate constituent parts of syllogisms, viz. propositions (*Int.*); and this book again with a treatise on the proximate constituent parts of propositions, i.e. words (*Cat.*). This, the most elementary book, was intended to be read first of all – though the scholastics themselves preferred to warm up with Porphyry's *Introduction to the Categories (Isagoge)*.

When scholasticism was in its infancy, several philosophers had subjected the *Categories* to unkind scrutiny, pointing out absurd doctrines, important omissions, internal inconsistencies and inconsistency with other Aristotelian writings. To a large extent this criticism determined the scholastic exegesis. The problems dealt with in the commentaries are very often those raised by the early critics. Many of the supposed deficiencies of the *Categories* could be explained away by showing that the criticism rested on a wrong interpretation of the text. But not all difficulties could be coped with in that way. Porphyry found a way to interpret the vices as virtues by appealing to Aristotle's concern for pedagogy. Thus the fact that Aristotle does not treat of quality immediately after substance but inserted the chapters on quantity and relation between substance and quality might seem odd both from a Stoic and from a Platonist point of view. Besides possible ontological reasons for Aristotle's order, Porphyry mentions that (1) there are more common characteristics between substance and quantity than between substance and quality; (2) in dealing with quantity Aristotle introduced the notions of big and small, which are relative terms; so, in order not to leave the reader in suspense, Aristotle decided to round off with a chapter on relation before going on to quality. Porphyry thus assigns a pedagogical motive to Aristotle, and Boethius accepts the explanation.[22] He also

<hr/>

propound, in dependence on Porphyry, because he [or: because his interpretation] is the least complicated and the plainest'. *in Int.*[2] 7: 'The book is entitled "On Interpretation". In composing our exposition of it we have drawn on Porphyry for the most part, though also on the rest, and have rendered [the borrowed material] in Latin. For in our opinion this expositor stands out both for keenness of insight and for [fine] presentation of the points in question'.

[21] Boeth. *in Isag.*[1] 12-15; *in Cat.* 161B-D; *in Int.*[2] 12 (cf. the scholia in *CAG* 4.5, p. xl). The Greek sources are numerous. See e.g. Simplicius *in Cat.* 14-15 & 18,14-16; Philoponus *in. An. Post.* 1-2.

[22] (1) Porph. *in Cat.* 100,21-3 and Boeth. *in Cat.* 202C. (2) Porph. 111,12-15 and Boeth. 217A; Porph. 127,3-7 and Boeth. 239A. A similar defence of Aristotle in Porph. 59,34-60,10 and Boeth. 163B-C.

follows Porphyry in the conviction that lack of agreement between the doctrine of the *Categories* and that of other books may be explained as due to pedagogical considerations. Thus they both say that when Aristotle ends his list of types of quality with the remark that there may be more than the ones in the list, this is not a sign of uncertainty, nor can he be blamed for not giving the better list that he has in the *Metaphysics*. The reason why he does not give it is that he does not wish to perplex the freshmen by introducing intricacies which they need not understand before they have reached a higher level.[23] Just in case anybody should be dissatisfied with this explanation, Boethius adds another one, this time not from Porphyry, according to which Aristotle said, 'And there may be other sorts than the ones I have listed' because he wanted to incite the reader to start thinking on his own instead of just being a passive recipient of learning.[24] Here, too, Boethius depicts Aristotle as a conscious pedagogue.

Porphyry held that Aristotle was also pedagogical in a philosophically more interesting way. The first book of the *Organon*, he held, is not a book on what there is. It is about an elementary matter, the rational classification of the words of the vocabulary which reflects our awareness of the sensible world. The categories with which Aristotle deals should be understood as widest predicates, 'predicates' here meaning words which we may apply to a thing, and primarily words which may function as names of sensible things. We do by abstraction form notions of (*post rem*) universals, but to say that a categorial common name like 'man' signifies a universal Man just means that there are some particular sensible things about which we may say, 'This is a man'.[25]

---

[23] Porph. *in Cat.* 134,25-9; Boeth. *in Cat.* 252B. A similar defence of Aristotle in Boeth. *in Cat.* 289C; cf. Simplicius *in Cat.* 427-8; Porphyry not available for comparison.

[24] Boeth. *in Cat.* 252C: 'There is also a further reason: to make us search for more qualities in order that he should be no mere teacher of his own [discoveries], but also one who incites us to find out something of our own.' Cf. Amm. *in Cat.* 88,20-2; Philop. *in Cat.* 156,8-11. Amm. and Philop. do not mention Porphyry's explanation. Simplicius *in Cat.* 264,2-4 has it, but does not mention the explanation of Amm. and Philop. Cf. Boeth. 294A-B where he uses a similar explanation, also found in Philop. *in Cat.* 205,26-8. Porph. and Amm. are not available for comparison in this place.

[25] See, in particular, Porph. *in Cat.* 56-8 and 90-1. Read 56,8-13 as follows: 'Every simple significative expression is called a "*katêgoria*" when it is spoken (*agoreuthêi*) and said of (*kata*) the thing signified. For example, let the thing be this particular stone which we feel or see: when we say about it that it is a stone, the expression "stone" is <a *katêgoria*, whereas the thing is> a *katêgorêma*. For it signifies such a thing and is spoken of (*agoreuetai kata*)

Porphyry had predecessors in the endeavour to make the *Categories* acceptable to Platonists by restricting its scope to the sensible world. But he was particularly insistent on the point, and Boethius followed him in this.

Critics of Aristotle had observed that Aristotle stood the world on its head by calling the sensible particulars *primary* substances. Porphyry would not deny that if Aristotle were doing basic metaphysics, this would indeed be standing the world on its head. But, he held, the point is that in the *Categories* Aristotle is not working on such a deep level. On the level on which he is working, it is perfectly reasonable to call sensible particulars primary substances while calling secondary the abstract universals whose only being consists in being predicable of the first ones, and to leave such intelligible entities as God or Mind totally out of account. Boethius agrees.[26] That he did not only copy but also understand this Porphyrian view may be inferred from the fact that he manages to say the same things as his source without reproducing it *verbatim*. He even manages to improve upon the master's formulations. Thus it is Boethius who says that 'secondary substances do not have their being except in being predicable' and that 'what causes secondary substances to be is nothing but their predicability of primary substances'. Porphyry uses a less pregnant formulation, saying that the particular animals and men are the causes of being for the commonly predicated ones.[27]

So Aristotle was right in abstaining from deeper matters when introducing people to philosophy. Porphyry extended the principle of abstention from deeper matters and concern for the novices from being a

the particular thing that is the stone.' Cf. Simpl. *in Cat*. 11,2-3 and 17,5-7. Boethius does not reproduce the two crucial passages on the meaning of *katêgoria, katêgorêma, katêgoreisthai* (Porph. *in Cat*. 56,6-13 and 58,16-18). Yet cf. Boeth. *in Cat*. 162D: 'Since there are ten primary sorts of things, there also had to be ten simple words that might be said of the things underlying them; for whatever signifies is said of the thing it signifies.' *Syll. Hyp*. p. 210 (Obertello): 'The categorical proposition, then, [viz. "man is an animal"] makes us realise that an actual man (*ipse homo*) is an animal, i.e. may receive the name of "animal". ... So the categorical proposition is a declaration to the effect that the thing which it puts in the role of subject is a recipient of the name of the thing predicated'. *Introd. Syll. Cat*. 768C: 'the subject is that which receives the expression of the predicate.' See also Boeth. *in Cat*. 243C where he is eager to make it clear that the fact that genus is entailed by species means that: 'Wherever there is a species, the name of its genus also turns up without delay; but where a genus is, the word for some species does not necessarily follow.' The words immediately before strongly resemble Iamblichus, ap. Simpl. *in Cat*. 230,32-231,1; but *ubicumque-sequitur* is not paralleled there. Porphyry is not available for comparison.

26 Porph. *in Cat*. 90-1. Boethius *in Cat*. 183-4.

27 Boeth. *in Cat*. 185D: 'Secondary substances are such that whereas they are not in a subject they are said of a subject. Hence they do not possess their being except by being predicated of something. Now, secondary substances are predicated of primary ones. Hence, what causes secondary substances to be is their predicability (*praedicatio*) of primary substances.' Porph. *in Cat*. 90,33-91, 1: 'The particular animals ... which in fact are the causes of being for the commonly predicated ones.'

principle of interpreting Aristotle's logic into a rule guiding his own activity as a commentator – at least when he was writing for beginners, as was the case when he composed his *Introduction to the Categories* and the extant commentary on the same work. On the whole, he remains faithful to the programme announced in the beginning of the *Introduction*: to give a concise account of Peripatetic lore from a logical point of view, abstaining from the deeper issues, such as the mode of being of universals, keeping in mind that he is writing an introduction.[28] Though Boethius, when commenting on this passage, could not quite keep himself from telling what Porphyry abstained from saying,[29] he elsewhere makes the Porphyrian programme his own.

In fact, Porphyry tried to make Aristotelian logic function on a minimum of assumptions, notably these:[30] (1) that man can recognise certain individuals in the sensible world; (2) that man can name these individuals; (3) that man can recognise a similarity between several individuals; (4) that man can decide to use a certain sound as a name of any individual which is similar to others in respect of a certain feature; (5) that man can recognise a similarity between certain names; (6) that man can decide to use a certain sound to name any individual name which is similar to others in respect of a certain feature.

These are the basic assumptions needed for an interpretation of the *Categories*. They allow for the creation of our primary object-language with its universal names, the classification of these names in ten categories, and for the creation of a second-order language, which is the subject of *de Interpretatione* and which is necessary for talking about the first-order language which is the subject of the *Categories*.

Some more assumptions are needed to deal with propositions. These are basic: (7) that any two men confronted with the same sense-data will isolate the same individuals and recognise the same similarities; (8) that the thoughts or 'concepts' to which these 'recognitions' give rise can be stored and recalled to consciousness when required; (9) that simple concepts can be combined into complex ones; (10) that man can invent words indicating the internal syntax of complex concepts; (11) that one man can teach another to use words in the same way as himself; (12) that by uttering the words associated with the simple or complex concept presently actualised in him one man can actualise the same concept in a fellow-man who speaks the same language. These further assumptions allow men to communicate with each other by means of propositions analysable into subject, predicate and their mutual relations, without the need of pointing at the object of discourse.

Of course, this is not the whole story, but Porphyry did his best to

---

[28] Porph. *Isag.* 1.

[29] Boeth. *in Isag.*[1] 24ff, *in Isag.*[2] 159ff.

[30] cf. S. Ebbesen, *CLCAG*, 1,141ff. It is pertinent to notice that Boeth. *in Int.*[2] is one of the really important sources for Porphyry's thought.

explain Aristotelian logic without a host of other assumptions, and he tried to be a good pedagogue by not introducing an assumption before it was needed. Thus, in spite of the crucial role of concepts in his Aristotelian semantics, he did not formally introduce concepts in the little commentary on the *Categories*. Concepts could wait until the reader got to the *de Interpretatione*. Boethius followed him in this. But he did more than just follow Porphyry.

Boethius demonstrates his understanding of Porphyry's thought by moving the presentation of the fundamental theory about the origin of our language to the very beginning of his commentary on the *Categories*. Porphyry operated with two labellings of things, two 'impositions of names'.[31] By the first imposition man has created his object-language, by the second his meta-language. Using and presenting the model requires some delicacy. For instance, it may be wise to de-personalise the first impositor as much as possible so as not to end up with one of the following ridiculous scenarios (with which some people have ended up):

(a) One wise impositor at some time decided what things ought to be called.

(b) A congress of terminologists convened to invent language. Having done so, they went home to meet again at a later time in order to perform the second imposition.[32]

Boethius avoids these absurdities. Porphyry had de-personalised the impositor by calling him 'man himself', not 'some man'.[33] Boethius achieves the same by saying that only the race of men could put names on things and that the human mind applied words to the things.[34] On the other hand, it is equally absurd to let an abstract mind perform the naming. Some particular man must have been the first to say 'man'. So it is reasonable enough when Boethius – not quoting Porphyry – speaks of the man who first said 'man'.[35] It is less reasonable that he sometimes (not in the commentary on the *Categories*) suggests that the imposition must have resembled a christening ceremony, the impositor saying, 'Let this be called a man'.[36] Apart from the fact that experience shows that there are other ways of introducing new words, the picture Boethius paints of the imposition ceremony is based on the unnecessarily strong and unconvincing claim that all names start as proper names. The model of the first imposition is designed to show that our use of generic names is dependent on a confrontation with the sensible particularised world. To

[31] Porph. *in Cat.* 57-8.
[32] See S. Ebbesen, op. cit., 1,178.
[33] Porph. *in Cat.* 57,21.
[34] Boeth. *in Cat.* 159A. Cf. *in Int*[2] 55,1-7.
[35] ibid. 183D.
[36] Boeth. *in Int.*[1] 46; *in Int.*[2] 64; cf. next note. Boethius may have had Greek models for the christening ceremony. Cf. *Anonymous Commentary on Aristotle's De Interpretatione* (Codex Parisinus Graecus 2064), L. Tarán (ed.), Meisenheim 1978, 3 (= Beiträge zur klass. Philol. 95).

avoid solipsism, the imposition must in some way be a public event, but there is no need to deny the possibility of a telescoped procedure, so that the impositor can say, 'Let such a thing be called a horse'. Boethius himself may on second thoughts have found the christening ceremony unconvincing. In the first version of his opuscule on categorical syllogisms, the Aristotelian claim that the nominative is more truly a name than the oblique cases of nouns is defended with the remark that the man who first introduced the word *circus* probably said, 'Let this be called *circus*'.[37] In the revised version, in which he does much to eradicate crude expression and thought, this explanation has been dropped. Instead we find the rather more sophisticated remark that since we start by sensing things which are present to us, and it is clear that men have assigned their words to the things which we perceive with a sensation in the present, it is reasonable to say that properly speaking verbs always have present signification, so that Aristotle's characterisation of past and future verb forms as non-verbs is justified.[38]

On the whole, then, Boethius' account of the theory of imposition is good. Moreover, he puts the notion of second imposition words, or names of names, to use in a place in which his main source did not. Discussing the transitivity of predication he has to deal with the example 'Man is a species, Socrates is a man, *ergo* Socrates is a species.' Boethius solves the paralogism by pointing out that 'species' does not occur in the definition of man, and so 'man is a species' cannot be a predication 'in quid'. No, he says, the fact is that in this proposition the function of 'species' is to indicate that 'man' is predicable of individuals only 'and ["species"] is, in a sense, a name of names'.[39] That is, the proposition may be paraphrased as 'the word "man" is predicable of individuals only', and 'species' is the name of those names which are predicable of individuals only. Boethius owes this solution of the paralogism to a Greek thinker,[40] but not to Porphyry's minor commentary on the *Categories*. His departure from the usual source probably means that he found the explanation attractive – as indeed it is in the theoretical framework within which he is working.

The cautious formulation that genus and species are 'in a sense (*quodammodo*)' names of names may indicate his own and/or his source's reluctance to call 'species' a name of names because that expression was primarily used of the designations of the parts of speech – noun and verb.[41] But there may also have been a more serious reason for his cautiousness.

At this point, after so many kind words about Boethius' intelligence, I

[37] Boeth. *Syll. Cat.* 796A; cf. preceding note.
[38] Boeth., *Intr. Syll. Cat.* 765D-766A. Notice that in *Intr. Syll. Cat.* Boethius is less dependent on his Greek source(s) than in *Syll. Cat.* Thus he expands the sections on the parts of speech, 796C-D, so as to present the whole *Latin* inventory of eight parts, one being interjections; see 766B-C.
[39] Boeth. *in Cat.* 176D-177A.
[40] Possibly Iamblichus. See Dexippus *in Cat.* 26; cf. S. Ebbesen, op. cit., 1, 231.
[41] See Boeth. *in Cat.* 159B-C, corresponding to Porph. *in Cat.* 57,29-58,3.

wish to make a digression about an intricate matter which he did not manage to sort out and which shows a limitation of his ability to use in one place what he had learned in another context.

When on his own, Boethius was not much at ease when having to explain the sort of relations that obtain between such non-categorial terms as 'species' and such categorial terms as 'man'. This is very clear in his two works on topical argumentation (*in Topica Ciceronis, de Differentiis Topicis*). For these he had no good Greek sources but had to produce his own mixture of a Greek theory which he knew from Themistius – an eloquent man, but not the greatest of philosophers – and of Roman rhetorical tradition. The result is astonishing in several respects. One cause of wonder is the total absence from these works of the notion of names of names, although it would appear to be highly relevant in the context, as some of Boethius' medieval commentators saw.[42] For in the topical works he operates with second-level words or concepts (it is not quite clear which), such as genus, species, definition. Associated with each of these is a set of axioms, such as 'That to which the definition of the genus does not apply is not a species of that of which the definition in question is a definition.' This particular axiom is supposed to bail for the soundness of the inference, 'An animal is an animated sensible substance, a tree is not an animated sensible substance, *ergo* a tree is no animal.' Directly the argument is supposed to hinge on the axiom, indirectly on the notion of definition. In other words, to decide the question whether trees are animals we may construct an argument founded on the notion of definition and on a particular instance of a definition, the definition of animal.[43] But Boethius has a worry.[44] Are not definition and definiendum really the same thing? Did not the definiendum, animal, occur as a term in the proposition we wanted to prove? Is not then our use of the definition of animal a case of using a term to prove something about itself? To explain that nothing is wrong Boethius uses singularly obscure language, a vice to which he was not addicted. I think what he wants to say is that the definition 'animate sensible substance' may be considered in three ways: (1) as the thing or the sign of a thing which is really identical with animal though notionally different; (2) as a phrase; in this sense the definition is also a thing 'in so far as phrases are things'; (3) as a definition; it is in this last sense that it is a *locus* (*topos*), i.e. a source of arguments (*sedes argumentorum, aphormê epikheirêmatôn*), and in this sense it is not a thing. This is suggestive, but it certainly does not attest to a clarified conception of the semantics of non-categorial terms.

Boethius knew next to nothing about Stoic logic. Porphyry in his Aristotle commentaries often compared Stoic terminology and tenets with Aristotle's. Boethius rarely bothered to include such passages in his own

---

[42] See N.J. Green-Pedersen, *The Tradition of the Topics in the Middle Ages*, Munich 1984.
[43] Boeth. *Diff. Top.* 2, 1187A-B.
[44] Boeth. *in Top. Cic.* 3, 1083Cff; 1091B; cf. 1,1055ff. I owe my awareness of the problems of these passages to N.J. Green-Pedersen, op. cit.

commentaries. He found them both irrelevant and obscure.[45] Real knowledge of Stoic logic had disappeared long before his time, but fragments – often distorted fragments – of Stoic theory would occur in all sorts of technical literature, not least in rhetorical writings. I think Boethius' confusion about the status of definitions was occasioned or increased by his use of a source that contained some distorted version of a Stoic distinction between corporeal and incorporeal entities, such as words vs. their meanings; or between incorporeal somethings (*tina*) and nothings (*outina*), such as predicates vs. universals.

Boethius' works on topics also contain a distinction between *argumentatio*, which is a proof qua (pronunciation of a) string of words, and *argumentum*, which is the sense of the *argumentatio*.[46] This must reflect a Stoic distinction between an incorporeal *epikheirêma* and a corporeal *epikheirêsis*, comparable to many other Stoic distinctions between corporeal entities with names in *-ia* or *-sis* and their incorporeal effects or meanings which have names in *-ma*.[47] The purpose of the distinction was no longer clear to Boethius.[48] Only very tentatively would I suggest that there may be a connection between the two detached fragments of Stoic theory. The original idea may have been that just as physical *topos* (place) is an incorporeal something, so is a *topos* in argumentation theory. Its contents are other incorporeal somethings, viz. *argumenta* (*epikheirêmata*), which constitute the meaning of *argumentationes* (*epikheirêseis*), our verbal formulations of proof.

[45] See Boeth. *in Int.*[2] 24; 71; 201.

[46] Boeth. *in Top. Cic.* 1,1050B; 1053A-1054A; *Diff. Top.* 1174D; 1183A.

[47] cf. e.g. *katorthôsis-katorthôrma*, v. Arnim, *SVF* III nos. 85 and 524. *ôpheleia-ôphelêma, harmatia-harmatêma* are other examples. This sort of distinction also underlies Porphyry's between *katêgoria, katêgorêma* (see n. 25 above).

[48] This appears both from the fact that he makes little use of the distinction and from the discussion in *in Top. Cic.* 1,1053A-1054A. The first evidence of the distinction *argumentum-argumentatio* is Cicero *Part. Or.* 45: 'you seem to be looking for argumentation, i.e., the unfolding of argument.' Cf. Cic. *Inv.* 1. 40,74. See also Fortunatianus *Ars Rh.* 2, ¶23 and 28 (= Halm, *Rh. Lat. Min.* 115; 118); Victorinus *in Rh. Cic.* 1,29; 31; 40 (= Halm, op. cit., 231; 232; 240; 247); Cassiodorus *Inst.* 2, p. 105 (Mynors). I have not found the distinction between *epikheirêma* and *epikheirêsis* in any Greek source. But notice the quotation of Porphyry in Syrianus' commentaries on Hermogenes, Rabe, *Rh. Gr.* 16.1, p. 93 and 16.2, p. 14: 'Speech has a soul (*psukhê*), as it were, and a body. The discovery of the concepts may justly be considered the soul of speech, their externalisation (*hermêneia*) its body.' Compare Boeth. *Diff. Top.* 1, 1174D: 'However the argument and argumentation are not the same. For the force (*vis*) of what is stated (*sententia*) and the structural property (*ratio*) which resides in an utterance (*oratio*) when something in doubt is being proved is called the argument; the actual externalisation (*elocutio*, = *hermêneia*) is called argumentation. Therefore, argument is the power [or: virtue (*virtus*)] and sense [or: mind (*mens*, = *nous* or *psukhê*?)] of the argumentation and is what is stated, whereas argumentation is the unfolding in utterance of the argument.' Similarly *in Top. Cic.* 1,1053B: 'For either the externalisation and the very string of propositions ... is called argumentation, whereas the sense (*mens*) and statement (*sententia*) involved in the syllogism is called argument.' Syrianus also has a definition of *epikheirêma* closely related to the Ciceronian/Boethian. Compare Boeth. *Diff. Top.* 1174D: 'An argument is a *ratio* that provides faith in a matter about which doubt has been raised' with Syrianus, op. cit. 16.1,57 'an argument (*epikheirêma*) is a *logos* adduced to produce faith in the question at hand'.

Boethius understood Porphyry much better than he understood the Stoics. He understood Porphyry's de-ontologising of logic and his economy of assumptions so well that on occasion he refused to follow his teacher when the master forgot his own principles.

Porphyry suggests that the order in which Aristotle deals with the principal categories, viz. substance – quantity – relation – quality, may be due to the fact that (1) being a body is prior to being a qualified body, and being a body implies having dimensions, and so implies having quantity; (2) when the dimensions pre-subsist, bigger and smaller, which are terms of a relation, accrue to them. Boethius reproduces this explanation. But he performs a tiny change. The statement that the relation of bigger and smaller accrues to the *pre-subsisting* dimensions becomes, 'quantity being posited we also have the relation of bigger and smaller'.[49] The removal of the ontologically loaded word 'pre-subsisting' may be significant.

Porphyry sinned in an even graver way against his own principles when he suggested that Aristotle was wrong in claiming that the known may exist prior to the knowledge of it. Perhaps, Porphyry said, it is best not to look at knowledge as something residing in men, but as residing in the nature of the things that may be known, since the eternal mind understands all things that are, whereas the knowledge of the separate things always descends to men. So that when there is something sensible, there is a universal sensation; and when there is something that may be known, there is a universal knowledge, the terms of the relation thus being simultaneous.[50]

Porphyry here uses the Neoplatonist device of grounding the possibility of communication between distinct entities in a higher-level union of these distinct entities. And he introduces the eternal mind so conspicuously absent from the rest of his exegesis of Aristotle's logic. Boethius deserts his main source at this point. Only at the end of a longish defence of Aristotle's opinion does he mention that some, including Porphyry, disagree, and then goes on to quote Porphyry, excusing himself for doing so with the remark that this will not take up much space.[51] But the work he quotes from is not his usual source, Porphyry's minor commentary on the *Categories*. It must be the big *Categories* commentary, addressed *ad Gedalium*. The quotation is likely to be second-hand, but this is immaterial. The question is: what did Boethius gain by switching source? Apparently very little, for the quotation says much the same as the minor commentary and there is no appreciable gain in terms of brevity. Yet he gains one thing: he avoids

[49] Porph. *in Cat.* 100; 111; 127, matched by Boeth. *in Cat.* 202B-C; 216D; 239A. Compare Porph. 111,9-10 'when length, width and depth presubsist the bigger and the smaller accrue to them, and they are relative', with Boeth. 216D 'quantity being posited the bigger [*maius*, Migne's text has '*magis*'] or smaller must be. Therefore, as relation immediately follows upon quantity, it was correct to put the relatives next in order after quantity.'

[50] Porph. *in Cat.* 120,33-121,3.

[51] Boeth. *in Cat.* 233B-D.

introducing the Eternal Mind in a work of logic, for the extract from the big commentary contains no mention of the Eternal Mind.

But is it really so remarkable that Boethius is Porphyrian, and sometimes a bit more than Porphyry himself? Yes, it is. For not everybody was so. In particular Iamblichus was not. He had introduced the two-level commentary, consisting for one part of the pedestrian Porphyrian exposition, for another of an 'intellectual' interpretation of the same matters. Iamblichus had the peculiar idea that Aristotle had plagiarised the Pythagorean Archytas when writing the *Categories*, and that the true interpretation of the doctrine of categories had to be Pythagorean. Boethius knew of the existence of Iamblichus' commentary.[52] We cannot be certain that he had read it. But if he had not, he had read some other commentary depending on Iamblichus, for he knew the sort of philosophising about the categories which it contained. And he liked it.

In his own commentary Boethius, after presenting Porphyry's explanation of what the *Categories* is about, adds that he has chosen to follow Porphyry because he is so easy to understand for a beginner in philosophy. But, says Boethius, I have in mind to write another work in which I shall treat of three questions, one of which is what the *Categories* is about. The explanation that I shall give there will be very different from the one I give here, much profounder and in accordance with the advanced theory of the Pythagoreans.[53]

It is not obvious what the other two questions are that Boethius intended to write of elsewhere. Various solutions have been proffered.[54] I would like to point out that there are two more references in Boethius' commentary to a future work. In one place he promises to discuss the

---

[52] See ibid. 162A; 224D and 225B.

[53] ibid. 160A-B. Migne's text is corrupt. De Rijk, op. cit. (n. 7 above) 133 quotes a Brussels MS. I here translate the text of MS Thott 168, 2⁰, fols 2v-3 in the Royal Library of Copenhagen. In the essentials, there is agreement with the Brussels MS: 'But we have in mind to discuss three questions, one of which is what the *Categories* is about and there we shall enumerate the interpretations that different people have put forward and tell which one we agree with. Nobody ought to be surprised that it will be in conflict with the interpretation proffered here, when he sees how much profounder the new one is so that it could not have been properly grasped by the minds of the beginners for whose elementary instruction we have written the present work. We must, then, use an elementary (*mediocris*) exposition to stimulate and, as it were, line up at the very doorstep of this discipline those whom we prepare to admit to this interpretation. So, the reader of both works will realise that the reason for our change of interpretation is that there the interpretation offered in the other exposition is tuned to Pythagorean science and perfect doctrine, whereas here it is tuned to the simple [mental] motions of beginners.'

[54] De Rijk, op. cit., 137 suggests *skopos, khreia, epigraphê*. A scholiast in MS Thott 168, 2⁰, fol. 2v says: 'This should not be understood as if he had produced another exposition, for what he promises here is what he clearly expounds in part 1 of the second edition of [his commentary on] *Peri hermeneias*, where in fact his closing remark is: "For the question what this book is about and concerning its title and the matter of its certain attribution to Aristotle, the above must suffice".' These last words in quotes come from Boeth. *in Int.*² 13,9-11. Above '*diversorum sententiis*' the scholiast wrote: *Aspasii, Alexandri, Theophrasti, Aristotelis, Andronici*. The scholiast is hardly right in thinking that Boethius is referring to *in Int*² 7-13, but it is very probable that Boethius there used some of the material he had intended for use in the promised work.

authenticity of the work on categories that Iamblichus believed to be by
the old Pythagorean Archytas, the contemporary of Plato.[55] In another
place he promises a refutation of people who criticise Aristotle's list of
categories for being too long, too short, or badly ordered.[56] These may be
the two missing questions. At any rate, there is every reason to believe
that Boethius wanted to treat them in the same work as the first one.

These passages show that Boethius had a clear notion of levels of
interpretation and that his exclusion of Neoplatonic speculation from
the elementary commentaries was deliberate. But isn't he cheating his
readers by offering them an interpretation which he himself considers
only second-best? Hasn't he a better defence for his procedure than the
claim that the profound theory is too difficult for novices? I think he has,
though he does not directly confront the question. He does, however, in his
Introduction to the Categorical Syllogisms, tell his readers not to think
that in teaching them logic and its way of dealing with language he wants
them to unlearn the grammar they were taught at school. What the
reader is invited to do is to consider the same matter from a new angle
which gives a profounder understanding. Looking at the constituents of
speech from a grammatical and a logical point of view may be compared
to looking at a line or a surface from a mathematical and a physical point
of view. The several disciplines which study the same object stand in no
conflict. On the contrary, he says, a true understanding of nature can only
arise as a result of using more than one approach.[57]

A similar attitude to the relation between logic and profounder theories
would hold that Aristotelian logic as interpreted by Porphyry is a
perfectly legitimate and useful discipline. We must have a theory of the
linguistic behaviour associated with our awareness of the sensible world,
and it is an advantage if this theory carries few ontological assumptions.
The profounder theory adds a new dimension to our understanding of the
world. It does not render the shallow theory superfluous. What was the
profound work to be like? I think we have enough information to gain an
impression of what a true Pythagorean interpretation of the categories

---

[55] Boeth. *in Cat.* 162A.

[56] ibid. 180C.

[57] Boeth. *Introd. Cat. Syll.* 761D-762C. Notice that 761D *Idem namque* – 762C *explicata
cognitio* is a replacement of the original exhortation to look up Boethius' Greek models; *Syll.
Cat.* 794C (I quote from MS Thott 166,2⁰ fol. 1v: 'And, if we are really not good enough for
those people, then they had better taste the works (*commentarii*) from which we have drawn
this. Attracted by their agreeable taste of subtlety those people, unbridled and untamed
lovers of polemics though they are, may find peace in accepting the unassailable authorities
of the ancients. But anyone without knowledge of the Greek language must invest an effort
in [the reading of] our works or similar ones, if such there are. Hence the law which this
preface lays down is that nobody may enter our court as a spectator if he intends to blame us
because he will not understand. But in order not to waste our time with empty prefaces, let
us start as soon as we have repelled the danger lest somebody blame our style for its
sterility. We do not seek the complexitites of eloquence, we seek to make ourselves plain; if
we manage to do that, we have achieved our aim, no matter how unrefined our language
may be.'

would be for Boethius. The story would run more or less like this:[58]

Philosophy is the love of wisdom, and this wisdom is the divine mind, which may also be called the primordial number. It contains the multitude of intellectual ideas but is characterised by non-distinction between mind, mental grasping and the mentally grasped. It gives the measures of being to all things. On this exalted level there is no need of names. But on the lower level of soul it is different. The soul is not the things themselves. It has 'pictures' of the things. These pictures are concepts or names. They exhibit the things as structured by the primordial number which (possibly by means of oppositions like even/odd) has structured the things in the perfect number of ten categories – ten like the fingers of the hands and the toes of the feet. The bottom is reached when the soul's immaterial names are embodied in matter, in sound. Only wise men who see the Mind and the nature of things can choose the appropriate matter for the name-forms or meanings, and thus perform this final act in the process that creates human language. But even wise men do not always see the same aspects of the things to be named. They are like artists painting the same motif. Even good artists produce different pictures. Consequently it is no wonder that different peoples may have different words for the same thing, or even that the same people may have more than one name for the same thing. The various names are the expression of the givers of names attending to different aspects of the forms of things. Language is 'by positing' (*thesei*) in the sense that the phonic stuff constituting the matter of each name was chosen by somebody. By nature (*phusei*) in the sense that the matter was not chosen at random but in imitation of the form to be conveyed by it. And thus there is a path leading back from material names to concepts and thence to things themselves and the original unity. Following that path the philosopher complies with Pythagoras' admonition *hepou theôi* (follow God).

[58] That, broadly speaking, 'Pythagorean' must mean 'after the manner of Iamblichus' is obvious, as pointed out by De Rijk, op. cit., 136ff. A more precise idea of what Boethius would understand by 'Pythagorean' in connection with the *Categories* may be obtained from the following observations. (a) Simplicius and Syrianus connect the list of exactly ten categories with Pythagorean speculation (Archytas). See Simpl. *in Cat.* 13,21-3; 51,3-4; 68,22-8 (= Ps.-Archytas, Szlezák (ed.), 57); Syrianus *in Hermogenis P. staseôn* (Rabe, *Rh. Gr.* 16.2) 58. So does Nicomachus *Intr. Arithm.* 2.22 (pp. 122-3 Hoche): 'The number 10, most perfect, as the Pythagoreans think, in accordance with which the ten relations received their quantity, as we saw a moment ago, and the ten so-called categories, and the divisions and relations of the extremities of our hands and feet, and lots of other things.' Boeth. *Inst. Arithm.* 2.41 (p. 139 Friedl.) expands this as follows: '... because of the perfection of the number 10, as the Pythagoreans thought. ... Therefore it is obviously the Pythagorean 10 that we find in the Aristotelian, and still earlier in Archytas', division of the ten categories. Well, Plato too, who took such interest in Pythagoras, uses the same system of division [*secundum eandem disputationem dividit*; presumably, *kata ton auton logon*, and thus an indication that this addition to Nicomachus comes from a Greek source], and Archytas the Pythagorean established these ten categories before Aristotle, though some doubt this. The ten partitions of our limbs and a host of other things have the same origin, but there is no need to spell it all out in detail.' (b) Boethius' contrasting Porphyry's

Darkness fell over the world of learning soon after Boethius' death. But his writings survived and were influential in the early phases of the medieval renaissance of philosophical studies. By keeping, for the most part, a clear distinction between the pedestrian and the profound level of interpretation, and by only handing the first down to posterity, Boethius greatly contributed to the sanity of medieval logic. Contrast this passage from Iamblichus:[59]

Since the power of the one from which [i.e. the one] everything that has quantity is engendered extends self-identical all through things and limits each thing by proceeding from itself, insofar as it extends totally indivisibly all through things, it establishes the continuous, and insofar as it exercises its procession as one, indivisible procession without delimitation. But insofar as it makes a stop in its procession at each of the forms and insofar as it limits each of them and makes each of them one, insofar does it produce the discrete. In virtue of the one and most principal cause which simultaneously comprises these two acts, it produces the two quanta. And in virtue of its total identity everywhere, both in each of the parts and in them all, it effects the continuous, but in virtue of the identity of each of them to themselves and of its being in its totality in each one it engenders

---

interpretation with the profounder Pythagorean one presupposes that the latter treats the categories as real, intelligible entities. And so it did according to Simpl. *in Cat.* 68,22-8; 91,14ff. (c) Simplicius and Dexippus consider it a hall-mark of Pythagorean exegesis of the *Categories* to hold that there is a natural link between things and names. See Simpl. *in Cat.* 13,21-6; 40,5-13; 105,3-4; Dexippus *in Cat.* 16,33-17,3 (notice the kick at Iamblichus in 17,4-6). (d) Proclus' exposition of Pythagorean semantics in his scholia on *Cratylus* 16 (ed. Pasquali pp. 5-6) is very closely related to the (Iamblichean) account of semantics in Simpl. *in Cat.* 12,12-13,11. That semantics does postulate the natural link between names and things, and introduces the notion of original unity in the (Divine) Mind. It also links up perfectly with the distinction between two senses of *phusei* presented in Proclus, op. cit., 17, pp. 7-8 Pasquali and Amm. *in Int.* 34ff. (e) Boeth. *in Int.*[2] 21-3, actually sketches this sort of semantics, though without attributing it to any particular school. A central passage, 22,6-13: 'But if you go back to nature and consider it carefully, you will realise that when there is a thing, there is also the concept of it – if not among men, at least in him who in the divinity of his own substance is ignorant of nothing in the thing's own nature. And, if there is a concept, there is also a word. But if there is a word, its letters are there; they may be unknown but this does not affect the nature of the word'. Cf. L.M. de Rijk, 'Boèce logicien et philosophe: ses positions sémantiques et sa métaphysique de l'être', in L. Obertello (ed.), *Congresso internazionale di studi Boeziani – Atti*, Roma 1981, 141-56. (f) From Nicomachus' *Arithm.* 1 1-6, which Boethius himself had rendered in Latin, he would know to connect the theory of divine exemplar ideas with the name of Pythagoras, and also the 'Pythagorean' explanation of what philosophy is. This explanation occurs with ascription to Pythagoras in Amm. *in Isag.* 9,7-23, in a list of definitions of philosophy. The corresponding passage in Boeth. *in Isag.*[1] 7, contains no list, but just the 'Pythagorean' explanation, without ascription. (g) Addressing Philosophy, Boethius in the *Consolation* 1 pr. 4,38-9 says: 'Day after day you keep dropping the Pythagorean motto, "Follow God" into my ears and my thoughts. It was not fitting for me to seek the protection of the most abject spirits when you were preparing me for such excellence that you might make me similar to God.' (h) The passage on levels of cognition in *Cons.* 5 pr. 4,25ff is consistent both with the 'Pythagorean' semantics and with Boethius' programme of not penetrating to the profoundest level when writing about logic for beginners.

[59] ap. Simpl. *in Cat.* 135,10-26.

the discrete. And in virtue of the mutual union of the intelligible quanta it establishes the continuous; but in virtue of their mutually separated union it establishes the discrete. And by virtue of its static act it creates the discrete, by virtue of its proceeding act it creates the continuous. Since, then, it is both static and proceeds, it engenders both. For the power of the intelligible measures simultaneously contains both those quanta which are static and those which proceed, in one and the same.

By not giving the early medieval logicians a Pythagorean commentary on the *Categories* Boethius saved them from being led astray by such gibberish.

CHAPTER SEVENTEEN

An unpublished funeral oration on Anna Comnena

Robert Browning

The Byzantinist has one advantage over the student of classical antiquity – unless the latter happens to be a papyrologist. With a little diligence and a minimum of good luck he can easily unearth unpublished texts and find himself producing an *editio princeps*. And however often one has turned over the leaves of a manuscript and laboriously read words which have remained unread for perhaps five centuries or more, it never loses its thrill. Yet one must admit that the advantage is less than it seems. The classical scholar's texts are usually worth reading from some point of view, while what the Byzantinist finds is so often empty rhetorical verbiage. Byzantine funeral orations are notorious for their lack of information on the life of the deceased. Yet they never tell us absolutely nothing if we read them alertly, and they are sometimes remarkably informative on the ideas and values of the times. When the subject is a major figure of medieval Greek literature about the details of whose life we are very much in the dark, even the most trifling addition to our knowledge is welcome. It is this thought which encourages me to present a hitherto unknown Byzantine writer of the middle of the twelfth century – George Tornikes, Metropolitan of Ephesus – and to dwell in particular on his funeral oration on Anna Comnena.

I shall try in my remarks to avoid involvement in technicalities of dating and prosopography which are of exclusively Byzantine interest. George Tornikes, Metropolitan of Ephesus, is in fact not a wholly unknown figure. Six of his letters were published by Spyridon Lampros in 1879 in his edition of the works of Michael Choniates, Metropolitan of Athens, to whom he wrongly supposed these letters to be addressed. And the same scholar thirty-seven years later described in some detail the unique manuscript of Tornikes' works (*Neos Hellenomnemon* 13, 1916, 13-22). His description has been superseded only in the last few months by that in the magnificent first volume of the new catalogue of the Vienna Greek manuscripts by Herbert Hunger. Yet the great reference works on Byzantine literature – those of Krumbacher and Beck – do not mention him. Historians of the period, like Chalandon and Paolo Lamma, pass him over in silence. And even the diligent Brockhoff, in his dissertation on the history of Ephesus in the Middle Ages (Jena 1905), fails to list him among the bishops of that city. On the few occasions when he is mentioned, he is tacitly or explicitly identified with a namesake who was professor of Rhetoric in the Patriarchal School in Constantinople at the end of the twelfth century. Indeed it is to this mistaken identity that we owe the publication of the six letters by Lampros more than eighty years ago.

The corpus of Tornikes' works survives in a single manuscript of the early fourteenth century, now in the National Library in Vienna, which is a treasure-house of unique twelfth-century texts, cod. Vindob. phil. graec. 321. The corpus comprises twenty-five letters to named and usually easily identifiable addressees, three *prooemia* to inaugural or ceremonial lectures delivered by Tornikes at the Patriarchal School, a confession of faith made in connection with a well-known theological controversy in the middle fifties of the twelfth century, a letter drafted for the emperor Manuel I to Pope Alexander III, and a very long funeral oration on Anna Comnena, with which I am now principally concerned. None of these texts has been published except in trifling excerpts.

From his works one can gather something of Tornikes' life and career. On his father's side he belonged to a wealthy Macedonian or Thracian family, allegedly of Armenian origin, which in 1047 provided an unsuccessful claimant to the imperial throne. His mother was a niece of an archbishop of Bulgaria, perhaps of the great Theophylact. We hear of a brother named Leo, who was for a time in Athens, doubtless on government service, and of a cousin Euthymius, his special protégé, who held a junior appointment on the staff of the Patriarch. As such posts were generally the prelude to a distinguished ecclesiastical career, we may tentatively identify this Euthymius with Euthymius Tornikes, bishop of Patrae, who was expelled from his see by the Latins in 1204. This prelate was a nephew of Euthymius Malakes, bishop of Neae Patrae, theologian and scholar, and lifelong friend of Eustathius, for whom he composed a still surviving funeral oration. So George Tornikes may also have been related to Malakes and have known Eustathius as a young man.

We do not know when he was born, nor much about his early life, except that he was an intimate of Anna Comnena and her family during her long years of retirement from public life after the death of her father Alexius Comnenus in 1118. He seems to have been a member of the literary and scholarly circle gathered round her, of which I shall have more to say later. He probably also held junior teaching posts in the Patriarchal School. At any rate in 1146-7 we find him appointed *didaskalos tou psaltêros*, the junior of the three Professors of Theology, and we have the proem to the inaugural lecture which he delivered on that occasion. Unfortunately, unlike many inaugural lectures of Byzantine teachers, it tells us nothing of Tornikes' earlier career, but consists largely of laudations of the Patriarch Cosmas II Atticus, to whom he owed his appointment. Some years later he became *didaskalos tou euangeliou* and head of the Patriarchal School, and later still, but probably before the end of 1154, he was appointed *hupomnêmatographos* and so became responsible for drafting the official documents issued by the Patriarch. Literary skill and a command of rhetoric were essential qualifications for such a post in the twelfth century, just as they were indispensable to the corresponding official in the imperial service, the Keeper of the Inkstand (*ho epi tou kanikleiou*). At this point in his rapid career Tornikes could reasonably look forward to an archbishopric in the provinces; this was the usual reward of a successful career in the patriarchal School or in the personal staff of the Patriarch. But he seems to have got on the wrong side in the complex ecclesiastical politics of the time, and we have a number of despondent letters from this period describing the hostility shown to his former patron, the Patriarch Cosmas II Atticus, whose right to a Christian burial he stoutly defended when the former Patriarch was accused not only of showing undue sympathy towards members of the imperial family then in disgrace, but also of being a crypto-Bogomil. The leader of the opposition to Tornikes at this time was his colleague Soterichus Panteugenes, with whom was associated his successor as Director of the Patriarchal School, Michael *ho tou Thessalonikês*. Tornikes got his revenge in time, when Panteugenes and Michael were condemned in one of the most celebrated heresy trials of the century. But in the meantime he suffered a setback. In due course, however, probably after a change of patriarchs in 1154, his chance came. He was put on the shortlist for the Archbishopric of Corinth – the vacancy was possibly due to the death of Gregory of Corinth, though the chronological problems are complex – but withdrew on the advice of a highly placed and no doubt well-informed friend. A little later, possibly in the second half of 1155, he was appointed Metropolitan of Ephesus. Like so many others who had spent their lives in the brilliant and sophisticated but narrow world of the capital, he found the transference to a position of high responsibility in the provinces a traumatic experience. His letters from Ephesus, like those of Michael Choniates from Athens, Michael Italicus from Philippopolis, Basil Pediadites from Corfu, are marked by self-pity and lack of sympathy towards the provincials. Captured by the Seljuks in 1090, recaptured by the Byzantines shortly afterwards, harried by pirates, particularly the notorious Čaqa, occupied by the Crusaders in 1147, Ephesus was but a shadow of its former self. We hear in Tornikes' letters of pieces of mosaic falling on the bishop's head as he officiated in the great church of St John the Theologian, around which the medieval town had grown up. Heresy was rife. The local population was ignorant and unfriendly. The Byzantine governor and his court were at Philadelphia, at the end of a long journey over the mountains. In several of his letters Tornikes talks of leaving his diocese and returning to the capital, but they cannot be readily dated. He was probably still in Ephesus in May 1157, and he may have remained there for years. In early summer 1166, however, we find him entrusted by Manuel I with the drafting of a reply to a letter from Pope Alexander III, in the course of negotiations of which we learn something in Boson's contemporary Life of that Pope. He must then have been in Constantinople, enjoying the closest confidence of the emperor. This is his last appearance on the stage of history. By February 1170 the Metropolitan of Ephesus is one Nicolaus.

So much for the man. Now to his funeral oration on Anna Comnena. I propose to say something first on the biographical information which it furnishes, then on the light it throws on the intellectual life of the period, but it will not be easy to keep the two themes clearly separate. But first of all a word on the construction of the speech. The overall pattern is that established in antiquity for a *basilikos logos* – *prooimion, patris, genos, genesis, anatrophê, paideia, epitêdeumata, praxeis* (classified under the four virtues), *tukhêi* – the rules are most clearly formulated by Menander. But there is interference from a different genre, the *epitaphios logos*. The fact that the subject is a woman in any case strains the pattern of the *basilikos logos*. And Tornikes' verbosity, as well his personal involvement, lead to an almost independent development of certain of the constituent parts. So the final result is not only very long – 13,000 to 14,000 words, only slightly shorter than Isocrates' *Panathenaicus* – but also somewhat complex. Tornikes begins by apologising for the delay in the delivery of his oration and expressing his astonishment that no one else in Constantinople has delivered a monody on the princess, the subject being so unique. He then turns to the praise of her parents, Alexius I and Irene Ducas. Then come Anna's birth, upbringing and education, her appearance, her betrothal to Constantine Ducas and his untimely death. Then the account of her subsequent betrothal to Nicephorus Bryennius leads to a long digression on the virtues and exploits of the princess's husband. Next comes a long development on Anna's devotion to her mother and the lessons she learned from her. The theme of her care for her parents leads to the account of the death of her father, and the change which it brought about in Anna's circumstances. Her misfortunes and the constancy with which she met them are described with a wealth of literary imagery – the Homeric cormorant, the wimple of Leucothea, etc. – but little precision. Next comes an account of how she spent her enforced retirement in intellectual pursuits, and gathered about her a group of scholars whose work she inspired and directed, and of her own philosophical views – these are expounded at great length. Embedded in this section is an account of the deaths of her mother and her husband. Then Tornikes speaks of Anna's literary work, her letters – which do not seem to have survived – and her *History*. By a skilful transition – her wide technical competence, her knowledge of medicine, both theoretical and practical, her care of the sick, her care of her sister during her illness – he leads to the story of the princess's last illness, her taking of the veil, and her death. He concludes with a development on Anna's daughter – probably Irene, with whom he was in correspondence – and on the many groups and classes who will sincerely mourn her loss.

Anna Comnena was born in the Porphyry Chamber of the Great Palace at dawn on Saturday, 2 December 1083. The date of her death is unknown: probably after 1148 is the nearest one can get on the internal evidence of her *History*, and the narrative sources for the middle of the twelfth century say nothing about her. The new text gives a little more precision, but not much more. It was delivered, says the title, when Tornikes was still *hupomnêmatographos*. This, as we have seen, gives a date before the beginning of 1156, and some years after 1147. Some time had elapsed, he says, since the princess's death. The impression conveyed to the reader is that he is thinking of months rather than years. I should be inclined to date Anna's death to the years 1153-5. Father J. Darrouzès informs me in a letter that he has independently reached the same conclusion. Perhaps we get some confirmation from a long passage in which the speaker compares Anna's relationship to the brilliant men of her age with that of a comet to the fixed stars. In both cases the novelty of the event attracts attention. Now Halley's comet put in one of its regular appearances in April 1145, and was visible from Constantinople; in February 1147 there was another comet, visible the world over; and finally in May 1155 a comet appeared, visible throughout Europe. I should like to think that men's eyes had been raised to it in wonderment just before our oration was delivered.

In any case, Anna must have been over seventy years of age, and have spent some thirty-five years in retirement in her apartments in the monastery *tês Kekharitômenês* when she died. She preserved to the last, says Tornikes, her rosy complexion. We might at this point glance at our author's description of the princess's appearance, the only one to survive, and one of the few eye-witness descriptions of living persons in Byzantine literature (see Appendix to this chapter on p. 404, extract 1).

Anna's own account of her education is celebrated (*Alexiad*, pr. 2; 15,7 *fin.*) And she continually thanks her parents for having taken such care over it. The story we find in the oration is slightly different, and perhaps more interesting. Anna was trained by her parents in virtue, but not in *logoi*. They did not object to her studying philosophy, which could be safely christianised and in any case tended to moral improvement, but they were strongly opposed to her studying its essential forerunner, grammar, which could not be christianised and was morally neutral to say the least. It was dangerous enough for men, far more so for women – and let us remember that Anna was no more than thirteen years old at this time. However, the princess outwitted the vigilance of her parents by taking private lessons in *grammatikê* from one of the palace eunuchs, like a maiden having a clandestine assignation with her lover (see Appendix, p. 404, extract 2). Later, after her marriage to Nicephorus Bryennius, she continued her education openly, studying grammar under a palace eunuch – apparently a different one this time – and philosophy under philosophers who combined eloquence, a philosophical ethos, and old age. The final stage in her education was after her father's death and her own retirement from public life, when she gathered around her some of the most learned men of her time, and with them studied Aristotle,

Plato, Euclid and Ptolemy – except such of his doctrines as Christianity rejects – rhetoric and history.

Anna Comnena is eloquent on her woes in her *History*, but she never makes it clear exactly what they were. We know from other sources that she spent the latter part of her life, after the death of her father, in the convent *tês Kekharitômenês* in Constantinople in semi-retirement, though of course she did not actually become a nun until she was on her death-bed – a fact which we learn from the present oration. The chronicler John Zonaras, whose history ends with the year 1118, tells us in some detail how Anna, who hated her younger brother John II, and still hoped to place the imperial crown on the head of her able, but good-natured and unambitious, husband Nicephorus Bryennius, quarrelled bitterly with her brother over their father's death-bed, and was the prime mover in a plot to assassinate him shortly after his accession (Zonaras, 18,28-9). The same story is told by Nicetas Choniates, writing at the beginning of the thirteenth century. If true, it would be sufficient explanation of the obscurity in which the rest of Anna's life was passed. Anna's own account of the death of her father gives an idyllic picture of a united family, though she does mention that John went off to the Great Palace before their father had breathed his last. And Anna's striking coldness towards her brother, whom she scarcely mentions in her *History*, has often attracted attention. Zonaras' story cannot be dated, unfortunately. We know that he was still alive and working on his great compilation of Canon Law in 1159, but his Chronicle may have been completed long before that. What does Tornikes, an intimate friend of the family, have to say? He was clearly aware of an account of the events discreditable to Anna, and implies that it had obtained wide credence, though of course he somewhat baldly denies it (see Appendix, p. 405, extract 3). The probability is that he had the text of Zonaras before him. This is not a very convincing defence of Anna, but then perhaps a funeral oration was not the place for polemical discussion of the events of more than a generation before.

Anna's nephew Manuel I, whom she perhaps scarcely knew, seems to have done nothing after his accession in 1143 to heal the breach with his formidable sexagenarian aunt. He gets a single brief and cold mention in this speech. In any case Anna and Manuel would never have seen eye to eye. Manuel was a Latinophile and a womaniser, and he was an enthusiastic believer in astrology, a science in defence of which he wrote a treatise. The condemnation of astrology which Tornikes in the present speech attributes to Anna may well have been directed mainly at her brilliant but erratic imperial nephew. So far as it is possible to date Manuel's defence of astrology, it is certainly later than 1147, and was probably written not long before 1156.

When death finally came to the princess as she was engaged in consoling one of her sisters – we do not know which – after a recent bereavement, she had been cut off from the sophisticated world of the court for thirty-five years. But she had not been out of contact with the intellectual movement of the time. It was in the closing years of her retirement, as we know, that she composed the history of her father's reign. The present oration furnishes precious information on another of her activities, her philosophical circle. Let us look once again at the passage in question (see Appendix, p. 405, extract 4). It seems that Anna not only studied herself – a procedure which would involve lectures or supervisions by specialists – but also organised and inspired, and no doubt paid for, the work of others. In particular we hear of the encouragement of Aristotelian commentators, and especially of the exegesis of works on which no commentary had survived from antiquity. And the name of Michael of Ephesus is mentioned as one who engaged in these activities under Anna's patronage.

Now the long series of commentaries on the works of Aristotle, which begins in the first century BC with Andronikos, the rediscoverer of the Aristotelian corpus, continues without a significant break down to Stephanus of Alexandria and his pupils David and Elias in the seventh century.[1] Then, with the loss to the Arabs of the school of Alexandria, the tradition seems to dry up. John Damascene in the eighth century was profoundly influenced by Aristotle and his commentators, but by his time it had become a closed body of thought; there was no further exegesis or development. Surprisingly, exegesis of Aristotle begins again in the eleventh or twelfth century with two men whose work survives, Eustratius, Metropolitan of Nicaea, and Michael of Ephesus. The former commented upon certain books of the *Nicomachean Ethics* and sections of the Organon, the latter on other books of the *Ethics*, sections of the Organon, the *Rhetoric*, the *Physics*, the *Politics*, and a number of the zoological and anthropological works. Eustratius is a well-known figure, a pupil of John Italus, who made a brilliant career in the Church, wrote many works of dogmatic and polemical theology, took part in the discussion with Petrus Chrysolanus in 1112, and found himself charged with heresy in 1117 as a result of an anti-Armenian tract which he had composed. He recanted, but was probably suspended for life. We do not know when he died. The date cited in the handbooks, c. 1120, is the result of a somewhat labile construction by Draeseke.[2] The date of his birth is equally unknown; it could be as late as 1060. As for Michael of Ephesus, nothing at all is known of his life, and up to now all that could be done by way of dating him was eleventh/twelfth century. Tatakis in his recent book on Byzantine philosophy supposes Michael to be a contemporary of John Italus and a predecessor of Eustratius.

The present text fills out the picture in much more detail. Michael of Ephesus' commentaries belong to the years of Anna's retirement after 1118. And they were probably completed by 1138, since after that year Anna was mainly engaged in the composition of her *History*, originally intended as a sequel to that written by her late husband. Karl Praechter

[1] [For differing views on the relations of these three philosophers, see Chapters 14 and 1 – Ed.]

[2] *Byzantinische Zeitschrift* 5, 1896, 319-36.

in a well-known paper[3] remarks that anyone looking at the list of works of Aristotle commented upon in late antiquity or early Byzantine times is struck by three gaps – the *Politics*, the *Rhetoric*, and the zoological and anthropological works. Eight hundred years before Praechter wrote these words, the same point seems to have struck Anna Comnena, who had the resources and the connections to remedy the shortcoming. Michael of Ephesus was breaking entirely new ground in his commentaries on the zoological and anthropological works and on the *Rhetoric* and the *Politics*. And he was doing it as part of a co-operative scholarly undertaking conceived and guided by Anna Comnena. The list of his own commentaries which he gives illustrates how systematically the plan of Anna or of her advisers was being carried out.[4]

What of Eustratius? In her *History* Anna speaks of him with high praise (14,8). In the proem to his commentary on *EN* 1 he tells us that it was composed at the behest of a highly placed personage whom he does not name. And in the proem to that on *EN* 6 he addresses his patron as *basilis theosebês, basilis philologê, basilis philagathê kai philokalê*. So far as I can discover, the identity of this princess – the word need not mean the wife of a reigning emperor in Byzantine usage – has never been cleared up. It is very tempting, and an obvious working hypothesis, to suppose that she was Anna Comnena, and that Eustratius' exegetical work belongs to the years of his theological disgrace. In the commentary on *EN* 6 he speaks of himself as an old man, for what that is worth. And it is significant that he was apparently asked to comment only on *EN* 1 and 6, while the other books of the *Nicomachean Ethics* were commented on by Michael of Ephesus and possibly by a nebulous Aspasius[5] – there is some variation in the titles in the manuscripts. No part of the *Ethics* was the object of comment by more than one of these scholars. This suggests that their commentaries were all prepared as part of the same co-operative enterprise. It may well be that Eustratius was the real inspirer of the whole project.

If some measure of probability can be accorded to our hypothesis thus far, Anna Comnena played a role in the revival of Aristotelian scholarship in the Byzantine world. It has long been a commonplace that the renaissance of Aristotelian exegesis depended ultimately on the renewed interest in and grasp of the ancient philosophical tradition displayed by men like Michael Psellus and John Italus in the eleventh century. But this remains a vague formulation. The tendency of Psellus and John Italus was Platonist or Neoplatonist rather than Aristotelian. The detailed connection and organisational link is missing. The more one examines Byzantine literature, the more one becomes convinced that it never appears spontaneously; it needs a salon, patronage, institutionalised forms. We know of some of the literary circles of the earlier twelfth century. The Patriarchal

---

[3] K. Praechter, review of *Michaelis Ephesii In libros De partibus animalium ... Commentaria*, M. Hayduck (ed.), *CAG* 22.2, in *Göttingische gelehrte Anzeigen* 168, 1906, 861-907.

[4] *Göttingische gelehrte Anzeigen* 22, 149, 8ff.

[5] [In Chapter 18, Mercken credits the second-century Aspasius – Ed.]

School housed one such circle, whose interests, theology apart, lay in the fields of grammar, rhetoric and belles-lettres; Michael Italicus is one of its leading figures. Another centred upon the sebastocratorissa Irene, widow of Manuel's elder brother Andronicus. Poetry was one of its main interests; innumerable occasion l poems of Theodore Prodromus can be connected with it; Tzetzes commented on Hesiod and Homer and wrote his *Theogony* for Irene; and she was the patroness and dedicatee of Constantine Manasses' verse chronicle. We can now add to these Anna Comnena's philosophical circle, numbering among its members Michael of Ephesus and probably Eustratius of Nicaea. It is worth recalling in this connection that it was in Constantinople in the thirties of the twelfth century that James of Venice became acquainted with the *Physics*, the *Sophistici Elenchi*, and other works of Aristotle, which he subsequently translated into Latin.[6] It has been assumed that he found them studied in the University. But we must now reckon with the possibility that he had contact with Anna Comnena's Aristotelian circle. It may be significant that the *Sophistici Elenchi*, one of the works translated by James of Venice, was first commented upon by Michael of Ephesus. It may well be, too, that other works of philosophical and mathematical exegesis will prove to have been composed under Anna's watchful eye in the suite in the *Kekharitômenê* convent, at the head of a valley overlooking the tranquil waters of the Golden Horn. One would look in the first place among the nameless Byzantine scholiasts on Euclid and Ptolemy, who continued the tradition of Proclus and Simplicius. John Tzetzes' unpublished commentary on the *Canons* of Ptolemy, in cod. Paris. gr. 2162, was probably composed too late to qualify, but one cannot be certain.

In so far as one can attach political labels to such things, Anna Comnena's circle belonged to the 'outs'. She herself was in semi-disgrace to the end of her days; Tornikes' complaint that no one but himself had thought of commemorating her death bears this out. Eustratius was a man whose career was finished; the Patriarch Cosmas II Atticus, who promoted Tornikes, and whom Tornikes defended after his death, was dismissed after just over a year in office, charged not only with Bogomil sympathies, but also with supporting Manuel's disgruntled relatives.

From time to time in her history Anna mentions this or that point of philosophy. However, the long account of her tenets given by George Tornikes provides a more comprehensive view than we can derive from the *History*. I shall outline the main points briefly, as they are not of much importance in themselves. Anna may not have really had much of a head for philosophy, Tornikes was probably no philosopher, and I am certainly quite incompetent in this sphere. Anna sees as her task to fit the tradition of ancient philosophy to the requirements of Christian dogma. The series of syntheses which had been made in the past no longer satisfy her entirely. And the tradition of ancient philosophy means to her, as to

---

[6] cf. L. Minio-Paluello, *Traditio* 8, 1952, 265-304.

all Byzantines, Aristotle and Plato, both seen through the spectacles of commentators of late antiquity, who were either pagan Neoplatonists like Simplicius, or Aristotelian heretics like John Philoponus. In general, she says, she finds Aristotle most satisfying. But she objects to his *agenêsia* (significantly the word seems first attested in Simplicius), that is, to an uncreated universe which leaves no room for providence and in which everything must be *automaton*. This is precisely the point in dispute between the schools of Athens and Alexandria in the early sixth century, which led John Philoponus in 529 to publish his *de Aeternitate Mundi contra Proclum*. To avoid this difficulty she accepted Plato's *dêmiourgos*; but she rejected totally *to par' autôi tôn ideôn mêkhanêma*, the Aristotelian criticism of which she regarded as valid. She admired Plato and his followers, the Neoplatonists, and approved many of their doctrines, such as that of the *anousion agathon*, but preferred Christian explanations of such matters, particularly those of Pseudo-Dionysius the Areopagite. However, she borrowed from the *Timaeus* the circles of the other and the same – men had been confusing themselves by interpreting the *Timaeus* literally for a millennium – and she accepted Plato's doctrine of the divisions of the soul, but of course rejected his metempsychosis. From Aristotle she borrowed the concept of entelechy (actuality). She favoured a double entelechy (*dittê entelekheia*) in regard to the soul – this points to her familiarity with the second book of the *de Anima* – and she frequently illustrated this by the analogies of the lyre-player and the steersman. This leads to another passage of the *de Anima* which, unfortunately for Anna, modern authorities generally regard as a momentary lapse on the part of Aristotle. But John Philoponus in his commentary took it seriously, and the word for steersman used by Tornikes is Philoponus' and not Aristotle's. And both the topic and the imagery alike figure in the surviving writings of Michael Psellus and John Italus. Above all, she was determined to find a physics and metaphysics which would not destroy the basis of ethics, and this to Anna meant an after-life in which our actions are judged, rewarded, and punished. Belief in destiny – *heimarmenê* – was to her something worthy of beasts rather than men. It is significant that it was precisely the *Physics* and *Metaphysics* which were neglected in the orthodox Christian – Aristotelian synthesis represented by Leontius of Byzantium and John Damascene.

I doubt if much can be made of Tornikes' garbled and rhetorical account. But it is clear that Anna and her colleagues were bent on constructing a philosophical system, and not merely on glossing texts. They were not alone in this in the twelfth century. Michael Anchialus, the future Patriarch, was appointed Professor of Philosophy – *hupatos tôn philosophôn* – about 1165, after the office had apparently been in abeyance for some time. In his inaugural lecture, which I have edited elsewhere,[7] he lays great emphasis upon the study of Aristotle and upon

[7] *Balkan Studies* (Thessalonika), 2, 1961, 173-214.

the support which a somewhat eclectic Aristotelianism can give to religion. He attacks at great length the followers of pagan theology, who believed matter to be uncreated. This is just the point which gave offence to Anna. And it is also, we recall, one of the charges made in 1082 against John Italus, who was also accused of reviving the errors of ancient philosophers on the nature of the soul, and of regarding profane literature as a fountain of truth. In 1156 Soterichus Panteugenes, whom we have already met briefly as an enemy of Tornikes, was condemned, together with a number of leading men of letters and teachers in the Patriarchal School, for heretical interpretation of the liturgy of the Eucharist. Nicolaus of Methone, the leading theologian of the age, expressly connected the heresy of Panteugenes with the Platonic doctrine of Ideas, which, he declared, had been refuted by Aristotle. And Nicolaus was no novice in philosophy. He wrote, probably before 1156, an *anaptuxis tês theologikês stoikheiôseôs Proklou* in which he says that he is arguing against men of his own age, who call themselves Christians, but who are befuddled by pagan learning, and so *epiprosthen tôn oikeiôn tithentai ta allotria*. It has been plausibly suggested, too, that Michael Glycas the chronicler, whose heretical doctrines began to attract attention early in the reign of Manuel I, was trying to construct a systematic cosmology of neoplatonising character.

System-building was not the monopoly of hellenisers and heretics at this time. Euthymius Zigabenus wrote his *Dogmatic Panoply* and Nicetas Acominatus his *Treasury of Orthodoxy* to combat the rationalist heresies so attractive to the twelfth-century mind. Neilus Doxopatres, an exalted functionary on the patriarchal staff, who became a monk and went off to Norman Sicily shortly before 1143, composed a great dogmatic *summa*, on a scale quite unprecedented in the Byzantine world. It was in five books, of which only the first two – comprising between them 466 chapters – survive unpublished.

In a book written seventy years ago[8] Fyodor Uspenskij argued that throughout the twelfth century a long argument went on between Nominalists and Realists in the Byzantine world, parallel to and not unconnected with that going on at the same time in the Latin world. By and large the Realists lean on Plato, the Nominalists on Aristotle.

We need a new study of the ground covered by Uspenskij seventy years ago. The time is scarcely ripe yet. Too many of the relevant texts still slumber unread in the dust of libraries. But we can begin to see why the tradition of Aristotelian exegesis was taken up again so vigorously after a lapse of nearly four centuries. And this unpromising-looking funeral oration gives a glimpse of the commentators at their work. To be quite fair, Anna Comnena and her circle were probably not quite the first to revive the tradition. Theodore of Smyrna, successor of John Italus as *hupatos tôn philosophôn*, who survived until the closing years of Alexius

---

[8] F. Uspenskij, *Ocherki po istorii vizantijskoj obrazovannosti*, St Petersburg 1891 (1892), 146-245.

I's reign, if not longer, and who appears among the intelligentsia of the underworld in that lively Byzantine satire the *Timarion*, had composed an exposition of the physical doctrines of the ancients, in which he seems to have dealt with Aristotle at some length. His work is unpublished. But this was only a small beginning. Without the resources at Anna's command the movement might well have petered out. In fact more than a century and a half elapsed before the next great 'wave' of Aristotelian commentaries in Byzantium. We clearly owe much to the drive and inspiration of this astonishing lady, whose memory is enshrined not only in the immortal history of her father's reign, but also in the austere volumes of the *Commentaria in Aristotelem Graeca*.[9]

Appendix

1. Her eyes, of well-proportioned size and shining with happiness, neither constantly moving and turning about – the signs of an unstable and giddy soul – nor immoderately motionless and sluggish – the marks of a slothful disposition – moved with liveliness and ease when she wished to survey her surroundings, but were more often steady and fixed. Her eyebrows were curved like the rainbow; her nose was straight and slightly curved towards her lip, protruding slightly and harmoniously; her lips were compressed like rosebuds, recalling the scarlet cord of the Song of Songs. Her whole complexion was white as wool, while her cheeks were tinged with a rosy blush, which she retained into old age. Her whole countenance formed a well-rounded circle, as if traced with a compass. Her head was firmly set upon her backbone by a neck of proportionate length, her shoulders did not heave irregularly, her feet were agile, her hands even more so. All her members were fair in themselves and fair in relation to one an other. Her body was like a lyre or a well-tempered lute, a good instrument fashioned for a good soul (fol. 25r).

2. As for profane learning, they suspected it of being insidious, just as wise mothers of children often distrust match-makers, lest they inspire in maidens dishonourable passions. For they admired and welcomed the subtlety of its logical procedures and the virtuosity of its dialectic, as well as its manifest revelation of the secrets of nature, and, among some of its practitioners (the understanding) of the creation of the universe by the Prime Mover and his providence, as revealed to them by God. But the literary study which precedes these disciplines, the principal object of which is poetry and its subject-matter polytheism, or rather atheism and fables recounting the ill-starred loves of gods, the violation of virgins, the abduction of youths, and other exploits as disgraceful in word as in deed, this study they rightly thought dangerous even for men, and for women

[9] Since this article was first published, the surviving works of George Tornikes have been edited for the first time by Father J. Darrouzès in *Georges et Démétrios Tornikès: lettres et discours*, Paris 1970. The translation in the Appendix is from Darrouzès text, not from that printed in the original article.

and girls excessively insidious, and believed that their eyes and ears should remain undefiled by them, since it is through these that passions enter the soul.

Such were their thoughts, truly worthy of imperial persons and followers of Christ. But she – for she listened attentively to those who gave displays of their wisdom every day before her father the Emperor, and was roused to emulation by them – what did she do? She knew the judgment of her parents concerning profane wisdom and accepted it. But as soldiers who have learnt of an ambush laid by the enemy but cannot return home by any other route brave their ambuscade, after arming themselves well and preparing themselves to hold out with courage to the end, so she armed herself against the deceitful fictions and the stories of dishonourable passions and braced the weakness of her soul so that it might not be taken by surprise or carried away by the magic potion of Circe or the songs of the Sirens. She closed and opened her ears in accordance with the guidance of reason and, advancing with Odysseus' magic herb, braved grammar and poetry, taking care not to be detected by her parents, and surreptitiously and with caution taking lessons from eunuch servants who were not ignorant of such matters. And like a maiden who takes a furtive glance at her bridegroom through some chink, so she had furtive meetings with her beloved grammar (fol. 24v).

3. But his son, who was also Emperor, while his father was still breathing, took up the sceptre of power and went off to the palace, as indeed he had to do, since time presses in such situations, and many unexpected claimants to imperial power plot against an Emperor's heirs if there is the least hesitation. She however, who according to those who say anything lightly was her brother's rival for power, although she knew that her father had just left this world, forgot, along with her children and her husband, the imperial title and joined with her mother in mourning, as they sat alone on the floor with bared heads around the Emperor instead of the chamberlains, the officers, and the company of valorous guardsmen (fol. 27v).

4. So she gathered together all the most eminent representatives of the logical sciences – and they were numerous and remarkable. For this was one of the achievements of the age of Alexios, that among those who taught the young by daily exercises he honoured the most distinguished by gifts and imperial dignities, which were given to men of letters as to others. First were those who were philosophers by their knowledge and their way of life, making this their prime goal rather than money-making or commerce, wealth or office, but rather gathering knowledge from books and spreading it in turn among the souls of those who desired it, and pouring into their ears great wisdom in simple words. Then came those who were at one and the same time men of the world and philosophers and eloquent of tongue, combining wealth of knowledge with elegance of exposition, teachers as brilliant by the content of their thought as by its

outward expression. By these men she was initiated into such of the doctrines of the Stagirite and Plato, Euclid and Ptolemy, as are not banished from society by the laws of the Christians. Neither did she reject political or epideictic oratory, nor did she disdain the utility of history, which provides the subject-matter for rhetoric and most of its verisimilitude. For she lived with poetry, wept with the tragedians and laughed with the comedians, refreshing herself from her philosophical labours by such distractions; some things she laughed at, others she lamented and wept over; she praised the laughter of Democritus and admired no less the tears of Heraclitus. The works which philosophers of our time addressed to her bear witness to her love of learning, works concerning those writings of Aristotle on which commentaries had not been written until her time, but the explanation of which was transmitted orally in every kind of form, without certitude and with little zeal. For books are an inviolable storehouse of words, and writing is an indestructible memorial of thought, while the ear is often violated by oblivion as by robbers. I have myself heard the wise man from Ephesus attribute the cause of his blindness to her, because he spent sleepless nights over commentaries on Aristotle at her command, whence came the damage done to his eyes by candles through desiccation (fol. 29v).

CHAPTER EIGHTEEN

The Greek commentators on Aristotle's *Ethics*

H.P.F. Mercken

The main commentaries

I shall examine the most important of the Greek commentaries on Aristotle's *Nicomachean Ethics*. One is a composite commentary (*CAG* 19.1, 158-86, and 20 G. Heylbut (ed.), 1889 and 1892; *CAG* 22.3, M. Hayduck (ed.), 1901), compiled in twelfth-century Constantinople, and translated into Latin in thirteenth-century England by Robert Grosseteste. Although the date of compilation is late, the composite work incorporates some of the earliest Greek commentaries on Aristotle that we possess, produced by Aspasius and other Peripatetics in the second century AD. This early commentary is juxtaposed with twelfth-century work, including that of Eustratius of Nicaea and Michael of Ephesus. The compilation is all the more significant because of the shortage of commentary on Aristotle's *Ethics* from the heyday of commentary writing which stretches from Alexander in the third century AD to Simplicius in the sixth.

There are further commentaries by Aspasius on Books 1 to 4 and part of Book 7 of the *Nicomachean Ethics* (*CAG* 19.1, G. Heylbut (ed.), 1889, 1-157).

The remaining Greek literature, which I shall not discuss, consists of: (i) an epitome of Aristotle, including his ethics, written by Arius Didymus in the first century BC, and partly preserved by Stobaeus.[1] (ii) Alexander of Aphrodisias, *Ethical Problems* (*CAG* suppl. 2.2, I. Bruns (ed.), 1892, translated by Robert W. Sharples, 1989), from the beginning of the third century AD, not in commentary form. (iii) Pseudo-Andronicus of Rhodes *On Emotions* (*Peri Pathôn*), also translated by Grosseteste, found in MS Peterhouse 116, A. Glibert-Thirry (ed.), *Pseudo-Andronicus de Rhodes PERI PATHÔN*, Édition critique du texte grec et de la traduction latine médiévale, *Corpus Latinum Commentariorum in Aristotelem Graecorum* (*CLCAG*), supp. 2, Leiden 1977. (iv) *Paraphrase of the Whole Philosophy of Aristotle* by Georgius Pachymerius from around 1300. (v) The paraphrase commentary ascribed unreliably in one MS to the otherwise

---

[1] cf. P. Moraux, *Der Aristotelismus bei den Griechen*, vol. 1, Berlin and New York 1973, 316-434: 'Areios Didymos, der Abriss der aristotelischen Ethik.'

unknown Heliodorus of Prusa (*CAG* 19.2, G. Heylbut (ed.), 1889), which may date from any time up to 1366.[2]

The contents of the composite commentary are diverse: commentaries on Books 1 and 6 by Eustratius, metropolitan bishop of Nicaea, in the years marking the transition from the eleventh to the twelfth century; anonymous scholia on Books 2, 3, 4, and 5, probably from the last quarter of the second century AD; another commentary on Book 5, as well as one on Books 9 and 10, by Michael of Ephesus, professor at Constantinople and contemporary of Eustratius; an anonymous commentary on Book 7, which is in all likelihood even later than those by Eustratius and Michael; finally a commentary on Book 8 by Aspasius, a renowned Peripatetic of the first half of the second century of our era. The composite commentary thus comprises texts from five authors, spread over eleven centuries: Aspasius, Michael of Ephesus, Eustratius of Nicaea, and two anonymous scholiasts.

There has been one earlier edition, the Aldine edition of 1536: *Eustratiou kai allôn tinôn episêmôn hupomnêmata eis ta deka tôn tou Aristotelous Éthikôn Nikomakheiôn biblia meta tou hupokeimenou ...*, with colophon: *Venetiis, in aedibus haeredum Aldi Manutii, et Andreae Asulani soceri, mense Julio. M.D.XXXVI.* It lacks the anonymous scholia on Book 5.

The extant Greek manuscripts containing the commentaries of Eustratius 'with others' can be divided into two main classes, the first of which contains basically the compilation which Grosseteste translated; the second class, lacking the early anonymous scholia, contains in their stead most or all of the remaining commentary of Aspasius.[3]

The Greek manuscripts of the composite commentary with the early anonymous scholia

It is a curious fact that there are only two extant Greek manuscripts with exactly the compilation which Grosseteste must have had in his possession. They are Oxford, Corpus Christi College 106 and Oxford New College 240/241. Being the only ones to contain the anonymous scholia on Book 5, they have consequently been used for the edition of these scholia by Heylbut, who gave them the *sigla* F and G, respectively.

There are, in addition, two manuscripts which differ only from the former and from Grosseteste's (lost) manuscript by the omission of the anonymous scholia on Book 5. This omission may have been justified by the consideration that Michael of Ephesus had incorporated most of these glosses in his commentary on the same book. These manuscripts are Milan 95 Ambrosianus B sup. and Paris Coislinianus 161. The latter is the only manuscript on which Heylbut, who gave it the *siglum* B, based his edition, for which he also used the Aldine edition. The Aldine edition

[2] cf. R.A. Gauthier, in R.A. Gauthier and J.Y. Jolif, *Aristote, L'Éthique à Nicomaque*[2], Louvain and Paris 1970, Introduction, 106-7.

[3] See G. Heylbut, *CAG* 19.1, v-vii, and 20, v-ix.

contains the same text as Coislinianus 161 (=B). Heylbut gave it the *siglum* a.

The Greek manuscripts of the composite commentary with the remaining commentary of Aspasius

Of Aspasius' commentary on the *Ethics*, only two parts have survived, viz. one on Books 1-4 and one on the greater part of Books 7 and 8.

The Greek manuscripts containing Eustratius 'with others' of the second class differ from those of the first in the following ways:

(1) They do not contain the older anonymous glosses on Books 2-5.

(2) They add the commentary of Aspasius on Books 1-4 after Eustratius on Book 1.[4]

(3) They add *capita moralia*, taken from the *Quaestiones*, attributed to Alexander of Aphrodisias,[5] after Eustratius on Book 6.

(4) They add Aspasius on Book 7 after the anonymous scholia on the same book, with the exception of Vatican gr. 269 and Paris gr. 1927. The omission in these two manuscripts may have been influenced by the consideration that Aspasius' commentary on Book 7 covers only the second half of that book.

To this second class belong Florence Laurentianus gr. 85,1 (=N); Modena gr. 197 (II.G.4); and Berlin (*ex collectione Carolii Morbii*) fol. 58,59 (Acc. 1889, 304).[6] I deliberately count also the incomplete manuscripts Vatican Barberinus gr. 223 (formerly II 44); Leiden Vossianus fol. n. 12; Vatican gr. 269 II; and Paris gr. 1927 in this class, because they also conform to the description of that class in so far as they can exhibit it, that is, only partially.

Finally, Vatican gr. 320 is fragmentary in that it contains only the commentary of Michael of Ephesus on Books 9 and 10.

In summary, all extant Greek manuscripts mentioned, in so far as they are complete, contain Eustratius on Books 1 and 6, Michael on Books 5, 9, and 10, the recent anonymous scholiast on Book 7, and Aspasius on Book 8; one main class contains in addition the anonymous glosses on Books 2, 3, and 4 (and 5 for the manuscripts F and G); the other main class contains instead (again in so far as the manuscripts are complete) *capita moralia* of Alexander of Aphrodisias and the whole of the extant commentary of Aspasius minus the first folio (except on Book 7 in two manuscripts, Vat. gr. 269 and Paris gr. 1927).

One cannot but wholeheartedly agreed with V. Rose that the second class of manuscripts containing Eustratius 'with others' resulted from a

---

[4] The text of this commentary is acephalous. It starts with *tên dialektikên enioi ephasan* ... on p. 3,11 of Heylbut's edition (*CAG* 19.1) and follows immediately upon Eustratius' commentary. As a result, the presence of Aspasius' commentary on Book 1 in these MSS has often been overlooked. Heylbut himself omits it in his description of Laurentianus gr. 85,1, on p. vii of *CAG* 20.

[5] I. Bruns (ed.), *Supplementum Aristotelicum* 2 pars 2, Berlin 1892, 117-63.

[6] The last MS is not mentioned in the *Praefatio* of *CAG* 19.1.

deliberate substitution of Aspasius for the anonymous glosses, and that the first class of manuscripts (and hence the translation of Grosseteste) represents the original compilation. The only part of Aspasius' commentary which belongs to the original compilation is that on Book 8. The decisive argument is that the text of this book in the manuscripts of the compilation deviates considerably from the one in the manuscripts containing Aspasius' commentary alone, whereas the text of the other books of Aspasius' commentary, whenever present in the manuscripts of the compilation (that is, in the second class of these manuscripts), is very close to that in the manuscripts containing Aspasius' commentary alone, the main difference being that the latter's text is not acephalous.[7]

The Renaissance translation of the composite commentary

In 1541 Giovanni Bernardo Feliciano published in Venice a new translation of the *Nicomachean Ethics* and of the Greek commentaries. He included the same items Grosseteste translated, with the exception of the anonymous scholia on Book 5, but adding some parts from Aspasius. Feliciano mixed the anonymous scholia on Books 2-4 with those of Aspasius on the same books. He attributed the worthless scholia on Book 7 to Aspasius and the commentary of Michael of Ephesus on Books 9 and 10 to Eustratius, while mentioning that some attributed these to Michael. He did not include a translation of Aspasius on Books 1 and 7.

Later editions are Basel, 1542; Paris (Roigny), 1543; Venice (heres Hier. Scoti), 1589; and Helmstadt (Sam. Rachelius), 1662. They contain practically the same text, although the Paris edition shows some corrections, including emendations based on the Greek text.

Eustratius on Books 1 and 6

Eustratius is the best known of our commentators.[8] He was born c. 1050 and died c. 1120, as Draeseke has conclusively argued. He received an education in philosophy from John Italus, the well known successor of

[7] V. Rose, 'Ueber die griechischen Commentare zur Ethik des Aristoteles', *Hermes* 5, 1871, 71 and 73. Rose's article (61-113) contains a wealth of information and is amazingly accurate, especially if one considers the time at which it was written. One can only regret that until recently subsequent scholars, in particular the editors of the Greek commentaries, have not made sufficient use of it.

[8] For the whole compilation, see F. Schleiermacher, 'Ueber die griechischen Scholien zur Nikomachischen Ethik des Aristoteles', *Sämmtliche Werke*, Abt. 3, Bd. 2, Berlin 1838, 309-26; V. Rose, 'Ueber die griechischen Commentare zur Ethik des Aristoteles', *Hermes* 5, 1871, 61-113; and R.A. Gauthier in R.A. Gauthier and J.Y. Jolif, op. cit. in n. 2, 100-5 and 121. For Eustratius, see J. Draeseke, 'Zu Eustratios von Nikaea', *Byzantinische Zeitschrift* 5, 1896, 319-36; S. Salaville, 'Philosophie et théologie ou épisodes scolastiques à Byzance de 1059 à 1117', *Échos d'Orient* 29, 1930, 132-56; P. Joannou, 'Eustrate de Nicée. Trois pièces inédites de son procès (1117)', *Revue des Études Byzantines* 10, 1952, 24-34; id., 'Die Definition des Seins bei Eustratios von Nikaia. Die Universalienlehre in der byzantinischen Theologie im XI. Jh.', *Byzantinische Zeitschrift* 47, 1954, 258-368; id., 'Der Nominalismus und die menschliche Psychologie Christi. Das Semeioma gegen Eustratios von Nikaia

Psellus as the head of the school of Constantinople (*hupatos tôn philosophôn*). John Italus, whose interest in Aristotle counterbalanced the Platonic tendency of Psellus, was much admired by his contemporaries for his dialectical ability, but his attempts to apply philosophical reasoning to the mysteries of Christian revelation led to his downfall. A synod in 1082 condemned nine articles, which he admitted having defended, as being filled with pagan atheism, forbade him to teach either privately or publicly, and relegated him to a monastery. The *synodicon* of Orthodoxy Sunday (first Sunday of Lent) retains eleven *anathemata* against John Italus and his doctrines, the first of which is directed against his attempts to discuss dialectically the mystery of the Incarnation and of the hypostatic union of two natures in Christ. Eustratius, who was merely a deacon at the time, and principal (*proximos*) of the school of Sporakin, is cited with other disciples of John Italus, all of whom succeeded in convincing the synod of their innocence in the matter at hand and signed a letter in which they anathematised their master's heretical doctrines.

Eustratius soon became an influential figure. Only a few years after the trial of Italus, he wrote a dialogue and a treatise on the question of the Icons against Leon, metropolitan bishop of Chalcedon. Leon had been relentless in accusing Emperor Alexius I Comnenus of sacrilege and iconoclasm, for the latter had caused sacred vases and golden and silver ornaments of church gates to be melted down for coin to sustain his wars. For this Alexius had obtained the consent of the clergy. Eustratius earned the emperor's favour and protection by writing against Leon, and his own election to the metropolitan seat of Nicaea was no doubt due to his connection with the emperor.

In 1111, Eustratius, as an official court theologian, expounded with others in the presence of Alexius the Byzantine position against Petrus Grossolanus, archbishop of Milan and representative of Pope Paschalis II, during one of the many fruitless attempts to reconcile East and West after the schism of 1054. Eustratius' position against the use of unleavened bread for Mass and against the doctrine teaching the 'procession' (*proodos*) of the Holy Ghost *from* the Son is found in several small *opuscula* which originated during these discussions.

In 1114, Eustratius accompanied Alexius to his summer residence in Philippopoli, where the emperor, duly supported by Eustratius, conducted a series of conferences against the monophysite heresy of the 'Armenians, Manicheans, or Bogomils'. Eustratius on this occasion wrote a dialectical discourse against the Armenian Tigranes on the two natures of Christ, a model of its kind, and the rough draft of two treatises on the same subject. The latter two were based on a text of St Cyril of Alexandria

---

(1117)', *Byzantinische Zeitschrift* 47, 1954, 369-78; id., 'Le sort des évêques hérétiques réconciliés. Un discours inédit de Nicétas de Serres contre Eustrate de Nicée', *Byzantion* 28, 1958, 1-30; K. Giocarinis, 'Eustratius of Nicaea's defense of the doctrine of Ideas', *Franciscan Studies* 24, 1964, 159-204; A.C. Lloyd, 'The Aristotelianism of Eustratios of Nicaea', *Aristoteles: Werk und Wirkung II*, J. Weisner (ed.) 1987, 341-51.

which Eustratius had explained in an unorthodox way. These *opuscula* were taken away from him – so he defended himself later – by some unknown person before they were finished; they were then copied and brought into circulation without his knowledge or consent. The theologians of the court thereupon accused Eustratius of heresy. He had defended the eternal subservience of the human element of Christ to God the Father. Trying to save his favourite, the emperor presided personally over the synod of April 17, 1117, together with the patriarch of Constantinople. There, Eustratius addressed himself to the emperor, the patriarch, and the synod in a written confession (*exomologêsis*), in which he told of the fate of the incriminated writings and revoked and condemned all errors in any form contained in them. They were, he explained apologetically, the result of his ignorance and carelessness, but he had never believed in them. A few days later the synod was urged by the patriarch to show clemency, but neither the effort of Alexius nor that of the patriarch could save Eustratius from suspension *a divinis* for life.

The arguments that won the case for his enemies are preserved in the discourse of Nicetas of Serrai at the last meeting of the synod: Eustratius was a heresiarch, founder of a new heresy, and for such there had never been a precedent of pardon, unless the point had not been defined by a Council, a condition which did not apply to Eustratius' case; moreover, the heresy had already been present in his first works on the question of the Icons, so that it was not true that he had never believed in it; finally, he had violated his signature on the letter anathematising John Italus' teaching.

Eustratius was suspended as a heresiarch in spite of imperial protection. One can only speculate about the political intrigues surrounding the trial, but the doctrinal implications are fairly clear. As in the case of John Italus, not only were specific doctrines condemned, but through them also a certain spirit. Of the twenty-four propositions summarising the errors found in Eustratius' two *libelli* against the Armenians, the last two are directly aimed at the use of dialectics in theology. The twenty-third condemned proposition affirms the necessity of relying on the power of dialectical reasoning (*tês tekhnês ton logon kai tês epistêmês tên epikheirêsin*) in order to speak truly about the Incarnation, whereas the last one reads: 'That Christ in all of his sacred and divine sayings reasons in Aristotelian syllogisms (*sullogizetai aristotelikôs*)'.

There is no doubt that the action was aimed at the dialectician in the theologian Eustratius, follower of John Italus. Eustratius had inherited from Italus the method of not relying on authorities – they are at most starting points for a dialectical discussion – but on formal syllogistic reasoning for solving doubtful problems. His dialogue on the question of the Icons presents Philosynethes (the friend of tradition) and Philalethes (the friend of truth) in what has all the characteristics of a scholastic debate, with questions and answers and a frequent recourse to syllogisms in their several forms. The two characters may well be interpreted as representing *in abstracto* the position of Leon and Eustratius, respectively.

The treatise on the same subject is an excellent example of how Eustratius uses dialectics in theology. It ends significantly with a formula stating that there is still more to say by means of arguments (*logismois*) that 'scratch' (*epixainousin*) the very problem, but that this will suffice to the intelligent.

The same dialectical method is characteristic of Eustratius' discourses against Petrus Grossolanus and of his treatise against the Armenians. This is in fact reflected in the title of the latter: 'Refutation of those who attribute one nature to Christ, our most true God, on the basis of logical, physical, and theological arguments, from which it is demonstrated necessarily (*ek logikôn kai phusikôn kai theologikôn epikheirêseôn ex hôn deiknutai anankaiôs*) that Christ, my Saviour, consists of two natures.' The work, which introduces itself as an 'exercise' on an already accepted truth, indeed contains pages and pages of sorites.

That Eustratius understood the accusation in this sense is brought out by a passage from his *exomologêsis*:

> He who says that one must syllogise about the indemonstrable principles of faith, and about those things about which the saints [the recognised Fathers of the Church] did not syllogise – as some have suspected us to say –, that he be rejected, not only as impious, but also as stupid and silly.

The very phrasing of this curious *anathema* betrays Eustratius' naturalistic bent of mind. He seems to allow for the possibility of an unintended heresy on his part, but not for that of having attempted a logical impossibility.

Eustratius, then, was a theologian whose use of philosophical arguments, especially of Aristotelian syllogisms, became detrimental to his career.

His surviving philosophical work, apart from a short scientific treatise, is limited to three commentaries, each of them explaining one book of a work of Aristotle: one on Book 2 of the *Posterior Analytics*,[9] one on Book 1 and one on Book 6 of the *Nicomachean Ethics*.

The scientific treatise concerns metereological, cosmological and astronomical matters and is addressed to 'the empress Lady Anna of Alania', the spouse of Michael VII Ducas, who himself had been a pupil of Psellus.[10] It was composed at her request. It is extant in two manuscripts, a Venetian and Parisian one. However, the Parisian MS lacks the beginning, has three chapters more than the Venetian one, and is on the whole more scientific in style and content than the latter. Since certain passages are similar to *loci* in Michael Psellus' *de Omnifaria Doctrina*

---

[9] *CAG* 21.1.

[10] Edited by Paola Polesso Schiavon, 'Un trattato inedito de meteorologia di Eustrazio di Nicea', *Rivista di studi bizantini e neoellenici*, n.s. 2-3 (xii-xiii), *Atti del primo congresso nazionale*, Ravenna, 23-5 maggio 1965, Rome 1965-6, 285-304.

and *Solutiones quaedam ad imperatorem Michaelem Ducan*, and the treatise shares with the *Solutiones* a common scheme of dividing the matter into short chapters and a dedication to a member of the imperial family, Psellus may be the direct source of Eustratius' little work. It looks as if the Parisian text is a collection of material that Eustratius found available at the Academy, whereas the Venetian version seems to be adapted to the requirements of educating the empress. Eustratius may have obtained the material in a number of ways, either as a student or specifically at the occasion of the empress's request. From all this it appears that the treatise probably belongs to Eustratius' early years and that he was acquainted with the Byzantine imperial family before the rise of Alexius I Comnenus. In any case, he was a person to whom women of that family would turn for instruction.

The commentary on the *Posterior Analytics* confirms Eustratius' interest in Aristotle's theory of syllogistic demonstration and continues the tradition of John Italus. The commentaries on the *Ethics* too reveal an acquaintance with Aristotle's logic, especially by frequently working out arguments in their explicit syllogistic form, often with their Aristotelian label of figure and mood attached to them.

This procedure, common to the commentaries on Books 1 and 6, marks Eustratius as the author of both. There is no doubt that they are the work of the same man, and that this man is Eustratius. This is well attested by the manuscript tradition. The generally accepted view has rightly ignored Schleiermacher's arguments against a common authorship of both partial commentaries on the *Ethics*. I mention them only because our Latin text provides us with the answer to Schleiermacher's strongest objection.

After having touched on some general differences between the two books, which can easily be explained by a lapse of years and by a growth in both knowledge and maturity of the author, Schleiermacher claimed to have found serious discrepancies in (a) the explanation of Aristotle's 'exoteric' *logoi* (*exôterikoi logoi*) given in the two commentaries and (b) their prologues. As regards (a), Book 1 (111,21ff) divides Aristotle's treatises into *acroamatic* and *exoteric* as follows: the former were written for the benefit of an audience, his pupils, whereas the latter were addressed to correspondents outside the school. Book 6 (298,30-31), however, explains that the *logoi* expressing the common view of the multitude outside the scientific tradition are called *exoteric* by Aristotle.

The second inconsistency (b), according to Schleiermacher, involves the prologue of both commentaries. Book 6, on the one hand, starts with a formal dedication in the usual, elaborate, highflown Byzantine style, in the second person, addressed to a God-fearing, *logos*-loving, goodness-and-beauty-loving *basilis* (royal lady). Robert Browning's hypothesis (see Chapter 17 above) that this was Anna Comnena, if not certain, is at least the best conjecture. Schleiermacher offered as candidates the queen of Cyprus and Maria of Alania, spouse of Michael VII Ducas, for whom Eustratius wrote the scientific treatise. But that work dates from his early youth.

In his dedication, Eustratius, conforming to the accepted literary canon, belittles himself as much as possible; he invokes his old age and recalls that some time ago (*pro khronou tinos*) the royal lady had requested from him an explanation of the first book of Aristotle's *Nicomachean Ethics*, which task he then performed in all due obedience. The prologue of Book 1, on the other hand, only mentions a certain person of the highest worth, who had requested the work; a refusal was out of the question, since this person had been a benefactor in many a difficulty. Eustratius could not have referred to the royal lady in this way, Schleiermacher argues, even if she had not wished to be named, and certainly not without some sort of apology, when he finally broke the silence in Book 6, for previously having mentioned her in such a remote manner.

The first argument can easily be disposed of. The lapse in time between the two commentaries may be held responsible for the fact that Eustratius did not recognise the expression 'the exoteric *logoi*' when he commented upon it for the second time. These are not two incompatible accounts of the technical expression 'exoteric *logoi*'. Only in Book 1 does the commentator understand the expression as denoting a class of Aristotle's works; in Book 6 he understand *logoi* in their most common sense of 'opinions' or 'arguments' and the expression 'the exoteric *logoi*' as referring to 'exoteric beliefs'.

The second argument is a serious one. Some curious facts emerge, however, with respect to the passage in Book 1 referring to the solicitor of the commentary (*in EN* 1,13-23). First, the reference is indeed surprisingly vague, a fact which remains puzzling even if Eustratius is not the author. Further, this is not an independent dedication or preface, but it is grammatically conjoined to a main sentence as a genitive absolute and in content interrupts the line of thought – which is to place, by way of a general introduction, Aristotle's *Ethics* in the framework of the whole of his philosophy. Finally, the passage is completely absent in Grosseteste's translation, and must have been lacking in his Greek manuscript.

There is no doubt, then, that this passage is an interpolation, an attempt to make the beginning of Book 1 conform to the dedication of Book 6.[11] It restricts the commentary to the first book of the *Nicomachean Ethics*, whereas at this point the introduction still envisages the whole of the *Ethics*. This conclusion is confirmed by the interpolation, equally unknown to Grosseteste, of the words *hou kai tên exêgêsin apêithêmetha* (*in EN* 4,9), 'an interpretation of which has been requested from us', referring to Book 1, to which at this point the commentary *is* restricted. Both references to a request for a commentary in the beginning of Book 1 are interpolations. The original text kept silent on that point.

This clarification of an otherwise puzzling fact illustrates how useful

---

[11] Thus V. Rose's intuition is vindicated: 'despite the alteration of the prologues which has to be assumed after a comparison of them' (op. cit., 70).

the comparison of the Greek text with the Latin translation of Grosseteste can be.

If Eustratius continued in his commentaries on the *Ethics* to make explicit use of the Aristotelian syllogistic forms, he nevertheless showed himself more a Platonist than an Aristotelian in his explanation.

This was made possible by the type of commentary Eustratius had chosen. His exegeses of Books 1 and 6 are commentaries in the fullest sense of the word. They are not primarily concerned with explaining particular passages, phrases, or words in the text, but with interpreting the very scope, design, and impact of Aristotle's *Ethics*. Eustratius interprets the work from his own theological-philosophical point of view, which is that of a Christian.

This Christian outlook pervades both commentaries. The prologue of Book 1 presents the Old Testament figures Abraham, Isaac, Jacob and Job as exemplary heads of of households, and Moses and Jesus Naue (Joshua) as exemplary statesmen. It contrasts the ancient sages (pagan thinkers) with 'ourselves' (Christians), where they 'call the end of human life happiness, whereas we call it beatitude'. It describes this end as the 'union with God in the indwelling One, which is called the flower of the Intellect by the great Dionysius'. Finally, the prologue concludes by invoking the assistance of 'the Cause of all good' in this (the commentary on Aristotle) as well as in all else. The commentary on the opening sentence of the *Nicomachean Ethics* reminds the reader that 'we are created after the image of God' and that it is 'our' aspiration to 'behold the Word and through It the Father', since 'nobody comes to the Father but through Me'. Other passages in Book 1 refer to the Christian martyrs and to the hermits;[12] the life of the latter is even identified with the 'life of contemplation' of *EN* 1095b19.[13] The prologue of Book 6 ends, as does its predecessor, by invoking God's assistance. The commentary on Book 6 contains a remarkable passage, several pages long, against the carnal philosophy of the 'pseudoprophet', Mohammed.[14]

Eustratius' Christian outlook, however, is cast in a philosophical mould. This philosophy can aptly be described as a 'Christian Neoplatonism'. Ethical growth is depicted as a journey upward, during which the soul goes through four stages:[15] (1) the moderation of passions; (2) the mortification of passions, leading to *'apatheia'*; (3) the participation in the Intellect; and (4) the union with God, who is the Primary Good, identified with 'the Good at which everything aims' of *EN* 1094a3.[16]

Eustratius sees the life of the passions, that is, the life of enjoyment or pleasure, as the natural life of the child, but one becomes practised in the moral virtues in order to leave that life behind for one of civic virtue, a

---

[12] *in EN* 35, 33-7 and 7, 9-12.
[13] cf. ibid. 7,9-12 with 34,23-8.
[14] ibid. 272,3-277,17.
[15] ibid. 4,25-38. See also below.
[16] ibid. 6,5-8.

middle stage between the life of the passions and that of contemplation. The *Nicomachean Ethics* is, for Eustratius, an exploration of the virtues of this middle sort of life, the life of the political man. To the following stages belong the 'purgative or purifying' life and the life of contemplation.[17] Aristotle provides only a few scattered hints in the earlier books, and devotes only a few chapters in Book 10 to describing the life of contemplation, the highest sort of life. Eustratius thus has relative freedom to wax neoplatonistically eloquent about man's pathway toward participation in the true intellect and in the uninterrupted activity of reason, and finally toward the mystical union with God.[18] Eustratius sees the life of the intellect as being particularly pursued by the Christian hermit, who seeks the happiness of unity with God 'in solitude'. When Aristotle comments at 1101b18, 'We call the most godlike men blessed and happy', Eustratius finds the occasion to say:

> These are the ones who have completely broken their relation with matter and found life outside the flesh and the world, above all visible things; their intellect is united with the divine natures; it converses with them and is exalted together with them; they live always in act, while reflecting the first light in an uninterrupted way.[19]

This strong support of the mystical and monastic life, in the context of a commentary on Aristotle's *Nicomachean Ethics*, was bound to influence western writers who already tended to see mysticism and monasticism in a favourable light.

Eustratius also develops a strong defence of Plato's theory of Forms, in the context of his commentary on *EN* 1.6.[20] He thinks that when Aristotle criticises the form of the Good in that chapter, he is inconsistent, since he has already conceded that there is 'a good at which all things aim', in the first chapter of the book. He clearly interprets Aristotle's rather semantic remark (the word 'good' means that at which something aims) as a definition of the *transcendent* Good. Later, Eustratius offers another definition of good: good as a quality of beings, good as the 'order' of beings; good is the universal ordering, the harmony, the cosmos; and evil is lack of order and disharmony.[21] The order of the universe, for the Neoplatonist, is found both in the immanent forms, taken to be identical to the Aristotelian species, genera, and perhaps categories, and in the *Logos* which transcends those forms. The link between the two meanings is given by Eustratius in a third definition of the good: the good of beings is a participation in the transcendent good: *participatio primi boni*. There is then, *pace* Aristotle (*EN* 1096a29-34), one science of all good things *qua* good, which is nothing other than metaphysics, the science of all beings

---

[17] ibid. 34,19-31.

[18] ibid. 4,25-8.

[19] ibid. 106,19-32; cf. 63,29-33.

[20] ibid. 39,24ff. See K. Giocarinis, 'Eustratius of Nicaea's defense of the doctrine of Ideas', 159-204.

[21] *in EN* 46,29-31.

qua being. Eustratius reserves for this science the name of 'theology'. The ultimate aim of the intellect is to know God, to know the order, and to participate fully in the universal unity.

As Eustratius sees it, Aristotle's criticisms of Plato are mistaken in that they impute to Plato transcendent *concepts*, universals in the Aristotelian sense, whereas Plato intended to assert the existence of *causes*. A.C. Lloyd attempted in a recent article to 'place' Eustratius in the whole of the Aristotelian tradition precisely with respect to his attitude towards the Platonic Ideas and more generally with respect to his view of universals:[22] 'Eustratius shows himself an able philosopher in the tradition passed on from Psellos to John Italos ... This consists in the standard combination of Aristotle and Neoplatonism, in which Aristotle's universals are concepts with a non-mental existence or *hupostasis* ... in the individual forms of individual substances and their accidents.' This interpretation of Aristotle – Lloyd calls it a form of 'conceptualism' – is, he claims rightly, not specially characteristic of the Neoplatonists: 'It would be difficult to find a philosophically trained Byzantine who did not take it for granted.' It originated with the Alexandrians, 'but Eustratius' version of the logico-metaphysical problem is in some respects more subtle' than theirs. 'No one acquainted with late Byzantine Aristotle commentators will look for originality in their suggestions', but 'in their style of exposition and their selection from traditional points of view.' Eustratius shows himself a follower of the Neoplatonists in keeping close to Proclus' *locus classicus*[23] of 'three ways of understanding' universals or 'wholes': (i) before the parts (*hôs pro tôn merôn*), (ii) out of the parts (*hôs ek tôn merôn*), (iii) in the part (*hôs en tôi merei*) and in defending 'not just the existence of the Ideas as archetypes but their function, explicit in Proclus, as efficient causes'.

Eustratius' commentary on *EN* 6 contains a further defence of Plato, namely, the defence of the Socratic definition of virtue as knowledge, against *EN* 1144b17-21. Here Eustratius explicitly refers to the 'Socrates' of Plato's *Republic*.[24]

To call Eustratius a 'Christian' Neoplatonist, however, is to deny that he was simply a Platonist or Plotinian Neoplatonist. His long and passionate defence of Plato in Book 1 concludes paradoxically: 'We do not say this as proponents of the Ideas, since those who wish to abolish the Ideas may have no difficulty refuting these words.' Eustratius no doubt felt that several aspects in regard to his exposition of Plato's theory of Ideas had to be reinterpreted in a Christian light, e.g. the place and

[22] A.C. Lloyd, op. cit. in n. 8 above. The author bases his account on the parallel passage of *in An. Post.*, CAG 21.1, 195,5ff and *in EN*, CAG 20, 40,22ff, but starts from the former commentary. He does not mention Giocarinis' article (op. cit.), which is restricted to *in EN*, but says that Eustratius there, in following ' "three ways of understanding wholes", ... uses some of his material (at 40,37-41,2) less well than in the *An. Post.* commentary (196,14-16) – if he is not plain confused.' Lloyd does refer to P. Joannou's work (see n. 8 above), adding some critical remarks to the latter's 'Die Definition des Seins ...'

[23] Proclus *Inst.* 67. Cf. Joannes Italos *Quaestiones Quodlibet*, P. Joannou (ed.), 7-8; 16-17.

[24] *in EN* 400,22-401,20.

function of the Demiurge, the relation of the Ideas to God, the relation of first being to the One, and the doctrine of emanation. He probably wanted to avoid the fate of Psellus, who had been accused of being a follower of Plato against Christ. Eustratius must have felt also that such a reinterpretation of Plato could hardly be undertaken in a commentary on Aristotle's *Ethics*. He agrees with Aristotle that the problem of the Idea of the Good is a metaphysical – Eustratius says 'theological' – one and falls outside the scope of ethics.

This leads to another observation concerning Eustratius as a commentator. Whereas he identifies, in a truly Platonic fashion, metaphysics and theology, he never so much as hints at a possible distinction between what has later been called 'speculative', 'philosophical', or 'natural' theology on the one hand and 'positive' theology, based on revelation, on the other.

To summarise, Eustratius' commentaries on Books 1 and 6 of the *Ethics* suffer from the typically Byzantine defect of being long-winded and verbose and they are not impressively systematic in structure, but they are very important as an interpretation of the *Nicomachean Ethics* from the point of view of a Christian Neoplatonist. By the same token, however, they are defective as a tool for a better understanding of Aristotle's genuine thoughts. Readers with different points of view have appreciated the work differently. Schleiermacher, for instance, has nothing but praise, while Gauthier finds much to blame.[25]

Such was the work and the life of the man whom Anna Comnena has described as 'skilled in the sacred and the profane sciences, more confident in dialectics than those who frequent the Stoa and the Academy'.[26]

The ancient anonymous scholia

The anonymous 'commentary' on Books 2, 3, 4 and 5 differs greatly from that of Eustratius. It is referred to in the book titles of the manuscripts as *skholia*. It is indeed a collection of scholia, that is to say explanatory notes of various content, which follow the text of the *Ethics* very closely, instead of a commentary concerned with the overall philosophical interpretation of the work. The scholia explain the meaning and use of certain words, give a wealth of historical and literary information by way of illustration (including quotations from classical sources, some of which are otherwise unknown or lost), or are philosophical in content – that is, they clarify an argument, explain technical notions, compare a Peripatetic thesis with or defend it against the view of a rival school: Plato, the Epicureans, the Stoics, or others. Scholia of the last type are especially useful for a better understanding of the text of Aristotle, since they are thoroughly Aristotelian in spirit. The scholia contain a considerable number of

[25] cf. R.A. Gauthier, *L'Éthique à Nicomaque*[2] ..., vol. 1, part 1, 105.
[26] Anna Comnena *Alexias* xiv,8.

references to Plato, who is often cited in support of Aristotle, to other works of Aristotle, to Theophrastus, and to the Stoics, who are openly attacked.

It is always difficult to date scholia. They may have accumulated over many years and be the work of several scholiasts; they are a collection of notes and excerpts from various sources. The evidence in this case, however, strongly suggests that the scholia on Books 2, 3, 4, and 5 were compiled by one man, or at least in one school, just before the end of the second century of our era. They show no Christian influence, except perhaps in Book 5, where one finds the three words 'So also Absalom' at the end of the story of Phoenix's liaison with his father's concubine.[27] They form, no doubt, a late gloss, which it was easy to add at the end of the paragraph.[28]

There are no quotations or references to any author later than Lucian. This negative argument finds a strong confirmation in a positive time index, contained in Book 5. The passage defends the Aristotelian doctrine that corporeal and external goods are to a degree necessary for happiness against the Stoic doctrine which stresses the all-sufficiency of virtue. In the very beginning of Book 4, the scholiast had already presented an argument against the division of virtue as the only good, vice as the only evil, and the rest, including wealth, as being neither good nor bad, but only potentially good or bad, depending on the use one makes of it. Here the doctrine of *ta adiaphora*, things indifferent, that is to say, intermediary between good and bad, is attacked again. Justice, whether distributive or retributive, must be useless for the proponents of the *adiaphora*-theory, 'among whom previously Aristonymus belonged, but *now* even some who pretend to be Platonists, while surreptitiously introducing this doctrine, among whom also *Atticus* appears to belong'.[29] The attacks on Aristotle by the Middle Platonist Atticus, including the above extreme doctrine, are well known from Eusebius. Atticus was active under Marcus Aurelius (AD 161-180).

The strict Aristotelian character of the scholia suggests also that their final form dates from the period before the school was to all intents and purposes absorbed in Neoplatonism; that is, before the end of the third century.

On the other hand, the references to Lucian and Atticus place the time of final composition of our 'commentary' definitely after Aspasius, the Peripatetic commentator of the first half of the second century. Since Aspasius' commentary has some material in common with the anonymous scholia, the latter must contain excerpts from the former, unless they have both drawn from a third source.

---

[27] *in EN* 229,22. For the story of Phoenix see: *Iliad* 9. 452; of Absalom: II Sam. 16:21-2.

[28] Rose's supposition (op. cit., 82) that this was an addition by Robert Grosseteste can only be understood by realising that he did not have access to the Greek text of the anonymous scholia on Book 5. Paul Moraux's remark, 'his statements about the origin of this addition would have to have been checked, however' (*Der Aristotelismus bei den Griechen*, vol. 2, 329 n. 146), has no ground.

[29] *in EN* 248,24-6 (italics mine).

The excerpts from Adrastus' monograph

A. Kenny suggested in 1987 the identification of the anonymous scholiast on Books 2-4 as Adrastus of Aphrodisias.[30] That Adrastus wrote a book on the *Nicomachean Ethics* is asserted by Athenaeus.[31] However, Adrastus lived in the first half of the second century and can hardly have made a reference to Atticus or have quoted Lucian. Moreover, the scholia are clearly a compilation from various sources. On the other hand, a good deal of them show unmistakably the characteristics ascribed to Adrastus' monograph, *Peri tôn kath' historian kai lexin zêtoumenôn* (*On historical and literary questions*), in that work. This has been abundantly shown by P. Moraux.[32]

Concerning Adrastus' chronology, Moraux has established that his commentary on Plato's *Timaeus* dates from before the year 147, whereas Galen's reference to the commentaries of Adrastus and Aspasius on Aristotle's *Categories* from about the middle of the century suggests that Adrastus was a perhaps younger contemporary of Aspasius'. This suggestion arises from the fact that he is named with, and before, Aspasius and that Galen 'heard' in his youth an unnamed pupil of the latter's in Pergamon.

Adrastus is best known for his influential commentary on the *Timaeus*, in which he incorporated contemporary theories of mathematical astronomy (eccentric spheres or epicycles) into the Platonic-Aristotelian cosmology, and for his *On the Order of Aristotle's Works*, quoted more than once by Simplicius and being chiefly philological in character. Nothing remains from his commentary on the *Categories*. Galen recommends it, together with that of Aspasius, for new students in philosophy, and Porphyry mentions that Plotinus used their *hupomnê- mata* among those of others, without explicitly mentioning the *Categories*. An important fragment from what in all likelihood was a commentary on Aristotle's *Physics* has been transmitted by Simplicius through Porphyry.

Adrastus' five books on Theophrastus' *Characters* and the sixth one on the *Nicomachean Ethics* of Aristotle have already been mentioned, together with their historical and literary nature. Moraux was rightly

[30] Anthony Kenny, *The Aristotelian Ethics. A study of the relationship between the Eudemian and Nicomachean Ethics of Aristotle*, Oxford 1978, 37 n. 3. Kenny overplays his hand in trying to make the anonymous scholia fit the report on Adrastus' work (see next note), for he first insinuates that Athenaeus speaks of *six* books of Aristotle's *Ethics* and then goes on to argue very cleverly that the second-century collection of scholia extended over exactly six books. The facts are that Athenaeus mentions only one book, be it a *sixth* one, of Adrastus on the *Nicomachean Ethics* and that only four books of the ancient anonymous scholia are extant.

[31] Athenaeus 15,673e-f: 'for our fine Adrastus has published five books on the historical and literary questions in Theophrastus' *Characters* and a sixth on those in the *Nicomachean Ethics* of Aristotle.'

[32] Paul Moraux, *Der Aristotelismus bei den Griechen* vol. 2, covers Adrastus, 294-332: chronology, 294-5; commentary on the *Timaeus*, 296-313; *On the Order of Aristotle's works*, 314-17; interpretation of Aristotle, 317-23; monograph on the *Ethics*, 323-30.

impressed by the richness and scholarly tenor of the anonymous scholia
that are of this kind, in contrast with the fairly indifferent character of
those that are not.

Moraux identified and described in detail the passages that qualify as
excerpts from Adrastus' work.[33] He did this by going through Heylbut's
Index nominum (and probably also the *Index verborum*) in so far as it refers
to the pages containing the anonymous scholia. These are the scholia
exhibiting a philological, literary or historical bias. They differ from those
that contain discussions with other schools of philosophy, offer philosophical analyses, or simply paraphrase Aristotle's text. The excerpts from
Adrastus show an interest in Atticism, a good acquaintance with Theophrastus' ethical works, but above all with Attic tragedy, with comedy, and
with historical sources.

In my further account of the ancient scholia book by book, I shall confine
myself to identifying the (groups of) scholia that may be considered as
excerpts from Adrastus' monograph. The reference to Lucian may be seen
as a later addition in an otherwise Adrastan context, but the one to Atticus
must belong to a scholion written entirely by the compiler himself.
Although nothing excludes the possibility that some gloss has been added
later on, the only evidence for such an addition is contained in the note on
Absalom.

The scholia on Book 2

The scholia on Book 2 have the following characteristics. First, they do
not form a comprehensive commentary. The text of the scholia is less
than twice the length of Aristotle's text, although each gloss gives a
rather detailed explanation of or comment on an expression in the text.
Secondly, two alternative explanations are often proffered. This suggests
a conflation of two scholia from different sources. Thirdly, there are
occurrences of a definition of a word being followed, a few pages later, by
the introduction of another definition, based on a different meaning. This
again suggests a compilation from different sources. Fourthly, sometimes
the same thought is repeated in different words, no doubt because the
scholiast had not perceived the identity in meaning or else wanted to
preserve the difference in form: another indication of a compilation from
different sources.

As to their content, the glosses frequently interpret the text of Aristotle
by adding a word or a phrase that was, supposedly, understood but not
expressed by Aristotle or that lays stress on an otherwise inconspicuous
expression of his. Other glosses give synonyms, offer definitions, or
explain by means of typically Aristotelian notions or principles.
Elsewhere concrete examples or literary quotations illustrate the

---

[33] 327-30.

meaning of the text. They are most likely taken from Adrastus.[34] Finally, the scholiast expresses several times approval of a thought or an expression in the *Ethics*.[35]

Plato is referred to three times, but the first reference is taken from Aristotle's text.[36] The scholiast remarks on the strength of *EN* 1104b24-5 that the doctrine which defines virtue as *apatheia* is older than the Stoa, and notes Aristotle's correction: virtue is not an unqualified *apatheia*, but a qualified one, that is, only in regard to faulty passions. Some Platonist is reported to have applauded the Stoic view as a Platonic thesis.[37]

On the whole, the short collection of scholia on Book 2 stays very close to both the letter and the spirit of Aristotle's text and shows some concern with the rival school of the Stoa. The attitude toward the Academy is ambiguous as was that of Aristotle himself: a mixture of admiration for Plato and criticism of the Platonists.

The scholia on Book 3

The scholia on Book 3, although more numerous than those on Book 2, have similar characteristics. However, the literary and historical references are, even in proportion, much more prominent. The scholiast has no doubt made extensive use of Adrastus' commentary.

In the first place, explanations are given for such references in the text of Aristotle. Alcmaeon killed his mother in Euripides' play (*EN* 1110a28) because his father had ordered it. The scholiast cites two different sources to explain why Alcmaeon obeyed the unusual order, thus revealing that he had no access to the text of the play: according to one source the motive was pity (not to distress his father), according to the other, which quotes a verse from the play, it was fear (to avoid his father's curses).[38] Aeschylus

---

[34] Moraux (329 n. 146) rightly judged that the attribution of the verses from *Iliad* 18.109-10 to Heraclitus (*in EN* 129,1-3) was a mistake of the copyist (probably the compiler) who was confused by the philosopher's name at 128,32 (in fact *EN* 2.3, 1105a8).

[35] e.g., *in EN* 122,9: *kalôs de touto* (good). The approval is often expressed by means of the words *kalôs* (good) (see also *in EN* 125,16 and 138,24), but not always: see for instance *in EN* 126,21: *panu anthrôpinôs* (very humane).

[36] *in EN* 127,5; 136,28; 137,8.

[37] ibid., 127,7.

[38] The whole scholion is probably Adrastus'. The text (*in EN* 142,22ff) is not very sound. Heylbut, following the Aldine edition (= *a*), drops *touton* (attested by B) before *hôi* on line 22, but Robert Grosseteste read *touton, phasin, hôi* (*hunc aiunt cui*). This is the commonly accepted view, against which the scholiast cites another authority (line 24). Heylbut has: *allôs. parentithetai ton <par'> Euripidêi Alkmaiôna hôs* .... Both *a* and B read *Euripidên*, the preposition is wanting in B. Again, Grosseteste seems to have had the correct reading: *allos palin tithetai ton par' Euripidêi Alkmaiôna hôs* ... (*Alius rursus ponit apud Euripidem Alcmeona ut* ...). What has happened is clear. The forgotten preposition, whose disappearance has been the cause of the accusative *Euripidên*, must have been corrected in the margin, from where it has been taken to replace *palin*. There are many disturbances in the text, for instance, the last three words of the preceding sentence are completely turned around in *a* and Grosseteste's original as against B, this time followed by Heylbut. That the scholiast and not just the second source is likely to be Adrastus is suggested by the construction *phasin*, which we find elsewhere used in similar circumstances, e.g. in the

is said to have divulged the Mysteries (*EN* 1111a10) in several of his plays, named by the scholiast, who refers to the historian Heraclides Ponticus for the story of Aeschylus' trial and acquittal and cites his epitaph. The error of Merope (*EN* 1111a12) is explained with reference to Euripides' lost play *Cresphon*. The Homeric quotations in Aristotle (*EN* 1116a23-6 and 34-5) are identified and completed.

Further, Aristotle's sayings are illustrated by concrete examples, most of which are mythological or historical: for instance, Zopyrus, Odysseus, and Dolon, each in a different way, did something distasteful in order to obtain a certain good, whereas Anaxarchus and Zeno bravely suffered torture without being swayed into committing a disgraceful act. The *Iliad* is a favourite source for such examples. Further quotations in various contexts are: one from a third lost play by Euripides, the *Erechtheus*; two from the comedian Epicharmus, one of them from a play called *Hêraklês ho para Pholôi*; one from Hesiod's *Hai megalai Éoiai*; one from Isocrates' *Panegyric*; and one from Lucian's *Somnium*. There is a reference to Pittacus, 'one of the seven wise men', and one to the lyric poet Tyrtaeus. A considerable number of historians are appealed to, among others Herodotus, Cephisodorus, Anaximenes, and Ephorus.

All the material discussed in the last two paragraphs, including the quotation from Lucian, coincides with whatever is known of Adrastus' interest in his book on Aristotle's *Nicomachean Ethics*. There are also several references to Plato. The most important one concerns Aristotle's argument that man is responsible either for both the good and the evil he does or for neither; that is, either both good and evil actions are done intentionally (*hekousiôs*) or neither are. The scholiast notes that this dilemma is directed against Plato. Thus, the Socratic paradox is ascribed to Plato himself.[39]

Whereas Epicharmus is quoted as placing man's good in labour, Callicles 'in Plato' and Epicurus are cited as placing it in pleasure. In this connection Protagoras' thesis of relativism is brought in, but the question is resolved in an Aristotelian manner: each person, according to his acquired *hexis*, will strive either after the genuine good or after a seeming good.[40] Also cited is Epicurus' division of desires into necessary and natural, not necessary and natural, and neither necessary nor natural,[41] but Aristotle is said to have used such a distinction before the Epicureans.

There are references to the *Topics* and to other works of Aristotle's, including one to his treatise *On Pleasure*,[42] probably his treatment of the subject in Book 10 of the *Nicomachean Ethics*.

---

discussion about the meaning of *ponêros* with the accent on the last syllable at *in EN* 1113b14 and of the Atticism *ponêros* with the accent on the first syllable, where we read *phasi ... alla phamen ...* (*in EN* 155,4-8).

[39] *in EN* 143,26ff.
[40] ibid. 153,19-154,8.
[41] ibid. 171, 23-8.
[42] ibid. 154,15-16.

One scholion appears to be a gloss on the one that precedes it: 'Fate (*to heimarmenon*) also would be classified by these people under nature, for it is neither unalterable nor necessary.'[43] The present quotation and many other discussions about nature reveal the preoccupation of the scholiast with the Stoa.

Earlier on, in the beginning of the book, a discussion on whether 'voluntary' and 'involuntary' have each one or more senses seems to reflect imperfectly a similar discussion that has found its way into problem 11 of the *Ethical Problems*, attributed to Alexander of Aphrodisias.[44]

Finally, there is a distinct interest in linguistic usage, especially in Atticism, e.g. when the use of *ponêros*, with the acute accent on the first syllable, is explained as an Atticism.[45] In the discussion on the meaning of *ouden pro ergou*, *EN* 1113b27, the Attic custom is appealed to, together with Isocrates.[46] Such passages again show Adrastus' hand.[47]

To sum up, the scholia on Book 3 show the same characteristics as those on Book 2; they contain, however, more references to and quotations from various literary and historical sources, most likely culled from Adrastus, and they are engaged in philosophical discussions, not only with the Stoa, but also with Plato, Epicurus, and several minor schools.

Concerning the philosophical interpretation of Aristotle's text, it is worth mentioning that F. Becchi has pointed out the positive role attributed by the anonymous scholiast to the passions in the constitution of moral virtue.[48] Becchi draws attention, for instance, to *in EN* 130,25: 'For passions (*pathê*) are the starting points for actions', which he contrasts with *EN* 1139a31, where deliberate choice (*proairesis*) is said to be the principle of action. We should see in this, he maintains, a functional adaptation of Aristotelianism in order successfully to answer rival theories. He cites similar passages in the *Magna Moralia*, Stobaeus, Aspasius and Alexander of Aphrodisias, and thinks on tenuous grounds that the change goes back to Theophrastus.[49] The scholion, however, does

---

[43] ibid. 150,2-4.

[44] See R.W. Sharples, 'Ambiguity and opposition: Alexander of Aphrodisias, *Ethical Problems* 11', *Bulletin of the Institute of Classical Studies* 32, 1985, 109-16.

[45] *in EN* 155,1-17. This passage contains already mentioned quotations from Hesiod and Epicharmus of Syracuse.

[46] From the *Panegyric*, as is already mentioned. The work is not named, however, probably because it was well known.

[47] We find the quotation from Lucian neatly tacked on the last of these scholia. If it is an addition from a pupil of Adrastus', some of the other 'Adrastan' notes may be his too.

[48] F. Becchi, 'Variazioni funzionali nei *Magna Moralia*: La virtù come impulso razionale al bene', *Prometheus* 6, 1980, 201-26, at 225. Becchi has developed the concept of 'functional Aristotelianism' in a series of articles in *Prometheus* between 1975 and 1983 on Peripatetic ethics, from the anonymous author of *Magna Moralia* to Plutarch's *de Virtute Morali*. This is an Aristotelianism that has adapted itself to the problems raised by its confronting rival schools. Becchi therefore questions the labelling of certain key notions in late Peripatetic ethical writings as Middle Platonist.

[49] It is doubtful that these philosophical discussions have their source in Adrastus, whereas the reference to the moral works of Theophrastus – the only hard evidence Becchi cites – concerns only the character of Simonides, in a scholion that is almost certainly from Adrastus (*in EN* 180,16-17).

not contradict 1139a31, because Aristotle himself stresses the dual
nature of deliberate choice (1113a11), a mixture of deliberation and
striving (*orexis*). The latter is the generic term for the activity (or its
faculty) of the irrational part of the soul that 'in a way partakes of reason
insofar as it listens to it and lets itself be persuaded by it' (1102b30). It is
this non-rational element that the scholiast calls passion (*pathos*), as is
clear from a scholion in Book 4 (*in EN* 180,24-5): 'deliberate choice is
deliberative striving (=*EN* 1113a11), and striving is a passion.' Aristotle
never calls striving (*orexis*) (nor willing, *boulêsis*) a passion, but its *species*
appetite (*epithumia*) definitely is one of the passions. To extend the scope
of passion to the whole domain of striving may be a matter of 'functional'
adaptation; it is certainly a question of interpretation.

The scholia on Book 4

The scholia on Book 4 resemble those on 2 and 3. The existence of two
scholia on 1126a21, 'For revenge quells anger' – the second one being out
of place – confirms the hypothesis that this commentary is also a
compilation of glosses from various sources. On the other hand, there are
signs that certain strings of scholia are the work of one scholiast, for
instance, the many references to the second book of the *Nicomachean
Ethics*: one scholiast seems constantly to have kept his eyes on the
summary treatment there of the subject matter of Book 4; and the
scholiast of *in EN* 178,30 explicitly refers to an earlier note of his on Book
3: 'As we also pointed out above in the section on courage ...'[50]
    The following information will give some idea of the kinds of scholia one
encounters here.
    Let us consider as a sample the first three glosses on Book 4.[51] The first
gloss, on *EN* 1119b21-6, is a methodological one: that, concerning which a
virtuous man is praised, is the subject matter (the-things-about-which: *ta
peri ha*) of his virtue, according to Aristotle; for instance, for liberality it is
the giving (and to an extent the acquisition) of money.
    The second gloss, on *EN* 1119b26-7, is a semantic one: *khrêma* means
properly (*kuriôs*) *nomisma* (money) but is also used loosely for *pragma*
(any act, deed, affair, or thing). The philological character of this gloss
points to Adrastus.
    The third gloss, on *EN* 1120a4-5, is a long and interesting one. It
explains *hôn de esti khreia* as meaning *hôn gar esti khrêsis* connects
khreia (use); with *khrômai* (I use); and establishes the difference between
khrêsis (use) and *to khrêsimon* (the useful): *how* we use something is its
use, whereas *what* we thus use is useful. The point, however, is not a
linguistic but a philosophical one. The subject matter of a virtue belongs
to the class of the useful, whereas virtue and vice belong to the class of
uses. The subject matter of each virtue is put to a good use if it is used

[50] *in EN* 168,5ff.
[51] ibid. 176-7.

well (*kalôs*) and to a bad use if used badly (*kakôs*). This invalidates the argument of those (the Stoics) who maintain that virtue alone is good and vice alone evil on the ground that no bad use can be made of virtue nor a good use of vice, but that wealth and other things – called potentially good – are neither good nor evil, on the ground that they can be used either way. According to the scholiast, the argument shows only that virtue is not evil and vice not a good. Moreover, it leads to the conclusion, not that wealth etc. are neither good nor evil, but that they are both. Finally, if what is used badly is either bad or neither good nor bad, Socrates, who was 'used badly' by the Athenians, would be either bad or neither good nor bad. This last note is probably an argument *ad hominem* against the Stoics, whose devotion to Socrates was well known. If this is the case, then the following lines are an addition: 'So would Anaxarchus, who was "badly used" by the tyrant Nicocreon; so also would Zeno', an echo taken from the gloss in Book 2 that connects the fate of these two philosophers.[52] Given the philosophical and polemical nature of this passage, it is most likely not taken from Adrastus as such, but it contains philological and historical material that is typical of his work.

One further gloss, also relating to the Stoics, seems to have two sources:[53]

(i) For not all *lupê* (grief, pain) nor all *pathos* (emotion, passion) is contrary to right reason, as some (*tines*) think, but one can also be grieved 'in the right way', that is, reasonably; but nothing that is done reasonably is sinful (*hêmartêmenon*).

(ii) This is the *lupê* which the Stoics instead of *lupê* call *sustolê* (contraction).

The gloss is on *EN* 1121a2: 'He will be grieved (*lupêsetai*), but moderately and in the right way.' The first part (i) contains the traditional complaint against the Stoics' attitude toward *pathos*, the word being understood in the Peripatetic sense; the second (ii) is a reply drawn from a Stoic source. The word *tines* in (i) is probably an emendation.

One gloss testifies to the existence of the variants *ê* (or) and *kai* (and) of *EN* 1126a28 in the early manuscript tradition of the *Ethics*.

An explanation of Aristotle's terms for 'avaricious people', to which the scholiast adds two terms of his own, and a further differentiation of the wicked man (*akolastos*) into eight types, each with its proper definition, show a Theophrastan interest in character types and terminology.[54] These scholia are almost certainly taken from Adrastus, as are all those on Book 4 that will be mentioned from here on, except those referring to Plato's *Republic*.

Various quotations from and references to comedians occur in two

---

[52] ibid. 143,1-3.
[53] ibid. 180,12-15.
[54] ibid. 182,25-9 and 6-13.

passages or scholia.[55] The first contains quotations from Ecphantides, 'the oldest poet of the ancients', and from Aristophanes' *Wasps*. It announces also a quotation from Myrtilus' *Titanopanes*, but the verses that follow are by Eupolis. Heylbut rightly suspects a lacuna here. The second passage quotes from Araros' *Kampuliôn* and from Plato Comicus' *Elders*, and refers to Aristophanes' *Thesmophoriazusae*. In addition to the comedians, it refers to Clitarchus, the glossographer, and to the historian Xenophon.

Elsewhere another historian, Callisthenes, is referred to *en têi prôtêi tôn Hellênikôn*,[56] and the poet Simonides is said to be remembered as a lover of money by Theophrastus in his *On Customs* and *On Wealth*.[57]

Finally, the glosses on Book 4 contain many references to Homer's *Iliad* and to Plato's *Republic*.

Kenny remarks that the last scholion on Book 4 'appears to promise a discussion of continence by Aristotle in the book after next, rather than as we would expect after two intervening books'.[58] However, the scholiast says only that Aristotle will discuss continence 'after the next book', adding: 'for he stretches out the whole treatise on justice over the book after this one.' The note is a simple paraphrase of Aristotle's closing sentence: 'Neither is continence a virtue, but something mixed. This will be shown later on. But let us now speak of justice.'

The scholia on Book 5

That the anonymous commentary on Book 5 is a compilation of scholia, like its predecessors, is clearly expressed in its title and is further substantiated by its selectiveness. Only certain phrases from Aristotle's text are explained or commented upon. There is, for instance, no introduction proper. The first gloss bypasses Aristotle's opening sentence and concentrates on the methodological implications of the second sentence. Another sign is again the occurrence of mutually exclusive explanations of one and the same notion or phrase – for instance, the twofold explanation of *EN* 1132b9, with the typical connective *ê houtôs* ('or thus:').[59] Finally, several glosses appear out of place.[60]

Stylistic elements, as well as matters of content, connect the scholia on

---

[55] ibid. 186,10-20 and 200,8-18.

[56] ibid. 189,13.

[57] See above.

[58] A. Kenny, *The Aristotelian Ethics*, Oxford 1978, 37.

[59] *in EN* 221,24.

[60] *in EN* 234 contains the same gloss twice with only slight variations (lines 7-18 correspond to 27-34) and *in EN* 254,28-255,1 belongs with *in EN* 254,12 (before *alla pleuritin*). That this is not just a matter of scribal errors is manifest from *in EN* 246,11, where the editor notes 'disturbed order' in his critical apparatus and refers to *in EN* 244,36. The gloss *in EN* 246 is obviously conceived in the way it appears there: words of two different passages are cited and commented upon together. The second part of the gloss cannot be detached and moved back. There is no 'disturbed order' in the sense of a mistake in the manuscript tradition. The only disturbing factor is that the earlier passage is already commented upon by another gloss. This shows the piecemeal character of the compilation.

Book 5 with those on 2 to 4. The use of 'such is what he says' (*in EN* 211,6) continues a practice which is found, for instance, in glosses on Book 4.[61] The frequent approval of Aristotle's expressions is another phenomenon that Book 5 has in common with preceding glosses.[62] I have already mentioned the scholion on Book 5 which attacks the Stoic indifferents-theory and related a similar gloss in the beginning of Book 4 to it.[63] This is the scholion that contains the time reference to the middle-Platonist Atticus.

The overall characteristics of these glosses show that they belong to the same compilation as those on Books 2 to 4: they contain a wealth of material, no doubt taken from Adrastus' work, as is obvious from the following examples. There are two quotations from Euripides.[64] Three lines are quoted from the elegiac poet Theognis in relation to the proverb of *EN* 1129b28-9 and the source of this information is given as Theophrastus' *On Customs*; but, the gloss continues, the same Theophrastus quotes this proverb in the first Book of his *Ethics* as occurring in Phocylides. Another scholion explains that Bias is 'one of the seven wise men' and cites two others, Pittacus of Mytilene and Chilo of Sparta, each with one of his famous sayings. One scholion refers by name to Aristotle's *Magna Moralia*, whereas another refers to the same work simply as *allakhou* (elsewhere). The former scholion also attributes the verse of *EN* 1132b27 to Hesiod and quotes the full sentence as it appeared in his *The Great Works*. There is also a reference to Aristotle's *Politics*.

The examples which Aristotle gives of what is just by convention in *EN* 1134b21ff are glossed as follows. The agreement between Sparta and Athens to fix the ransom for prisoners of war to one mina is illustrated by a quotation from the historian Androtion. That a goat but not two sheep shall be sacrificed is not attested by any historical account, according to the scholiast. Finally, that sacrifices be offered to Brasidas is said to be a decision of the citizens of Amphipolis, who celebrated him as a 'hero'.

The scholia on Book 5 again contain references to Homer's *Iliad*,[65] and to Plato's *Republic*. All of the scholia touched upon in the last three paragraphs may be traced back to Adrastus, with the exception of those referring to works of Plato and Aristotle.

Michael of Ephesus on Books 5, 9 and 10

Michael of Ephesus is the author of the second commentary on Book 5, as well as of the *skholai* on 9 and 10. This is attested by the titles in the

---

[61] *in EN* 202,18 and 203,14.

[62] As was mentioned in relation to Book 2, see above, n. 35. An example is *eulogôs prosethêke* (*in EN* 246,13). See also for Book 4: *in EN* 203,8.

[63] See above.

[64] *in EN* 240,29-30. They are said to belong to the *Bellerophon*, but Welcker thought they came from the *Alcmaeon* (Nauck *FTG*², 381, n. 2).

[65] For instance, the one to Phoenix's intercourse with his father's concubine, which is followed by the insertion 'So also Absalom'.

manuscript tradition and confirmed by the character of the commentaries themselves: they agree in method, style, language, and areas of interest with the other works of the same commentator.[66] Michael was a native of Ephesus, according to his own testimony in the commentary on Book 10 of the *Ethics* (first mentioned by Schleiermacher), where he calls Heraclitus a fellow citizen.[67]

Almost nothing is known of the man, apart from what can be found in or inferred from his own testimony, as Praechter remarks; and that information is very scarce and of little importance. As a result, the date of Michael of Ephesus' activity has been a matter of considerable puzzlement, until, in 1962, R. Browning drew the attention of the scholarly world to the funeral oration of Anna Comnena by a George Tornikès, metropolitan bishop of Ephesus.[68] In 1970 followed the edition and translation of the oration.[69]

The passage concerning Michael of Ephesus reads:[70]

> I myself heard the scholar from Ephesus impute to her the cause of his blindness, i.e. his having devoted entire nights without sleep to his commentaries on the words of Aristotle by her command; hence his eye-troubles, brought on by the candles through desiccation.

Quite rightly, Darrouzès notes:[71]

> The scholar of Ephesus (a native, not the metropolitan bishop) cannot be other than Michael, who in fact commented on *EN* 5, 9, 10, on the *Parva Naturalia*, on *PA*, *MA* and *IA*. The testimony of Tornikès, who knew the scholar personally and seems to treat him as no longer alive, allows us at least to fix Michael's activity in the first half of the [twelfth] century ...

This piece of evidence put an end to fruitless speculations concerning the dating of Michael's life and works. Still, it is worthwhile investigating why so competent a scholar as Praechter went wrong in his paper 'Michael von Ephesos und Psellos', which was mainly devoted to this subject. Praechter placed Michael's activity an entire century earlier, since he thought that most of his commentaries on Aristotle were written before 1040. He thought that they were used in, and so must precede, a certain anonymous summary of logic and of the four branches of the

---

[66] For Michael of Ephesus, see K. Praechter, review of *Michaelis Ephesii In libros De partibus animalium ... Commentaria*, M. Hayduck (ed.) *CAG* 22.2, in *Göttingische gelehrte Anzeigen* 168, 1906, 861-907; id., review of *Comm. in Ar. Graeca*, in *Byzantinische Zeitschrift* 18, 1909, 535-7 (= Chapter 2 above); id., 'Michael von Ephesos und Psellos', *Byzantische Zeitschrift* 31, 1931, 1-12.

[67] *in EN* 570,21.

[68] R. Browning, Chapter 17 above.

[69] Jean Darrouzès (ed.), *Georges et Démétrios Tornikès: Lettres et discours. Introduction, texte, analyses, traduction et notes*, Paris, CNRS, 1970, 220-323.

[70] 283,9-12, translated also at the end of Chapter 17.

[71] 282, n. 70.

quadrivium,[72] the oldest dated manuscript of which was completed in January 6548 (AD 1040). This summary (Anonymous Heiberg) contains passages which are textually identical with Michael's commentary on the *Sophistici Elenchi*. Anonymous Heiberg contains a number of expressions ('he says', 'he inferred') which show that the common passages are excerpts from a commentary on the *Sophistici Elenchi*. These expressions are present also in Michael's commentary, which moreover contains cross references and other characteristics, fully warranting the assumption that the common passages form an integral and therefore original part of it. The commentary in question is certainly Michael's work: it agrees in method, style, and language with his other commentaries on Aristotle.

Now, Michael refers explicitly in his commentary on the *Sophistici Elenchi* to his own commentaries on Aristotle's logic (more specifically the *Analytics* and the *Topics*), *Rhetoric* and *Physics*. Further, a comparison between the two shows that his commentary on the *Parva Naturalia* preceded the one on the *Sophistici Elenchi*. This, Praechter argued, is an important conclusion, since the commentary on the *Parva Naturalia* contains a list of commentaries on Aristotle which Michael had already written at that time, i.e. those on *de Partibus Animalium, de Motu Animalium, de Incessu Animalium, de Generatione Animalium*, and the second half of the *Metaphysics*, while promising a new one on *de Coloribus* (a spurious treatise). The inclusion of the commentary on the *Metaphysics* shows that Michael did not restrict himself here to Aristotle's physical works. It is therefore remarkable that he makes no mention of his work on the Organon or on the *Rhetoric*, let alone on the *Ethics* or the *Politics*. Praechter concluded that young Michael's first interest focused on physics and resulted in a group of commentaries on Aristotle's physical treatises, not including the *Physics*. The commentary on the *Physics* must have been written later. This first group includes also the commentary on the *Metaphysics*. A second group relates to the Organon – including at least the *Prior Analytics, Topics* and *Sophistici Elenchi – Rhetoric* and *Physics*. All these works, Praechter argued, must have been written some time before January 1040. The commentaries on the *Ethics* and *Politics*, written later, form a third group.

Praechter may be right about the internal relationship of Michael's work, but he was wrong to suppose that Anonymous Heiberg depended on Michael. By an exhaustive study of the origins of Michael's commentary, Sten Ebbesen has been able to distinguish earlier recensions by Michael of his commentary on the *Sophistici Elenchi*.[73] Taking these into account, Ebbesen has shown that Anonymous Heiberg does not depend on Michael, but that, at least in part, they draw from a common tradition of earlier scholia. Some of the scholia which they have in common were derived by Michael via Psellus' *Brevis Traditio*. Ebbesen does not exclude

---

[72] *Anonymi Logica et Quadrivium cum scholiis antiquis*, J.L. Heiberg (ed.) (Det Kgl. Danske Videnskabernes Selskab. Historisk-filolog. Meddelelser, xv,1), Copenhagen, 1929.

[73] Sten Ebbesen, *CLCAG* 7.1, 268-85 (V.14 Michael of Ephesus); see also Chapter 19 below.

the possibility that in other cases Michael drew on Anonymous Heiberg. But the important point is that the relation of dependency does not go the other way round, so that there is no need to date Michael earlier than Anonymous Heiberg.

Ebbesen's study incidentally reveals that Michael's technique in the *Sophistici Elenchi* commentary, like that in his *Ethics* commentary, is a painstaking compilation and editing of earlier scholia, motivated by nothing so much as the desire to elucidate Aristotle.

Tornikès' testimony situates Michael's *floruit* incontestably in the first half of the twelfth century. Taken together with its sequel, it contains also a strong hint that Michael, who, unlike Eustratius, certainly was no theologian, may have been a physician. Praechter refers to the surmise, in a book of literary history, that Michael followed the medical profession.[74] Consistent with this hypothesis, Praechter concedes, are Michael's interest in Aristotle's biological works, exceptional not only for his time but in the Aristotelian tradition as a whole, his personal observations in the areas of physiology and psychology, and especially various remarks on the activity of sight, not derived from Aristotle; although a passage in his commentary on *GA* implies that, at the time Michael wrote this, he was not (yet) a medical man.[75] It is of course not unthinkable that considerations of this kind are at the origin of the hypothesis. In any case, Michael's aetiology of his own eye-disease has a professional ring. Tornikès' next sentence reads surprisingly:[76]

> Moreover, she [= Anna Comnena] herself, although she did not yet make an exact investigation [*akribôsamenê*] of medicine – for she was putting off its detailed study [*analusin*] for the time being, and that because she was engaged in philosophy and preferred philosophy, the medicine of the soul, before that of the body – nevertheless organised [*sundietitheto*] the philosophical materials according to the most scientific canons of the other discipline.

It is hard to understand this sudden jump in Tornikès' train of thought – there has been no mention of medicine before – unless the last of the words he attributes to Michael suggested to him the notion of that profession; and that again is most unlikely if Michael had no part in it. Michael's remark, in one of his well known references to his celebrated but unnamed master, that he died from peripneumonia, also betrays a

---

[74] Praechter, 'Michaeli Ephesii in libros ...', 864, n. 2: 'In the literary history of Nicolas, III, p. 306, I find the remark whose source I do not know, that Michael was supposedly a doctor by calling.'

[75] ibid. 863-4. Cf. the remainder of n. 2, 864: 'That would fit well with the above explanation. The passage at p. 215, 30 gives, to be sure, an opposing indication, insofar as it shows that Michael was not a doctor at a certain time, at least. Michael reports here, 'one of my companions was a doctor'. Someone who practised the same occupations would not express it like that. One would have to expect, '... a companion was also a doctor by trade'.

[76] *Georges et Démétrios Tornikès: Lettres et discours*, 283.

medical interest.[77]

Michael, we have seen, was remarkable among Byzantine scholars for the scope of his interests. He commented on Aristotelian works which were all but ignored by other commentators as well as on those which were studied traditionally. To the former class belong the commentaries on *de Partibus Animalium, de Motu Animalium, de Incessu Animalium*,[78] the *Parva Naturalia*[79] and *de Generatione Animalium*[80] – all of which are physical treatises – as well as the only known Byzantine commentary on the *Politics*, of which but a few pages survive.[81] To the latter class belong the commentaries on the Organon, of which none but that on the *Sophistici Elenchi*[82] is preserved; on Books 6-14 of the *Metaphysics*,[83] if it is by Michael; and on Books 5, 9 and 10 of the *Nicomachean Ethics*. The commentaries on the *Physics* and the *Topics* are lost.

L. Tarán has mounted a powerful challenge to the widely accepted view that the commentary on *Metaphysics* 6-14 is by Michael. He argues that it was already used seven centuries earlier by Syrianus, and that it was written by a forger (pseudo-Alexander) who wanted it accepted as being the lost second part of Alexander's commentary on the *Metaphysics*.[84] On the other side there are three points to be made. Given Michael's work habits, it is not unlikely that the commentary we have is Michael's reworking of the forger's commentary incorporating independent material, for example from Alexander's *Problemata*. Secondly, it is not clear that we should dismiss as spurious the remark at the end of Michael's commentary on the *Parva Naturalia*: 'I also wrote on the *Metaphysics* from precisely (*autou*) 7 to 14 (see Michael, *in Parv. Nat.* 149,8-16). It is admittedly surprising that no commentary on Book 6 is mentioned, and that the commentary on 7-14 is mentioned as an afterthought, when it would have been in fact his most important work. But it is possible that Michael had not at the time finished the *Metaphysics* commentary. Hence the unexpected 'precisely' (*autou*), the

---

[77] *in Parva Nat.*, *CAG* 22.1, 142,5. See 'Michaeli Ephesii in libros ...', 902.

[78] M. Hayduck (ed.), *CAG* 12.2, Berlin, 1904. The last two works are translated into English in Anthony Preus, *Aristotle and Michael of Ephesus. On the Movement and Progression of Animals*, Hildesheim and New York, 1981.

[79] P. Wendland (ed.), *CAG* 22.1, Berlin, 1891.

[80] M. Hayduck (ed.), *CAG* 14.3 (wrongly attributed to Philoponus).

[81] In the form of scholia in a Berlin MS of the *Politics*, O. Immisch (ed.), *Aristoteles, Politica*, Teubner, 2nd edition 1929, xvii-xxi and 293-327, translated in Ernest Barker, *Social and Political Thought in Byzantium*, Oxford 1957. The scholia reflect, according to Immisch, not a historical or a political, but a philosophic commentary, with little originality, in the Neoplatonic style. 'But occasionally Michael addresses himself ... to questions of literary criticism; and occasionally, too, he refers ... to the conditions of his own time' (E. Barker, op. cit., 137).

[82] Max Wallies (ed.), *CAG* 2.3 (wrongly attributed to Alexander of Aphrodisias). Perhaps also fragments of a commentary on the *de Interpretatione*: see *CAG* 4.5, suppl., xlvff.

[83] M. Hayduck (ed.), *CAG* 1, 440ff (wrongly attributed to Alexander of Aphrodisias).

[84] Leonardo Tarán, 'Syrianus and Pseudo-Alexander's Commentary on Metaph. E-N', in Jürgen Wiesner (ed.), *Aristoteles: Werk und Wirkung*, vol. 2: *Kommentierung, Ueberlieferung, Nachleben*, Berlin and New York 1987, 215-32.

silence on Book 6 and the mention of this commentary as an afterthought. Finally, the ascription of the extant commentary to Alexander is easy to understand, since that reflects the forger's intentions, but the ascription by other sources to Michael is hard to explain, unless there were good grounds for it.

Michael's commentaries on the *Ethics* are according to his own word *skholai*, lectures or commentaries, written either with a view to or as a product of his teaching. In them he explains both the letter and the spirit of Aristotle's text, concerns himself with textual criticism, points out the connection between various passages, spells out arguments that are too succinct for direct comprehension, advances parallel texts, makes cross-references throughout the Aristotelian corpus, and refers also to other philosophers, especially to Plato.

In his commentary on Book 5 Michael follows almost step for step the anonymous scholia, which he often summarises or repeats in a different form, sometimes even borrowing literally. Michael's commentary on Book 5, while not adding anything essential to the anonymous scholia, fills in what they left without comment, supplies a short introduction but no concluding paragraph, and bears witness to a better text of the anonymous scholia than the one we actually possess.

Michael of Ephesus is above all known as an Aristotelian. His Aristotelianism manifests itself in many ways. He chooses the physical and other treatises of Aristotle to comment upon; he stays close to the text of Aristotle, which he explains with reference to its general import (*dianoia*) as well as to its detailed form (*lexis*); he makes a wide use of other works of the Stagirite; and he does not attempt to make Aristotle fit into a Neoplatonic strait jacket. Michael differs greatly from Eustratius on this account. Praechter contrasts Michael, the Aristotelian, with Psellus, the Platonist.

However, Michael's Aristotelianism is never a militant one. This point has never been made, so far as I know, but it deserves to be emphasised because the existing accounts tend to give the wrong impression. That his philosophical language is coloured by Neoplatonism, although much less so than that of his contemporaries, is a feature he shares with his age, but nowhere in his commentary on the *Ethics* does he show an interest in attacking Plato and the Platonists in the name of Aristotle and the Peripatetic school.

This is brought out by an analysis of the passages which explicitly mention Platonic doctrines and expressions. They fall roughly into three classes: (a) where Plato or Platonists are advanced in support of Aristotle; (b) where a specific Platonic usage is simply mentioned or an opposition between Platonism and Aristotelianism simply explained; and finally (c) where actual arguments against Platonic positions are given. Let us consider each of them separately.

(a) There are two passages in the commentary on Book 9[85] and five in

---

[85] *in EN* 483,3 and 515,30.

Book 10[86] where Plato is summoned in support of Aristotle. We may add to this the single quotation from Plotinus.[87] In none of these, however, does Michael attempt to force Aristotle into a Platonic mould. The doctrines defended are genuinely Aristotelian.

(b) In many places a Platonic usage or doctrine is simply stated or explained without any discussion.[88] Although in most of these passages Michael opposes Aristotle to Plato or the Platonists, whenever he does so, he simply states the opposition without supplying at that point an argument in favour of either of the opponents.

(c) Only two passages in Michael's commentary on the *Ethics* contain an explicit argument against Plato. The first, found in the commentary on Book 5,[89] is a *reductio ad absurdum*: if the gods possess virtue, they possess justice (in the Aristotelian sense), which implies in turn that they possess exterior goods. Michael refers to a similar argument 'elsewhere' which leads to the impossible conclusion that the gods are subject to passions. These arguments are entirely in line with Aristotle's concepts of justice and virtue in the *Ethica Nicomachea*, and are actually implied in *EN* 1178b11 and 1178b16, respectively. This is the only place in Michael's whole commentary on the *Ethics* that contains arguments against Plato which go beyond what is expressed in the text of Aristotle on which he is commenting. Even here, Michael does not proffer an independent argumentation of his own.

The second place containing an argument against Plato is *in EN* 542,27ff in the commentary on Book 10. Michael's attitude, however, becomes very clear when we consider the wider context, which includes also *in EN* 537,13.[90] Michael had here an excellent occasion to use Plato

[86] ibid. 537,13; 579,5 and 30; 598,23; and 616,35. On 537,13, see below under (c).

[87] *in EN* 529,21.

[88] They are three in relation to Book 5: (1) *in EN* 25,28-9, which notes the difference between Aristotle's and the Platonists' use of the word *adikein* (to treat unjustly): it is a synonym of *blaptein* (to harm) for Aristotle, but not for the Platonists; (2) *in EN* 47,17-18, where the belief that justice belongs to the gods, here implied by Aristotle's argument, is ascribed to Plato; (3) *in EN* 72,5-6, where Michael, explaining how Aristotle accounts in his own terms for Plato's doctrine of justice, explicitly quotes Plato's definition of justice as the parts of the soul doing their own job.

One in relation to Book 9: *in EN* 524,17, which simply states the opposition 'since ... for Plato pleasure and pain are not contraries'.

And ten in relation to Book 10: *in EN* 533,22 and 35, where the Platonists' use of compound nouns, formed by prefixing *t-* or *auto-* to an adjective, is explained and their identification of the One with the Good is stated; *in EN* 578,16, where it is alleged that the Peripatetics, unlike the Platonists, distinguish between moral and civil virtue; *in EN* 579,23, where the term *nous* (intellect), here used by Aristotle in the Platonic sense, is contrasted with the Platonic expression *zôê logikê* (rational life); *in EN* 585,10 and 13, as well as 601,4, which assert that the really happy man, according to Plato, does not need anybody nor anything else, since he possesses the source of happiness within his mind; *in EN* 619,15 and 19, as well as 620,4, where Plato is mentioned in connection with Aristotle's contention that nobody wrote an (adequate) work on politics before he started on it, and where his judgment, that some of what according to Plato would preserve the state would in fact be detrimental to it, is proffered as a matter of fact.

[89] *in EN* 66,5-9.

[90] See above.

as a target, since both Aristotelian passages involved (*EN* 1172b32-5 and 1173a15ff) are direct attacks on Plato, but Michael does not take this opportunity before *in EN* 542,27 and even then does not go beyond repeating the argument of Aristotle's text. Let us take the two passages in turn.

First Michael simply explains Plato's reversal of Eudoxus' argument (*EN* 1172b28), still keeping within the scope of the text commented upon. Then, however, he treats 1172b32ff as if it were actually an argument of Plato, although it is directed against the very notion of an absolute good. Nor does he understand 1173a15ff as the criticism of the *Philebus* which it is. He even misunderstands Aristotle's appeal to Plato's distinction between 'mixed' and 'unmixed' pleasure. This shows how little Michael knew Plato. Next, Michael explains at length Aristotle's argument that pleasure is not a movement, without so much as mentioning Plato. Then comes a surprise: 'Having said what moved Plato to call pleasure a movement, he (Aristotle) now argues against him and says what else convinced him (Plato) to call it a movement.' In the following lines Michael adds nothing to Aristotle's argumentation. He explains Plato's arguments with the same care as Aristotle's.

In conclusion, with the qualified exception of 5, 66,5-9,[91] Michael's attitude is clearly that of a commentator who attempts to explain what Aristotle says. Platonic doctrines, explicitly mentioned by Aristotle or understood by Michael as being alluded to by Aristotle, fall within the scope of such an explanation. Platonic doctrines or expressions, whenever Michael introduces them, serve to clarify the text. Nowhere does he venture an independent argument either for or against Plato. He even fails to discern some obvious attacks on Plato in the text of the *Ethics*.

The spirit in which Michael comments on Aristotle's *Ethics* is on the whole not unlike that exhibited in Albertus Magnus' commentaries on Aristotle, except that Michael does not sharply distinguish the scope of philosophy from that of theology: he does not even mention theology. Michael is obviously not interested in relating Aristotle to the dogma of the Church or to the Christian way of life, despite the impression left by the repeated reference to the friendship between St Gregory of Nazianzus and St Basil, by the equally repeated example of apostasy as an instance of what one should not do under any circumstances, and by the concluding apostrophe to the 'Lord and Creator, crucified out of an immense love for men'.

Anna Comnena's 'Aristotelians'

Robert Browning's findings (Chapter 17 above) on Anna Comnena's influence have been widely acclaimed by scholars. The one exception is Eva de Vries-van der Velden.[92] She finds the very idea unacceptable that

[91] See above.
[92] Eva de Vries-van der Velden, *Théodore Métochite, une réévaluation*, Amsterdam 1987, 111, n. 10.

Anna could have inspired an attempt at constructing a new philosophical system based on Aristotle rather than on Plato in order to obtain a synthesis of ancient philosophy and Christian dogma. This would have gone against the whole Byzantine tradition as well as against Anna's own attitude regarding Aristotle, expressed in her *History* and echoed in the funeral oration. Dr de Vries points out the absence of any theological concern in Michael's commentaries and underlines that the rhetorical style of a funeral oration does not promote exactitude. She believes that Tornikès, himself ignorant in philosophical matters, only wanted to praise Anna's general culture, which included an interest in philosophy. She thinks it possible that Anna requested some philosophers to procure her commentaries on Aristotle for her private information only.

We are indebted to Browning for his re-dating of Michael and his hypothesis on Eustratius, both of which give a role to Anna. The only question is how much we can infer from the evidence to which he has drawn attention. My own view is that the revival of Aristotelian scholarship did not go much beyond the activities of Michael and Eustratius, and that it was confined to exegesis, not extending to a revival of Aristotelian philosophy. Tornikès does not speak of a philosophical circle around Anna, and though the study of Aristotle is later emphasised around 1265 in the inaugural lecture of Michael Anchialis as head of the philosophy school (*hupatos tôn philosophôn*), the chair had been vacant for some years before that. It is not possible either to be sure about the extent of Michael's dependence on Anna, or to exclude the view of Praechter that Michael was a philosophy professor at the Academy founded by Constantine IX Monomachus, and of Barker that he wrote most of his commentaries there.[93] He could have started his work as a commentator before Anna contacted him, and, as Preus has argued,[94] he could have continued it after 1138, when she redirected her attention to work on her *Alexiad*.

The extent of Michael's work on the composite *Ethics* commentary is also hard to gauge. He certainly wrote the portions on Books 5, 9 and 10 himself. But he could also have been the person who planned the entire commentary and put it all together, including the makeshift portion on Book 7.[95]

The anonymous commentator on Book 7

The anonymous commentary on Book 7 has again the character of a formal commentary by one man, although the title refers to it as *skholia*.

One can but subscribe to Schleiermacher's verdict that it exceeds

---

[93] Karl Praechter, review of *CAG* 22.2 (Michael *in PA*), *Göttingische gelehrte Anzeigen* 22, 1906, 903ff (reprinted in his *Kleine Schriften*, H. Dörrie (ed.), 1973); Ernest Barker, *Social and Political Thought in Byzantium*, Oxford 1957, 136.

[94] Anthony Preus, *Aristotle and Michael of Ephesus, On the Movement and Progression of Animals*, Hildesheim and New York 1981, 10, n. 22. Preus, however, envisages a more extensive and vigorous circle around Anna Comnena.

[95] Sten Ebbesen in Chapter 19 below also considers it likely that he was the editor.

everything in poverty. It misinterprets passages that are quite clear in themselves. It lacks good taste as well as an elementary feeling for (classical) Greek, as is illustrated by the Latin word *karbônes* (for *anthrakes* – coals), and by the present tense of *phagein* (to eat).[96] The style is clumsy and marred by the endless repetition of *êtoi* (or) by means of which explanation is heaped upon explanation. Nor is the commentator afraid of repeating himself.

The language marks the composition as very late. Rose could only give Grosseteste's translation as a *terminus ante quem*. The commentary was evidently written with the sole purpose of filling the gap left by the commentaries I have already discussed. The subject matter of Book 7 (incontinence and pleasure) could appeal to a man Schleiermacher suspected might be a physician because of his manifest liking for examples from the medical field.

Aspasius on Book 8

Aspasius was a renowned Peripatetic teacher at the beginning of the second century.[97] His commentaries were still used by Plotinus in his school, as were those of two other Peripatetics, Adrastus and Alexander, both of Aphrodisias.[98] Galen advised a friend who requested a commentary on Aristotle's *Categories* from him to begin with reading those of Adrastus and Aspasius.[99] He himself in his youth had heard a pupil of Aspasius, the Peripatetic, lecture. Galen does not name this pupil but identifies him as a fellow-citizen, i.e. as originating from Pergamon.[100] Aspasius is not to be identified with his contemporary, the sophist Aspasius of Byblus, an Atticist rhetorician, nor with his namesake of Tyre, also a rhetorician, both mentioned in the *Suda*.[101]

Aspasius wrote formal commentaries on Aristotle: on the *Categories, de Interpretatione, Physics, de Caelo, de Sensu* and *Metaphysics*, none of which have survived, and on the *Nicomachean Ethics*. Of the latter we possess the elucidations of Books 1 to 4, part of Book 7, and most of Book 8.

Many gaps occur in the extant parts. Moraux attempts to show that the whole of our present-day text probably goes back to one incomplete and quite damaged exemplar that must have been discovered and copied in the late thirteenth or early fourteenth century (pp. 252-3). However,

---

[96] It also makes the verb agree in number with a neuter plural. Although this is common in sixth-century authors, it is not found in Michael or Eustratius, any more than in classical Greek.

[97] On Aspasius, see Paul Moraux, *Der Aristotelismus bei den Griechen*, vol. 2, 226-93, especially 249-93: 'G. Zur Nikomachischen Ethik: a) Ueberlieferung; b) Tendenz und Einordenung; c) Die kontroversen Bücher; d) Aspasios und sein Vorgänger; e) Philosophischer Standort.'

[98] Porph. *Vit. Plot.* 14,10-14.

[99] Galen 19, *de Libr. Propr.* 42,10-43,1 = *Scr. Min.* 2.118,17-119,2.

[100] Galen 5, *de Cogn. An. Morb.* 8, 41,17-42,2 = *Scr. Min* 1. 32, 5-7.

[101] *Pace* R. Hanquet, *Aspasius, sa vie, son oeuvre*, Diss. Louvain 1945, 12ff.

Aspasius' commentary on Book 8 in the Byzantine collection ends in the same tattered way as it does elsewhere. Hence, at least the tail-end mutilation dates from the twelfth century or before. That the Byzantine compiler obviously had no access to the remainder of Aspasius' commentary is another indication that the work had already fallen to pieces by that time. It is true that all the MSS that contain Aspasius on other Books beside 8 belong to the same tradition and that his commentary on Book 1, where it appears after Eustratius', is acephalous, i.e. derives from a copy with a defective beginning, but the latter does not have to be the archetype of that tradition. Nor do we have to ascribe the existing lacunae to this archetype, for the text of Book 8 that belongs to it, although differing from the one that occurs in the Byzantine compilation, is no less complete.

There is no reason to doubt that Aspasius' work covered the ten books of the *Nicomachean Ethics*. What remains of it is, in Gauthier's judgment, the most valuable legacy left by antiquity for the understanding of Aristotle's moral philosophy. Aspasius bears witness to a much older state of the text of the *Ethics* than that represented by our manuscripts, the oldest of which dates only from the tenth century.[102] His education and his ties with the Peripatetic tradition often enabled him to comprehend Aristotle's intentions accurately.[103] Gauthier, nevertheless, in his own commentary frequently points to traditional misinterpretations that originated with Aspasius. He reminds us that Aspasius was strongly influenced by the Stoics and that he was after all separated by five centuries from his master. The repeated emphasis on being in a natural state (*ekhein kata tên phusin*) as the standard for both friendship and virtue, which at the same time shows them to be rational (*kata ton logon*), is Stoic. The appreciation of virtue as the highest good, although tempered by the qualification 'after happiness', is also Stoic.

That Aspasius' language is coloured by Stoic expression has been noted by R. Hanquet.[104] It does not mean that he deliberately takes a Stoic position. As Moraux observes (p. 269), orthodox Aristotelians such as Alexander of Aphrodisias often use typical Stoic terms, without experiencing them as foreign elements. Stoic terminology had invaded the philosophical language of the time in such a way that its use is no evidence for a Stoic approach. In all great ethical questions, Moraux continues, Aspasius takes a position against the Stoa: external goods contribute to happiness; some passions are compatible with reason; the main species of passion are only pleasure and pain, to which fear and desire must be reduced; the virtuous man can suffer pain.

Aspasius' method is that of paraphrasing Aristotle in a clear, succinct

[102] Moraux notices, however, that for his commentaries on the *Physics* and *de Sensu* Aspasius possessed manuscripts with corrupt passages, some of which were the result of unscrupulous contemporary emendations (238-9; 244-5). His readings of the *Ethics* diverge less from our vulgate (257).

[103] R.A. Gauthier, *L'Éthique à Nicomaque*², vol. 1, part 1, 100.

[104] R. Hanquet, op. cit. in n. 101, 78-81.

manner. He keeps well to the point and abstains from introducing literary and historical information, a practice that characterises the anonymous scholia on Books 2 to 5. But he concerns himself with problems of textual criticism and attempts to elucidate the meaning of different variants.[105]

One interesting textual problem about which Aspasius has some information to offer is that of the so-called common Books 4-6 of the *Eudemian Ethics* (*EE*) which are the same as 5-7 of the *Nicomachean* (*EN*). Hans Gottschalk has shown[106] that Aspasius found the common books in his text of *EN*, but thought they had been transferred from *EE*, which he imagined to be by Aristotle's pupil Eudemus of Rhodes instead of by Aristotle himself, the transfer being designed to replace some lost books of *EN*. Kenny has further shown that at first it was *EE* rather than *EN* that was most often quoted and enjoyed the higher esteem.[107] But in Chapter 3 above Gottschalk challenges Kenny's view that it was Aspasius who initiated the change and transferred the common books.

Aspasius critically examines the definitions of passion given by Andronicus of Rhodes and by his pupil Boethus,[108] whom he contrasts with the ancient Peripatetics, none of whom give such a definition.[109] Occasional objections to Aristotle are always resolved. Some of these objections appear to come from an anti-Aristotelian source: those against the thesis that the absence of good birth, of good children and of beauty affect happiness; against the interpretation of irony as a vice, since Socrates possessed this quality; against the opinion that the high-minded person (*megalopsukhos*) would be ashamed of being the recipient of benefaction; and against the characteristic tendency of the same to remember benefits bestowed but to forget benefits received.[110] In his defence of *metriopatheia*, Aspasius rejoins the Aristotelian position of his time.

Moraux (pp. 255ff) wonders whether the relatively pure Aristotelianism of Aspasius is the result of his deliberately adhering to the orthodoxy of the school or of his understanding his task as an interpreter to be that of explaining the text of Aristotle as carefully as possible from the author's point of view. In several places in his commentary, Aspasius refers in the third person plural or by the pronoun *houtoi* (they) to

---

[105] Moraux gives a list of the passages discussing variants, 257, n. 101.

[106] H.B. Gottschalk, 'Aristotelian philosophy in the Roman world', in Wolfgang Haase (ed.), *Aufstieg und Niedergang der römischen Welt* II, 36.2, 1158.

[107] Anthony Kenny, *The Aristotelian Ethics*, Oxford 1978. Cf. also Moraux, op. cit. 257-61.

[108] Boethus the Athenian Peripatetic of the first century BC is not to be confused with Boethus the Stoic in the second century BC.

[109] *in EN* 44,20-4. For Aspasius' discussion of the definition of passions see also Moraux, 279-88; H.B. Gottschalk, op. cit. in n. 106, 1156-7; F. Becchi, 'Aspasio e i peripatetici posteriori. La formula definitoria della passione', *Prometheus* 9, 1983, 83-104; and Pier Luigi Donini, *Tre studi sull'aristotelismo nel II secolo D.C.*, Torino etc. 1974, 63-125: 'Capitulo II. Il platonismo medio e l'interpretazione dell'etica aristotelica', especially 100-104.

[110] Moraux, 267-8.

unnamed individuals who must have been Aristotelians.[111] Nowhere does he expressly present himself as belonging to the school, not even when he distinguishes the older from the younger Peripatetics. Moraux is inclined to consider Aspasius as formally an outsider, but with strong Aristotelian sympathies.

The *argumentum a silentio* is always tricky. Given that Aspasius was known in antiquity as a Peripatetic and that his doctrinal leanings are Aristotelian, the relative distance he appears to take from other Aristotelians may well be that of a contemporary interpreter against his predecessors in the same school. Moreover, he may find it a good pedagogical device not to proclaim himself too openly as a follower of the master whose texts he wants to clarify. Gottschalk still considers Aspasius as one of the few 'professed Aristotelians' of the first two centuries of the Roman Empire (p. 1080). He points out that Aspasius' criticism of Andronicus' and Boethus' definition of passion was inspired by a desire to purge the school teaching of accretions that resulted from Stoic influence, thus placing Aspasius within 'the trend towards a purer form of Aristotelianism' (p. 1158). What is important, in any case, is that Aspasius clearly saw it as his task to develop the content and meaning of Aristotle's text as carefully as possible from the author's point of view (p. 269) and, one should add, that he possessed the necessary professional equipment to accomplish that task well.

Aspasius' commentary on Book 8, the one incorporated in the composite commentary, survived in a mutilated form. It appears to be complete up to 180,8 *hekastôi gar*, where it breaks off abruptly. The passages covering *EN* 1159a35-b19, 1160a9-33 and 1160b21-1161a9 are missing. Moreover, from 180,10 onward, the commentary gradually acquires the character of disconnected *skholia*, becoming sparser and sparser toward the end, with the order of the text disturbed. The last five pages, approximately one-sixth of the commentary, cover one-third of Book 8.

Eustratius in Albertus Magnus and Bonaventure

I shall finish by returning to Eustratius, to see how his commentary, once translated into Latin by Grosseteste, was received by Albertus Magnus and Bonaventure.

Albertus Magnus commented on the *Nicomachean Ethics* twice; the first time about 1250-1252 in Cologne, the second time about 1267-1270, possibly in Strasbourg. There is a great difference between the two commentaries. The first time, Albert lectured on the newly translated complete text of Aristotle's *Ethics* at the freshly founded *studium generale* of his order. He chose the form used by the masters of the arts in Paris: an explanation of the *littera*, acompanied by *quaestiones*. We possess a *reportatio* (notes taken down by one or more students) of these

---

[111] *in EN* 2,16-3,2; 5,23-30; 10,29-32; 156,14-16.

lectures. It is likely that it was made by Thomas Aquinas.[112] Albert tries in these lectures to come to grips with a newly discovered text, aiming at exegesis and explanation, but not at the sort of interpretation which would fit Aristotle's theory into a thoroughly Christian ethics, as Eustratius had attempted to do. Here, for the first time, a sharp distinction between philosophy and theology is formulated, which was soon to be taken over by Thomas Aquinas. Albert also uses all the sources he can: among others, the recently translated Greek commentaries including Eustratius, Michael of Ephesus and the *notule* of Grosseteste; Averroes[113] and other materials from the Arabic tradition, especially Avicenna; and Nemesius, *de Natura Hominis* and John of Damascus, *de Fide Orthodoxa*.

The second time, almost twenty years later, when Albert 'felt himself to be an old man', he did not lecture on the *Ethics* but wrote a paraphrase of it, 'based on the Avicennan model, aimed at popularizing the texts of Aristotle, which many found too difficult'.[114] This was one of the last in a series of such commentaries on the works of the Stagirite. Whereas Albert was at pains to distinguish Aristotle's philosophical treatment of ethics from a theological one in his first commentary, here this distinction is taken for granted. He gives 'Aristotle's teaching a purely philosophical context', sees it 'in the light of other rationalist moral philosophy', that of 'the Stoics whose head was Socrates', in other words, the Greek Platonist school, which he combines with the Roman Stoics, quoting Plato, Cicero and Seneca all under the same category.[115]

Also in his second commentary, Albert takes over a great deal of the material from Eustratius and the other commentators. For example, he uses Eustratius' account of the theory of Ideas, stating the argument in the same order but more condensed, often using the Eustratius/ Grosseteste phrases, without attribution, except occasionally to the 'Commentator', who here is Eustratius, not Averroes. If we compare Albert lib. 1, tract. 5, cap. 12 with Eustratius *in EN* 40,4-14; 17-34, we find that Albert has extracted six different arguments from one page of Eustratius.

Thomas Aquinas learned about the Grosseteste translation of Eustratius 'and others' from Albert's Cologne lectures, but seems not to have had a copy of his own. Of course his interpretation owes a good deal to Albert, who developed those lectures relying on the Greek commentaries.[116]

We may possibly also trace the influence of Eustratius 'and others'

[112] Albertus Magnus, *Opera Omnia*, 14, *Super Ethica Commentum et Quaestiones*, W. Kübel (ed.), Münster, 2 vols, 1968-1970 and 1987.

[113] Averroes did not write a long commentary on the *Ethics*, only a middle commentary, completed in 1147 and translated by Herman the German, Toledo 1240.

[114] Jean Dunbabin, 'The two commentaries of Albertus Magnus on the Nicomachean Ethics', *Recherches de Théologie ancienne et médiévale* 30, 1963, 232-50.

[115] Dunbabin, op. cit., 246.

[116] See R.A. Gauthier, 'Appendix: St. Thomas et l'Éthique à Nicomaque', in Thomas Aquinas, *Opera Omnia*, vol. 48, Rome 1971, xviii.

through Albert to Bonaventure. In the middle of Lectio 6 of Book 1, in the first commentary, Albert says:

> These arguments of Aristotle necessarily work against Plato, if Plato posited one Idea of all good things as their generic or specific form, as we explained above; this is how Aristotle understands him. If, on the other hand, Plato meant one Idea, by virtue of which all things descend as likenesses from one first formal cause of all good things, as the Commentator says, then it is clear that Aristotle's arguments have no force (*quod rationes nihil valent*).[117]

The last words are also found in Bonaventure's famous anti-Aristotelian *Collationes in Hexaemeron* 6,2,[118] but the Seraphic Doctor does not make the restrictions which Albert makes. He completely agrees with Eustratius' criticism of Aristotle's attack on the Supreme Good as one Idea:

> Whence Aristotle is also the first man to attack these Ideas in the *Ethics*, where he says that the supreme Good cannot be an Idea. And his arguments have no force (*quod rationes nihil valent*); they have been solved by the Commentator.[119]

This is clearly a reference to Eustratius, not Averroes, and indeed to the argument which we have already discussed. In the thirteenth to fifteenth centuries, the designation 'the commentator', which normally applies to Averroes, is used in relation to the *Ethics* for Eustratius. And no doubt it was found reassuring that the commentator on that work was a Christian.

In his second commentary, Albert follows Eustratius more closely. He gives an affirmative answer to the question[120] whether this is the first good before which there is nothing, and which is the cause of good in all other things, and adds: 'but some Peripatetics have objected with sophistical objections (*sophistice*) to this'. Eustratius uses the word *sophistice* at least three times to describe Aristotle's criticism of Plato's doctrine of the Good. Albert then adduces the Stoics (= Platonists) to argue in favour of a *ratio boni* which is not a *ratio generis*, which would belong to all its subjects, but a *ratio principii*, under which all good things fall, but which transcends them.[121]

---

[117] Lib. 1, lectio 6, 27,40-5.

[118] Quaracchi edition, *Opera Omnia*, Florence, 5,361.

[119] *Collatio* 6.2, 361.

[120] Lib. 1, tract. 2, cap. 3.

[121] I am grateful to Professor G. Locke of the University of Leiden and the Catholic University of Nijmegen, to Dr S. Scott-Fleming of Linacre College, Oxford, and to Mr Robin Rollinger of Utrecht, who all read considerable portions of this chapter and helped to improve my English. I am particularly indebted to Professor Sorabji for his many helpful suggestions. The new material in this chapter will be included in my introduction to *CLCAG* VII 3 (forthcoming).

CHAPTER NINETEEN

Philoponus, 'Alexander' and the origins of medieval logic[1]

Sten Ebbesen

Some modern scholars, Richard Sorabji prominent among them, are building a heroon for John Philoponus, the man who courageously rebelled against Aristotelian physics and pointed out weaknesses in traditional arguments for the eternity of the world.[2] In my mythology he used to be of less than heroic stature; I used to think of him as a chimera, whose head would happily chew away at its own tail, for I knew him only as the author of some generally flaccid commentaries on the *Organon*[3] whose few interesting statements tend to be mutually inconsistent. But perhaps both views of Philoponus are right. Professor Sorabji's heroic inventor of a new physics is the mature scholar who furthermore is fired by a crusader's conviction that he is fighting for truth. My John Chimera is the diffident young assistant professor of logic charged with teaching a subject he has not quite mastered; he relies on notes taken during professor Ammonius' lectures, but they are none too good, for though Ammonius taught lots of logic classes in his time, he never managed to become really interested in the discipline. Like most of his contemporaries, he considered acquaintance with the *Organon* as only a stepping-stone on the way to real philosophy.

In antiquity the great era of logic was over by about 200 BC. Its next blossoming occurred in Western Europe between AD 1100 and 1400. In this chapter I shall contend that late ancient Greek scholastic writers on logic, Philoponus among them, in spite of their own minute status as logicians, not only gave important impulses to medieval scholastic logic in general, but more specifically contributed both to the rise of a nominalistic current which was strong in the twelfth and fourteenth

[1] This is a slightly revised version of a lecture given in Professor Sorabji's seminar at the London Institute of Classical Studies on 22 February 1988. It was not meant for publication and time did not permit a thorough revision to supply documentation for all claims. See the Bibliography on pp. 460-1 for further details of the authors cited in the footnotes.

[2] See in particular Sorabji (ed.) 1987.

[3] On the *Categories, Prior Analytics and Posterior Analytics*; published in *CAG* 13.1-3.

centuries, and to the rise of the realistic current which dominated the thirteenth century.

*

When I was as young as Philoponus perhaps was when he wrote his commentaries on Aristotle, that is in my early twenties, I embarked on a one-man crusade to rescue the glorious achievements of Byzantine logicians from the oblivion into which they had fallen. I was then working on an edition of a Latin logic book from about 1270; some quotations in it suggested use of a rather sophisticated Greek commentary on Aristotle's *Sophistici Elenchi*, probably by the old professor of Aristotelian philosophy, Alexander of Aphrodisias, who lived round AD 200. However, no manuscript could be found, whether of the Latin translation or of the Greek original. So to find out what was going on, I had to gather Latin fragments and to look for Greek counterparts by searching Byzantine sources for traces left by their use of Alexander. Once I had got that far in my considerations, the idea of an expedition to rescue the beautiful virgin, Logica Byzantina, was born. My reasoning was simple: Everybody who ever said anything about Byzantine philosophy describes it as essentially theology and if they mention logic at all, they agree that it was of no value, consisting of bad rehashes of the ancients. This is exactly the description that used to be given of Western European logic from the Middle Ages, before the research of this century showed it to be of a standard not reached again till very recently. So probably, if someone who does not wear the distorting spectacles of a late nineteenth-century scholar starts to look at the texts, he will find gold where the old philologists found dirt.

Simple and persuasive argumentation – but wrong. Old Busse and his companions in the late nineteenth century had been quite right in their evaluation of Byzantine logicians.

A fiasco, then, which became only more tragic when my research did not reveal traces of a lost work by Alexander. Instead, many footprints stopped at Philoponus' door. Still, I continued the study of those miserable Greek texts for more than a decade because it became clear that for all their lack of logical insight they had proved historically important, helping to start that most glorious era of logic research that lasted from about 1100 till about 1400.

The text I was editing twenty years ago consisted of '*quaestiones*' on Aristotles' *Sophistici Elenchi*,[4] composed by an unknown and mediocre master at Paris about 1270, i.e. about the end of Thomas Aquinas' life. By then, even mediocre Parisian masters were much better logicians than Philoponus or the run of Greek commentators. Nowhere in the ancient world was there anything like the university of Paris. Yet my Parisian master refers with deference to a Greek commentator, 'Alexander'.

[4] Incerti Auctores (1977).

In a discussion of the six fallacies that Aristotle says depend on features of language,[5] it carries the weight of an argument that according to Alexander some of them depend on an actual, some on a potential and some on a purely imaginary multiplicity of meaning.[6] A little research will establish that this division is first met with in a small essay[7] on language-dependent fallacies by the famous physician Galen in the second century and reappears in a commentary on the *Sophistici Elenchi* by Michael of Ephesus from about 1130.[8] This Greek item not only was standard doctrine in Western Europe between 1150 and 1500, it also created the framework for new theories.

In what sense exactly is 'flying planes can be dangerous' an ambiguous expression? When correctly pronounced it is not ambiguous at all – it is not even *it*. Either you have a sentence that points out the dangers threatening mankind from objects that do not stay on earth; or one that warns you about exercising a certain action which affects aeroplanes, whether paper-aeroplanes or real ones is not clear. Using the Galenic classification you say we have a case of potential duplicity of meaning in the case of 'flying planes'. Now, this catches an intuition that we are dealing with something that is close to being real ambiguity – so close that it cannot be written off as pure imagination, as something that only an ignorant person could think of as a case of ambiguity. How is this intuition to be spelled out in scientific language? Well, the name *'potential* ambiguity' provides a clue: a potency is actualised when matter is equipped with form. Why not think of the single words of the two sentences as the common, undifferentiated matter of both, which becomes actualised when certain suprasegmental features, intonation, pausation etc., are added? Why not, indeed? There you have got a theory of the relation between string of words and sentence, and one that may also be transferred to the relationship between phonemes and word. The theory I have just sketched developed in the thirteenth century from a germ that was just a few lines of a Greek scholium translated into Latin.[9]

I shall not bother you with the details here, but my research uncovered many references to and loans from 'Alexander' in Latin texts from about

[5] Arist. *SE* 4, 165b24-27.

[6] For Western sources that attribute this division to Alexander, see Ebbesen 1981a, vol. 2, 395ff.

[7] Galenus, *de Captionibus in Dictione*. Edition in Ebbesen 1981a, vol. 2. Discussion of the work in Ebbesen 1981a, vol. 1, 79-87 and 236-9.

[8] The final edition of Michael's commentary was edited by Wallies in *CAG* 2.3, as 'Alexandri quod fertur commentarium...'; in Ebbesen 1981a and some other publications I refer to it as 'Ps.-Alexander-1'. An earlier version, which I have baptised 'Ps.-Alexander-2', remains unedited, but there are some excerpts in the preface to *CAG* 2.3 and in Ebbesen 1981a, vol. 2. A table showing Michael's loans from Galen is found in Ebbesen 1981a, vol. 2, 3. Michael's text about the three sorts of multiplicity and a couple of Latin echos are printed in parallel columns in Ebbesen 1979, xxxii-xxxiii.

[9] For further discussion of Western theories about potential ambiguity, see Ebbesen 1981b.

1150 or later.[10] It proved impossible to accept the ascription of the Greek commentary to Alexander of Aphrodisias, whereas it proved to have had an uncanny resemblance to the commentary that Michael of Ephesus composed about 1130 and that Maximilian Wallies edited in *Commentaria in Aristotelem Graeca* 2.3 a century ago. I was able to chart the genesis of Michael's commentary,[11] and a remarkable feature of the Latin translation appeared: it seemed to contain some material from an early, some from a late, edition of Michael's work, and some material known to have been in his possession though left out in the final edition.[12]

Do not imagine, however, that Michael was fastidious. He could not afford to be, since none of the ancient *Elenchi*-commentaries had survived for him to pillage. He therefore vacuumed old books for useful passages that might serve as or in scholia on the *Elenchi*, then emptied the bag of the vacuum cleaner and called the rubbish-heap a commentary. The heap emits a characteristic smell. It smells of Philoponus and his age, for that was where Michael gathered many a crumb and formed his whole conception of his subject and his task.[13]

Let me now turn from the *Elenchi* to the *Posterior Analytics*, which also makes its appearance in the West around 1150. It took some time for it to become a regular item in the curriculum, and the earliest known Latin commentary on it is from about 1225, composed by the idiosyncratic bishop of whom Richard Southern recently painted an unforgettable portrait in his *Robert Grosseteste: the growth of an English mind in medieval Europe* – the man who used the incomes of England's richest diocese to keep up his own research collective; the man who at the end of his life went to Lyons to tell the pope that there were strong indications that the pope was Antichrist. Southern contrasts Grosseteste's grasp of what is going on in the *Posterior Analytics* with the superficial acquaintance displayed by the slightly older Alexander Neckham, who 'looked on it partly as a collection of logical puzzles disturbing the traditional study of logic, partly as a haphazard collection of scientific curiosities ripe for moralisation', and thus in a heavily moralising chapter about the stars tells his reader that

> Stars twinkle, as Aristotle says in his *Posterior Analytics*, because they are very distant from the earth. Other stars do not twinkle, because they are near. The same effect can be seen in a candle which does not twinkle when it

[10] The fragments of 'Alexander's' commentary on Arist. *SE* were published in Ebbesen 1981a, vol. 2, 331-535. I have found a few more since then, but none that gives important new information.

[11] Ebbesen 1981a, vol. 1, 268-85. There is also a summary of my findings in Ebbesen 1979, viii-xii.

[12] The evidence for this is scarcely conclusive, but while most Latin fragments match Michael's first edition best, one discussed in Ebbesen 1981a, vol. 3, 221 seems to reflect the final edition. A Latin text discussed in op. cit. 206 appears to echo a scholium from a collection (*Comm. II*) that Michael certainly knew though he did not include this particular item from it in his commentary.

[13] Thus Michael's preface to the *Elenchi* commentary is closely related to, and possibly derived from Philoponus' in his commentary on *Analytica Posteriora*, *CAG* 13.3.

is near, but only when it is far away. Similarly, the minds of the faithful who are far removed from earthly desires are radiant with the light of grace.[14]

Southern correctly notes that Neckham does not pay any attention to the form of the argument, which was Aristotle's only reason for mentioning the matter, and shows no interest in the scientific explanation of the phenomenon either. But he adds,

> And yet, in parenthesis, there is one genuine observation – whether Nequam's or borrowed we cannot tell, but it is not Aristotle's – he notices that a candle in the distance twinkles, but nearby it does not. This small observation brings us a little nearer to scientific 'experience', and to Grosseteste.[15]

It probably is true that Grosseteste had a better grasp of the *Posterior Analytics* than Neckham. And it is true that the candle-example brings us a little nearer to Grosseteste – but in quite another way than Southern thought. For the candle-example is borrowed from John Philoponus' commentary on the Aristotelian passage,[16] and Grosseteste also contains material from Philoponus – in fact, a whole page of his commentary is a literal translation of Philoponus.[17] The candle tells a story about a debt to the Greeks, not about English curiosity about nature. Research by Minio-Paluello, Bernard Dod and myself has unearthed a considerable number of citations and direct quotations of Philoponus' commentary on the *Posterior Analytics* in Latin works from the twelfth to thirteenth centuries. However, when the Westerners mention their source, they call him Alexander.[18]

It is much the same story with the *Prior Analytics*. It began to be studied only after the middle of the twelfth century. And again it turns

[14] Alexander Neckham *de Rerum Naturis* I.6; the translation is taken from Southern 1986, 154-5.

[15] Southern 1986, 155.

[16] Philoponus *in An. Post.* (*CAG* 13.3) 171,13ff. In a footnote on p. 155 Southern comments on similar casual reference to *An. Post.* in Neckham *de Nat. Rer.* II.22: 'pisces non respirant, ut ex doctrina Posteriorum Analecticorum liquet.' Southern says: 'There is in fact no mention of the respiration of fish in *An. Post.*, and this is not Aristotle's doctrine in those works (...) where he discusses the problem. Nequam's statement, therefore, is an illustration of the distorted way in which the ideas of works not yet fully available in translation circulated in the early thirteenth century.' Yes – but the distortion just represents the common medieval practice of crediting an *auctor* with saying what his text means according to the standard commentary. In *An. Post.* 1.13, 78b15ff Aristotle says that although the fact that a wall is no living being may be used to show that it does not breathe, this fact does not explain why it does not breathe, for while 'everything that breathes is a living being' is true, 'every living being breathes' is not. Aristotle does not tell his reader what living organisms do not breathe, but Philoponus, *in An. Post.* (*CAG* 13.3) 174,28-9 gives insects and fish as examples of such creatures.

[17] Rossi 1981, 142-3 = Philop. *in An. Post.* (*CAG* 13.3) 109-10.

[18] The most complete collection of fragments of the Latin 'Alexander'/Philoponus commentary on *An. Post.* is the one in Ebbesen 1976, 89ff with corrigenda in Ebbesen 1979, xxxix-xl. A few more are found in Dod 1970. There are others as well. For Grosseteste's use of the Greek material, cf. Rossi 1978 and 1981.

out that the first men to work on it had access to some Greek explanatory notes, possibly a whole commentary. And again it turns out that there is a very good match between Philoponus' commentary and the echoes of Greek scholia that we find in Latin works.[19]

You may feel relieved to learn that one of the books of the post-1150 *New Logic* came without Philoponean notes. Apart from one or two scholia by Alexander of Aphrodisias, Western exegetes depended for their understanding of the *Topics* on Boethius, and hence indirectly on Themistius.[20]

For the *Old Logic*, i.e. Porphyry's *Isagoge*, and Aristotle's *Categories* and *de Interpretatione*, early Western scholars neither had nor needed Greek commentaries. Their standard companions to these works were by Boethius, a contemporary of Philoponus', who had exploited Greek predecessors – Porphyry in particular – to the utmost.

Until c. 1150 only the three books of the *Old Logic* were read, for only they had Boethian commentaries (we must remember that not one Western scholar in a thousand knew Greek). The *New Logic*, i.e. the rest of the *Organon*, became accessible through a combination of digging up forgotten Boethian translations of Aristotle, making new ones, and providing the necessary guidance for the reader by translating Greek commentaries. Even though the masters of France were often great logicians, they needed help to find their way in the maze of *Logica Nova*. Thanks to the long Greek tradition of exegesis, a mediocre Greek could help a brilliant Frenchman.

The man who did the translations was James of Venice – Jacobus Veneticus Graecus.[21] We do not know where he lived at the time he did the work, nor whence he got the Greek manuscripts needed. But we do know that he was in Constantinople at least once. And we know one environment there where he could find all the material needed. It was a circle of scholars whom princess Anna Comnena had gathered in the first decades of the twelfth century to study Aristotle. Michael of Ephesus was one of them. I strongly suspect Michael let his friend James use his manuscripts, including some that were the working copies for his own commentaries.[22]

[19] The exact nature of the Greek material on the *Prior Analytics* that had been translated into Latin is still a matter for research. James Shiel, following a suggestion by L. Minio-Paluello, in a number of papers (1982, 1984a, 1984b) has defended the thesis that all the West had was the set of scholia found in MS Firenze BNC Conv. Soppr. J.6.34 (published in *Aristoteles Latinus* III) and that they are due to Boethius. In Ebbesen 1981c reasons are given for thinking there may have been more material than offered by the Florence MS. I also think that the identity of the translator cannot be determined with certainty before a more thorough search for traces of the Greek material in the Latin tradition has been carried out. As things are, the argument for Boethius is pretty strong. For the whole question, cf. Ebbesen 1987a, 290-1 n. 15 (= p. 376 of this volume).

[20] For the translated scholium or scholia on the *Topics*, see Ebbesen 1976, 118-20 and 1979, xli-xlii. For the Western tradition of exegesis of the *Topics*, see Green-Pedersen 1984.

[21] The fundamental study is Minio-Paluello 1952. Additional information about James's work as a translator may be found in the volumes of *Aristoteles Latinus*. For a handy list of translations of Aristotelian works into Latin, see Dod 1982.

[22] This would explain the curious relationship between 'Alexander's' comm. *in SE* and Michael's that I mentioned above. Moreover, it might explain how 'Alexander's' commentary

I mentioned earlier that Michael vacuumed old manuscripts to find notes for his *Elenchi* commentary. Indeed his whole method of work consisted in gathering whatever ancient materials he could lay hands on, putting them together, mending them and supplementing them, so as to produce something that could claim to be a companion to a whole work by Aristotle. He put together commentaries on the *Metaphysics* and the *Ethics* in this way too.[23] Why? The reason is as simple as it is terrible: there was no living philosophical tradition in Byzantium to draw on. No wonder the empire of Constantine lasted for only one millennium!

Ammonius and his pupils from the sixth century were the men a Byzantine scholar would primarily consult if he wanted to do some work on the *Organon*. Those men who made it possible for a small part of the ancient philosophical tradition to cross the border into the Christian age would be the authors or sources of much that James of Venice could find in Michael's study. By that route they acquired a rôle in the formation of Western scholasticism.

But the ground had been prepared by Boethius. This older contemporary of Philoponus was the man who first of all made a part of Aristotle's *Organon* accessible in faithful Latin translation and accompanied with adaptations of Greek commentaries. He gave the West such a basic course in ancient Aristotelian Scholasticism that when the educational boom arrived in the twelfth century it was natural to boost the progress of knowledge by acquiring more Aristotle with Greek commentaries rather than ask for more Plato. Just as Boethius made the West receptive to Philoponus and Michael, so the common origin of Western and Islamic philosophy in ancient Greek scholasticism made it possible for the West to acknowledge Avicenna and Averroes as people with a relevant message.

*

What, then, did the Greek scholastics do to the development of Western logic?

First, via Boethius, they equipped the West with a belief in the superiority of Aristotelian logic over any imaginable rival.

Secondly, via Boethius they taught the West to take it easy if it looked as if the ontology behind the logic was at loggerhead᷎ with the one implied by platonising theologians. If Boethius had not taugh᷎ ᷎he West

---

came to contain extracts from scholia on the *Ethics*, as some Latin texts suggest it did (see Ebbesen 1981a, vol. 3, 155-7); Michael himself at one time worked on the project of annotating the *Ethics*. The idea that James might have known Michael was first proposed by Browning 1962, 8 (p. 401 of this volume) in the paper that for the first time established that Michael lived in the twelfth century and worked under the patronage of Anna Comnena.

[23] This statement may need modification, but I consider it probable that the Byzantine commentary on Arist. *EN* that Robert Grosseteste translated was put together by Michael, the latest identifiable contributor to the work (cf. Mercken 1973). Michael certainly supplemented Alexander's commentary on *Metaphysics* 1-5 with scholia on 6-13, and he may at the same time have revised Alexander's work (cf. Ebbesen 1981a, vol. 1, 201).

that a logic for the language we use about the sensible world may recognise no paradigmatic universals, and yet be reconcilable with a strong form of realism which considers more than just the sensible world, the dominance of Augustinian theology in early medieval times might have made it impossible for Aristotelian logic to become established as a respected discipline.

Thirdly, via Boethius' logical monographs, they kindled an interest – untypical of themselves – in the art of argumentation, and also in logical analysis of questions in which no serious ontological principle seemed to be at stake.[24] It is not difficult to see that the ontological status of propositional contents is relevant to the truth of the principle that there is only one eternal thing, God himself, and also relevant to the question whether the patriarchs of the Old Covenant believed in the same articles of faith as Christians do. Though these were not favourite themes in late ancient times as they became in twelfth-century France, it is a sort of problem that is kindred in spirit to those that Simplicius, for example, would address about the ontological status of accidents or the like. But the Latin interest in how arguments work, whether there is some sort of warrant for non-syllogistic inferences of the type 'Socrates is a man, so he is an animal' or whether the principle that anything follows from an impossibility is valid – that is something that can only be understood with reference to the fact that Boethius' logical monographs, which are not representative of a major interest of the ancients, made up a major part of the set texts in early medieval schools.

Fourthly, they gave the West the first encouragement to embark on the wider reading of Aristotle from c. 1150 which resulted in the 'classical' scholasticism of the late thirteenth century with its important contributions to epistemology, ontology, psychology and several other -ologies plus general linguistics.

It is remarkable that the Greek scholia/commentaries on the *Prior* and *Posterior Analytics* and *Elenchi* seem to have had very scant diffusion in the thirteenth century, and the very same Grosseteste who copies a page from Philoponus does not to my knowledge repeat his predecessor's explanation of anything philosophically important. Though much research remains to be done to see what influence the Greek commentaries on *Ars Nova* exerted, the general picture is that they had a tremendous effect in starting a redirection of Western logic, but soon lost readers because they were unsuited (too jejune) for use once the train with Western scholars had acquired some speed down the new track. Little details, like the story about the twinkling candle, remained in margins of Aristotle's text as a reminder of the time when the Greek scholia were the only guide to the text.

*

[24] The best introduction to Latin medieval logic is still Pinborg 1972. Cf. also Kretzmann *et al.* 1982.

Among Boethius' logical monographs[25] the one on hypothetical syllogisms and the one about topics were particularly dear to the early Middle Ages. Boethius' *Topica* (or *de Differentiis Topicis*) shows how all arguments depend for their acceptability on certain axioms about genera, species, opposites and the like – the so-called topical differences. Topical axioms – or 'maxims', as Boethius calls them – may be like 'of whatever a species is predicated, of that the genus may be predicated'; the topical difference 'species' and the associated maxim makes 'since Socrates is a swine, Socrates is a beast' an excellent argument. There is a long and complicated history behind this piece of theory which is perhaps best understood in a Platonic light to the effect that 'genus', 'species' and the like are ideas, which may be unfolded in arguments. The first step in the unwrapping is the formulation of the maxims which reveal the mutual properties of these quite formal ideas. The next step consists in the formulation of some of the infinitely many arguments of which the maxims are the ultimate generalisations or forms – with a little good will and not making too much of the difference between conditional and declarative propositions you can see 'Socrates is a swine, therefore he is a beast' as an instance of the axiom 'of whatever a species is predicated, of that the genus is predicated'.[26] But Boethius does not say that his topical differences are Platonic ideas. He claims that they have a certain power which they may transfer to arguments, but he does not say what they are. The medievals tried to find an answer.

*

One most remarkable feature of early medieval philosophy in the eleventh and early twelfth centuries is the occurrence of very strong forms of nominalism, with the explicit claim that predication is a linguistic matter – a predicate is a word, not some sort of thing[27]– and that there is nothing universal except for words, not even universal concepts. Roscelin, Abélard's teacher and the object of Anselm's wrath, seems to have been a truculent nominalist. Mitigated, and more viable, forms of the position also occur. Thus Abélard's variety which introduces a special sort of non-thing, the status 'to be white', 'to be a man' etc., to account for the applicability of one word to a multitude of things. Later varieties tend to become conceptualistic – the primary universal is a concept, via its universality its companion word is universal. This latter form is particularly popular in the late Middle Ages, from the time of

---

[25] List of Boethius' works in Ebbesen 1987a, 286 = this volume p. 373.

[26] For Boethian theory and its background, see Ebbesen 1981a, vol. 1, 106-26; Green-Pedersen 1984, part 1.

[27] Thus, e.g., the anonymous and unedited late eleventh-century commentary on Boethius' *Diff. Top.* called 'Primum oportet' (see Green-Pedersen 1984) says: 'in quo destruuntur veteres qui praedicatum et subiectum dicunt res esse, non voces' – 'and thus the traditional view is refuted according to which predicate and subject are things, not words.'

Ockham and Buridan. But it is a continuation of the earlier forms in the sense that a main reason for introducing it was an acceptance of a logical tradition with twelfth-century roots which seemed to require an extensional semantics that only some sort of nominalism could provide. This logical tradition had been pushed somewhat in the background in the years 1200-1315, but had not quite disappeared.[28] While the metaphysical battles raged, logic hibernated, and got out again when realism in metaphysics had left all metaphysicians severely battered.

Now, thirteenth-century mainstream philosophy was heavily Aristotle-centred and owed a lot to the late ancient blend of Aristotelian and Platonic thought – though sometimes by devious routes, as via Avicenna or Averroes. Like so much late ancient philosophy it first produces an inextricable tangle of the real and the intelligible, then claims that there is a pure reality prior to the tangle, but screened from the gaze of mortals.

People with a robust sense of reality like to maintain that before the rise of thinking beings there was a real world, and one that would have been there even if there had not now been humans to think of it; and similarly that there are unknown realities now and after the extinction of intelligent life in the universe whose being there is independent of whether they are ever discovered by man or any other living organism; moreover, that things do not change their character for being studied or not, and that the things that we can study would neither be nor appear different to us if we were supplied with the extra powers needed to see those that we actually cannot see.

In the late thirteenth-century type of philosophy which is often styled 'modism' all objects grasped by thought are in some way real in the way they are thought – Socrates has singular, independent, actual, concrete reality; man has universal, concrete reality; humanity has universal, abstract reality. There are as many sorts of real things as we have angles from which to view them. Things are irreducibly intentional. Yet this exuberant ontology is reduced by introducing super-things, common natures. What is Socrates but human nature thought of in concretion and individually? What is man but human nature thought of in concretion and universally? What is humanity but human nature thought of in abstraction?[29]

The undifferentiated natures make up a kind of mind-independent world, but a strange one, consisting of non-existing things, each having less-than-numeric identity, as Duns Scotus said. Things which upon inspection by a created mind at least will or would manifest themselves as abstract or concrete, universal or particular according to the perspective chosen. Like eternity it is a world that by necessity disappears once you start to examine it – it is by definition inaccessible to examination in its pureness.

[28] cf. Ebbesen 1985.

[29] This presentation of modism is grossly over-simplified. Some idea of the actual complexity may be obtained from Ebbesen 1988. Some of the best studies of modistic logic and theory of science are found in Pinborg 1984.

As Ockham saw, whatever strange constructs theology may need to deal with the Trinity's peculiar way of being one, there is a simple way to avoid that sort of twilight world in philosophy by letting universality be a property of words and concepts only, and letting things come in one variety only: as numerically distinct. You may still feel uncomfortable about things that nobody sees, but if you want to make room for them in your ontology, you can do so without equipping them with the exotic property of being invisible when unmodified, a property that seems to belong to principles of things rather than to real things and thus, to speak in medieval terms, obscures the distinction between natures and God, between creature and creator. And, surely, the world is created and depends on God's will for whatever sort of being it possesses.

It is often held that there is a connection between fourteenth-century nominalism and a realisation that the notion of an omnipotent God, creator of a contingent universe, each particular thing in which is also contingent with respect to the whole, is difficult to reconcile with the notion of a universe, the singular objects or facts of which either reduce to being God himself because they are just principles seen in a certain light; or are all accessible to intellectual inspection thanks to their having also a universal mode of being apart from whatever other modes they may have.

But if this can with some plausibility be invoked as a major motive force behind fourteenth-century nominalism, I see no evidence that its predecessor about 1100 was similarly motivated. Nominalism looks implausible in a time when philosophers were raised on Boethius, one of those Neoplatonic Aristotelians of whose philosophy thirteenth-century modism was both historically and systematically a continuation. How could the early nominalism arise?

A first hint at an explanation is given if we turn our attention to ninth-century Byzantium, where Photius exhibits some extraordinarily nominalistic leanings in an essay occasioned by a reading of Porphyry's *Isagoge* with some late ancient commentary.[30] In contemporary France, you find not only strong forms of realism, as with Scotus Eriugena, but also a strong attack on such realism and the way it trades on the everyday sense of figurative expressions used in such formulas as 'species flow from genera', 'the more general engenders the less general' etc. The attack occurs in Ratramnus' *De anima ad Odonem*; some of Ratramnus' heaviest ammunition was supplied by Boethius' commentary on the *Isagoge*. Eleventh- and twelfth-century defences of nominalism often adduce supporting evidence from the *Categories*, the standard commentary on which was Boethius'.

Both to the ancients and to the early medievals, *Isagoge* and *Categories* belong together. They were read together and they were generally supposed to express the same doctrine, only in slightly different areas. Aristotle's book obviously was the more important one, so their

[30] Photius *Amphilochia* 77.

interpretation of the *Categories* was bound to determine what they would say about universals when commenting on Porphyry.

To see how late ancient exegesis of Porphyry and Aristotle could inspire nominalism, we should remember that the way the Neoplatonists made it possible for themselves to wear both a Platonic and an Aristotelian mask was by interpreting the *Categories* in a nominalistic-conceptualistic way, summarised in the statement that the work is about words qua significative of things and the slogan 'words signify things via concepts', plus the limitation that the theory of categories does not apply when we turn to higher levels than the sensible world. It will be convenient to remember that the discussion whether the subject of the *Categories* is words or things takes up much space in ancient commentaries.

We may also remember that Boethius in his commentary on the *Categories* follows Porphyry's on the same work in all essentials. He, in turn, was not only the first strong advocate of the word-qua-significative view, but also one of the last philosophers with some sympathetic interest in Stoic thought, though he may have known the school only at second hand. The Stoics were scarcely genuine nominalists; they did, however, reject universal things, substituting for universals some quasi-things that words signify, accepting as real only the particulars that words denote.

I believe that Stoic anti-realism via its influence on Porphyry and his on Boethius is part of the explanation why a nominalism could arise in the early Middle Ages. It should be kept in mind, though, that the medievals got the Stoic influence in a form which had obscured both the beauty and some of the difficulties of the original theory. Thus there is something fishy about Stoic particulars which is not quite so obvious in medieval nominalism. After all, Stoics accept just one substance, and so like all monists get into trouble when trying to find values of the x in their '$(x) Fx$' formulas. Bertrand Russell, having embraced a mathematical and hence, in his own words, incurably Platonic, logic, throughout his long life continued the search for an italicised a, a genuine individual to satisfy his propositional functions. The medievals did not quite escape the problem, *inter alia* because they had inherited Porphyry's definition of an individual as a unique set of properties. The problem was brought to consciousness in the fourteenth century, when it was shown that even Ockham-style nominalists actually operated with nothing or everything – non-descript thises – as carriers of properties or names.[31] But at least the problem could be more easily concealed in a tradition where, thanks to Aristotle, people were not quite strangers to the notion of an entity whose formal component is self-satisfying. A primary substance, in short.

However, this is not quite enough to explain the characteristics of early medieval nominalism. We should also not forget the theory of imposition of words, which came to the Middle Ages from Porphyry via Boethius. In short description it says that man has two different sorts of vocabulary: a

[31] For the late medieval recognition of the problem, see Ebbesen and Pinborg 1982, 120.

primary one created by naming sensible things; and a secondary one created by naming the names that belong in the object-language. 'Man' and 'rotund' are words of the first type, 'noun' and 'verb' of the second type.[32]

Boethius presents the theory of the two impositions in the introduction to his commentary on the *Categories*, but he never uses it for anything except in one place, where he shows that it can be used to solve a sophism which threatens the transitivity of predication. The sophism is 'Socrates is a man, man is a species, ergo Socrates is a species'. Boethius explains that the transitivity breaks down in the second premise, because there is no predication 'in quid': when we say 'man is a species', the function of 'species' is to indicate that 'man' is predicable of individuals only, and thus 'species' is 'in a way, a name of names'.[33]

It was not Boethius' idea to use the 'name-of-names' solution in this place, for it is also mentioned by Dexippus, that wonderfully unfaithful pupil of Iamblichus, always ready to deliver an unexpected kick at 'those who fancy the Pythagorean assumptions'.[34] In this case, though, he may owe the not particularly Pythagorean piece of doctrine to his teacher; or else his and Boethius' common source was Porphyry.

Anyhow, this little scholium – some five lines all told – was to be of tremendous importance.

*

So here is a recipe for a potent brew, which may release significant amounts of nominalism and hence should be labelled 'dangerous' and kept away from children and innocent people in general:

Take
    (1) Porphyry's own claim that his treatise on universals is an introduction to Aristotle's *Categories*.
Add
    (2) Boethius' reproduction of Porphyry's explanation that the *Categories* is a book about words
and
    (3) Boethius' reproduction of Porphyry's story about the two impositions
plus
    (4) Boethius' version of the Greek scholium about 'man is a species'.

Stir the whole thing and you start to realise that many of the statements in *Ars Vetus* and Boethius' commentaries make best sense if you take 'species' as a name of words.

[32] For more details, see the extract from Ebbesen 1981a, vol. 1, 141ff (reprinted above, pp. 146ff).

[33] For Boethius on imposition and names of names, see Ebbesen 1987a, 287-99 (reprinted in this volume, pp. 374-83). The Dexippus passage referred to below is in his comm. *in Cat.* (*CAG* 4.2) 26.

[34] Dexippus *in Cat.* 17.1ff.

Now add
>   (6) the Aristotelian claim of priority for primary substances, and
>   Boethius' emphatic endorsement of this (again echoing Porphyry).

Finally add
>   (7) Boethius' doctrine of topics, which cries for an answer to the question,
>   what ontological status do the topical differences have?

Stir the mixture once more, and the nominalistic vapours start pouring out
of the cauldron. For now you suddenly see that of course the topical
differences are words of the second imposition, that is names of those
words which are names of individual things. All of logic will work without
the assumption of universal entities except for the linguistic ones. A lot of
authoritative statements become understandable. You need not devise
strange explanations of why the auctores sometimes say that a universal
'is predicated', sometimes that it 'is said' or 'uttered'. If any universal,
hence any predicate, is a word, of course 'is said' or 'uttered' is a good
predicate of predicates.

If this last point sounds familiar, it's all right. Similar arguments are
related by Dexippus and other ancient commentators. But for all I know,
there was no true Aristotelian nominalism in ancient times, at most a
conceptualism with concepts abstracted from sets of similar objects.

In the late eleventh century, if not before, some Westerners took the
crucial step from exegesis to philosophical claim, and said: 'When *Isagoge,
Categories, Topics*, all make sense with a nominalistic interpretation,
nominalism is the truth.'[35]

The first, apparently rather crude versions came under heavy fire and
were succeeded by Abélard's more sophisticated variety. However, this too
disappeared before the end of the twelfth century. What did not disappear
so fast was a generally extensionalistic interpretation of predication,
where at least the subject term had to range over a non-empty set of
individuals for a proposition to be true.[36] Also the view that the
Aristotelian categories are primarily a classification of words survived.
Gilbert the Porretan saw things that way and noticed that the logical
behaviour of words differs according as they are used to speak about things
whose structure derives from nature – animals, plants etc., – things that
result from human decisions such as social positions and artefacts, or,
finally, things that belong in the sphere of rational and linguistic activity –
words, arguments etc. Hence he resolutely tripled the categories, reserv-
ing one set of ten categories for the natural vocabulary, one for the ethical,

---

[35] Most sources for early nominalism remain unedited. There are strong nominalist
tendencies in Garlandus Compotista and Anon. Comm. *in Boeth. Diff. Top.* 'Primum oportet'
(both c. 1050/1100). An account of (presumably early) nominalists' arguments is given in
Ps.-Rhabanus' commentary on Porphyry, in anonymous fragment in MS clm 29520/2 and
other sources as well. I owe my information about the early Latin Porphyry commentaries to
Y. Iwakuma who is preparing an edition.

[36] cf. Ebbesen 1981d.

and one for the rational-linguistic.[37]

When the new wave of Aristotelian texts arrived about 1150, the *Elenchi* and the Greek commentary on it were the first to achieve widespread attention. It caused some confusion that the treatment of fallacies was different from the traditional Western one, but at first the new material, which included for instance a version of the Stoic 'not someone' (*outis*) sophisma – an argument against crude Platonic realism – at first this new material just helped refine existing logic, including the so-called theory of supposition or theory of what a term stands for in given contexts.

*

However, a virus was spreading. The availability of Philoponus' commentary gave some people the courage to study the *Posterior Analytics*, and they were infected with yearning for a theory of knowledge and science, such as that book seemed to promise devoted readers, a theory vastly superior to anything the West had previously known.[38] Those infected with the disease would turn their backs on the world of particulars, and many were persuaded that the theory of which they expected so much bliss required acceptance of some sort of real universals to be the immutable objects of knowledge and verifiers of sentences about things with no present representatives. Avicenna persuaded almost everybody that this was what should be done, and though few gave in to rampant Platonism, many accepted some variant of the Avicennan distinction between existential and essential being, only the latter of which is required for objects of knowledge.

The thirteenth-century turn towards realism is epitomised in the way the subject of the *Categories* was redefined. It was now commonly said to be *(ens) dicibile (incomplexum) ordinabile in genere* 'that which is expressible, and simple, in its hierarchical ordering',[39] i.e. realities qua signifiable by words. Porphyry's definition 'words qua significative of things' had been stood on its head. The way was open for common natures to make their entry.

And now I have closed the circle. We are back in modistic times, waiting for an English mind, waiting for Ockham. Medieval logicians surpassed the ancients. But they were deeply influenced by the men from Porphyry to Philoponus; both in nominalistic periods and in realistic ones. The ancient scholastics were chimeras with an Aristotelian body barely managing to keep the Platonic head and the Stoic tail from either running in opposite directions or engaging in a deadly fight with each other. The medievals saw the monster from both ends.

---

[37] See Ebbesen *et al.* 1983; Jacobi 1987.

[38] The twelfth-century texts published in Ebbesen 1976 and 1979 are witnesses to the fascination that *An. Post.* with Philoponus' commentary could exert.

[39] So already in John Pagus' commentary on the *Categories* (MS Padova BU 1589), presumably dating from c. 1230.

Bibliography

Browning, Robert. 1962: 'An unpublished funeral oration on Anna Comnena', *Proceedings of the Cambridge Philological Society* 188 (n.s. 8) 1-12. Repr. in Browning 1977 and in this volume as Chapter 17.

Browning, Robert. 1977: *Studies on Byzantine History, Literature and Education.* Variorum: London.

Dod, Bernard G. 1970: *The Study of Aristotle's Posterior Analytics in the Twelfth and Thirteenth Centuries,* Unpublished B.Litt. thesis, Oxford.

Dod, Bernard G. 1982: 'Aristoteles Latinus', in N. Kretzmann, A. Kenny, J. Pinborg (eds), *The Cambridge History of Later Medieval Philosophy,* 46-79.

Ebbesen, Sten. 1976: 'Anonymus Aurelianensis II, Aristotle, Alexander, Porphyry and Boethius. Ancient Scholasticism and twelfth-century Western Europe', *CIMAGL* 16, 1-128.

Ebbesen, Sten. 1979: 'Anonymi Aurelianensis I Commentarium in Sophisticos Elenchos', *Cahiers de l'Institut du moyen âge grec et latin (CIMAGL),* University of Copenhagen, 34.

Ebbesen, Sten. 1981a: *Commentators and Commentaries on Aristotle's Sophistici Elenchi. A Study of Post-Aristotelian Ancient and Medieval Writings on Fallacies,* vols 1-3 = *Corpus Latinum Commentariorum in Aristotelem Graecorum (CLCAG)* 7.1-3, Leiden.

Ebbesen, Sten. 1981b: 'Suprasegmental phonemes in ancient and mediaeval logic', in H.A.G. Braakhuis *et al.* (eds), *English Logic and Semantics from the End of the Twelfth Century to the Time of Ockham and Burleigh. Acts of the 4th European Symposium on Mediaeval Logic and Semantics = Artistarium, Supplementa I,* Nijmegen, 331-59.

Ebbesen, Sten. 1981c: 'Analyzing syllogisms *or* Anonymus Aurelianensis III – the (presumably) earliest extant Latin commentary on the Prior Analytics, and its Greek model', *CIMAGL* 37, 1-20.

Ebbesen, Sten. 1981d: 'The present king of France wears hypothetical shoes with categorical laces. Twelfth-century writers on well-formedness', *Medioevo* 7, 91-113.

Ebbesen, Sten and Pinborg, Jan. 1982: 'Thott 581⁰ 4, or De ente rationis, De definitione accidentis, De probatione terminorum', in A. Maierù (ed.), *English Logic in Italy in the 14th and 15th Centuries. Acts of the 5th European Symposium on Medieval Logic and Semantics = History of Logic* I, Naples, 111-46.

Ebbesen, Sten, K.M. Fredborg and L.O. Nielsen (eds). 1983: 'Compendium logicae Porretanum ex codice Oxoniensi Collegii Corporis Christi 250: a manual of Porretan doctrine by a pupil of Gilbert's', *CIMAGL* 46.

Ebbesen, Sten. 1985: 'OXYNAT: a theory about the origins of British logic', in P.O. Lewry (ed.), *The Rise of British Logic, Acts of the Sixth European Symposium on Medieval Logic and Semantics = Papers in Medieval Studies* 7, Toronto, 1-17.

Ebbesen, Sten. 1987a: 'Boethius as an Aristotelian scholar', in J. Wiesner (ed.), *Aristoteles: Werk und Wirkung* 2, Berlin and NY, 286-311. Repr. in this volume as Chapter 16.

Ebbesen, Sten. 1987b: 'The way fallacies were treated in scholastic logic', *CIMAGL* 55, 107-34.

Ebbesen, Sten. 1988: 'Concrete accidental terms: late thirteenth-century debates about problems relating to such terms as "album" ', in N. Kretzmann (ed.), *Meaning and Inference in Medieval Philosophy,* Dordrecht, 104-74.

Garlandus Compotista. 1959: *Dialectica*, L.M. de Rijk (ed.), Wijsgerige teksten en studies 3, Assen.

Green-Pedersen, Niels Jørgen. 1984: *The Tradition of the Topics in the Middle Ages*, Munich.

Incerti Auctores. 1977: *Quaestiones super Sophisticos Elenchos*, ed. S. Ebbesen. Corpus Philosophorum Danicorum Medii Aevi VII, Copenhagen.

Jacobi, Klaus. 1987: 'Kategorien der Sittenlehre. Gedanken zur Sprache der Moral in einem Logik-Kompendium des 12. Jahrhunderts', in Beckmann, J.P. *et al.* (eds), *Philosophie im Mittelalter. Entwicklungslinien und Paradigmen*, Hamburg, 103-24.

Kretzmann, N., A. Kenny, J. Pinborg (eds). 1982: *The Cambridge History of Later Medieval Philosophy*, Cambridge.

Mercken, H.P.F. 1973: *The Greek Commentaries on the Nicomachean Ethics of Aristotle* I = *Corpus Latinum Commentariorum in Aristotelem Graecorum* 6.1, Leiden.

Minio-Paluello, Lorenzo. 1952: 'Iacobus Veneticus Grecus: canonist and translator of Aristotle', *Traditio* 8, 265-304. Repr. in *Opuscula, The Latin Aristotle*, Amsterdam 1972.

Photius. 1986: *Epistulae et Amphilochia* 5, L.G. Westerink (ed.), Leipzig.

Pinborg, Jan. 1972: *Logik und Semantik im Mittelalter*, Stuttgart and Bad Cannstatt.

Pinborg, Jan. 1984: *Medieval Semantics. Selected Studies on Medieval Logic and Grammar*, London.

Ratramne de Corbie. 1952. *Liber de anima ad Odonem Bellovacensem*, D.C. Lambot (ed.), Analecta Mediaevalia Namurcensia 2, Namur and Lille.

Rossi, Pietro. 1978: 'Tracce della versione latina di un commento greco ai Secondi Analitici nel Commentarius in Posteriorum Analyticorum libros di Roberto Grossatesta', *Rivista di filosofia neo-scolastica* 70, 433-9.

Rossi, Pietro (ed.). 1981: *Robertus Grosseteste, Commentarius in Posteriorum Analyticorum libros* = Testi e studi per il 'Corpus Philosophorum Medii Aevi' II, Firenze.

Shiel, James. 1982: 'A recent discovery: Boethius' notes on the Prior Analytics', *Vivarium* 20, 128-41.

Shiel, James. 1984a: 'A set of Greek reference signs in the Florentine ms. of Boethius' translation of the Prior Analytics', *Scriptorium* 38, 327-42.

Shiel, James. 1984b: 'Aristoteles Latinus III: Scholiorum in Analytica Priora supplementa', *Bulletin de philosophie médiévale édité par la SIEPM* 26, 119-26.

Sorabji, Richard (ed.). 1987: *Philoponus and the Rejection of Aristotelian Science*, London.

Southern, Richard W. 1986. *Robert Grosseteste: the growth of an English mind in medieval Europe*, Oxford.

CHAPTER TWENTY

Aristotle's doctrine of abstraction in the commentators

Ian Mueller

1. Universals

Discussions of mathematical ontology are frequently blurred by the assertion that mathematics or science generally is about universals. Consider the following geometric proposition:

(1) If *ABC* and *DEF* are two triangles with equal sides *AB, DE* and *BC, EF*, and equal angles *ABC, DEF*, then the sides *AC, DF* are also equal.

In one sense we may say that this proposition and any other general proposition is 'about' universals: it enunciates a consequence of being a triangle. But there is another, *prima facie* more straightforward sense of 'about' in which (1) is not about being a triangle, but about triangles, not about universals, but about mathematical objects, as I shall call them.[1] This sense of 'to be about' can perhaps be paraphrased as 'to presuppose as existing'.[2] Although there is a tendency for individuals to hold analogous views about universals and mathematical objects, there is no necessary connection between the two issues. One might, for example, be

---

[1] Most of the ancients, including Aristotle, speak of mathematics and mathematical objects generally, but carry on their discussion in terms of geometry in ways not always easily generalisable to include arithmetic. It is convenient to follow them by using the word 'mathematics' and 'mathematical objects', but much of what is said will be most easily understood in terms of geometry.

[2] The notion of 'presupposition of existence' I have in mind is clearly formulated by W.V.O. Quine in his frequently reprinted paper 'On what there is', in *From a Logical Point of View*, Cambridge Mass. 1953, 1-19. I, however, would like to use this notion more intuitively than he does without presupposing the representation of a theory or proposition in the first order predicate calculus or insisting on Quine's monolithic conception of existence based on the use of bound variables in a first-order theory. From my point of view it would be coherent to say that a theory expressed in the vocabulary of Aristotle's syllogistic was about universals, and even to go on to say that the universals are not real entities, e.g. not substances. Worrying about these subtler issues would obscure my main points.

I should also mention that in translations from the Greek concerning this topic I render *peri* as 'about' without any intention of imposing an interpretation on the passage translated.

a realist about universals and yet think that the triangles mentioned in (1) are mental constructions or fictions, or be a nominalist and yet think that there are real triangles (defined, say, by points in space).

I shall take for granted that mathematics is about universals in the first sense I have mentioned, or, as I shall say, mathematics concerns universals, since I do not think there would be serious disagreement on this topic among the ancient commentators and their associates. However, like Aristotle and Plato themselves, and like many modern commentators, they are not always clear about the distinction between mathematical universals and mathematical objects. I do not, of course, mean that they do not make the distinction clearly in some contexts, but only that at crucial points they violate it, invoking truths about universals to justify what seem to be claims about mathematical objects or vice versa. Since I am primarily interested in the treatment of mathematical objects, I shall focus on discussions of them, but it is impossible to avoid introducing material on universals, since they intrude so frequently into these discussions.

2. Aristotle's account of mathematical objects

It seems to me that there are four main interpretations of Aristotle's account of mathematical objects. According to one interpretation, there are no such objects for him since he believes geometry to be about universals. I shall not discuss this alternative, which although thoroughly in line with the doctrine of science of the *Analytics*, hardly fits with the things Aristotle says about mathematical objects in his major discussions of them in *Physics* 2.2 and *Metaphysics* 13.3. I shall simply sketch the remaining alternatives and the major difficulties they face.

> Alternative 1. Mathematical objects are physical objects which the mathematician studies by leaving out of account their mathematically irrelevant properties. On this interpretation, which seems to be gaining in popularity[3] (if one can speak about popularity in such rarefied matters), the only difference between mathematics and, say, physics is the properties studied and left out of account by students in the two fields: the mathematician worries about the shape of the earth, but not its weight; the physicist studies the weight of the earth, but not the distribution of crops over its surface. This interpretation is, I believe, foreign to most Neoplatonists, who take for granted that physical things do not satisfy the definitions of mathematics.[4]

> Alternative 2. Mathematical objects are embodied in pure extension underlying physical objects; the geometer's abstraction of non-geometric properties enables him to apprehend these things which satisfy the

[3] The view is put forward by Jonathan Lear in 'Aristotle's philosophy of mathematics,' *Philosophical Review* 91, 1982, 161-92.

[4] I am inclined to think Aristotle also takes this position, but he is not at all explicit about it.

mathematician's definitions. This interpretation, which I have espoused,[5] has the disadvantage of assigning to Aristotle a theory about which one might expect him to have been more explicit if he held it.

Alternative 3. Mathematical objects exist only in the mind of the mathematician who reasons about triangles, angles, etc., which he conceives separately from matter. This interpretation, which I think one can say is that of at least the majority of the commentators, has not found much explicit support in modern scholarship[6] because of the generally accepted view that Aristotle's conception of knowledge is too realistic to allow for such a mentalistic account of mathematics.

My major reason for going through these alternatives is to make clear in advance that the commentators' interpretation of Aristotle is certainly disputable and probably wrong. However, I am much less interested in the question of the correctness of their interpretation than in the question of its origins and development.

3. Ammonius and Philoponus

At 55,23ff of his commentary on the *de Anima* Philoponus distinguishes three factors in natural things, form, matter, and the cause of the presence of form in matter, and five *methodoi* for dealing with them, physics, particular *tekhnai* (technologies), dialectic, mathematics, and first philosophy. The first two of these *methodoi* deal with all three factors, the last three with form only, first philosophy with forms completely separate from matter, dialectic with the formal causes of things in matter, but not as cause. Here is Philoponus on mathematics:

> The mathematician also deals with forms which are inseparable from matter, not with all, but only with those which can be separated by thought (*epinoia*). These are the so-called common sensibles, such as magnitudes and figures. For it is not possible to separate the form of flesh or bone and things of this kind from matter even in *epinoia*. For if one has conceived softness and moistness and ruddiness and whatever else gives form to flesh, one will have also simultaneously conceived the appropriate matter, so that if one abstracts the matter one also abstracts these things. Therefore, the mathematician gives definitions of the *per se* (essential) forms capable of abstraction; without taking matter into account, he gives these definitions in and of themselves. Consequently in a definition he does not mention the cause either. For if he defined the cause, he would certainly also have taken the matter into account. Since, then, he doesn't discuss matter, he doesn't mention the cause either. For example: What is a triangle? A figure

---

[5] 'Aristotle on geometric objects', in Jonathan Barnes, Malcolm Schofield, Richard Sorabji (eds), *Articles on Aristotle*, vol. 3, London 1979, 96-107.

[6] By 'explicit support' I mean only detailed interpretations and defences. Many general accounts of Aristotle include brief descriptions of his philosophy of mathematics which I would classify under alternative 3. See, for example, Abraham Edel, *Aristotle and his Philosophy*, Chapel Hill 1982, 106: 'Mathematics in [Aristotle's] view deals with the features of things that can be separated in thought (that is, abstracted) and held separate.'

contained by three straight lines. What is a circle? A figure contained by one line. In these definitions matter is not mentioned and therefore neither is a cause through which a specific form is in a specific matter. Consequently, the mathematician will give [only] the causes for the features which necessarily belong to figures (*ta sumptômata ta kath' hauta sumbainonta tois skhêmasi*); for example, he will say why the triangle has angles equal to two right angles. (*in DA* 57,28-58,6)

Philoponus is here quite clearly dependent on Ammonius, who expresses very much the same view in his commentary on Porphyry's *Isagoge* (11,22-13,7). Ammonius makes the following correlation between the parts of philosophy and the entities they study:

theology: things entirely separate from matter in *hupostasis* (existence) and in the *epinoia* of them;
physics: things entirely inseparate from matter both in *hupostasis* and in the *epinoia* of them;
mathematics: things separate in one respect (*kata ti*), not separate in another.

And he explains the character of mathematics as follows:

For a circle or a square and such things cannot exist (*hupostênai*) by themselves separate from some matter, and therefore they are inseparable from matter; but when we see a wooden or copper or stone circle we get an impression of the form of the circle itself in our *dianoia* (discursive thought), and we maintain such impressions by themselves apart from matter (just as wax receives the impression of a signet without also receiving any of the matter); and therefore it is separable from the matter in the sense that it is separated in *epinoia*. (*in Isag.* 11,31-12,6)

Ammonius introduces another trichotomy related to but not identical with the distinction among the parts of philosophy in his commentary on Porphyry's *Isagoge* (39,14ff), taking up a question Porphyry (1,9-14) had set aside as requiring too deep and lengthy a discussion, namely the question of the ontological status of genera and species (*eidê*). By the end of Ammonius' explanation the term *eidos* seems to have taken on its more general sense of form:

Consider a signet ring with a certain image (*ektupôma*), e.g., of Achilles, and several wax tablets, and let the signet be impressed on the tablets. Someone later seeing the tablets will know that they are all derived from one image; let him be said to have the replica (*tupos*) which is the image in the *dianoia*. The image (*sphragis*) in the signet is said to be prior to the many, that in the tablets is said to be in the many, and that in the *dianoia* of the replicator is said to be derived from (*epi*) the many and posterior to them. Let the same thing be conceived in the case of genera and species.... There is an *eidos* in the Demiurge [Plato's Creator] like the *tupos* in the signet, and it is said to be prior to the many and separate from matter. And there is also the *eidos* of human in each human, like the images in the tablets, and it is said to be in the many and inseparable from matter. And when we see that all individual humans have the form of human, as we reach the posterior [image] by seeing the tablets, we replicate this *eidos* in our *dianoia*; and this is said to be derived from or after the many and posterior to them. Such *eidê* are separable from bodies, since they exist not in body, but in soul, but they are not absolutely separable; for they cannot be apprehended *per se* as Plato supposes the *eidê* prior to the many to be. (*in Isag.* 41,13-20, 42,6-16)

I will call the doctrine of mathematical objects expressed by Philoponus and Ammonius abstractionism because commentators expounding it frequently refer to mathematical objects as abstractions (*ta ex aphaireseôs*). My impression is that Ammonius and Philoponus accept abstractionism, i.e. think it is a correct account of mathematics. As is well-known, the form of a commentary does not always make it possible to infer acceptance from failure to criticise, but I believe the importance of this fact can be exaggerated. Simplicius certainly manages to convey his own views on most subjects, and Philoponus does so often enough to provide good grounds for thinking he accepts ideas he doesn't criticise.[7]

4. Alexander

It seems reasonably certain that the doctrine of abstractionism can be traced back to Alexander of Aphrodisias, who made it authoritative as an interpretation of Aristotle and authoritative for later philosophers who made heavy use of what they took to be Aristotelian ideas in their own philosophising. The evidence in the surviving texts for Alexander's views is not as clear as one would like, but I think the general tenor of it is unmistakable. Perhaps the most explicit statement of abstractionism comes in the commentary on the *Metaphysics* (52,15-19) where Alexander says that mathematical objects do not exist *per se*, but by *epinoia*: 'for matter and motion are separated from enmattered things, with respect to which and with which mathematical objects have their existence, and mathematical objects are left ...'[8] There are several other passages in which Alexander associates mathematical objects with *epinoia*. In his commentary on the *de Sensu* (111,17-19) he explains that he means by a mathematical body something that doesn't exist in its own right, but is apprehended by *epinoia* separate from sensible properties. He appears to assert much the same view at 52,13-16 of *in Metaph.*, and the view is ascribed to him by Philoponus (*in GC* 77, 8-15).[9]

Perhaps the strongest (and strangest) evidence that Alexander adopted

---

[7] For a discussion of this point from a different perspective see H.J. Blumenthal, Chapter 13 above.

[8] See also *in Metaph.* 201,4-11.

[9] Another text in the same vein is a report of Philoponus (*in An. Post.* 181,11ff), who

an abstractionist conception of mathematics comes in Simplicius' discussion of *Physics* 4.1, 208b22-5, a part of Aristotle's list of the considerations which lead to the belief that there is such a thing as place. The first is the fact of *antimetastasis* (things taking each other's place), the second that of natural place. In discussing the second Aristotle insists that differences of natural place are not just differences in position (*thesis*) relative to us. He then says:

> This is shown also by the objects of mathematics: without being in any place (*topos*), they none the less have a right and left corresponding to their position (*thesis*) in relation to us, suggesting that things which are only so described through their position do not by nature have a right and left (*hôs ta monon legomena dia thesin ouk ekhonta phusei toutôn hekaston*).

This is presumably the text read by Simplicius and adopted by Ross.[10] It would seem that Aristotle wants to affirm the reality of natural place by pointing out the contrast between the natural or absolute place of real things and the relative place of geometric objects: when a geometer speaks of drawing a straight line between two points, he takes no account of direction; he does not say that one point is above or below or behind or to the right of the other.

Simplicius tells us at *in Phys.* 526,16-18 that Alexander emended the text starting from *hôs* to *hôste monon noeisthai autôn tên thesin* (so that their position is merely conceived in the mind), claiming that Aristotle's point is to make clear that their position in relation to us (*hê pros hêmas thesis*) is a position in thought (*hê kat' epinoian*), and explaining, 'if mathematical objects do not have[11] their principle *per se*, they could not have their position (*thesis*) *per se*'. Simplicius adds that Alexander's purpose is to make clear that Aristotle's remark about the place of mathematical objects is not an independent consideration but merely a way of reinforcing the belief in natural place. However, Simplicius also says that Alexander at one time believed the remark to be an independent consideration, and tells us that it would then be paraphrased thus: 'if mathematical objects, although not in place naturally, nevertheless occupy different places with respect to us, it is evident that place is something; for things which are by *thesis*

---

describes Alexander as saying that 'geometry uses only forms without substrata.' The parallel statement in Themistius' presentation of the same passage says more explicitly that geometric forms exist in physical bodies and are separated by the mathematician: 'Geometry uses only the form of straight line, which is not *per se* but always in some substance; for the straight is in either air or stone or wood or something else. But the geometer examines the straight not as in one these things, but *per se*' (*in Phys.* 29,20-3).

[10] Ross, however, places the comma after *thesin*, a reading he thinks to be 'equally likely' as the 'quite likely' one I have adopted. Simplicius divides his discussion of the passage where I have placed the comma.

[11] Reading *ekhei* for *esti* at 526,20; cf. 526,21.

(= convention) are derived from things which are by nature, as imagined things are derived from sensible ones.' Presumably, Simplicius' paraphrase is derived from Alexander, and is based on the text read by Simplicius, the second sentence of the paraphrase being a rendering of the final clause of the passage. It is hard to know how much to make of the comparison with the relation between imagined and sensible things, but it is the only trace of a conception of mathematical objects as being brought into existence mentally in the first reading. However, Alexander's second reading is not only mentalistic, it involves a radical alteration of the text with, as far as we can tell, no manuscript authority. Simplicius rightly rejects the alteration, but he manages to hold on to a mentalistic reading.[12]

Alexander may also have been a major contributor to the tendency to run together mathematical objects and universals.[13] In his *de Anima* Alexander distinguishes between *per se* forms, which are identical with *nous* (intellect) when they are known by it, and enmattered forms which *nous* grasps by separating them from their matter; from this process only a partial identification results because 'the thing known has its being in some matter' (87,24-8; 88,10-16). Alexander connects this doctrine with mathematics in the following passage:

> In the case of enmattered forms there is no *nous* of them when they are not known since their *hupostasis* (existence) is in being known. For universals and what is common [in their case] have their *huparxis* (being) in enmattered particulars; they become common and universal when they are known separate from matter, and *nous* exists when they are known. If they were not to be known, they would no longer be, so that these things are destroyed when they are separated from knowing *nous*, since their being is in being known. And abstractions, such as the objects of mathematics, are similar to these things. (*Mant.* 90,2-10)

There is, of course, no way to determine the precise degree of similarity which Alexander has in mind. However, it seems to me likely that he thinks that abstractions are separated from matter and exist only when they are known, but I am not at all sure whether he means to say that abstractions are universals. The doctrine that enmattered forms exist separately as universals only when they are known makes reasonable sense as an interpretation of Aristotle, but if abstractions were also universals of this sort for Aristotle, it is not immediately clear what difference Aristotle would be bringing out by using the word 'abstractions'

---

[12] One other passage suggesting that Alexander is a source for the abstractionist interpretation is *in Metaph.* 199,19-22 where he says that, unlike mathematical objects, the objects of physics are not abstractions because 'it is impossible to separate by *epinoia* substance from physical body'.

[13] For a discussion of some difficult passages bearing on Alexander's treatment of universals see Martin M. Tweedale, 'Alexander of Aphrodisias' views on universals', *Phronesis* 29, 1984, 279-303.

for mathematical objects. On the other hand, if for Alexander the difference between abstractions and separated forms lies only in the contrast between being particular and being universal, one would expect him to focus more on the step of generalisation in the process of separating forms. That is to say, one would expect a clear marking of the stages enmattered form, separated particular form, separated universal form, rather than a running together of the last two steps.[14]

5. Syrianus

Aristotle's theory of mathematical objects was clearly anti-Platonic in motivation, and *prima facie* abstractionism would seem difficult to reconcile with the central role assigned to mathematics in philosophical education in the *Republic*. Here is how Philoponus attempts to reconcile them:

> Mathematical objects ... have an immaterial *ousia* (essence) even if they don't have an immaterial *huparxis* (being), so that becoming accustomed to act in relation to these things and advancing in an immaterial way, one will reach things which are entirely separate from matter, I mean divine things. Therefore Plotinus says, 'Let the young be led through mathematics to get them used to immaterial nature (*pros sunethismon tês asômatou phuseôs*).' (*in DA* 3,8-13)

Philoponus here quotes part of a sentence from *Ennead* 1.3.3; Plotinus actually recommends the study of mathematics as a preliminary to dialectic to get people used to incorporeal thought and belief (*pros sunethismon katanoêseôs kai pisteôs asômatou*), and there is, I think, no clear evidence that he would understand mathematical objects in the way Philoponus and Ammonius do. At least as early as Ammonius, the phrase quoted by Philoponus became a kind of slogan, repeated again and again.[15] However, it seems to me that the abstractionist conception of

---

[14] For a discussion of the running together of these steps see Paul Moraux, *Alexandre d'Aphrodise: Exégète de la Noétique d'Aristote, Bibliothèque de la Faculté de Philosophie et Lettres de l'Université de Liège* 99, Liège and Paris 1942, 69-71.

Alexander does distinguish universals and the objects of a science at *in Metaph.* 199,35-9, when he writes, 'Every science and *tekhnê* is about the universal, which is eternal and is not sensible. For even if one applies sciences and *tekhnai* to sensibles, they are not about sensibles. But although they are about universals and such things, they deal with (*pragmateuesthai peri*) sensibles, not as sensibles and particulars, but as such and such and sharing in the common.' (I read *metekhonta* for *metekhei* in line 39.)

[15] I have found versions of it in the following places. Iamblichus *Comm. Math.* 55,19 (without naming Plotinus), Ammonius *in Isag.* 12,25-7, Proclus *in Eucl.* 20,21-2, Philoponus *in Cat.* 6,15-16, *in DA* 3,12-13, and *in Nic.* 1 and 27, Simplicius *in Phys.* 14,4 (without naming Plotinus), Asclepius *in Metaph.* 98,7-8, 104,13-15 (both without naming Plotinus), and 151,4-6, Olympiodorus *Proleg.* 9,27-10,2, David *Proleg.* 59,17-19, and [Galen] *de Part. Phil.* 7, 19-20.

It is interesting to note that Alexander gives essentially the same defence of the study of mathematics as that offered by Philoponus in the name of Plotinus, although he uses an Aristotelian rather than a Neoplatonic conceptual framework: 'For geometry does not just

mathematics really provides an inadequate account of the role of mathematics in philosophical ascent. This was certainly Syrianus' view, and I now want to discuss some of the things he says about abstractionism in his commentary on the *Metaphysics*.

At 3.2, 996a12 of the *Metaphysics* Aristotle introduces as one of the puzzles (*aporiai*) to be discussed the question whether mathematical objects are substances and, if so, whether they are separate from or inherent in sensibles. Commenting on this passage, Syrianus (12,28ff) affirms their substantiality, and continues,

> For one can see figure and number and natural surface and its limits in the sensible activities of nature; and these things also exist in our imagination and opinion, whether they are taken by abstraction from sensibles, as Aristotle thinks, or whether they are completed by us from the substantial forms of the soul. These imagined and opined things participate in being, but they are not substances; they should be referred to quantity or quality or another category. But the substantial *logoi* of the soul which contain these things are substances. But if one were to consider the paradigms of these things in *nous* or among intelligibles, he would see number and figure and magnitude itself counted among the most primary substances. (*in Metaph.* 12,29-13,3)

Syrianus here invokes a standard Neoplatonic hierarchy:

Nous – forms
Soul – *logoi* of the forms
Physical world – embodiments of the *logoi* in matter

However, below soul and probably above the physical world Syrianus inserts imagination[16] and mathematical objects corresponding to it. Here he admits as options the possibility that these objects come to be by

theorise about sensibles but about things arising from sense and intelligibles... Furthermore, geometry accustoms young people to theorise about lines and planes and solids on their own (*idiai*), and none of these things are sensible. For being able to separate from one another by *logos* things which differ from one another in substance but cannot be separate from one another in *hupostasis* or *huparxis* is most necessary for philosophy. For this is the way one apprehends the principles of natural things, matter and form. For these two things are inseparable in *hupostasis*' (Alexander *in An. Pr.* 4,3-14).

[16] I will not discuss opinion here because I am not sure how much can be made of Syrianus' mention of it. I know of only one analogue. In an intriguing passage (*in Eucl.* 94,19ff) in his discussion of Euclid's definition of point Proclus gives his answer to the problem of how the geometer can imagine a partless point since the imagination receives things in shapes and part by part (*morphotikôs kai meristôs*). He then turns to the interpretation of the allegedly Pythagorean definition of the point as a unit with position, and explains the difference between the point and the unit indicated by this definition: 'When they speak of a unit having position, I think they are indicating that the unit and number (I mean monadic [as opposed to eidetic] number) has its *hupostasis* in *doxa* (opinion); and therefore in each soul each number, e.g. 5 and 7, is one and not many and free of figure or adventitious form. But the point comes forth (*proteinetai*) in imagination and comes to be in a kind of place ...' (*in Eucl.* 95,26-96,7). Obviously the suggestion in this paragraph is that *doxa* is to arithmetic as imagination is to geometry, but unfortunately

abstraction from sensibles or as a kind of completion of things in the soul. Elsewhere he leaves no doubt that he favours the latter alternative, which he associates with Plato and the Pythagoreans. I have in mind particularly two other passages in which Syrianus comments on Aristotle's criticism of realistic conceptions of mathematical objects and puts forward his own account.

In the first, Syrianus is dealing with a general passage (*Metaph*. 13.2, 1077a14-20) in which Aristotle dismisses the attempt to treat mathematical objects as separate entities. Syrianus (91,20) introduces the distinction between the universal which is cause of the sensible and the universal which is generated posterior to it, and says that there are similarly two kinds of magnitude, the one in dianoetic *logos*, which is cause of the existence of the imagined form, the other by abstraction from the sensible. The absence of a reference to the universal (or magnitude) in sensibles is presumably to be explained by its irrelevance to the topic of mathematics. Syrianus goes on to deny that abstracted things are the concern of geometry on the grounds that we do not perceive anything with the accuracy, character, and independence of matter exhibited by the objects which the geometer discusses.

> Geometry deals with imagined things insofar as they coexist with the substantial *logoi* of the *dianoia*, which also provides the cause of demonstration; or rather geometry wants to deal with the partless *logoi* of the soul, but is too weak to use *noêseis* not involving imagination and so spreads out the *logoi* into imagined and extended figures and magnitudes, and studies the *logoi* in them. (*in Metaph*. 91,29-34)

Syrianus continues by comparing the geometer's use of imagination to his use of diagrams; just as one would not say that the geometer is proving things about his diagrams, so one should not say he is proving things about the imagined figures. The strongest evidence for this is that proof is of the universal, but every imagined thing exists as an individual.

In the other passage (95,29ff), Syrianus takes on those who try to avoid his claim that abstractionism is incompatible with the accuracy of geometric figures by saying that 'we add what is lacking and make them more accurate'. Syrianus asks where we get our ability to do this unless there are pre-existing *logoi* in our soul. He adds, presumably having in mind the abstractionist doctrine that mathematics does study sensibles in a way,[17] that adding things will make the abstractions less rather than more accurate. Syrianus admits that we can derive images of things from sensibles, but again insists that our making them more accurate depends on the pre-existent *logoi*. And it is the sense of approximation to these *logoi* which makes mathematics an appropriate vehicle of philosophical

---

Proclus does not develop the comparison, and we possess no discussion of arithmetic analogous to *in Eucl*.

[17] In *Metaph*. 13.3 Aristotle uses the slogan 'sensibles not as sensibles' to characterise the things studied by mathematics.

ascent. Syrianus also concedes that we are reminded of the Forms by sensibles, but distinguishes this from asserting that the *dianoia* introduces a Form derived from them. Concern with sensibles only blinds the soul, and such blinding is certainly the result of dealing with abstractions.[18] He continues by arguing that abstractionism makes the relation of mathematics to knowledge of the forms like the relationship between the rhetoric teacher's artificial speeches and real legal arguments: there are, indeed, similarities, but the fundamental contrast between the real and the artificial remains. Such a view cannot explain the ascent of our soul nor why mathematics is comparable to a bridge leading us from sensibles to intelligibles, nor why it isn't better to deal with sensible magnitude in the way in which it is rather than in a way in which it neither is nor can be.

The fullest development of Syrianus' position on geometric reasoning is given by his pupil Proclus in his commentary on book 1 of Euclid's *Elements* (notably at 48,1-57,8, which includes a strong attack on abstractionism).[19] According to this view, the geometer deals with forms or *logoi* in the *dianoia*, but he does so by projecting images of them into his imagination. These images are perfect embodiments of geometric definitions because they are derived from the forms, as they could not be if they were somehow put together out of sense perceptions. Equally, geometry can play its Platonic role of bridge or ladder leading from the sensible to the intelligible world because it is the study of these projections from the higher world.

There is a clear sense in which abstractionism is the opposite or converse of the doctrine of Syrianus and Proclus, which I will call projectionism. In abstractionism the objects of mathematics are derived from sense perceptions of such features of things as their shapes, but these perceived features are somehow mentally separated from their material substratum, this separation from matter being what makes mathematics a suitable bridge to the intelligible world. However, there do not seem to be any important differences in the metaphysical or epistemological underpinnings of abstractionism and projectionism. Proponents of both accept the idea that there are forms and *logoi* which exist prior to sensibles and forms or mathematical objects which are derived from sensibles. This is brought out clearly in Philoponus' characterisation of the first philosopher which immediately follows the passage I quoted at the beginning of this chapter:

> But the first philosopher will discuss forms which are entirely separate from matter. For there are in our soul *logoi* of the enmattered forms, and these also exist transcendentally (*exêirêmenoi*) in demiurgic *nous*. And of the things in our soul those in the imagination are extended, those in the rational part of the soul are partless and unextended. And the geometer discusses the extended forms in the imagination; for he uses imagination as

[18] In this connection Syrianus attacks Alexander for saying that a person moulds intelligibles by himself (*noêta atta heautêi anaplasasa*).

[19] I discuss Proclus' views in my paper 'Mathematics and philosophy in Proclus' commentary on Book 1 of Euclid's *Elements*', in Jean Pépin and H.D. Saffrey (eds), *Proclus, Lecteur et Interprète des Anciens*, Paris 1987, 305-18. What I say about Proclus in this chapter is based on the more extended discussion in that paper.

a drawing board, acting by way of division (*meristôs*) and measuring and
dividing intervals. (*in DA* 58,6-13)

However, the shared vocabulary and metaphysical apparatus should not
lead us to suppose a shared conception of mathematical objects. Nor
should we think that for Philoponus the imagination is the projection
screen of Syrianus and Proclus. For elsewhere Philoponus says of the
imagination that it is included in and has its source in perception (*in DA*
78,24-6), and 'takes *tupoi* (imprints) of sensibles from *aisthêsis* (sense
perception) and weaves them together inside itself' (*in DA* 5,38-6,1).

Philoponus and Ammonius do not, I think, have anything to say on the
question of the accuracy of abstractions, an issue on which Syrianus
focuses much of his attack. Their silence may be due to the inability to
respond to the criticism, but I suspect that other factors are involved.
There survive slight traces of attempts to argue that sensible things do
satisfy mathematical definitions, e.g. that the division between a shaded
and a lighted area is a perceptible breadthless length,[20] but the evidence
does not suggest that this position was developed fully or widely accepted.
Another, presumably more widely accepted position, which might even be
taken for granted, would be that separation from matter by itself yields
perfection, i.e. that matter is the source of the failure of sensible objects to
satisfy mathematical definitions. A final important factor is the failure to
distinguish the conception of abstraction as leading to the apprehension
of particular shapes separate from their physical embodiment and as
leading to the apprehension of universals.

6. Simplicius[21]

Although the word 'imagination' occurs in my last quotation from
Philoponus, he, Ammonius and Alexander more frequently use the word
epinoia in connection with mathematics, a word suggesting that

[20] Philoponus *in Cat.* 85,8-86,1. Analogous material is found in Proclus *in Eucl.* 100,5-19
(cf. 114,20-5) and [Heron] *Deff.* 16,5-11 (cf. 20,18-22). In the light of Syrianus'
characterisation of Alexander's view of mathematical objects (see n. 18), it is perhaps
interesting to note that Philoponus characterises his considerations as showing that the
notion that there is such a thing as breadthless length is not an *anaplasma* (moulding) of
our *dianoia* but something in the nature of things.

[21] In my discussion of Simplicius I use only the *de Anima* commentary traditionally
ascribed to him. The authorship of this commentary has been placed in doubt by F. Bossier
and C. Steel in 'Priscianus Lydus en de "In de anima" van Pseudo(?)-Simplicius', *Tijdschrift
voor Filosofie* 34, 1972, 761-822. For arguments minimising the doctrinal significance of
their assignment of the commentary to Priscianus see Ilsetraut Hadot, *Le problème du
néoplatonisme Alexandrin: Hiéroclès et Simplicius*, Paris 1978, 193-202 and Chapter 12
above, and for sceptical arguments concerning the reassignment see H.J. Blumenthal, 'The
psychology of (?) Simplicius' commentary on the *de Anima*,' in H.J. Blumenthal and A.C.
Lloyd (eds), *Soul and the Structure of Being in Late Neoplatonism*, Liverpool 1982, 73-5 with
the discussion on 94-5. Since I make no major use of the undisputed commentaries of
Simplicius, nothing I say turns on the authorship of the *de Anima* commentary, and it
seems simplest to use Simplicius' name in discussing it.

mathematical objects are purely mental.[22] Imagination plays a much more prominent role in Simplicius' discussions of abstraction in his *de Anima* commentary, discussions which offer other interests as well. Commenting on a passage (3.4, 429b18) in which Aristotle invokes the distinction between *to euthei einai* (the form of straightness) and *to euthu* (the straight line) and uses the word 'abstractions' (*ta en aphairesei*), Simplicius says,

> Aristotle usually believes and says that mathematical objects are abstractions, in this differing from the Pythagoreans who investigate the *logoi* which are projective of the mathematical *tupoi* in the imagination and are substantial in the corporeal life of the soul. However, Aristotle says that the *mathêmata* (objects of mathematics)[23] are in the imagined *tupoi* themselves, concerning which the mathematicians in truth carry on all their business. The Pythagoreans, looking to the living *logoi* which are projective of the *tupoi*, suppose *mathêmata* to be substances. However, Aristotle denies that the *tupoi* are substances, and says they arise from abstraction in that the soul receives them because of their imitation of sensible things. Therefore also, the soul does not project them by its own activity. (*in DA* 233,7-17)

Here the contrast between Aristotelian and Pythagorean conceptions of mathematics is made explicit, but the primary contrast does not relate to the distinction between abstractions and projections, but to that between concern with images believed to be derived from sense perception and concern with the *logoi* which are projective of images not believed to be so derived. Simplicius goes on to argue that the accuracy of mathematical objects shows they are projected from within, although he concedes that such projection is impossible without apprehension of sensibles. However, his main concern is to explicate the distinction between *to euthu* (the imagined straight line) and *to euthei einai* (the form of straightness).

Simplicius might appear to be siding straightforwardly with Syrianus and Proclus here, but another passage (276,28ff) in which he proposes to explain Aristotle's notion of abstraction suggests a more complicated situation. Simplicius first recalls the way Aristotle distinguishes between mathematics and physics in Book 2 of the *Physics*:

> The mathematician who investigates the *kath' hauta sumbebêkota* (essential accidents) such as figures, magnitudes, motions, numbers and consonant ratios, needs perception itself for his apprehension. The physicist

---

[22] Another word frequently used in connection with abstractionist discussions of mathematics is *logos*, the sense being that mathematical objects are separated by an act of definition.

[23] Simplicius here follows a standard practice among later authors of using *mathêmata* as synonymous with *mathêmatika*, as Philoponus announces he himself does at *in DA* 3,8-9. Compare Plato's specification of the highest *mathêma* as the Idea of the Good. (*Republic* 6, 505A. I thank Hayden Ausland for this reference and for a correction in one of my translations.)

investigates both the shapes and their consequences which attach
appropriately to substances, [making use of] causes of both the forms and of
the compound substances themselves as substances. Therefore the subject
of physics is a kind of philosophy since it deals with substance, and knows
things which have causes on the basis of their causes. However,
mathematics is not [a kind of philosophy], but, as Plato says, it resembles a
bridge. For, as the same philosopher declares, there is a beginning for it
which the mathematician does not know and therefore does not know about
the middle things or the conclusion from them,[24] because he leaves out the
causes by not investigating substances. For the absolutely authoritative
cause is substance or a cause stronger than this. (*in DA* 276,28-277,1)

Here Simplicius assigns the role of bridge to a mathematics which he
concedes to be at best a minimal form of knowledge. However, he then
goes on to contrast the mathematics he has just described with what the
Pythagoreans call mathematics:

I am now speaking of mathematics not in the manner of the Pythagoreans
who investigate the living *logoi* which are productive by projection of
extensions and figures, whether in natural bodies or imaginations (for that
is philosophy), but of the whole treatment itself of the projected things, e.g.
figures and magnitudes and motions, which Aristotle usually calls
abstractions. (*in DA* 277,1-6)

Thus for Simplicius the contrast between mathematics as viewed by
Aristotle and mathematics as viewed by the Pythagoreans is the contrast
between mathematics and a kind of philosophy. Simplicius gives nothing
but a general characterisation of Pythagorean philosophy, but I think it is
certain that he has in mind the kind of mystical and symbolic
interpretation of mathematical concepts which we associate with
Pythagoreanism and Neopythagoreanism and which we find in such
Neoplatonists as Syrianus and Iamblichus. Simplicius next returns to the
topic of mathematics, stressing the imaginary and non-substantial
character of mathematical objects, and giving examples of mathematical
statements to substantiate his claim: all the radii of any circle are equal;
all the circles about a single pole move together; every even-times even
number is divisible down to the unit; and every 2:1 ratio is composed of
4:3 and 3:2. He then repeats his claim about the insubstantial character
of the objects of ordinary mathematics, but quite suddenly denies the
adequacy of the account he has assigned to Aristotle both because
imagined things transcend sensibles in accuracy and because the activity
involved in mathematical reasoning is incompatible with mere passive
reception through sense. At this point it would appear that Simplicius
has contradicted himself, first accepting and then rejecting Aristotle's
account of mathematical objects as abstractions. But in his summary he

---

[24] *arkhê ... autêi ... ha mê oide, mesa de kai teleutê ex hôn mê oide*, obviously a
remembrance of Plato *Republic* 7, 533C3-4, but Plato nowhere compares mathematics to a
bridge.

makes it clear that he accepts Aristotle's account for ordinary mathematics, but rejects it for another form of reasoning, which presumably is, or includes, Pythagorean mathematics:

> It has been said then what abstractions are, namely mathematical objects, and not the causes of things like substances, but extended things and *sumbebêkota* (accidents). The reason for the name is that they are not investigated as they exist, i.e. with substance, but without it by those the majority of people usually call mathematicians. Perception and imagination are the modes of apprehension co-ordinated with these sensible and imagined *sumbebêkota*. For these modes of apprehension make judgments about *sumbebêkota*, but not about substance; for *logos* and *nous* apprehend substance.... The *tupoi* which come to the imagination from sensibles are not substances. Such things are not only ... investigated by the co-ordinated modes of apprehension, but also by our *nous*, sometimes interwoven with imagination and sensation and acting only concerning them without apprehension of their substances. (Some people call this mathematical *nous*, deriving the name from the person the many customarily call a mathematician.) But sometimes *nous* does not attend to these things but to their substantial causes, the formal and the composite, and subsequently grasps the *sumbebêkota* which are caused in terms of their causes, this stronger *nous* apprehending substances. (277,30-278,6)

I am not sure I understand Simplicius' position fully and I certainly do not see how it could be worked out with complete consistency. However, it appears to me that he wants to treat abstractionism as a correct account of ordinary mathematics, to which he also wants to assign the Platonic role of bridge or ladder. To this extent he seems to agree with Philoponus and Ammonius, although he seems to place more emphasis on the role of imagination in this mathematics than they do. Syrianus denies that a mathematics based on abstraction can play this role, and espouses a projectionist doctrine according to which real mathematics deals with *logoi* by projecting them into the imagination. Simplicius admits the validity of this subject, but makes it into a form of philosophy as opposed to (ordinary) mathematics.

It is not entirely clear whether Syrianus thought of projectionism as applying to both ordinary and Pythagorean mathematics or only to ordinary mathematics. It seems undeniable that Proclus intended it to apply to both since he defends projectionism in a commentary on ordinary geometry, although he also invokes a number of Pythagorean ideas in the commentary; it is also quite certain that he considered mathematics so described to be the Platonic bridge. But I am inclined to think that Syrianus thought of projectionism rather as an account only of Pythagorean mathematics of the kind labelled philosophy by Simplicius. Certainly in the *Metaphysics* commentary he shows much more interest in this sort of thing than in ordinary mathematics. And in one passage (101,22-103,12) he dismisses Aristotle's account of mathematics in favour of the genuine opinions of the Pythagoreans, the subjects of which he proceeds to list. The list is a fairly close approximation to a table of

contents of Iamblichus *de Communi Mathematica Scientia*, and at the
end of it Syrianus refers the person eager to learn more to the work of
Nicomachus and Iamblichus, the latter of whom is said to provide
constructions and proofs and more intelligible apprehensions (*noerôterai
epibolai*). No modern, or at least none with a background in analytic
philosophy, would describe the contents of *Comm. Math.* in terms of
constructions and proofs, although the word 'intelligible' might be
appropriate as long as the Neoplatonic meaning were borne in mind. The
important point is that *Comm. Math.* is a work of Pythagorean
philosophy in Simplicius' sense. Indeed, like Simplicius, Iamblichus
insists on the difference between Pythagorean and ordinary
mathematics:

> Pythagorean mathematics is not like the mathematics pursued by the
> many. For the latter is largely technical (*tekhnikos*) and does not have a
> single goal, or aim at the beautiful and good, but Pythagorean mathematics
> is pre-eminently theoretical; it leads its *theôrêmata* toward one end,
> adapting all its assertions to the beautiful and good, and using them to
> conduce to being. (*Comm. Math.* 91,3-11)

The similarities between *Comm. Math.* and the first prologue of
Proclus' Euclid commentary have often been noted, but I believe it can be
shown that the two texts diverge precisely in Proclus' dropping of many of
the most Pythagorean features of *Comm. Math.*[25] There are clear
suggestions of projectionism in *Comm. Math.* (see especially 33,19-34,18),
but whether or not Iamblichus is the originator of the doctrine, he seems
to be our earliest source, and I would guess he was an important source
for the combination of projectionism and glorification of Pythagorean
mathematics we find in Syrianus. I would claim that Proclus transforms
projectionism into a philosophy of ordinary mathematics, although he by
no means abandons completely his teacher Syrianus' view of the
profundity of the Pythagoreans. Simplicius, on the other hand, seems to
restrict projectionism to Pythagorean mathematics, while conceding the
validity of abstractionism as an account of ordinary mathematics.

7. Porphyry

In this last main section I want to argue that Porphyry was an
abstractionist. His being one would help explain the acceptance of the
doctrine by later Neoplatonists. However, the evidence in his case is
rather sparse. One piece is provided by Proclus, who remarks explicitly
on the divergence of his projectionism from Porphyry's account of
geometry (*in Eucl.* 56,23-57,4), although he does not tell us what
Porphyry's account was. Moreover, Proclus' acknowledged borrowings
from Porphyry in the Euclid commentary all relate to quite ordinary

---

[25] For details of the argument see my paper 'Iamblichus and Proclus' Euclid commentary',
Hermes 115, 1987, 334-48 .

geometric arguments or terminological points, having nothing to do with Pythagorean mathematics. Porphyry's distance from the Pythagorean-ising of Iamblichus and Syrianus is perhaps most strongly confirmed by his commentary on Ptolemy's *Harmonics*, in which he completely accepts Ptolemy's criticisms of the arbitrary procedures of the Pythagoreans. Finally in the same commentary there is an interesting passage (13,15-14,28) in which Porphyry comments on Ptolemy's statement that the criteria in harmonics are hearing and *logos*, hearing for matter and what is passive, *logos* for the form and cause.

In his comment Porphyry introduces the notion of 'psychic matter', pointing out that all the underpinnings are immediate matter for the superstructure (*panta ta hupobebêkota prosekhôs hulai tôn epanabebêko-tôn*). He illustrates this relation by contrasting external and superior *nous* with the *nous* which it uses as matter in its own activity. The correspond-ence with Iamblichus, Syrianus, and Proclus is here quite clear, but Porphyry goes on to give a highly Aristotelian account of judgment in which the soul is said to 'tear off' (*apospan*) forms from matter. He describes an epistemological sequence consisting of *aisthêsis* (perception), *antilêpsis* (apprehension), and then doxastic *hupolêpsis* (conception), in which what has been received is written down for the soul through *logos*, as if on a writing tablet. After these things comes imagination, which does not copy sense impressions exactly, but introduces accuracy into the images[26] and presents them to the soul as *ennoiai* (concepts), which, when they are made firm, produce *epistêmê* (scientific understanding), which in turn 'lights up' *nous* (intellect). This account of the activating of *nous* remains 'Platonic' because the activation is a stimulation to recall rather than an implanting of something new,[27] but the mechanism is purely Aristotelian in substance. Particularly important for the philosophy of mathematics is the fact that imagination produces 'accurate' images. Porphyry does not mention mathematics and so does not say that the images of imagination satisfy the conditions of mathematical definitions, but it does not seem unreasonable to read this notion into what he does say.

8. Summary

In this paper I have argued for the following account of the treatment of abstractionism in later antiquity:

(1) Alexander established abstractionism as an interpretation of

---

[26] The text here is difficult: *tritê d'esti ... phantasia ouk arkoumenê tôi tês prosagoreuseôs eidei kai tôi tês anagraphês, all' honper tropon hoi tous katapleontas eikonizontes ê kata tous tois sumbolois parakolonthountas tên akribeian tês homoiotêtos eklogizonta; houtô kai hautê tou pragmatos hapasan tên morphên eklogizomenê, hopotan touton ton tropon akribôsêi, tote apetheto en têi psukhêi to eidos.* (13,29-14,3, using a textual correction of Bengt Alexanderson, *Textual Remarks on Ptolemy's Harmonica and Porphyry's Commentary, Studia Graeca et Latina Gothoburgensa* 27, Göteborg 1969, 20.)

[27] See on this point W. Theiler's review of Düring's editions of Ptolemy's *Harmonics* and Porphyry's commentary, *Göttingische gelehrte Anzeigen* 198, 1936, 203.

Aristotle's philosophy of mathematics. Alexander's account was accepted, with insignificant variations, as an interpretation by all subsequent philosophers.

(2) The doctrine of abstractionism was accepted as a true account of ordinary mathematics by Porphyry, Ammonius, and Philoponus, who saw ordinary mathematics as a Platonic bridge from the sensible to the intelligible world.

(3) Iamblichus put forward the doctrine of projectionism as an account of Pythagorean mathematics, which he glorified at the expense of ordinary mathematics; he was followed by Syrianus, but Proclus transformed projectionism into an account of ordinary mathematics to which he restored its Platonic role.

(4) Simplicius accepted the 'Porphyrean' position on ordinary mathematics, but elevated Pythagorean mathematics, of which he thinks projectionism provides the correct account, to the level of philosophy.[28]

[28] This paper was written while the author held a fellowship from the American National Endowment for the Humanities. It was revised as a result of discussion after presentations at the Institute of Classical Studies in London and the West Coast Colloquium on Ancient Philosophy in Berkeley.

'Aristotle and Alexander of Aphrodisias' by Ulocrino

Donald R. Morrison

This charming small Renaissance plaquette is also rather mysterious.[1] The only precise fact we know is that it was produced by the same hand as certain other plaquettes, some of which are signed with the name 'Ulocrino'. Who Ulocrino was, and exactly why, when and where he carved this plaquette, no one knows.

An ingenious suggestion concerning Ulocrino's identity was made a hundred years ago by Molinier in his comprehensive catalogue of plaquettes.[2] Noting that the name 'Ulocrino' has no meaning in Italian, he proposed that the word is a hybrid word-play, formed from the Greek *oulos* and the Latin *crinis*, meaning 'curly-haired', the Italian for which is *riccio*, and the Latin *crispus*. Word-games of this sort were much loved in the Renaissance, and it happens that there was a celebrated sculptor active in Padua at the time, Andrea Briosco, who was called 'Riccio' because of his curly hair, and who himself signed a medal 'Crispus'. Therefore Molinier proposed to identify the mysterious Ulocrino with the well-known sculptor Andrea Riccio. This sort of story ought to be true; but Molinier himself noted that Ulocrino's style is somewhat different from Riccio's, and the identification has been firmly rejected by J. Pope-Henessey on that ground.[3]

So we are left with nothing but a name and a small corpus of plaquettes. This is enough to give us a context: for on grounds of style and subject-matter the plaquettes can be safely placed in Padua or Venice and dated between, say, 1485 and 1530. And much was happening in Padua and Venice during this period which helps explain the production of a plaquette devoted to Aristotle and Alexander of Aphrodisias. The iconography is remarkable, because the subject-matter of most Italian plaquettes from the period is religious, or else mythological or allegorical. Such subjects as a portrait of St Jerome or a scene of Apollo and Marsyas are easy to find – Ulocrino himself did both – but the portrait of an

---

[1] A rectangular bronze plaquette with brown patina. Dimensions approx. 72 x 55mm. Examples are found in the Dahlem Museum, Berlin; the Victoria and Albert Museum, London; the Museo Correr, Venice; and the National Gallery of Art, Washington, DC.

[2] Molinier 1886, p. 176.

[3] Pope-Henessey 1964, p. 77.

historical person from antiquity is unusual.

However, at Padua and Venice during this period interest in Aristotle and in his greatest Greek commentator, Alexander of Aphrodisias, was strong and growing. The first Italian printed edition of Aristotle's complete works (in Latin translation) was produced at Venice in 1483. The Latin translation of Alexander's *de Anima* was first printed in Venice in 1495, and by 1520 it had been reprinted five times.[4] After years of lecturing on the subject, in 1516 the Paduan philosopher Pietro Pomponazzi published his most famous work, *de Immortalitate Animi*, in which he explicitly defended Alexander's views. Pomponazzi's book provoked furious opposition, and he published two further works in its defence. As for Alexander's commentaries on Aristotle, they were gradually published, in Greek, in Venice between 1513 and 1536.

The translator of Alexander's *de Anima*, Girolamo Donati, was an early patron of Andrea Riccio. Pope-Henessey suggests that this connection between the publication of Alexander's *de Anima* in 1495 and the circle of Paduan sculptors makes it tempting to link our plaquette with this event.[5] The thought is tempting – and for the intellectual historian, tantalising. Since Alexander's *de Anima* contains the controversial doctrines on the soul which gave Paduan Alexandrism its distinctive character, to connect the plaquette with the first printing of this work would tie it with a major event in intellectual history. However that may be, a more cautious and secure conclusion is that Ulocrino's plaquette 'Aristotle and Alexander of Aphrodisias' arose out of a growing fascination with Aristotle and his commentator Alexander in Venice and Padua during the period 1485-1530. Ulocrino's charming plaquette can stand for us today as a symbol of this movement.

The prototype of the scene in 'Aristotle and Alexander of Aphrodisias' is the magnificent hand-illuminated frontispiece to volume 1 of the Pierpont Morgan Library's copy of the 1483 Latin Aristotle, probably by Girolamo da Cremona.[6] Many features of the scene on the frontispiece, which shows Aristotle speaking to Averroes, are echoed in Ulocrino's plaquette. In both scenes, a seated Aristotle speaks to a turbaned philosopher in the setting of a country landscape. In both, his right arm is raised and extended while his left arm is held lower, roughly parallel to his left leg. Both scenes include a large hill on the horizon between the two figures,

[4] Edward Cranz, 'Alexander of Aphrodisias', in Kristeller 1960, pp. 184ff.

[5] Pope-Henessey 1964, pp. 77-8.

[6] A colour reproduction of that frontispiece is most easily found in Alexander 1977, plate 17, with bibiliography, pp. 31-2. Pope-Henessey reports (1964, p. 77) that the closest analogies to this scene occur in the illustrations to Zoppino's *Vite de philosophi moralissimi* (a translation of Diogenes Laertius), Venice 1521. Unfortunately, I have not yet been able to see these illustrations. Therefore the conclusions drawn in the remainder of this note must be conditioned by a warning that the question whether Ulocrino based his plaquette directly upon the Morgan Aristotle, or rather upon one or more intermediates, remains open.

and both show buildings – human habitation – on the hill and also lower down to its right. In both scenes a smaller hill in the middle ground curves downward from the right edge of the image to disappear behind Aristotle's left shoulder.

Some of the differences between the two images are the result of Ulocrino's successful efforts to adapt the horizontal format of the scene in the Morgan frontispiece to the vertical format of his plaquette. The tree along the right-hand side of the plaquette (which replaces a cave), the greater proximity of the two figures, and Alexander's standing posture (Averroes is seated) are all to be explained in this way. One difference may reflect Girolamo's greater subtlety (he is undeniably the greater artist); his villas, barely visible in the background, are replaced by Ulocrino's more intrusive fortified buildings.

One change Ulocrino made in his prototype is puzzling. What is the meaning of the hare in the right foreground? Fertility? Aristotle's biological interests?

Other differences can be explained as reflecting Ulocrino's changed conception of the scene. Girolamo's figures are old, and have the wisdom and nobility of age. Ulocrino's figures are nearly as subtly portrayed (bronze relief does not permit the detail of painting), but they have a more rugged and youthful aspect. This greater ruggedness is due to the broader, less delicate shapes of both hats; both men's shorter, less pointed beards, and the plain bronze colour of the beards, replacing their snowy whiteness in Girolamo's image. Girolamo's Aristotle is the wise old man who wrote *Metaphysics* 12; Ulocrino's Aristotle is the younger dialectician and scientist who wrote the *Topics* and studied fishes off Lesbos.

Another significant change Ulocrino made is in the commentator's activity. Averroes is seated in front of an open book, with an inked quill in his right hand. He is writing down the words or ideas which he hears from Aristotle, and the book in front of him is his commentary. The scene recalls portrayals of the inspiration of the Evangelists. By contrast, Ulocrino's Alexander has no quill. He holds a book and concentrates his gaze on the page while Aristotle speaks. It is *possible* that Alexander here is holding his commentary, and that he has returned to Aristotle in a worried state to ask whether in a certain passage he had actually got it right. But by far the more likely explanation is that the book Alexander holds is Aristotle's text itself, and he is staring at a puzzling phrase or sentence while Aristotle explains its meaning. Ulocrino's image emphasises the commentator's puzzlement and the difficulty of Aristotle's text. By contrast, the focus on inspiration in Girolamo's image makes the process of writing the commentary seem effortless. Thus we may say that Girolamo's scene portrays the myth projected by a naive reader: 'This commentary reads as if its author had been under the direct inspiration of the Master.' Ulocrino changes this to present the ultimate fantasy of a commentator: 'If only I could have the Author in front of me and get him to explain this passage himself.' The spirit behind Ulocrino's plaquette is more secular, and reveals a greater sensitivity to the experience of writing a commentary.[7]

Bibliography

Alexander, J.J.G. *Italian Renaissance Illuminations*, New York 1977.

Bange, E.F. *Die italienischen Bronzen der Renaissance und des Barock*, zweiter Teil: *Reliefs und Plaketten*, Berlin and Leipzig 1922.

Bode, W. von. *Berliner Museen: Amtliche Berichte* 29, 1907-8.

Cott, National Gallery of Art, Washington (DC). *Renaissance Bronzes, Statuettes, Reliefs and Plaquettes, Medals and Coins from the Kress Collection*, Washington, DC 1951.

Jacobsen, E. 'Plaketten im Museo Correr zu Venedig', *Repertorium für Kunstwissenschaft* 16, 1893, pp. 54-75.

Kristeller, P. *Mediaeval and Renaissance Latin Translations and Commentaries* I, 1960.

Lazari, *Notizia della Raccolta Correr di Venezia*, 1859.

Maclagan, E. *Victoria and Albert Museum: Catalogue of Italian Plaquettes*, London 1924.

Migeon, *Les Arts* 80, 1908.

Molinier, E. *Les Plaquettes: Catalogue raisonné*, 2 vols, Paris 1886.

Planiscig, L. *Andrea Riccio*, Vienna 1927.

Panvini Rosati, F. *Italienische Medaillen und Plaketten von der Frührenaissance bis zum Ende des Barock*, Cologne 1966.

Panvini Rosati, F. *Medaglie e Placchette italiane dal Renascimento al XVIII secolo*, Rome 1968.

Pope-Henessey, J. 'The Italian Plaquette', *Proceedings of the British Academy*, 1964, pp. 63-76.

Pope-Henessey, J. *Renaissance Bronzes from the Samuel H. Kress Collection*, London 1965.

Ricci, *The Gustav Dreyfus Collection: reliefs and plaquettes*, Oxford 1931.

[7] Further bibliography: Lazari 1859, p. 198, n. 1050 (n. 50); Jacobsen 1893, p. 62; Migeon 1908, p. 27; Bange 1922, p. 58, n. 427, plate 40; Bode 1907, col. 252; Maclagan 1924, p. 27; Planiscig 1927, p. 316 (fig. 358); Ricci 1931, p. 125, n. 160; Cott 1951, p. 150; Pope-Henessey 1965, p. 72, n. 243, fig. 348; Panvini Rosati 1966, p. 98, n. 12; Panvini Rosati 1968, pp. 68-9, n. 12, fig. 12.

Select Bibliography of Secondary Literature

A bibliography on the commentators prepared by Titos Christodoulou with the help of many hands, is being built up on computer at King's College, London. The bibliography that follows is a selection by John Ellis of the most important items. Any works of a general character are grouped at the beginning of each section.

RE = Pauly-Wissowa (eds), *Real-Encyclopädie der classischen Altertumswissenschaft*, Stuttgart.

General

Blumenthal, H.J., 'Plotinus in Later Platonism', in H.J. Blumenthal & R.A. Markus (eds), *Neoplatonism and Early Christian Thought. Essays in Honour of A.H. Armstrong*, London 1981, 212-22.

Blumenthal, H.J., 'Neoplatonic elements in the *de Anima* commentaries', Chapter 13 above, repr. with revisions from *Phronesis* 21, 1976, 64-87.

Brandis, C.A., 'Über Aristoteles Rhetorik und die griechischen Ausleger derselben', *Philologus* 4, 1849, 34ff.

Brink, K.O., 'Peripatos', *RE* Suppl. 7, 1940, cols 938ff.

Burnett, C., *Commentaries and Glosses to Aristotelian Logical Texts: the Syriac, Arabic and European tradition*, forthcoming.

Diels, H. (ed.), *Commentaria in Aristotelem Graeca (CAG)*, Berlin 1892-1909, see the introductions.

Festugière, A.J., 'Modes de composition des commentaires de Proclus', *Museum Helveticum* 20, 1963, 77-100; repr. in his *Études de philosophie grecque*, Paris 1971, 551-74.

Festugière, A.-J., 'L'ordre de lecture des dialogues de Platon aux Ve-VIe siècles', *Museum Helveticum* 26, 1969, 281-96; repr. in his *Études de philosophie grecque*, Paris 1971, 535-50.

Glucker, J., *Antiochus and the Late Academy*, Hypomnemata 56, Göttingen 1978.

Hadot, I., 'Les *Introductions* aux commentaires exégétiques chez les auteurs néoplatoniciens et les auteurs chrétiens', to be included in her French translation of Simplicius *in Cat.*, vol. 1; also in M. Tardieu, *Les règles de l'interpretation*, Paris 1987.

Hadot, I., 'La division néoplatonicienne des écrits d'Aristote', in J. Wiesner (ed.), *Aristoteles: Werk und Wirkung, Paul Moraux gewidmet*, vol. 2, Berlin-New York 1987, 249-85.

Hadot, P., 'Les divisions des parties de la philosophie dans l'antiquité', *Museum Helveticum* 36, 1979, 201-23; unpublished English translation by Victor Caston.

Hadot, P., 'The harmony of Plotinus and Aristotle according to Porphyry', Chapter 6 above, translated from *Atti del Convegno Internazionale sul tema Plotino e il*

Neoplatonismo in Oriente e Occidente (Roma 5-9 ottobre 1970), Accademia dei Lincei, Rome 1974, 31-47.

Lamberz, E., 'Proklos und die Form des philosophischen Kommentars', in J. Pépin & H.D. Saffrey (eds), *Proclus. Lecteur et interprète des Anciens*, Paris 1987.

Lynch, J.P., *Aristotle's School. A Study of a Greek Educational Institution*, Berkeley-Los Angeles 1972.

Mercati, G., 'Fra i commentatori greci di Aristotele', in *Mélanges d'archéologie et d'histoire* 35, 1915, 191-219; repr. in *Opere Minori III*, Rome 1937, 458-67.

Moraux, P., 'La critique d'authenticité chez les commentateurs grecs d'Aristote', in *Mélanges Mansel* 1, Ankara 1974, 265-88.

Moraux, P., *D'Aristote à Bessarion: trois études sur l'histoire et la transmission de l'aristotélisme grec*, Laval, Quebec 1970.

Müller, C.W., 'Die neuplatonischen Aristoteleskommentatoren über die Ursachen der Pseudepigraphie', *Rheinisches Museum* 112, 1969, 120-6.

Plezia, M., *De Commentariis Isagogicis*, Cracow 1947.

Praechter, K., Review of *Commentaria in Aristotelem Graeca*, Chapter 2 above, repr. from 'Die griechischen Aristoteleskommentatoren', *Byzantinische Zeitschrift* 18, 1909, 516-38.

Praechter, K., 'Richtungen und Schulen im Neuplatonismus', *Genethliakon für Carl Robert*, Berlin 1910, 105-55; repr. in *Kleine Schriften*, H. Dörrie (ed.), Collectanea 7, Hildesheim-New York 1973, 165-216.

Richard, M., 'Apo phônês' (in French – unpublished English translation by Victor Caston), *Byzantion* 20, 1950, 191-222.

Sorabji, R., 'The ancient commentators on Aristotle', Chapter 1 above.

Sorabji, R. (ed.), The Ancient Commentators on Aristotle, a series of English translations with introductions and indexes, London-Ithaca N.Y. 1987-.

Tannery, P., 'Sur la période finale de la philosophie grecque', *Revue philosophique* 42, 1896, 226-87.

Tarán, L., 'Amicus Plato sed magis amica veritas. From Plato and Aristotle to Cervantes', *Antike und Abendland* 30, 1984, 93-124.

Todd, R.B., 'Galenic medical ideas in the Greek Aristotelian Commentators', *Symbolae Osloenses* 52, 1977, 117-34.

Usener, H., Review of *CAG*, *Göttingische gelehrte Anzeigen*, 1892, 1001-22.

Westerink, L.G., 'Academic practice about 500 A.D. in Alexandria', unpublished paper delivered to Dumbarton Oaks conference.

Westerink, L.G., 'Ein astrologisches Kolleg aus dem Jahre 564', *Byzantinische Zeitschrift* 64, 1971, 6-21; repr. in his *Texts and Studies in Neoplatonism and Byzantine Literature*, Amsterdam 1980, 279-94.

Westerink, L.G., *Anonymous Prolegomena to Platonic Philosophy*, Amsterdam 1962; pp. ix-xxxii repr. with the revisions prepared for the new Budé edition in Chapter 14 above.

Individual commentators

Adrastus

Gottschalk, H.B, 'The earliest Aristotelian commentators', Chapter 3 above, repr. with revisions from W. Haase (ed.), *Aufstieg und Niedergang der römischen Welt*, II, 36.2, Berlin 1987, 1079-174.

Gottschalk, H.B., Review of P. Moraux, *Der Aristotelismus*, vol. 2, in *Liverpool Classical Monthly* 10.8, 1985, 122-8.

Immisch, O., '*Attikoi exegetai*', *Philologus* 63, 1904, 31-40.

Kenny, A., *The Aristotelian Ethics*, Oxford 1978.
Mercken, H.P.F., 'The Greek commentaries on Aristotle's *Ethics*', Chapter 18 above, revised from 'Introduction', Corpus Latinum Commentariorum in Aristotelem Graecorum 6.1.
Moraux, P., *Der Aristotelismus bei den Griechen von Andronikos bis Alexander von Aphrodisias*, vol. 2, Der Aristotelismus im I. und II. Jh. n. Chr., Peripatoi 6, Berlin-New York 1984, 294-332.

Alexander of Aphrodisias

Berti, E., 'Alessandro di Afrodisia', in *Enciclopedia di Filosofia* 1.2, Florence 1967, cols 171-2.
Gercke, A., 'Alexander von Aphrodisias', *RE* 1, cols 1453-5.
Lloyd, A.C., 'Alexander of Aphrodisias', in P. Edwards (ed.), *Encyclopedia of Philosophy*, New York-London 1967, 73.
Merlan, P., 'Alexander of Aphrodisias', in C.S. Gillispie (ed.), *Dictionary of Scientific Biography*, New York 1970, 117-20.
Mueller, Ian, 'Stoic and Peripatetic logic', *Archiv für Geschichte der Philosophie* 51, 1969, 173-87.
Nardi, B., 'Alessandro di Afrodisia', *Enciclopedia Cattolica*, vol. 1, Vatican City 1968, 778-80.
Sharples, R.W., 'The school of Alexander?', Chapter 4 above.
Sharples, R.W., 'Alexander of Aphrodisias, scholasticism and innovation', in W. Haase (ed.), *Aufstieg und Niedergang der römischen Welt*, II, 36.2, Berlin 1987, 1176-243.
Steinschneider, M., 'Zu Alexander von Aphrodisias', *Magazin für die Wissenschaft des Judentums* 14, 1887, 190-5.

*

Bazán, B.C., 'L'authenticité du "de Intellectu" attribué à Alexandre d'Aphrodise', *Revue philosophique de Louvain* 71, 1973, 468-87.
Blumenthal, H.J., 'Alexander of Aphrodisias in the later Greek commentaries on Aristotle's *de Anima*', in J. Wiesner (ed.), *Aristoteles: Werk und Wirkung, Paul Moraux gewidmet*, vol. 2, Berlin-New York 1987, 90-106.
Blumenthal, H.J., 'Plotinus Ennead IV.3.20-21 and its sources – Alexander, Aristotle and others', *Archiv für Geschichte der Philosophie* 50, 1968, 254-61.
Coutant, V.C., *Alexander of Aphrodisias, Commentary on Book IV of Aristotle's Meteorologica*, diss., Columbia 1936; reviewed by B. Einarson in *Classical Weekly* 31, 1937, 33.
Cranz, F.E., 'Alexander Aphrodisiensis', in P.O. Kristeller & F.E. Cranz (eds), *Catalogus Translationum et Commentariorum, Medieval and Renaissance Latin Translations and Commentaries*, Washington D.C., vol. 1, 1960, 77-135; 2, 1971, 411-22.
Cranz, F.E., 'The prefaces to the Greek editions and Latin translations of Alexander of Aphrodisias, 1450-1575', *Proceedings of the American Philosophical Society* 102, 1958, 510-46.
Dietrich, A., 'Die arabische Version einer unbekannten Schrift des Alexander von Aphrodisias über die Differentia specifica', *Nachrichten der Akademie der Wissenschaften in Göttingen*, 1964, 85-148.
Donini, P.L., *Tre studi sull'Aristotelismo nel II secolo D. C.*, Historica, Politica, Philosophica 7, Turin 1974.

Donini, P.L., 'L'anima e gli elementi nel "de Anima" di Alessandro di Afrodisia', *Atti della Accademia delle Scienze di Torino*, Classe di Scienze Morali, Storiche e Filologiche 105, 1970-71, 61-107.

Donini, P.L., 'Il de Anima di Alessandro di Afrodisia e Michele Efesio', *Rivista di Filologia e di Instruzione Classica* 96, 1968, 316-23.

Ebbesen, S., *Commentators and Commentaries on Aristotle's Sophistici Elenchi. A Study of Post-Aristotelian and Medieval Writings on Fallacies*, 3 vols, Corpus Latinum Commentariorum in Aristotelem Graecorum 7.1-3, Leiden 1981.

Ess, J. van, 'Über einige neue fragmente des Alexander von Aphrodisias in arabischer Übersetzung', *Der Islam* 42, 1966, 148-68.

Finnegan, J., 'Al-Farabi et le "Peri Nou" d'Alexandre d'Aphrodise', *Mélanges L. Massignon*, 1957, 133-52.

Freudenthal, J., 'Die durch Averroes erhaltenen Fragmente Alexanders zur Metaphysik des Aristoteles untersucht und übersetzt', *Abhandlung der (k.) preussischen Akademie der Wissenschaften*, Berlin 1884.

Gätje, H., 'Die Schrift des Alexander von Aphrodisias über das Sahen' (with G. Losseren), *Studien zur Überlieferung der aristotelischen Psychologie im Islam*, Annales Universitatis Saraviensis 11, Heidelberg 1971, 140-72.

Gätje, H., 'Die arabische Übersetzung der Schrift des Alexander von Afrodisias über die Farbe', *Nachrichten der Academie der Wissenschaften in Göttingen*, 1967, 341-82.

Gätje, H., 'Zur arabischen Überlieferung des Alexander von Aphrodisias', *Zeitschrift der deutschen morgenländischen Gesellschaft* 116, 1966, 255-78.

Genequand, C., 'L'objet de la métaphysique selon Alexandre d'Aphrodise', *Museum Helveticum* 36, 1979, 48-57.

Hager, F.P., 'Die Aristotelesinterpretation des Alexander von Aphrodisias und die Aristoteleskritik Plotins bezüglich der Lehre vom Geist', *Archiv für Geschichte der Philosophie* 46, 1964, 174-87.

Hamelin, O., *La théorie de l'intellect d'après Aristote et ses commentateurs*, posthumous ed. E. Barbotin, Paris 1953.

Lloyd, A.C., 'The significance of Alexander's theory of universals', in *Proceedings of the World Congress on Aristotle*, vol. 1, Athens 1981, 155-9.

Madigan, A.S.J., 'Alexander of Aphrodisias, the book of Ethical Problems', in W. Haase (ed.), *Aufstieg und Niedergang der römischen Welt*, II, 36.2, Berlin 1987, 1260-79.

Merlan, P., 'Zwei Untersuchungen zu Alexander von Aphrodisias', *Philologus* 113, 1969, 85-91.

Mignucci, M., 'Puzzles about identity, Aristotle and his Greek commentators', in J. Wiesner (ed.), *Aristoteles: Werk und Wirkung, Paul Moraux gewidmet*, vol. 1, Berlin 1985, 57-97.

Moraux, P., *Le commentaire d'Alexandre d'Aphrodise aux Secondes Analytiques d'Aristote*, Peripatoi 13, Berlin 1979. Review by E. Berti, *Archiv für Geschichte der Philosophie* 63, 1981, 84-6.

Moraux, P., *Alexandre d'Aphrodise: exégète de la noétique d'Aristote*, Liège-Paris 1942.

Pinès, S., *'Omne quod movetur necesse est ab aliquo moveri*, a refutation of Galen by Alexander of Aphrodisias and the theory of motion', *Isis* 52, 1961, 21-54.

Rescher, N. & Marmura, M., *Alexander of Aphrodisias. The Refutation by Alexander of Aphrodisias of Galen's Treatise of the Theory of Motion*, Islamabad (Islamic Research Institute), 1965.

Rist, J.M., 'On tracking Alexander of Aphrodisias', *Archiv für Geschichte der Philosophie* 48, 1966, 82-90.

Ruland, H.-J., 'Die arabische Übersetzung der Schrift des Alexander von Aphrodisias über das Wachstum (Quaestio I 5)', *Nachrichten der Akademie der Wissenschaften in Göttingen*, 1981, 51-74.

Ruland, H.-J., 'Zwei arabische Fassungen der Abhandlung des Alexander von Aphrodisias über die universalia (Quaestio I 11a)', *Nachrichten der Akademie der Wissenschaften in Göttingen*, 1979, 243-74.

Ruland, H.-J., 'Die arabische Übersetzung der Schrift des Alexander von Aphrodisias über die Sinneswahrnehmung', *Nachrichten der Akademie der Wissenschaften in Göttingen*, 1978, 159-225.

Ruland, H.-J., *Die arabische Fassungen von zwei Schriften des Alexander von Aphrodisias: Über die Vorsehung und über das liberum arbitrium*, diss., Saarbrücken 1976.

Schroeder, F.M., 'Light and the active intellect in Alexander and Plotinus', *Hermes* 112, 1984, 239-48.

Schroeder, F.M., 'The potential or material intellect and the authorship of the de Intellectu: a reply to B.C. Bazán', *Symbolae Osloenses* 57, 1982, 115-25.

Schroeder, F.M., 'The analogy of the active intellect to light in the de Anima of Alexander of Aphrodisias', *Hermes* 109, 1981, 215-25.

Sharples, R.W., 'Ambiguity and opposition, Alexander of Aphrodisias on "Ethical Problems" ', *Bulletin of the Institute of Classical Studies* 32, 1985, 109-16.

Sharples, R.W., 'The Unmoved Mover and the motion of the heavens in Alexander of Aphrodisias', *Apeiron* 17, 1983, 62-6.

Sharples, R.W., *Alexander of Aphrodisias on Fate*, London 1983.

Sorabji, R., *Matter, Space and Motion* (ch. 8), London-Ithaca, N.Y. 1988.

Strohmaier, G., 'al-Iskandar al-Afrudisi', in G. van Donzel et al. (eds), *Encyclopedia of Islam²*, vol. 4, Leiden 1978, 129f.

Théry, G., *Autour du décret de 1210: II. Alexandre d'Aphrodise: apercu sur l'influence de sa noétique*, Bibliothèque thomiste 7, Kain 1926.

Thillet, P., 'Matérialisme et théorie de l'âme et de l'intellect chez Alexandre d'Aphrodise', *Revue philosophique de la France et de l'étranger* 171, 1981, 5-24.

Thurot, C., 'Alexandre d'Aphrodisias, Commentaire sur le traité d'Aristote "De Sensu et Sensibili" ', *Notices et extraits des MSS de la bibliothèque nationale* 25, 1875, no. 2.

Todd, R.B., 'The de Intellectu attributed to Alexander of Aphrodisias. Translation, Introduction and Commentary', in R.B. Todd & F.M. Shroeder (eds), *The Greek Aristotelian Commentators on the Active Intellect*, Toronto, forthcoming.

Todd, R.B., *Alexander of Aphrodisias on Stoic Physics*, Leiden 1976.

Todd, R.B., 'Lexicographical notes on Alexander of Aphrodisias' philosophical terminology', *Glotta* 52, 1974, 207-15.

Tweedale, M.M., 'Alexander of Aphrodisias' views on universals', *Phronesis* 29, 1984, 279-303.

Verbeke, G, 'Aristotle's Metaphysics as viewed by the ancient Greek commentators', in D.J. O'Meara (ed.), *Studies in Aristotle*, Washington, D.C. 1981, 107-27.

Wallies, M., 'Die griechischen Ausleger der aristotelesichen Topik', *Wissenschaftliche Beilage zum Programm des Sophien–Gymnasiums zu Berlin* 65, 1891, 1-27.

Ammonius son of Hermeias

Anton, J.P., 'Ancient interpretations of Aristotle's doctrine of homonyma', *Journal of the History of Philosophy* 7, 1969, 1-18.

Isaak, I., *Le Peri hermeneias en Occident de Boèce à Saint Thomas. Histoire littéraire d'un traité d'Aristote*, Bibliothèque thomiste 29, Paris 1953; includes the first 10 chapters of William of Moerbeke's translation, pp. 160-9.

Merlan, P., 'Ammonius Hermiae, Zacharias Scholasticus and Boethius', *Greek, Roman and Byzantine Studies* 9, 1968, 143-203.

Noica, C., *Ammonius, Stephanus. Comentarii la Tratatul Despre Interpretare al lui Aristotel, însotite de Textul Comentat, Traducere, Curînt înainte, note si Comentariu*, Bucarest 1971.

Noica, C., *Porfir, Dexip, Ammonius. Comentarii la Categoriile lui Aristotel, însotite de Textul Comentat Traducere, Curînt înainte si Note*, Bucarest 1968.

Saffrey, H.D., 'Le chrétien Jean Philopon et la survivance de l'école d'Alexandrie au VIe siècle', *Revue des études grecques* 67, 1954, 396-410.

Sheppard, Anne, 'Proclus' philosophical method of exegesis, the use of Aristotle and the Stoics in the Commentary on the Cratylus', in J. Pépin & P. Saffrey (eds), *Proclus. Lecteur et interprète des Anciens*, Paris 1987, 137-51.

Sorabji. R., 'Infinite power impressed, the transformation of Aristotle's physics and theology', Chapter 9 above (fuller version in *Matter, Space and Motion*, London-Ithaca N.Y. 1988).

Sorabji, R., *Time, Creation and the Continuum*, London-Ithaca N.Y. 1983, ch. 16.

Verrycken, K., 'The metaphysics of Ammonius son of Hermeias', Chapter 10 above.

Westerink, L.G., *Anonymous Prolegomena to Platonic Philosophy*, Amsterdam 1962, pp. ix-xxxii repr. with the revisions prepared for the new Budé edition as Chapter 14 above.

Andronicus

Düring, I., *Aristotle in the Ancient Biographical Tradition*, Göteborg 1957.

Düring, I., 'Notes on the history of the transmission of Aristotle's writings', *Göteborg Högskulas Arsskrift* 56, 1950, 3, 35-70.

Gottschalk, H.B., 'Aristotelian philosophy in the Roman world from the time of Cicero to the end of the second century A.D.', in W. Haase (ed.), *Aufstieg und Niedergang der römischen Welt*, II, 36.2, Berlin 1987, 1079-174; part. repr. with revisions as Chapter 3 above.

Littig, Fr., *Andronikos von Rhodos* (3 vols), Erlangen 1, 1890; 2, 1894; 3, 1985.

Moraux, P., *Der Aristotelismus bei den Griechen von Andronikos bis Alexander von Aphrodisias*, vol. 1, Die Renaissance des Aristotelismus im I. Jh. v. Chr., Section 2: 'Andronikos von Rhodos', Peripatoi 5, Berlin 1973, 97-141.

Plezia, M., *De Andronici Rhodii Studiis Aristotelicis, Polska Academia Uniectnosci*, Archiwum Filologiczne, no. 20, Cracow 1946.

Shute, R., *On the History of the Process by which the Aristotelian Writings Arrived at their Present Form*, Oxford 1888.

Asclepius

Kremer, K., *Der Metaphysikbegriff in den Aristoteles-Kommentaren der Ammonius-Schule*, Beiträge zur Geschichte der Philosophie und Theologie des Mittelalters 39, 1, Münster 1961.

Madigan, A., 'Syrianus and Asclepius on forms and intermediates in Plato and Aristotle', *Journal of the History of Philosophy* 24, 1986, 49-71.

Tarán, L., 'Asclepius of Tralles' commentary to Nicomachus' Introduction to Arithmetic', *Transactions of the American Philosophical Society*, n.s. 59, 1969, 8.

Verrycken, K., 'The metaphysics of Ammonius son of Hermeias', Chapter 10 above.
Westerink, L.G., 'Deux commentaires sur Nicomaque, Asclépius et Jean Philopon', *Revue des études grecques* 77, 1964, 526-35; repr. in his *Texts and Studies in Neoplatonism and Byzantine Literature*, Amsterdam 1980, 101-10.

Aspasius

Gercke, A., 'Aspasios', *RE* 2, 1896, cols 1722-3.
Überweg, F., 'Aspasius', *Grundriss der Geschichte der Philosophie*, vol. 1, 562, 177.
Zahlfleisch, J., 'Aspasio', *Enciclopedia di Filosofia*, vol. 1, col. 507.

*

Becchi, F., 'Aspasio e i peripatetici posteriori, la formula definitiva della passione', *Prometheus* 9, 1983, 83-104.
Gauthier, R.-A., 'Introduction', in R.A. Gauthier & J.Y. Jolif (eds), *L'Éthique à Nicomaque. Introduction, traduction et commentaire*, 2nd ed., vol. 1, part 1, Paris 1970, 100-5, 121.
Gottschalk, H.B., 'Aristotelian philosophy in the Roman world from the time of Cicero to the end of the second century A.D.', in W. Haase (ed.), *Aufstieg und Niedergang der römischen Welt*, II, 36.2, Berlin 1987, 1079-174, part repr. with revisions as Chapter 3 above.
Hanquet, R., *Aspasius, sa vie, son oeuvre, sa pensée*, diss., Louvain 1945.
Kenny, A., *The Aristotelian Ethics*, Oxford 1978.
Mercken, H.P.F., 'The Greek commentaries on Aristotle's *Ethics*', Chapter 18 above, repr. with revisions from Introduction to Corpus Latinum Commentariorum in Aristotelem Graecorum 6.1.
Moraux, P., *Der Aristotelismus bei den Griechen von Andronikos bis Alexander von Aphrodisias*, vol. 2, *Der Aristotelismus im I. und II. Jh. n. Chr.*, Peripatoi 6, Berlin-New York 1984, esp. 226-93.
Rose, V., 'Über die griechischen Kommentare zur Ethik des Aristoteles', *Hermes* 5, 1871, 61-113.
Schleiermacher, F., 'Über die griechischen Scholien zur Nicomachischen Ethik des Aristoteles', *Sammtliche Werke*, section 3, vol. 2, Berlin 1838, 309-26.

Boethius

Bieler, L. (ed.), 'Praefatio' and 'Bibliographia', in *Boethii Philosophiae Consolatio*, ed. 2a, Turnholt 1989.
Cappuyns, M., 'Boèce', *DAGE* 9, 1939.
Chadwick, H., *Boethius. The Consolations of Music, Logic, Theology, and Philosophy*, Oxford 1981.
Fuhrmann, M. & Gruber, J. (eds), *Boethius*, Wege der Forschung 483, Darmstadt 1984.
Liebeschütz, H., 'Boethius and the legacy of antiquity', in A.H. Armstrong (ed.), *The Cambridge History of Later Greek and Early Medieval Philosophy*, Cambridge 1967, 538-64.
Minio-Paluello, L., 'Boethius', *Dictionary of Scientific Biography* 2, 1970, 228-36.
Minio-Paluello, L., 'Boethius', article in *Encyclopaedia Britannica*, 1968.
Obertello, L., *Severino Boezio*, 2 vols, Genoa 1974.

492   *Select Bibliography*

Shiel, J., 'Boethius' commentaries on Aristotle', Chapter 15 above, revised from *Medieval and Renaissance Studies* 4, 1958, 217-44.

*

Barnes, J., 'Boethius and the study of logic', in M. Gibson (ed.), *Boethius. His Life, Thought and Influence*, Oxford 1981, 73-89.

Bidez, J., 'Boèce et Porphyre', *Comptes rendus de l'académie des inscriptions et des belles lettres*, 1922, 345-50.

Courcelle, P., *Late Latin Writers and their Greek Sources*, Cambridge, Mass. 1969; translated from *Les lettres grecques en Occident, de Macrobe à Cassiodore*, 2nd ed., Paris 1948.

Dürr, K., *The Propositional Logic of Boethius*, Studies in Logic and the Foundations of Mathematics, Amsterdam 1951.

Ebbesen, S., 'Boethius as an Aristotelian commentator', Chapter 16 above; repr. from J. Wiesner (ed.), *Aristoteles: Werk und Wirkung, Paul Moraux gewidmet*, vol. 2, Berlin-New York 1987, 286-311.

Ebbesen, S., 'Analyzing syllogisms, or Anonymus Aurelianensis III – the (presumably) earliest extant Latin commentary on the Prior Analytics, and its Greek model', *Cahiers de l'Institut du moyen-âge grec et latin* 37, Copenhagen 1981, 1-20.

Ebbesen, S., *Commentators and Commentaries on Aristotle's Sophistici Elenchi. A Study of Post-Aristotelian and Medieval Writings on Fallacies*, 3 vols, Corpus Latinum Commentariorum in Aristotelem Graecorum 7.1-3, Leiden 1981.

Ebbesen, S., 'Anonymus Aurelianensis II, Aristotle, Alexander, Porphyry and Boethius: ancient scholasticism and twelfth-century Western Europe. With an edition of the Tractatus de Paralogismis', *Cahiers de l'Institut du moyen-âge grec et latin* 16, Copenhagen 1976, 1-128.

Gersh, S., *Middle Platonism and Neoplatonism. The Latin Tradition*, 2 vols, Notre Dame 1986, ch. 9.

Gibson, M. (ed), *Boethius. His Life, Thought and Influence*, Oxford 1981.

Hadot, P., 'Un fragment du commentaire perdu de Boèce sur les Catégories d'Aristote dans le codex Bernensis 363', *Archives d'histoire doctrinale et littéraire du moyen-âge* 26, 1959, 11-27.

Isaak, I., *Le Peri hermeneias en Occident de Boèce à Saint Thomas. Histoire littéraire d'un traité d'Aristote*, Bibliothèque thomiste 29, Paris 1953; includes the first 10 chapters of William of Moerbeke's translation, pp. 160-9.

Kretzmann, N., 'Boethius and the truth about tomorrow's sea battle', in L.M. de Rijk & H.A.G. Braakhuis (eds), *Logos and Pragma. Essays in honour of Prof. G. Nuchelmans*, Artistarium suppl. 3, Nijmegen 1987, 63-97.

Kretzmann, N., '*Nos ipsi principia sumus*: Boethius and the basis of contingency', in T. Rudavsky (ed.), *Divine Omniscience and Omnipotence in Medieval Philosophy: Islamic, Jewish and Christian perspectives*, Synthese Historical Library 25, Dordrecht 1985.

Magee, J., *Boethius on Signification and Mind*, forthcoming, Leiden 1989.

Minio-Paluello, L., *Opuscula, the Latin Aristotle*, Amsterdam 1972.

Minio-Paluello, L., 'Praefationes' in *Aristoteles Latinus* 1.1-5 and (B. Dod, ed.) 1.6-7, Paris 1966; includes Boethius' translations of *Isagoge, Cat., Int., An. Pr., Top., SE*.

Minio-Paluello, L., 'Les traductions et les commentaires aristotéliciennes de Boèce', *Studia Patristica II*, Texte und Untersuchungen zur Geschichte der altchristlichen Literatur 64, 1957, 358-65.

Minio-Paluello, L., 'A Latin commentary (?translated by Boethius) on the Prior

Analytics and its Greek sources', *Journal of Hellenic Studies* 77, 1957, part 1, 93-102.

Nuchelmans, G., *Theories of the Proposition. Ancient and Medieval Conceptions of the Bearers of Truth and Falsity*, Amsterdam 1973.

Obertello, L. (ed.), *Atti di Congresso Internazionale di Studi Boeziani*, Roma 1981.

Prior, A.N., 'The logic of negative terms in Boethius', *Franciscan Studies* 13, 1953, 1-16.

Rijk, L.M. de, 'On Boethius' notion of being: a chapter of Boethian semantics', in N. Kretzmann (ed.), *Meaning and Inference in Medieval Philosophy. Studies in Memory of Jan Pinborg*, Synthese Historical Library 32, Dordrecht 1988, 1-29.

Rijk, L.M. de, 'Boèce logicien et philosophe, ses positions et sa métaphysique de l'être', in L. Obertello (ed.), *Congresso Internazionale di Studi Boeziani – Atti*, Roma 1981, 141-56.

Rijk, L.M. de, *Logica Modernorum*, Assen, vol. 1, 1962; vol. 2, 1967.

Rijk, L.M. de, 'On the chronology of Boethius' works on logic', *Vivarium* 2, 1964, 1-49, 122-62.

Shiel, J., '*Religio Grammatici*', *Matrix* 10, 1990.

Shiel, J., 'The Greek copy of Porphyrios' Isagoge used by Boethius', in J. Wiesner (ed.), *Aristoteles: Werk und Wirkung, Paul Moraux gewidmet*, vol. 2, Berlin-New York 1987, 312-40.

Shiel, J., 'A recent discovery, Boethius' notes on the Prior Analytics', *Vivarium* 20, 1982, 128-41.

Shiel, J., 'Boethius and Eudemus', *Vivarium* 12, 1974, 14-17.

Shiel, J., 'Boethius', article in *Encyclopaedia Britannica*, 1974.

Shiel, J., 'Boethius and Andronicus of Rhodes', *Vigiliae Christianae* 11, 1957, 179-85.

Solmsen, F., 'Boethius and the history of the Organon', *American Journal of Philology* 31, 1944, 69-74.

Stump, E., 'Boethius' works on the Topics', *Vivarium* 12, 1974, 77-93.

Damascius

Chaignet, A., *Damascius le Diadoque*, Paris 1898.

Heitz, E., *Der Philosoph Damascius*, Freiburg i. Br. 1884.

Kroll, W., 'Damaskios', *RE* 4, 2, 1901, cols 2039-42.

Strömberg, R., 'Damascius, his personality and importance', *Eranos* 44, 1946, 175-92.

Westerink, L. & Combès, J., 'Introduction' in Damascius, *Traité des premiers principes*, vol. 1, Budé edition, Paris 1986, xxxvi-xli.

Westerink, L.G., *The Greek Commentaries on Plato's Phaedo*, vol. 2, Damascius, Amsterdam 1977.

Westerink, L.G., 'Damascius, commentateur de Platon', in *Le néoplatonisme*, Actes du Colloque de Royaumont 9-13 Juin, 1969, Paris 1971, 253-60.

David

Aversatjan, S., 'David l'Invincible et sa doctrine philosophique', *Revue des études arméniennes* 15, 1981, 33-43.

Benakis, L., 'David der Armenier in der Werken der byzantinischen Kommentatoren des Aristoteles', in *David the Invincible. The Great Philosopher of Ancient Armenia*, Yerevan 1983, 558-70. Also in Armenian, in *Patma – Banasirakan Handen* (Yerevan) 1, 1981, 46-55.

Select Bibliography

Dörrie, H., 'David', *RE* 4, 1901, cols 2232-3.
Kendall, B. & Thomson, R.W., *Definitions and Divisions of Philosophy by David the Invincible Philosopher*, Armenian Texts and Studies 5, California 1983.
Khostikian, M., *David der Philosoph*, Bern 1907.
Neumann, C., 'Mémoire sur la vie et des ouvrages de David, philosophe arménien du Ve siècle de notre ère', *Nouveau journal asiatique* 3, 1829, 49-86, 97-157; repr. Paris 1921.
Praechter, K., David Prolegomena (*CAG* 18, 2.5. 34,6ff.), *Hermes* 1911, 316-17.
Praechter, K., review of *Prolegomena* and *in Isagogem* (*CAG*), *Göttingische gelehrte Anzeigen* 170, Göttingen 1908.
Rose, V., *Leben des Heiligen David von Salonika, griechisch nach der einzigen bisher aufgefundenen Handschrift herausgeg. Mit Beziehung auf David Invictus Philosophus*, Berlin 1887.
Sanjian, A.K. (ed.), *David Anhaght*, the Invincible Philosopher*, Atlanta, Georgia 1986.
Westerink, L.G., *Anonymous Prolegomena to Platonic Philosophy*, Amsterdam 1962; new edition in preparation; pp. ix-xxxii repr. with the revisions prepared for the new Budé edition in Chapter 14 above.

Dexippus

Anton, J.P., 'Ancient interpretations of Aristotle's doctrine of homonyma', *Journal of the History of Philosophy* 7, 1969, 1-18.
Boeft, J. den, 'Desippo', *Enciclopedia di Filosofia*, vol. 2, cols 391-2.
Busse, A., 'Der Historiker und der Philosoph Dexippus', *Hermes* 23, 1888, 402-9.
Kroll, W., 'Dexippos', in *RE* 5, 1913, cols 293-4.

*

Aubenque, P., 'Plotin et Dexippe, exégètes des Catégories d'Aristote', in C. Rutten & A. Motte (eds), *Aristotelica. Mélanges offerts à Marcel de Corte*, Brussels-Liège 1985, 7-40.
Hadot, P., 'The harmony of Plotinus and Aristotle according to Porphyry', Chapter 6 above, translated from *Atti del Convegno Internazionale sul tema Plotino e il Neoplatonismo in Oriente e Occidente* (Roma 5-9 ottobre 1970), Accademia Nazionale dei Lincei, Rome 1974, 31-47.
Henry, P., 'Trois apories orales de Plotin sur les Catégories', *Zetesis, Mélanges de Strycker*, Anvers 1973, 234-65.
Noica, C., *Porfir, Dexip, Ammonius. Comentarii la Categoriile lui Aristotel, însotite de Textul Comentat Traducere, Curînt înainte si Note*, Bucarest 1968.
Usener, H., Review of L. Spengel (*CAG* edition of Dexippus), *Litterar. Centralblatt*, 1860, 124-5.

Elias

Anton, J.P., 'Ancient interpretations of Aristotle's doctrine of homonyma', *Journal of the History of Philosophy* 7, 1969, 1-18.
Blumenthal, H.J, 'Pseudo-Elias and the Isagoge commentaries again', *Rheinisches Museum* 124, 1981, 188-92.
Ebbesen, S., *Commentators and Commentaries on Aristotle's Sophistici Elenchi. A Study of Post-Aristotelian and Medieval Writings on Fallacies*, 3 vols, Corpus Latinorum Commentariorum in Aristotelem Graecorum 7.1-3, Leiden 1981.

Marcovich, M., Pseudo-Elias on Heraclitus, *American Journal of Philology* 96, 1975, 31-4.

Westerink, L.G. (ed.), 'Elias on the Prior Analytics', *Mnemosyne* 14, 1961, 126-39; repr. in his *Texts and Studies in Neoplatonism and Byzantine Literature*, Amsterdam 1980, 59-72.

Westerink, L.G., 'Elias und Plotin', *Byzantinische Zeitschrift* 57, 1964, 26-32; repr. in his *Texts and Studies in Neoplatonism and Byzantine Literature*, Amsterdam 1980, 93-9.

Westerink, L.G., *Pseudo-Elias (Pseudo-David), Lectures on Porphyry's Isagoge*, Amsterdam 1967.

Westerink, L.G., *Anonymous Prolegomena to Platonic Philosophy*, Amsterdam 1962; new edition in preparation; pp. x-xxxii repr. with the revisions prepared for the new Budé edition in Chapter 14 above.

Eustratius

Dräseke, J., 'Zu Eustratius von Nikaea', *Byzantinische Zeitschrift* 5, 1896, 319-36.

Martini, E., 'Eustratius, Metropolit von Nicaea', in *RE* 6, 1, 1907, col. 1490-1.

*

Gauthier, R.-A., 'Introduction', in R.A. Gauthier & J.Y. Jolif, *L'Éthique à Nicomaque. Introduction, traduction et commentaire*, vol. 1, part 1, 2nd ed., Paris 1970, 100-5, 121.

Giocarinis, K., 'Eustratius of Nicaea's defence of the doctrine of Ideas', *Franciscan Studies* 24, 1964, 159-204.

Ioannou, P., 'Die Definition des Seins bei Eustratius von Nicaea. Die Universalien-lehre in der byzantinischen Theologie im XI Jahrhundert', *Byzantinische Zeitschrift* 47, 1954, 258-368.

Lloyd, A.C., 'The Aristotelianism of Eustratius of Nicaea', in J. Wiesner (ed.), *Aristoteles: Werk und Wirkung, Paul Moraux gewidmet*, vol. 2, Berlin-New York 1987, 341-51.

Mercken, H.P.F., 'The Greek commentaries on Aristotle's *Ethics*', Chapter 18 above, repr. with revisions from 'Introduction', Corpus Latinum Commentariorum in Aristotelem Graecorum 6.1.

Rose, V., 'Über die griechischen Kommentare zur Ethik des Aristoteles', *Hermes* 5, 1871, 61-113.

Rossi, P., 'Tracce della versione latina di un commento greco ai Secondi Analitici nel Commentarius in Posteriorium Analyticorum di Grossatesta', *Rivista di Filosofia Neoscolastica*, 1978, 433-9.

Iamblichus

Bidez, J., 'Le philosophe Jamblique et son école', *Revue des études grecques* 323, 1919, 29-40.

Dalsgaard-Larsen, B., *Jamblique de Chalcis: exégète et philosophe*, 2 vols, Århus 1972.

Dillon, J., 'Iamblichus of Chalcis (c. 240-325 A.D.)', in W. Haase (ed.), *Aufstieg und Niedergang der römischen Welt*, II, 36.2, Berlin 1987, 862-909.

Kroll, W., 'Iamblichus', *RE* 10, 1, 1914, cols 649-51.

*

Blumenthal, H.J., 'Did Iamblichus write a commentary on the de Anima?', *Hermes* 102, 1974, 540-56.

Dalsgaard-Larsen, B., 'La place de Jamblique dans la philosophie antique tardive', in H. Dörrie (ed.), *De Jamblique à Proclus*, Entretiens sur l'antiquité classique 21, Vandoeuvres-Genève 1975, 1-34.

Hadot, P., 'The harmony of Plotinus and Aristotle according to Porphyry', Chapter 6 above, translated from *Atti del Convegno Internazionale sul tema Plotino e il Neoplatonismo in Oriente e Occidente* (Roma 5-9 ottobre 1970), Accademia dei Lincei, Rome 1974, 31-47.

Hoffmann, P., 'Jamblique exégète du pythagoricien Archytas: trois originalités d'une doctrine du temps', *Les études philosophiques* 1980, 307-23.

Whittaker, J., 'The historical background of Proclus' doctrine of the "authupostata"', in H. Dörrie (ed.), *De Jamblique à Proclus*, Entretiens sur l'antiquité classique 21, Vandoeuvres-Genève 1975, 193-230.

Michael of Ephesus

Browning, R., 'An unpublished funeral oration on Anna Comnena', Chapter 17 above, repr. with revisions from *Proceedings of the Cambridge Philological Society* 188, 1962, 1-12.

Donini, P.L., 'Il de Anima di Alessandro di Afrodisia e Michele Efesio', *Rivista di Filologia e di Instruzione Classica* 96, 1968, 316-23.

Ebbesen, S., 'Philoponus, "Alexander" and the origins of medieval logic', Chapter 19 above.

Ebbesen, S., *Commentators and Commentaries on Aristotle's Sophistici Elenchi. A Study of Post-Aristotelian and Medieval Writings on Fallacies*, 3 vols, Corpus Latinum Commentariorum in Aristotelem Graecorum 7.1-3, Leiden 1981.

Ebbesen, S., 'Boethius, Jacobus Veneticus, Michael Ephesius and "Alexander"', *Cahiers de l'Institut du moyen-âge grec et latin* 34, Copenhagen 1979, 5-13.

Giordano, D., 'Michele di Efeso', *Enciclopedia di Filosofia* vol. 4, col. 624.

Mercken, H.P.F., 'The Greek commentaries on Aristotle's *Ethics*', Chapter 18 above, repr. with revisions from 'Introduction', Corpus Latinum Commentariorum in Aristotelem Graecorum 6.1.

Praechter, K., 'Michael von Ephesos und Psellos', *Byzantinische Zeitschrift* 31, 1931, 1-12.

Praechter, K., review of Hayduck 1904, *CAG* 22.2 (*Michael Ephesii In Libros De Partibus Animalium Commentaria*), *Göttingische gelehrte Anzeigen* 168, 1906, 861-907.

Preus, A., 'Michael of Ephesus on Aristotle IA and MA', in *Proceedings of the 1978 World Congress on Aristotle*, vol. 2, Athens 1981, 21-30.

Preus, A., *Aristotle and Michael of Ephesus on the Movement and Progression of Animals*, Hildesheim-New York 1981.

Olympiodorus

Anton, J.P., 'Ancient interpretations of Aristotle's doctrine of homonyma', *Journal of the History of Philosophy* 7, 1969, 1-18.

Beutler, R., 'Olympiodorus (13)', *RE* 18, 2, 1949, cols 207-27.

Blumenthal, H.J., review of Westerink, *The Greek Commentaries on Plato's Phaedo*, *Mnemosyne* 33, 1980, 411-14.

Norvin, W., *Olympiodoros fra Alexandria og hans Commentar til Platons Phaidon*, Copenhagen 1915.

Praechter, K., 'Olympiodor und Kedren', *Byzantinische Zeitschrift* 12, 1903, 224-30.

Vancourt, R., *Les derniers commentateurs alexandrins d'Aristote: l'école d'Olympiodore, Étienne d'Alexandrie*, Lille 1941.

Westerink, L.G., *The Greek Commentaries on Plato's Phaedo*, vol. 1, *Olympiodorus*, Amsterdam 1973.

Westerink, L.G., *Anonymous Prolegomena to Platonic Philosophy*, Amsterdam 1962; new edition in preparation; pp. x-xxxii repr. with the revisions prepared for the new Budé edition in Chapter 14 above.

Philoponus

Böhm, W., *Johannes Philoponos. Grammatikos von Alexandrien*, Munich-Paderborn-Vienna 1967.

Gudeman, A. & Kroll, W., 'Ioannes (Nr. 21, Ioannes Philoponus)', in *RE* 9, 2, 1916, cols 1764-95.

Saffrey, H.D., 'Le chrétien Jean Philopon et la survivance de l'école d'Alexandrie au VIe siècle', *Revue des études grecques* 67, 1954, 396-410.

Sorabji, R., 'John Philoponus', in R. Sorabji (ed.), *Philoponus and the Rejection of Aristotelian Science*, London-Ithaca N.Y. 1987, 1-40.

Verrycken, K., 'The development of Philoponus' thought and its chronology', Chapter 11 above.

*

Blumenthal, H.J., 'Philoponus – John: Alexandrian Platonist', *Hermes* 114, 1986, 314-35.

Blumenthal, H.J., 'Body and soul in Philoponus', *Monist* 69, 1986, 370-82.

Blumenthal, H.J., 'John Philoponus and Stephanus of Alexandria: two Neoplatonist Christian commentators on Aristotle?', in D.J. O'Meara (ed.), *Neoplatonism and Christian Thought*, Norfolk 1982, 54-66; 244-6.

Davidson, H.A., *Proofs for Eternity, Creation and the Existence of God in Medieval Islamic and Jewish Philosophy*, New York-Oxford 1987.

Davidson, H.A., 'John Philoponus as a source of Medieval Islamic and Jewish proofs of creation', *Journal of the American Oriental Society* 89, 1969, 357-91.

Ebbesen, S., 'Philoponus, "Alexander" and the origins of medieval logic', Chapter 19 above.

Endress, G., *The Works of Yaḥyâ ibn 'Adi*, Wiesbaden 1977.

Évrard, É., 'Jean Philopon, la ténèbre originelle et la création du monde', in C. Rutten & A. Motte (eds), *Aristotelica, Mélanges offerts à Marcel de Corte*, Brussels-Liège 1985, 177-88.

Évrard, É., 'Jean Philopon, son commentaire sur Nicomaque et ses rapports avec Ammonius', *Revue des études grecques* 78, 1965, 592-8.

Évrard, É., *L'école d'Olympiodore et la composition du commentaire à la Physique de Jean Philopon*, diss., Liège 1957.

Évrard, É., 'Les convictions religieuses de Jean Philopon et la date de son commentaire aux Météorologiques', *Bulletin de l'academie royale de Belgique*, Classe des lettres et sciences politiques et morales 5 ser. 39, 1953, 299-357.

Grant, E., 'Aristotle, Philoponus, Avempace and Galileo's Pisan dynamics', *Centaurus* 11, 1965, 79-95.

Kraemer, J.L., 'A lost passage from Philoponus' Contra Aristotelem in Arabic translation (Simpl. de Caelo, I, 3, 270b5-11)', *Journal of the American Oriental*

Society 85, 1965, 318-27.

Mahdi, M., 'Alfarabi against Philoponus', *Journal of Near Eastern Studies* 26, 1967, 233-60.

McGuire, J.E., 'Philoponus on Physics ii 1, *phusis, hormê emphutos* and the motion of simple bodies', *Ancient Philosophy* 5, 1985, 241-67.

Moody, E.A., 'Galileo and Avempace, the dynamics of the leaning tower experiment', *Journal of the History of Ideas* 13, 1951, 163-93; 375-422.

Pinès, S., 'Un précurseur bagdadien de la théorie de l'impetus', *Isis* 44, 1953, 246-51; repr. in Pinès, S., *Studies in Arabic Versions of Greek Texts and in Medieval Science*, vol. 2, Leiden-Jerusalem 1986, 418-22.

Pinès, S., 'An Arabic summary of a lost work of John Philoponus', *Israel Oriental Studies* 2, 1972, 320-52; repr. in S. Pinès, *Studies in Arabic Versions of Greek Texts and in Medieval Science*, vol. 2, Leiden-Jerusalem 1986, 294-326.

Pinès, S., 'La dynamique d'Ibn Bajja', in *Mélanges Alexandre Koyré* 1, Paris, 1964, 442-68.

Pinès, S., 'Études sur Awhad al-Zamân Abu' l-Barakât al-Baghdâdî', *Revue des études juives* n.s. 3, 1938, 3-64 and n.s. 4, 1938, 1-33.

Pinès, S., 'Les précurseurs musulmans de la théorie de l'impetus', *Archeion* 21, 1938, 298-306.

Riet, A. van, 'Fragments de l'original grec du de Intellectu de Philopon dans une compilation de Sophonias', *Revue philosophique de Louvain* 63, 1965, 5-40.

Rossi, P., 'Tracce della versione latina di un commento greco ai Secondi Analitici nel Commentarius in Posteriorium Analyticorum di Grossatesta', *Rivista di Filosofia Neoscolastica* 1978, 433-9.

Sambursky, S. & Pinès, S., *The Concept of Time in Late Neoplatonism. Texts with Translation, Introduction and Notes*, Jerusalem 1981; repr. Leiden 1987.

Sambursky, S., *The Concept of Place in Late Neoplatonism. Texts with Translation, Introduction and Notes*, Jerusalem 1982.

Sambursky, S., 'Philoponus, John', in P. Edwards (ed.), *The Encyclopaedia of Philosophy* vol. 6, New York 1967, 156-7.

Sambursky, S., *The Physical World of Late Antiquity*, London 1962.

Schmitt, C.B., *Gianfrancesco Pico della Mirandola (1469-1533) and his Critique of Aristotle*, The Hague 1967.

Sorabji, R., *Matter, Space and Motion* (chs 2, 14, 15), London-Ithaca N.Y. 1988.

Sorabji., R. (ed.), *Philoponus and the Rejection of Aristotelian Science*, London-Ithaca N.Y. 1987.

Sorabji, R., *Time, Creation and the Continuum*, London-Ithaca N.Y. 1983 (ch. 14).

Steinschneider, M., 'Johannes Philoponus bei den Arabern', in 'Al-Farabi-Alpharabius, des arabischen Philosophen Leben und Schriften', *Mémoires de l'academie impériale des sciences de St. Petersbourg*, series 7, 13, 4, 1869, 152-76; 220-4; 250-2.

Tannery, P., 'Philoponus', *Philosophie ancienne*, Mémoires scientifiques publiées par J.L. Heiberg 7, Paris 1925, 318-20.

Todd, R.B., 'Philosophy and medicine in John Philoponus' commentary on Aristotle's de Anima', *Dumbarton Oaks Papers*, 38, 1984, 103-20.

Todd, R.B., 'Some concepts in physical theory in John Philoponus' Aristotelian commentaries', *Archiv für Begriffsgeschichte* 24, 1980, 151-70.

Verbeke, G., 'Levels of human thinking in Philoponus', in C. Laga, J.A. Munitz, L. van Rompay (eds), *After Chalcedon. Studies in Theology and Church History offered to Professor Albert van Roey for his seventieth birthday*, Louvain 1986, 451-70.

Verbeke, G., 'Some later Neoplatonic views on divine creation and the eternity of the world', in D.J. O'Meara (ed.), *Neoplatonism and Christian Thought*, Norfolk 1982, 45-53 and 241-4.

Verbeke, G., *Jean Philopon. Commentaire sur le de Anima d'Aristote, traduction de Guillaume de Moerbeke*, Corpus Latinum Commentariorum in Aristotelem Graecorum 3, Louvain-Paris 1966.

Westerink, L.G., 'Deux commentaires sur Nicomaque, Asclépius et Jean Philopon', *Revue des études grecques* 77, 1964, 526-35; repr. in his *Texts and Studies in Neoplatonism and Byzantine Literature*, Amsterdam 1980, 101-10.

Wieland, W. 'Zur Raumtheorie des Johannes Philoponus', in E. Fries (ed.), *Festschrift für J. Klein*, Göttingen 1967, 114-35.

Wieland, W., 'Die Ewigkeit der Welt (der Streit zwischen Joannes Philoponus und Simplicius)', in D. Heinrich, W. Schulz, K.H. Volkmann-Schluck (eds), *Die Gegenwart der Griechen im neueren Denken, Festschrift für H.-G. Gadamer zum 60. Geburtstag*, Tübingen 1960, 291-316.

Wildberg, C., *John Philoponus' Criticism of Aristotle's Theory of Aether*, Berlin 1988.

Wildberg, C., *Philoponus, Against Aristotle on the Eternity of the World*, London-Ithaca N.Y. 1987.

Wohlwill, E., 'Ein Vorgänger Galileis im 6. Jahrhundert', *Verhandlungen der Gesellschaft deutscher Naturforscher und Ärzte* 77, part 2, 1905, 80-2; repr. in *Physicalische Zeitschrift* 7, 1906, 23-32.

Wolff, M., *Geschichte der Impetustheorie. Untersuchungen zum Ursprung der klassischen Mechanik*, Frankfurt 1978.

Wolff, M., *Fallgesetz und Massebegriff. Zwei wissenschaftshistorische Untersuchungen zur Kosmologie des Johannes Philoponus*, Quellen und Studien zur Geschichte der Philosophie 21, Berlin 1971.

Porphyry

Beutler, R., 'Porphyrios', *RE* 32, 1, 1953, cols 175-313.

Bidez, J., *Vie de Porphyre*, Gent-Leipzig, 1913.

Ebbesen, S., 'Porphyry's legacy to logic: a reconstruction', Chapter 7 above, repr. from S. Ebbesen, *Commentators and Commentaries on Aristotle's Sophistici Elenchi. A Study of Post-Aristotelian and Medieval Writings on Fallacies*, 3 vols, Corpus Latinum Commentariorum in Aristotelem Graecorum 7.1-3, Leiden 1981; 7.1, 133-70.

Evangeliou, C.C., *Aristotle's Categories and Porphyry*, Philosophia Antiqua 48, Leiden 1988.

Evangeliou, C., 'Aristotle's doctrine of predicables and Porphyry's Isagoge', *Journal of the History of Philosophy* 23, 1985, 15-34.

Finnegan, J., 'Avicenna's refutation of Porphyrius', in *Avicenna Commemoration Volume*, Calcutta 1956, 187-203.

Hadot, P., 'The harmony of Plotinus and Aristotle according to Porphyry', Chapter 6 above, translated from *Atti del Convegno Internazionale sul tema Plotino e il Neoplatonismo in Oriente e Occidente* (Roma 5-9 ottobre 1970), Accademia Nazionale dei Lincei, Rome 1974, 31-47.

Hadot, P., *Porphyre et Victorinus*, Paris 1968.

Lloyd, A.C., 'Neoplatonic logic and Aristotelian logic', *Phronesis* 1, 1955-6, 58-72, 146-60.

Moraux, P., 'Porphyre, commentateur de la Physique d'Aristote', in C. Rutten & A. Motte (eds), *Aristotelica. Mélanges offerts à Marcel de Corte*, Brussels-Liège 1985, 227-39.

Noica, C., *Porfir, Dexip, Ammonius. Comentarii la Categoriile lui Aristotel, însotite de Textul Comentat Traducere, Curînt înainte si Note*, Bucarest 1968.

Romano, F., *Porfirio e la Fisica Aristotelica*, Catania 1985.

Romano, F., *Porfirio di Tiro. Filosofia e Cultura nel III secolo D.C.*, Catania 1979.

Smith, A., 'Porphyrian studies since 1913', in W. Haase (ed.), *Aufstieg und Niedergang der römischen Welt*, II, 36.2, Berlin 1987, 717-73.

Smith, A., *Porphyry's Place in Neoplatonic Tradition. A Study in Post-Plotinian Neoplatonism*, The Hague, 1974.

Proclus

Beutler, R., 'Proklos', *RE* 23, 1, 1957, cols 186-247.

Blumenthal, H.J., 'Plutarch's exposition of the de Anima and the psychology of Proclus', in H. Dörrie (ed.), *De Jamblique à Proclus*, Entretiens sur l'antiquité classique 21, Vandoeuvres-Genève 1975, 123-47.

Festugière, A.-J, 'L'ordre de lecture des dialogues de Platon aux Ve/VIe siècles', *Museum Helveticum* 26, 1969, 281-96; repr. in his *Études de philosophie grecque*, Paris 1971, 535-50.

Hadot, I., 'Les introductions aux commentaires exégétiques chez les auteurs néoplatoniciens et les auteurs chrétiens', to be included in her French translation of *Simplicius In Categorias*, vol. 1; also in M. Tardieu, *Les règles de l'interpretation*, Paris 1987.

Hadot, P., 'Les divisions des parties de la philosophie dans l'antiquité', *Museum Helveticum* 36, 1979, 201-23; English translation by Victor Caston, unpublished.

Sheppard, Anne, 'Proclus' philosophical method of exegesis: the use of Aristotle and the Stoics in the Commentary on the Cratylus', in J. Pépin & H.D. Saffrey (eds), *Proclus. Lecteur et interprète des Anciens*, Paris 1987, 137-51.

Sorabji. R., 'Infinite power impressed, the transformation of Aristotle's physics and theology', Chapter 9 above (fuller version in his *Matter, Space and Motion*, London-Ithaca N.Y. 1988, ch. 15).

Steel, Carlos, 'Proclus et Aristote sur la causalité efficiente de l'intellect divin', in J. Pépin & H.D. Saffrey (eds), *Proclus. Lecteur et interprète des Anciens*, Paris 1987.

Westerink, L.G., 'Proclus, Procopius, Psellus', *Mnemosyne* 3, 1941/42, 275-80.

Westerink, L.G. & Saffrey, H.D., *Proclus, Théologie platonicienne*, Budé edition, vol. 1-4, 1968-87; introductions.

Whittaker, J., 'The historical background of Proclus' doctrine of the "authu-postata" ', in H. Dörrie (ed.), *De Jamblique à Proclus*, Entretiens sur l'antiquité classique 21, Vandoeuvres-Genève 1975, 193-230.

Whittaker, J., 'Varia Procliana', *Greek, Roman and Byzantine Studies* 14, 1973, 425-32.

Simplicius

Dodds, E.R., 'Simplicius', *Oxford Classical Dictionary*, Oxford 1970.

Hadot, I., 'The life and work of Simplicius in Greek and Arabic sources', Chapter 12 above, translated from following entry.

Hadot, I. (ed.), *Simplicius, sa vie, son oeuvre, sa survie*, Peripatoi 15, Berlin 1987.

Hadot, I., *Le problème du néoplatonisme alexandrin: Hiéroclès et Simplicius*, Paris 1978.

Lloyd, A.C., 'Simplicius', in P. Edwards (ed.), *Encyclopaedia of Philosophy*, vol. 7, 1967, 448-9.

Praechter, K., 'Simplikios', *RE* 3 A, 1 (Zweite Reihe), 1927, cols 204-13.

Verbeke, G., 'Simplicius', *Dictionary of Scientific Biography* 12, 1975, 440-3.

*

Becker, O., 'Formallogisches und mathematisches in griechischen philosophischen Texten', *Philologus* 100, 1956, 108-12.

Becker, O., 'Zum Text eines mathematischen Beweises im eudemischen Bericht über die Quadraturen der Möndchen durch Hippokrates von Chios bei Simplikios (Arist. Phys. S. 66 Diels)', *Philologus* 99, 1955, 312-16.

Blumenthal, H.J., 'The psychology of (?) Simplicius' commentary on the de Anima', in H.J. Blumenthal & A.C. Lloyd (eds), *Soul and the Structure of Being in Late Neoplatonism*, Liverpool 1982, 73-93.

Blumenthal, H.J., 'Neoplatonic elements in the *de Anima* commentaries', Chapter 13 above, repr. with revisions from *Phronesis* 21, 1976, 64-87.

Bossier, F. and Steel, C., 'Priscianus Lydus en de In de Anima van Pseudo (?) Simplicius', *Tijdschrift voor Filosofie* 34, 1972, 761-822.

Cameron, A., 'The last days of the Academy at Athens', *Proceedings of the Cambridge Philological Society* 195, 1969, 7-29; French abridgment, 'Le fin de l'académie', in *Le néoplatonisme*, Actes du colloque de Royaumont 9-13 Juin 1969, Paris, 1971, 281-90.

Clagett, M., 'A thirteenth-century fragment of Simplicius' commentary on the *Physics* of Aristotle, Quadratura per lunulas', in J.H. Mundy, R.W. Emery & B.N. Nelson (eds), *Essays in Medieval Life and Thought presented in honour of A.P. Evans*, New York 1955, 99-108.

Gätje, H., 'Simplikios in der arabischen Überlieferung', *Der Islam* 59, 1982, 6-31.

Hadot, I., *Simplicius, commentaire sur les Catégories, traduction commentée sous la direction d'Ilsetraut Hadot*, 1 (Introduction, first part), 3 (commentary on the first chapter of the *Categories*), Leiden 1989.

Hadot, I., 'La vie et l'oeuvre de Simplicius d'après des sources grecques et arabes', in id. (ed.), *Simplicius, sa vie, son oeuvre, sa survie*, Berlin 1987, 3-29.

Hadot, I., 'La doctrine de Simplicius sur l'âme raisonnable humaine dans le commentaire sur le *Manuel* d'Epictète', in H.J. Blumenthal & A.C. Lloyd (eds), *Soul and the Structure of Being in Late Neoplatonism*, Liverpool 1982, 46-70.

Hoffmann, P., 'Catégories et langage selon Simplicius – la question du "skopos" du traité aristotélicien des Catégories', in I. Hadot (ed.), *Simplicius, sa vie, son oeuvre, sa survie*, Berlin-New York 1987, 61-90.

Hoffmann, P., 'Simplicius' polemics. Some aspects of Simplicius' polemical writings against John Philoponus, from invective to a reaffirmation of the transcendency of the heavens', in R. Sorabji (ed.), *Philoponus and the Rejection of Aristotelian Science*, London-Ithaca N.Y. 1987, 57-83.

Hoffmann, P., 'Sens et dénomination. Homonymie, analogie, métaphore selon le commentaire de Simplicius sur les Catégories d'Aristote', *École pratique des hautes études annuaire* 93, 1984-85, 343-56.

Hoffmann, P., 'Les catégories "où" et "quand" chez Aristote et Simplicius', in P. Aubenque (ed.), *Concepts et catégories dans la pensée antique*, Paris 1980, 217-45.

Hoffmann, P., 'Simplicius: Corollarium de Loco', in *L'astronomie dans l'antiquité classique*, Actes du colloque tenu à l'Université de Toulouse-Le Mirail, 21-33 Oct. 1977, Paris 1979, 143-63.

Meyer, H., *Das Corollarium de Tempore des Simplikios und die Aporien des Aristoteles zur Zeit*, Monographien zur Naturphilosophie 8, Meisenheim am Glan 1969.

Montoya Saenz, J., 'Interpretacion por Simplicio de la teoria aristotelica del "Nous" ', *Annales del Seminario del Metafisico*, Madrid 1968, 75-95.

Sabra, A.I., 'Simplicius' proof of Euclid's parallels postulate', *Journal of the Warburg and Courtauld Institutes* 32, 1969, 1-24.

Sambursky, S. & Pinès, S., *The Concept of Time in Late Neoplatonism. Texts with Translation, Introduction and Notes*, Jerusalem 1981; repr. Leiden 1987.

Sambursky, S., *The Concept of Place in Late Neoplatonism. Texts with Translation, Introduction and Notes*, Jerusalem 1982.

Sonderegger, E., *Simplikios. Über die Zeit: Ein Kommentar zum Corollarium de Tempore*, Hypomnemata 70, Göttingen 1982.

Sorabji, R., *Matter, Space and Motion*, London-Ithaca N.Y. 1988, chs 1 and 12.

Sorabji, R., *Time, Creation and the Continuum*, London-Ithaca N.Y. 1983, ch. 5.

Steel, C., *The Changing Self. A Study on the Soul in Later Neoplatonism, Iamblichus, Damascius and Priscianus*, Brussels 1978.

Tardieu, M., *Coutumes nautiques mésopotamiennes chez Simplicius*, forthcoming.

Tardieu, M., 'Les calendriers en usage à Ḥarrân d'après les sources arabes et le commentaire de Simplicius à la *Physique* d'Aristote', in I. Hadot (ed.), *Simplicius, sa vie, son oeuvre, sa survie*, Berlin-New York 1987, 40-57.

Tardieu, M., 'Ṣâbiens coraniques et "Ṣâbiens" de Ḥarrân', *Journal asiatique* 274, 1986, 1-44.

Tsouyopoulos N., 'Die Entstehung physikalischer Terminologie aus der neoplatonischen Metaphysik', *Archiv für Begriffsgeschichte* 13, 1969, 7-33.

Vamvoukakis N., 'Les catégories aristotéliciennes vues par Simplicius', in P. Aubenque (ed.), *Concepts et catégories dans la pensée antique*, Paris 1980, 253-69.

Verbeke, G., 'Ort und Raum nach Aristoteles und Simplicius. Eine philosophische topologie', in J. von Irmscher & I. Mueller (eds), *Aristoteles als Wissenschaftstheoretiker*, Berlin 1983, 113-22.

Verbeke, G., 'Le commentaire de Simplicius sur les *Catégories*', *Revue philosophique de Louvain* 70, 1972, 279-82.

Wieland, W., 'Die Ewigkeit der Welt (der Streit zwischen Joannes Philoponus und Simplicius)', in D. Heinrich, W. Schulz, K.H. Volkmann-Schluck (eds), *Die Gegenwart der Griechen im neueren Denken, Festschrift für H.-G. Gadamer zum 60. Geburtstag*, Tübingen 1960, 291-316.

Zahlfleisch, J., 'Einige Bemerkung zur Corollarien des Simplicius in seinem Kommentar zu Aristoteles *Physik*', *Archiv für Geschichte der Philosophie* 15, n.s. 8, 1902, 186-213.

Zahlfleisch, J., 'Die polemik des Simplicius gegen Alexander und andere in dem Kommentar des ersteren zu der aristotelischen Schrift de Caelo dargestelt', *Archiv für Geschichte der Philosophie* 10, n.s. 3, 1897, 191-227.

Zahlfleisch, J, 'Die Polemik des Simplicius gegen Aristoteles *Physik* 4, 1-15 über den Raum dargestelt', *Archiv für Geschichte der Philosophie* 10, 1897, 85-109.

Stephanus

Lumpe, A., 'Stephanos von Alexandrie und Kaizer Herakleios', *Classical and Medieval Dissertationes* 9, 1973, 150-9.

Usener, H., 'De Stephano Alexandrino', *Bonner Lektionskatal*, Sommer 1879, Bonn, 1880; repr. in his *Kleine Schriften* 3, Leipzig-Berlin 1914, 247-322.

Blumenthal, H.J., 'John Philoponus and Stephanus of Alexandria, two Neoplatonist Christian commentators on Aristotle?', in D.J. O'Meara (ed.), *Neoplatonism and Christian Thought*, Norfolk 1982, 54-66; 244-6.

Ebbesen, S., *Commentators and Commentaries on Aristotle's Sophistici Elenchi. A Study of Post-Aristotelian and Medieval Writings on Fallacies*, 3 vols, Corpus Latinum Commentariorum in Aristotelem Graecorum 7.1-3, Leiden 1981 (in 7.1, pp. 133-70, vocabulary); pp. 133-70 repr. as 'Porphyry's legacy to logic: a reconstruction', Chapter 7 above.

Noica, C., *Ammonius, Stephanus. Comentarii la Tratatul Despre Interpretare al lui Aristotel, însotite de Textul Comentat, Traducere, Curînt înainte, note si Comentariu*, Bucarest 1971.

Roueché, Mossman, 'The definitions of philosophy and a new fragment of Stephanus of Alexandria', in preparation.

Roueché, Mossman, 'Byzantine philosophical texts of the seventh century', *Jahrbuch der Oesterreichischen Byzantinistik* 23, 1974, 61-76.

Vancourt, R., *Les derniers commentateurs alexandrins d'Aristote: l'école d'Olympiodore, Étienne d'Alexandrie*, Lille 1941.

Westerink, L.G., *Pseudo-Elias (Pseudo-David), Lectures on Porphyry's Isagoge*, Amsterdam 1967.

Syrianus

Cardullo, L., 'Siriano nella storiografia filosofica moderna e contemporanea', *Siculorum Gymnasium* n.s. 40, 1987, 71-182.

Cardullo, L., 'Syrianus' lost commentaries on Aristotle', *Bulletin of the Institute of Classical Studies* 33, 1986, 112-24.

Kremer, K., *Der Metaphysikbegriff in den Aristoteles-Kommentaren der Ammonius-Schule*, Beiträge zur Geschichte der Philosophie und Theologie des Mittelalters 39, 1, Münster 1961.

Madigan, A., 'Syrianus and Asclepius on forms and intermediates in Plato and Aristotle', *Journal of the History of Philosophy* 24, 1986, 49-71.

O'Meara, D.J., 'Le problème de la métaphysique dans l'antiquité tardive', *Freiburger Zeitschrift für Theologie und Philosophie* 23, 1986, 3-22.

Praechter, K., 'Syrianos' (1), in *RE* 4 A, 2, 1932, cols 1728-75.

Praechter, K., Review of Kroll, *Syrianus in Metaphysica*, *CAG* 6, *Göttingische gelehrte Anzeigen* 1903; repr. in his *Kleine Schriften*, H. Dörrie (ed.), Hildesheim 1973, 246-63.

Saffrey, H.D., 'How did Syrianus regard Aristotle?', Chapter 8 above, trans. from J. Wiesner (ed.), *Aristoteles: Werk und Wirkung, Paul Moraux gewidmet*, vol. 2, Berlin-New York 1987, 205-14.

Sheppard, Anne, 'Monad and dyad as cosmic principles in Syrianus', in H.J. Blumenthal & A.C. Lloyd (eds), *Soul and the Structure of Being in Late Neoplatonism*, Liverpool 1982, 1-14.

Sorabji, R., *Matter, Space and Motion*, London-Ithaca N.Y. 1988.

Themistius

Blumenthal, H.J., 'Themistius: the last Peripatetic commentator on Aristotle?', Chapter 5 above; repr. from G. Bowersock et al. (eds), *Arktouros, Hellenic Studies presented to B. Knox*, Berlin 1979, 391-400.

Stegemann, W., 'Themistius', *RE* 5, 1934, cols 1642-80.

Verbeke, G., 'Themistius', *Dictionary of Scientific Biography* 13, 1976, 307-9.

*

Badawi, A., *La transmission de la philosophie grecque au monde arabe*, Paris 1968, 100-4, 166-80 (French translation of Themistius' 'Reply to Maximus on the reduction of the second and third syllogistic figures to the first').

Blumenthal, H.J., 'Photius on Themistius (Cod.74): did Themistius write commentaries on Aristotle?', *Hermes* 107, 1979, 178-82.

Brown, H.V.B, 'Avicenna and the Christian philosophers in Baghdad', in S.M. Stern et al. (eds), *Islamic Philosophy and the Classical Tradition, Essays presented to Richard Walzer*, Oriental Studies 5, Oxford 1972, 35-48.

Browne, G. M., 'Ad Themistium Arabum', *Illinois Classical Studies* 11, 1986, 223-45.

Frank, R.M., 'Some textual notes of the oriental versions of Themistius' paraphrase of Book 1 of the Metaphysics', *Cahiers de Byrsá* 8, 1958-9, 215-30.

Lyons, M.C. (ed.), *Themistius Paraphrasis in libros Aristotelis de Anima*, London 1973.

Lyons, M.C., 'An Arabic translation of the commentary of Themistius', *Bulletin of the School of Oriental and African Studies* 17, 1955, 426-35.

Mahoney, E.P., 'Neoplatonism, the Greek commentators and Renaissance Aristotelianism', in D.J. O' Meara (ed.), *Neoplatonism and Christian Thought*, Norfolk 1982, 169-84, 264-82.

Mahoney, E.P., 'Themistius and the Agent Intellect in James of Viterbo and other thirteenth-century philosophers', *Augustiniana* 23, 1973, 422-67.

Mattock, J.N., 'The supposed epitome by Themistius of Aristotle's zoological works', *Akten des VII Kongress für Arabistik und Islamwissenschaften*, 260-7.

Minio-Paluello, L. (ed.), *Aristoteles Latinus* 1.1-5, Paris 1961; includes *Pseudo-Augustini Paraphrasis Themistiana*.

Moraux, P., 'Le "de Anima" dans la tradition grecque. Quelques aspects de l'interprétation du traité, de Théophraste à Thémistius', in G.E.R. Lloyd & G.E.L Owen (eds), *Aristotle on Mind and the Senses*, Cambridge 1978, 281-324.

O'Donnell, J.R., 'Themistius' paraphrasis of the Posterior Analytics in Gerard of Cremona's translation', *Mediaeval Studies* 20, 1958, 239-315.

Pinès, S., 'Some distinctive metaphysical conceptions in Themistius' commentary on Book Lambda and their place in the history of philosophy', in J. Wiesner (ed.), *Aristoteles: Werk und Wirkung, Paul Moraux gewidmet*, vol. 2, Berlin-New York 1987, 177-206.

Rose, V., 'Über eine angebliche Paraphrase des Themistius', *Hermes* 2, 1867, 212.

Schroeder, F.M., 'Themistius' paraphrase of Aristotle de Anima III, 4-8', in R.B. Todd & F.M. Schroeder (eds), *Two Greek Commentators on the Active Intellect*, Pontifical Institute, Toronto, forthcoming.

Steel, C., 'Des commentaires d'Aristote par Thémistius?', *Revue philosophique de Louvain* 71, 1973, 669-80.

Todd, R.B. & Shroeder, F.M., *Two Greek Aristotelian Commentators on the Active Intellect*, Pontifical Institute, Toronto, forthcoming.

Todd, R.B., 'Themistius and the traditional intepretation of Aristotle's theory of phantasia', *Acta Classica* 24, 1981, 49-59.

Verbeke, G., *Thémistius. Commentaire sur le traité de l'âme d'Aristote*, Paris 1957 (with an introduction), Corpus Latinum Commentariorum in Aristotelem Graecorum 1.

Zimmermann, F.W. & Brown, H.V.B., Review of A. Badawi, *Commentaires sur Aristote perdus en grec et autres épitres*, Beirut 1971, 'Neue arabischen Übersetzungen aus dem Bereich der spätantiken griechischen Philosophie', *Der Islam* 50, 1973, 313-24.

Philosophical subjects

Logic

General

Benakis, L., 'Commentaries and commentators on the logical works of Aristotle in Byzantium', in R. Claussen & R. Daube-Schackat (eds), *Gedankenzeichen. Festschrift für Klaus Oehler*, Tübingen 1988, 3-12.

Brandis, C.A., 'Über die Reihenfolge der Bücher des aristotelischen Organons und ihre griechischen Ausleger', *Abh. Akad. Berlin*, 1833, 249-99.

Dürr, K., *The Propositional Logic of Boethius*, Studies in Logic and the Foundations of Mathematics, Amsterdam 1951.

Ebbesen, S., 'Ancient scholastic logic as the source of medieval scholastic logic', in N. Kretzmann, A. Kenny & J. Pinborg (eds), *The Cambridge History of Later Medieval Philosophy*, Cambridge 1982, 101-27.

Ebbesen, S., 'Philoponus, "Alexander" and the origins of medieval logic', Chapter 19 above.

Ebbesen, S., *Commentators and Commentaries on Aristotle's Sophistici Elenchi. A Study of Post-Aristotelian and Medieval Writings on Fallacies*, 3 vols, Corpus Latinum Commentariorum in Aristotelem Graecorum 7.1-3, Leiden 1981.

Ebbesen, S., 'The contribution of the Greek Commentators on the Organon to the formation of Western scholasticism', in *Proceedings of the 1978 World Congress on Aristotle*, vol. 1, Athens 1981, 183-6.

Ebbesen, S., 'Anonymus Aurelianensis II, Aristotle, Alexander, Porphyry and Boethius; ancient scholasticism and twelfth-century Western Europe. With an edition of the Tractatus de Paralogismis', *Cahiers de l'Institut du moyen-âge grec et latin* 16, Copenhagen 1976, 1-128.

Kneale, W. & M., *The Development of Logic*, Oxford 1962.

Lloyd, A.C., 'Neoplatonic logic and Aristotelian logic', *Phronesis* 1, 1955-56, 58-72, 146-60.

Mueller, Ian, 'Stoic and Peripatetic logic', *Archiv für Geschichte der Philosophie* 51, 1969, 173-87.

Rijk, L.M. de, 'Boèce logicien et philosophe, ses positions et sa métaphysique de l'être', in L. Obertello (ed.), *Congresso Internazionale di Studi Boeziani – Atti*, Roma 1981, 141-56.

Rijk, L.M. de, *Logica Modernorum*, Assen, vol. 1, 1962; vol. 2, 1967.

Solmsen, F., 'Boethius and the history of the Organon', *American Journal of Philology* 31, 1944, 69-74.

Isagoge and Categories

Anton, J.P., 'Ancient interpretations of Aristotle's doctrine of homonyma', *Journal of the History of Philosophy* 7, 1969, 1-18.

Aubenque, P., 'Plotin et Dexippe, exégètes des Categories d'Aristote', in C. Rutten & A. Motte (eds), *Aristotelica. Mélanges offerts à Marcel de Corte*, Brussels-Liège 1985, 7-40.

Blumenthal, H.J., 'Pseudo-Elias and the Isagoge commentaries again', *Rheinisches Museum* 124, 1981, 188-92.

Evangeliou, C., *Aristotle's Categories and Porphyry*, Philosophia Antiqua 48, Leiden 1988.

Evangeliou, C., 'The Plotinian reduction of Aristotle's Categories', *Ancient Philosophy* 7, 1987, 147-62.

Evangeliou, C., 'Aristotle's doctrine of predicables and Porphyry's Isagoge', *Journal of the History of Philosophy* 23, 1985, 15-34.

Gottschalk, H.B., 'The earliest Aristotelian commentators', Chapter 3 above, repr. with revisions from W. Haase (ed.), *Aufstieg und Niedergang der römischen Welt*, II, 36.2, Berlin 1987, 1079-174.

Hadot, P., 'The harmony of Plotinus and Aristotle according to Porphyry', Chapter 6 above, translated from *Atti del Convegno Internazionale sul tema Plotino e il Neoplatonismo in Oriente e Occidente* (Roma 5-9 ottobre 1970), Accademia Nazionale dei Lincei, Rome 1974, 31-47.

Hadot, P., 'Un fragment du commentaire perdu de Boèce sur les Catégories d'Aristote dans le codex Bernensis 363', *Archives d'histoire doctrinale et littéraire du moyen-âge* 26, 1959, 11-27.

Henry, P., 'Trois apories orales de Plotin sur les Catégories', *Zetesis. Mélanges de Strycker*, Anvers 1973, 234-65.

Hoffmann, P., 'Catégories et langage selon Simplicius – la question du "skopos" du traité aristotélicien des Catégories', in I. Hadot (ed.), *Simplicius, sa vie, son oeuvre, sa survie*, Berlin-New York 1987, 61-90.

Hoffmann, P., 'Sens et dénomination. Homonymie, analogie, métaphore selon le commentaire de Simplicius sur les Catégories d'Aristote', *École pratique des hautes études annuaire* 93, 1984-85, 343-56.

Hoffmann, P., 'Les catégories "où" et "quand" chez Aristote et Simplicius', in P. Aubenque (ed.), *Concepts et catégories dans la pensée antique*, Paris 1980, 217-45.

Luna, C., 'La relation chez Simplicius', in I. Hadot (ed.), *Simplicius, sa vie, son oeuvre, sa survie*, Berlin-New York 1987, 113-47.

Marcovich, M., 'Pseudo-Elias on Heraclitus', *American Journal of Philology* 96, 1975, 31-4.

Mignucci, M., 'Aristotle's definitions of relatives in Categories 7', *Phronesis* 31, 1986, 101-27.

Noica, C., *Porfir, Dexip, Ammonius. Comentarii la Categoriile lui Aristotel, însotite de Textul Comentat Traducere, Curînt înainte si Note*, Bucarest 1968.

Plezia, M., *De Commentariis Isagogicis*, Cracow 1947.

Praechter, K., review of *Prolegomena* and *in Isagogem (CAG)*, *Göttingische gelehrte Anzeigen* 170, Göttingen 1908.

Strange, S.K., 'Plotinus, Porphyry and the Neoplatonic interpretation of the Categories', in W. Haase (ed.), *Aufstieg und Niedergang der römischen Welt*, II, 36.2, Berlin 1987, 955-74.

Usener, H., Review of L. Spengel (*CAG* edition of Dexippus), *Litterar. Centralblatt*, 1860, 124-5.

Vamvoukakis N., 'Les catégories aristotéliciennes vues par Simplicius', in P. Aubenque (ed.), *Concepts et catégories dans la pensée antique*, Paris 1980, 253-69.

Verbeke, G., 'Le commentaire de Simplicius sur les Catégories', *Revue philosophique de Louvain* 70, 1972, 279-82.

Westerink, L.G., *Pseudo-Elias (Pseudo-David), Lectures on Porphyry's Isagoge*, Amsterdam 1967.

Wurm, K., *Substanz und Qualität: ein Beitrag zur Interpretation der plotinischen Traktat VI 1, 2 und 3*, Berlin 1973.

de Interpretatione

Arens, H., *Aristotle's Theory of Language and its Tradition*, Amsterdam Studies in the Theory and History of Linguistic Science 29, Amsterdam 1984.

Busse, A., *Die neuplatonischen Ausleger der Isagoge des Porphyrius* (repeated with addition in *CAG* 18.2), Berlin 1892.

Hoffmann, J.G.E., *de Hermeneuticis apud Syros Aristotelis*, Leipzig 1869.

Isaak, I., *Le Peri hermeneias en Occident, de Boèce à Saint Thomas. Histoire littéraire d'un traité d'Aristote*, Bibliothèque thomiste 29, Paris 1953; includes the first 10 chapters of William of Moerbeke's translation, pp. 160-9.

Kustas, G.L., *Studies in Byzantine Rhetoric* [pp. 101-26, *The Commentators on Aristotle's Categories and on Porphyry's Isagoge*], Analecta Vlatadon 17, Thessaloniki 1973.

Noica, C., *Ammonius, Stephanus. Comentarii la Tratatul Despre Interpretare al lui Aristotel, însotite de Textul Comentat, Traducere, Curînt înainte, note si Comentariu*, Bucarest 1971.

Nuchelmans, G., *Theories of the Proposition. Ancient and Medieval Conceptions of the Bearers of Truth and Falsity*, Amsterdam 1973.

Prior, A.N., 'The logic of negative terms in Boethius', *Franciscan Studies* 13, 1953, 1-16.

Sheppard, Anne, 'Proclus' philosophical method of exegesis: the use of Aristotle and the Stoics in the Commentary on the Cratylus', in J. Pépin & P. Saffrey (eds), *Proclus. Lecteur et interprète des Anciens*, Paris 1987, 137-51.

Sullivan, M.W., *Apuleian Logic. The Nature, Sources and Influences of Apuleius' Peri Hermeneias*, Amsterdam 1967.

Tarán, L., *Anonymous' Commentary on Aristotle's de Interpretatione (Codex Parisinus Graecus 2064)*, Beiträge zür Klassische Philologie 95, Meisenheim am Glan 1978.

Zimmermann, F., *Al-Farabi's Commentary and Short Treatise on Aristotle's de Interpretatione*, translated with Introduction and Notes, Oxford 1981.

Analytics

Ebbesen, S., 'Analyzing syllogisms, or Anonymous Aurelianensis III – the (presumably) earliest extant Latin commentary on the Prior Analytics, and its Greek model', *Cahiers de l'Institut du moyen-âge grec et latin* 37, Copenhagen 1981, 1-20.

Lee, T.-S., *Die griechische Tradition der aristotelischen Syllogistik in der Spätantike, eine Untersuchung über die Kommentare zu den Analytica Priora von Alexander Aphrodisiensis, Ammonius und Philoponus*, Hypomnemata 79, Göttingen 1984.

Minio-Paluello, L., 'A Latin commentary (?translated by Boethius) on the Prior Analytics and its Greek sources', *Journal of Hellenic Studies* 77, 1957, part 1, 93-102.

Moraux, P., *Le commentaire d'Alexandre d'Aphrodise aux Secondes Analytiques d'Aristote*, Peripatoi 13, Berlin 1979. Review by E. Berti, *Archiv für Geschichte der Philosophie* 63, 1981, 84-6.

O'Donnell, J.R., 'Themistius' paraphrasis of the Posterior Analytics in Gerard of Cremona's translation', *Mediaeval Studies* 20, 1958, 239-315.

Rossi, P., 'Tracce della versione latina di un commento greco ai Secondi Analitici nel Commentarius in Posteriorium Analyticorum di Grossatesta', *Rivista di Filosofia Neoscolastica* 1978, 433-9.

Shiel, J., 'A recent discovery, Boethius' notes on the Prior Analytics', *Vivarium* 20, 1982, 128-41.

Westerink, L.G. (ed.), 'Elias on the Prior Analytics', *Mnemosyne* 14, 1961, 126-39;

repr. in his *Texts and Studies in Neoplatonism and Byzantine Literature*, Amsterdam 1980, 59-72.

Topics and Sophistici Elenchi

Ebbesen, S., 'The theory of *loci* in Antiquity and the Middle Ages', in K. Jacobi (ed.), *Acts of the Eighth European Symposium on Medieval Logic and Semantics*, Munich, forthcoming.

Ebbesen, S., *Commentators and Commentaries on Aristotle's Sophistici Elenchi. A Study of Post-Aristotelian and Medieval Writings on Fallacies*, 3 vols, Corpus Latinum Commentariorum in Aristotelem Graecorum 7.1-3, Leiden 1981.

Edlow, R.B., *Galen on language and ambiguity; an English translation of Galen's De captionibus, with introduction, text and commentary*, Philosophia Antiqua 31, Leiden 1977.

Green-Pedersen, N.J., *The Tradition of the Topics in the Middle Ages: the commentaries on Aristotle's and Boethius' Topics*, Analytica, Munich 1984.

Stump, E., 'Boethius works on the Topics', *Vivarium* 12, 1974, 77-93.

Wallies, M., 'Die griechischen Ausleger der aristotelischen Topik', *Wissenschaftliche Beilage zum Programm des Sophien–Gymnasiums zu Berlin* 65, 1891, 1-27.

Metaphysics

Benakis, L., 'The problem of general concepts in Neoplatonism and Byzantine thought', in D.J. O'Meara (ed.), *Neoplatonism and Christian Thought*, Norfolk 1982, 75-86, 248-9.

Frank, R.M., 'Some textual notes of the oriental versions of Themistius' paraphrase of Book 1 of the Metaphysics', *Cahiers de Byrsá* 8, 1958-9, 215-30.

Freudenthal, J., 'Die durch Averroes erhaltenen Fragmente Alexanders zur Metaphysik des Aristoteles untersucht und übersetzt', *Abhandlung der (k.) preussischen Akademie der Wissenschaften*, Berlin, 1884.

Giocarinis, K., 'Eustratius of Nicaea's defence of the doctrine of Ideas', *Franciscan Studies* 24, 1964, 159-204.

Ioannou, P., 'Die Definition des Seins bei Eustratius von Nicaea. Die Universalienlehre in der Byzantinischen Theologie im XI Jahrhundert', *Byzantinische Zeitschrift* 47, 1954, 258-368.

Lloyd, A.C., 'The significance of Alexander's theory of universals', in *Proceedings of the World Congress on Aristotle*, vol. 1, Athens 1981, 155-9.

Madigan, A., 'Syrianus and Asclepius on forms and intermediates in Plato and Aristotle', *Journal of the History of Philosophy* 24, 1986, 49-71.

Mignucci, M., 'Puzzles about identity, Aristotle and his Greek commentators', in J. Wiesner (ed.), *Aristoteles: Werk und Wirkung, Paul Moraux gewidmet*, vol. 1, Berlin-New York 1985, 57-97.

Mueller, I., 'Aristotle's doctrine of abstraction in the commentators', Chapter 20 above.

O'Meara, D.J., 'Le problème de la métaphysique dans l'antiquité tardive', *Freiburger Zeitschrift für Theologie und Philosophie* 23, 1986, 3-22.

Pinès, S., 'Some distinctive metaphysical conceptions in Themistius' commentary on Book Lambda and their place in the history of philosophy', in J. Wiesner (ed.), *Aristoteles: Werk und Wirkung, Paul Moraux gewidmet*, vol. 2, Berlin-New York 1987, 177-206.

Pinès, S., 'Les limites de la métaphysique selon Al-Farabi, Ibn-Bassa et Maimonides: sources et antithèses de ces doctrines chez Alexandre d'Aphrodise et chez Thémistius', *Sprache und Erkenntnis im Mittelalter* 1, Miscellanea Medievalia 13.1, Berlin-New York 1981.

Ruland, H.-J., 'Zwei arabische Fassungen der Abhandlung des Alexander von Aphrodisias über die universalia (Quaestio I 11a)', *Nachrichten der Akademie der Wissenschaften in Göttingen*, 1979, 243-74.

Saffrey, H.D., 'How did Syrianus regard Aristotle?', Chapter 8 above, transl. from J. Wiesner (ed.), *Aristoteles: Werk und Wirkung, Paul Moraux gewidmet*, vol. 2, Berlin-New York 1987, 205-14.

Tarán, L., 'Syrianus and Pseudo-Alexander's commentary on Metaphysics E-N', in J. Wiesner (ed.), *Aristoteles: Werk und Wirkung, Paul Moraux gewidmet*, vol. 2, Berlin-New York 1987, 215-32.

Tweedale, M.M., 'Alexander of Aphrodisias' views on universals', *Phronesis* 29, 1984, 279-303.

Verbeke, G., 'Aristotle's Metaphysics as viewed by the ancient Greek commentators', in D.J. O' Meara (ed.), *Studies in Aristotle*, Washington, D.C. 1981, 107-27.

Physics and Mathematics

Becker, O., 'Formallogisches und Mathematisches in griechischen philosophischen Texten', *Philologus* 100, 1956, 108-12.

Becker, O., 'Zum Text eines mathematischen Beweises im eudemischen Bericht über die Quadraturen der Möndchen durch Hippokrates von Chios bei Simplikios (Arist. *Phys*. S. 66 Diels)', *Philologus* 99, 1955, 313-16.

Christensen de Groot, J., 'Philoponus on de Anima 2.5, Physics 3.3 and the propagation of light', *Phronesis* 28, 1983, 177-96.

Clagett, M., 'A thirteenth-century fragment of Simplicius' commentary on the *Physics* of Aristotle, Quadratura per lunulas', in J.H. Mundy, R.W. Emery & B.N. Nelson (eds), *Essays in Medieval Life and Thought presented in honour of A.P. Evans*, New York 1955, 99-108.

Coutant, V.C., *Alexander of Aphrodisias, Commentary on Book IV of Aristotle's Meteorologica*, diss. Columbia, 1936; reviewed by B. Einarson in *Classical Weekly* 31, 1937, 33.

Davidson, H.A., 'The principle that a finite body can contain only a finite power', S. Stein & R. Loewe (eds), *Studies in Jewish Religious and Intellectual History Presented to Alexander Altmann*, Alabama 1979, 75-92.

Davidson, H.A., 'John Philoponus as a source of Medieval Islamic and Jewish proofs of creation', *Journal of the American Oriental Society* 89, 1969, 357-91.

Duhem, P.L., *Le système du monde I and II. Histoire des doctrines cosmologiques de Platon à Copernique*, Paris 1913-17; repr. 1 Paris 1954; 2 Paris 1974.

Évrard, É, 'Les convictions religieuses de Jean Philopon et la date de son commentaire aux Météorologiques', *Bulletin de l'academie royale de Belgique*, Classe des lettres et sciences politiques et morales 5, ser. 39, 1953, 299-357.

Fazzo, S., Alessandro d'Afrodisia e Tolomeo: Aristotelismo e astrologia fra il II e il III Secolo D.C.', *Rivista di storia della filosofia* 4, 1988, 627-49.

Genequand, C., 'Quelques aspects de l'idée de nature d'Aristote à Al-Ghazali', *Revue de théologie et de philosophie* 116, 1984, 105-29.

Grant, E., 'Aristotle, Philoponus, Avempace and Galileo's Pisan dynamics', *Centaurus* 11, 1965, 79-95.

Hoffmann, P., 'Paratasis. De la description aspectuelle des verbes grecs à la définition du temps dans le néoplatonisme tardif', *Revue des études grecques* 96, 1983, 1-26.

Hoffmann, P., 'Jamblique exégète du pythagoricien Archytas: trois originalités d'une doctrine du temps', *Les études philosophiques*, 1980, 307-23.

Hoffmann, P., 'Simplicius, Corollarium de Loco', *L'astronomie dans l'antiquité classique*, Actes du Colloque tenu à l'Université de Toulouse-Le Mirail, 21-33 Oct. 1977, Paris 1979, 143-63.

Judson, L., 'God or Nature? Philoponus on generability and perishability', in R. Sorabji (ed.), *Philoponus and the Rejection of Aristotelian Science*, London-Ithaca N.Y. 1987, 179-96.

Kraemer, J.L., 'A lost passage from Philoponus' Contra Aristotelem in arabic translation (Simpl. de Caelo, I, 3, 270b5-11)', *Journal of the American Oriental Society* 85, 1965, 318-27.

Lucchetta, G.A., *Una Fisica Senza Matematica, Democrito, Aristotele, Filopono*, Trento 1978.

Mahdi, M., 'Alfarabi against Philoponus', *Journal of Near Eastern Studies* 26, 1967, 233-60.

McGuire, J.E., 'Philoponus on Physics ii 1, *phusis, hormê emphutos* and the motion of simple bodies', *Ancient Philosophy* 5, 1985, 241-67.

Meyer, H., *Das Corollarium de Tempore des Simplikios und die Aporien des Aristoteles zur Zeit*, Monographien zur Naturphilosophie 8, Meisenheim am Glan 1969.

Moody, E.A., 'Galileo and Avempace, the dynamics of the leaning tower experiment', *Journal of the History of Ideas* 13, 1951, 163-93; 375-422.

Moraux, P., 'Porphyre, commentateur de la Physique d'Aristote', in C. Rutten & A. Motte (eds), *Aristotelica. Mélanges offerts à Marcel de Corte*, Brussels-Liège 1985, 227-39.

Moraux, P., 'Notes sur la tradition indirecte du de Caelo d'Aristote', *Hermes* 82, 1954, 145-82.

Mueller, I., 'Aristotle's doctrine of abstraction in the commentators', Chapter 20 above.

Pinès, S., 'An Arabic summary of a lost work of John Philoponus', *Israel Oriental Studies* 2, 1972, 320-52; repr. in S. Pinès, *Studies in Arabic Versions of Greek Texts and in Medieval Science*, vol. 2, Leiden-Jerusalem 1986, 294-326.

Pinès, S., 'La dynamique d'Ibn Bajja', in *Mélanges Alexandre Koyré* I, Paris, 1964, 442-68; repr. in S. Pinès, *Studies in Arabic Versions of Greek Texts and in Medieval Science*, vol. 2, Leiden-Jerusalem 1986, 440-66.

Pinès, S., 'Les précurseurs musulmans de la théorie de l'impetus', *Archeion* 21, 1938, 298-306; repr. in S. Pinès, *Studies in Arabic Versions of Greek Texts and in Medieval Science*, vol. 2, Leiden-Jerusalem 1986, 409-17.

Pinès, S., '*Omne quod movetur necesse est ab aliquo moveri*, a refutation of Galen by Alexander of Aphrodisias and the theory of motion', *Isis* 52, 1961, 21-54; repr. in S. Pinès, *Studies in Arabic Versions of Greek Texts and in Medieval Science*, vol. 2, Leiden-Jerusalem 1986, 218-51.

Pinès, S., 'Un précurseur bagdadien de la théorie de l'impetus', *Isis* 44, 1953, 246-51; repr. in S. Pinès, *Studies in Arabic Versions of Greek Texts and in Medieval Science*, vol. 2, Leiden-Jerusalem 1986, 418-22.

Pinès, S., 'A tenth-century philosophical correspondence', *Proceedings of the American Academy for Jewish Research* 24, 1955, 103-36; repr. in A. Hyman (ed.), *Essays in Medieval Jewish and Islamic Philosophy*, New York 1977, 357-90.

Pinès, S., 'Études sur Awhad al-Zamân Abu' l-Barakât al-Baghdâdî', *Revue des études juives* n.s. 3, 1938, 3-64 and n.s. 4, 1938, 1-33.

Rescher, N. & Marmura, M., *Alexander of Aphrodisias, the Refutation by*

Alexander of Aphrodisias of Galen's Treatise of the Theory of Motion, Islamabad (Islamic Research Institute) 1965.

Romano, F., *Porfirio e la Fisica Aristotelica*, Catania 1985.

Ruland, H.-J., 'Die arabische Übersetzung der Schrift des Alexander von Aphrodisias über das Wachstum (Quaestio I 5)', *Nachrichten der Akademie der Wissenschaften in Göttingen*, 1981, 51-74.

Sabra, A.I., 'Simplicius' proof of Euclid's parallels postulate', *Journal of the Warburg and Courtauld Institutes* 32, 1969, 1-24.

Sambursky, S. & Pinès, S., *The Concept of Time in Late Neoplatonism. Texts with Translation, Introduction and Notes*, Jerusalem 1981; repr. Leiden 1987.

Sambursky, S., *The Concept of Place in Late Neoplatonism. Texts with Translation, Introduction and Notes*, Jerusalem 1982.

Sambursky, S., *The Physical World of Late Antiquity*, London 1962.

Schmitt, C.B., *Gianfrancesco Pico della Mirandola (1469-1533) and his Critique of Aristotle*, The Hague 1967.

Sedley, D., 'Philoponus' conception of space', in R. Sorabji (ed.), *Philoponus and the Rejection of Aristotelian Science*, London-Ithaca N.Y. 1987, 140-53.

Sharples, R.W., 'The Unmoved Mover and the motion of the heavens in Alexander of Aphrodisias', *Apeiron* 17, 1983, 62-6.

Sharples, R.W., *Alexander of Aphrodisias on Fate*, London 1983.

Sonderegger, E., *Simplikios. Über die Zeit: Ein Kommentar zum Corollarium de Tempore*, Hypomnemata 70, Göttingen 1982.

Sorabji, R., *Matter, Space and Motion*, London-Ithaca N.Y. 1988.

Sorabji. R., 'Infinite power impressed, the transformation of Aristotle's physics and theology', Chapter 9 above (fuller version in his *Matter, Space and Motion*, London-Ithaca N.Y. 1988, ch. 15).

Sorabji, R. (ed.), *Philoponus and the Rejection of Aristotelian Science*, London-Ithaca N.Y. 1987.

Sorabji, R., *Time, Creation and the Continuum*, London-Ithaca N.Y. 1983.

Steel, C., 'Proclus et Aristote sur la causalité efficiente de l'intellect divin', in J. Pépin & H.D. Saffrey (eds), *Proclus. Lecteur et interprète des Anciens*, Paris 1987.

Todd, R.B., 'Some concepts in physical theory in John Philoponus' Aristotelian commentaries', *Archiv für Begriffsgeschichte* 24, 1980, 151-70.

Todd, R.B., *Alexander of Aphrodisias on Stoic Physics*, Leiden 1976.

Verbeke, G., 'Ort und Raum nach Aristoteles und Simplicius. Eine philosophische topologie', in J. von Irmscher & I. Mueller (eds), *Aristoteles als Wissenschaftstheoretiker*, Berlin 1983, 113-22.

Verbeke, G., 'Some later neoplatonic views on divine creation and the eternity of the world', in D.J. O'Meara (ed.), *Neoplatonism and Christian Thought*, Norfolk 1982, 45-53 and 241-4.

Verbeke, G., 'La physique d'Aristote et les anciens commentateurs grecs', in *Proceedings of the 1978 World Congress on Aristotle*, vol. 1, Athens 1981, 187-92.

Wieland, W., 'Zur Raumtheorie des Johannes Philoponus', in E. Fries (ed.), *Festschrift für J. Klein*, Göttingen 1967, 114-35.

Wieland, W., 'Die Ewigkeit der Welt (der Streit zwischen Joannes Philoponus und Simplicius)', in D. Heinrich, W. Schulz, K.H. Volkmann-Schluck (eds), *Die Gegenwart der Griechen im neueren Denken, Festschrift für H.-G. Gadamer zum 60. Geburtstag*, Tübingen 1960, 291-316.

Wildberg, C., *John Philoponus' Criticism of Aristotle's Theory of Aether*, Peripatoi 18, Berlin 1988.

Wildberg, C., *Philoponus, Against Aristotle on the Eternity of the World*, London-Ithaca N.Y. 1987.

Wohlwill, E., 'Ein Vorgänger Galileis im 6. Jahrhundert', *Verhandlungen der Gesellschaft deutscher Naturforscher und Ärzte* 77, part 2, 1905, 80-2; repr. in *Physicalische Zeitschrift* 7, 1906, 23-32.

Wolff, M., 'Philoponus and the rise of preclassical dynamics', in R. Sorabji, (ed.), *Philoponus and the Rejection of Aristotelian Science*, London-Ithaca N.Y. 1987, 84-120.

Wolff, M., *Geschichte der Impetustheorie. Untersuchungen zum Ursprung der klassischen Mechanik*, Frankfurt 1978.

Wolff, M., *Fallgesetz und Massebegriff. Zwei wissenschaftshistorische Untersuchungen zur Kosmologie des Johannes Philoponus*, Quellen und Studien zur Geschichte der Philosophie 21, Berlin 1971.

Wolfson, H.A., *The Philosophy of the Kalam*, Cambridge Mass. 1976.

Wolfson, H.A., 'The problem of the souls of the spheres from the Byzantine commentaries on Aristotle through the Arabs and St Thomas to Kepler', *Dumbarton Oaks Papers* 16, 1965, 67-93.

Wolfson, H.A., 'The Kalam arguments for creation in Saadia, Averroes, Maimonides and St Thomas', *Saadia Anniversary Volume, American Academy of Jewish Research, Texts and Studies* 2, New York 1943, 197-245.

Wolfson, H.A., *Crescas' Critique of Aristotle. Problems in Aristotle's Physics in Jewish and Arabic Philosophy*, Cambridge Mass. 1929.

Zahlfleisch, J., 'Einige Bemerkungen zur Corollarien des Simplicius in seinem Kommentar zu Aristoteles *Physik*', *Archiv für Geschichte der Philosophie* 15, n.s. 8, 1902, 186-213.

Zahlfleisch, J., 'Die polemik des Simplicius gegen Alexander und andere in dem Kommentar des ersteren zu der aristotelischen Schrift *de Caelo* dargestelt', *Archiv für Geschichte der Philosophie* 10, n.s. 3, 1897, 191-227.

Zahlfleisch, J., 'Die Polemik des Simplicius gegen Aristoteles *Physik* 4, 1-15 über den Raum dargestelt', *Archiv für Geschichte der Philosophie* 10, 1897, 85-109.

Zimmermann, F., 'Philoponus' impetus theory in the Arabic tradition', in R. Sorabji (ed.), *Philoponus and the Rejection of Aristotelian Science*, London-Ithaca N.Y. 1987, 121-9.

Psychology

General

Blumenthal, H.J., 'Alexander of Aphrodisias in the later Greek commentaries on Aristotle's *de Anima*', in J. Wiesner (ed.), *Aristoteles: Werk und Wirkung, Paul Moraux gewidmet*, vol. 2, Berlin-New York 1987, 90-106.

Blumenthal, H.J., 'The psychology of (?) Simplicius' commentary on the *de Anima*', in H.J. Blumenthal & A.C. Lloyd (eds), *Soul and the Structure of Being in Late Neoplatonism*, Liverpool 1982, 73-93.

Blumenthal, H.J., 'Neoplatonic interpretations of Aristotelian phantasia', *Review of Metaphysics* 31, 1977, 242-57.

Blumenthal, H.J., 'Neoplatonic elements in the *de Anima* commentaries', Chapter 13 above, repr. with revisions from *Phronesis* 21, 1976, 64-87.

Blumenthal, H.J., 'Plutarch's exposition of the *de Anima* and the psychology of Proclus', in H. Dörrie (ed.), *De Jamblique à Proclus*, Entretiens sur l'antiquité classique 21, Vandoeuvres-Genève 1975, 123-47.

Blumenthal, H.J., 'Did Iamblichus write a commentary on the *de Anima*?', *Hermes* 102, 1974, 540-56.

Donini, P.L., 'L'anima e gli elementi nel "de Anima" di Alessandro di Afrodisia',

Atti della Accademia delle Scienze di Torino, Classe di Scienze Morali, Storiche e Filologiche 105, 1970-71, 61-107.

Donini, P.L., 'Il de Anima di Alessandro di Afrodisia e Michele Efesio', *Rivista di Filologia e di Instruzione Classica* 96, 1968, 316-23.

Gätje, H., 'Die Shrift des Alexander von Aphrodisias über das Sahen' (with G. Losseren), *Studien zur Überlieferung der aristotelischen Psychologie im Islam*, Annales Universitatis Saraviensis 11, Heidelberg 1971, 140-72.

Gätje, H., 'Die arabische Übersetzung der Schrift des Alexander von Afrodisias über die Farbe', *Nachrichten der Academie der Wissenschaften in Göttingen*, 1967, 341-82.

Gauthier, R., Introduction to Thomas Aquinas *Opera Omnia*, Leonine Edition 45.1, 1984.

Hager, F.P., 'Die Aristotelesinterpretation des Alexander von Aphrodisias und die Aristoteleskritik Plotins bezüglich der Lehre vom Geist', *Archiv für Geschichte der Philosophie* 46, 1964, 174-87.

Lyons, M.C., 'An Arabic translation of the commentary of Themistius', *Bulletin of the School of Oriental and African Studies* 17, 1955, 426-35.

Moraux, P., 'Le "de Anima" dans la tradition grecque. Quelques aspects de l'interprétation du traité, de Théophraste à Thémistius', in G.E.R. Lloyd & G.E.L. Owen (eds), *Aristotle on Mind and the Senses*, Cambridge 1978, 281-324.

Ruland, H.-J., 'Die arabische Übersetzung der Schrift des Alexander von Aphrodisias über die Sinneswahrnehmung', *Nachrichten der Akademie der Wissenschaften in Göttingen*, 1978, 159-225.

Sorabji, R., 'From physiology to intentionality', in M. Nussbaum & A. Rorty (eds), *Aristotle's de Anima*, Oxford 1989.

Steel, C., *The Changing Self. A Study on the Soul in Later Neoplatonism, Iamblichus, Damascius and Priscianus*, Brussels 1978.

Todd, R.B., 'Themistius and the traditional interpretation of Aristotle's theory of phantasia', *Acta Classica* 24, 1981, 49-59.

Verbeke, G., 'Levels of human thinking in Philoponus', in C. Laga, J.A. Munitz, L. van Rompay (eds), *After Chalcedon, Studies in Theology and Church History offered to Professor Albert van Roey for his seventieth birthday*, Louvain 1986, 451-70.

Intellect

Balleriaux, O., *Thémistius. Son interpretation de la noétique aristotélicienne*, diss., Liège 1941.

Davidson, H.A., 'Al-Farabi and Avicenna on the active intellect', *Viator* 3, 1972, 109-78.

Finnegan, J., 'Al-Farabi et le "Peri Nou" d'Alexandre d'Aphrodise', *Mélanges L. Massignon*, 1957, 133-52.

Grünaz, A., *Die Abhandlung Alexanders von Aphrodisias über den Intellect. Aus handschriftlichen Quellen zum ersten Male herausgegeben und durch die Abhandlung, Die Nuslehre Alexanders von Aphrodisias und ihr Einfluss auf die arabisch-jüdische Philosophie des Mittelalters eingeleitet*, Berlin 1886.

Hadot, I., 'La doctrine de Simplicius sur l'âme raisonnable humaine dans le commentaire sur le *Manuel* d'Epictète', in H.J. Blumenthal & A.C. Lloyd (eds), *Soul and the Structure of Being in Late Neoplatonism*, Liverpool 1982, 46-70.

Hamelin, O., *La théorie de l'intellect d'après Aristote et ses commentateurs*, posthumous ed. E. Barbotin, Paris 1953.

Hicks, R.D., *Introduction to Aristotle's De Anima*, Cambridge 1907.

Jolivet, J., *L'intellect selon Al-Kindi*, Leiden 1971.

Hyman, A., 'Aristotle's theory of the intellect and its interpretation by Averroes', in D.J. O'Meara (ed.), *Studies in Aristotle*, Washington D.C. 1981, 161-90.

Kurfess, H., *Zur Geschichte der Erklärung der aristotelischen Lehre vom sogenannten 'Nous Poietikos' und 'Pathetikos'*, diss., Tübingen 1911.

Mahoney, E.P., 'Themistius and the Agent Intellect in James of Viterbo and other thirteenth-century philosophers', *Augustiniana* 23, 1973, 422-67.

Montoya Saenz, J., 'Interpretacion por Simplicio de la teoria aristotelica del "Nous" ', *Annales del Seminario del Metafisico*, Madrid 1968, 75-95.

Moraux, P., *Alexandre d'Aphrodise: exégète de la noétique d'Aristote*, Liège-Paris 1942.

Nardi, B., 'Il commento di Simplicio al de Anima nelle controversie della Fine del secolo XVe al secolo XVI', in his *Saggi dell' Aristotelismo Padovano dal Secolo XIV al XVI*, Florence 1958, 365-42.

Riet, A. van, 'Fragments de l'originel grec du de Intellectu de Philopon dans une compilation de Sophonias', *Revue philosophique de Louvain* 63, 1965, 5-40.

Schroeder, F.M., 'Light and the active intellect in Alexander and Plotinus', *Hermes* 112, 1984, 239-48.

Schroeder, F.M., 'The potential or material intellect and the authorship of the de Intellectu, a reply to B.C. Bazán', *Symbolae Osloenses* 57, 1982, 115-25.

Schroeder, F.M., 'The analogy of the active intellect to light in the de Anima of Alexander of Aphrodisias', *Hermes* 109, 1981, 215-25.

Théry, G., *Autour du décret de 1210: I. David de Dinant. Étude sur son panthéisme matérialiste*, Bibliothèque thomiste 7, Kain 1926.

Thillet, P., 'Matérialisme et théorie de l'âme et de l'intellect chez Alexandre d'Aphrodise', *Revue philosophique de la France et de l'étranger* 171, 1981, 5-24.

Todd, R.B. & Shroeder, F.M., *Two Greek Aristotelian Commentators on the Active Intellect*, Pontifical Institute, Toronto, forthcoming.

Verbeke, G., 'Levels of human thinking in Philoponus', in C. Laga, J.A. Munitz, L. van Rompay (eds), *After Chalcedon. Studies in Theology and Church History offered to Professor Albert van Roey for his seventieth birthday*, Louvain 1986, 451-70.

Wilpert, P., 'Die Ausgestaltung der aristotelischen Lehre vom Intellectus agens bei den griechischen Kommentatoren und in der Scholastik des 13. Jahrhunderts', *Aus der Geisteswelt des Mittelalters. Festschrift für M. Grabmann*, Beiträge zur Geschichte der Philosophie und Theologie des Mittelalters, supp. vol. 3 i, 1935, 447-62.

History of the commentaries
(Subjects in this section appear in roughly chronological order)

The early commentators

Accatino, P., 'Alessandro di Afrodisia e Aristotele di Mitilene', *Elenchos* 6, 1985, 67-74.

Arnim, H. von, 'Herminos' (2), *RE* 8, 1, 1913, col 835.

Arnim, H. von, 'Boethos' (4), *RE* 3, 1, 1899, cols 601-3.

Becchi, F., 'Aspasio e i peripatetici posteriori, la formula definitiva della passione', *Prometheus* 9, 1983, 83-104.

Brink, K.O., 'Peripatos', *RE* Suppl. 7, 1940, cols 899-949.

Busse, A., 'Peripatos und Peripatetiker', *Hermes* 61, 1926, 335-42.

Capelle, W., 'Lukios' (1), *RE* 13, 2, 1927, cols 1791-7.

Dalsgaard-Larsen, B., *Jamblique de Chalcis: exégète et philosophe*, 2 vols, Århus 1972.

Donini, P.L., *Le scuole, l'anima, l'impero: la filosofia antica da Antioco a Plotino*, Turin 1982.

Donini, P.L., *Tre studi sull'Aristotelismo nel II secolo D.C.*, Historica, Politica, Philosophica 7, Turin 1974.

Drossaart Lulofs, H.J., *Nicolaus Damascenus on the Philosophy of Aristotle*, Philosophia Antiqua 13, Leiden 1965; 2nd ed. 1969.

Drossaart Lulofs, H.J., 'Aristotle, Bar Hebraeus and Nicolaos Damascenus on animals', in A. Gotthelf (ed.), *Aristotle on Nature and Living Things*, Pittsburg-Bristol 1986, 345-57.

Düring, I., *Aristotle in the Ancient Biographical Tradition*, Göteborg 1957.

Fritz, K. von, 'Nikostratos' (26), *RE* 13, 1, 1936, 547-51.

Gercke, A., 'Alexandros (von Aigai)' (2), *RE* 1, 2, col. 1452.

Gercke, A., 'Boethos' (9), *RE* 3, 1, 1899, cols 603-4.

Glucker, J., *Antiochus and the Late Academy*, Hypomnemata 56, Göttingen 1978.

Gottschalk, H.B., 'The earliest Aristotelian commentators', Chapter 3 above, repr. with revisions from W. Haase (ed.), *Aufstieg und Niedergang der römischen Welt*, II, 36.2, Berlin 1987, 1079-174.

Gottschalk, H.B., 'Boethus' psychology and the Neoplatonists', *Phronesis* 31, 1986, 243-57.

Gottschalk, H.B., review of P. Moraux, *Der Aristotelismus*, vol. 2, in *Liverpool Classical Monthly* 10.8, 1985, 122-8.

Huby, P.M., 'An excerpt from Boethus of Sidon's commentary on the Categories?', *Classical Quarterly* 31, 1981, 398-40.

Littig, Fr., *Andronikos von Rhodos* (3 vols), Erlangen 1, 1890; 2, 1894; 3, 1985.

Moraux, P., 'Diogène Laërce et le Peripatos', *Elenchos* 7, 1986, 247-94.

Moraux, P., *Der Aristotelismus bei den Griechen: von Andronikos bis Alexander von Aphrodisias*, vol. 1, *Die Renaissance des Aristotelismus im I. Jh. v. Chr.*, Peripatoi 5, Berlin-New York 1973; vol. 2, *Der Aristotelismus im I. und II. Jh. n. Chr.*, Peripatoi 6, Berlin-New York 1984.

Moraux, P., 'Die Anfänge der griechischen Aristoteles-Interpretation', *Proceedings of the 1978 World Congress on Aristotle*, vol. 1, Athens 1981, 95-100.

Moraux, P., 'Einige Aspekte des Aristotelismus von Andronikos bis Alexander von Aphrodisias', in J. Burian & L. Vidman (eds), *Antiquitas Graeco-Romana et Tempora Nostra*, Prague 1968, 203-8.

Moraux, P., 'L'expose de la philosophie d'Aristote chez Diogene Laërce', *Revue philosophique de Louvain* 47, 1949, 5-43.

Plezia, M., *De Andronici Rhodii Studiis Aristotelicis*, Polska Academia Unmiectnosci, Archiwum Filologiczne 20, Cracow 1946.

Praechter, K., 'Nikostratos der Platoniker', *Hermes* 57, 1922, 481-517; repr. in his *Kleine Schriften*, H. Dörrie (ed.), Collectanea 7, Hildesheim-New York 1973, 101-37.

Sullivan, M.W., *Apuleian Logic. The Nature, Sources and Influences of Apuleius' Peri Hermeneias*, Amsterdam 1967.

Tarán, L., review of Paul Moraux, *Der Aristotelismus*, vol. 1, *Gnomon* 46, 1981, 721-50.

Wacholder, B.Z., *Nikolaos of Damascus*, Berkeley 1962.

School of Athens

Beutler, R., 'Plutarchos von Athen', *RE* 21, 1, 1951, cols 962-75.
Cameron, A., 'The last days of the Academy at Athens', *Proceedings of the Cambridge Philological Society* 195, 1969, 7-29; French abridgment, 'Le fin de l'académie' in *Le néoplatonisme*, Actes du colloque de Royaumont 9-13 Juin, 1969, Paris, 1971, 281-90.
Cameron, A., 'Iamblichus at Athens', *Athenaeum* 45, 1967, 143-53.
Évrard, É., 'Le maitre de Plutarque d'Athènes et les origines du néoplatonisme athénien', *L'antiquité classique* 29, 1960, 108-33; 'Plutarque, Jamblique, Porphyre', ibid., 392-406.
Frantz, Alison, 'Pagan philosophers in Christian Athens', *Proceedings of the American Philosophical Society* 119, 1975, 29-38.
Immisch, O., '*Attikoi exegetai*', *Philologus* 63, 1904, 31-40.
Tardieu, M., 'Les calendriers en usage à Ḥarrân d'après les sources arabes et le commentaire de Simplicius à la *Physique* d'Aristote', in I. Hadot (ed.), *Simplicius, sa vie, son oeuvre, sa survie*, Berlin-New York 1987, 40-57.
Tardieu, M., 'Ṣâbiens coraniques et "Ṣâbiens" de Ḥarrân', *Journal asiatique* 274, 1986, 1-44.
Westerink, L.G. & Saffrey, H.D., *Proclus. Théologie platonicienne*, Budé edition, vol. 1, Paris 1968; introduction.

School of Alexandria

Blumenthal, H.J., 'Pseudo-Elias and the Isagoge commentaries again', *Rheinisches Museum* 124, 1981, 188-92.
Évrard, É., *L'école d'Olympiodore et la composition du commentaire à la Physique de Jean Philopon*, diss., Liège 1957.
Kremer, K., 'Die Anschauung der Ammonius (Hermeiou)-Schule über den Wirklichkeitscharacter des Intelligiblen. Über einen Beitrag der Spätantike zur platonisch-aristotelischen Metaphysik', *Philosophisches Jahrbuch* 69, 1961, 46-63.
Kremer, K., *Der Metaphysikbegriff in den Aristoteles-Kommentaren der Ammonius-Schule*, Beiträge zur Geschichte der Philosophie und Theologie des Mittelalters 39, 1, Münster 1961.
Marcovich, M., 'Pseudo-Elias on Heraclitus', *American Journal of Philology* 96, 1975, 31-4.
Meyerhof, M., 'La fin de l'école d'Alexandrie d'après quelques auteurs arabes', *Archeion* 15, 1933, 1-15.
Meyerhof, M., 'Von Alexandrien nach Bagdad', *Sitzungsberichte der preussischen Akademie der Wissenschaften*, 1930, 389-429.
Praechter, K., 'Hermeias', *RE* 8, 1, 1913, cols 516-38.
Roueché, Mossman, 'The definitions of philosophy and a new fragment of Stephanus of Alexandria', in preparation.
Saffrey, H.D., 'Le chrétien Jean Philopon et la survivance de l'école d'Alexandrie au VIe siècle', *Revue des études grecques* 67, 1954, 396-410.
Simon, Jules, *Histoire de l'école d'alexandrie*, 2 vols, Paris 1843-45.
Tarán, L., *Anonymous Commentary on Aristotle's de Interpretatione (Codex Parisinus Graecus 2064)*, Beiträge zur Klassische Philologie 95, Meisenheim am Glan 1978.
Vacherot, E., *Histoire critique de l'école d'Alexandrie*, 2 vols, Paris 1846-51.
Vancourt, R., *Les derniers commentateurs alexandrins d'Aristote: l'école*

d'Olympiodore, Étienne d'Alexandrie, Lille 1941.

Westerink, L.G., 'Academic practice about 500 A.D. in Alexandria', unpublished paper delivered to Dumbarton Oaks conference.

Westerink, L.G., *The Greek Commentaries on Plato's Phaedo*, vol. 1, Olympiodorus, Amsterdam 1973.

Westerink, L.G., 'Ein astrologisches Kolleg aus dem Jahre 564', *Byzantinische Zeitschrift* 64, 1971, 6-21.

Westerink, L.G., Pseudo-Elias (Pseudo-David), *Lectures on Porphyry's Isagoge*, Amsterdam 1967.

Westerink, L.G., *Anonymous Prolegomena to Platonic Philosophy*, Amsterdam 1962; new edition in preparation; pp. ix-xxxii repr. with the revisions prepared for the new Budé edition in Chapter 14 above.

The Arab tradition

Badawi, A., *Commentaires sur Aristote perdus en grec et autres épitres*, Beirut 1971.

Badawi, A., *La transmission de la philosophie grecque au monde arabe*, Études de philosophie médiévale 56, Paris 1968.

Baumstark, A., *Aristoteles bei den Syrern vom V bis VIII Jahrhundert*, Leipzig 1900.

Booth, E.G.T., *Aristotelian Aporetic Ontology in Islamic and Christian Thinkers*, Cambridge 1983.

Brown, H.V.B, 'Avicenna and the Christian philosophers in Baghdad', in S.M. Stern et al. (eds), *Islamic Philosophy and the Classical Tradition, Essays presented to Richard Walzer*, Oriental Studies 5, Oxford 1972, 35-48.

Browne, G.M., 'Ad Themistium Arabum', *Illinois Classical Studies* 11, 1986, 223-45.

Craig, W.L., *The Kalam Cosmological Argument*, London 1979.

Daiber, H., *Ein Kompendium der Aristotelischen Meteorologie in der Fassung des Hunain ibn Isḥâq*, Amsterdam 1975.

Davidson, H.A., *Proofs for Eternity, Creation and the Existence of God in Medieval Islamic and Jewish Philosophy*, New York-Oxford 1987.

Davidson, H.A., 'The principle that a finite body can contain only a finite power', in S. Stein & R. Loewe (eds), *Studies in Jewish Religious and Intellectual History Presented to Alexander Altmann*, Alabama 1979, 75-92.

Davidson, H.A., 'Al-Farabi and Avicenna on the active intellect', *Mediaeval and Renaissance Studies* 3, 1972, 109-78.

Davidson, H.A., *Averroes' Middle Commentary on Porphyry's Isagoge and on Aristotle's Categoriae*, Cambridge Mass. 1969.

Davidson, H.A., 'Philoponus as a source of Medieval Islamic and Jewish proofs of creation', *Journal of the American Oriental Society* 89, 1969, 357-91.

Endress, G., *The Works of Yahyâ ibn 'Adi*, Wiesbaden 1977.

Fakhry, M., 'The "antinomy" of the eternity of the world in Averroes, Maimonides and Aquinas', *Le Muséon* 66, 1953, 139-55.

Feldman, S., 'The theory of eternal creation in Hasdai Crescas and some of his predecessors', *Medieval and Renaissance Studies* 11, 1980, 289-320.

Finnegan, J., 'Al-Farabi et le "Peri Nou" d'Alexandre d'Aphrodise', *Mélanges L. Massignon*, 1957, 133-52.

Finnegan, J., 'Avicenna's refutation of Porphyrius', in *Avicenna Commemoration Volume*, Calcutta 1956, 187-203.

Frank, R.M., 'Some textual notes of the oriental versions of Themistius' paraphrase of Book 1 of the Metaphysics', *Cahiers de Byrsá* 8, 1958-9, 215-30.

Gabrieli, F., 'Plotino e Porfirio in un eresiografo musulmano', *La Parola del Passato* 1, 1946, 338-46.

Gätje, H., 'Simplikios in der arabischen Überlieferung', *Der Islam* 59, 1982, 6-31.

Gätje, H., *Studien zur Überlieferung des Aristotelischen Psychologie im Islam*, Annales Universitatis Saraviensis 11, Heidelberg 1971.

Gätje, H., 'Zur arabischen Überlieferung des Alexander von Aphrodisias', *Zeitschrift der deutschen morgenländischen Gesellschaft* 116, 1966, 255-78.

Gauthier, R., Introduction to Thomas Aquinas *Opera Omnia*, Leonine Edition 45.1, 1984.

Genequand, C., 'Quelques aspects de l'idée de la nature d'Aristote à Al-Ghazali', *Revue de théologie et de philosophie* 116, 1984, 105-9.

Ghorab, A.A., 'The Greek commentators on Aristotle quoted in Al-Almiri's 'As-sa 'âda Wa'l-is'âd', in S.M. Stern et al. (eds), *Islamic Philosophy and the Classical Tradition. Essays presented to R. Walzer on his 70th birthday*, Oxford 1972, 77-88.

Grant, E., 'Aristotle, Philoponus, Avempace and Galileo's Pisan dynamics', *Centaurus* 11, 1965, 79-95.

Lyons, M.C., 'An Arabic translation of the commentary of Themistius', *Bulletin of the School of Oriental and African Studies* 17, 1955, 426-35.

Madkour, I., *L'Organon d'Aristote dans le monde arabe*, Paris 1969.

Mahdi, M., 'Alfarabi against Philoponus', *Journal of Near Eastern Studies* 26, 1967, 233-60.

Moody, E.A., 'Galileo and Avempace, the dynamics of the leaning tower experiment', *Journal of the History of Ideas* 13, 1951, 163-93; 375-422.

Peters, F.E., *Aristoteles Arabus. The Oriental Translations and Commentaries on the Aristotelian Corpus*, Monographs on Mediterranean Antiquity 2, Leiden 1968.

Pinès, S., 'Les précurseurs musulmans de la théorie de l'impetus', *Archeion* 21, 1938, 298-306; repr. in S. Pinès (ed.), *Studies in Arabic Versions of Greek Texts and in Medieval Science*, vol. 2, Leiden-Jerusalem 1986, 409-17.

Pinès, S., 'Les textes arabes dits plotiniens et le "courant porphyrien" dans le néoplatonisme grec', in *Le néoplatonisme*, Actes du Colloque de Royaumont 9-13 Juin 1969, Paris 1971, 303-17; repr. in S. Pinès, *Studies in Arabic Versions of Greek Texts and in Medieval Science*, vol. 2, Leiden-Jerusalem 1986, 264-77.

Pinès, S., 'The spiritual force permeating the Cosmos according to a passage in the Treatise on the Principles of the All ascribed to Alexander of Aphrodisias', in S. Pinès, *Studies in Arabic Versions of Greek Texts and in Medieval Science*, vol. 2, Leiden-Jerusalem 1986, 252-5.

Pinès, S., 'Un précurseur bagdadien de la théorie de l'impetus', *Isis* 44, 1953, 246-51; repr. in S. Pinès, *Studies in Arabic Versions of Greek Texts and in Medieval Science*, vol. 2, Leiden-Jerusalem 1986, 418-22.

Pinès, S., Les limites de la Métaphysique selon Al-Farabi, Ibn-Bassa et Maimonides; sources et antithèses de ces doctrines chez Alexandre d'Aphrodise et chez Themistius, *Sprache und Erkenntnis im Mittelalter* 1, Miscellanea Medievalia 13.1, Berlin-New York 1981.

Pinès, S., '*Omne quod movetur necesse est ab aliquo moveri*, a refutation of Galen by Alexander of Aphrodisias and the theory of motion', *Isis* 52, 1961, 21-54.

Rescher, N. & Marmura, M., *Alexander of Aphrodisias. The Refutation by Alexander of Aphrodisias of Galen's Treatise of the Theory of Motion*, Islamabad (Islamic Research Institute), 1965.

Rescher, N., *Al-Farabi's Short Commentary on Aristotle's Prior Analytics*, Pittsburgh 1963.

Sorabji, R., 'Infinite power impressed, the transformation of Aristotle's physics and theology', Chapter 9 above (fuller version in his *Matter, Space and Motion*, London-Ithaca N.Y. 1988, ch. 15).

Steinschneider, M., 'Johannes Philoponus bei den Arabern', in 'Al-Farabi-Alpharabius, des arabischen Philosophen Leben und Schriften', *Mémoires de l'academie impériale des sciences de St. Petersbourg*, series 7, 13, 4, 1869, 152-76; 220-4; 250-2.

Steinschneider, M., *Die arabischen Übersetzungen aus dem Griechischen*, Leipzig 1893; repr. Graz 1960.

Stern, S.M., ' "The first in thought is the last in action", the history of a saying attributed to Aristotle', *Journal of Semitic Studies* 7, 1962, 234-52.

Tardieu, M., 'Şâbiens coraniques et "Şâbiens" de Harrân', *Journal asiatique* 274, 1986, 1-44.

Thillet, P., 'Indices porphyriens dans la théologie d'Aristote', *Le néoplatonisme*, Actes du Colloque de Royaumont 9-13 Juin, 1969, Paris 1971, 293-302.

Ullmann, M., *Die Natur- und Geheimwissenschaften in Islam*, Leiden 1972.

Walzer, R., 'Porphyry and the Arabic tradition', in *Porphyry the Philosopher*, Entretiens sur l'antiquité classique 12, Vandoeuvres-Genève 1966, 273-97.

Walzer, R., *Greek into Arabic*, Oxford 1962.

Wenrich, J.G., *De auctorum graecorum versionibus et commentariis syriacis, arabicis, armenicis, persisque*, Leipzig 1842.

Wolfson, H.A., *The Philosophy of the Kalam*, Cambridge Mass. 1976.

Wolfson, H.A., 'The problem of the souls of the spheres from the Byzantine commentaries on Aristotle through the Arabs and St Thomas to Kepler', *Dumbarton Oaks Papers* 16, 1965, 67-93.

Wolfson, H.A., 'The Kalam arguments for creation in Saadia, Averroes, Maimonides and St Thomas', in *Saadia Anniversary Volume, American Academy of Jewish Research, Texts and Studies* 2, New York 1943, 197-245.

Wolfson, H.A., *Crescas' Critique of Aristotle. Problems in Aristotle's Physics in Jewish and Arabic Philosophy*, Cambridge Mass. 1929.

Zimmermann, F., 'Philoponus' impetus theory in the Arabic tradition', in R. Sorabji (ed.), *Philoponus and the Rejection of Aristotelian Science*, London-Ithaca N.Y. 1987, 121-9.

Zimmermann, F., *Al-Farabi's Commentary and Short Treatise on Aristotle's de Interpretatione*, translated with Introduction and Notes, Oxford 1981.

Zimmermann, F. & Brown, H.V.B., Review of A. Badawi, *Commentaires sur Aristote perdus en grec et autres épitres*, Beirut 1971, 'Neue arabischen Übersetzungen aus dem Bereich der spätantiken griechischen Philosophie', *Der Islam* 50, 1973, 313-24.

Middle and Late Byzantium

Benakis, L., 'Commentaries and commentators on the logical works of Aristotle in Byzantium', in R. Claussen & R. Daube-Schackat (eds), *Gedankenzeichen. Festschrift für Klaus Oehler*, Tübingen 1988, 3-12.

Benakis, L., 'Grundbibliographie zum Aristoteles-Studium in Byzanz', in J. Wiesner (ed.), *Aristoteles: Werk und Wirkung, Paul Moraux gewidmet*, vol. 2, Berlin-New York 1987, 352-79.

Benakis, L., 'The problem of general concepts in Neoplatonism and Byzantine thought', in D.J. O'Meara (ed.), *Neoplatonism and Christian Thought*, Norfolk 1982, 75-86, 248-9.

Benakis, L., 'Studien zu den Aristoteles Kommentaren des Michael Psellos 1. Ein unedierte Kommentar zur Physik des Aristoteles von Michael Psellos 2. Die aristotelischen Begriffe "Physis", "Materie", "Form" nach Michael Psellos', *Archiv für Geschichte der Philosophie* 43, 1961, 215-38; 44, 1962, 33-61.

Browning, R., 'An unpublished funeral oration on Anna Comnena', Chapter 17 above, repr. with revisions from *Proceedings of the Cambridge Philological Society* 188, 1962, 1-12.

Dräseke, J., 'Zu Michael Psellos', *Zeitschrift für wissenschaftliche Theologie* 32, 1899, 303-30.

Ebbesen, S., 'Philoponus, "Alexander" and the origins of medieval logic', Chapter 19 above.

Ebbesen, S., 'Boethius, Jacobus Veneticus, Michael Ephesius and "Alexander"', *Cahiers de l'Institut du moyen-âge grec et latin* 34, Copenhagen 1979, v-xiii.

Ebbesen, S., 'Anonymus Aurelianensis II, Aristotle, Alexander, Porphyry and Boethius: ancient scholasticism and twelfth-century Western Europe. With an edition of the Tractatus de Paralogismis', *Cahiers de l'Institut du moyen-âge grec et latin* 16, Copenhagen 1976, 1-128.

Ebbesen, S., '*Ho Psellos kai hoi Sophistikoi Elenchoi*', *Byzantina* 5, 1973, 429-44.

Hunger, H., *Die hochsprachliche profane Literatur der Byzantiner*, Munich 1978; cf. esp. vol. 1, 11-41, Platonismus und Aristotelismus in Byzanz, 54-62; Bibliography, Handbuch der Altertumswissenschaften 12, Byzantinisches Handbuch 5.

Krumbacher, K., *Geshichte der byzantinischen Litteratur von Justinian bis zum Ende des Oströmischen Reiches (527-1453)*, Handbuch der klassischen Altertumswissenschaft 9, 1, Fortleben des Aristoteles, 2nd ed. Munich 1897, 430ff.

Lackner, W., 'Zum Lehrbuch der Physik des Nikephoros Blemmydes', *Byzantinische Forschungen* 4, 1972, 157-69.

Moraux, P., *D'Aristote à Bessarion: trois études sur l'histoire et la transmission de l'aristotélisme grec*, Laval, Quebec 1970.

Oehler, K., 'Aristotle in Byzantium', *Greek, Roman and Byzantine Studies* 5, 1964, 133-46; German transl. by P. Moraux, *Aristoteles in der neuren Forschung*, Darmstadt 1968, 381-99; reprinted in K. Oehler, *Antike Philosophie und byzantinisches Mittelalter*, Munich 1969, 272-86.

Roueché, Mossman, 'A middle Byzantine handbook of logical terminology', *Jahrbuch der Oesterreichischen Byzantinistik* 29, 1980, 71-98.

Roueché, Mossman, 'Byzantine philosophical texts of the seventh century', *Jahrbuch der Oesterreichischen Byzantinistik* 23, 1974, 61-76.

Tarán, L., Review of K. Oehler, *Antike Philosophie und byzantinisches Mittelalter*, *Gnomon* 46, 1974, 534-47.

Tatakis, B.N., 'La philosophie byzantine', in E. Brehier, *Histoire de la philosophie*, suppl. 2, Paris 1949, 161-210; repr. 1959.

Wolfson, H.A., 'The problem of the souls of the spheres from the Byzantine commentaries on Aristotle through the Arabs and St Thomas to Kepler', *Dumbarton Oaks Papers* 16, 1965, 67-93.

Zervos, C., *Un philosophe néoplatonicien du XIe siècle, Michael Psellos, sa vie, son oeuvre, ses luttes philosophiques, son influence*, diss., University of Paris, Paris 1920; repr. New York 1973.

Translation into Latin
(see also Boethius)

Allan, D.J., 'Medieval versions of Aristotle, de Caelo, and of the Commentary of Simplicius', *Mediaeval and Renaissance Studies* 2, 1950, 82-120.

Bossier, F. & Brams, J. (ed.), *Méthodes de traduction et problèmes de chronologie. Recueil d'articles sur Moerbeke*, Louvain 1988.

Bossier, F., 'Traductions latines et influences du commentaire in de Caelo en Occident (XIIIe-XIVe siècle)', in I. Hadot (ed.), *Simplicius, sa vie, son oeuvre, sa survie*, Berlin-New York 1987, 289-325.

Courcelle, P., *Late Latin Writers and their Greek Sources*, Cambridge, Mass. 1969; translated from *Les lettres grecques en Occident, de Macrobe à Cassiodore*, 2nd ed., Paris 1948.

Cranz, F.E., 'Alexander Aphrodisiensis', in P.O. Kristeller & F.E. Cranz (eds), *Catalogus Translationum et Commentariorum, Medieval and Renaissance Latin Translations and Commentaries*, Washington D.C., vol. 1, 1960, 77-135; vol. 2, 1971, 411-22.

Cranz, F.E., 'The prefaces to the Greek editions and Latin translations of Alexander of Aphrodisias, 1450-1575', *Proceedings of the American Philosophical Society* 102, 1958, 510-46.

Ebbesen, S., 'Philoponus, "Alexander" and the origins of medieval logic', Chapter 19 above.

Ebbesen, S., 'Analyzing syllogisms, or Anonymous Aurelianensis III – the (presumably) earliest extant Latin commentary on the *Prior Analytics*, and its Greek model', *Cahiers de l'Institut du moyen-âge grec et latin* 37, Copenhagen 1981, 1-20.

Ebbesen, S., *Commentators and Commentaries on Aristotle's Sophistici Elenchi. A Study of Post-Aristotelian and Medieval Writings on Fallacies*, 3 vols, Corpus Latinum Commentariorum in Aristotelem Graecorum 7.1-3, Leiden 1981.

Ebbesen, S., 'Anonymus Aurelianensis II, Aristotle, Alexander, Porphyry and Boethius; ancient scholasticism and twelfth-century Western Europe. With an edition of the Tractatus de Paralogismis', *Cahiers de l'Institut du moyen-âge grec et latin* 16, Copenhagen 1976, 1-128.

Gersh, S., *Middle Platonism and Neoplatonism. The Latin Tradition*, 2 vols, Notre Dame 1986.

Gilson, E., *History of Christian Philosophy in the Middle Ages*, London 1955.

Grabmann, M., *Guglielmo di Moerbeke O.P., il Traduttore delle Opere di Aristotele* (I Papi del Duecento e l'Aristotelismo, II.), Miscellanea Historiae Pontificae XI.20, Rome 1946.

Grabmann, M., *Die Aristoteleskommentare des Heinrich von Brüssel und die Einfluss Alberts des Grossen auf die mittelalterlichen Aristoteleserklärung*, Sitzungsberichte der bayerischen Akademie der Wissenschaften, Munich 1943.

Grabmann, M., *Mittelalterliche lateinische Übersetzungen von Schriften der Aristoteles-Kommentatoren Johannes Philoponos, Alexander von Aphrodisias und Themistios*, Sitzungsberichte der bayerischen Akademie der Wissenschaften, Munich 1929.

Hadot, P., *Marius Victorinus*, Paris 1971.

Hadot, P., *Porphyre et Victorinus*, Paris 1968.

Isaak, I., *Le Peri hermeneias en Occident de Boèce à Saint Thomas. Histoire littéraire d'un traité d'Aristote*, Bibliothèque thomiste 29, Paris 1953; includes the first 10 chapters of William of Moerbeke's translation, pp. 160-9.

Jolivet, J., 'The Arab inheritance', in P. Dronke (ed.), *A History of Twelfth-Century Philosophy*, Cambridge 1988.

Jourdain, A., *Recherches critiques sur l'âge et l'origine des traductions latines d'Aristote et sur des commentateurs grecs ou arabes employés par les docteurs scholastiques*, new ed. revised and expanded by C. Jourdain (from original 1819), Paris 1843.

Kristeller, P.O. & Cranz, F.G. (eds), *Catalogus Translationum et Commentariorum, Medieval and Renaissance Latin Translations and Commentaries*, Washington D.C., vol. 1, 1960; vol. 2, 1971.

Lohr, C.H., 'Aristotle in the West; some recent works', *Traditio* 25, 1969, 417-31.

McEvoy, J., *The Philosophy of Robert Grosseteste*, Oxford 1982.

Mercken, H.P.F., 'The Greek commentaries on Aristotle's *Ethics*', Chapter 18 above, revised from 'Introduction', Corpus Latinum Commentariorum in Aristotelem Graecorum 6.1.

Minio-Paluello, L., *Opuscula, the Latin Aristotle*, Amsterdam 1972.

Minio-Paluello, L., 'Giacomo Veneto e l'Aristotelismo latino', in Pertuzi (ed.), *Venezia e l'Oriento fra tardo Medioevo e Rinascimento*, Florence 1966, 53-74; repr. in his *Opuscula, the Latin Aristotle*, Amsterdam 1972.

Minio-Paluello, L., 'Jacobus Veneticus Graecus, canonist and translator of Aristotle', *Traditio* 8, 1952, 265-304; repr. in his *Opuscula, the Latin Aristotle*, Amsterdam 1972.

Moraux, P., *D'Aristote à Bessarion: trois études sur l'histoire et la transmission de l'aristotélisme grec*, Laval, Quebec 1970.

Oehler, K., *Antike Philosophie und byzantisches Mittelalter*, Munich 1969, ch. 13, 'Aristotle in Byzantium'; repr. from *Greek, Roman and Byzantine Studies* 5, 1964, 133-46.

Rossi, P., 'Tracce della versione latina di un commento greco ai Secondi Analitici nel Commentarius in Posteriorium Analyticorum di Grossatesta', *Rivista di Filosofia Neoscolastica*, 1978, 433-9.

Shiel, J., *Aristoteles Latinus III: Scholiorum in Analytica priora supplementa*, Bulletin de la Société internationale pour l'étude de la philosophie médiévale 26, 1984, 119-26.

Shiel, J., 'The Latin Aristotle', *Medium Aevum* 42, 1973, 147-52.

Steenberghen, F. van, *Aristotle in the West. The Origins of Latin Aristotelianism*, translation of the Louvain 1955 edition, *Aristote en Occident. Les origines de l'Aristotélisme parisien*, by L. Johnston, New York 1970.

Steinschneider, M., *Die europäischen Übersetzungen aus dem arabischen bis Mitte des 17 Jahrhunderts*; repr. Graz 1956.

Théry, G., *Autour du décret de 1210: I. David de Dinant. Étude sur son panthéisme matérialiste*, Bibliothèque thomiste 7, Kain 1926.

Thillet, P., *Alexandre d'Aphrodise, de Fato ad Imperatores, version de Guillaume de Moerbeke*, Études de philosophie médiévale 51, Paris 1963.

Verbeke, G., *Thémistius, Commentaire sur le traité de l'âme d'Aristote*, Corpus Latinum Commentariorum in Aristotelem Graecorum 1, Paris 1957 (with an introduction).

Verbeke, G. (ed.), *Corpus Latinum Commentariorum in Aristotelem Graecorum, the Medieval Latin translations of the commentaries*, Paris 1957-.

The Renaissance

Grant, E., 'Aristotle, Philoponus, Avempace and Galileo's Pisan dynamics', *Centaurus* 11, 1965, 79-95.

Kristeller, P.O. & Cranz, F.G. (eds), *Catalogus Translationum et Commentariorum, Medieval and Renaissance Latin Translations and Commentaries*,

Washington D.C., vol. 1, 1960; vol. 2, 1971.

Kristeller, P.O., 'Paduan Averroism and Alexandrism in the light of recent studies', *Aristotelismo padovano e filosofia aristotelica*, Atti del XII congresso internazionale di filosofia IX, Florence 1960, 147-155; repr. in his *Renaissance Thought* 2, New York 1965, 111-18.

Lohr, C.H., 'Comment. d'Aristote au moyen-âge', *Vestigia* 2, Fribourg 1988-.

Lohr, C.H., 'Renaissance Latin Aristotle commentaries', *Studies in the Renaissance* 21, 1974; *Renaissance Quarterly* 28, 1975; 29, 1976; 30, 1977, 681-741; 31, 1978, 532-603; 32, 1979, 529-80; 33, 1980, 623-74; 35, 1982, 164-76.

Lohr, C.H. (ed.), *Commentaria in Aristotelem Graeca, versiones Latinae, the Renaissance Latin Translations Reprinted*, Frankfurt 1978-.

Mahoney, E.P., 'Marcilio Ficino's influence on Nicoleto Vernia, Augustino Nifo and Marcantonio Zimara', in Gian Carlo Giamparini (ed.), *Marcilio Ficino e il Ritorno di Platone*, Padua 1986, 509-31.

Mahoney, E.P., 'Philosophy and science in Nicoleto Vernia and Augustino Nifo', in Antonino Poppi (ed.), *Scienza e Filosofia all' Universita di Padova nel Quattrocento*, Padua 1985, 135-202.

Mahoney, E.P., 'Neoplatonism, the Greek commentators and Renaissance Aristotelianism', in D.J. O'Meara (ed.), *Neoplatonism and Christian Thought*, Norfolk 1982, 169-84, 264-82.

Mahoney, E.P., 'Nicoletto Vernia on the soul and immortality', in E.P. Mahoney (ed.), *Renaissance Essays in Honour of P.O. Kristeller*, Leiden 1976, 144-53.

Mahoney, E.P., 'Themistius and the agent intellect in James of Viterbo and other thirteenth-century philosophers', *Augustiniana* 23, 1973, 422-67.

Moody, E.A., 'Galileo and Avempace, the dynamics of the leaning tower experiment', *Journal of the History of Ideas* 13, 1951, 163-93; 375-422.

Nardi, B., 'Alessandrismo', *Enciclopedia Cattolica*, Vatican City 1968, vol. 1, 778f.

Nardi, B., 'Il commento di Simplicio al de Anima nelle controversie della fine del secolo XVe al secolo XVI', *Archivio di Filosofia*, 1951, 139-206; repr. in his *Saggi sull'Aristotelismo Padovano dal Secolo XIV al XVI*, Florence, 1958, 365-442.

Schmitt, C.B., 'Philoponus' commentary on Aristotle's *Physics* in the sixteenth century', in R. Sorabji (ed.), *Philoponus and the Rejection of Aristotelian Science*, London-Ithaca N.Y. 1987, 210-27.

Schmitt, C.B., *Aristotle and the Renaissance*, Cambridge, Mass.-London 1983.

Schmitt, C.B., *Gianfrancesco Pico della Mirandola (1469-1533) and his Critique of Aristotle*, The Hague 1967.

Manuscripts

Argyropoulos, R.D. & Caras, I., *Inventaire des manuscrits grecs d'Aristote et de ses commentateurs. Contribution à l'histoire du texte d'Aristote. Supplement*, Paris 1980.

Canart, P., 'Manuscrits d'Aristote et de ses commentateurs sur papier occidental ancien', in J. Wiesner (ed.), *Aristoteles: Werk und Wirkung, Paul Moraux gewidmet*, vol. 2, Berlin-New York 1987, 418-33.

Harlfinger, D. & Wiesner, J., 'Die griechischen Handschriften des Aristoteles und seiner Kommentatoren', *Scriptorium* 18, 1964, 238-57.

Hoffmann, P., Review of R.D. Argyropoulos and I. Caras, *Inventaire des manuscrits grecs d'Aristote*, *Revue des études anciennes* 83, 1981, 352-6.

Huby, P.M., 'The transmission of Aristotle's writings and the places where copies of his works existed', *Classica et Mediaevalia* 30, 1969, 241-57.

Minio-Paluello, L. (ed.), *Aristoteles Latinus. Codices. Supplementa*, Paris 1961.

Mioni, E., 'Manoscritti Graeci-Veneti di Aristotele e Commentatori', in C. Mango, *Catalogo Manoscritti e stampe venete dell'Aristotelismo e Averroismo*, Venice 1958.

Moraux, P. et al., *Aristoteles Graecus I-*, Berlin 1976-.

Thillet, P., 'Les MSS grecs d'Aristote et de ses commentateurs', *Bulletin de l'association Guillaume Budé*, 1963, 351-5.

Wartelle, A., *Inventaire des manuscrits grecs d'Aristote et de ses commentateurs*, Paris 1963. Supplement by R.D. Argyropoulos & I. Caras, Paris 1980. Corrections by D. Harlfinger & J. Wiesner, 'Die griechischen Handschriften des Aristoteles und seiner Kommentatoren', *Scriptorium* 18, 1963, 238-57.

Index Locorum

This index is to the commentaries on Aristotle included in *CAG* plus the works by Boethius and ps.-Elias listed below after the abbreviations.

The following abbreviations are used in this index:

in An. Post.	*in Analytica Posteriora*
in An. Pr.	*in Analytica Priora*
in Cael.	*in de Caelo*
in Cat.	*in Categoriae*
in DA	*in de Anima*
in EN	*in Ethica Nicomachea*
in GA	*in de Generatione Animalium*
in GC	*in de Generatione et Corruptione*
in HA	*in Historia Animalium*
in IA	*in de Incessu Animalium*
in Int.	*in de Interpretatione*
in Isag.	*in Porphyrii Isagogen*
in Metaph.	*in Metaphysica*
in Meteor.	*in Meteorologica*
in MA	*in de Motu Animalium*
in PA	*in de Partibus Animalium*
in Phys.	*in Physica*
in SE	*in de Sophisticis Elenchis*
in Sens.	*in de Sensu et Sensibilia*
in Top.	*in Topica*
Proleg.	*Prolegomena*

Full references for these works, for individual authors, are given on pp. 26-8 of this volume, with the exception of the following:

Boethius, *in Cat.*: *Patrologia Latina* (Migne) 64, 159-294.
Boethius, *in Int.*[1] (=ed. prima, in vol. 1) and *in Int.*[2] (=ed. secunda, in vol. 2): *Boethii commentarii in librum Aristotelis peri Hermeneias*, Meiser (ed.), Teubner 1877-80.
Boethius, *in Isag.*[1] (=ed. prima) and *in Isag.*[2] (=ed. secunda): *Anicii Manlii Severini Boethii In Isagogen Porphyrii commenta*, S. Brandt (ed.), Vienna and Leipzig 1906 (Corpus Scriptorum Ecclesiasticorum Latinorum 48).
ps.-Elias, *in Isag.*: *Pseudo-Elias (Pseudo-David), Lectures on Porphyry's Isagoge*, L.G. Westerink (ed.), Amsterdam 1967.

References to the pages of this volume appear in **bold** type.

256; 157,5-6, **256**; 178,21-2, **256**; 199,4-6, **255**; 206,2-4, **255**; 280,21-4, **256**; 282,23-7, **255**; 286,7, **185**; 288,19-289,22, **255**; 290,12-13, **255**; 290,24-5, **255**; 291,21-3, **255**; 296,14-17, **255**; 296,14-298,8, **255**; 296,19-21, **236**; 297,15-24, **224**; 299,18-19, **255**; 299,22, **255**; 299,25, **255**; 300,1-3, **255**; 300,7-8, **255**; 301,28-9, **256**; 312,17-18, **255**

in Meteor., **13, 231, 234, 241-3, 257-8, 264-5, 326-7**; 8,13, **242**; 9,8, **242**; 11,24-37, **258**; 12,24-32, **258**; 12,30-1, **258**; 15,23, **242**; 22,8, **242**; 23,22, **242**; 43,7, **242**; 43,37, **242**; 47,30, **242**; 48,14, **242**; 53,26-7, **241**; 61,16, **242**; 63,8-9, **242**; 71,3-4, **241**; 77,23, **242**; 78,31, **242**; 79,31, **242**; 82,17, **242**; 86,18-19, **242**; 91,3, **261**; 96,22, **242**; 106,9, **261**; 110,13, **242**; 118,25-6, **242**

in Phys., **8, 13, 17, 48, 122, 231, 234-5, 239-58, 261, 264-5, 273, 326**; 1,17, **245**; 1,23-4, **245**; 2,21-2, **248**; 2,25-7, **247**; 5,21-5, **214**; 9,23-10,2, **235**; 15,29-30, **235**; 15,30, **245**; 16,2, **235**; 16,8, **235**; 22,13-15, **236**; 54,8-55,26, **245, 249**; 55,20-2, **254**; 55,24-6, **249, 252-4**; 55,25, **249**; 55,26, **249, 253**; 81,25, **92**; 111,19ff., **106**; 128,22-31, **235**; 152,5-7, **245**; 156,10-12, **235**; 156,16-17, **253**; 162,12-20, **219**; 163,2-12, **236**; 173,21-6, **98**; 187,6-9, **236**; 189,10-26, **185**; 189,13-17, **224**; 191,1-2, **249**; 191,9-192,2, **245, 249**; 191,34-192,1, **249**; 191,34-192,2, **249**; 219,19-22, **235**; 220,20-5, **235**; 225,4-226,11, **4**; 236,29-237,4, **245**; 240,18-19, **185**; 250,28, **250**; 298,6-10, **224**; 298,6-12, **245**; 303,1-5, **245**; 303,18-25, **245**; 303,24-5, **245**; 304,5-10, **224**; 340,7-9, **248**; 340,12-13, **248**; 340,31, **235**; 346,8-9, **248**; 347,10-11, **248**; 362,21-5, **245**; 384,29-385,11, **196**; 405,3-7, **245**; 405,28-9, **248**; 408,14-15, **248**; 410,21-4, **245**; 414,21-2, **250**; 428,23-430,10, **245, 249, 254**; 430,9-10, **249, 254**; 438,5-6, **245**; 438,9-10, **235**; 440,16-17, **247**; 444,5-6, **247**; 447,18-20,

247; 448,20-1, **247**; 454,23-4, **247**; 456,17-458,31, **245**; 456,17-459,1, **249**; 458,15-6, **249**; 458,30-1, **244, 249**; 463,3-4, **247**; 467,1-468,4, **245**; 467,1-468,7, **249**; 484,15-19, **245**; 490,14, **236**; 497,8-9, **245**; 499,26, **247**; 499,26-7, **247**; 500,28-9, **248**; 526,20-3, **247**; 536,6-7, **247**; 539,5-6, **247**; 542,17-18, **247**; 542,18, **247**; 542,36, **247**; 543,1-4, **247**; 546,16-17, **247**; 555,25-7, **247**; 557,8-585,4, **246, 249**; 563,20-5, **246**; 563,22-5, **247**; 567,29-33, **246**; 583,13-585,4, **239**; 584,14, **248**; 592,16-32, **246, 249**; 601,12-13, **245**; 606,25-675,11, **247**; 611,16, **248**; 619,1-4, **248**; 619,10-13, **249**; 632,4-634,2, **247, 249**; 639,3-643,8, **247, 249**; 639,7-9, **244, 249, 253**; 639,7-10, **249**; 640,23-5, **249**; 641,13-642,20, **196**; 644,16-22, **198**; 661,9-12, **248**; 675,12-695,8, **247, 249**; 675,21-9, **247**; 677,9-686,29, **248**; 677,9-689,25, **247**; 685,23-686,29, **248**; 686,12-17, **248**; 686,16-17, **248**; 689,4-16, **248**; 689,26-694,27, **247-8**; 690,34-691,5, **196**; 693,30, **248**; 695,9-702,9, **247**; 697,26, **248**; 703,16-17, **239**; 705,21-2, **250**; 747,1-3, **245**; 761,34-762,9, **249**; 762,2-9, **245**; 762,7-9, **244, 251**; 762,8-9, **248-9**; 777,11-12, **245**; 797,23-6, **246**; 812,22-3, **246**; 812,23, **246**; 820,30-2, **246**; 820,30-821,4, **246**; 823,16-20, **246**; 824,22-5, **246**; 832,17-18, **246**; 838,14-15, **245**; 838,20-1, **246**; 838,28-33, **246**; 859,30, **245**; 870,2-9, **246**; 870,3-8, **246**; 873,1-2, **246**; 889,17-23, **246**; 890,2-3, **246**; 890,7, **246**; 891,33-892,24, **246**; 891,35, **246**; 892,7, **246**; 892,18, **246**; 893,6-9, **246**; 893,6-28, **245**; 894,8-10, **246**; 894,26, **246**; 897,23-7, **246**; 898,2-4, **245**; 905,19-21, **246**; 906,38-9, **246**; 906,38-40, **246**

Philoponus (?)
in An. Post. 2 421,3-4, **148**
in DA 3, **47, 123, 182, 311-14, 317, 322, 340**; 448,6-7, **341**; 450,8ff., **123**; 450,27-33, **123**; 457,24-5, **342**; 470,18, **95**; 490,18ff., **318**; 508,19-25,

General Index

DATE DUE
